BUSINESS REVIEW BOOKS

Finance

SEVENTH EDITION

Ehsan Nikbakht, D.B.A., C.F.A.
Professor of Finance
Frank G. Zarb School of Business
Hofstra University

A. A. Groppelli, Ph.D.
Former Professor of Finance
Frank G. Zarb School of Business
Hofstra University

BARRON'S

Published by Kaplan, Inc., d/b/a Barron's Educational Series
750 Third Avenue
New York, NY 10017
www.barronseduc.com

Library of Congress Catalog Card Number 2018936894

ISBN: 978-1-4380-1036-6

9 8 7 6 5 4 3 2

Kaplan, Inc., d/b/a Barron's Educational Series print books are available at
special quantity discounts to use for sales promotions, employee premiums, or
educational purposes. For more information or to purchase books, please call the
Simon & Schuster special sales department at 866-506-1949.

CONTENTS

INTRODUCTION TO INVESTMENT POLICY:
CAPITAL BUDGETING

INVESTING, FINANCING, AND DIVIDEND DECISIONS

SHORT- AND LONG-TERM CAPITAL SOURCES

INTRODUCTION TO FINANCIAL ANALYSIS

MANAGING WORKING CAPITAL

ANALYZING FINANCIAL STATEMENTS

SPECIAL TOPICS

PREFACE

Finance is among the most dynamic and evolving subjects in applied business disciplines. For persons and entities engaged in the practical conduct of businesses, a knowledge of finance is essential. In turn, academicians are constantly developing new concepts and updating their theories to keep abreast of the rapid changes taking place in financial markets. Financial software is continuing to advance and become more sophisticated, and provides the users with the extensive data files and mathematical tools to help develop decision-making relationships. The Internet has continued to become an integral part of the way a firm conducts its business. New instruments such as financial derivatives, although criticized as contributing to the recent debt crisis, are still used by investors to hedge against risk in the market. Globalization of the firm has continued and introduced a new dimension into our thinking regarding the solution of finance problems.

Finance is a highly technical discipline, yet our main purpose in writing and revising this book is to keep the explanations as simple as possible. As a result, we believe that this book, with its new revisions, will provide the reader with a sound understanding of the fundamentals of finance while making learning an easy and enjoyable experience.

The book is designed primarily for students enrolled in introductory finance courses and for persons in business who need a basic knowledge of finance to run firms efficiently, converse more intelligently, and make better and profitable investment decisions. We have made extensive use of tables, numerical examples, and graphs to explain theories and practical business applications.

The book covers the following major areas of finance:

1. The kind of knowledge and background needed by corporate managers.

2. Discussion and application of the time value of money and risk/return analysis as a basis for making investment decisions and for determining the valuation of stocks, bonds, and other assets.

3. Methods of capital budgeting and techniques to show how to forecast cash flows, discount them over time, and project the profitability of various projects.

4. How firms make investment decisions with respect to the cost of capital, and how these decisions affect the firm's value, its capital structure, and its dividend policy.

5. Financial derivatives, including options, futures, swaps, and how these instruments are used in hedging against risks and potential losses.

6. Financial planning and controlling operations by employing strategies to monitor accounts receivable, accounts payable, and inventories, and to manage cash.

7. Short- and long-term capital, such as leases and convertibles. How interest rates are determined, and methods of financing new issues of stocks and bonds are discussed.

8. Special topics, including mergers, IPOs, and the growing importance of international finance in the firm's decision-making process.

9. Financial software and the Internet as management tools.

NEW FEATURES OF THE SEVENTH EDITION

What has prompted us to revise and publish a new edition (the 7th edition) is the evolution and changes in taxation, as well as the important trends in financial databases and technology—both in academia and industry.

As a result, in this edition we have revised and reported, in chronological order, the tax rates of 2011 and 2016, and the proposed tax rates for 2018. Various numerical examples have been presented. It is important for finance students to see the trend and evolution of the changes in fiscal policy.

In Chapter 3, we have shown the sequential changes and updates from 2011 to 2016 and the recent proposal for 2018. The changes in fiscal policy demonstrate how economic policies (in terms of fiscal policies) evolve over time. It is our prediction that the newly approved tax plan will also be periodically adjusted and new provisions will be added in the forthcoming years. At the time of writing this book, there is already discussion in the media and among policy makers for possible adjustments. For example, in 2018, the maximum deductions for real estate property taxes plus the state and local income taxes cannot exceed $10,000 per couple, which may put the residents of some states in an unexpected situation. Be prepared for a set of future changes, following the publication of this book, in the rates and provisions that are stated in this edition. Fiscal policy is a dynamic act; it gets revised periodically.

In Chapter 20, we wrote a complete new chapter on financial software and databases. It is important for finance students to become familiar with financial technology as financial algorithms and information technology (IT) evolve. At the Zarb School of Business at Hofstra University, we have 34 fully functional Bloomberg Terminals with access to significant sources and databases. One of the authors of this book has been teaching investment courses using widely popular financial databases as partially listed in Chapter 20.

When needed, editorial and further clarifications were also made in other remaining chapters of this seventh edition.

The authors take full responsibility for any errors that may appear in this textbook. Our intent is to keep the explanations as simple as possible, but wherever necessary, coverage is enhanced to facilitate comprehension. The authors wish to thank the anonymous reviewer for his or her constructive feedback and suggestions. We thank our research assistant, Michael Rooney, and acknowledge his diligent contributions to update materials including tax tables and new Internet tools. The contributions of our assistants Rachelle Fabre and Michael Motazedi are highly appreciated. We also express our gratitude to our editor, Bruce B. Morris, for his patience, advice and support, which helped ensure the successful publication of this seventh edition.

Ehsan Nikbakht and A. A. Groppelli

INTRODUCTION

1

WHAT IS FINANCE ALL ABOUT?

KEY TERMS

agency costs costs incurred to resolve conflicts between managers, stockholders, and bondholders

finance the application of a series of financial and economic principles to maximize a firm's wealth and the value of its stock

financial planning projecting cash requirements, setting up guidelines to control costs, establishing future sales and profit targets, deciding the best allocation of scarce funds, and developing alternative strategies in case existing plans do not work out

global firm a firm with asset investments and operations on a worldwide basis

macro factors broad economic and financial developments that impact the sales and profits of the firm

micro decisions internal decisions by a firm that influence the outcome of sales, help control costs, and determine pricing policies

outsourcing a firm decides to invest and produce products abroad (or rely on imports) instead of building plants in the United States to produce these products

risk/return trade-off the required rate of return that justifies making an investment, given a level of risk

wealth maximization contribution to the value of a firm by selecting those investments that have the best risk/return trade-off

Finance is the application of a number of financial and economic principles to maximize the wealth or overall value of a business. More specifically, by employing net present value (time discounted cash flows minus the original costs) to measure profitability, a firm maximizes wealth by investing in projects and acquiring assets whose combined returns yield the highest possible profits at the least risk. No one really knows when maximum wealth is achieved, though it is assumed to be the ultimate goal of every firm. One way of finding out the wealth of a firm is through the price of its common stock. When the price of a firm's shares increases, it is said that the wealth of the firm's shareholders has increased. Why do stock prices reflect a firm's ability to create and increase wealth? Because the stock market is a very efficient mechanism. Therefore, stock prices capture very quickly all available information as well as the outlook for future changes in the wealth of the firm. The market is even more efficient today because investors are better informed and managers use better methods and more effective strategies to telegraph their performance. The proliferation of computers has provided a platform for selecting the best investment alternatives. Of course, the advent of the **Internet** has revolutionized ways to search, gather, and disseminate information upon which sounder business decisions are made.

Today, financial managers have available many sophisticated tools to solve difficult business problems. That was not always the case in the past. Before 1970, the emphasis was on new ways of achieving effective working capital management, improving methods for maintaining financial records, and interpreting balance sheets and income statements. Recent advances in the field of finance have given managers better tools to make sound investment decisions. With the aid of new methods to measure risk and return, corporations can apply more effective ways to achieve optimal allocation of scarce resources. The emergence of financial derivatives markets permit managers to hedge against risk. The ability to simulate strategies allows a firm to select the best projects, which leads to the maximization of the wealth of a firm.

Knowledge of finance should not be limited to treasurers, controllers, and financial planners. In any firm, if the accountants, statisticians, and marketers have an appreciation and understanding of the principles of finance, they will be able to participate more effectively in the decision-making process. Different departments should participate in the final plans made by the finance division.

ADAPTING TO CHANGES

Finance is part science, part art. **Financial analysis** provides a means of making flexible and correct investment decisions at the appropriate and most advantageous time. When financial managers succeed, they help improve the value of the firm's shares.

A manager gives favorable signals to investors by establishing a record of sound financial statements with returns that are growing rapidly and steadily at a minimum level of risk. Why are the right signals so necessary? Because *stockholders (investors) ultimately determine the market value of the firm as reflected in the prices of the securities it issues.* If the firm has a good record, and investors believe that its record will continue, valuation will be high. Conversely, a poor record, with expectations of unfavorable returns and high risk levels, will produce a low valuation.

To be successful, financial managers have to deal with the changes constantly occurring in the field of finance. They must adopt more sophisticated methods so they can plan better in an increasingly competitive climate. They need to deal effectively with constant change inside and outside the company. In short, managers are responsible for recognizing and responding to changing financial environments.

There is a growing need for timing new product introductions correctly, for delivering products and services that meet current and developing needs, and for ensuring that decisions are backed up by alternative plans. Changes in research efforts and production are sometimes called for to ensure that new products meet the challenges of an increasingly competitive marketplace.

BUILDING AN IMAGE

Many times the most successful financial plans do not receive the attention they should get mainly because managers fail to publicize them or "blow their own horns." In the past, this information was conveyed to security analysts who, in turn, advised investors of new developments taking place in a firm. But this approach was too selective and reached only a few investors. Usually, company officials propagated this information through the newspapers, television, and quarterly and annual reports. At best, this information was sporadic and lacked immediacy.

The aim should be to disseminate new information as quickly as possible, reaching a large number of investors. The Internet has and will become an effective vehicle for achieving this goal. The firm should seek to make investments in those fields that investors associate with growth and glamour, and have great profit potential. Unfortunately, many good, financially sound companies are identified with low valuation areas. Good products do not receive the recognition they deserve. The idea would be to direct investors' attention to the most attractive areas of the firm to ensure a better valuation. The firm may want investors to know that it is shifting to more attractive areas of growth and profitability. The firm's responsibility to stockholders is to create the best image possible. Recently, a successful strategy has been to employ "tracking stocks." This strategy consists of issuing new stock to represent that part of the firm's assets that have the best financial outlook. In this way, investors can identify the stock with similar high valuation areas and will give the price of a **tracking stock** the full valuation it deserves.

Managers should give this concept of image building more attention when acquiring new companies, adding new product lines, or giving research new direction. This part of investment strategy, whether it is real or illusory, should be ever present in the minds of managers when they expect to change the investor's perception of the investments' potential of the firm's stock.

• THE MANAGER AS AN AGENT

At one time or another, most people have had occasion to hire agents to take care of a specific matter. In doing so, responsibility is delegated to another person. For example, when suing for damages, individuals may represent themselves or may hire a lawyer to plead their case in court. As an agent, the lawyer is given the assignment to get the highest possible award. And so it is with stockholders when they delegate the task of running a firm to a financial manager who acts as an agent of the company. Obviously, the goal is to achieve the highest value of a share of stock for the firm's owners. But there are no standard rules that indicate which course of action should be followed by managers to achieve this. The ultimate guideline is how investors perceive the actions of managers. A good way to motivate managers is to offer them lucrative stock options linked to performance.

POLICY CONFLICTS

In general, managers should seek to use sound investment policies that minimize **risk**. However, some managers interpret their mission differently. As agents, they envision their role as one of avoiding big mistakes. As a result, these agents may overlook good growth opportunities with acceptable levels of risk. This conflict between agent and stockholders is unlikely to produce the best results.

There is no guarantee that managers, acting as agents, will make the appropriate decisions and take the best course of action. For example, in assessing the risks of different projects against their expected returns, managers may concentrate on only certain investments, failing to diversify the assets of the firm to achieve a lower risk level.

About 10 years ago we witnessed cases of outright fraud, falsification of financial statements, and mismanagement by firms like Enron, Adelphia Communications, and Worldcom. Part of the blame for these failures was the inability of the board of directors to insist on the implementation of acceptable standards of conduct and governance. Fortunately, the majority of executives in the United States are responsible individuals.

Agents are often caught in the middle by trying to satisfy two major factions: the creditors and the stockholders. This consideration is especially important when debt becomes an important source of financing. Creditors impose certain constraints on the firm, such as limiting dividend payments when profits are too low, and otherwise force the managers to maintain the liquidity of the firm at a given level to ensure repayment of loans. In trying to satisfy the claims and restrictions imposed by these creditors, financial managers may have to devote too much attention to creditors and not enough attention to stockholders. This conflict can make managers less efficient and prevent them from taking advantage of the best opportunities.

There are no easy answers to ensure compatibility between agents and their stockholders. It is up to the stockholders—acting through the board of directors—to hire the right managers and to make sure they are properly compensated. This means meeting the market price to attract the right talent. Offering stock to these managers also helps ensure that they will seek to maximize the value of the firm's shares.

In any event, capable managers have the right judgment and instincts to know what policies to implement and when to implement them. They know when to raise funds and how to control assets. Correct decisions are translated into favorable signals to investors, usually resulting in a higher valuation of the firm's common stock.

YOU SHOULD REMEMBER

If there is one problem that enters into the decision-making process, it is the uncertainty and the risk aspects of investments. When a firm makes investment decisions, it automatically attempts to put together (invest in) the best asset mix. This means utilizing the best quality assets in the most efficient way so that they will yield the fastest and least risky returns in the future. In addition, the firm must be concerned with the way it generates internal and external funds, since too much outstanding stock can cause earnings-per-share dilution, and too much debt can increase the financial riskiness and fixed loan commitments of the firm. Proper utilization of these factors, however, can produce a higher valuation for the firm. Consequently, it is important for financial managers to adopt a balanced financing policy so that investors can be assured that their invested funds are well managed and safe.

• RISK VERSUS PROFITS

Profit maximization is a short-term objective and is less important than maximizing the wealth of the firm. A firm can achieve high profits in the short run simply by cutting corners. In other words, managers can delay charging off some expenses, they can defer buying expensive albeit cost-effective equipment, and they can lay off some of their most productive high-salaried workers. These shortsighted decisions can lower costs and raise profits temporarily. Furthermore, high profits may be obtained by investing in highly uncertain and risky projects. In the long run, these chancy projects can weaken the competitive position of a firm and lower the value of its stock. Therefore, attempts to maximize profits may prove inconsistent with the goal to maximize the wealth of the firm, which calls for attaining the highest expected return at the lowest risk level.

In finance, higher risks are generally associated with higher possible gains—but there is also a greater chance of loss. The same principle applies to Aunt Jane or John Doe. Both would like to strike it rich, but they know that to do so they must be willing to face the dangers of heavy losses. Aunt Jane and John Doe are aware that it is safer to purchase a U.S. Treasury bill than to buy pork belly contracts. The chances of incurring losses from owning a treasury bill are slim indeed, while pork belly contracts could mean high gains or large losses.

Managers are faced with a similar dilemma. Some projects may be more profitable than others, but the risk associated with them could be too high and might jeopardize the solvency of the firm. This situation is analogous to gamblers who insist on betting on long-shot horses. Although the payout is great if the long-shot wins, the chances are that these gamblers will be consistent losers. Bettors who play to "show" or put their money on the favorite horse have a better chance of winning, but their gains will be lower. The same applies to the policies adopted by managers. There is a constant conflict between engaging in highly profitable ventures and maintaining a sound financial status. These managerial decisions involve a compromise between taking excessive risks to maximize profits and making investments that will probably result in lower risk and lower profitability—but will lead to a sound financial posture for the firm.

Let's elaborate on these points. Investment decisions involve comparing the future projected returns, generated by investments, with the risk faced by these undertakings. This fundamental decision rests on the well-known **risk/return trade-off** principle, which is shown in Figure 1-1. Basically, the relationship in Figure 1-1 says: A decision to invest in a low-risk project (A) will yield a low return (A'), and a high-risk project (B) should produce a higher return (B') to justify its implementation.

The only way to evaluate the contribution of various investments to the wealth of the firm is to adjust the future returns of each investment for risk. For example, suppose you have two projects, A and B. Both projects generate the same series of future returns, but project A is less risky than project B. Which is the best project and which will increase the wealth of the firm most? Obviously, it is project A.

Therefore, the goal of a manager is to maximize the value of the firm or its stock. This is accomplished by investing in those projects that have the best risk/return trade-off.

THE LONG-RANGE VIEW

Management can, in the short run, gain high profits by buying inferior materials and hiring poorly trained or unskilled workers. This decision may temporarily yield lower costs and lower prices than those charged by competitors. The first results may be higher profits. These shortsighted policies, however, tend to produce long-range problems. Inferior machinery produces more than the usual number of rejects. Machinery breakdowns become more frequent, costs of repairs mount, and fewer products meet quality standards. The outcome is likely to damage the image of the firm, affecting the price of the firm's stock adversely. The better course of action is to incur the added expense of maintaining quality control, thereby reducing the potential risk of unfavorable feedback from investors.

High profits gained at the expense of increased risk generally produce unsatisfactory reactions by stockholders and investors in the long run. Investors generally give more value to earnings generated by a firm with a steady profit record than to the same level of earnings generated by a firm in highly risky investments with a widely fluctuating earnings record.

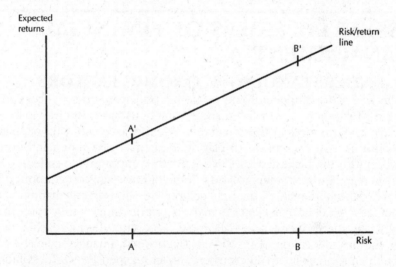

Figure 1-1 Relationship Between Risk and Expected Returns

As a result, the objective of profit maximization may conflict with that of the maximization of wealth. Attempts to increase profits beyond a certain level may mean the taking of greater than necessary risks and may also impair, to some extent, the ability of the firm to maintain solvency. **Wealth maximization** implies a constant concern with risk. This goal may not be achieved if the firm pursues a policy of short-term profit maximization.

There are many tools for accomplishing the maximization of wealth, among them the understanding and application of the principles of economics, accounting, finance, and related disciplines.

YOU SHOULD REMEMBER

The primary goal of a financial manager is to maximize the wealth of stockholders. Maximizing profits is a short-term goal that does not address itself to some key factors, one of which is an acceptable risk level. The goal to maximize wealth may conflict with the aim to optimize profits in the short run, but wealth maximization should always be the primary consideration. When striving for this goal, we should apply the risk/return trade-off principle.

ESSENTIAL SKILLS OF FINANCIAL MANAGEMENT

• UNDERSTANDING ECONOMIC FACTORS

Almost everyone applies some economic principles on one occasion or another. Take the case of a flea market. Most of us have either gone to one or have been vendors at these markets. Whether one is buying or selling, it is obvious that the vendors displaying the items most in demand usually wind up with the biggest sales. Price is another important consideration. If it is too high, few customers will buy. Some of these simple economic principles are useful in making the right sell/buy decisions in any market.

Similarly, financial managers can make better decisions if they apply these basic economic principles. For example, economic theory teaches us to seek the best allocation of resources. To this end, financial managers are given the responsibility to find the best and least expensive sources of funds and to invest these funds into the best and most efficient mix of assets. In doing so, they try to find the mix of available resources that will achieve the highest return at the least risk within the confines of an expected change in the economic climate. Good financial management has a sound grasp of the way economic and financial principles impact the profitability of the firm.

MICROECONOMIC FACTORS

Financial managers do a better job when they understand how to respond effectively to changes in supply, demand, and prices (firm-related **micro factors**), as well as to the more general and overall economic factors (**macro factors**). Learning to deal with these factors provides important tools for effective financial planning.

When making investment decisions, financial managers consider the effects of changing supply, demand, and price conditions on the firm's performance. Understanding the nature of these factors helps managers make the most advantageous operating decisions. Also, managers should determine when it is best to issue stock, bonds, or other financial instruments.

The sale of products at a profit depends heavily on how well managers are able to analyze and interpret supply and demand conditions. Supply considerations relate specifically to the control of production costs, where the key element is to hold costs down so that prices can be set at competitive levels. The best machinery must be bought; and the most productive workers available must be hired. The goal is to squeeze out the biggest possible profit under given supply conditions. Maintaining a low-cost operation will enable the firm to charge competitive prices for its products and maintain its market share while still obtaining a reasonable return.

Knowledge of economic principles can be useful in generating the highest sales possible. Understanding and appropriately responding to changes in demand allows financial managers to take full advantage of market conditions. To accomplish this, the best managers develop and adopt reliable, workable statistical techniques that forecast demand and pinpoint when directional changes in sales take place.

This task, however, is not an easy one. Economic factors cannot be forecast with any degree of accuracy, and many projections are subject to large errors. Good managers, however, can modify forecasts of supply and demand to make them come reasonably close to the actual results. In other words, good financial managers know when to raise and/or lower prices. If demand estimates are high, they institute actions to avoid overproduction and excessive inventories. Therefore, while all managers are faced with forecasting problems, the good ones can deal effectively with difficult situations.

Assuming that demand and prices can be forecast fairly accurately, the next step is to make a decision on the kind of plant and equipment needed to produce goods at the cheapest cost. Obviously, this decision calls for a great deal of judgment regarding the efficiency of different types of equipment and whether or not—or when—this equipment might become outdated. The choice of one machine over another involves considering the risks associated with each machine and how fast it is likely to become obsolete. This risk decision must also consider that future shifts in demand can make a particular machine useless. These are some of the important microeconomic questions which financial managers must answer.

MACROECONOMIC FACTORS

Peoples' decisions are influenced by changing economic conditions. By reading the newspapers and listening, people develop a sense about the economic climate. If it seems to be deteriorating, consumers tend to cut spending and become more conservative in their buying habits. Conversely, when conditions improve, people are likely to loosen their purse strings. These reactions to changing external economic (macro) forces, such as rising or declining business activity and changes in tax laws, influence the decisions made by a firm.

When business is expanding, a firm increases its investment and production. It pulls in its horns when faced by a business contraction. The important thing is to be able to detect when these changes in activity are likely to occur. This is why financial management relies on internal and external models that forecast expected business activity in future months and years. A firm must also develop a flexible strategy to deal with major shifts in demographics, changes in legislation or tax laws, and new technological breakthroughs. It behooves managers to engage in financial planning so that they can be armed with different alternatives under different economic conditions.

Failure—or success—in dealing with macroeconomic problems can have an impact on the price of the firm's shares.

TIMING OF ECONOMIC DECISIONS

Most consumers know that one can get a good buy on a product once the demand for it fades. This kind of timing can pay off handsomely. Christmas greeting cards, for example, sell for half price right after the holidays.

In the same way, the successful manager instinctively knows how to react in a timely fashion to changes in supply, demand, and price conditions. Buying raw materials at low prices can give a cost advantage to a firm. Conversely, if investments are undertaken and demand does not increase as expected, a firm may expand too early, getting stuck with large inventories and an underutilized capacity. The way financial managers time their decisions with respect to changing microeconomic factors can be reflected in higher or lower prices of the company's stock.

Equally valued is the ability to time decisions dealing with changing macroeconomic factors properly. Knowledgeable managers have the judgment to be able to take full advantage of profitable opportunities at reasonable risks when general business activity is expanding. It is important, therefore, for financial managers not only to forecast levels of business and related activities accurately, but also to make sound judgments with respect to expected changes in the direction of related macro and micro factors.

Financial managers must make sure that their decisions to invest or not to invest, to raise capital or not to raise capital, are justified. To do this they must judge the future direction of interest rates, the behavior of stock prices, the expected changes in overall business activity, the anticipated rate of inflation, the status of financial markets, and even the trend of foreign exchange rates. Wrong timing in regard to any of these factors can mean higher costs of generating funds in financial markets. If corporate managers misjudge the business cycle at the peak, they may get stuck with unwanted and costly inventories. A decision to increase capital expenditures and to produce more at the peak of a business cycle could lead to excess inventory once demand contracts. By correctly timing a rise in the rate of inflation, managers can make better judgments about purchasing raw materials at low prices, building inventories, buying equipment at the most advantageous terms, and raising funds at the right time.

Proper timing of these factors also reduces volatility and the uncertainty of future profits.

• IMPORTANCE OF ACCOUNTING

Financial managers rely on accountants to prepare income and balance sheet statements that provide information on the profitability and the financial status of a firm. The Financial Accounting Standards Board's statement number 95 now requires firms to report a current Statement of Cash Flows. This statement provides a detailed analysis of the way cash is generated and traces how cash is utilized in the conduct of all phases of a business. As a result, this statement supplies another important financial tool to managers who seek to control and understand the external factors and internal policies that can influence the cash flows of the firm.

Financial statements help managers to make business decisions involving the best use of cash, the attainment of efficient operations, the optimal allocation of funds among assets, and the effective financing of investment and operations. The interpretation of financial statements is achieved partly by using financial ratios, pro forma statements, sources and uses of funds and cash budgets.

It should be pointed out that the managers of a firm are supplied with more detailed statistical information than appears in published financial statements. These data are especially important in developing cash flow concepts for evaluating the relative merits of different investment projects. This information permits managers to determine incremental cash flows (an approach that looks at the net returns a given project generates in comparison with alternative investments), thus enabling them to make more accurate assessments of the profitabilities of specific investments. It is the responsibility of managers to direct their accountants to prepare internal statements that include this information so that they can make the best investment decisions possible.

YOU SHOULD REMEMBER

Managers should learn how to time and forecast, as accurately as possible, changes in basic micro- and macroeconomic factors. They should make good use of accountants, who supply the financial statements that enable managers to monitor the performance of the firm. In other words, the best managers know how to use all available tools and how to piece together different sources of information to achieve the most effective investment strategies and objectives for the firm.

GLOBALIZATION OF THE FIRM

Most large corporations operate on a global basis and with good reason: investing abroad has proven to be highly profitable. Decisions to build plants and produce goods abroad are also motivated by the lure of low-cost labor and the easy transfer of highly efficient technology that gives competitive price advantages to foreign operations.

As domestic demand reaches maturation, the search for new markets leads corporations to invest and sell abroad. The trend to develop a presence abroad is also motivated by a desire to hedge against risks. Because economic activity diverges from one country to the next, diversification abroad tends to dampen the overall fluctuations of sales and earnings, thus reducing the risk exposure of a corporation. Unfortunately, the advantages of this covariance principle are not as great as they were in the past. Fortunately, the advent of new financial instruments, including financial derivatives, such as futures and swap agreements, provide managers with new tools for hedging and minimizing foreign risks.

The emergence of foreign industrial powers, like Japan, South Korea, and China, has intensified competition while it opens new opportunities for American firms to import lower-priced goods for sale in the domestic market. This not only saves the domestic firm the need to invest in new capacity, but it also allows it to share in the technological advances of that country.

DECISION-MAKING CHALLENGES

Globalization means that managers are faced with new challenges in decision making. What works in the domestic market may not work in foreign countries. Foreign subsidiaries are called on to seek ways to protect asset values by employing hedges and instruments, such as futures, options, and swaps, which may not enter into the domestic equation. More specifically, the managements for foreign subsidiaries and operations should institute policies to protect the value of inventories and account receivables. Safeguarding earnings against exchange rate risk should be a continuous concern. That means constant vigilance and keeping abreast with economic and financial trends as they affect the earnings of a multinational firm.

The question arises whether a foreign subsidiary should pay dividends to the parent company. In the United States, intercorporate dividends are partially exempt from taxation but repatriated dividends are fully taxed. There are also important cost of capital considerations. Sometimes the costs of borrowing in foreign countries is lower than in the United States. Some foreign governments subsidize loans used for direct investment purposes. In addition, the debt of a foreign subsidiary is often guaranteed by the parent company. Therefore, the attitude toward debt financing differs abroad. Because of these protective measures, the debt-to-equity ratio abroad is higher than in the United States. As a result, there is less concern with financial distress and a better chance for taking advantage of financial leverage. Currency depreciation is an ever-present danger and can play havoc with the value of assets. That is why managers must consider selling assets when faced by a probable foreign currency depreciation, and hold back payment of liabilities in this situation.

Expanding abroad requires that managers learn hedging techniques to minimize exchange rate risks. Also, when employing capital budgeting procedures to measure the relative risk/return merits of foreign projects, managers should keep in mind the need to adjust cash flows for changes in exhange rates. Don't forget the role of the Internet, which serves as a useful vehicle for matching buyers and sellers involved in forward contracts and swap agreements.

It is evident that managers of multinational corporations face many more challenges when they consider investing abroad. Although the opportunities are still attractive, more attention must be given to the risk/return trade-off principle when assessing the merits of foreign investments. Globalization of the firm will continue to provide highly profitable opportunities to domestic firms, but this movement requires careful decision making and highly skillful financial management.

YOU SHOULD REMEMBER

Firms expand globally to improve profits, increase their growth potential, and gain from an exchange of technology. Globalization can mean diversification and less risk. There are risks, such as currency devaluations and global crises; however, in the long run, foreign operations can provide lower costs of production and sometimes lower costs of borrowing. The closer link between countries has caused firms to become more sensitive to financial and fiscal crises. That is why managers must not overextend themselves abroad.

Globalization means developing plans to protect assets from deterioration in value, and it means knowing how to hedge against foreign risks by employing futures and swaps. Obviously, managers should make adjustments for differences in discount rates in capital budgeting, and efforts should be made to determine how unequal tax laws, legal rules, and accounting standards can affect performance. It should be recognized that domestic standards involving capital structure, cost of capital, and dividend policies require different treatment abroad than they do domestically. While foreign investments can be attractive, managers should not ignore the new set of risks associated with expanding on a global basis.

IMPLICATIONS OF OUTSOURCING

Outsourcing occurs when domestic firms invest and produce goods in foreign countries or when these firms choose to rely on imports rather than build domestic plants and produce these goods domestically. Low-labor-cost countries, like China, open up new investment opportunities for American corporations. Growing competitive pressures are forcing domestic firms to invest abroad or to import cheap foreign products. These developments have altered the decision-making process.

One major factor responsible for outsourcing is the ease with which technology can be transferred abroad. China and other Asian countries can claim technological parity while enjoying low costs of production. No wonder American companies have a difficult time competing. That is why outsourcing is such an attractive investment option. When evaluating the merits of outsourcing, a corporate manager is forced to make several decisions.

1. Invest and produce domestically or move a plant overseas.

2. Import cheaper foreign goods to take advantage of low labor and other costs or shift to more capital-intensive and technologically advanced operations.

3. Invest abroad in order to gain access to new rapidly growing foreign markets.

Decisions to invest domestically are justified when the firm has a technological advantage or the goods it produces are capital-intensive. However, substituting imports for domestic investments in plant and equipment means that the firm may forfeit the cash flows it would generate from depreciation. In this case a firm must compare the benefits from low-cost imports against the loss of cash flows originating in depreciation charge offs. The firm may also have to weigh the probable benefits derived from internal research efforts as opposed to the benefits obtained from outsourcing. Learning how to work with probability models will help a manager to evaluate the relative merits of outsourcing compared to domestic investments.

Outsourcing relieves managers from having to purchase raw materials or to hedge against the risk that the prices of these raw materials will increase. An outsourcing firm does not have to incur the high costs of pension plans, health benefits, pollution control, and worker safety. Some risks such as technological obsolescence and unforeseen changes in demand become less important with outsourcing. These and other advantages make outsourcing an attractive option.

Let's examine the case of a U.S. manufacturer who has a domestic subsidiary that supplies it with parts. The firm can either upgrade the facilities of the subsidiary, cut costs, and increase productivity, or move the plant overseas. The costs of moving abroad must take into account the cost of abandoning the plant of the subsidiary. Given these choices, what options are available to the firm? One course of action would be to increase research spending for the development of new products and to raise the efficiency of the subsidiary's plant. But even if research efforts are successful, the benefits may be ephemeral because foreign manufacturers are good copiers and tend to ignore patent protection rules. Another alternative is to invest and shift production to new facilities that are highly capital-intensive. The cost of this move may be too high. Staying in the forefront of technology should help the firm to remain competitive. Don't overlook the fact that rapid growth abroad, in the long run, will put upward pressure on the cost structure of other countries, which should help to level the competitive playing field. Meanwhile, given global cost disparities among countries, outsourcing will continue to play an important role in business decision making.

PUBLIC RESPONSIBILITY AND FINANCIAL MANAGEMENT

Finance is a very challenging and rewarding field. It is an exciting area because financial managers are given the responsibility to plan the future growth and direction of a firm—which can greatly affect the community in which it is based. Many of the tools and techniques for solving financial problems are discussed in the following chapters of this book. One must bear in mind, however, that these models and methods provide only a starting point. The decisions reached by a financial manager ultimately represent a blend of theoretical, technical, and judgmental matters that must reflect the concerns of society.

BENEFITS AND OBLIGATIONS TO SOCIETY

All of us grumble occasionally about government regulations, but as good citizens we abide by the law. Voting on election day may take some of our time, but it is a civic duty and right that citizens exercise for the good of society. We go on jury duty even though it takes us away from more productive business endeavors, because we know this is a necessary function if our legal system is to work.

Business firms are faced by similar obligations to society. Though they search for ways to be profitable and achieve the highest wealth, financial managers must accept certain compromises that may impede them from obtaining the highest wealth possible. For example, a firm may be prevented from selecting certain production methods because the government says they cause too much pollution. In other words, firms have obligations to society that can interfere with their profit motives. Social, moral, environmental, and ethical considerations are part of the investment decision process and cannot be ignored by financial planners.

The burdens of these costs fall unevenly on different firms. Some firms, especially large corporations, have more resources to deal with these problems. And it seems logical to assume that the most profitable and financially strong corporations should incur a greater share of these social costs. Pollution abatement, enforcement of safety standards, and improved sanitary conditions can reduce employee absences and raise labor productivity. Therefore, a firm can deal with social and legal constraints satisfactorily without critically impairing its ability to maximize the price of its stock.

BENEFITS AND OBLIGATIONS TO THE FIRM

Within this framework, financial managers have certain obligations to those who entrust them with the running of the firm. They must have a clear sense of ethics and must avoid payoffs or other forms of personal gain. Managers should not engage in practices that can damage the image of the firm, but should participate as much as possible in social activities to demonstrate that they are cognizant of the importance of the community and those who buy their products or services. Financial managers should also ensure that all environmental and legal standards necessary to ensure the health and safety of the community and of the workers are met.

The gender issue should also be a concern of the corporation. This calls for setting up guidelines on the treatment of women and how to avoid sexual harassment. Although it is a known fact that many women are paid less than men for doing the same jobs, there is little justification for this differential treatment. A firm has the responsibility to address the gender issue and strive to remedy inequities of this kind.

More specifically, if financial managers work in a vacuum and are concerned only with monetary gains, they may overlook other equally important aspects necessary for maintaining a high public opinion of their firms. By allocating funds for the social betterment of employees and the community, managers will attract customers and a more stable shareholder following. Obviously, the costs of social programs must be tempered by the financial ability of the firm to engage in these less-profitable endeavors. Certain socially desirable policies—hiring minorities, providing for worker safety, and refusing to invest in specific profitable ventures because they fail to meet democratic principles—should be part of the financial decision process. Although there may be a conflict between promoting socially responsible programs and the profit motive, maintaining some concern for social needs when pursuing the goal of maximizing the wealth of the firm is a prime responsibility of a firm.

YOU SHOULD REMEMBER

Financial managers must reconcile social and environmental requirements with profit-making motives. Adherence to social values may not produce the most efficient use of assets or the lowest costs, but it will enhance the image of the firm. Looking after the interests of minorities, setting up training facilities, caring for the safety and the welfare of workers, and dealing effectively with gender issues can produce long-term benefits in the form of higher productivity and more harmonious relationships between labor and management.

GOALS OF FINANCIAL PLANNING

A good manager knows how to use the factors just discussed in arriving at final decisions. Financial managers are charged with the primary responsibility of maximizing the price of the firm's shares while holding risk at the lowest level possible. In order to achieve these goals, a manager must determine which investments will provide the highest profits at least risk. Once this decision is reached, the next step involves the selection of optimal ways to finance these investments.

Planning to achieve the best results should be flexible, allowing for alternative strategies to replace existing plans should financial and economic developments diverge from an expected pattern. Furthermore, **financial planning** involves proper timing of investments in order to avoid over-expansion and inefficient use of resources. Optimal use of available funds means exploring different options and selecting those that provide the greatest overall value. It also means adopting effective ways of determining how much to borrow in order to reduce financing risks. The financing used to raise funds should include safety features that will allow managers to refinance when market conditions become favorable.

After a financial decision has been made, there must be constant vigilance and monitoring of developments. If the original plan falls short of expectations, early recognition and remedial action become necessary. Those who delay in taking appropriate action pay the price for poor management. This price is exacted by the market (and the investment community), which in the aggregate represents a highly efficient judge of performance. Poor or inflexible managers are accountable to competitive forces and to the marketplace, where valuation becomes the ultimate determinant of successful or unsuccessful financial management.

That is why it is important to keep abreast of new advances in the modern theory of finance as well as of developments taking place in the financial markets. Finance has emerged as an important discipline that requires constant updating of old and refining of new concepts. The latest advances in valuation methods can help to make better decisions. The emergence of new financial instruments, such as financial futures, options, and other contingency liability claims, provides managers with more sophisticated and effective methods for evaluating and, when necessary, altering financial decisions.

KNOW THE CONCEPTS

DO YOU KNOW THE BASICS?

1. What do financial managers try to maximize, and what is their second objective?

2. In trying to achieve optimum profits, what may a firm ignore?

3. State the kinds of assurances that investors and creditors seek from a firm.

4. What environmental considerations prevent the firm from achieving the best results in terms of cost control and profitability? Explain what this means.

5. What are some of the micro- and macroeconomic factors that influence the decisions of a firm?

6. What kinds of conflicts confront the financial manager as an agent of the firm? How can a firm attract the best managers?

7. What three accounting statements help the manager monitor a firm's performance? What can the balance sheet tell the firm about its assets and financial structure?

8. In what way can statistics be used to help managers succeed?

9. What are some of the nonfinancial aspects of the manager's role in society, such as responsibility toward workers, treatment of minorities, and dealing with gender problems?

10. What happens when the firm issues either too much debt or too much common stock?

11. Does knowledge of financial theory and statistical approaches give a manager all the answers in solving financial problems? Explain.

12. Besides maximizing the wealth of the firm, what are some of the other goals of financial management?

13. Why do firms seek global exposure?

14. What kinds of different decisions are faced by a global firm?

15. What are some of the advantages of outsourcing? What are some of the problems it creates for the firm?

TERMS FOR STUDY

agency costs	micro factors
finance	outsourcing
financial analysis	risk
financial planning	risk/return trade-off
global firm	tracking stock
Internet	wealth maximization
macro factors	

ANSWERS

KNOW THE CONCEPTS

1. The primary objective of financial managers is to maximize the wealth of the firm or the price of the firm's stock. A secondary objective is to maximize earnings per share.

2. In striving for optimum profits, a firm may overlook risk. In other words, investment decisions based on high profits can cause profits to disappear or fluctuate excessively; this could lead to insolvency, a great deal of uncertainty, and a decline in the price of the firm's stock.

3. Investors are looking for the highest returns at the lowest risk. Creditors want to be assured that the firm maintains a sound financial structure and that its policies ensure payment of interest and repayment of principal. Creditors don't want the firm to take unnecessary chances, which could lead to insolvency.

4. Firms must try to minimize such environmental hazards as air and water pollution. By buying pollution equipment, a firm allocates funds to unproductive and unprofitable equipment. In doing so, it cannot achieve the highest financial returns but it will enhance its image.

5. Firm-related micro factors are mainly supply, demand, and prices. Macro factors are external in nature and include the business cycle, the rate of inflation, trends in the financial field, and changes in foreign exchange rates. Correct timing and forecasting of these macro factors are essential.

6. By acting as agents, managers may adopt conservative approaches to avoid making big mistakes. They may be forced to reconcile the different aims of stockholders and creditors. In trying to meet the constraints imposed on the firm by creditors, agents may not be able to devote enough time and effort to achieve maximization of the firm's wealth. Agents may not be willing to assume the added risks of certain projects even though such investments may more than adequately compensate the firm for the risks incurred.

  The best managers can be attracted to the firm in two ways: first, by offering them attractive compensation and, second, by giving them options to buy stock in the firm as an incentive to make decisions that will raise the market value of shares.

7. The income statement, the balance sheet, and the statement of cash flows. The balance sheet tells the firm how it is allocating its funds to various assets and how the firm generates funds from internal and external sources. The income statement is concerned with sales, costs, and profits. The statement of cash flows traces cash inflows and outflows for operating, investing, and financing purposes.

8. Statistics provide the tools for comparing the financial status of the firm with that of other companies and of its own industry. Statistical techniques are invaluable for projecting the returns and relative risks of different investments. They can be used to simulate the outcome of investments, given different assumptions. Statistics can help managers to monitor operations and to time borrowings, purchases of goods, and capacity expansion.

9. Financial managers must be ethical and seek to interact with the community. They must conform to environmental, legal, health, and safety standards. In this connection, they should avoid investments in ventures that transgress democratic principles and should seek to hire minorities. In other words, a balance should be struck between attempts to maximize wealth and the attainment of social betterment. A firm should also establish rules to prevent sexual harassment and to eliminate salary differentials based on gender or race.

10. Risk increases and the firm fails to take full advantage of the various sources of funds. In this case, the cost of issuing debt or stock will eventually increase.

11. Financial theory is a starting point. It merely provides some tools which cannot substitute for experience and judgment. However, despite its limitations, theory helps to explain the financial process and shows how to avoid pitfalls in making investment decisions.

12. Besides having the responsibility of maximizing the price of a company's shares at the least risk possible, a manager must adopt flexible financing methods in order to control costs. Furthermore, when implementing a plan, constant monitoring is required, and when the plan fails to achieve the desired goal, a new strategy should be adopted.

13. Firms seek global exposure because they wish to increase growth, diversify risk, gain from new technology exchanges, lower costs of labor, and benefit from cheap imports. However, they must be aware of certain risks such as exchange rate devaluations, expropriations, and the potential losses in the value of assets.

14. Managers have to be aware of the different tax laws and legal aspects in foreign countries. They should take advantage of lower interest rates when borrowing abroad. It is also important to consider differences in discount rates between domestic and foreign projects involving similar projects. Strategies should be adopted to protect against losses in current assets and liabilities. The interpretation of the D/E ratio can differ significantly in various countries calling for a different attitude toward debt risk and insolvency. Managers must learn to employ financial derivatives as hedges against currency rate changes. Among the most popular derivatives are futures and swaps. Also, because managers face an exchange rate risk, they have to adjust the projected cash flows of a

foreign project for expected changes in currency values and they must adopt strategies to protect the values of working capital assets.

Repatriation of earnings is not simple because of losses that a firm can incur in currency translations. Furthermore, managers cannot employ the same standards of accounting. They should be cognizant of the differences in capital structure interpretations because abroad, high D/E ratios are more acceptable than in the domestic market. Although there are many benefits in globalizing, a prudent policy is advised to avoid overexposure in weak currency countries.

15. By outsourcing a firm can avoid technological obsolescence. The firm does not have to incur the costs of pollution control and worker safety. If the existing capacity mix fails to match changing demand, outsourcing can fill the deficiency gap. Above all, the firm benefits from low labor and other costs. In contrast, the firm is faced with new risks such as adverse changes in exchange rates. Loss of depreciation cash flows is a real possibility. Foreign investments may be subject to expropriation.

2
BUSINESS TYPES AND TAXATION METHODS

KEY TERMS

accelerated depreciation a method of depreciation whereby more of the asset base is depreciated in the earlier years

active income income generated from a trade or business in which an investor actively and materially participates, unlike *passive income*, which is generated from a trade or business in which the taxpayer "does not materially participate."

capital gain profit from the resale of an asset (selling price minus book value)

capital asset a real and tangible asset such as real estate or machinery

cash flow a measure of a company's liquidity, consisting of net income plus noncash expenditures (such as depreciation charges)

financial asset assets that are not real on their own; for example, bonds, stocks, certificates of deposit

inflation-adjusted tax brackets annual income tax brackets that increase by an assumed rate of inflation. The ratio was 1.7% from 1998–1999

marginal tax rate a rate a taxpayer pays on his or her last unit of income

Modified Accelerated Cost Recovery System (MACRS) a depreciation method in which assets are classified according to their specifications and to the number of years over which they can be depreciated

S corporation small business with a corporate form but in which all profits (and losses) are passed through to the shareholders, as in a partnership

triple tax a situation where taxes are paid three times: income tax on corporate income, tax on stockholders' dividends, and tax on dividend income of the firm from its outside investment

BUSINESS ORGANIZATIONS FOR OPERATIONS AND TAX PURPOSES

Business organizations in the United States can be classified into three main types with different implications in terms of liabilities and tax treatment: **proprietorships**, **partnerships**, **and corporations**. The general characteristics of each type of organization are explained in this section.

PROPRIETORSHIP

A **proprietorship** is the oldest form of organization for a business owned by only one individual. Anyone with money can buy basic working tools and start a proprietorship to produce goods or offer services thought to be marketable.

A main advantage of a proprietorship is its easy formation process. The formation of a proprietorship doesn't require the approval of any regulatory agency. Once the working conditions of the business are present, the sole proprietorship is in existence. (The only exception is that certain professions require a license in order to practice.) Another advantage is the straightforward taxation method used for proprietorships: The proprietor's income is simply included on the owner's individual tax return each year.

A main disadvantage of this form of organization is that the owner is responsible for the entire liability of the proprietorship. Since the owner has unlimited liability, personal properties that are not used in the business may be lost to creditors.

Another disadvantage is that a proprietorship can't use organized capital markets—such as stock and bond markets—to raise needed capital. A proprietorship therefore has limited opportunities for growth because its capital can be expanded only so far. **Capital**, in the form of either debt or equity, is the means to buy assets and expand a company. Since a proprietorship cannot raise equity capital by outside means, it cannot enjoy the benefits of continuous growth.

Although more than 80% of the businesses in the United States are proprietorships, they represent only 10% of the total sales in the marketplace! The reason? *Proprietorships are small business with limited means to finance operations and limited resources to compete and survive in the market.*

PARTNERSHIP

A **partnership** is a form of business organization in which two or more individuals are the owners. A partnership can be viewed as a proprietorship with more than one owner.

There are two kinds of partners: general partners and limited partners. General partners have unlimited liability in running a business, but limited partners are liable only up to the amount of their investments or for a specified amount of money. In a **general partnership**, all partners have unlimited liability. In a **limited partnership**, there is at least one limited partner in the business.

Business publications such as the *Wall Street Journal* often contain advertisements for limited partners in real estate businesses. In such a case, an individual typically invests a certain amount of money in a partnership for the purpose of building a shopping center, buying or leasing a rental property, or purchasing land. The profits of the partnership are divided among the limited and general partners according to predetermined ratios. Since the risk of a limited partner is confided to the loss of the investment, his or her portion of the total profit is usually less than that of a general partner. In order to bring more capital to some undertakings, particularly lucrative real estate ventures, existing general partners may sometimes offer nearly equal shares of profits to new limited partners.

CORPORATION

The third form of organization is the **corporation**, which, in terms of dollars, dominates today's business world. A corporation can be formed by a person or a group of persons. The "personality" of the corporation, under the law, is totally separate from its owners. Precisely speaking, a corporation, is a "legal entity"; therefore, the corporation, rather than the owners, is responsible for paying all debts.

Because of the legal status of a corporation, the owners have limited liability and can't lose more than their invested money. Unlike a proprietor, the owners of a corporation do not have to withdraw from their personal savings or sell their personal belongings to satisfy creditors if the corporation goes bankrupt. An owner of a corporation is called a stockholder or shareholder.

The purpose of a corporation is to increase the wealth of stockholders, who elect a board of directors from among themselves and from people outside the corporation to set general guidelines for the corporation. If the corporation is relatively large, the board hires managers to work as agents of the stockholders. Managers have a responsibility to set long-range corporate strategy, which specifies the objectives that the corporation must achieve in the future. Managers have other responsibilities, including hiring employees, purchasing assets, borrowing money, issuing stock, controlling the work of other employees, and reporting the status of the corporation to the board of directors and stockholders on a periodic basis. Figure 2-1 illustrates the basic organization of a corporation.

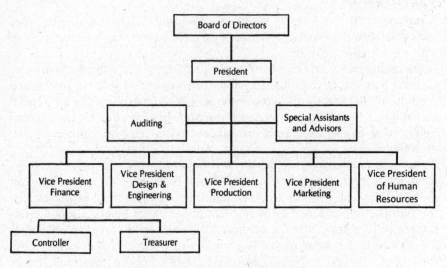

Figure 2-1 A Typical Corporate Organization

YOU SHOULD REMEMBER

The three major forms of business organizations are proprietorships, partnerships, and corporations. An owner of a proprietorship or a general partnership has unlimited liability, but the liabilities of shareholders in a limited partnership or a corporation do not exceed the value of their investments. Unlike a proprietorship or a partnership, a business corporation is a "legal entity" separate from its owners.

Proprietorships and partnerships are small firms with very limited ways to raise capital and to expand operations. While more than 80% of U.S. business firms are either proprietorships or partnerships, they have a market share of only 10% of the national economy.

BASICS OF TAXATION

The U.S. tax law has been revised many times in the last 20 years. The current tax system is the outcome of many revisions including the Economic Recovery Act of 1981, the Tax Equity and Fiscal Responsibility Act of 1982, the Tax Reform Act of 1984, the Tax Reform Act of 1986, the Omnibus Budget Reconciliation Act of 1993, and the Tax Reform Act of 1996. A number of other revisions and amendments after the year 2000 have affected the existing tax laws with different economic reasons behind each amendment. A basic knowledge of taxation is needed for a financial analyst to measure the impact of tax rates on financial decisions. Without a good understanding of taxation, we may not be able to arrive at correct decisions in evaluating non-mutually exclusive projects, deciding on leasing versus buying, determining dividend policy, identifying alternative sources of financing, and analyzing other cases related to finance and investment. In the following sections, we will introduce the basic concepts of taxation and illustrate how the existing tax law works in the case of individuals and corporations.

- ## *EVOLUTION AND EXAMPLES OF FEDERAL INCOME TAX FOR INDIVIDUALS: 2011, 2016, AND 2018 (NEW PLAN)*

Prior to the Tax Reform Act of 1986, individuals were taxed at 15 progressive tax rates from 11% to 50%. In 1986 the tax structure was reduced to two basic brackets, 15% and 28% with an intermittent rate of 33% for a certain mid-level income. For example, a single return taxpayer would pay 33% on the income between $17,851 and $43,150; beyond that level a lower rate of 28% would be in effect. Because of the intermittent rate of 33%, the previous tax systems were called **progressive-and-regressive** in the sense that mid-level incomes were taxed at the highest rate of 33%. The progressive-regressive aspect of the tax system turned into a **progressive system** (higher rates for higher income) in 1993 following a series of amendments based on the Omnibus Budget Reconciliation Act of 1993.

Since 1993 a number of changes in tax law have affected the tax brackets on different individual taxpayers. In the area of federal income taxation, following is a list of the major tax components (tax variables) that often divide policymakers' views on how individuals should be taxed; therefore, the tax variables change from one year to another.

- **Inflation-adjusted tax brackets.** These adjustments revise the low and high boundaries of different tax brackets. See Table 2-1 to compare how tax brackets have changed between 2010 and 2011.
- **Basic standard deductions.** The basic standard deduction amounts for 2011 are as follows:
  - Head of Household—$8,500
  - Married taxpayers filing jointly and qualifying widow(er)s—$11,600
  - Married taxpayers filing separately—$5,800
  - Single—$5,800

The standard deduction amount for an individual who may be claimed as a dependent by another taxpayer may not exceed the greater of $950 or the sum of $300 and the individual's earned income.

- **Personal exemptions.** The amount one can deduct for each exemption has increased by $50 from $3,650 in 2010 to $3,700 in 2011. One begins to lose all or part of the benefit of exemptions if the adjusted gross income is above a certain amount. The amount at which the phaseout depends on the taxpayer's filing status. For 2011, the phaseout begins at:
- $127,175 for married persons filing separately
- $169,550 for single individuals
- $211,950 for heads of households
- $254,350 for married persons filing jointly or qualifying widow(er)s

Other areas of taxation that are constantly under debate and revisions are filing requirements, types and limits of deductibles, tax shelters (including different forms of investment retirement accounts), depreciation tables, definition of capital gains, the tax rate of capital gains, and self-employment taxes.

Table 2-1 (on pages 31–32) illustrates the tax rates for four possible individual tax situations: single, married filing jointly, head of household, and married filing separately as of 2011. The current individual tax rates are 10%, 15%, 25%, 28%, 33%, and 35%.

DO NOT CONFUSE MARGINAL TAX RATE AND AVERAGE TAX RATE

The distinction between marginal and average tax rates is important in financial decision making. Suppose you are a single taxpayer and report $60,000 as taxable income. You pay 15% on the first $34,500 and 25% on the remaining income. In this case, your **marginal tax rate** (the highest rate you pay on additional income) is 25%. To calculate the average tax rate precisely, let's see how much tax you owe on the entire income (refer to Table 2-1):

$$25\% \times (\$60,000 - \$34,500) = \$6,375$$
$$\text{Total taxes} = \$4,750 + \$6,375 = \$11,125$$
$$\text{Average tax rate} = \$11,125/\$60,000 = 0.1854 \text{ or } 18.54\%$$

As you see, the average tax rate is the percentage of total taxes paid on total taxable income. The marginal tax rate is the only relevant tax rate in financial decision making. Suppose Bob and Betty are married; they file their tax forms separately, and each earns a taxable income of $125,000. Looking at Table 2-1, the marginal tax rate for each spouse is 33%. In other words, for every $100 worth of extra income, each pays $33 income taxes excluding state and other taxes.

Table 2–1 Comparing Marginal Tax Rates on Individual Taxable Income

2011 Tax Rate Schedule				
Single				
Taxable income is over	But not over	The tax is	Plus	Of the amount over
$0	$8,500	$0.00	10%	$0
8,550	34,500	850.00	15%	8,500
34,500	83,600	4,750.00	25%	34,500
83,600	174,400	17,025.00	28%	83,600
174,800	379,150	42,449.00	33%	174,400
379,150		110,016.50	35%	379,150
Married Filing Jointly Qualifying Widow(er)				
Taxable income is over	But not over	The tax is	Plus	Of the amount over
$0	$17,000	$0.00	10%	$0
17,000	69,000	1,700.00	15%	17,000
69,000	139,350	9,500.00	25%	69,000
139,350	212,300	27,087.50	28%	139,350
212,300	379,150	47,513.00	33%	212,300
379,150		102,574.00	35%	379,150
Head of Household				
Taxable income is over	But not over	The tax is	Plus	Of the amount over
$0	12,150	$0.00	10%	$0
12,150	46,250	1,215.00	15%	12,150
46,250	119,400	6,330.00	25%	46,250
119,400	193,350	24,617.50	28%	119,400
193,350	379,150	45,323.50	33%	193,350
379,150		106,637.50	35%	379,150
Married Filing Separately				
Taxable income is over	But not over	The tax is	Plus	Of the amount over
$0	$8,500	$0.00	10%	$0
8,500	34,500	850.00	15%	8,500
34,500	69,675	4,750.00	25%	34,500
69,675	106,150	13,543.75	28%	69,675
106,150	189,575	23,756.75	33%	106,150
189,575		51,287.00	35%	189,575

2011 Tax Rate Schedule

Single

Taxable income is over	But not over	The tax is	Plus	Of the amount over
$0	$8,375	$0.00	10%	$0
8,375	34,000	837.50	15%	8,375
34,000	82,400	4,681.25	25%	34,000
82,400	171,850	16,781.25	28%	82,400
171,850	373,650	41,827.25	33%	171,850
373,650		108,421.25	35%	373,650

Married Filing Jointly
Qualifying Widow(er)

Taxable income is over	But not over	The tax is	Plus	Of the amount over
$0	$16,750	$0.00	10%	$0
16,750	68,000	1,675.00	15%	16,750
68,000	137,300	9,362.50	25%	68,000
137,300	209,250	26,687.50	28%	137,300
209,250	373,650	46,833.50	33%	209,250
373,650		101,085.50	35%	373,650

Head of Household

Taxable income is over	But not over	The tax is	Plus	Of the amount over
$0	$11,950	$0.00	10%	$0
11,950	45,550	1,195.00	15%	11,950
45,550	117,650	6,235.00	25%	45,550
117,650	190,550	24,260.00	28%	117,650
190,550	373,650	44,672.00	33%	190,550
373,650		105,095.00	35%	373,650

Married Filing Separately

Taxable income is over	But not over	The tax is	Plus	Of the amount over
$0	$8,500	$0.00	10%	$0
8,375	34,000	837.50	15%	8,375
34,000	68,650	4,861.25	25%	34,000
68,650	104,625	13,343.75	28%	68,650
104,625	186,825	23,416.75	33%	104,625
186,825		50,542.75	35%	186,825

What are the implications of the marginal tax rate? Bob and Betty may argue that with a federal tax rate of almost 33%, and assuming 10% state taxes, they have to pay nearly half of their new earnings (43%) to the federal and state governments. This 43% rate (federal plus state) ignores other possible deductions. Therefore, Bob and Betty may reconsider any offers that may bring them additional income. This is true because in a progressive taxable income system, *the higher the marginal tax rate, the less will remain as a disposable income to the person.* One way in which you can reduce the negative impact of a higher marginal tax rate is through tax planning for more legitimate and substantiated tax deductions so that a person can lower his or her average tax rate. The following schematic shows an interaction of the income level, marginal tax rate, legitimate deductions, and the average tax rate:

Higher income → Higher marginal tax rate → More legitimate deductions needed → Lower average tax rate

Tax deductions and their impact on the average tax rate are discussed later in this chapter.

EXAMPLE TO COMPUTE TAXABLE INCOME

To arrive at taxable income, we must go through three steps. First we need to determine the total income. Total income includes all kinds of income minus certain exclusions such as interest from tax-exempt securities and some Social Security benefits. Second, the total income should be reduced by certain adjustments such as IRA deductions (if eligible), contributions to other acceptable retirement plans, alimony payments, and penalties in early withdrawals of savings. The balance is called the **adjusted gross income**. Third, subtract the standard deductions or the itemized deductions (whichever is higher) and the total exemptions from the adjusted gross income; the remaining figure is taxable income on which we must pay taxes.

Example: Determining the Amount of Taxable Income

PROBLEM   Alice and Larry have a total income of $60,000. They have made a $5,000 contribution to an acceptable self-employed retirement plant and have also paid a $500 penalty on an early withdrawal of a certificate of deposit from their bank. Including their children, they are entitled to four personal exemptions (assuming $3,700). Their total itemized deductions are $12,000. What is the taxable income of Alice and Larry?

SOLUTION   Adjusted gross income = Total income – Adjustments

$$= \$60,000 - 5,000 - 500$$
$$= \$54,500$$

Taxable Income = Adjusted gross income – Deductions – Exemptions

$$= 54,500 - 12,000 - (3,700 \times 4)$$
$$= \$27,700$$

In this example, Alice and Larry will pay taxes on $29,000.

STANDARD DEDUCTIONS VERSUS ITEMIZED DEDUCTIONS

Once the adjusted gross income is computed, a taxpayer has the choice of taking a fixed amount of deductions as stated by law or reporting a detailed itemized list of deductions. As a rational person, the taxpayer should compute and compare both amounts and claim the higher amount. The itemized deductions, subject to limits, include medical and dental expenses, state and local income taxes, real estate taxes, home mortgage interest, some other interest expenses, gifts to charity, casualty and theft losses, job-related expenses, and a broad category of miscellaneous expenses.

Itemized deductions have been severely limited. For instance, medical expenses that are not reimbursed by insurance companies may be deductible to the extent that they exceed 7.5% of the adjusted gross income. For instance, a taxpayer with an adjusted gross income of $60,000 is not entitled to any medical deduction before he or she pays $4,500 of medical expenses ($60,000 × 0.075). If total expenses are $6,000, deductions would be $1,500 ($6,000 – $4,500); assuming a marginal tax rate of 25%, the tax benefit of this deduction is only $375 ($1,500 × 0.25). Stated differently, a tax payer in a 28% tax bracket, with an adjusted gross income of $60,000 who pays $4,500 for medical expenses, receives only $375 in the form of a tax benefit. Interest expenses, except interest expenses on home mortgage, are nondeductible. An exception to this rule is the interest on one's principal residence or a second residence; the deduction however is limited to the interest on a mortgage no greater than the home's purchase price plus the cost of home improvement. If the extra debt on the principal or second residence is used for educational or medical purposes, interest expenses may also be considered deductible.

CAPITAL GAINS AND LOSSES

By definition, if a capital asset is sold above its book value, a **capital gain** is realized; if the asset is sold for less than the book value, there is a capital loss. A **capital asset** could be a real asset, such as real estate, or a **financial asset**, such as stocks and bonds. One of the most controversial provisions of the Tax Reform Act of 1986 was the elimination of the long-term capital gain deduction. Under previous tax law, a capital gain of $1,000 on an asset that an investor had owned for 6 months or longer was exempt by 60%. Because that maximum tax bracket in the previous system was 50%, the most an individual had to pay on long-term capital gains was only 20% (0.50 × (1 – 0.60)). In the existing system, there is no capital gains deduction; therefore, capital gains and ordinary income (wages, salaries, rent, etc.) are taxed at the same rates. The maximum tax rate on capital gains is 28%. The highest tax rate on a net capital gain is generally 15%. There are three exceptions:

1. The taxable part of a gain from qualified small business stock is taxed at a maximum 28% rate.

2. Net capital gain from selling collectibles such as coins or art is taxed at a maximum 28% rate.

3. The part of any net capital gains from selling Section 1250 real property that is due to depreciation is taxed at a maximum 25% rate.

PASSIVE INCOME VERSUS ACTIVE INCOME

The current tax law makes a distinction between **passive income** and **active income**. What is the difference between the two? Passive income is generated from a trade or business in which the taxpayer "does not materially participate." With certain exceptions, investments in rental properties and limited partnerships are defined as passive. Investments in which a taxpayer is continuously and rigorously involved are called active. Why does this distinction matter? The answer is that a taxpayer cannot deduct a passive loss from his or her salary, portfolio income, or business income. Passive losses are deducible to the extent that there is a new income from passive activities. A dollar loss from one limited partnership can be deducted from a dollar net income of another passive investment. If there is no income from any other passive investment, either passive losses should be carried forward to a future year or their deductible expenses should be itemized, although itemized deductions are severely limited in the current tax law. The capital gain provision does not exist, and the maximum capital gain rate is 28%. Passive losses cannot be deducted from ordinary and portfolio income. The only exception is for people who, on a small scale, actively engage in owning and managing a real estate property. A maximum deductible loss in this case is $25,000, and it is proportionally phased out for people with income between $100,000 and $150,000 annually.

The tax rates changed in 2016. Below are the major changes that were approved in 2016. The personal income taxes for 2017, as of writing this revised edition, will be based on the following rates:

Basic Standard Deductions for 2017	
Head of Households	$9,300
Single	$6,300
Married, Filing Separately	$6,300
Married, Filing Jointly	$12,600
Qualifying Widow(er)	$12,600

Tax Rate Schedule to Apply for 2017				
Single				
Taxable Income is over	But not over	The tax is	Plus	Of the amount over
$0	$9,275	$0	10%	$0
$9,275	$37,650	$927.50	15%	$9,275
$37,650	$91,150	$5,183.75	25%	$37,650
$91,150	$190,150	$18,558.75	28%	$91,150
$190,150	$413,350	$46,278.75	33%	$190,150
$413,350	$415,050	$119,934.50	35%	$413,350
$415,050		$120,539.75	39.6%	$415,050
Married Filing Jointly OR Qualifying Widow(er)				
Taxable Income is over	But not over	The tax is	Plus	Of the amount over
$0	$18,550	$0	10%	$0
$18,550	$75,300	$1,855.00	15%	$18,550
$75,300	$151,900	$10,367.50	25%	$75,300
$151,900	$231,450	$29,517.50	28%	$151,900
$231,450	$413,350	$51,791.50	33%	$231,450
$413,350	$466,950	$111,818.50	35%	$413,350
$466,950		$130,578.50	39.6%	$466,950
Married Filing Separately				
Taxable Income is over	But not over	The tax is	Plus	Of the amount over
$0	$9,275	$0	10%	$0
$9,275	$37,650	$927.50	15%	$9,275
$37,650	$75,390	$5,183.75	25%	$37,650
$75,390	$115,725	$14,758.75	28%	$75,390
$115,725	$206,675	$25,895.75	33%	$115,725
$206,675	$233,475	$55,909.25	35%	$206,675
$233,475		$65,289.25	39.6%	$233,475

Head of Household				
Taxable Income is over	But not over	The tax is	Plus	Of the amount over
$0	$13,250	$0	10%	$0
$13,250	$50,400	$1,325.00	15%	$13,250
$50,400	$130,150	$6,897.50	25%	$50,400
$130,150	$210,800	$26,835.00	28%	$130,150
$210,800	$413,350	$49,417.00	33%	$210,800
$413,350	$441,000	$116,258.50	35%	$413,350
$441,000		$125,936.00	39.6%	$441,000

PROPOSED TAX PLAN FOR 2018

At the time of writing this chapter, Congress was in the process of drafting a major tax reform. Backed by President Trump, the proposed tax bill would cut the corporate tax rate from 35% to 20%. In December 2017, it was approved at 21%. The belief is that this tax cut will lead to an increase in domestic investment, investment corporations bringing revenues from foreign countries back to the United States, as will the allowance of the repatriation of profits earned overseas at a lower tax rate. According to the Joint Committee on Taxation, the proposed tax cut creates a $1.4 trillion extra in tax revenues. Republicans believe the tax cuts will pay for themselves through a revitalized economy and are targeting 3% growth in GDP per year for the next decade; however, most economists believe this to be unrealistic. President Trump's plan also lowers the minimum tax rate for small businesses to 25%, which includes sole proprietorships, partnerships, and S corporations. Another aspect that could be beneficial to businesses is the immediate write-off of depreciated assets, instead of a long-term depreciable schedule.

Proposed tax reform is also expected to simplify the personal tax bracket from the existing seven brackets to just three: 10%, 25%, and 35%. There is a possibility of the addition of a fourth tax bracket, for "high-income earners," of 39.6% on income above $1,000,000. The bill further proposes the elimination of the alternative minimum tax, which was discussed at length earlier in the chapter. The proposed plan seeks to double the standard deduction while eliminating personal exemptions. Itemized deductions may also be eliminated, except for those on mortgage interest, charitable contributions, and retirement savings. Most theorize that, through these cuts and elimination of itemized deductions, the tax rate for most tax payers will increase slightly, especially if a taxpayer has a large amount of itemized deductions.

Furthermore, Trump proposes to eliminate the estate tax, which currently contributes approximately $17 billion.

A Final Tax Schedule approved in December 2017, effective in the year 2018 and thereafter

As reported in the IRS documents, below is a final tax schedule for single and joint filings for 2018, as approved by Congress:

Tax Rate	Income Brackets (Individuals)	Income Brackets (Joint)
10%	$0–$9,525	$0–$19,050
12%	$9,526–$38,700	$19,051–$77,400
22%	$38,701–$82,500	$77,401–$165,000
24%	$82,501–$157,500	$165,001–$315,000
32%	$157,501–$200,000	$315,001–$400,000
35%	$200,001–$500,000	$400,001–$600,000
37%	$500,001 and Up	$600,001 and Up

YOU SHOULD REMEMBER

Fiscal policy is a dynamic act; it evolves with two main purposes: boost economic growth and maintain fairness in tax obligations. In a nutshell, the Omnibus Reconciliation Act of 1993 was followed by tax modifications of 1996 and 2000. Five progressive rates were incorporated. Note that the marginal tax rate (the tax paid on the last dollar earned) is the only relevant factor to consider in both personal and corporate finance decisions. Further changes were made in 2011 and are still effective in 2017. As of December 2017, a major tax law passed in which the corporate tax rate was reduced to 21%. The marginal personal tax rates will be 10%, 12%, 22%, 24%, 32%, 35%, and 37%, effective in 2018. Along with other limitations on deductions and changes in personal exemptions, among other things, the new tax structure has significantly changed with the hope of more economic growth. The economic and social consequences of such massive changes are not clear yet.

• *CORPORATE TAXATION*

Corporations are responsible to compute and pay taxes on earnings. Earnings are computed as net sales minus all expenses and noncash expenditures, including depreciation, amortization, and depletion. Tangible assets are depreciated; intangible assets such as patents, bonds discounts, and bonds premium are amortized; and natural resources are depleted. The costs of depreciation, amortization, and depletion are subtracted from sales. Dividends are paid from earnings available after all taxes are paid. The current system of corporate taxation can be called **progressive-regressive-progressive**, meaning that the tax rate increases up to a point then declines in the mid-level, and again increases over a taxable income of $10 million. This system was passed by Congress through the Omnibus Budget Reconciliation Act of 1993, signed by President Clinton in August 1993, and became retroactive from the beginning of 1993. The following tax rates are for corporate taxable incomes as of December 2011:

Tax Rate	Marginal Corporate Tax Rates	The tax is:
15%	Up to $50,000	15% of the amount over $0
25%	$50,001 to $75,000	$7,500 plus 25% over $50,000
34%	$75,001 to $100,000	$13,750 plus 34% over $75,000
39%	$100,001 to $335,000	$22,250 plus 39% over $100,000
34%	$335,001 to $10,000,000	$1,139,000 plus 34% over $335,000
35%	$10,000,001 to $15,000,000	$3,400,000 plus 35% over $10,000,000
38%	$15,000,001 to $18,333,333	$5,151,000 plus 38% over $15,000,000
35%	Over $18,333,333	35% of the amount over $0

The preceding rates apply to the **ordinary income** (profit from regular operations) of a firm. Should a firm sell an asset used in operations for more than the book value (original value minus all previous depreciations), then the company has a capital gain on which it must pay taxes at ordinary income tax rates (specified previously) with a maximum rate of 39%. If the sale price is less than the book value, then the company declares a capital loss, which becomes tax deductible following certain tax rules. If the firm cannot or does not want to deduct all or part of the capital of loss in one year, it may carry the tax loss forward up to 15 years and/or backward up to 3 years.

TAXES ON DIVIDENDS RECEIVED BY CORPORATIONS

In addition to their main functions, corporations may participate as investors in the capital market. They may invest in financial securities of other corporations or institutions. Because corporations pay taxes on their income and stockholders also pay taxes on distributed dividends, the law permits an exemption of 70% of the dividends that corporations receive on their investment outside the company. In other words, corporations pay taxes on 30% of their **dividend income**. Because the maximum corporate tax rate is 39%, the effective highest rate in dividends is 11.7% (0.39 × 0.30).

Taxes on a corporation's dividend income, which is in addition to taxes a corporation pays on its earnings and that stockholders pay on their dividends, are usually called a **triple tax**. The rationale for a 70% tax exemption of the dividend income of corporations is basically to minimize the effects of a triple tax.

Example: Computing Total Tax Liability of a Corporation

PROBLEM   The KAT Company has $450,000 in sales revenue, of which 40% is the cost of goods sold. Other costs include selling expenses of $17,000, administrative expenses of $10,000, interest expenses of $6,000, and depreciation charges of $12,000. In addition, the company has equal capital gains income of $85,000 and capital losses of $75,000 from the resale of equipment. A dividend income is $55,000. Determine the total tax liability of the KAT Company.

SOLUTION   Using an income-statement format, the taxable income of the company is computed as follows:

Sales	$450,000
Dividend Income	16,500
Capital gain income of net capital losses ($85,000 – $75,000)	10,000
Cost of goods sold (40% of $450,000)	(180,000)
Selling expenses	(17,000)
Administrative expenses	(10,000)
Interest expenses	(6,000)
Depreciation	(12,000)
Taxable income	$251,500

On the taxable income of $251,500, we calculate the tax liability of the firm as follows:

15% on the first $50,000 (0.15 × 50,000)	$7,500
25% on the next $25,000 (0.25 × 25,000)	6,250
34% on the next $25,000 (0.34 × 25,000)	8,500
39% on the remaining $151,500 (0.39 × 151,500)	59,085
Total tax liability	$81,335

Note: the marginal tax rate of the firm is 39%; however, the average tax rate is 32% ($81,335/$251,500).

• *BASICS OF DEPRECIATION*

Depreciation is the allocation, for accounting and tax purposes, of the purchase costs of fixed assets (such as machinery and equipment) over a number of years. Since depreciation is a major expense, it has a significant effect on the net income of the firm. **Overdepreciation** (depreciating more than the purchase price) of assets decreases the net income of the firm, and **underdepreciation** (depreciating less than the purchase price) increases it. In simple terms, then, when a company depreciates an asset at more than the normal rate, total expenses go up and lower profits are reported. Therefore, profits vary depending on the method of depreciation used in preparing financial statements.

To prevent inconsistent use of depreciation methods by different companies from one year to another, the Internal Revenue Service (IRS) requires all firms to depreciate their assets based on certain procedures approved by Congress. However, firms can use different depreciation methods in various internal or external reports, or for evaluation of their own performance.

A company or individual cannot depreciate an asset more than its original price. In other words, an asset purchased for $100 can be depreciated for no more than $100. This may sound unreasonable because annual rates of inflation can sometimes raise the price of an asset above its initial price.

Unfortunately, the existing depreciation laws ignore inflation and limit the total depreciation charges to the purchase price and installation cost.

• *MAJOR METHODS OF DEPRECIATION*

An asset can be depreciated in several ways. Although IRS regulations require a certain method for tax purposes, management can use different depreciation methods for internal evaluation and other nontax purposes. The major methods of depreciation are the accelerated cost recovery system and the straight-line, sum-of-the-years'-digits, and double-declining balance methods.

MODIFIED ACCELERATED COST RECOVERY SYSTEM (MACRS)

In the **Modified Accelerated Cost Recovery System (MACRS)**, all properties, except real estate, are classified into several groups for the purpose of depreciation; 3-year, 5-year, and 7-year properties are listed in Table 2-2. Depreciation life for residential real estate is 27½ years and for nonresidential, 31½ years. The precise application of MACRS is cumbersome and may deviate our attention from finance, the focus of this book. Therefore, throughout the examples, we will use a simplified MACRS table for more common assets of 3, 5, and 7 years. Annual factors of depreciation for these assets are presented in Table 2-3. For example, an asset with a 3-year depreciable life is depreciated at 33% of its cost in the first year, 44% in the second year, 15% in the third year (and the residual of 8% in the fourth year).

An important point to keep in mind is that depreciation is a noncash expenditure, in the sense that the firm does not pay cash for depreciation as it does for wages and salaries. Depreciation reduces taxable income; therefore, it produces additional cash flows for the company. **Cash flow** is the sum of net earnings and depreciation.

Table 2–2   Property Classes for Depreciation

Example of Property	Normal Recovery Period
Research equipment and special tools	3 years
Computers	5 years
Office furniture	7 years

Table 2–3 Annual Depreciation Factors

3-Year Asset		5-Year Asset		7-Year Asset	
Year	%	Year	%	Year	%
1	33	1	20	1	14
2	44	2	32	2	24
3	15	3	19	3	17
4*	8	4	12	4	12
		5	12	5	9
		6*	5	6	9
				7	9
				8*	6

*Because of a double-declining balance (discussed later), a small portion of the value of the asset carries forward beyond the years 3, 5, and 7 in the table.

As depreciation charges increase, the cash flow of the firm improves, providing more funds for further business activities. Because depreciation has a favorable effect on the cash flow and the activities of the firm, Congress passed the MACRS, under which assets are depreciated at faster rates than they were under the previous system.

Tax relief in the business sector also means decreased government revenue and an increased budget deficit. Supply-side economists, however, argue that tax relief stimulates the economy, generates new business activities, and increases the profits of firms. Once profits in the business sector have increased, they say, the government will have a broader tax base from which to collect taxes. From a supply-side economic view, then, the MACRS not only increases business sector profits, but also improves government tax revenues in the long run. To prove this theory, of course, would require a staggering amount of research.

STRAIGHT-LINE METHOD

In the **straight-line method**, information about the purchase price of the asset, the life of the asset, and its **salvage value** (or scrap value) is required. Annual depreciation charges are calculated by using the following formula:

$$\text{Annual depreciation} = \frac{\text{Purchasing costs} - \text{Salvage value}}{\text{Number of years the asset will be used}}$$

Example: Calculating Straight-Line Depreciation

PROBLEM   Determine the annual depreciation of a piece of equipment with a useful life of 5 years, a purchase price of $62,000, and a salvage value of $12,000.

SOLUTION $\text{Annual depreciation} = \dfrac{\$62,000 - \$12,000}{5 \text{ years}} = \$10,000 \text{ per year}$

In this method, it is assumed that the asset is used at a constant rate over its useful life.

The straight-line method is recommended for performance evaluation of various departments in the same company or for comparison of company performance from one year to another.

SUM-OF-THE-YEARS'-DIGITS METHOD

In the **sum-of-the-years'-digits** method, it is assumed that the asset is used more often either in the earlier part or the later part of its useful life. The procedure to figure out annual depreciation charges contains three steps:

1. Add all the digits of the years of depreciation together.

2. Make annual fractions of the sum so that the first year's numerator is the highest digit, the second year's numerator is the next highest digit, and so on.

3. Multiply the fraction for each year by the value of the asset to get the depreciation charges for that particular year.

Take a look at the following example; this method is really a lot easier than it seems.

Example: Calculating Sum-of-the-Years'-Digits Depreciation

PROBLEM   Suppose the purchase cost of an asset, after the salvage value, is $62,000, and the useful life of the asset is 3 years. Find the depreciation amount for each year of its useful life.

SOLUTION   In this case, the sum of the years' digits (3 years) is $1 + 2 + 3$, or 6. The fractions for years 1 to 3 are ⅚, ⅔, and ⅙, respectively. The annual depreciation charges are computed as follows, using these fractions:

$$\text{Depreciation of first year} = \tfrac{3}{6} \times \$62,000 = \$31,000$$
$$\text{Depreciation of second year} = \tfrac{2}{6} \times \$62,000 = \$20,666$$
$$\text{Depreciation of third year} = \tfrac{1}{6} \times \$62,000 = \$10,333$$

This method of computation (the *accelerating* method) is appropriate when the management of a company believes that the asset is used more in the first half of its life. If the asset is used more in the later part of its useful life, the order of the fractions has merely to be reversed (the *decelerating* method):

$$\text{Depreciation of first year} = \frac{1}{6} \times \$62,000 = \$10,333$$
$$\text{Depreciation of second year} = \frac{2}{6} \times \$62,000 = \$20,666$$
$$\text{Depreciation of third year} = \frac{3}{6} \times \$62,000 = \$31,000$$

DOUBLE-DECLINING BALANCE METHOD

In the **double-declining balance method**, which was popular before the ACRS became mandatory, the firm uses an annual depreciation ratio equal to double the straight-line ratio. This ratio is multiplied by the book value (undepreciated balance) of the asset to get depreciation charges for that particular year.

Example: Calculating Double-Declining Balance Depreciation

PROBLEM Suppose the purchase cost of an asset is $80,000 and its useful life is 5 years. Find the depreciation amount for each year of useful life.

SOLUTION The annual straight-line ratio is $\frac{1}{5}$, or 20%. Twice this is 40%. Annual depreciation charges are calculated in Table 2-4, using the ratio of 40%.

Table 2–4   Double-Declining Balance Depreciation Method

Year	Depreciation Ratio (%) (R)	Book Value (undepreciated balance) (dollars) (B)	Annual Depreciation Charges (dollars) (R)(B)
1	40	80,000	32,000
2	40	48,000	19,200
3	40	28,800	11,520
4	40	17,280	6,912
5	40	10,368	4,147

NOTE: In the double-declining balance method, the salvage value is not subtracted from the purchase cost. In this example, the total depreciation charges are $73,779, which can be computed from Table 2–4 ($32,000 + $19,000 + $11,520 + $6,912 + $4,147 = $73,779). When $73,779 is subtracted from the purchase cost of $80,000, the undepreciated amount remaining—which can be considered the salvage value of the asset—is $6,221.

• *S CORPORATIONS AND TAX ADVANTAGES*

Certain businesses that adopt the organization of a corporation are not subject to corporate income tax regulations. This type of organization is called an **S corporation**. A basic reason to apply for S corporation status is to enjoy the corporate benefit of limited liability and meantime pay taxes at individual rates like a proprietorship. Thus, the tax advantage of an S Corporation is that dividends are taxed only once. A regular corporation pays taxes before dividends are paid, and then shareholders pay income taxes on the same dividends. This can be avoided if an S corporation is formed. Owners of an S corporation combine their business and personal income, subtract business losses, and pay taxes only once. Note that like an individual taxpayer, an S corporation is also entitled to a $3,000 capital loss deduction against its business or personal income. Of course, before applying for S corporation status, taxes should be estimated for a regular corporation and compared to taxes on an S corporation, in order to determine which status is more advantageous.

Among main requirements for the formation of an S corporation are: the firm must be domestic, have only one class of stock, and be owned by no more than 35 shareholders. Financial institutions and most insurance companies, no matter how small, cannot apply to become an S corporation.

Note that losses from passive investments cannot be deducted from the ordinary income of a passive investor. The IRS is extremely careful in screening those passive investors that inadvertently deduct passive losses on an annual basis. An investor must satisfy certain rules of active investment before those losses can be declared; otherwise, the losses should be added to the asset base (the total cost of acquisition) and subtracted from the sales proceeds of the asset at the time of sale. This tax provision has a lot of implications in the current environment as many real estate investments generate losses. Those yearly losses, unless proved to be active, cannot benefit from year-to-year tax shelters. There is a double whammy; not only current passive losses are not deductible, the sales proceeds may not be high enough to generate profit to benefit from tax deductions. This issue is part of the current real estate investment malaise at the time of revising this section!

• *SMALL BUSINESS ADMINISTRATION (SBA)*

The **Small Business Administration (SBA)** is a federal agency established in 1935 whose purpose is to help small businesses. The SBA offers three types of loans: direct loans, participation loans, and economic opportunity loans. *Direct loans* are available to small businesses that have no source of financing. *Participation loans* are offered by a local bank or financial institution but are guaranteed by the SBA. *Economic opportunity loans* are generally given to minority individuals who own and run small businesses.

Interest rates on SBA loans are usually lower than those on regular commercial loans.

YOU SHOULD REMEMBER

For 2017, we have six different tax rates that apply to eight different levels of corporate taxable income: 15% up to $50,000, 25% up to $75,000, 34% up to $100,000, 39% up to $335,000, 34% up to $10,000,000, 35% up to $15,000,000, 38% up to $18,333,333 and 35% over $18,333,333. Most firms receive a 70% exemption on the dividend income they receive for holding other firms' stocks; this reduces the triple taxation effect. In the Modified Accelerated Cost Recovery System (MACRS), all properties, except real estate, are categorized into several groups for the purpose of depreciation. Even though IRS laws and guidelines must be followed in terms of the depreciation methods used for tax purposes, firms may use different depreciation methods for the internal evaluation of their operations. The most common methods of depreciation are straight-line, sum-of-the-years'-digits, and the double-declining balance.

Passive investment losses are not deductible from the ordinary income of investors.

KNOW THE CONCEPTS

DO YOU KNOW THE BASICS?

1. What are the three types of business organizations? Define them.
2. Name the major tax acts that changed tax laws in the 1980s and 1990s.
3. What are the personal income tax progressive rates for 2018?
4. What are current corporate tax rates?
5. How are capital gains and ordinary income taxed in the current tax system?
6. What major tax changes may we expect in the future?
7. What is the MACRS depreciation procedure for an asset with a useful life of 5 years?
8. Is a firm allowed to use the straight-line depreciation method?
9. How are capital losses treated in the new tax law?
10. What percentage of dividend income received by a corporation is subject to tax?

11. Is investment in real estate considered active or passive?

12. At what level of income is a person *not* entitled to any passive loss from investment in real estate, no matter how actively he/she is involved in managing his/her rental property?

13. Are corporations entitled to investment tax credit?

14. A corporation has 40 owners. They like to pay taxes as individuals, but they do not want to give up their limited liability status. What is your advice?

TERMS FOR STUDY

Active income
Capital
Capital asset
Capital gains
Cash flow
Corporation
Depreciation
Dividend income
Double-declining balance method
Financial asset
General partnership
Inflation-adjusted tax brackets
Investment tax credit
Limited partnership
Marginal tax rate

Modified Accelerated Cost
   Recovery System (MACRS)
Ordinary income
Overdepreciation
Partnership
Proprietorship
Salvage value
S corporation (Subchapter S
   Corporation)
Small Business Administration
   (SBA)
Straight-line method
Sum-of-the-years'-digits method
Triple tax
Underdepreciation

PRACTICAL APPLICATION

COMPUTATIONAL PROBLEMS

1. Calculate the annual depreciation charges, assuming no salvage value and depreciation life of 3 years, for an asset bought for $200,000 using the following four methods:

   a. Straight-line

   b. Sum-of-years'-digits (accelerating)

   c. Double-declining

   d. MACRS

2. XYZ Corporation sells personal computers. During the past year, the company's sales were $2,400,000. The combined cost of goods sold and operating expenses were 62.5% of sales. In addition, the company paid $20,000 in interest on a bank loan and $30,000 in preferred stock dividends. The firm also received $25,000 in dividend income and sold land for $70,000. The land was purchased 2 years ago at a cost of $55,000. Calculate XYZ's tax liability. Find the average tax rate and marginal tax rate.

3. On January 1, 2004, NAC Co. purchased a machine for $77,000. The machine has an estimated salvage value of $5,000 and a useful life of 5 years. Compute the annual depreciation charge over the machine's lifetime using the double-declining balance method.

4. ABC Company receives $20,000 of dividend income from XYZ Company. ABC is entitled to $7,000 deductible from its taxable income. If this company's marginal tax rate is 35%:

   a. Calculate the taxes on total dividends.

   b. Find the effective tax rate on the intercorporate dividend payment.

5. XYZ, Inc. has $700,000 in sales revenue, of which 70% is the cost of goods sold. Other costs are selling expenses of $12,000, and depreciation charges of $17,000. The company also has capital gains income of $70,000 from the resale of an old machine and has received a dividend income of $60,000. Calculate the total tax liability of XYZ, Inc.

6. Mary Sue Co. purchased a piece of equipment for $362,500, a salvage value of $25,000, and useful life of 25 years. Determine the annual depreciation.

7. Samantha and Alex have a total net income of $165,000. They both made a $25,000 contribution to a retirement plan and have also paid a $1,500 penalty on an early withdrawal of a certificate of deposit from their bank. Including their child, they are entitled to three personal exemptions ($3,700 each as of now). Their total itemized deductions are $16,250. What is the taxable income of Samantha and Alex?

8. The future net earnings of the XYZ Co. are estimated as follows:

Year	1	2	3	4	5
Net earnings:	$100,000	$150,000	$200,000	$250,000	$300,000

   Assets worth $400,000 will be depreciated using the MACRS method for the next 5 years. Determine the annual cash flows for those years.

9. XYZ Co. purchased a tractor trailer for $89,000, with a useful life of 4 years and a salvage value of $9,000. Find the accelerated depreciation amount for each year of the useful life using the sum-of-year's-digits method.

10. Mario's Painting Company has $640,000 in sales revenue, of which 60% is the cost of goods sold. Other costs include selling expenses of $19,000, administrative expenses of $11,000, interest expenses of $9,000, and depreciation charges of $14,000. In addition, the company has equal capital gains income of $80,000 and capital losses of $60,000 from the resale of equipment. A dividend income is $40,000. Determine the total tax liability of the company.

11. John J. has $150,000 adjusted taxable income. He has $40,000 tax losses on renting an apartment located in Myrtle Beach, South Carolina. This property is run by a management company and John J. has a job as computer analyst. He is in a 30% tax bracket. What are the tax benefits of $40,000 tax loss on his rental property?

Note: The following problems are related to the new 2018 tax policy and tax rates:

12. What is the desired effect that the new corporate tax rate will have on corporations?

13. Chelsea is a middle-aged woman working in marketing, while her husband, John, is an engineer. Chelsea makes $75,000 per year, while her husband makes $160,000. Should Chelsea and her husband file separately or jointly in order to pay the least amount of taxes on their income?

14. In 2017, Company ABC had a taxable income of $7.5 million, which resulted in the company paying $2.625 million in corporate taxes. Assuming 5% growth in taxable income over the next year, how much will Company ABC pay in taxes in 2018?

15. An individual makes $85,000 in 2018, with tax deductions of $10,000. How much does this person pay in taxes?

16. Michael is very involved in the community and often donates both time and money to charity. Over the course of 2018, Michael donated $6,500 toward various charitable donations, while incurring travel costs of $450 while volunteering. With an annual salary of $160,000, what is Michael's tax rate? Assuming no other deductions, how much is Michael saving in taxes by donating?

ANSWERS

KNOW THE CONCEPTS

1. The three types of business organizations are proprietorships, partnerships, and corporations. A proprietorship is owned by one individual. A partnership is owned by more than one person. A corporation can be formed by a person or a group of persons; the identity or "persona" of the corporation is totally separate from those of the owners.

2. The Economic Recovery Tax Act of 1981, the Tax Equity and Fiscal Responsibility Act of 1982, the Tax Reform Act of 1984, the Tax Reform Act of 1986, and the Omnibus Budget Reconciliation Act of 1993.

3. Below are the progressive personal income tax rates for 2018.

   10%, 12%, 22%, 24%, 32%, 35%, and 37%

4. 15%, 25%, 34%, 39%, 35%, and 38%.

5. The same, like ordinary income.

6. The capital gain tax provision may come back again.

7. 20%, 32%, 19%, 12%, 12%, and 5% (Total 100%)

8. Yes, for internal purposes.

9. In the case of individuals, capital losses may be offset against other ordinary income up to a limit, with the balance carried forward.

10. 30%

11. Passive

12. $150,000

13. Not in the current tax system. Investment tax credit, like capital gains deductions, could be the subject of a future debate among legislators.

14. Number of shareholders should be reduced to 35, if possible.

PRACTICAL APPLICATION

1.

Depreciation Method	Year 1	Year 2	Year 3
Straight-line	$ 66,666	$66,666	$66,666
Sum-of-the-years'-digits	$100,000	$66,666	$33,333
Double-declining	$133,333	$44,444	$14,815
MACRS	$ 66,000	$88,000	$30,000

2.

Sales	$ 2,400,000
Cost of goods and operating expenses (62.5% of sales)	$ (1,500,000)
Interest Expenses	$ (20,000)
Ordinary Income	$ 880,000
Plus: Capital gain ($70,000 – $55,000)	$ 15,000
Taxable dividend income after 80% exemption	$ 7,500
Total taxable income	$ 902,500

Taxes = (50,000 × 0.15) + (25,000 × 0.25) + (25,000 × 0.34) + (235,000 × 0.39) + (567,600 × 0.34)

= $7,500 + 6,250 + 8,500 + 91,650 + 192,950 = 306,850

Average tax rate = $\dfrac{306,850}{902,500}$ = 0.34 or 34%

In this case, the marginal tax rate is 34% and the average tax rate is also 34%.

3.

Year	Depreciation Ratio, R (%)	Book Value (Undepreciated Balance), B ($)	Annual (Depreciation Charges), R × B ($)
1	40	77,000	30,800
2	40	46,200	18,480
3	40	27,720	11,088
4	40	16,632	6,652.80
5	40	9,979.20	3,991.68

4.

  a. $(0.35 \times \$20,000) \times (1 - 0.70) = \$2,100$.

  b. 30% × 35% = 10.5%, which is the same as $2,100/$20,000.

5.

Sales	$700,000
Cost of goods sold (70% of sales)	($490,000)
Selling expenses	($60,000)
Administrative expenses	($18,000)
Interest expenses	($12,000)
Depreciation	($17,000)
Ordinary income	$103,000
Plus: Capital gain	$70,000
Taxable income	$173,000

Taxes = ($50,000 × 0.15) + ($25,000 × 0.25) + ($25,000 × 0.34) +
      ($73,000 × 0.39)
    = $7,500 + $6,250 + $8,500 + $28,470 = $50,720

Taxes on dividends = ($60,000 × 0.30 × 0.39) = $7,020
Total taxes = $50,720 + $7,020 = $57,740

6. Annual depreciation $= \dfrac{\$362,500 - \$25,000}{25 \text{ years}} = \$13,500$ per year

7. Adjusted gross income = Total income – Adjustments
                  = $165,000 – $25,000 – $1,500
                  = $138,500

Taxable Income = Adjusted gross income – Deductions – Exemptions
          = $138,500 – $16,250 – ($3,700 × 3)
          = $111,150

Samantha and Alex will pay taxes on $111,150.

8.

Year	Net Earnings ($)	Depreciation ($)	Cash Flow ($)
1	100,000	80,000	180,000
2	150,000	128,000	278,000
3	200,000	76,000	276,000
4	250,000	48,000	298,000
5	300,000	48,000	348,000

NOTE: Cash Flow = Net earnings + Depreciation

9.

Depreciation of first year	4/10 × $80,000 = $32,000
Depreciation of second year	3/10 × $80,000 = $24,000
Depreciation of third year	2/10 × $80,000 = $16,000
Depreciation of fourth year	1/10 × $80,000 = $ 8,000

10.

Sales	$640,000
Dividend income (30% of $40,000)	12,000
Capital gains income of net capital losses ($80,000 − $60,000)	20,000
Cost of goods sold (60% of $640,000)	(384,000)
Selling expenses	(19,000)
Administrative expenses	(11,000)
Interest expenses	(9,000)
Depreciation	(14,000)
Taxable income	$235,000

On the taxable income of $235,000, we calculate the tax liability of the firm as follows:

15% on the first $50,000 (0.15 × 50,000)	$7,500
25% on the next $25,000 (0.25 ×25,000)	$6,250
34% on the next $25,000 (0.34 ×25,000)	$8,500
39% on the remaining $135,000 (0.39 × 135,000)	$52,650
Total tax liability	$74,900

Note: The marginal tax rate of the firm is 39%; however, the average tax rate is 32% ($74,900/$235,000).

11. The tax benefits are zero. John J. is not an active investor. He should add the $40,000 tax losses to the asset base and then subtract from the sales proceeds at the time of sale.

12. With a lower corporate tax rate, corporations would be able to generate greater net income, as they are paying less in taxes each year. This extra capital would be used to finance projects that they would otherwise not undertake. Having a lower tax rate, and more cash on hand, would also lower the required ROI for new projects. The desired effect is more rapid growth and more spending power for both corporations and citizens.

13. If Chelsea and John file jointly, their combined income is $235,000, which means they will get taxed at a rate of 24%:

$$\$235,000 \times 24\% = \$56,400$$

However, if Chelsea and her husband file separately, their taxes will be the following:

Chelsea: $75,000 × 22% = $16,500
John: $160,000 × 32% = $51,200
$67,700

Therefore, Chelsea and John should file jointly in order to pay less taxes.

14. $7,500,000 × (1+5%) = $7,875,000 in taxable income
$7,875,000 × (21%) = $1,753,750 paid in corporate taxes in 2018

Company ABC will pay less in taxes in 2018 versus 2017, despite increasing their taxable income by 5%.

15. $85,000 – $10,000 = $75,000 in taxable income
$75,000 × (22%) = $16,500 paid in taxes

16. With Deductions:
$160,000 – $6,500 – $450 = $153,050 in taxable income
$153,050 × (24%) = $36,732 paid in taxes

Without Deductions:
$160,000 × (.32) = $51,200 paid in taxes

Savings: $51,200 – ($36,732 + $6,500 + $450) = $7,518 in savings

VALUATION (TIME AND RISK)

3

THE VALUE OF MONEY OVER TIME

WHY THE VALUE OF MONEY CHANGES OVER TIME

The old saying "A bird in the hand is worth two in the bush" makes a great deal of sense when applied to finance. In monetary terms, it means that cash today is worth more than cash in the future. In other words, the value of money changes over time. Investors have a natural preference for cash now rather than later, so they can *increase* its value. This, of course, is a major goal of a financial manager. Aside from this basic reason why cash now is worth more than cash later, you should also be aware of factors that *decrease* the value of money over time. Three important reasons why the value of money decreases progressively over time are as follows:

1. Inflation

2. Risk

3. Preference for Liquidity

INFLATION

Inflation refers to a general price increase in the economy. When prices increase, the value of a dollar decreases, and since prices are expected to rise in the future, the value of a dollar in future years will be less than it is today. In other words, the purchasing power of a dollar today is higher than it will be tomorrow because rising prices will diminish the value of that dollar. Therefore, it is possible to buy more goods with one dollar a year from now than two years from now, and so on.

Example: Inflation

If general prices increased by 5% annually, the purchasing power of one dollar today would be 5% less one year from now. In other words, $1.00 today would depreciate in value to $0.95 one year from now. If consumers could buy 100 pins with a dollar today, they would be able to buy only 95 pins a year from now. Simply stated, the higher the rate of inflation, and the longer the period of time involved, the less a given amount of money will be worth in the future.

RISK

Risk, or uncertainty about the future, also causes a decline in the value of money. Because the future is uncertain, risk increases with time. Most people wish to avoid risk, so they value cash today more than the promise of cash in the future. Most people are willing to give up cash for promised cash only if properly compensated for the risk they are asked to take.

No one can predict with certainty either the future of the U.S. economy or economic and financial trends in other parts of the world. It is impossible to predict accurately whether money invested today will be available tomorrow. There is no assurance that a financially sound firm will remain so in the years ahead. Investors cannot be guaranteed dividends or price appreciation in stocks they purchase, nor can they be completely certain that the interest and principal on fixed-income securities will be paid as agreed by the issuer. Financial analysts or sophisticated investors, no matter how competent they are, cannot be assured that the returns they project from a given investment will turn out as originally visualized.

Since uncertainty increases the further one looks into the future, risk also increases—and the value of money promised in the future diminishes accordingly.

PREFERENCE FOR LIQUIDITY

Liquidity is important to an investor or a firm. Liquidity refers to how easily assets can be converted into cash. Cash, government bonds, and other marketable **securities** (company assets guaranteed to lenders to ensure repayment of a loan) increase the liquidity of a firm. By the same token, fixed assets such as plant and equipment are not considered very liquid. Investors have a **preference for liquidity**; that is, they prefer to hold ready cash for unexpected emergencies and financial claims rather than commit funds into future-yielding assets. If they do give up current liquidity by buying assets that promise future returns, they are trading an assured cash asset for a riskier future asset. The trade will take place only if the promised rewards of the future assets are sufficiently high to warrant taking the risk.

When lenders or investors give up cash for very risky future returns, they require high premiums, or returns, on their invested cash to compensate for less liquidity. Conversely, when they invest in low-risk assets, the premiums they expect in return are relatively low.

Example: Liquidity versus Future Returns

If a person deposits cash in a bank that is FDIC insured, she will be willing to accept 5% interest, whereas if she buys the long-term bond of an unknown company, a higher rate of interest, say 15%, would be required. In both cases, cash, or 100% liquidity, is given up, and the return must compensate for the risk.

It is clearly essential for lenders or investors to know how much their cash investments will grow so they can determine whether their investments are worthwhile. Borrowers also want to know how much, and over what period of time, they will have to repay the lenders, and whether the returns from these borrowed funds will be greater than the costs of borrowing. This all boils down to the concept of future value, as determined by the compound rate of interest, and the present value of future returns once they are adjusted for risk.

YOU SHOULD REMEMBER

Aside from the fact that money invested wisely today will yield a return in the future (a fact that creates a natural investor desire for cash today), money loses value over time because of inflation, risk, and preference for cash. The concept that the value of a dollar today is more than the value of a dollar tomorrow is central to financial theory.

FUTURE VALUE AND COMPOUND INTEREST

Any reasonable investment or commitment of cash must provide for an increase in value over time. Given the amount of cash that you want to commit, you can find out how much that cash value will increase in the future once the expected rate of return is known. This calculation is called finding the **future value** of an investment.

Example: Future Value after One Year

Suppose an investor saves $100. This cash is deposited in the bank at a 10% annual interest rate. After one year the investor will have the original $100 plus $10 in interest:

$$\text{Original deposit} + \text{Interest on deposit} = FV$$
$$\$100 \quad + \quad (10\%)(\$100) \quad = \$110$$

At the time of deposit the $100 was worth 100%, or $100. Since the bank promised to pay an additional 10%, the future value of the $100 one year from now is equal to $110 ($100 plus 10).

Calculating future value for one year is perfectly straightforward, but what happens when someone wants to know how much money will be in an account after 20 years? Luckily, there is an easy formula to calculate future values:

$$FV = P(1 + R)^N$$

where FV = future value
  P = initial deposit (principal)
  R = annual rate of interest
  N = number of years

Example: Future Value after Any Number of Years

The equation just introduced can be used for any number of years. Here are two instances involving a $100 deposit at a 10% interest rate:

1 Year on Deposit	2 Years on Deposit
$FV = P(1 + R)^1$	$FV = P(1 + R)^2$
$FV = \$100(1 + .10)$	$FV = \$100(1 + .10)^2$
$FV = \$100(1.10)$	$FV = \$100(1.10)(1.10)$
$FV = \$110$	$FV = \$121$

If the preceding example had involved 10 years, you would have had to calculate $(1.10)^{10}$, which is equal to 2.594. So the future value of $100 in 10 years would be $100(2.594), or $259.40. Note that each year the cash value increases, not by 10% of the original $100, but by 10% of each subsequently higher amount. In other words, you earn interest not only on your initial deposit, but also on your interest:

Original $100 \times 1.10 = 110 future value (*FV*) after 1 year

$110 \times 1.10 = 121 *FV* after 2 years

$121 \times 1.10 = 133 *FV* after 3 years

This method of computing future value is cumbersome. Fortunately, future value tables are available to speed the computations. These tables calculate all of the factors $(1 + R)^N$ for a given number of years. If the rate of interest is known, you can easily find the factor by which to multiply the original cash investment to obtain the future value.

Table 3-1 shows what is known as a Future Value Interest Factor (*FVIF*). It is a highly useful tool for obtaining different values related to future values.

USING FUTURE VALUE TABLES

Reading the future value table is fairly simple. Suppose you wish to find the *FV* of an original investment of $100 over a 3-year period at 10% interest. Look up the factor (1.33), and multiply it by the original investment: $100(1.33) = $133. If the intent is to find out how fast an investment will grow over 3 years, just deduct 1.00 from the factor and you get the total percentage increase (1.33 − 1.00 = .33, or 33%). In other words, a $100 investment that grows to $133 in 3 years represents an increase in value of 33%.

If your goal is to find out the annual rate of compound interest that applies to an investment of $100 which is expected to grow 33% in 3 years, all that is required is to locate the factor (133%, or 1.000 + .33 = 1.33) by going to the third year and finding 1.33. By looking up the column, you find that the rate of interest for a $100 investment expected to grow 33% in 3 years is 10%. Conversely, if you want to find out how many years it will take for an investment growing at 10% annually to increase 33%, merely look up 10% and the factor 1.33, and then move your eyes horizontally along the row to obtain the corresponding time of 3 years.

ANNUITY

An **annuity** is a series of equal payments (or receipts) made at any regular interval of time. An annuity can be a payment or an investment each year, each half-year (semiannually), each quarter, or each month. Examples are the monthly mortgage payments on a house, quarterly investments in a trust account for a child's future education, and periodic loan payments.

FV factors can be used to find the total future value of an annuity. Even long-term annuities can be handled easily in this manner.

Example: Using FV Factors to Calculate Annuities

PROBLEM   Find the total future value of payments for a $100 annuity paid once a year over a period of 4 years. Assume 10% compound interest.

Table 3–1   Future Value of $1 After *n* Periods

Periods	Interest Rate											
	1%	2%	3%	4%	5%	6%	7%	8%	9%	10%	11%	12%
1	1.0100	1.0200	1.0300	1.0400	1.0500	1.0600	1.0700	1.0800	1.0900	1.1000	1.1100	1.1200
2	1.0201	1.0404	1.0609	1.0816	1.1025	1.1236	1.1449	1.1664	1.1881	1.2100	1.2321	1.2544
3	1.0303	1.0612	1.0927	1.1249	1.1576	1.1910	1.2250	1.2597	1.2950	1.3310	1.3676	1.4049
4	1.0406	1.0824	1.1255	1.1699	1.2155	1.2625	1.3108	1.3605	1.4116	1.4641	1.5181	1.5735
5	1.0510	1.1041	1.1593	1.2167	1.2763	1.3382	1.4026	1.4693	1.5386	1.6105	1.6851	1.7623
6	1.0615	1.1261	1.1941	1.2653	1.3401	1.4185	1.5007	1.5869	1.6771	1.7716	1.8704	1.9738
7	1.0721	1.1487	1.2299	1.3159	1.4071	1.5036	1.6058	1.7138	1.8280	1.9487	2.0762	2.2107
8	1.0829	1.1717	1.2668	1.3686	1.4775	1.5939	1.7182	1.8509	1.9926	2.1436	2.3045	2.4760
9	1.0937	1.1951	1.3048	1.4233	1.5513	1.6895	1.8385	1.9990	2.1719	2.3580	2.5580	2.7731
10	1.1046	1.2190	1.3439	1.4802	1.6289	1.7909	1.9672	2.1589	2.3674	2.5937	2.8394	3.1059
11	1.1157	1.2434	1.3842	1.5395	1.7103	1.8983	2.1049	2.3316	2.5804	2.8531	3.1518	3.4786
12	1.1268	1.2682	1.4258	1.6010	1.7959	2.0122	2.2522	2.5182	2.8127	3.1384	3.4985	3.8960
13	1.1381	1.2936	1.4685	1.6651	1.8857	2.1329	2.4098	2.7196	3.0658	3.4523	3.8833	4.3635
14	1.1495	1.3195	1.5126	1.7317	1.9799	2.2609	2.5785	2.9372	3.3417	3.7975	4.3104	4.8871
15	1.1610	1.3459	1.5580	1.8009	2.0789	2.3966	2.7590	3.1722	3.6425	4.1773	4.7846	5.4736
16	1.1726	1.3728	1.6047	1.8730	2.1829	2.5404	2.9522	3.4259	3.9703	4.5950	5.3109	6.1304
17	1.1843	1.4002	1.6529	1.9479	2.2920	2.6928	3.1588	3.7000	4.3276	5.0545	5.8951	6.8660
18	1.1962	1.4283	1.7024	2.0258	2.4066	2.8543	3.3799	3.9960	4.7171	5.5599	6.5436	7.6900
19	1.2081	1.4568	1.7535	2.1069	2.5270	3.0256	3.6165	4.3157	5.1417	6.1159	7.2633	8.6128
20	1.2202	1.4860	1.8061	2.1911	2.6533	3.2071	3.8697	4.6610	5.6044	6.725	8.0623	9.6463
21	1.2324	1.5157	1.8603	2.2788	2.7860	3.3996	4.1406	5.0338	6.1088	7.4003	8.9492	10.804
22	1.2447	1.5460	1.9161	2.3699	2.9253	3.6035	4.4304	5.4365	6.6586	8.1403	9.9336	12.100
23	1.2572	1.5769	1.9736	2.4647	3.0715	3.8198	4.7405	5.8714	7.2579	8.9543	11.026	13.552
24	1.2697	1.6084	2.0328	2.5633	3.2251	4.0489	5.0724	6.3412	7.9111	9.8497	12.239	15.179

SOLUTION   Finding the total future value of this series of payments is a relatively easy task. All you have to do is sum up the future value factors for the number of years that cover the annuity. From the *FV* table, then, the factor for a 4-year annuity at a 10% compound interest rate would be 1.000 + 1.100 + 1.210 + 1.331, or 4.641. In

4 years, annuity payments of $100 would be worth $100(4.641), or $464.10.

The equation that represents the future value of an annuity is

$$FV_a = P(1+R)^1 + P(1+R)^2 + P(1+R)^3 + \cdots + P(1+R)^{N-1}$$

This equation can be simplified into

$$FV_a = P \times \left[\frac{(1+R)^N - 1}{R} \right]$$
$$= P \times FVIFA_{R,N}$$

where FV_a = Future value of an annuity
P = Payment
R = Annual rate of interest
N = Number of periods
$FVIFA_{R,N}$ = annuity factor, or future value interest annuity factor.

EXAMPLE: Let us calculate the future value of a $100 annuity over a period of 4 years with a 10% compound interest rate using the future value of an annuity formula.

SOLUTION: P = $100 per year
N = 4 years
R = 10%

$$FV_a = 100 \times \left[\frac{(1+0.10)^4 - 1}{0.10} \right]$$
$$= 100 \times 4.641$$
$$= \$464.10$$

USING FUTURE VALUE ANNUITY TABLES

Future annuity tables merely simplify your computations by adding up the interim compound interest rate factors and providing you with a single factor ($FVI_{R,N}FA$), future value interest annuity factor.

Then you can easily use the FV_a formula as follows;

$$FV_a = P \times FVIFA_{R,N}$$

Table 3-2 is a sample future value annuity table. Using the figures from the preceding example, you can find the 4-year annuity factor, or 4.641, from the table.

Table 3–2 Future Value Interest Factor Annuity

Period	1%	2%	3%	4%	5%	6%	7%	8%	9%	10%
1	1.000	1.000	1.000	1.000	1.000	1.000	1.000	1.000	1.000	1.000
2	2.010	2.020	2.030	2.040	2.050	2.060	2.070	2.080	2.090	2.100
3	3.030	3.060	3.091	3.122	3.152	3.184	3.215	3.246	3.278	3.310
4	4.060	4.122	4.184	4.246	4.310	4.375	4.440	4.506	4.573	4.641
5	5.101	5.204	5.309	5.416	5.526	5.637	5.751	5.867	5.985	6.105
6	6.152	6.308	6.468	6.633	6.802	6.975	7.153	7.336	7.523	7.716
7	7.214	7.434	7.662	7.898	8.142	8.394	8.654	8.923	9.200	9.487
8	8.286	8.583	8.892	9.214	9.549	9.897	10.260	10.637	11.028	11.436
9	9.368	9.755	10.159	10.583	11.027	11.491	11.978	12.488	13.021	13.579
10	10.462	10.950	11.464	12.006	12.578	13.181	13.816	14.487	15.193	15.937
11	11.567	12.169	12.808	13.486	14.207	14.972	15.784	16.645	17.560	18.531
12	12.682	13.412	14.192	15.026	15.917	16.870	17.888	18.977	20.141	21.384
13	13.809	14.680	15.618	16.627	17.713	18.882	20.141	21.495	22.953	24.523
14	14.947	15.974	17.086	18.292	19.598	21.015	22.550	24.215	26.019	27.975
15	16.097	17.293	18.599	20.023	21.578	23.276	25.129	27.152	29.361	31.772
16	17.258	18.639	20.157	21.824	23.657	25.672	27.888	30.324	33.003	35.949
17	18.430	20.012	21.761	23.697	25.840	28.213	30.840	33.750	36.973	40.544
18	19.614	21.412	23.414	25.645	28.132	30.905	33.999	37.450	41.301	45.599
19	20.811	22.840	25.117	27.671	30.539	33.760	37.379	41.446	46.018	51.158
20	22.019	24.297	26.870	29.778	33.066	36.785	40.995	45.762	51.159	57.274
21	23.239	25.783	28.676	31.969	35.719	39.992	44.865	50.422	56.764	64.002
22	24.471	27.299	30.536	34.248	38.505	43.392	49.005	55.456	62.872	71.402
23	25.716	28.845	32.452	36.618	41.430	46.995	53.435	60.893	69.531	79.542
24	26.973	30.421	34.426	39.082	44.501	50.815	58.176	66.764	76.789	88.496
25	28.243	32.030	36.459	41.645	47.726	54.864	63.248	73.105	84.699	98.346
30	34.784	40.567	47.575	56.084	66.438	79.057	94.459	113.282	136.305	164.491
40	48.885	60.401	75.400	95.024	120.797	154.758	199.630	259.052	337.872	442.580
50	64.461	84.577	112.794	152.664	209.341	290.325	406.516	573.756	815.051	1163.865

YOU SHOULD REMEMBER

There are two ways to determine the future value of a deposit: using a formula and using a future value table. The formula for the future value is

$$FV_N = P(1 + R)^N$$

where FV_N = future value in period N
 P = initial deposit (principal)
 R = annual rate of interest
 N = number of periods

If you want to use the table, multiply your initial deposit by the value of *FVIF*. In the case of annuities, you should multiply the amount of annuity by the value of *FVIFA* available in the table.

PRESENT VALUE AND DISCOUNT RATES

Why is present value of crucial interest to financial people? The answer is that it provides them with a basis for comparing the profitability of different projects or investments over a period of years. **Present value**, therefore, is the cash value of future returns or income once a discount (capitalization) rate has been applied to it. The **discount**, or **capitalization**, **rate** is an interest rate applied to a series of future payments to adjust for risk and the uncertainty of the time factor.

ADJUSTING FOR RISK

To calculate present value, a discount rate must be determined that takes into consideration how much risk is associated with each project or investment. Risk levels follow a simple rule:

High risk means a high discount (capitalization) rate, and low risk means a low discount rate.

For example, if an investor decides that the discount rate assigned to a stock should be 5%, another stock having double this risk will have a discount rate of 10%.

Once the risk level is determined, the next step is to adjust returns or future income for the uncertainty of time. Generally speaking, the following principles apply to evaluating discount rates.

Evaluating Discount Rates

1. Between two future incomes, the one that will take longer to reach maturity should have a higher discount rate.

2. The lower the perceived risk, the lower the discount rate should be.

3. If general interest rates in the market rise, the discount rate should increase also.

Risk can decline because of a more favorable business outlook, the prospect of declining inflation and interest rates, or less uncertain economic conditions. As risk declines, the present value of future income will increase, as illustrated in Table 3-3.

Table 3–3   Inverse Relationship between Present Value and Risk

Future Income (3 years from now) (dollars)	Discount Rate (%)	PV of $1 in 3 Years	PV of Future Income (dollars)
1,000	15 (high risk)	.658	658
1,000	10 (average risk)	.751	751
1,000	5 (low risk)	.864	864

ADJUSTING FOR TIME

The present value of any future returns declines the further out into the future you look. Obviously, this procedure employs a mathematical adjustment for the time value of money. As it turns out, the principle involved is not a difficult one to grasp—*the present value of future returns is merely the reverse of future value compounding.*

An arithmetic illustration will provide a better understanding of this principle. Assume you wish to find out the present value of $1,000 3 years from now, and you expect the level of risk associated with the project to be 10% annually. Thus, if

$$FV = P(1 + R)^N$$

then

$$PV = \frac{FV}{(1+R)^N}$$

It is evident from Table 3-1 that the factors increase as time passes and as the compound interest rate rises. You can observe that, if these factors are plugged into the denominator in the last equation, the present value of $1,000 3 years hence is

$$\frac{\$1,000}{(1+.10)^3} = \$751$$

How was this value found? Simply by multiplying 1.10 three times (1.10 × 1.10 × 1.10 = 1.33), and using this factor to discount:

$$\frac{\$1,000}{1.33} = \$751$$

The present value table saves all the work required to compute the different *PV* factors. This table indicates, for example, that the values decrease the longer the time period considered, and that these values also decline as the discount rate increases. The table merely indicates the factor which, when multiplied by a future value, will yield the present value. A sample present value table is available in Table 3-4.

It is evident that, if you had two projects with the same costs and same economic lives but different risk factors, it would be possible to find out their present values and then determine which is more favorable. Capital budgeting evaluation, which is designed to determine the relative merits of projects or investments, employs the present value concept as a guideline. The whole idea is to discount the future returns by a level of risk plus the uncertainty of time. The present value method accomplishes this objective.

USING PRESENT VALUE TABLES

In the last illustration, in which you had to find the present value of $1,000 3 years hence, all you had to do was look up the length of time and its corresponding present value factor at a given discount rate in Table 3-4. This factor is shown to be .751. To obtain the present value of $1,000 3 years from now at a discount rate of 10%, calculate the product of the present value times the factor ($1,000 × .751 = $751), which is the same amount you obtained using the long method.

The present value table obviously saves investors and financial managers a great deal of time. Note that when the discount rate declines the present value increases, and that when it increases the present value decreases. It should be clear by now that the present value concept is an important tool in making investment and other financial decisions.

Table 3–4   Present Value of $1

Discount Rate

Periods	1%	2%	3%	4%	5%	6%	7%	8%	9%	10%	11%	12%
1	.99010	.98039	.97087	.96154	.95238	.94340	.93458	.92593	.91743	.90909	.90090	.89286
2	.98030	.96117	.94260	.92456	.90703	.89000	.87344	.85734	.84168	.82645	.81162	.79719
3	.97059	.94232	.91514	.88900	.86384	.83962	.81630	.79383	.77218	.75131	.73119	.71178
4	.96098	.92385	.88849	.85480	.82270	.79209	.76290	.73503	.70843	.68301	.65873	.63552
5	.95147	.90573	.86261	.82193	.78353	.74726	.71299	.68058	.64993	.62092	.59345	.56743
6	.94204	.88797	.83748	.79031	.74622	.70496	.66634	.63017	.59627	.56447	.53464	.50663
7	.93272	.87056	.81309	.75992	.71068	.66506	.62275	.58349	.54703	.51316	.48166	.45235
8	.92348	.85349	.78941	.73069	.67684	.62741	.58201	.54027	.50187	.46651	.43393	.40388
9	.91434	.83675	.76642	.70259	.64461	.59190	.54393	.50025	.46043	.42410	.39092	.36061
10	.90529	.82035	.74409	.67556	.61391	.55839	.50835	.46319	.42241	.38554	.35218	.32197
11	.89632	.80426	.72242	.64958	.58468	.52679	.47509	.42888	.38753	.35049	.31728	.28748
12	.88745	.78849	.70138	.62460	.55684	.49697	.44401	.39711	.35553	.31683	.28584	.25667
13	.87866	.77303	.68095	.60057	.53032	.46884	.41496	.36770	.32618	.28966	.25751	.22917
14	.86996	.75787	.66112	.57747	.50507	.44230	.38782	.34046	.29925	.26333	.23199	.20462
15	.86135	.74301	.64186	.55526	.48102	.41726	.36245	.31524	.27454	.23939	.20900	.18270
16	.85282	.72845	.62317	.53391	.45811	.39365	.33873	.29189	.25187	.21763	.18829	.16312
17	.84438	.71416	.60502	.51337	.43630	.37136	.31657	.27027	.23107	.19784	.16963	.14564
18	.83602	.70016	.58739	.49363	.41552	.35034	.29586	.25025	.21199	.17986	.15282	.13004
19	.82774	.68643	.57029	.47464	.39573	.33051	.27651	.23171	.19449	.16351	.13768	.11611
20	.81954	.67297	.55367	.45639	.37689	.31180	.25842	.21455	.17843	.14864	.12403	.10367
21	.81143	.65978	.53755	.43883	.35894	.29415	.24151	.19866	.16370	.13513	.11174	.09256
22	.80340	.64684	.52189	.42195	.34185	.27750	.22571	.18394	.15018	.12285	.10067	.08264
23	.79544	.63414	.50669	.40573	.32557	.26180	.21095	.17031	.13778	.11168	.09069	.07379
24	.78757	.62172	.49193	.39012	.31007	.24698	.19715	.15770	.12640	.10153	.08170	.06588

• *PRESENT VALUE OF AN ANNUITY*

When financial managers are faced by a steady and constant stream of future payments or receipts, and they want to evaluate the present value of these figures, they can do two things:

1. Calculate the present value of each future year by discounting each payment or receipt with its appropriate present value factor. This is a long and redundant method.

2. Calculate the *PV* annuity of future cash flows by employing a present value annuity factor. This is the short and easy method.

An example will help show you which method is easier. Assume you expect a cash flow of $100 in the next 3 years and wish to find out the *PV* of these cash flows given a discount rate, or risk level, of 10%.

In the long method of calculation you would look up the factors in the *PV* table, derive the *PV* for each $100 in the next 3 years, and sum the products:

Year	Cash Flow	PVIF (10%)	Present Value
1	$100	.909	$ 90.90
2	100	.826	82.60
3	100	.751	75.10
	Total	2.486	$248.60

Recall that when *FV* annuities were discussed it was pointed out that annuity factors represent the summation of the future value factors. The same principle applies in calculating the present value annuity for an equal series of future cash flows. All that you have to do is add up the *PV* factors for the period under analysis and apply this total annuity factor to the cash flow for any year. Mathematically, the equation for *PV* annuity is

$$PV_a = \frac{A}{(1+R)^N}$$

where PV_a = present value of an annuity
A = amount of annuity
R = discount rate
N = number of years or periods

Example: Calculating Present Values of Annuities—The Long Way

PROBLEM   Calculate the present value of a $100 annuity for a 3-year period. Assume a discount rate of 10%.

SOLUTION

$$\text{Present value of 1st payment } = \frac{\$100}{(1+.10)^1} = \$90.90$$

$$\text{Present value of 2nd payment } = \frac{\$100}{(1+.10)^2} = \$82.60$$

$$\text{Present value of 3rd payment } = \frac{\$100}{(1+.10)^3} = \$75.10$$

$$\text{Present value of all three payments } = \$90.90 + \$82.60 + \$75.10$$
$$= \$248.60$$

The above calculations show that the three payments of $100 each are currently worth only $248.60 if the discount rate is 10%. This is exactly what discounting is all about. The difference between $300 and $248.60 is called the time value of money, or the total discount.

The equation that represents the present value of an annuity is

$$PV_a = \frac{P}{(1+R)^1} + \frac{P}{(1+R)^2} + \frac{P}{(1+R)^3} + \ldots\ldots + \frac{P}{(1+R)^N}$$

This equation can be simplified into

$$PV_a = P \times \left[\frac{1}{R} - \frac{1}{R(1+R)^N} \right]$$
$$= P \times PVIFA_{R,N}$$

where PV_a = Present value of an annuity
P = Payment
R = Annual rate of interest
N = Number of periods
$PVIFA_{R,N}$ = Present value interest annuity factor.

USING PRESENT VALUE ANNUITY TABLES

Instead of having to go through laborious calculations, a table has been set up that sums the PV factors. Table 3-5 is a present value annuity interest factor table, and it is relatively easy to read. Assume that you contemplate buying stock A, which will return $1,000 annually over 5 years, and stock B, which will return $1,025 yearly during the same period. You wish to find out which annuity is the better investment. A security analyst tells you that stock A is discounted at 10% and stock B at 12%. To compare the PV annuities of these two stocks all you have to do is go to the annuity table and look up the present value interest factor annuity (PVIFA) for these two streams of returns. At 10% in 5 years the factor is 3.7908 and at 12% it is 3.6048. Given these factors you can calculate the PV of the two stocks:

$$PV_{stock\,A} = \$1,000(3.791) = \$3,791$$
$$PV_{stock\,B} = \$1,025(3.605) = \$3,695$$

After adjusting, or discounting, these cash flow annuities it is evident that stock B, which will return less than stock A, is less attractive on a risk/reward basis.

• *PRESENT VALUE OF VARIABLE CASH FLOWS*

Suppose a firm expects to receive the following varying amounts of money over the next 4 years:

Year	Cash Flow
1	$1,000
2	1,200
3	1,500
4	900

The present value of this mixed cash flow is simply the sum of the present values of the four individual cash flows. If the discount rate is 10%, then the present value of such a mixed cash flow will be $3,642.43:

Year	Cash Flow	PVIF (see Table 3–4)	Present Value
1	$1,000	.9091	$ 909.10
2	1,200	.8264	991.68
3	1,500	.7513	1,126.95
4	900	.6830	614.70
		Present value of 4-year cash flow =	$ 3,642.43

• *PRESENT VALUE OF PERPETUITIES*

A perpetuity is an annuity forever! Stated otherwise, a **perpetuity** is a certain amount of money that will be paid at regular periods of time permanently. Dividends on a preferred stock or benefits from an education endowment fund may be viewed as examples of perpetuities.

Table 3–5   Present Value Interest Factor Annuities

Periods						Discount Rate						
	1%	2%	3%	4%	5%	6%	7%	8%	9%	10%	11%	12%
1	.9901	.9804	.9709	.9615	.9524	.9434	.9346	.9259	.9174	.9091	.9009	.8929
2	1.9704	1.9416	1.9135	1.8861	1.8594	1.8334	1.8080	1.7833	1.7591	1.7355	1.7125	1.6901
3	2.9410	2.8839	2.8286	2.7751	2.7233	2.6730	2.6243	2.5771	2.5313	2.4868	2.4437	2.4018
4	3.9020	3.8077	3.7171	3.6299	3.5459	3.4651	3.3872	3.3121	3.2397	3.1699	3.1024	3.0374
5	4.8535	4.7134	4.5797	4.4518	4.3295	4.2123	4.1002	3.9927	3.8896	3.7908	3.6959	3.6048
6	5.7955	5.6014	5.4172	5.2421	5.0757	4.9173	4.7665	4.6229	4.4859	4.3553	4.2305	4.1114
7	6.7282	6.4720	6.2302	6.0020	5.7863	5.5824	5.3893	5.2064	5.0329	4.8684	4.7122	4.5638
8	7.6517	7.3254	7.0196	6.7327	6.4632	6.2098	5.9713	5.7466	5.5348	5.3349	5.1461	4.9676
9	8.5661	8.1622	7.7861	7.4353	7.1078	6.8017	6.5152	6.2469	5.9852	5.7590	5.5370	5.3282
10	9.4714	8.9825	8.7302	8.1109	7.7217	7.3601	7.0236	6.7101	6.4176	6.1446	5.8892	5.6502
11	10.3677	9.7868	9.2526	8.7604	8.3064	7.8868	7.4987	7.1389	6.8052	6.4951	6.2065	5.9377
12	11.2552	10.5753	9.9539	9.3850	8.8632	8.3838	7.9427	7.5361	7.1607	6.8137	6.4924	6.1944
13	12.1338	11.3483	10.6349	9.9856	9.3935	8.8527	8.3576	7.9038	7.4869	7.1034	6.7499	6.4235
14	13.0038	12.1062	11.2960	10.5631	9.8986	9.2950	8.7454	8.2442	7.7861	7.3667	6.9819	6.6282
15	13.8651	12.8492	11.9379	11.1183	10.3796	9.7122	9.1079	8.5595	8.0607	7.6061	7.1909	6.8109
16	14.7180	13.5777	12.5610	11.6522	10.8377	10.1059	9.4466	8.8514	8.3125	7.8237	7.3792	6.9740
17	15.5624	14.2918	13.1660	12.1656	11.2740	10.4772	9.7632	9.1216	8.5436	8.0215	7.5488	7.1196
18	16.3984	14.9920	13.7534	12.6592	11.6895	10.8276	10.0591	9.3719	8.7556	8.2014	7.7016	7.2497
19	17.2261	15.2684	14.3237	13.1339	12.0853	11.1581	10.3356	9.6036	8.9501	8.3649	7.8393	7.3650
20	18.0457	16.3514	14.8774	13.5903	12.4622	11.4699	10.5940	9.8181	9.1285	8.5136	7.9633	7.4694
21	18.8571	17.0111	15.4149	14.0291	12.8211	11.7640	10.8355	10.0168	9.2922	8.6487	8.0751	7.5620
22	19.6605	17.6581	15.9368	14.4511	13.1630	12.0416	11.0612	10.2007	9.4424	8.7715	8.1757	7.6446
23	20.4559	18.2921	16.4435	14.8568	13.4885	12.3033	11.2722	10.3710	9.5802	8.8832	8.2664	7.7184
24	21.2435	18.9139	16.9355	15.2469	13.7986	12.5503	11.4693	10.5287	9.7066	8.9847	8.3481	7.7843

The present value of a perpetuity is the sum of the present value of infinite payments.

$$PV_p = \frac{D_1}{(1+R)^1} + \frac{D_2}{(1+R)^2} + \frac{D_3}{(1+R)^3} + \dots + \frac{D_\infty}{(1+R)^\infty}$$

where PV_p = present value of a perpetuity
$\quad\quad D$ = amount of regular payment
$\quad\quad R$ = discount factor
$\quad\quad \infty$ = infinity

Do you have to solve this unpleasant-looking equation to determine PV_p in the case of perpetuities? No! Mathematicians have proved that the answer to this equation is much simpler than you might think. The compact but precise equation for the present value of a perpetuity is

$$PV_p = \frac{D}{R}$$

For instance, the present value of a $2 perpetuity discounted at 8% is

$$PV_p = \frac{2}{.08} = \$25$$

YOU SHOULD REMEMBER

There are two ways to determine the present value of a future income: using a simple formula and using a present value table. The formula for the present value is

$$PV = \frac{FV_N}{(1+R)^N}$$

where PV = present value of a future income
 FV_N = future income in period N
 R = interest or discount rate
 N = number of years or periods

If you want to use the table, multiply your future income by the value of *PVIF*. In the case of annuities, multiply the amount of annuity by the value of *PVIFA* as available in the table.

INTERIM-YEAR COMPOUNDING

So far, it has been assumed for the sake of simplicity that interest is compounded only once a year. But this sort of simplicity rarely occurs in actual practice. Happily, the general tables and equations with which you have become familiar are unaffected by changes in the frequency of compounding. And the factors that *are* affected—interest rate (R) and period (N)—are easily adjusted.

If an interest rate is 10% annually, it is clear that the semiannual rate is 5%, and the quarterly rate 2.5%. Therefore, if you want to determine the annual interest on an investment that pays 10% annual interest compounded semiannually, you would look in the proper table for a 5% interest rate, *but for two periods of time*. Accordingly, interest compounded quarterly can be calculated using a 2.5% interest rate for four periods of time.

If *m* is the number of times interest is compounded in a year, future values can be calculated by

$$FV_N = P\left(1+\frac{R}{m}\right)^{mN}$$

For instance, the future value of $100, compounded monthly at an annual rate of 12%, after 2 years is determined as follows:

$$FV_2 = \$100\left(1 + \frac{.12}{12}\right)^{(12)(2)} = \$100(1.01)^{24} = \$12,700$$

Example 1: Interim-Year Compounding

PROBLEM   Assume you deposit $100 in a bank that pays 8% interest compounded quarterly. This means that at the end of each quarter your deposit gets bigger and interest is paid on the original deposit plus any accrued interest. How much will your bankbook show at the end of 1 year?

SOLUTION   Using 2% as the interest rate $\left(\frac{8\%}{4} = 2\%\right)$, compound as follows:

1st quarter: $100.00 × 1.02 = $102.00
2nd quarter: $102.00 × 1.02 = $104.04
3rd quarter: $104.04 × 1.02 = $106.12
4th quarter: $106.12 × 1.02 = $108.24

At the beginning of the following year the bankbook will record a total of $108.24 on deposit.

It is easier, however, to use the future value table to compute the final value of the deposit. Since the time involves 4 periods, look up 4 periods (years) in the table at 2% and find that the *FV* factor is 1.0824. As a result, the figure on deposit in the bank at the beginning of the following year equals $108.24 (or 100 × 1.0824). One point requires clarification. *It is important to remember when using the tables that the figure in the first column is not necessarily the number of years. It is the number of time periods—and the other columns give the interest rate for each time period.*

Example 2: Interim-Year Compounding

PROBLEM   Determine the future value after 2 years of $100 deposited today if the annual interest rate is 12% and interest is compounded monthly.

SOLUTION   There are 12 months in a year; therefore, *N*, the number of periods, is 24 (2 years × 12 months). Since interest is compounded monthly, *R*, the monthly compounding rate, is 1% (12% ÷ 12 months). Looking through Table 3-1, you can find that the future value of $1 after 24 periods at the rate of 1% is $1.27. The future value of $100 is, therefore, $127 (1.27 × $100).

CALCULATING GROWTH RATES

Knowing growth rates can be very valuable. They can give you the rates of annual returns that can be obtained from any given shares of stock. These rates can then be compared to the annual return rates of other assets to find out if they are faster or slower.

You can use present value or future value tables to find out the annual growth rates of revenues, earnings, dividends, and so on. Suppose the dividend per share has been $2, $2.10, $2.40, and $3.04 from year 1 to year 4, respectively. What is the annual rate of growth of this stream of dividends?

The first step is to find out the total percentage growth in the above series of dividends. This can be done in the following manner:

$$\frac{FV}{PV} = \frac{3.04}{2.00} = 1.520$$

The value 1.520 is the factor to look up in the *FV* table corresponding to 4 years; the annual rate of growth obtained is approximately 11%. The procedure for computing rates of growth, then, is:

1. Divide the terminal value by the first figure in the series.

2. For the given number of years (or periods), find the rate in the future value table that corresponds with the value you calculated in Step 1.

YOU SHOULD REMEMBER

In actual practice, interest rates are usually compounded more often than once a year. If *m* is the number of times that interest is compounded in a year, the future value (*FV*) of an initial deposit (*P*) at an interest rate of *R* after *N* years is calculated as follows:

$$FV = P\left(1 + \frac{R}{m}\right)^{mN}$$

To determine the rate of growth, divide the terminal value by the first value in the series to get a figure. Then, for the given number of years (or periods), find the growth rate in the future value table that corresponds with that particular figure.

KNOW THE CONCEPTS

DO YOU KNOW THE BASICS?

1. Is a dollar today worth more than a dollar next year if the annual rate of inflation is zero?

2. Does preference for liquidity increase or decrease the cash value of a future income? Explain in your own words.

3. Which offer would you rather accept: an investment paying 10% compounded annually, or an investment paying 10% compounded quarterly?

4. Give two examples of common annuities.

5. What happens to present values when the interest is compounded more frequently?

TERMS FOR STUDY

annuity
capitalization rate
discount rate
future value
inflation
liquidity

perpetuity
preference for liquidity
present value
risk
securities

PRACTICAL APPLICATION

COMPUTATIONAL PROBLEMS

1. Using the basic formula for future value, determine how much an investor will collect after 5 years if $1 is deposited and is compounded annually at the rate of 8%.

2. Using the future value table, determine the future value of $500 invested for 8 years if the rate of interest is 12% compounded annually.

3. What is the future value of a $250 annuity at the end of the next 5 years if the annual compounding rate is 10%?

4. The future value of an annuity after 4 years is $4,000. If the annual compounding interest rate is 8%, what is the value of each annuity payment?

5. A government bond can be converted to $25,000 at maturity 10 years from now. What is the value of this bond if the discount rate in the bond market is 9%? (Ignore interest payments on the bond.)

6. Which alternative do you prefer: $4,500 cash or $1,200 each year for a period of 4 years? Assume a discount rate of 10% annually.

7. You have borrowed $6,000 from the ABC Bank for a period of 4 years. The annual interest rate is 12%. Can you determine your annual repayment of the loan? (Hint: $6,000 is the present value of your annual loan repayment.)

8. Determine the future value of $1,200 after 4 years under the following assumptions:
   (a) Interest is compounded annually at 12%.
   (b) Interest is compounded semiannually at 12%.
   (c) Interest is compounded quarterly at 16%.
   (d) Interest is compounded monthly at 24%.

9. A share of preferred stock is usually viewed as a perpetuity. If the annual dividend of a preferred stock is $5 and the discount rate is 10%, what is the value of that preferred stock? (Hint: Calculate the present value of a $5 perpetuity.)

10. Suppose a bond will give you $100 annual interest forever. Can you determine the present value of such a perpetuity? (Assume an annual discount rate of 12%.)

11. You are planning to lease a BMW and trying to make a choice between two options: You can lease the car either for a $4,200 initial payment and $610 monthly payments for 36 months or for an $8,160 initial payment and $495 monthly payments for 36 months. Assume that the discount rate is 1% per month and compounded monthly.
   (a) Calculate the total payments for the first option ignoring the time value of money concept.
   (b) Calculate the total payments for the second option ignoring the time value of money concept.
   (c) Which option would you choose according to the results in (a) and (b)?
   (d) Calculate the present value of the first option.
   (e) Calculate the present value of the second option.
   (f) After the present value calculations, which option would you choose?

12. New York lottery is offering a new lotto. Winners can pick their own price where they can win either $15,000 a year for the next 10 years or $10,000 a year forever. Assuming that the discount rate is 12% a year, calculate the present value of both options.

13. Your spouse and you have decided to put aside $7,500 a year for retirement. Assuming that you can earn 9% interest on your investment, what would be the total amount in your account after 32 years?

14. You are estimating that the price of a trip around the world will be $30,000 in 10 years from now. How much should you put aside each year in order to save for this trip? Assume the interest rate is 10%.

15. You have learned that you have inherited a bank account from your grandfather who had deposited $350 into the account 95 years ago. The account has been receiving 7% interest annually.

    (a) How much money have you inherited from your grandfather?

    (b) How much money would you have received if your grandfather has negotiated the interest rate to be 9%?

16. If a $500 investment earns an interest rate of 6%, approximately how many years will it take to double? How long will it take if the investment earns an interest rate of 15%?

17. You are planning to retire in 20 years, and at that time you will need $2 million. How much will you have to save at the end of each year for the next 20 years to meet that goal, if the interest rate is 6.5%?

18. You are planning on purchasing a house for $450,000. You will have to put down 15% in the form of a down payment. You then plan on financing the rest at 6.5% for a thirty-year mortgage. Calculate the PV after the down payment and the monthly payments.

19. You have $1,000, and today you want to invest it. The bank makes an agreement with you that it will pay you $1,500 in 5 years. With the information provided, what is the interest rate that you will be receiving on this investment?

20. Today is July 21, 2011. There is a bond that will mature on December 23, 2020. The bond has a face value of $1,000 and an annual coupon rate of 8% being paid semiannually. This bond is trading at Bloomberg terminal at $1,020 with a market rate at 6%. What is the fair price? Should I buy this bond?

21. You are planning on purchasing a condo for $750,000 with 10% down payment. In order to finance the remaining balance, you have two options: A) you can borrow at 7% fixed 30-year mortgage or B) borrow at 5% fixed 15-year mortgage. Calculate the difference between the two options.

22. You are a winner from the lottery drawing, and you will now receive $60,000 each year, which will continue forever. However, the first payment will be made immediately. What is the current value of your lottery winnings if interest rate is 8%?

23. You have the following cash flow information; you are to calculate the net PV of this cash flow at 10%.

Year	Cash Flow
0	–10,000
1	5,000
2	3,000
3	–2,000
4	4,500
5	500

24. You have a bond with an annual coupon of 5% (paid and discounted annually) with a maturity of six years from now. What is the approximate price of this bond four years from now (price in year 4) if the interest rate goes up to 12% in year 4?

ANSWERS

KNOW THE CONCEPTS

1. No. If the inflation rate is zero, a dollar today and a dollar next year have the same purchasing power.

2. As preference for liquidity goes up, the cash value of future income declines because future income becomes less certain and less desirable.

3. The investment paying 10% compounded quarterly is preferable because the interest paid will be greater.

4. Mortgage or home loans; pension funds.

5. The value declines.

PRACTICAL APPLICATION

1. $\$1(1.08)^5 = \$1.469$

2. $500 (*FVIF* of 12%, 8 yrs) = $500(2.476) = $1,238

3. $250 (*FVIFA* of 10%, 5 yrs) = $250(6.1051) = $1,526

4. $4,000 (*PVIFA* of 8%, 4 yrs) = $4,000(4.506) = $888

5. $25,000 (*PVIF* of 9%, 10 yrs) = $25,000(.4224) = $10,560

6. $1,200 (*PVIFA* of 10%, 4 yrs) = $1,200(3.1699) = $3,803 Therefore, $4,500 cash is preferred.

7. $6,000 (*PVIFA* of 12%, 4 yrs) = $\dfrac{\$6,000}{3.0373} = \$1,975$

8. (a) $1,200 (*FVIF* of 12%, 4 yrs)
= $1,200(1.5735) = $1,888
  (b) $1,200 (*FVIF* of 6%, 8 periods) = $1,200(1.5938) = $1,912
  (c) $1,200 (*FVIF* of 4%, 16 periods) = $1,200(1.873) = $2,247
  (d) $1,200 (*FVIF* of 2%, 48 periods) = $1,200(2.587) = $3,104

9. $\dfrac{\$5}{.10} = \$50$

10. $\dfrac{\$100}{.12} = \$833$

11. (a) $4,200 + 36 \times 610 = \$26,160$

(b) $8,160 + 36 \times 495 = \$25,980$

(c) Option 2, since the total payments is less than option 1.

(d) $4,200 + \$610$ (*PVIFA* of 1%, 36 months) $= \$4,200 + \$610$

$$\left[\frac{1}{0.01} - \frac{1}{0.01(1+0.01)^{36}} \right]$$

$$= \$4,200 + \$610 \times 30.107$$
$$= \$22,565.27$$

(e) $8,160 + \$495$ (*PVIFA* of 1%, 36 months) $= \$8,160 + \$495$

$$\left[\frac{1}{0.01} - \frac{1}{0.01(1+0.01)^{36}} \right]$$

$$= \$8160 + \$495 \times 30.107$$
$$= \$23,062.97$$

(f) Option 1

12. *PV* ($15,000 a year for 10 years)
$$= \$15,000 \times \left[\frac{1}{0.12} - \frac{1}{0.12(1+0.12)^{10}} \right]$$
$$= \$15,000 \times 5.6503$$
$$= \$84,754.50$$

PV ($10,000 a year forever)
$$= \$10,000/0.12$$
$$= \$83,333.33$$

13. $7,500 (*FVIFA* of 9%, 32 years)
$$= \$7,500 \times \left[\frac{(1+0.09)^{32}-1}{0.09} \right]$$
$$= \$7,500 \times 164.03$$
$$= \$1,230,277.40$$

14. $30,000 = \text{Yearly savings} \times FVI_{R=0.10,N=10}FA$
Yearly saving $= \$30,000 / 15.937$
$$= \$1,882.41$$

15. (a) $100 (*FVIFA* of 7%, 95 years) $= \$100 \times (1 + 0.07)^{95}$
$$= \$350 \times 618.67$$
$$= \$216,534.50$$

(b) $100 (*FVIFA* of 9%, 95 years) $= \$100 \times (1 + 0.09)^{95}$
$$= \$350 \times 3593.49$$
$$= \$1,257,721.50$$

16. Use your calculator: $6 = I/Y$; $5,000 = PV$; $10,000 = FV$; $0 = PMT$; **CPT = N**
Answer = 12 years (rounded); Do the same for 15%; the answer is 5
years (rounded.)
Note: If you use equations, instead of the calculator, you would
get the same answers. Please do if you want to verify your answers
through equations.

17. $FVA_n = PMT \dfrac{(1 + R)^n - 1}{R}$

$$2,000,000 = PMT \left(\dfrac{(1.065)^{20} - 1}{0.065} \right)$$

$$\dfrac{2,000,000}{38.8253} = \dfrac{PMT (38.8253)}{38.8253}$$

$$\$51,512.79 = PMT$$

18. 15% of $450,000 = $67,500 down payment

$450,000 − $67,500 = $382,500 PV

$N = 30*12 = 360$
$I/Y(R) = 6.5/12$
$PV = -382,500$
$FV = 0$
$PMT = \$2,417.66$

19. $FV = PV * (1+r)^n$

$1500 = 1000 * (1 + r)^5$
$1000 = 1000$
$1.5^{1/5} = (1 + r)^{5*(1/5)}$
$1.5^{0.2} = 1 + r$
$1.0845 = 1 + r$
$-1 \quad = -1 + r$
$.0845 = r$
$8.45\% = r$

20. 80% of $1,000 = $80

$80/2 = $40 paid semiannually
$N = 19$; $(6/2 = 3)$ $R = 3$; $PMT = \$40$; $FV = 1000$ $\boxed{PV = \$1,423.23}$

21. 10% of $750,000 = $75,000

$750,000 − $75,000 = $675,000 PV

Enter each option in a financial calculator:

Option A: $PV = -675,000$; $I/Y(R) = 7\%/12$; $N = 30*12 = 360$;
$CPT\ PMT = \$4,490.79$

Option B: $PV = -675{,}000$; I/Y $(R) = 5\%/12$; $N = 15*12 = 180$;
   CPT $PMT = \$5{,}337.86$

The difference between Option B and Option A is:
$5{,}337.86 - 4{,}490.79 = \$847.07$

22. $\dfrac{60{,}000}{.08} = \$750{,}000$

$\$750{,}000 + \$60{,}000 = \$810{,}000$

PV_p = present value of perpetuity
$PV = PV_p + PV$ of 6000 at time 0.
$PV = 60{,}000 + 60{,}000/0.08 = \$810{,}000$

23. To solve for this problem enter it into a financial calculator.
1st press $\boxed{CF}$ then press $\boxed{2^{nd}}$ $\boxed{CE/C}$

Then press

CF0 = –10,000	$\boxed{enter}$ $\boxed{\downarrow}$
C01 = 5,000	$\boxed{enter}$ $\boxed{\downarrow}$
F01 = 1.00	$\boxed{enter}$ $\boxed{\downarrow}$
C02 = 3,000	$\boxed{enter}$ $\boxed{\downarrow}$
F02 = 1.00	$\boxed{enter}$ $\boxed{\downarrow}$
C03 = –2,000	$\boxed{enter}$ $\boxed{\downarrow}$
F03 = 1.00	$\boxed{enter}$ $\boxed{\downarrow}$
C04 = 4,500	$\boxed{enter}$ $\boxed{\downarrow}$
F04 = 1.00	$\boxed{enter}$ $\boxed{\downarrow}$
C05 = 500	$\boxed{enter}$ $\boxed{\downarrow}$
F01 = 1.00	$\boxed{enter}$ $\boxed{\downarrow}$

Then press $\boxed{NPV}$ enter 10% for $I(R)$ and then press $\boxed{CPT}$ $\boxed{NPV}$ = –1,093.82

24. To solve this problem enter into the financial calculator:

$PMT = 1{,}000*5\% = \$50$
$N = 6 - 4 = 2$
$I/Y = 12$
$FV = 1{,}000$
$\boxed{CPT}$ $\boxed{PV}$ = –881.70

4

RISK AND RETURN

KEY TERMS

arbitrage pricing theory (APT) an alternate method for determining the required rate of return of an asset. That rate of return is a function of several factors. Price equilibrium among assets is maintained by arbitrage

beta the risk observed in a security relative to the risk of a market portfolio (Since market risk equals 1.0, assets with betas >1 are riskier than assets with betas <1.)

coefficient of variation a statistical ratio that measures the volatility of an asset's return relative to its risk

covariance method for calculating the way returns move relative to one another in a portfolio (The more different the movements between assets, the less the risk.)

efficient frontier an upward sloping curve that matches different portfolio risk levels with corresponding optimal returns

efficient market a thesis that maintains that the market incorporates all information. New information causes stock prices to change; consequently, stock prices represent fair values

risk the degree of time uncertainty and volatility involved with a project or investment

risk/return trade-off the relationship between the riskiness of an investment and its expected returns

security market line (SML) the security market line compares the risk of a security (beta) to its required rate of return

standard deviation a measure of the dispersion of returns (their volatility) away from an expected return

volatility the fluctuations that occur away from a common denominator such as the mean, or expected value (The greater the volatility in returns, the greater the risk.)

RELATIONSHIP BETWEEN RISK AND RETURN

Risk and return are the foundations upon which rational and intelligent investment decisions are made. Broadly speaking, **risk** is a measure of the volatility, or uncertainty of returns, and **returns** are the expected receipts or cash flows anticipated from any investment.

The following example may help explain the meaning of risk. Everyone knows that deposits at a savings bank are safer than money bet on a horse race. Bank deposits yield a steady but low rate of interest year by year and are insured by the Federal Deposit Insurance Corporation (FDIC). There is a high degree of confidence that these returns and the original deposit will be paid back. The returns from bank deposits don't fluctuate very much, and for this reason they are considered to be safe and to have a low degree of risk. On the other hand, when people gamble they don't know the outcome. They may win big, but they can also lose everything. Returns from horse betting are highly uncertain, very volatile, and subject to a high degree of risk. When two investments yield the same returns, the final choice will be based on the evaluation of the riskiness of each project. The project having the lower risk will be selected.

WHY DIFFERENT INVESTMENTS PAY DIFFERENT RETURNS

Some investments pay a high return, and others a low return. Certainly, you can't expect a high return from a "sure thing." But it is reasonable to demand a high return when asked to invest money in an uncertain or risky venture. In other words, investors must be properly compensated for the risks they take.

RELATIONSHIP BETWEEN RISK AND RETURN

The return on your money should be proportional to the risk involved. Risk is a measure of the volatility of returns and the uncertainty of future outcomes.

Risk is the degree of uncertainty associated with an investment. The more volatile the returns from an investment, the greater its risk. When two projects have the same expected returns, choose the one with the least risk.

Low risk is associated with low returns and high risk with high returns. The relationship between risk and expected returns is illustrated in Figure 4-1. At zero risk investors will get Y_1 returns, at X_1 risk they will get Y_2 returns, and at X_2 risk they will get Y_3 returns. Figure 4-1 presents the trade-off between risk and expected returns. Under normal circumstances, low risk will bring low returns and high risk is associated with high returns.

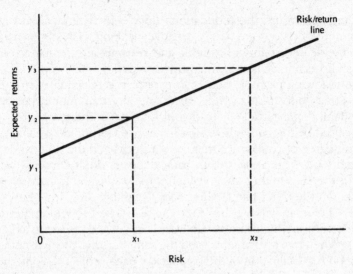

Figure 4-1 Relationship between Risk and Return

In finance, risk is measured by the degree of volatility associated with expected returns. **Volatility** is the amount of fluctuation that occurs in a series of figures as they deviate from a representative average. For example, the average of the series 1, 2, 3 is 2, and the average of the series 1, 3, 5 is 3. The second series is considered more volatile than the first series of figures. The higher the volatility, then, the higher the level of risk.

Another factor that adds to risk is time. Present cash is worth more to investors than future cash. When an investor lends money, there is always the risk or uncertainty that the loan may not be repaid. To get lenders to take the risk of parting with their cash, lenders have to be properly compensated. An example should help explain this principle.

Example: Risk and Return

Assume an individual has $10,000 in cash. If $1,000 is lent or invested, the individual gives up the safety of cash for an uncertain future return a year from today and might ask for a $100 return to lend this initial $1,000. The return is equivalent to 10% ($100 ÷ $1,000).

The investor now becomes more reluctant to part with additional cash. If asked to lend an additional $1,000, the investor might ask for a $110 return to overcome a growing reluctance to give up the safety of cash and to assume the growing risk of a future return. The rate of return on the additional investment of $1,000 is 11% ($110 ÷ $1,000). The total rate of return on both investments would be 10.5% ($210 ÷ $2,000).

The principle is that the future is riskier than the present. As more cash is invested, risk increases, and investors want to be compensated for taking this extra risk. In other words, the required rate of return (discount rate) increases with the growing risk of tying up more funds in an asset that promises a future return.

As demonstrated in subsequent chapters, *the key to all valuation and capital budgeting decisions is the analysis of risk and return.* Capital budgeting decisions involve adjusting future expected returns for risk and comparing these returns with the cost of a project. In this way, it is possible to determine whether or not a project is acceptable, and whether it is more or less profitable than some other project.

YOU SHOULD REMEMBER

There is a trade-off between risk and return. Generally, the more risk, the higher the expected return, and the lower the risk, the lower the expected return. Also, the longer the time money is at risk, the greater the return required.

• *MEASURING RETURN*

A company invests funds to make a profit and to gain a return. We can say, therefore, that the decision to invest is to generate earnings. These earnings are translated into two returns:

1. Appreciation in the price of the company's stock

2. A series of dividend payments made possible by these earnings.

Many times it is not possible to determine the future returns of the investment in a project. There simply are no data available. In finance, it is theoretically possible to employ a proxy. That is, one should be able to find a stock that has the same features as the project under investigation, calculate the expected returns of this stock, and then assume these returns will reflect the returns of the project. Mathematically, the expected returns of a stock used as a proxy for evaluating a project are obtained as follows:

$$\frac{\text{Expected}}{\text{return}} = \frac{\text{Dividend} + \text{Capital appreciation}}{\text{Value of stock in period } (t-1)} = \frac{D_t + (P_t - P_{(t-1)})}{P_{t-1}}$$

where D_t = dividend in current year
P_t = price of stock in current year
P_{t-1} = price of stock in previous year
t = period of time

Using this formula to calculate expected returns, we can obtain a series of annual **dividend yields** and the **capital appreciation** of the stock. Let's see how these returns are computed if we assume that the dividend (D_t) equals $1, the previous period stock price ($P_t - 1$) was $10, and the current price (P_t) is $11.

$$\text{Rate of returns} = \frac{\$1.00}{\$10.00} + \frac{(\$11 - \$10)}{\$10.00} = 20\%$$

Suppose we calculate the rates of returns for a number of years, and find that in poor economic times they average 10%, in normal business times they are 20%, and in boom times they average 30%. The likelihood is that these returns will fall in a range of 10% to 30%, but the actual figure depends on economic conditions. If we can establish the probable future economic climate, we can obtain an expected value. After asking some economists and other experts, it is decided that there is a 30% chance for a poor economy, a 40% chance we will have a normal economy, and a 30% chance for a booming economy.

The parameters are available for calculating the expected return, of the range of returns, by using the following formula:

$$\overline{K} = \sum_{t=1}^{N} K_1 P_1$$

Given our three scenarios of poor (p), normal (n), and boom (b) periods, the preceding equation can be expanded as follows:

$$\overline{K} = K_p P_p + K_n P_n + K_b P_b$$

where $\overline{K}$ = expected returns
K_1 or (K_p, K_n, K_b) = returns in poor periods (K_p), returns in normal periods (K_n), and returns in boom periods (K_b)
P_1 or (P_p, P_n, P_b) = probabilities in poor periods (P_p), probabilities in normal periods (P_n), and probabilities in boom periods (P_b)

The expected return of the three returns in this example are calculated as shown in Table 4-1. This probable expected return of .20 becomes the benchmark for calculating the deviations of actual values away from the expected value and, therefore, determines the risk of a project.

Table 4–1   Calculating Expected Returns by Using Probabilities

Expected Economic Conditions	Actual Returns (K)	Probabilities (P)	K × P
Poor	10%	.30	.03
Normal	20%	.40	.08
Boom	30%	.30	.09
		Expected Return $\overline{K}$	.20

• *MEASURING RISK*

Risk is defined as the deviation of expected outcomes from a mean or expected value. It can also be regarded as the chance of incurring a loss or gain by investing in an asset or project. The chances of making a profit or incurring a loss can be high or low depending on the degree of risk (variability of expected returns) associated with a given investment.

The simplest way to analyze risk is to break it down into two components: the *level of risk* and the *risk of time*. Why is this distinction necessary? The answer is: Investment decisions are based on the calculation of the present value of **cash flows** generated by the investment. To obtain the present value of a series of future cash flows, we must first establish the degree of risk (discount rate) of a project. And second, since these cash flows are generated over a number of future years, we must take into account the time value of money.

THE LEVEL OF RISK

The level of risk can be determined by comparing the risk of one asset to that of another. For example, the risk associated with AT&T is generally much less than that for a small firm. In other words, some firms have a low degree of risk while others have a high degree of risk. This is important because low-risk firms can borrow funds more cheaply than high-risk firms. Their discount rate or required rate of return is lower, which means that a return for the low-risk firm gets a better valuation in the marketplace than the same return generated by a high-risk firm.

The chances of getting back an investment in AT&T stock are much better than they are for an unknown small company. Usually, it is easier to forecast the returns of a low-risk company than to forecast the returns of a high-risk company. Why? Because the volatility of the low-risk company's returns are usually small, whereas the returns of high-risk companies are subject to high volatility.

THE RISK OF TIME

In financial jargon, risk is an increasing function of time. In other words, the longer funds remain invested, the greater is the risk involved. If the investment has no chance of loss and is made for a very short period, it is called risk-free. If a longer time period is considered, though, a premium must be paid to lenders for assuming this time risk. Therefore, the usual procedure is to divide total risk into a risk-free rate and a risk premium.

Total risk = Risk-free rate + Risk premium

The **risk-free rate** is the interest rate paid on assets that provide a sure return, like U.S. treasury bills, which come due in 90 days and are backed by the federal government's guarantee to pay on maturity. This risk-free rate provides the benchmark for measuring how risky other assets are. A **risk premium** is the required rate of return of an asset over and above the risk-free rate. Because long-term government securities mature years from now, they have a higher risk premium than one-year government notes. You can see that this kind of risk rating helps investors to measure the relative time risks of different assets.

The way to measure the risk of a project (or company) is to calculate the volatility of the expected returns of that project. If the expected returns are highly volatile, the chances of knowing the outcome will be less than when returns fluctuate in a narrow range. For example, in Figure 4-2 the returns of Company A are more volatile than those of Company B. Investors would feel more confident in judging the outcome of Company B's return than those of Company A.

The following illustration should help to explain why the analysis of risk is so important. Let us assume investors are evaluating two companies (A and B), one a low-risk company (A) and the other a high-risk company (B). Investors estimate that both companies will generate returns of $1.00 and $1.50 per share over the next two years. Low-risk Company A is assigned a 10% discount rate and high-risk Company B a 20% discount rate. The discounted present values of these two companies are

$$PV_a = \frac{1.00}{(1.10)^1} + \frac{1.50}{(1.10)^2} = \$2.15$$

$$PV_b = \frac{1.00}{(1.20)^1} + \frac{1.50}{(1.20)^2} = \$1.87$$

All other things being equal, investors will find the earnings of Company A more attractive than those of Company B.

Since the risk-free rate provides a benchmark, the risk premiums of more risky assets can be measured as the difference between the total risk of different assets and the risk-free rate. This measurement is shown in Table 4-2 for government securities differing in the time to maturity.

Table 4–2   How Risk Changes Over Time

	Time to Maturity	Risk-Free Rate (%)	Risk Premium (%)	Total Risk (%)
Treasury bills	90 days	5	0	5
Government notes	1 year	5	2	7
Government bonds	20 years	5	4	9
Corporate bonds	20 years	5	5	10

This ranking of risk levels helps to evaluate the relative merits of assets. A study of the returns of these assets would indicate that the prices of short-term securities are less volatile than those of long-term securities. The chances of default are smaller for short-term securities than for long-term securities. Consequently, the risk assigned to them is less than for longer term and less certain securities.

The same principle applies in measuring the riskiness of other assets. The volatility of the returns of any asset measures the level of risk. The wider dispersion of Company A's returns in Figure 4-2 indicates that there is a greater chance that an estimate will fall either below or above the straight line. This range is unwieldy to work with and makes the merits of investments more difficult to evaluate. Some judgment must be applied in order to help bring the range down to a more manageable single figure. To do this, it is necessary to assign probabilities to the different estimated values in the range. These probabilities, of course, must add up to 1.00.

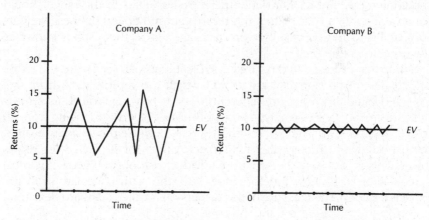

Figure 4-2 Volatility of Returns for Company A and Company B
Note: Company A and Company B have same percentage scale of returns and EV = expected value.

CALCULATING EXPECTED RETURNS AND RISKS OF UNCERTAIN PROJECTS

ASSIGNING PROBABILITIES

Probabilities help us to determine the likelihood or chance of an event occurring. Some probabilities can be obtained from actual observations. For example, the risk of getting heads or tails from a coin can be readily measured by flipping it many times and finding out the actual outcomes. On the other hand, there are instances—such as the introduction of a new product—when the outcome is highly uncertain. In these cases, there usually is no past experience to draw on. The manager must make a judgment as to the probable outcome. Because the future returns from the new product are highly uncertain, a manager will work with the assumption that projected returns will probably fall within a particular range. The more uncertain the outcome, the bigger the range. Since it is difficult to interpret returns from a range, managers assign weights or probabilities to the values in the range in order to bring the figures in the range down to a single and more manageable figure. One way this can be done is to apply the formula we have already encountered.

$$\overline{K} = K_p P_p + K_n P_n + K_b P_b$$

Table 4-3 compares the returns of Project A with the returns of Project B. Project A's returns fluctuate within a narrower range than Project B's. Based on subjective judgments, it is assumed that the most likely outcome should get a weight of 50% while the extreme values in the range should get a value of 25% each. When the returns are multiplied by these weights (probabilities) and the resulting products are added, the result is known as the expected value $(\overline{E}_R)$.

Notice that the expected returns in Project A and Project B are the same, or 320. The dispersions (or range over which the returns vary) from this expected value, however, are different for each project. Project A's returns range from 100 to 500, whereas Project B has a dispersion ranging from 80 to 600. What does this mean? It indicates that, because the volatility around the expected return is smaller for Project A than for Project B, its risk is lower. This is precisely the way the individual risk of each project is measured—namely, by how much or how little the returns deviate from the expected values. The measure of this dispersion is called standard deviation.

YOU SHOULD REMEMBER

In the securities market, a stock's returns consist of capital gains plus dividend yield. These stock returns can serve as a proxy for a project's return.

The valuation of securities and the determination of the merits of investments involve the use of risk and return concepts. Managers will invest as long as discounted future returns exceed the cost of the original investment. Risk has two components: the level of risk and the uncertainty of time. The level of risk is measured by a discount rate and the time risk by a discounting process, which adjusts future return for the increased risk of time.

STANDARD DEVIATION AS A MEASURE OF RISK

One common way to measure the risk of an asset is to calculate its deviation from a mean or an expected return. Since the expected returns of both projects in Table 4-3 are the same (320), it is evident that the higher dispersion of Project B (100-500 for A versus 80-600 for B) implies that B project is riskier than A. By assuming that all values are distributed normally—that the returns are distributed equally between the higher and lower sides of expected returns—it is possible to measure the volatility of returns for each project and, in turn, to measure their comparative risk. This can be done, for Project A, by subtracting the actual returns (100, 333, and 500) in the range from the expected return (K) of 320: $(K - K)$. The values derived from these calculations are then squared to eliminate the problem of minus signs. In a world of uncertainty, probabilities are assigned to each deviation to obtain a single representative value, which is called **variance**. The square root of variance is none other than the **standard deviation**.

**Table 4–3 Obtaining Expected Values by Assigning Probabilities
to Projected Returns**

Probable Outcome	Projected Return (K)	Weight or Probability (p)	Probably Return (K × p)
Project A			
Pessimistic	100	.20	20
Most likely	333	.60	200
Optimistic	500	.20	100
		1.00	320 ($\bar{E}_R$)
Project B			
Pessimistic	80	.25	20
Most likely	300	.50	150
Optimistic	600	.25	150
		1.00	320 ($\bar{E}_R$)

$\bar{E}_R$ = Expected returns.

$$\text{Standard deviation } (\sigma) = \sqrt{\sum_{t=1}^{N}(K-\overline{K})^2 P_i}$$

where N = number of observations
t = time periods
$\overline{K}$ = expected returns
P_t = probabilities of returns
K = actual returns

Table 4-4 presents a simple example that shows how the standard deviation of Project A is computed.

Table 4–4 Calculating the Standard Deviation of Project A's Returns

i	K	$\overline{K}$	$(K-\overline{K})$	$(K-\overline{K})^2$	P_i (probabilities)	$(K-\overline{K})^2 P_i$
1	100	320	−220	48,400	.20	9,680
2	333	320	+ 13	169	.60	101
3	500	320	+180	32,400	.20	6,480
						Variance = 16,261

Standard deviation of Project A = $\sqrt{\text{variance}}$ or $\sqrt{16,261}$ = 128. Using the same approach, the standard deviation of Project B (see Table 4-3 for figures) is 185.

What does all this mean? First, you must assume that the probability distribution is normal. This implies that half the values in the distribution are likely to fall below the expected value and half to fall above the expected value. The closer a distribution is to the expected value, the more likely it is that the actual outcomes will be closer to the mean or expected value. Chances will be higher that the outcomes will be close to the expected value in a narrow distribution than in a wide distribution.

As Figure 4-3 shows, probability distributions for both A and B are normal, but B has a wider dispersion away from the expected value. Consequently, the distribution for B is considered riskier than the distribution for A. Note: Both probability distributions have the same expected value, but A has a narrower distribution, indicating less volatility relative to the expected value and hence less risk.

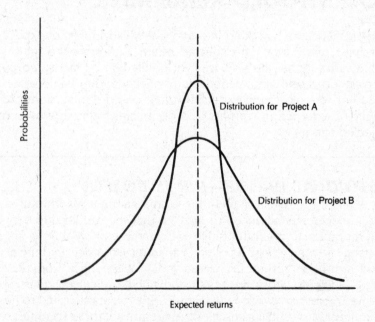

Figure 4-3 Normal Probability Distributions of Two Projects, A and B

In finance, it is statistically acceptable to assume that probability distributions are normally bell-shaped because this assumption facilitates the calculation of expected outcomes. For example, statisticians have discovered that in cases involving normal distributions one can expect 68% of the outcomes or returns to fall within plus or minus one standard deviation of the expected value. In the preceding example, when you subtract and add one standard deviation (128) from the expected return of 320, the result will be a range of 192 to 448. This range indicates that, in 68 out of 100 times, you can expect returns to fall within the range of 192 to 448. When two standard deviations (256) are used, practically all of the values in the distribution (or 95%) should fall within a range of 64 to 576. The accepted procedure is to work with one standard deviation.

Table 4-4 indicates that the standard deviation of Project B is 185. In the case of Project B, a deviation of plus or minus one standard deviation produces a range of 135 to 505, which is wider than the 192 to 448 range for Project A. Given these parameters, the risk of Project A can be compared to that of Project B. They have the same expected return, but because Project A has a smaller dispersion around the expected value—its standard deviation is lower—its risk is lower than that of Project B.

YOU SHOULD REMEMBER

Risk is measured by taking into account the variability of expected returns away from an expected return. The more the returns fluctuate, the higher the risk. This variability can be measured by using standard deviation. When returns are uncertain, the accepted procedure for calculating expected values and probable standard deviations is to assign weights or probabilities to the figures in a projected range.

HISTORICAL PROOF—R/R IS POSITIVE

Having outlined the statistical methods for measuring risk and returns, no tangible evidence was advanced to indicate that the relationship between risk and return is a direct and positive one. To this end, we refer to a study by Ibbotson and Sinquefield. These two academicians calculated the actual historical returns of several broad categories of securities from 1926 to 1988 (see Table 4-5). Stock returns were defined as dividends plus capital gains while the returns of fixed-income securities were calculated to be the sum of interest plus capital gains. Once the returns of these securities were obtained, their corresponding standard deviations were calculated and the results analyzed. The historical results support precisely what was discussed before.

Table 4–5   Risk and Returns of Selected Securities 1926–1988

	Average Annual Returns (%)	Standard Deviations
Small stocks	17.8	35.6
Common stocks	12.1	20.0
Long-term corporate bonds	5.3	8.4
Long-term government bonds	4.7	8.5
U.S. Treasury bills	3.6	4.7

As one would expect, small speculative or unseasoned companies, as well as common stocks, in general, recorded the highest risk (standard deviations) and returns. Obviously, part of this pattern reflects the fluctuations in the earnings of stocks without the guarantees of repayment of principle in case of default. Bonds were less risky than stocks, according to a comparison of their standard deviations, but their returns were also lower. The low-time risk of U.S. Treasury bills constitutes an additional factor responsible for the low risk and low returns of these government securities. Based on this historical evidence, sufficient proof has been supplied to support the concept that the relationship between risk and return is a direct and positive one.

COEFFICIENT OF VARIATION: THE RISK/RETURN TRADE-OFF

What if the expected returns of one project differ from those of another project? In this case, it is difficult to compare absolute measures of dispersion as provided by standard deviation. The way to deal with this problem is to determine the risk of a project relative to its expected returns. This measure is called the **coefficient of variation**, or **risk/return trade-off ratio**. It is calculated as follows:

$$\text{Coefficient of variation } (CV) = \frac{\text{Standard deviation of returns}}{\text{Expected returns}} = \frac{\sigma}{K}$$

Example: Calculating the Risk/Return Trade-off

PROBLEM   Interpret the risk/return trade-off by using the figures calculated in the preceding example, where the standard deviations are 128 and 185 for Projects A and B, respectively.

SOLUTION   Expected returns in both cases are 320. The coefficients of variation (*CV*) for the two projects are:

$$CV \text{ of Project A: } \frac{128}{320} = .40$$

$$CV \text{ or Project B: } \frac{185}{320} = .58$$

Even though Project A's expected return is the same as Project B's, the risk or standard deviation of Project A is lower, and it has a better risk/return trade-off ratio.

When the coefficients of variation of different projects are compared, the lower the *CV*, the better the project from a risk/return trade-off point of view. Project A is a better investment because, despite having the same expected return, it has a lower risk than Project B. Therefore, Project A is better than Project B.

YOU SHOULD REMEMBER

In order to compare the risk/return trade-offs of different investments, it is necessary to state these values on a relative basis. The coefficient of variation, which represents the standard deviation divided by the expected return, accomplishes this feat. The lower the value of the coefficient of variation, the better the merits of an investment from a risk/return standpoint.

• *PORTFOLIO RISK*

So far, risk and return have been analyzed for individual projects. Firms, however, invest in a number of projects and investors usually have a number of securities in their portfolios. Presumably, these investments are made with the goal in mind to maximize returns and minimize risk. It is important, therefore, to consider the risk/return characteristics of individual assets as well as their specific contributions to the risk and returns of a given **portfolio** (the sum total of a firm's or investor's assets).

The approach to measuring the risk and returns of a portfolio starts with the calculations of the standard deviations and expected returns of each security in the portfolio. This procedure was discussed previously in this chapter. The objective is to spread the risk among several assets or securities, thereby reducing overall risk.

There are two ways this can be done. One way is to diversify by adding more securities to the portfolio, and the other way is to search for securities whose returns move differently from the returns of the securities (assets) already in the portfolio. Up to a certain point, adding more assets and securities to a portfolio can reduce risk. What risk? **Diversifiable risk**. Attention should be called to the fact that total risk is divided into two components.

Total risk = Diversifiable risk + Non-diversifiable risk

As shown in Figure 4-4, when more assets are added to a portfolio, the only risk that is reduced is diversifiable risk. There is a catch, however. If investors add securities that have the same patterns of dispersion and movement as the securities already in the portfolio, risk will remain unchanged. The idea is to find securities that move differently.

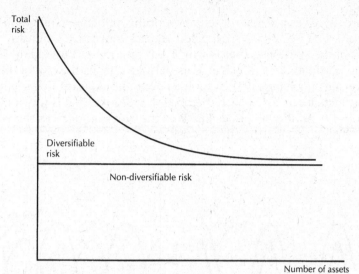

Figure 4–4 Risk Reduction Via Diversification

COVARIANCE PRINCIPLE

The search for securities that move differently is made easier by the use of a measure called **covariance.** Covariance is a statistical method used to compare the movements of two variables—or, in our case, the returns of projects in a portfolio.

A proxy for covariance, which limits the values within a range of + 1.0 and – 1.0, is called coefficient of correlation (R). It tells us how closely asset returns correlate or move relative to one another. If they move exactly the same way, the (R) has a value of + 1.0. If they move exactly in opposite directions, (R) has a value of – 1.0. When asset returns do not correlate with one another, the (R) equals zero. The mathematical formula for the **correlation coefficient** involving two assets is

$$P_{a,b} = \frac{\sum_{T=1}^{N}(K_a - \bar{K}_a)(K_b - \bar{K}_b)/N}{\sigma_a\sigma_b} = \frac{\text{Covariance }(a,b)}{\sigma_a\sigma_b}$$

This formula measures the volatility ($K - \bar{K}$) of asset A relative to asset B (in the numerator), and the covariance between the two assets is standardized by the product of the two assets' standard deviations (in the denominator).

Figure 4-5 gives a visual presentation of this principle. The graph to the left shows that security A's expected returns move the same way as the returns of the portfolio. That is why it has an $R = +1.0$. Adding security A to the portfolio does not change its volatility, hence the risk of this portfolio remains unchanged. The graph to the right indicates that security B's returns fluctuate inversely with the portfolio returns. That is why it has an R value of -1.0. Adding securities like B to the portfolio reduces the volatility of the portfolio, hence lowering its risk.

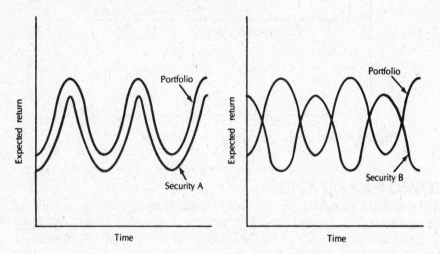

Figure 4–5 Covariance and Its Role in Reducing Risk

It is important to understand how risk changes in a portfolio context. Corporate managers should be aware that by diversifying the mix of their assets, they can reduce the risk to the firm, thus helping to reduce costs of borrowing.

These portfolio considerations play a key role in the decision-making process. For example, some investors who wish to lower their risk exposure may consider adding stocks and bonds to their portfolios because the prices of these two types of securities usually move in opposite directions over a complete business cycle.

To gain a better understanding of portfolio theory and to keep the explanation as simple as possible, we restrict the discussion to a two-securities portfolio. The first step is to determine the risk and return of a portfolio. This can be achieved by employing two basic equations. One equation calculates portfolio risk (or standard deviation), and the other equation determines the expected return. The equation to measure portfolio risk follows:

Portfolio risk or standard deviation (σ_{ab})

$$\sigma_{ab} = \sqrt{W_a^2\ \sigma_a^2 + W_b^2\ \sigma_b^2 + 2W_a W_b\ p_{ab}\ \sigma_a \sigma_b}$$

In the above equation the standard deviation (σ) reflects the risk associated with each security in the portfolio. The letter (W) represents the proportion (%) that a security contributes to the total value of the portfolio. Covariance ($p_{ab}\ \sigma_a\ \sigma_b$) determines the way securities fluctuate relative to each other. Note that as the covariance changes from a positive value of 1.0 to a negative value approaching −1.0 (security returns move in opposite directions), the portfolio's risk diminishes.

The other equation calculates the expected return of the portfolio as follows:

Portfolio expected return (Er_{ab})

$$(Er_{ab}) = (W_a\ Er_a) + (W_b\ Er_b)$$

The expected return of the portfolio is obtained by summing up the weighted returns of each security in the portfolio. The above two equations establish the basis for measuring the risk/returns of a number of portfolios that have different security mixes. By expanding the foregoing equations to include a number of securities, it is possible to construct mathematically a series of efficient portfolios whose mixes of securities provide the highest possible expected returns for different levels of risk. After constructing a number of these portfolios and calculating their respective risks and returns, we come up with a curve called the **efficient frontier**. This curve serves as a benchmark for comparing the performance of a given portfolio to the optimal portfolio. An efficient frontier is illustrated graphically in Figure 4-6 where risk A has a corresponding optimal return X. The level of risk B should yield a return equal to Y. Notice that since B risk > A risk, then X return < Y return. Provided with these risk/return alternatives, an investor should decide how much risk to assume and then proceed to construct a portfolio that will yield an optimal expected return.

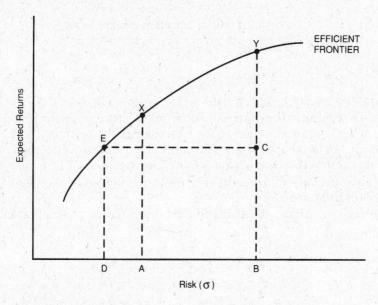

Figure 4–6 Portfolio Theory and the Efficient Frontier

Assume the investor wants to take risk B and constructs a portfolio that yields returns equal to C. The performance of this portfolio is subnormal. The investor can improve the performance of the portfolio in two ways. First, there are other securities available that yield higher returns at risk level B. So, all the investor has to do is find these securities, change the mix of the portfolio, and increase the return to Y. The investor's other option is to diversify the portfolio and change its mix by adding new securities with returns that fluctuate differently than the securities in the existing portfolio. In this way it will be possible for the investor to achieve the same returns as C (see Point E, which is equal to C) but at a much lower risk level (see point D).

In the field of corporate finance, it is more difficult to change the mix or diversify the asset or project composition of a firm. Theoretically, managers have a very large number of projects to review and are able to develop an efficient frontier. Since a firm's risk is partly determined by its industry and related factors, a manager will be faced by a certain degree of risk which he or she must accept and handle. Given this level of risk, managers have an expected return target to shoot for, namely, point Y on the efficient frontier. Assume the portfolio of projects yields expected returns of C, which represents a subnormal performance. This performance can be improved simply by restructuring the portfolio to add either projects with higher returns or projects with different covariances than in the original portfolio. Generally, therefore, the basic principles of portfolio theory provide a benchmark for making intelligent investment decisions that will improve performance, help raise returns at the least risk, and promote the maximization of stockholders' wealth.

YOU SHOULD REMEMBER

The risk of a single asset is greater than the risk of a portfolio of assets. The more assets you have, the more you spread the risk. This is known as diversification. The addition of new assets to a portfolio will reduce its variability or diversifiable risk. When the movements of the returns of new assets are different from the movements of assets in an existing portfolio, the total risk of the portfolio is reduced. The relationship between the movements of various assets is studied by a statistical measure called covariance. A standardized covariance is the correlation coefficient, which varies from −1.0 to +1.0. New assets with a correlation coefficient of +1.0 move similarly to the portfolio and will not help reduce risk. As the correlation coefficient declines from +1.0 to −1.0, portfolio risk also declines. Managers can improve the firm's performance by understanding and applying the principles that underlie portfolio theory, using the efficient frontier as a benchmark or reference. Also, there is historical proof to indicate that the risk/return relationship is a positive one.

MEASURING RISK AND RETURN WITH THE CAPITAL ASSET PRICING MODEL (CAPM)

Measuring risk is not an easy task, partly because of the many factors to be considered. The mathematics of risk include knowledge of probability theory and understanding of how portfolio risks and returns are brought together into a meaningful model. Attempts have been made to simplify the measurement of risk, and one of the more successful efforts has been the development of the **Capital Asset Pricing Model (CAPM)**, a model that relates predicted undiversifiable risks to the expected returns of a project. Although the CAPM is more readily applicable to security analysis, it can be employed to evaluate the risk/return merits of investments and assets at the corporate level.

The CAPM starts by dividing risk into two major components: diversifiable risk and nondiversifiable risk. The premise is that there is a close relationship between the returns of individual securities and the returns of the market. These returns, whether for a given stock or for the market, consist of capital gains plus dividend yields. It has been established by academicians that the stock market is a highly efficient vehicle because it quickly incorporates all available information. If so, the volatility of the market provides a common denominator for evaluating the degrees of risk of individual assets and securities. This degree of risk is determined by finding out how sensitive the returns of a stock are to the returns of the market. In this way, you employ a common index that measures the sensitivity of the individual stocks against a common index—namely, the market. If a stock's returns move up and down more than the market returns, the stock is said to be more risky than the market. When a stock's returns move up and down less than market returns, the stock is said to be less risky than the market. It is possible, therefore, to classify the risks of different securities simply by relating them to the common market index.

Example: Finding the Sensitivity of a Stock to the Market

PROBLEM   An investor calculates that the volatility of market returns (σ_m) averaged 5% annually over the past 10 years. When the volatility of the returns (σ_s) of three stocks is computed, the investor finds that stock A's standard deviation is 10%, stock B is 5%, and stock C is 3%. Using the market as a common denominator, compare these standard deviations to the market and determine the risk sensitivities of each stock.

SOLUTION   The sensitivity of these stocks to the market can be computed using the formula

$$\frac{\text{Volatility of stock returns } (\sigma_s)}{\text{Volatility of market returns } (\sigma_m)} = \text{Sensitivity}$$

$$\text{Stock A} = \frac{.10}{.05} = 2.00$$

$$\text{Stock B} = \frac{.05}{.05} = 1.00$$

$$\text{Stock C} = \frac{.03}{.05} = .60$$

According to this formula, stock A is more sensitive (hence, more risky) than the market, stock B has the same sensitivity (hence, as risky) as the market, and stock C is less sensitive (hence, less risky) than the market.

The CAPM uses a more sophisticated approach than the simple arithmetic example outlined here, but the concept is very similar.

THE BETA COEFFICIENT

The three characteristic lines in Figure 4-7 can be calculated mathematically, but they simply represent the relationship between stock returns and market returns. The slope, or slant, of each line is called **beta** (β), and it is precisely this beta that measures the sensitivity or risk of a stock (R_s) compared to the market return (K_m). Statistically, the equation, known as the characteristic line, which describes this relationship, is

$$R_s = a + \beta K_m + e$$

$$\text{where } \beta = \text{beta coefficient (slope)}$$
$$K_m = \text{market return}$$
$$R_s = \text{return of stock}$$
$$a = \text{constant}$$
$$e = \text{error term}$$

Let us assume that the monthly returns of stock A were correlated with the monthly returns of a market indicator like the Standard & Poor's 500 Composite Index. If one uses the Standard equation $R_s = a + \beta (K_m) + e$, the characteristic lines of three securities A, B and C are as follows (CAPM assumes a and $e = 0$).

$$R_a = 0 + 2.0 \ (K_m) + 0$$
$$R_b = 0 + 1.0 \ (K_m) + 0$$
$$R_c = 0 + 0.6 \ (K_m) + 0$$

As shown graphically in Figure 4-7, the beta values (2.0, 1.0, 0.6) in each equation are the crucial factors. These so-called betas are relative measures of undiversifiable risk associated with the returns of a stock relative to the returns of the market index. Suppose we solve for R_a R_b and R_c by estimating a market return of 10%. The expected returns of each stock would be:

$$R_a = 20\%$$
$$R_b = 10\%$$
$$R_c = 6\%$$

Instead of using a characteristic line to calculate beta, this risk value can be calculated as follows:

$$\text{Beta} = \frac{\sigma_a}{\sigma_m} P_{a,m}$$

Therefore, given the standard deviations of stocks A, B, and C and the market (σ_m) shown below plus a coefficient of correlation ($P_{a,m}$), beta can be determined in this alternate way. (Assume the coefficient of correlation value equals 1.0.)

$$\sigma_a = .10$$
$$\sigma_b = .05$$
$$\sigma_c = .03$$
$$\sigma_m = .05$$

The beta of each stock is equal to

$$\text{Beta of Stock A} = \frac{.10}{.05} \times 1.0 = 2.0$$

$$\text{Beta of Stock B} = \frac{.05}{.05} \times 1.0 = 1.0$$

$$\text{Beta of Stock C} = \frac{.03}{.05} \times 1.0 = .6$$

These betas are the same as the ones derived from the characteristic line equations. The only factor we must consider is the coefficient of correlation. It is clear that the lower the coefficient, the lower the nondiversifiable risk or beta.

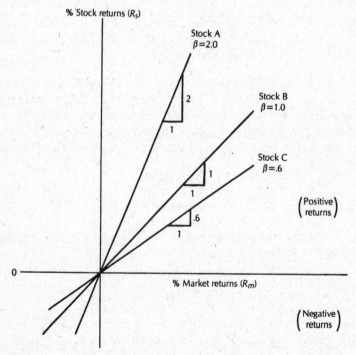

Figure 4–7 Using the CAPM to Compute Betas (βs) of Individual Stocks

When stock returns, correlated against market returns, produce a line with a 45° angle, this implies a 1-to-1 relationship. Stated another way, a 1% change in market returns produces a 1% change in stock returns. The co-movement between the returns of a stock (R_s) and market (K_m) is perfect when the beta has a value of 1.0. When using beta analysis, then, the obvious starting point for comparing risk among securities or assets is a beta of 1.0. Security B, with a 1.0 beta, will move up and down at the same rate as the market, and it has the same nondiversifiable risk as the market. Security C, with a .6 beta, moves up and down less than the market, and has a lower risk than the market. And Security A, with a 2.0 beta, moves up and down more than the market and is said to have a higher risk than the market.

It is evident that the CAPM provides an easy way to compare the various risk levels of individual stocks. An important precondition, though, is that the dispersion around the representative line is not large. If the dispersion is large, there are additional sources of risk to be considered, and the market alone may not be a good measure of the risk of an individual security.

Furthermore, theoreticians have engaged in a lively controversy centering on the nature of the market index. Some academicians claim that no one knows what the true market indicator is, and therefore, a good measure of nondiversifiable risk cannot be obtained. In practice, however, it is acceptable to employ well-known market indexes, such as the Standard & Poor's 500 Composite Stock Index, as proxies for the true market index.

CAPM furnishes an alternative measure of risk in contrast to standard deviation. The next step is to employ beta to obtain a corresponding required rate of return. This can be done by using the security market line (SML) principle.

YOU SHOULD REMEMBER

The capital asset pricing model (CAPM) compares or correlates individual stock returns with market returns. The market is a standard or common denominator for deriving what is known as nondiversifiable risk, sometimes also called systematic risk. The measure of the sensitivity of a stock to the market is called beta (β). If the beta of the market equals 1.0, all securities having betas greater than 1.0 are riskier than the market, and securities with assigned betas of less than 1.0 are less risky than the market. In constructing a portfolio, investors who select low-beta stocks are likely to achieve a lower overall return than those who select stocks with higher and therefore riskier betas.

THE SECURITY MARKET LINE (SML)

In the earlier part of this chapter it was shown that the required rate of return for an asset consists of the sum of the riskless rate plus a risk premium.

In beta analysis, the risk premium consists of the market return minus the risk-free rate $(K_m - R_F)$ multiplied by the security's index of nondiversifiable risk, or beta. You now have the tools to undertake the risk/return analysis of a security when the market is the standard for measuring risk. In other words, given the risk level of market returns we can calculate the corresponding rates of return of a stock by using the following security market line (SML) equation.

$$RRR_s = R_F \div (K_m - R_F)\, \beta_s$$

where RRR_s = required rate of return of a stock
R_F = risk-free rate
K_m = average return of the market
β_s = beta or nondiversifiable risk

With the foregoing data, the required rate of return is easily found:

$$RRR_s = .05 + (.10 - .05)1.2 = 11\%$$

This 11% figure means that any stock with a risk, or beta, of 1.2 should return 11%. A return lower than 11% makes the stock unattractive, and it should be sold. A return greater than 11% means the stock is undervalued and should be bought. Selling and buying by investors, therefore, will cause stock prices to move up or down until the returns gravitate to an equilibrium point on the SML. This relationship is presented in Figure 4-8 in the form of a **security market line (SML),** which is a graphical presentation of the CAPM.

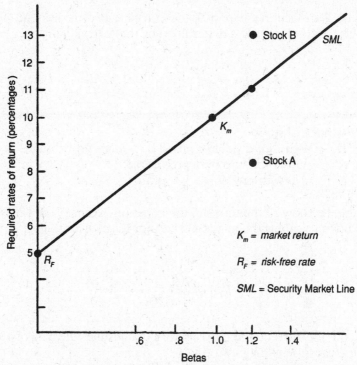

Figure 4–8 The Security Market Line (SML) as a Benchmark for Determining the Required Rates of Returns Given Different Betas

Note that various required rates of return can be found if the SML and the betas of the different securities are known. A stock with a beta of .8 would have a RRR_s of 9%, and a stock with a beta of 1.2 would have a required rate of return of 11%.

The security market line provides a basis for evaluating the relative merits of securities. For example, assume that stock B offers returns of 13% when the SML line calls for 11%. This stock is undervalued and will be bought. The opposite occurs in the case of stock A. At a beta of 1.2, stock A should return 11%, but if the actual returns of this stock were 8%, stock A should be sold because it is not a bargain.

If the goal is to keep risk at a low level, then stocks having low betas should be included in the portfolio. Conversely, if the goal is to achieve a higher return, investors should add stocks that have high betas. Clearly, the advantage of employing the CAPM in conjunction with the security market line is simplicity.

The CAPM is a highly useful tool for evaluating securities because it supplies a required rate of return (discount rate) that can be employed to determine the value of securities.

As will be discussed in Chapter 5, the constant growth dividend model says that the price of a stock is determined by the following formula:

$$P_s = \frac{D_1}{K_s - G}$$

where P_s = price of stock
D_1 = current dividends raised by 1-year's growth rate
K_s = discount rate or degree of risk
G = growth rate of stock's returns

Assuming we know all the terms in the equation except K, the CAPM can be called upon to supply the missing risk factor to solve for the price of the stock.

$$P_s = \frac{D_1}{RRR_s - G}$$

RRR_s stands for the required rate of return that justifies the beta of a stock or project ($RRR_s = R_f + (K_m - K_f)\, \beta_s$).

The CAPM and SML equation can also be used to adjust the cash flow of projects for the degree of risk and risk over time of projects to determine their present values and their profitability as shown below

$$NPV = \sum_{t=1}^{N} \frac{CF_t}{(1 + RRR_s)^t} - I$$

where CF_t = future revenues of a project
I = original cost of project
RRR_s = discount rate
NPV = net present value

The first part of the equation on the right-hand side calls for calculating the present value of future cash flows using the discount rate (RRR_s) or required rate of return derived from CAPM. We can observe that CAPM provides us with a required rate of return that serves as the discount rate to adjust future returns for risk.

YOU SHOULD REMEMBER

The CAPM model starts with a risk-free rate, and then adds a premium consisting of the market returns plus an adjustment called beta, or nondiversifiable risk. The SML approach calculates the rate of return an investor should be getting for a security having a given beta. When the actual return offered by a security is lower than this rate, it means investors are getting less than they are supposed to; hence, the security is overvalued. When actual returns are higher than the required rate of return, investors are getting a bonus over what they should get, which means the security is a bargain. Furthermore, by providing a discount rate, the SML method helps investors to determine the present value and the profitability of investments.

KEEPING THE CAPM AND SML IN PERSPECTIVE

In the final analysis, whether you calculate risk by using standard deviation or by using beta, both systems provide a basis for determining the valuations of securities and other assets.

The CAPM and SML approaches, however, are not free of problems. There may be other, more important factors besides the market that influence the returns of a security. In this case, beta would not be a good measure of risk. Also, using historical data may not be an appropriate way to calculate expected returns. Some academicians have pointed out that the CAPM and SML approaches are weak because the stock market indexes, like the Standard and Poor's 500 Composite Index, are merely proxies and do not represent the true market index. Others say that the calculation of CAPM values is based on past historical data, while the model is based on expected values. Consequently, historical betas cannot serve as a basis for establishing the true required rate of return for a security.

In addition, recent empirical studies like the one by Fama and French indicate that the market indicator shows little correlation with expected returns and, therefore, cannot serve as a common denominator for determining the betas (nondiversifiable risk) and the SML. They have found that measures, such as size and the ratio of book value to price are more suitable indicators of stock returns. That would mean that beta and CAPM, as we know it, are no longer valid. In response to these criticisms, we point out that the CAPM concept is still valid but calls for the search of more appropriate common measures to obtain acceptable and more workable betas.

The CAPM approach provides only a rough approximation, but it still represents an alternate tool for determining the risk/return trade-off and the ultimate pricing of assets. The only thing we need to do is to discover which relationship or combination of factors can serve as the common representative measure.

ARBITRAGE PRICING THEORY

The Capital Asset Pricing Model (CAPM) establishes a positive relationship between beta (risk) and expected returns with the market being the single common factor as a point of reference. Following strong criticism launched against CAPM, an alternative approach labeled **Arbitrage Pricing Theory (APT)** has been proposed to explain risk and return. APT states that the expected returns of securities are influenced by a number of industry and financially related factors. This model claims to give a broader explanation of the positive relationship between risks and returns.

The APT model implies that the returns of a security are determined by all the projected information available to investors. This information includes the unexpected part of an event such as new discoveries, changes in interest rates, inflation, industrial production, earnings announcements, and so forth. Only unexpected factors influence stock price changes, while expected events are already discounted by the market.

Each stock reacts differently to a projected factor's event and its sensitivity to that factor is captured in the beta coefficients assigned to each factor. Beta, therefore, measures the response of a stock's returns to a factor. The relationship between expected returns and a factor can be either positive or negative. That will determine the plus or minus sign assigned to the corresponding betas. For example, usually a positive sign can be expected when a change in industrial production is anticipated, whereas a negative sign could emerge when expected inflation causes costs of production to increase without compensating price increases.

Putting these observations into a three-factor equation, we come up with the following:

$$Er_{ab} = a + B_a F_a + B_b F_b + B_c F_c + e$$

where Er_{ab} = expected return
a = alpha
B_a, B_b, B_c = betas related to each factor
F_a, F_b, F_c = projected change in factors
e = error term representing specific risk or influences that are not relevant in this relationship

The specific effects of the (e) component, which represents unsystematic risk, are diversified away when the returns are those of a very large portfolio. What counts in this equation are the projected values of each factor, the size of the betas assigned to each factor (which tells us how important that factor is in the relationship), and the signs of the betas, which reveal whether the impact of the factor is a negative or a positive one.

We now have a correlation ready to be solved. After estimating the change expected in each factor, we can obtain an expected return for the stock. This expected return becomes the basis for comparing the pricing of assets. Because the market is efficient, there are no mispriced securities. Otherwise, arbitrage takes place to bring the price back to its true equilibrium value.

Should the return of a security exceed the APT required return, it will be considered undervalued. Arbitrageurs will buy the stock until the return moves back to the APT equilibrium rate of return. If the return falls below the APT estimated required rate of return, the stock will be sold until the return becomes equal to the APT estimated return.

This, then, is the way the APT model works. It represents an alternative method for determining the pricing of assets.

APT VERSUS CAPM

APT considers a number of factors while CAPM takes into account only one factor, a market index. When the only factor in the APT model is the market index, both models are very similar. However, it would seem logical to assume that a multifactor model produces more realistic results.

In the case of APT, when securities are mispriced, only a small number of arbitrageurs are needed to reestablish equilibrium. CAPM envisions that all investors spot and trade in mispriced securities to bring about equilibrium pricing of an asset. Furthermore, the APT model is subject to less restrictive assumptions, such as the necessity that returns follow a normal probability distribution, the identification of a true market index, and so forth.

Both models assume a linear relationship between risk and return, which may not be the case. Despite the market being very efficient, it is not realistic to expect that it is the representative measure of all the factors influencing the pricing of assets.

The APT model, however, runs into several problems. It not only involves highly complex mathematical formulations requiring enormous calculations, but the results of APT change as sample size, from which factors are selected, increases. There are sign problems to deal with. Analysts using APT run into severe statistical problems such as multicolinearity among factors and the tendency of one or two factors to dominate the relationship.

Despite these criticisms, APT provides additional insights into the way assets are priced and kept at equilibrium levels. From a corporation's standpoint, APT can serve as a model for establishing the required rate of return, or discount rate, that can then be employed in capital budgeting decisions.

YOU SHOULD REMEMBER

APT is an alternative method for calculating the required rate of return of a firm (discount rate). Like CAPM, it relies on the risk-return relationship, but allows for the inclusion of several factors and their unanticipated outcomes. A normal regression approach is used to calculate the required rate of return. APT is like CAPM if the only factor is the market index. However, it runs into many statistical problems such as sampling distortions, proper selection of factors, plus multicolinearity among factors. The computations are enormous and complex. APT, however, has less restrictive assumptions than CAPM, but both help us to understand how we can determine the discount rate of a firm.

• *TAKING ADVANTAGE OF THE EFFICIENT MARKET*

By having a good understanding of the mechanism involved in the determination of stock prices, corporate managers should be able to implement strategies designed to increase the wealth of the firm and in some cases minimize adverse stock price reactions to unfavorable news. Knowing how to take advantage of the efficient market is an important consideration if the goal is to minimize risk and maximize returns.

The **efficient market** theory states that current stock prices reflect all available information. Investors and the market react favorably or unfavorably to new information and events. This is what causes stock prices to change. New information impacts the existing market perception of the risk and returns of a firm's stock. Given this situation, it is up to managers to implement investment plans and supply new information that translates into a favorable valuation. Any information that alters investors' views toward expected cash flows (returns) and the discount rate (risk) of a firm results in a change of the price of a stock.

Investors acknowledge companies that follow sound accounting practices, publish strong balance sheets, and establish earnings growth supported by cost controls and effective policies. A good balance sheet and strong, steady earnings growth is the kind of information that investors associate with low risk and are willing to assign a high valuation to a stock. Managers should be conscious of the need to continuously convince investors that the firm's research is the best technologically, the products unique and differentiated from those marketed by competitors. This involves establishing a solid image and trust so that new information reported by the company is quickly incorporated into the price of its stock.

Cosmetic approaches to mask underlying weaknesses in financial statements are quickly detected with a resulting damage to the credibility of the firm. A case in point is to rely on operating leases instead of financing investments by issuing debt. These leases are not recorded on the balance sheet, except in a footnote. They distort the true debt obligations of a firm but do not escape the notice of well-trained analysts. Attempts to doctor financial statements by delaying expense charges are quickly noticed. This kind of information tarnishes the image of a firm and serves only to downgrade the valuation of a firm's stock.

Early announcements of the potential of forthcoming new products can benefit a firm and its stock. Supplying Wall Street and the public at large with details about the synergistic benefits of a merger are likely to make a favorable impression. The Internet should help clarify misconceptions about rumors and the effect of faulty products on earnings. The best policy is to come clean.

Managers who understand the workings of the efficient market are now willing to issue advance warnings of a shortfall in earnings expectations in order to allow the market to discount, in an orderly fashion, this unfavorable news. Good results can be achieved by making the public aware of arrangements with other firms to exchange technology. It pays to spell out in detail the gains obtainable from integrating the technology of other firms that will lead to greater efficiency or market advantage. Don't fail to inform the public about charitable contributions, funding to support community development projects, efforts to control pollution, or new policies designed to hire minorities and women.

There are many strategies a firm can adopt to improve its image. New systems of communication and the Internet have increased exponentially the amount and speed by which new information becomes incorporated into the pricing of stocks. Knowing how the efficient market works provides managers with better means of transmitting relevant information, which can favorably impact the price of the firm's stock.

YOU SHOULD REMEMBER

The efficient market thesis states that all information is incorporated into the prices of stocks, and therefore, these prices represent fair values. A good understanding of the efficient market can help improve a firm's image and avoid unfavorable investor attitudes. Managers should supply quick and favorable information about future expected changes. A firm should devote more time toward improving its image.

• *DIVISIONAL RISK AND RETURNS*

Value Line Service, Merrill Lynch, and Standard & Poor's publish the betas of a large number of corporations. Due to the wide differences in product and divisional composition of corporations, a comparison of the systematic risks of these firms is of limited value. Also, it is a well-known fact that the beta explains only a part of the risk associated with a company. This is why we find many corporations having the same betas, while the market valuations, such as the P/E of their stocks, differ markedly. The returns of some companies may have the same standard deviations, but their growth rates may vary significantly. Comprehension of the process of risk determination and valuation extend into the analysis of exposures to uncertain international markets, and evaluation of the soundness of balance sheets. Capital structures vary, and so do the cost structures of income statements.

The efficient market incorporates all available information in stock prices. Some of this information consists of the analysis of risk differences assigned to major product lines and divisions of corporations. Breaking down the risk of various corporate components facilitates the comparisons of the betas of these components with the betas of other firms. Also, chief executive officers of a company, being responsible for overseeing divisional performances, will find this segmented approach to risk measurement a guide for tracing shifts in risk taking by divisions. A shift to riskier projects is quickly perceived by the efficient market resulting in a change to a higher required rate of return for projects.

When a firm employs the standard Net Present Value approach, the cash flows of all projects are discounted by the overall required rate of return of the firm. This approach fails to take into account differences in the risk of individual projects and divisions. For these reasons, a segmentation approach to calculating betas can shed more light on the kind of information picked up by the market. Furthermore, it might alert managers to take precautionary steps to minimize excessive risk taken by divisions.

Based on these observations, product and divisional beta analysis makes a great deal of sense. To simplify the presentation, assume a corporation has two major divisions (A and B). The present values of these two divisions represent the value of the firm.

$$PV_{ab} = PV_a + PV_b$$

Where PV_a = present value of division A
PV_b = present value of division B
PV_{ab} = sum of present value of divisions A and B

The present values of these two divisions is obtained by discounting the cash flows that each product is expected to generate in the future. Each discount rate should reflect the unique systematic risk of that division. That means obtaining betas for each division, which are likely to differ. In our case, assume Division A is less risky than Division B. Consequently, if both divisions generate the same returns, the *PV* of Division A's cash flows will be worth more than the present value of Division B. Immediately, the significance of risk differences can be observed. Therefore, the next step is to calculate betas of each division by using the formulas:

$$\beta_a = \frac{\sigma_a}{\sigma_m} P_a, m \qquad \beta_b = \frac{\sigma_b}{\sigma_m} P_b, m$$

Given this measure of systematic risk, we proceed to determine the required rate of returns (discounted rates) for each division based on the following equation:

$$RRR_s = R_f + (R_m - R_f) \beta_s$$

Assume these two steps yield the following results shown in the following table:

	Present Values	Betas	Required Rate of Returns (%)
Division A	$2,000	1.0 (β_a)	8
Division B	$2,500	2.0 (β_b)	12

Suppose the risk free is 5% and market returns are 9%. Notice that the systematic risk of Division A is lower than Division B; therefore, the required rate of return of A is lower than B. The market recognizes this. This means money allocation to Division B must generate higher returns than Division A to justify a given investment. The required rate of return and the beta of this corporation is simply the weighted sum of these measures as shown below:

$$\beta_{ab} = 1.0 \frac{\$2,000}{\$2,000 + \$2,500} + 2.0 \frac{\$2,500}{\$2,000 + \$2,500} = 1.55$$

The required rate of return or its discount rate is

$$RRR_{ab} = .05 + (.09 - .05)\, 1.55 = .112 \text{ or } 11.2\%$$

Should the decision be made to allocate a larger proportion of funds to Division B and less to Division A, such a move could only be justified if Division B generated substantially higher projected cash flows. At the same time, the market is likely to recognize this greater exposure to risk and may downgrade the valuation of the stock.

Segmentation of beta analysis gives managers a better understanding of the potential changes in risk. Vigilance is called for to prevent excessive risk taking that might impair the ability of the firm to maximize wealth. Given that corporations have several divisions, the beta and opportunity cost of a multidivision firm is easily calculated simply by following the above steps to obtain the betas and required rates of return of each division. Then, applying the weighted procedure shown above, we can determine the overall beta and required rate of return for the corporation.

The importance of dissecting risk by product and division becomes clear. This type of information is crucial when managers are asked to seek the best combination of risks and returns.

YOU SHOULD REMEMBER

Some corporations calculate the NPV of projects or divisions by assigning the WACC of the firm as a discount rate. Unfortunately, a firm is composed of several product lines or divisions that are subject to unique risks and returns. A better way to assess the riskiness of a firm is to calculate separate betas and required rates of return for each division. In this way, we obtain a more accurate measure of the risk-adjusted profitability of each component that makes up the aggregate firm. This approach establishes a better basis for determining how to allocate scarce resources in the quest for raising the value of the firm.

SOURCES OF RISK

Now that we know how to measure risk and returns, a few comments will help us understand how some factors influence the volatility of expected returns. Some of these sources of risk include the general economic climate, political developments, industry trends, firm-specific factors, inflation, and international sources of risk.

As we have already discussed, the cash flows generated by investments depend partly on external business activity. The state of the economy produces changes in risk and return. An expanding economy means increased demand for products, rising productivity, and the benefits of economies of scale. These developments increase expected cash flows but eventually lead to capacity problems, rising inflation, and increased cost of borrowing. The risk of a downturn must be considered in making investment decisions and in forecasting cash flows as well as assessing the changing risks of projects. An economy going into a contraction phase will affect cash flows adversely and magnify the volatility of returns. Profits diminish as demand declines and diseconomies of scale sets in. So, it is clear that a major source of changes in risk and return is the general state of the economy.

Political developments can help or hinder the generation of cash flows and they can alter the risk aspects of companies and projects. For example, the health care reform program of the Clinton administration in 1993 has changed the potential outlook for drug companies. Since their price advantage was threatened by this new legislation, the risks facing these companies increased, and this increased risk was reflected in a lower valuation of the stocks. A change in the political climate can alter the expected cash flows projected by corporations because the degree of risk changes. Such things as an increase in the corporate tax rate, stricter pollution regulations, a new tax on cigarettes, and the passage of NAFTA in 1994, for example, can have a significant impact on the profits and the risks faced by firms. In some areas, however, increased spending by the government, such as the nationalization of health care, has a beneficial influence on the returns of some companies. In contrast, cutbacks in defense spending have put firms producing military goods at greater risk. Therefore, the past in many cases may be less valuable as a guideline of future risks. This is why the assignment of probabilities to the projected cash flows permits managers greater flexibility in reviewing existing and making new investment decisions.

Inflation is a source of risk that can affect the profitability and the risk of projects. A sudden increase in inflation may be detrimental to cash flows partly because the costs of goods sold may rise faster than the prices charged by a firm. Inflation raises the initial cost of investments and lowers the projected profits of projects. Protections against inflation risks might call for the buying of futures contracts to lock in current prices. Or, it may require managers to purchase raw materials in advance, as well as move up the time schedule used to issue debt for financing projects. The inflation premium forces nominal interest rates to increase, and this results in higher additional costs of borrowing. Finding out how sensitive a company is to changes in inflation can lead to the implementation of strategies that will minimize risk and safeguard potential returns.

Industry and company risk are crucial to developing successful investment policies. Risk faced in this area include things that are common to an industry and that cannot be avoided. For example, the aluminum industry is subject to high fixed costs, and its profitability is significantly affected by changes in capacity utilization. A low capacity use means low profit margins and high capacity use means high profit margins. This risk is inherent to the industry. It makes the swings in cash flows become more volatile because of these industry-specific factors.

The firm is also subject to certain unique risks that will affect its expected returns, such as failure to invest in up-to-date technology and to modernize. This could mean lower efficiency and higher costs than competition. Different projects have different risks associated with them, which must be considered when evaluating their potential risk-adjusted cash flows.

Firms are also becoming more concerned with environmental and social risks, and these risks are playing a more important role in management decisions. For example, restrictive government legislation regarding all forms of pollution force firms to make nonproductive, albeit essential, investments to control air and water contamination. Investments of this kind can affect the potential returns and cash flows of a firm. In some industries, capital spending for pollution-abatement equipment is high and places a growing financial burden on these industries. Firms that ignore these commitments or damage the environment can be faced with heavy fines and costly lawsuits, as is evident in the Exxon-Valdez, the Union Carbide, and the Three Mile Island incidents. Environmental risks require firms to implement more safeguards and preventive measures that, although costly, help to improve the overall life of the community and the nation.

Firms are part of the social fabric of the areas in which they operate. It is their responsibility to play an active and positive role toward improving the social climate. Large firms, in particular, should set aside funds to retrain displaced workers. The recent trend toward downsizing the workforce challenges managers to develop more effective ways to deal with problems without creating undue hardship. Managers should address themselves to correcting sexual and minority discrimination in the workplace and in the marketplace. The indirect and direct risks include a deteriorating image and the loss of customers.

A new challenge and growing social risk is universal health legislation, which may impose a heavy burden on smaller firms with limited resources. Large firms can minimize the high costs of health care insurance with group plans, but smaller firms will be taxed by the added risks of providing these services and may not have the ability to operate at acceptable profit levels. Managers will continue to encounter a growing number of environmental and social risks in the future. It is their responsibility to search for more effective ways to deal with these risks than they have in the past.

And finally, we have the global aspects of risk, which can influence the fortunes of any company. These international risks can originate in changing exports' activities and the costs of imports because economic and market activities abroad may not follow the same pattern as the domestic market. U.S. multinational corporations that have investments abroad are subject to certain risks not faced by domestically based corporations. These foreign risks include the danger of expropriation, adverse changes in the political climate, and above all, the fluctuating foreign exchange rate. An appreciation of the value of the dollar relative to other currencies could lead to lower repatriated earnings for foreign subsidiaries, but imports might be cheaper, lowering the costs of production of domestic operations. There are several ways to hedge against the dangers that accompany changes in the exchange rates, namely, adopting accounting strategies to minimize the exposure to risk and employing futures and forward contracts to avoid exchange rate risk.

We can see that external risk and return relationships represent a complex interaction of forces, which must be considered as part of the investment strategy of a firm if it expects to minimize its risks and maximize its returns.

THE HIGHLIGHT OF
THE BLACK–LITTERMAN MODEL

The purpose of the traditional mean-variance optimization (maximizing return for a given risk) of Harry Markowitz is to determine an optimal asset allocation from a given set of securities. The inputs required for this model are the expected rates of return, the volatility of securities, and the interaction among securities measured by their covariance. The final output is a curve (efficient frontier) on which the best and feasible portfolios lie. The main property of an efficient portfolio is its lowest risk for a given level of expected return. The traditional approach of Markowitz was later extended and streamlined by William Sharpe in his CAPM (capital asset pricing model) as explained before. Yet, there are a number of limitations behind this traditional model as observed by practitioners:

In practice, investors and managers do not have access to or are not interested in *all* securities. Only a subset of the universe of the securities is the domain of their consideration. The interaction among securities (the historical variance-covariance table) cannot be computed easily all the time. The variance–covariance structures for the same group of securities could be constructed differently by different analysts. The computed asset allocation weights (how much to invest in each asset) are quite sensitive to the data used. For example, a change in the expected rates of return may lead to a totally different asset allocation in the traditional model. The result would be a huge estimation error in the traditional model many practitioners often complain.

To alleviate the above limitations of the traditional approach, Black–Litterman proposed a sophisticated sequential model, which can be summarized as follows:

Step 1: Find a global index or a well-diversified portfolio that is market-cap based (i.e., value weighted like S&P 500 or Russell 3000 Index.)

Step 2: Assume the rate of the return of the selected index as constant.

Step 3: The asset allocation of the securities in the index should be assumed as if it is at equilibrium.

Step 4: Compute the expected rates of return of the securities in the index.

Step 5: Adjust those computed rates of return based on your own expectations of the market, the industry, and firm. **Note this flexibility was missing in the traditional approach.** You may use any quantitative or qualitative methods to make those adjustments as often as necessary. Unlike other models, the Black–Litterman model puts you in "the driver's seat"; revise your expectations as long as you can adjust it based on observing the current and future trends in the market.

Step 6: Based on those adjustments, recompute the new revised equilibrium returns.

Step 7: Now, you are ready to run the mean-variance optimization (determine your efficient portfolio) as if you are conducting the traditional approach.

YOU SHOULD REMEMBER

Some factors that affect the risk and return of a firm include business activity, political developments, industry factors, and international exposure. Changing economic conditions influence the demand for products, costs of production, and cost of borrowing. Changes in tax legislation, health care reform, and spending by the government can influence the outcome of cash flows and their volatility. Firms are also faced with specific industry, technological, social, environmental, and competitive risks against which they must protect themselves. International exposure brings with it new risks including the danger of expropriation and losses due to adverse changes in exchange rates. It is fine to be able to measure risk, but managers must know how to cope with a number of external and internal risk forces if they expect to maximize the wealth of a firm.

KNOW THE CONCEPTS

DO YOU KNOW THE BASICS?

1. Under conditions of uncertainty, what kind of weights are used to determine the expected value and risk of an investment?

2. If the dispersion of the returns of Project A is large and that for Project B is narrow, which is the riskier project and why?

3. Define standard deviation, and calculate the range within which you can estimate that 68% of the returns will fall within plus or minus one standard deviation. Assume standard deviation equals 10 and the mean or expected return equals 100.

4. Why would you want to use the coefficient of variation to evaluate the merits of two different projects?

5. How does diversification reduce risk? Is it better for the co-movement of the assets in a portfolio to be positive or negative? Why?

6. Why is the market a standard measure of nondiversifiable risk?

7. Given three securities, what do betas of 1.0, .8, and 1.4 tell us about the nondiversifiable risk of each security?

8. Explain how the SML approach can be a useful tool in calculating the net present value of a project.

9. A security's returns, when related to the returns of the market, produce a nondiversifiable line that has a 45° angle. What does this imply?

10. What are some of the weaknesses connected with the beta and SML methods for determining the required rate of return of a security?

11. Define the efficient frontier and explain what can be done to improve a portfolio's expected return that has fallen below the efficient frontier.

12. Given the risk-free rate, cite the other component of total risk and indicate how this helps to measure differences in the risks of various projects.

13. Cite some major sources of risk and indicate the strategy a firm can adopt to cope with these risks.

14. How does APT work? Compare it to CAPM.

15. Describe the efficient market thesis and indicate how a manager can take advantage of this development.

TERMS FOR STUDY

APT	portfolio
beta	probabilities
capital appreciation	return
Capital Asset Pricing Model (CAPM)	risk
cash flow	risk-free rate
coefficient of variation	risk premium
correlation coefficient	risk/return trade-off
covariance	security market line (SML)
diversifiable risk	standard deviation
dividend yield	variance
efficient frontier	volatility
efficient market	

PRACTICAL APPLICATION

COMPUTATIONAL PROBLEMS

1. Calculate the standard deviation of returns based on the following information:

   Returns: 1, 2, 3
   Probabilities: .25, .50, .25
   Expected return: 2

   Give the range that covers a 95% confidence level of the returns or outcomes.

2. Calculate the required rate of return of a security, using the SML approach, if the risk-free rate is 8%, the market returns 12%, and the beta of the stock is 1.5. Is this security under- or overvalued if its actual return is 9%?

3. Given the following information on assets A and B, calculate their expected returns and which asset provides a better risk/return trade-off?

Project A		Project B	
Probability	Return	Probability	Return
.10	10	.15	9
.20	12	.35	13
.40	17	.35	16
.20	22	.15	20
.10	24		

4. If the risk-free rate is 6% and the market return is 10%, calculate the required rates of return for the following investments:

Security	Beta
A	.53
B	1.35
C	.85
D	1.05

5. Stock A, which has a beta of 1.2, is currently selling for $50 per share and will pay a dividend of $2.50 per share this year. On the basis of the company's strong growth, you expect the stock price to be $54 per share at the end of 1 year. The current risk-free rate is 7%, and the market return is 13%. Calculate the stock's required rate of return. Should you purchase the stock?

6. Suppose a 3-year project generates the following cash flows:

1	$1,000
2	$2,000
3	$3,000

If this project has the same characteristics as stock A in Problem 5, then determine the present value of the cash flows of this project.

7. Rodex Company has two divisions (A and B). You look up the betas of comparable stocks traded on the stock exchange. Division A has a beta of 1.0 and Division B a beta of 1.5. The risk-free rate is 4% and the market return is estimated at 12%. You calculate the present value of Division A as $10,000 and that of B as $10,000. Determine the required rate of return of divisions A and B (use CAPM) and the combined betas of the two divisions. Employ as weights the relative importance (proportions, %) of each division's present value to obtain the sum of the two present values. If the average cost of capital of the firm is .14, what kind of biases would have resulted in the divisional present value had the firm's discount rate been applied to compute them?

ANSWERS

KNOW THE CONCEPTS

1. The weights used to determine the expected returns and risk are called probabilities.

2. Project B is less risky than Project A because its volatility, as measured by standard deviation, is lower than Project A's. The more returns fluctuate, the greater the uncertainty of a project and the greater its risk.

3. Standard deviation measures the deviation of actual values from an expected value or the mean of historical observations. It is a measure of risk. When the standard deviation is 10 and the expected returns are 100, the range of the distribution is

   (assume $1 \pm \sigma$) 90 to 110

4. It is not possible to compare risk with absolute numbers. A relative measure, such as the coefficient of variation σ/K, provides the basis for comparing the risk/return trade-off between different projects.

5. Diversification reduces risk because the risk is spread among a greater number of assets. A negative covariation is better than a positive one, because different movements of assets in a portfolio tend to dampen its overall fluctuations.

6. The market is a highly efficient vehicle that contains all available information. Therefore, market risk establishes a common indicator against which the nondiversifiable risks of all other securities can be compared.

7. A beta of 1.0 means that a security has the same risk as the market. A beta of .8 indicates that a security is less risky than the market. Conversely, securities with betas of 1.4 are more risky and volatile than the market indicator.

8. The SML equation provides the Required Rate of Returns (RRR_s) of an asset. This is equivalent to the discount rate. By knowing the initial cost of a project and its discounted future returns, one can determine the *NPV* of the project as follows: (*PV* of returns—Initial cost).

9. When the returns of a security are correlated to the returns of the market and a characteristic line emerges having a 45° angle, this implies a one-to-one relationship. In other words, security returns move the same way as market returns. The beta of this relationship is equal to 1.0. A 45° angle implies that the security has the same risk characteristics as the market index.

10. Weaknesses of the beta and SML approaches include:

    (a) There is no true market index that can be used as a benchmark for comparison purposes.

(b) Historical patterns are not representative of future required rates of return.

(c) If the dispersion around the characteristic line is too wide, the line is not representative of the relationship. Consequently, beta is also a poor measure of the nondiversifiable risk of a security.

11. The efficient frontier is a curve that determines the maximum or optimal expected returns of portfolios at different levels of risk. If a portfolio's expected returns fall below the efficient frontier, a manager can diversify the portfolio mix in two ways. First, the manager can find securities with higher returns to increase the expected returns at a given risk level. Second, it is possible to diversify the portfolio by adding securities that have covariance values of zero or −1.0. This will reduce the risk of the portfolio while maintaining the same expected return.

12. Total risk is composed of the risk-free rate plus a risk premium. The more risky a project, the greater its risk premium because this is the additional return required to justify undertaking an investment. Suppose K_f is equal to 5%, we might compare a lower-risk Project A to the higher-risk Project B by saying

$$\text{Project A total risk} = .05 + .05 = 10\%$$
$$\text{Project B total risk} = .05 + .10 = 15\%$$

The discount rate of A is lower than that of B. If these two projects had the same series of returns, the risk adjusted cash flow of A would be better than B.

13. Some of the major sources of risk are economic activity, industry factors, political changes, and international developments. Firms can hedge against some of these risks by buying futures and forward contracts to avoid exchange rate risk. They can time their borrowings in the early stages of a business cycle expansion, and they can adopt new technology to maintain control over costs and prevent competitive loss of market share. To deal with government spending shifts, the firm should attempt to change its product mix to soften the blow of spending cutbacks.

14. APT is mainly a model for determining the required rate of return of an asset. This model establishes a fair value of a stock and any market deviation from this fair value is brought back to equilibrium through the process of arbitrage. Unlike CAPM, the expected return in an APT model is usually a function of the unexpected outcome of several macro factors. CAPM is subject to more restrictive assumptions and relies on one factor—a true market index, which no one has been able to identify. APT encounters sampling and multicolinearity problems. It also seems to select only one or two factors, which usually are the same ones. Besides the enormous computations involved, APT helps to

explain only a small part of the underlying events that determine asset pricing. Yet, it has helped us to understand more clearly the process by which assets are valued.

15. The efficient market theory states that all good and bad news about a company helps to determine the price of a firm's stock. Only new information can produce a change in the price of a stock. If so, then corporations should avoid attempts to mask weaknesses in their financial statements. Doctoring accounting results is quickly discovered and can damage the image of a firm. To take advantage of the efficient market, managers should be willing to reveal favorable developments as soon as possible. They should also be willing to admit mistakes and take corrective action. Understanding how the efficient market affects the price of a stock helps managers to adopt beneficial strategies that will help raise the price of a firm's stock.

PRACTICAL APPLICATION

1. $\sqrt{.50} = 0.71$

   A mean of 2 and $\pm 2\sigma$ will mean a range of +.58 to 3.42.

2. $RRR_s = .08 + (0.12 - .08)\ 1.5$
   $ = .08 + .06 = .14,\ \text{or } 14\%$
   If the actual return of this security is 9%, it is overvalued.

3. (a) Expected returns

Project A	Project B
.10 × 10 = 1.00	.15 × 9 = 1.35
.20 × 12 = 2.40	.35 × 13 = 4.55
.40 × 17 = 6.80	.35 × 16 = 5.60
.20 × 22 = 4.40	.15 × 20 = 3.00
.10 × 24 = 2.40	$E(R)_B = 14.50\%$
$E(R)_A = 17.00\%$	

   (b) Standard deviations

Project A		Project B	
$(10 - 17)^2 \times .10 =$	4.90	$(9 - 14.5)^2 \times .15 =$	4.5375
$(12 - 17)^2 \times .20 =$	5.00	$(13 - 14.5)^2 \times .35 =$	.7875
$(17 - 17)^2 \times .40 =$	0	$(16 - 14.5)^2 \times .35 =$	.7875
$(22 - 17)^2 \times .20 =$	5.00	$(20 - 14.5)^2 \times .15 =$	4.5375
$(24 - 17)^2 \times .10 =$	4.90	$\sigma_B^2 =$	10.65
$\sigma_A^2 =$	19.8	$\sigma_B =$	3.26
$\sigma_A =$	4.45		

(c) Coefficients of variation

$$CV_A = \frac{4.45}{17.00} = .26 \qquad CV_B = \frac{3.26}{14.50} = .22$$

Stock B has a lower risk per unit of return.

4. *Security*   *Required Rate of Return*

A $.06 + .53(.10 - .06) = 8.12\%$

B $.06 + 1.35(.10 - .06) = 11.4\%$

C $.06 + .85(.10 - .06) = 9.4\%$

D $.06 + 1.05(.10 - .06) = 10.2\%$

5. Expected rate of return $= \dfrac{2.50 + (54 - 50)}{50} = 13\%$

Required rate of return $= .07 + 1.2(.13 - .07) = 14.2\%$
Since the required rate of return exceeds the expected rate of return, Stock A is overvalued and you should not purchase it.

6. *PV* project equals the sum of the discounted cash flows. If the discount rate of Stock A is 14.3%, then

$$PV \text{ Project} = \frac{\$1,000}{(1.142)^1} + \frac{\$2,000}{(1.142)^2} + \frac{\$3,000}{(1.142)^3}$$

or

$$= \$875.65 + \$1,533.55 + \$2,014.29 = \$4,423.49$$

7. Division A $RRR_a = .04 + (.12 - .04)\, 1.0 = .12$
Division B $RRR_b = .04 + (.12 - .04)\, 1.5 = .16$

Weighted average:
Discount rate of
Division A and B $= (.50 \times .12) + (.50 \times .16) = .14$
First, we notice that the cash flows of Division B (unadjusted for risk) are growing faster than Division A. Second, by applying the firm's overall .14% cost of capital to discount the cash flows of each division, the present value of Division A would have been understated and Division B's present value would have been overstated.

5

VALUATION METHODS

KEY TERMS

bond a long-term debt security issued by a borrower, either a public or private institution

coupon rate the rate of interest received by a bondholder on an annual, semiannual, or quarterly basis

Distress debt a security in government entities or companies that are already in default, under bankruptcy protection, or heading toward default

equity the dollar value of the total assets after subtracted from debt

face value the value of a bond at maturity; also called the nominal, or par, value

free cash flows net income adjusted for all noncash expenditures as well as estimated increases or decreases in capital expenditures and working capital

junior debt a type of debt that has a lower priority or ranking than another debt claim within the same asset or property; usually unsecured; also known as subordinate debt

liquidity the degree of the ability for a security to be bought and sold on the market without its share price being affected

P/E ratio the price of stock divided by either the current or expected earnings per share

senior debt debt with a higher ranking or priority than all subordinate or junior debt in the same asset or property

z-score statistical index or variable used to a predict a firm's potential probability of financial problem or bankruptcy

THE CONCEPT OF VALUE

The value of an asset, such as a share of common stock or a bond, is influenced by three major factors: cash flow of the asset, growth rate of the cash flow, and risk or uncertainty of the cash flow.

An increase in the amount of cash flow tends to raise the price of an asset. Conversely, the price declines if cash flow becomes more uncertain. These relationships are fundamental to the valuation of an asset. Accordingly, the responsibility of a financial officer is to increase cash flows as much as possible while controlling risk.

The **cash flow** of a share of common stock or preferred stock is measured by its annual dividend and the change in its stock price. The cash flow of a **bond**, which is a long-term debt security issued by a borrower, is the amount of interest received by a bondholder in a year plus the change in its price. Since profits raise the price of an asset and risk reduces the price, all of the following three conditions are required for a continuous increase in the value of any asset:

1. The asset must continuously produce cash flow.

2. Cash flow must have a positive rate of growth (i.e., cash flow must increase over time).

3. Risk must be controlled.

Of the three factors, estimation of risk is the most difficult task. As a result, the subject of risk in the valuation of an asset should receive more attention when the outlook for the economy becomes more uncertain. In Chapters 3 and 4, it was discussed that the discount rate reflects risk, or uncertainty of the future income. To find the current price of an asset, then, future cash flows must be discounted back to present value at an appropriate rate to reflect each aspect of risk. Therefore, the price of an asset is the same as the present value of its future cash flows.

Price of an asset = Present value of its future cash flows

In order to obtain the present value of future cash flows (returns), you must sum an estimated series of net incomes and depreciations for a number of years in the future. These cash flows are then adjusted for risk to determine their present value.

In Chapter 5, it will be shown that the value of common stocks, preferred stocks, and bonds can be estimated by discounting or by calculating the present value of the future returns that these securities are expected to generate.

YOU SHOULD REMEMBER

The value of an asset is defined as the present value of all future cash flows associated with that particular asset.

• *VALUATION OF BONDS*

As previously stated, the value of an asset is equal to the present value of its future cash flows. This rule can be applied to any financial asset, including a bond. The U.S. government regularly borrows from the public by issuing government bonds to cover its budget deficit. Corporations issue bonds to raise the capital required to expand their operations. In this manner, the U.S. government and borrowing corporations commit themselves to pay a certain amount of money in interest to bondholders on an annual, semiannual, or quarterly basis. The amount of interest to be received is the **coupon rate** stated on each bond certificate. Other information found on a bond certificate include the maturity date, the face value, and the number of times interest is paid each year. The **maturity date** is the date when the issuer must pay the investor the full price of the bond, thus retiring the debt. The **face value** of a bond is the price of the bond at maturity. When these figures are available, the value of the bond can easily be determined.

How to Determine the Value of a Bond

1. Calculate the present value of interest payments.

2. Calculate the present value of the face value.

3. Add the two present values.

Note that both the interest and the face value must be discounted at the market rate (the rate at which similar bonds are discounted).

Example: Determining the Value of a Bond

PROBLEM The ABC Co. has issued a 5-year bond with a face value of $1,000 at a coupon rate of 10%. Interest is paid annually, and the discount rate for similar bonds in the market is 12%. Determine the value of the bond.

SOLUTION To determine the value of this bond, you first discount the annual interest of $100 (10% $\times$ $1,000 = $100) at a discount rate of 12% for 5 years. Next, discount the face value of $1,000 at 12% for 5 years and add the two present values;

$$\text{Bond Value} = \left[\frac{100}{(1+12\%)^1} + \frac{100}{(1+12\%)^2} + \frac{100}{(1+12\%)^3} \right.$$
$$(V_b)$$

$$\left. + \frac{100}{(1+12\%)^4} + \frac{100}{(1+12\%)^5} \right]$$

$$+ \left[\frac{1,000}{(1+12\%)^5} \right] = \textit{Stop!} \text{ Don't work this out by hand.}$$

The answer to this equation can easily be determined by the use of the present value tables in Chapter 3:

$$\$100(PVIFA) + \$1,000(PVIF) = \$100(3.604) + \$1,000(.567)$$
$$\text{12\%, 5 yr} \qquad \text{12\%, 5 yr}$$
$$= \$360 + \$567 = \$927$$

where $PVIFA$ = present value interest factor annuity
$PVIF$ = present value interest factor

The value of this bond is $927. In other words, an investor would pay $927 for the bond.

A general formula to calculate the value of bonds can be written as

$$V_b = I(PVIFA_{k,n}) + F(PVIF_{k,n})$$

where V_b = value of the bond
I = interest in each time period
F = face value of the bond
k = discount rate
n = number of periods

The values for the $PVIFA$ (present value interest factor annuity) are available in their corresponding tables in Chapter 3. Note that in the preceding example, the value of the bond is only $927—which is below the face value of $1,000. Since the 12% discount rate in the market is higher than the 10% coupon rate, the bond sells at a discount. The bond would sell at a premium if the discount rate were below the coupon rate. For instance, at a discount rate of 8%, the price of this bond would be $1,079:

$$V_b = 100 \ (PVIFA) + 1,000(PVIF) = 100(3.99) + 1,000(.68) = 1079$$
$$\quad\quad 8\%, 5 \text{ yr} \quad\quad\quad 8\%, 5 \text{ yr}$$

When the interest rate in the market falls, interest received on old bonds is more than interest on new bonds because of the lower coupon rates. Therefore, old bonds sell at a higher price (premium). The price of a bond moves inversely with the interest rate in the market. If the interest rate rises, the price of a bond with a lower coupon rate declines. This inverse relationship between interest rate and price holds also in the cases of preferred and common stock.

• VALUATION OF PREFERRED STOCK

Holders of preferred stock receive a fixed dividend from the issuing companies on a regular basis. There is no maturity date on preferred stock; therefore, a share of preferred stock can be considered a perpetuity, as discussed in Chapter 3. The value of a preferred stock can also be determined by discounting the present value of its dividends over an infinite period of time:

$$V_p = \frac{D}{(1+K)^1} + \frac{D}{(1+K)^2} + \frac{D}{(1+K)^3} + \cdots + \frac{D}{(1+K)^\infty}$$

where V_p = market value of preferred stock
$\quad\quad D$ = constant dividend
$\quad\quad K$ = discount rate

This equation can be rewritten as a simple perpetuity formula:

$$V_p = \frac{D}{K}$$

With this simple equation, the value of a preferred stock can be determined once information about dividends and the discount rate is available. What a straightforward solution to a very important problem!

Example: Determining the Value of Preferred Stock

PROBLEM   The XYZ Co. issues preferred stock, each share paying an annual dividend of $2. The discount rate of similar preferred stock in the market is 10%. Determine the value of a share of preferred stock issued by this company.

SOLUTION   The price of the preferred stock is calculated simply:

$$V_p = \frac{D}{K} = \frac{\$2}{.10} = \$20$$

Although the annual dividends of preferred stock are constant, the price of the stock can change over time. The price of a preferred stock will increase if the market discount rate goes down. By the same token, an increase in the discount rate will lower the price of a preferred stock. For instance, if the discount rate in the preceding example rises to 15%, the preferred stock of the XYZ Co. is worth only $13.33:

$$V_p = \frac{D}{K} = \frac{\$2}{.15} = 13.33$$

• *VALUATION OF COMMON STOCK*

Buyers of common stock invest in the ownership of the issuing company, that is, they become owners of the company. Dividends on common stock are not guaranteed. Each company's dividend policy depends on the firm's profitability and the availability of funds. Dividends paid in one year may be more or less than dividends paid in a previous year. In some years, no dividend may be paid at all.

Over time, the annual dividend per share may remain fixed, may grow at a constant rate, or may rise at a relatively high rate for a few years and then grow at a constant rate. Because of all these possibilities, calculation of the price of common stock calls for careful projection of future dividends. Since a company is considered to operate forever, the price of common stock is not influenced by the number of years an investor wants to maintain ownership.

The price of common stock is largely determined by three factors: the annual dividends, growth of dividends, and discount rate. The rate at which future dividends are to be discounted is called the required rate of return. If a company has a high level of risk, a high required rate of return is expected by investors. To encourage investors to invest their money in a risky venture, a higher payoff must be offered. The following are the procedures to determine the value of common stock in three possible cases:

VALUING STOCK WITH NO DIVIDEND GROWTH

With D as a constant annual dividend and K_s as a required rate of return, the price of common stock, denoted as P_0, can be determined by discounting future dividends at K_s:

$$P_0 = \frac{D_1}{(1+K_s)^1} + \frac{D_2}{(1+K_s)^2} + \frac{D_3}{(1+K_s)^3} + \cdots + \frac{D_\infty}{(1+K_s)^\infty}$$

Note that this is the same familiar equation you used earlier for preferred stock. The only difference is the required rate of return (K_s) of common stock, which depends on the risk of that particular common stock. The equation can be simplified further as

$$P_0 = \frac{D}{K_s}$$

Example: Common Stock with No Dividend Growth

PROBLEM   A company pays an annual dividend of $3 per share, expects no growth in future dividends, and has a required rate of return of 12%. What should the price of its common stock be?

SOLUTION $P_0 = \frac{\$3}{.12} = \$25$

VALUING STOCK WITH CONSTANT DIVIDEND GROWTH

Dividends of a firm may increase at a fixed rate on an annual basis. For example, if the latest dividend was $2 and dividends grow at an annual rate of 5%, the dividend in the next year will be $2.10:

$$\$2(1 + .05) = \$2(1.05)^1 = \$2.10$$

The dividend in the second year will be $2.21:

$$\$2(1 + .05)(1 + .05) = \$2(1.05)^2 = \$2.21$$

The pattern, of course, continues with future years.

The price of common stock with a constant rate of growth can also be determined if future dividends are discounted at the required rate of return:

$$P_0 = \frac{D_0(1+g)^1}{(1+K_s)^1} + \frac{D_0(1+g)^2}{(1+K_s)^2} + \frac{D_0(1+g)^3}{(1+K_s)^3} + \cdots + \frac{D_0(1+g)^\infty}{(1+K_s)^\infty}$$

In this equation, $D_0(1 + g)^1$ is the dividend in year 1, $D_0(1 + g)^2$ is the dividend in year 2, and so on. Don't be scared of too many calculations. Professor Myron J. Gordon, a pioneer in the field of finance, made the above equation simple and workable:

$$P_0 = \frac{D_0(1+g)}{K_s - g} \text{ or } \frac{D_1}{K_s - g}$$

where D_0 = latest dividend paid per share
D_1 = expected dividend per share in year 1
K_s = required rate of return
g = growth rate of dividends

This equation is often referred to in financial literature as the Gordon model.

Example: Common Stock with Constant Dividend Growth

PROBLEM The latest dividend per share paid by a company was $1.80. The company is expected to raise its annual dividends at a rate of 6%. Assuming that the required rate of return is 11%, estimate the stock price.

SOLUTION Using the Gordon model, calculate the price of the common stock as follows:

$$P_0 = \frac{D_0(1+g)}{K_s-g} = \frac{\$1.80(1+.06)}{.11-.06} = \frac{\$1.91}{.05} = \$38.16$$

As in the cases of bonds and preferred stock, the price of common stock will decline if the discount rate, K_s, goes up. For instance, the price of a share of common stock in the preceding example would have been only $21.22 if K_s had increased to 15%.

$$P_0 = \frac{D_0(1+g)}{K_s-g} = \frac{\$1.80(1+.06)}{.15-.06} = \frac{\$1.91}{0.09} = \$21.22$$

Also, note that the price of the stock will increase as the growth rate (g) increases and that the price will decrease as g decreases.

VALUING STOCK WITH UNUSUAL DIVIDEND GROWTH

A firm may have an unusual growth rate of dividends in the first few years and then maintain a normal and constant rate of growth. In this case, the question is how to estimate the stock price when dividends grow at different rates during two periods of time. This problem can easily be solved if we apply the same principle of valuation used for the preceding cases: The price of a financial asset is the present value of its future income.

When a common stock has two or more different growth rates of dividend, future dividends must be projected separately. These projected dividends must be discounted back to present, and finally all of the present values are added together. A numerical approach will clarify the procedure:

Example: Common Stock with Unusual Dividend Growth

PROBLEM The Profitable Co. paid an annual dividend per share of $4 last year. It is expected that dividends will grow at an annual rate of 20% for the next 3 years and then drop to a normal growth rate of 6%. Assuming a required rate of return of 12%, estimate the price of the common stock today. To help solve this problem, use the future incomes shown in the table.

Year	Income	PVIF at 12%	Present Value of Income
1	$D_1 =$ $4.80	.8929	$ 4.29
2	$D_2 =$ 5.76	.7972	4.59
3	$D_3 =$ 6.91	.7118	4.92
	$P_3 =$ 122.08	.7118	86.90
			Total PV = $100.70

SOLUTION   In the table D_1, D_2, and D_3 or dividends in years 1, 2, and 3, respectively—are expected to grow at an annual rate of 20%. The stock price in year 3 (P_3) is calculated as follows:

$$P_3 = \frac{D_3(1+g)}{K_s - g} = \frac{\$6.91(1.06)}{.12 - .06} = \$122.08$$

Note that, when determining the stock price in a particular year with the Gordon model, the dividend in the following year must be used. Since the growth rate of dividends is constant (6%) after the third year, the Gordon model is used to estimate P_3. The next step is to discount all future income (D_1, D_2, D_3, and P_3) at a given rate of 12%. When the discounted values are summed, the price of the stock is estimated (see the table) to be $100.70.

USING PRICE MULTIPLES

A price multiple is a ratio of comparing two financial variables. Examples of price multiples are Price to Earnings Per Share (EPS), Price to Sales Per Share, and Price to Book Value Per Share. Note that any financial variable could be compared to the price; however, the relationship should not be arbitrary. The ratio should be conceptually meaningful. Otherwise, the multiple would be an arithmetic value with no financial meaning. Once a multiple is computed, it is usually compared to a benchmark (the industry or a group of competitors) or analyzed over a period of time to observe historical fluctuations. Drawing on the concept of a single price, two competing firms of identical financial profiles (having equal assets, capital structure, etc.) should maintain similar multiples of Price to EPS. Based on this logic, a financial analyst may decide that a stock is overpriced or underpriced if its multiple is out of an acceptable range. To determine if a multiple is justified, the fundamentals of the company including cash flows, dividends, sales, and beta should be evaluated. Following are the most common price multiples that analysts use for the purpose of stock or company valuation.

P/E RATIO

The *P/E* ratio is the relationship between the current price and expected earnings per share. Since earnings determine the value of any asset, it is natural to measure the price versus the expected earnings. The *P/E* ratio is widely accepted as a determinant of the long-term return on the stock. Note that the *P/E* ratio is the inverse of an earning yield:

$$P/E = 1/(E/P)$$

Although the *P/E* ratio is a popular and useful indicator, an analyst should be cautious about the *P/E* ratio when EPS is negative. The *P/E* ratio of a negative yielding firm is meaningless. An analyst must be careful about the fluctuation of a *P/E* ratio. Therefore, *P/E* ratios must be used over a period of time with a particular attention to its volatility (standard deviation). An often asked question is whether the latest EPS (historical) or an expected EPS (forward) should be used in the denominator of the *P/E* ratio. Ideally, an expected value should be applied. However, if an analyst is not comfortable in forecasting a future EPS, it is prudent that the average of the latest values of EPS be plugged into the denominator.

Example:

XYZ has reported $16 million in earnings in year 2005. An analyst forecasts an EPS of 50 cents per share in the year 2006. This company has 20 million shares outstanding, trading at $8 per share. How do we calculate the *P/E* ratio of this company using historical EPS versus expected EPS. In this case, we can simply divide the current price by the expected EPS and determine the EPS. The answer is $8/.50 = 16. It means, using estimated data, the current price is 16 times what an investor expects to earn over the next period. Whereas, using the historical data, the EPS would be different. The answer is 10 as computed below:

$$EPS = \$16,000,000/20,000,000 \text{ shares} = 0.80$$
$$P/E \text{ ratio} = \$8/0.80 = 10$$

Regardless of which method one uses, the analysis should be made consistent, using the same method, over a period of time and compared to the industry.

YOU SHOULD REMEMBER

To determine the price of a bond, its future interest income and principal value must be discounted separately and then added together. The price of preferred stock can be estimated by calculating the present value of annual dividends, as in the case of perpetuities. The valuation of common stock can be estimated using three conditions: no growth rate of dividends, constant growth rate of dividends, and unusual growth rates of dividends.

USING THE CAPM IN VALUATION METHODS

In the preceding sections, the value of an asset was defined as the present value of its future income. It was also assumed that the discount rate was given in all cases. This is not a realistic assumption in practice. Therefore, the CAPM discussed in Chapter 4 can be used to estimate a required rate of return for valuation of a common stock.

The formula for the CAPM is

$$K_s = R_f + \beta(\bar{K}_m - R_f)$$

where K_s = required rate of return
R_f = risk-free rate (such as the return on U.S. treasury bills)
β = beta coefficient of the company
K_m = return on a market portfolio

Once K_s (required rate of returns) is computed, the future income is discounted at that rate.

Example: Using the CAPM for Valuation

PROBLEM   The beta of a company is 1.50, the return on the Dow Jones portfolio is 12%, U.S. treasury bills currently yield 9%, the company has historically maintained a growth rate of 6% in dividends, and investors expect to receive a $3 dividend per share in the next year. Using the available data, determine the current price per share.

SOLUTION   In solving this problem, the Gordon model can be used directly if the required rate of return (K_s) is given:

$$P_0 = \frac{D_1}{K_s - g} = \frac{3}{K_s - 6\%}$$

K_s, which is a missing value in the above equation, can be derived by the use of the CAPM, for which all necessary data are available:

$$K_s = R_f + \beta(\bar{K}_m - R_f) = .09 + 1.50(.12 - .09) = 13.5\%$$

Inserting 13.5% as the value of K_s in the Gordon model, the current price per share in this example would be $40:

$$P_0 = \frac{\$3}{.135 - .06} = \$40$$

The use of the CAPM is recommended, of course, in valuation of common stocks for which reliable betas are available. If the beta is not available, the estimated price could be considerably biased.

Prices estimated by using the CAPM may also be different from actual market prices. If the difference is significant, the undervalued stock should be purchased and the overvalued stock should be sold. Undervalued stocks have actual prices lower than the CAPM estimates; overvalued stocks are sold at prices above the CAPM estimates.

FREE CASH FLOW

Free cash flow is defined as the funds available to the company but not required for investment projects. Free cash flow is computed after satisfying all the capital requirements, working capital, and financial needs. Since not all firms pay dividends, free cash flow could be used as a reliable cash flow indicator for valuing a firm.

Firms, irrespective of capital components and dividend payments, may use free cash flow to determine their market values. It is important to remember that the free cash flow method should not be used for valuation if the company has a negative free cash flow. High-growth capital-intensive companies, with expenditures exceeding cash inflow, may not use this method for valuation. In general, the following firms may use the free cash flow in place of other methods of valuation:

1. Firms with no dividend history.

2. Firms whose dividends are not tied to earnings. There are firms that dig into capital merely to maintain dividends. On the other hand, there are

firms that have significant amounts of cash but choose not to use cash for paying dividends. A number of high-technology firms belong to this category.

3. Firms with reliable free cash flow for a number of years.

Once the value of the free cash flow is computed, the value of the company's equity is the present value of the expected future *free cash flow* discounted at the *required return on equity*.

Example:

Suppose the free cash flow of a firm is estimated to be $1,000,000. This firm has 1,000,000 shares outstanding. Free cash flow is expected to grow at a constant annual rate of 4%. Based on the capital asset pricing model, the discount rate is determined to be 12%. What is the value of this share based on free cash flow? To solve this problem, first we determine the free cash flow per share which is $1 ($1,000,000/1,000,000 shares =1). Using the constant growth model from previous sections, the value of a share of this company is

Price = Expected free cash flow per share next year/(Discount rate − Growth rate)
Price = 1 (1 + 4%)/(12% − 4%) = 1.04/0.08 = $13

Note that, if this stock is trading below $13, and if the analyst is confident about the estimates, this stock is a **buy recommendation** based on a free cash flow analysis.

FREE CASH FLOWS TO EQUITY HOLDERS AND FREE CASH FLOWS TO THE FIRM

Free cash flows may be computed for either the equity holders or the entire firm as formulated below:

Free Cash Flows to Equity Holders (FCFE) = Net Income + Noncash Expenditures including depreciation − Capital Expenditures − Increase in Working Capital − Payments for Debt Principals + New Debts Issued

Free Cash Flows to the Firm (FCFF) = Earnings Before Interest and Taxes (1 − Tax Rate) + Noncash expenditures including depreciation − Increase in Capital Expenditures − Increase in Working Capital − Increase in other assets

When the FCFE is discounted, the cost of equity (as computed by CAPM) should be used as a discount rate. In the case of FCFF, the weighted average cost of capital (WACC) for both debt and equity should be selected as the discount rate. For valuation of equity, the FCFE discounted at the CAPM rate is often recommended.

DISTRESSED DEBT

A distressed debt security is a security of an entity that is currently in default, under bankruptcy protection, or in the process of going to default. While there is no true definition of distressed debt, generally any fixed-income instrument with a yield to maturity of over 1,000 basis above the risk-free rate is normally thought of as distressed debt. The most traditional way of classifying securities is through rating agencies such as Moody Investor Services and the Standard and Poor's. They rate these securities on a 10-grade scheme. For example, the rating of CCC and below can be labeled as "**distressed**," "**might be in default**," or "**in default**." Different rating agencies use different rating systems and definitions. The rating agencies do not attempt to give any information if the trading prices of these securities are fair or economically justified. There are other characteristics common with most distressed debt. These securities usually sell at a huge discount trading for less than a dollar. There are a large number of different securities that can be considered distressed debt. These securities may include bank loans, bonds of various seniority, leases, trade claims, and even preferred stocks. So one may wonder what happens to the common stockholders of a company that files for bankruptcy. Unless there is a potential short sale, these equity holders' shares are usually worthless.

Typical factors used to determine distressed debt are price, the character of the borrower or the obligator, whether the entity is in bankruptcy or reorganization, and the rating assigned by the rating agencies. Distressed debt doesn't behave like traditional asset classes of debt and equity. Below are among the major differentiating features:

   a. Vulture funds that invest in risk assets may require as high as 20% in their investment in distressed debts to compensate for both the systematic and unique risks associated with distressed debts.
   b. Returns on distressed debts are negatively correlated with the economy, hence called "countercyclical." After all, in good times, there are fewer cases of bankruptcies and financial distress.
   c. Prospective entities that may go through stressed debt have signs of weak management, underinvestment and undercapitalization (not enough commitment to growth), poor client services, and fluctuating assets, liabilities, and equity on their balance sheet.

Below is a hypothetical simple scenario where a company may easily end up with stressed debt on their balance sheet: Ambitious Ltd, a firm in high technology, has determined to borrow $15 million in debt at an average cost of 9% from various sources to finance a domestic project or expand its operations internationally. The management estimates that newly generated funds lead to a sufficient return on investment (ROI) of, let's say, 14 to pay the debt as well as generate additional value for the firm of +5%; namely,

ROI minus the average cost of debt. Should these estimates not be realized, and the bonds come due, the firm may easily become in default, either for Chapter 13 (reorganization) or Chapter 7 (full bankruptcy). The outcome is simply an outstanding debt classified as "distressed!"

PROSPECTIVE INVESTORS IN DISTRESSED DEBT

Investing in distressed debt is not appropriate for the individual investor for four reasons. The risk of loss is incredibly high when it comes to distress debt securities. The second is that an individual investor is at a disadvantage when it comes to information. This disadvantage is due to the number of professional market participants. The third reason is that since the average trading block of a distressed security is so large that it becomes extremely hard to diversify your portfolio unless the individual is extremely wealthy. Due to the risk level of distressed debt securities, diversification is necessary and puts an individual investor at a disadvantage. Most blocks trade between 1 and 5 million, and if one needs to invest in a number of securities, the capital outlay is very large for one single investor. The fourth reason is due to illiquidity of distressed debt securities. Since these securities are so illiquid, even if you invest on a modest scale, the large transaction costs cause it to be difficult to earn a proper risk adjusted return. When looking at these reasons, most people who want to invest in these types of securities are advised to invest in a hedge fund or a mutual fund.

Bankruptcies in the United States were extremely high in the 2000 era, and there were many opportunities to invest in distress debt securities. During the financial collapse, there was another abundance of opportunities to invest. In 2009 the number of bankruptcies in the United States was around 2,050, and the trend has decreased by an incredible number. In 2010 and 2011 the number of bankruptcies in the United States was 550 and 440, respectively. This drop in bankruptcies may signal that these opportunities are shrinking. No one can predict the future, but from looking at past data, there will be many opportunities available today and will continue in the future. From history we will notice that there are always periods of high default rates due to economic performance, quantity of low-grade bonds, and capital market liquidity. We will talk about why these variables can cause an increase the chances of default. Various research reports show that here is a correlation between the amount of low-grade bonds and the future default rates. Since lower rated bonds have a higher chance of default, it is logical to assume that the more lower grade bonds are available, a higher chance of default is expected. For example, if there are 1 million low-grade bonds available in the current year and there are 1.5 million low-grade bonds expected in the next year, we can expect the default rate to be higher in the following year.

SENIOR VERSUS JUNIOR DEBT

There are two main classes of debt called senior and junior debt. They each are different, and each has its own advantages. We will describe each in some detail to get a fuller understanding of these terms. Junior debt is a type of debt that has a lower priority or ranking than another debt claim within the same asset or property. Junior debt is usually unsecured, and it is also known by the name of subordinate debt. Senior debt is debt with a higher ranking or priority than all subordinate or junior debt in the same asset or property. For example someone can have two home mortgages called the first and second mortgages. The first mortgage is considered the senior debt, and the second is called subordinate debt. One may wonder why this is important; it matters if the borrowers default on their obligations. If the home goes into foreclosure, then the proceeds of selling the house go to the senior debt. If there is anything left over, it goes to the second debt. This has important considerations because the holder of junior debt may not get paid at all and bears the most risk. We will do a numerical example to fully understand the complications. Joe buys a house for $300,000 by getting a first mortgage from Bank A for $200,000 and second mortgage from Bank B for $100,000. Joe then defaults on his loans and is forced to sell the home for $250,000 due to a tough housing market. Bank A will get its full $200,000 principal back, but Bank B will only get $50,000 out of its $100,000 loan. As you can see in these types of situations, you would rather be Bank A than Bank B.

LEGAL RESTRUCTURING AND VALUATION

A distressed debt investor must always assess how the debt restructuring process will affect his or her investment. The two most common approaches to the process are in-court proceedings (ICP) and out-of-court proceedings (OCP). The OCP is the most preferred type of approach to an investor and the company. It is preferred because of the cost involved with the proceedings when they are in court. The ICP is a long process. Plus is when vendors hear the firm is in court, the supply chain of the firm is negatively affected. During an out-of-court proceeding, the most significant creditors either renegotiate their obligations by changing their terms or willingly exchange their financial interests. These creditors can change their terms by lowering their interest rates or extending their maturities of the debt. Sometimes this is not feasible, and the other route must be taken. An exchange of financial interests is exchanging the old bonds for a combination of new bonds with less principal, with some type of equity or cash.

Valuation of distressed debt is complicated; it is more of an art than science. Yet, there are several methods to price distressed debt, mostly using classic models of discounted cash flows. The problem with using discount models is its sensitivity to future cash flow projections of the firm. Most distressed debt investors do not use this approach; they use the earnings before interest, taxes, and depreciation (EBITDA Multiple Approach).

To use the EBITDA Multiple Approach, we need to calculate the annual EBITDA and assume a multiple in line with industry and market conditions. To find the value of a firm, we multiply the annual EBITDA by the multiple together. For example, if the annual EBITDA calculated is $100 and the multiple is 7, then the distressed debt is worth $700. Using a 5% margin of error, to be conservative in our computations, the minimum value (called the "floor") would be $655; namely, $700 multiplied by (1–5%.) There are limitations in using this approach:

a. EBITDA is not the best proxy for cash flows
b. EBITDA does not reflect working capital
c. EBITDA does not adjust for capital expenditures
d. EBITDA ignores the time value of money
e. EBITDA may ignore whether the firm is operating under normal conditions
f. EBITDA totally ignores probability and scenario analyses; it is only one static number

There have been a number of models predicting the value and the probability of a firm going to be financially distressed. Among the classic models is the one developed by Professor Edward Altman for his z-score model. The z-score model attempts to predict future bankruptcy using different accounting ratios and market-priced data. For example, the z-scores of less than 1.81 have been shown to predict bankruptcy two years in advance before they occur. The z-scores greater than 3 are indicative of having good credit strength. In its most basic format, below is a multiple regression model for the z-score:

$$Z = a + b_1 X_1 + b_2 X_2 + b_3 X_3 + b_4 X_4$$

Where "a" is a constant value and the independent variables of X_1 to X_4 are predictors of financial distress, such as the ratios of working capital to total assets, retained earnings to total assets, EBIT/Total assets, and market equity to book value. This is a flexible model where the value of EBITDA can also be normalized and incorporated in the model in place of another variable or as an additional indicator. Logistic regression is another popular technique, which is beyond the scope of this chapter.

YOU SHOULD REMEMBER

The Capital Asset Pricing Model (CAPM) can be used to determine the required rate of return in the valuation of common stock. In the Gordon model, the value of K_s (required rate of return) may be unknown. In this case, a financial analyst may determine K_s by the use of the Capital Asset Pricing Model and then use it in the valuation equation:

$$P_0 = \frac{D_1}{K_s - g}$$

where P_0 = stock price to be estimated
D_1 = dividend in year 1
K_s = required rate of return
g = annual growth rate of dividends

KNOW THE CONCEPTS

DO YOU KNOW THE BASICS?

1. What information do you need to determine the value of the following assets?
   (a) Bonds
   (b) Preferred stock
   (c) Common stock

2. Is it possible that the prices you calculate for bonds and stocks are different from actual market prices? Why?

3. What is the general definition of the value of an asset?

4. What happens to the value of a bond if its coupon rate is less than the discount rate required for bonds of similar risk?

5. How can the Capital Asset Pricing Model be used in valuation methods?

TERMS FOR STUDY

bond	face value
cash flow	maturity date
coupon rate	

PRACTICAL APPLICATION

COMPUTATIONAL PROBLEMS

1. How much will you pay for a 5-year, $1,000-denomination bond if the coupon rate is 10% and interest is paid semiannually? Assume that similar bonds are currently discounted at 12%.

2. How much will you pay for a share of a preferred stock with an annual dividend of $5? Similar preferred stocks are discounted at 13%.

3. Does the value of the preferred stock in Problem 2 change if you know that you will sell your shares next year? Why?

4. The earnings and common stock dividends of Steady Co. have been growing at an annual rate of 7%. The rate of growth is expected to remain unchanged for the foreseeable future. The latest annual dividend per share was $2.50. Determine the value of a share of Steady's common stock with each of the following required rates of return:

   (a) 10%
   (b) 12%
   (c) 20%
   (d) 5%

5. Using the CAPM and the following data, determine the value of a share of Public Utility Co.:

   • The latest annual dividend paid by Public Utility Co. is $1.50.

   • Growth is constant at an annual rate of 4%.

   • The beta of Public Utility Co. is 1.20.

   • The rate of return on a market portfolio is 14%.

   • The rate of return on U.S. treasury bills is 9%.

6. The chairman of World Food Corporation announced that the firm's dividends will grow at a rate of 18% for the next 3 years, and that thereafter the annual rate of growth is expected to be only 6%. The annual dividend per share is estimated to be $4 in the next year. If a required rate of return of 15% is assumed, what is the highest price you are willing to pay for a share of World Food Corporation's common stock?

7. A bond, with a face value of $150, is paying $25 coupons annually. The bond will mature in 10 years and the market rate of interest is 10%.

   (a) What is the current price of the bond?
   (b) Is the bond selling at premium or discount?

8. The last dividend paid by stock A was $2 per share. With a 9% required rate of return, calculate the market value of this stock if the growth rate is:
   (a) No growth
   (b) 2% growth
   (c) 5% growth

9. Stock B has paid an annual dividend of $5 per share this year. Analysts estimate that the growth rate of the dividends will be 5%. The required rate of return for the company is 9%. What would be the change in the stock price if the company invests in a business that will increase the growth rate as well as the required rate of return by an additional 2%?

10. Computerplus company already paid $6 dividend per share this year and expects the dividends to grow 10% annually for the next four years and 7% annually thereafter. If the company decides to invest in a new technology, it estimates that the dividends will not increase for the next 5 years but the growth rate of the dividends will be 11% thereafter. Required rate of return for the stock is 17%. In order to maximize the shareholder value, should the company invest in the new technology or not?

11. Today a stock is trading for $10.50. The last dividend paid was $1 and, the required rate of return is 12%. What should the growth rate of this firm be?

12. A 10-year bond was issued by a firm with a coupon rate of 12%. Maturity value is $1,000. What is the value of this bond to an investor who requires a rate of return of 10%?

13. Apple preferred stocks have a par value of $20 and pay 9% preferred dividend. The required rate of interest (or required rate of return) is 7%. What is the price you would be willing to pay for Apple preferred stocks?

14. ABC Company is expected to pay a dividend of $10 in year 1, $5 in year 2, and $5 in year 3. Starting in year 4, it will pay a dividend of $1, which is expected to grow at the rate of 10% each year. What is the price that you would be willing to pay if the required rate of return was 13%?

15. You are planning to borrow $460,000 for 30 years at an interest rate of 6%, and it will be paid monthly. What will be the monthly payment?

16. Bowling Lanes Co. is expected to pay dividends of $2.50, $3.00, and $4.00 in the next three years. D_1 = $2.50, D_2 = $3.00, D_3 = $4.00, respectively. After three years the expected constant growth rate of the dividend is 4% per year indefinitely. The required rate of return is 14% for a shareholder to invest in Bowling Lanes Co. common stock. What is the value of this stock today?

ANSWERS

KNOW THE CONCEPTS

1. The information required to evaluate bonds, preferred stock, and common stock is as follows:
   (a) *Bonds:* coupon rate, face value, maturity, discount rate, and time between interest payments
   (b) *Preferred stock:* dividends paid in each period, discount rate
   (c) *Common stock:* expected dividend next year, required rate of return, rate of growth of dividends

2. Yes. The actual market prices may be more or less because of other factors not considered in the formulas.

3. The value of any asset is defined as the present value of the asset's expected future cash flows.

4. Since the price of a bond moves inversely with the market interest rate, the bond price declines and the bond sells at a discount.

5. The CAPM formula calculates the required rate of return for a common stock, which is the discount rate used to find the present value of the stock's dividend stream.

PRACTICAL APPLICATION

1. $50 (*PVIFA*) + $1,000 (*PVIF*) = $50(7.3601) + $1,000(.5584) = $926
   6%, 10 periods   12%, 10 periods

2. $\dfrac{\$5}{.13} = \$38.46$

3. No. The assumption is that dividends are paid in perpetuity (forever). Once you have sold the stock, somebody else will own it. Therefore, price has nothing to do with the time period an investor holds the stock.

4. $P_0 = D_1/(K_s - g)$; Note: $D_1 = D_0 (1 + g)$

   (a) $\dfrac{\$2.50(1.07)}{.10 - .07} = \$89.17$

   (b) $\dfrac{\$2.50(1.07)}{.12 - .07} = \$53.50$

   (c) $\dfrac{\$2.50(1.07)}{.20 - .07} = \$20.58$

   (d) $\dfrac{\$2.50(1.07)}{.05 - .07} = -\$133.75$

   Answer (d) is not acceptable because the price is negative—which does not make sense!

5. $K_s = R_f + \beta (K_m - R_f) = .09 + 1.20(.14 - .09) = .15$

$$P_0 = \frac{D_1}{(K_s - g)} = \$1.50(1.04) \div (.15 - .04) = \$14.18$$

6. $D_1 = \$4$
$D_2 = \$4(1.18) = \$4.72$
$D_3 = \$4.72(1.18) = \$5.57$
$D_4 = \$5.57(1.06) = \$5.90$

$$P_3 = \frac{D_3(1 + g)}{(K_s - g)} = \frac{\$5.90}{(.15 - .06)} = \$65.56$$

Value of stock $= (PV\,of\,D_1) + (PV\,of\,D_2)$
$\qquad\qquad\quad + (PV\,of\,D_3) + (PV\,of\,P_3)$
$\qquad\qquad = \$4(.8696) + \$4.72(.7561)$
$\qquad\qquad\quad + \$5.57\,(.6575) + \$65.56\,(.6575)$
$\qquad\qquad = \$53.82$

7. (a) $25\,(PVIFA\,of\,10\%,\,10\,years) + \$150(PV\,10\%,\,10\,years) = \$25 \times$
6.1446 $+ \$150 \times 0.38554 = 153.615 + 57.831 = \$211.446$

(b) Premium

8. (a) $\dfrac{\$2}{0.09} = \$22.22$

(b) $\dfrac{\$2}{0.09 - 0.02} = \$28.57$

(c) $\dfrac{\$2}{0.09 - 0.05} = \$50$

9. $5 dividend (5% growth, required rate of return 9%) $=$

$$\frac{\$5}{0.09 - 0.05} = \$125$$

$5 dividend (7% growth, required rate of return 11%) $=$

$$\frac{\$5}{0.11 - 0.07} = \$125$$

There would not be any change.

10. $6 dividend (10% growth for 4 years, 7% thereafter)

$D_1 = \$6 \times 1.10 = \$6.60$
$D_2 = \$6.60 \times 1.10 = \$7.26$
$D_3 = \$7.26 \times 1.10 = \$7.98$
$D_4 = \$7.98 \times 1.10 = \$8.78$

$$P_4 = \frac{D_4(1 + g)}{(K_s - g)} = \frac{9.3946}{0.10} = \$93.94$$

Value of stock = $(PV\ of\ D_1) + (PV\ of\ D_2) + (PV\ of\ D_3) + (PV\ of\ D_4)$
$+ (PV\ of\ P_4)$
$= 6.60\ (0.855) + 7.26\ (0.731) + 7.98\ (0.624) + 8.78$
$(0.534) + 93.94\ (0.534)$
$= 5.643 + 5.307 + 4.979 + 4.689 + 50.164$
$\sim = \$70.78$

$6 dividend (no growth for 5 years, 11% thereafter)

$D_1 = \$6$
$D_2 = \$6$
$D_3 = \$6$
$D_4 = \$6$
$D_5 = \$6$

$$P_5 = \frac{D_5(1 + g)}{(K_s - g)} = \frac{6.66}{0.06} = \$111$$

Value of stock = $(PV\ of\ D_1) + (PV\ of\ D_2) + (PV\ of\ D_3) + (PV\ of\ D_4)$
$+ (PV\ of\ P_4)$
$= 6\ (0.855) + 6\ (0.731) + 6\ (0.624) + 6\ (0.534) + 6$
$(0.456) + 111\ (0.456)$
$= 6\ (0.855 + 0.731 + 0.624 + 0.534 + 0.456) + 111$
(0.456)
$= 6\ (3.2) + 111\ (0.456)$
$\sim = \$69.82$

Do not invest in the technology.

11. $P_0 = \dfrac{D_0(1+g)}{K-g}$

$10.50 = \dfrac{1(1+g)}{.12-g}$

$\dfrac{10.50}{1} = \dfrac{(1+g)}{.12-g}$

$1 + g = 10.50\ (.12 - g)$
$1 + g = 1.26 - 10.50g$
$11.5g = .26$
$g = .26/11.5 = .0226 = 2.26$
$g = 2.26$

12. $V_d = \left(120\dfrac{1-(1+.10)^{-10}}{0.10}\right)+\dfrac{1000}{(1.10)^{10}}$

$$737.35 + 385.54 = \$1,129.89$$

13. D_p = 9% of \$20 = \$1.80

$P_o = \dfrac{1.80}{0.07} = \$25.71$

If Apple preferred stock is priced below \$25.71, invest. If it is above \$25.71, do not invest.

14. $D_1 = \$10$, $D_2 = \$5$, $D_3 = \$5$, $D_4 = \dfrac{1.00}{.13-.10} = \$33.33$

$P_0 = \dfrac{10}{1.13^1} + \dfrac{5}{1.13^2} + \dfrac{5}{1.13^3} + \dfrac{33.33}{1.13^3} = \$39.34$

15. $\dfrac{6\%}{12} = 0.5$ per month

$$460,000 = PMT\left(\dfrac{1-(1.005)^{-360}}{0.005}\right)$$

$$460,000 = PMT \, (166.7916)$$
$$\dfrac{}{166.7916} \qquad \dfrac{}{166.7916}$$

$$\$2,757.93 = PMT$$

16.

Year	D	PV@14
1	\$2.50	\$2.19
2	3.00	2.31
3	4.00	2.70
Price at Year 3	\$41.60	28.08
Price today		\$35.28

$P_1 = \dfrac{2.50}{1.14^1} = \$2.19$

$\dfrac{4(1.04)}{0.14-0.04} = \$41.60$

INTRODUCTION TO INVESTMENT POLICY: CAPITAL BUDGETING

6

CAPITAL BUDGETING: PRELIMINARY STEPS

WHAT IS CAPITAL BUDGETING?

Capital budgeting is a required managerial tool. One duty of a financial manager is to choose investments with satisfactory cash flows and rates of return. Therefore, a financial manager must be able to decide whether or not an investment is worth undertaking and be able to choose intelligently between two or more alternatives. To do this, a sound procedure to evaluate, compare, and select projects is needed. This procedure is called **capital budgeting**.

EFFICIENT USE OF A LIMITED RESOURCE

In the form of either debt or equity, capital is a very limited resource. There is a limit to the volume of credit that the banking system can create in the economy. Commercial banks and other lending institutions have limited deposits from which they can lend money to individuals, corporations, and governments. In addition, the Federal Reserve System requires each bank to maintain part of its deposits as reserves. Having limited resources to lend, lending institutions are selective in extending loans to their customers. But even if a bank were to extend unlimited loans to a company, the management of that company would need to consider the impact that increasing loans would have on the overall cost of financing.

In reality, any firm has limited borrowing resources that should be allocated among the best investment alternatives. One might argue that a company can issue an almost unlimited amount of common stock to raise capital. Increasing the number of shares of company stock, however, will serve only to distribute the same amount of equity among a greater number of shareholders. In other words, as the number of shares of a company increases, the company ownership of the individual stockholder may proportionally decrease.

The argument that capital is a limited resource is true of any form of capital, whether debt or equity (short-term or long-term, common stock) or retained earnings, accounts payable or notes payable, and so on. Even the best-known firm in an industry or a community can increase its borrowing up to a certain limit. Once this point has been reached, the firm will either be denied more credit or be charged a higher interest rate, making borrowing a less desirable way to raise capital.

Faced with limited sources of capital, management should carefully decide whether or not a particular project is economically acceptable. In the case of more than one project, management must identify the projects that will contribute most to profits and, consequently, to the value (or wealth) of the firm. This, in essence, is the basis of capital budgeting.

CURRENT EXPENDITURES AND CAPITAL EXPENDITURES

A firm makes two types of expenditures: current and capital. **Current expenditures** are short term and completely written off in the same year that the expenses occur. Examples of current expenditures are wages, salaries, cost of raw materials, and various administrative expenses. **Capital expenditures** are long term, and are **amortized** (their value is gradually reduced) over a period of years according to IRS regulations (discussed previously in Chapter 2). Examples of capital expenditures include an outlay of $100,000 for a new building or machinery, the purchase of a personal computer for business purposes, the purchase of patent rights from an inventor, expenditures for research and development, and so on. For the purposes of this chapter, only capital expenditures will be discussed.

Types of Capital Expenditures

1. New machines and equipment bought for new purposes. In order to expand business operations, firms often buy new equipment. According to IRS regulations, light-duty trucks, different models of automobiles, research and development equipment, and relatively inexpensive equip-

ment are depreciated over a period of 3 years. Other machinery tools are depreciated over 5 years. Public utility capital expenditures generally have a recovery period of 10 or 15 years.

2. Replacement of existing machines. To increase efficiency, management may decide to sell existing still-functioning equipment and replace it with current models. Capital budgeting for replacement projects is concerned not only with the cost of new machines but also with the revenue from the sale of old machines and the tax effects from this sale. Examples later in the chapter will clarify this point.

3. Mandatory projects. With the rise of consumerism, **mandatory projects** are becoming a major component of capital expenditures. These investments are required by law to maintain the safety of consumers and workers as well as a healthy environment.

4. Other capital expenditures. This category encompasses various other long-term investments, such as purchasing land, expanding office buildings, and buying patent rights.

YOU SHOULD REMEMBER

Capital budgeting is investment decision-making as to whether or not a project is worth undertaking. Capital budgeting is basically concerned with the justification of capital expenditures.

Current expenditures are short term and are completely written off in the same year that expenses occur. Capital expenditures are long term and are amortized over a period of years as required by the IRS.

DETERMINING INITIAL COSTS

The first important step in deciding whether a project should be accepted is the calculation of its initial cost. The **initial cost,** or cost of initial investment, is simply the actual cost of starting an investment. Once managers know how much it costs to run a project, they can compare the initial investment with future benefits and make a judgment as to whether or not the project is worth undertaking. To determine the cost of the initial investment, financial analysts answer the following questions:

- What is the invoice price of new items (machinery, equipment, services, etc.)?

- What are the additional expenses, such as costs of packing, delivery, installation, and inspection?
- What is the revenue from the sale of existing machinery, if it needs to be replaced?
- How much tax should be paid on the sale of the existing machinery?

Table 6-1 should be used as a checklist to determine the initial cost of a project.

Table 6–1 Calculating the Initial Cost of a Project

Initial Expense	Amount	Initial Revenue	Amount
Price of new items	xx	Revenue from sale of existing machinery	xx
Additional expenses		Tax credit on sale of	
packing and delivery	xx	existing machinery at	
installation	xx	loss	xx
inspection	xx		
other	xx		
Taxes on sale of existing machinery	xx		
Change in net working capital	xx	Total initial revenue	xx
Total initial expense	xx	Initial cost of project*	xx

*Initial cost of project = Total initial expense – Total initial revenue

Example 1: Determining Initial Costs

PROBLEM   XYZ Co. is planning to buy new machinery for $200,000. The machinery has a depreciation life of 5 years. As a result of buying the new machinery, XYZ Co. will sell the existing machinery at $50,000. The existing machinery was purchased 3 years ago for $100,000. The company must pay $4,000 for delivery and $9,000 for installation of the new machinery. As a financial analyst, determine the initial cost of the project. Assume tax rates of 34%. Net working capital does not change.

**Table 6–2 XYZ Co.—Calculation of the Initial Cost
of Buying New Machinery**

Initial Expense	Amount	Initial Revenue	Amount
Price of new item	$200,000	Revenue from sale of existing machinery	$50,000
Additional expenses		Tax credit on sale of	
packing and delivery	$4,000	existing machinery	
installation	9,000	at loss	0
inspection	0		
other	0		
Taxes on sale of existing machinery	$7,140		
Change in net working capital			————
Total expenses	$220,140	Total revenue	50,000
		Total expenses	220,140
		Net Cost	$170,140

As shown in Table 6-2, the total initial expenses are $220,140: including $200,000 for new machinery, $4,000 for packing and delivery, $9,000 for installation, and $7,140 for taxes on the sale of the existing machinery.

Taxes of $7,140 are determined as follows: Since the existing machinery was sold below the original price of $100,000, there is capital gains. The company should pay 34% ordinary tax on any sale price over the book value. Since the existing machinery was purchased 3 years ago, it has been depreciated as follows:

Depreciation in year 1: $(.20)($100,000) = $20,000$
Depreciation in year 2: $(.32)($100,000) = 32,000$
Depreciation in year 3: $(.19)($100,000) = \underline{19,000}$
Total depreciation $= \overline{$71,000}$

Therefore, the book value of the machinery is $29,000 ($100,000 – $71,000).

Since the machinery has been sold at $50,000, the company has a recaptured depreciation of $21,000. (Remember that **recaptured depreciation** is the difference between the selling price—excluding capital gain—and the book value.) Paying 34% tax on the recaptured depreciation, XYZ Co. should pay 34% of $21,000, which equals $7,140 as reported. (See Table 6-2.)

The total initial revenue is $50,000. Subtracting the total initial revenue of $50,000 from the total initial expenses of $220,140, XYZ Co. will invest $170,140 as the initial cost of this project.

Example 2: Determining Initial Costs

PROBLEM   What would be the initial cost of the project in the preceding example if the existing machinery was sold at $20,000? Assume that all other information remains unchanged.

SOLUTION

Table 6–3   XYZ Co.—Calculation of the Initial Cost of Buying New Machinery

Initial Expense	Amount	Initial Revenue	Amount
Price of new item	$200,000	Revenue from sale of existing machinery	$20,000
Additional expenses		Tax credit on sale of	
packing and delivery	4,000	existing machinery at	
installation	9,000	loss	3,060
inspection	0		
other	0		
Taxes on sale of existing			
machinery	0	Total revenue	23,060
Total expenses	$213,000	Total expenses	213,000
		Net Cost	$189,940

Since the old machinery is sold below the book value, there is a loss of $9,000 ($29,000 book value minus $20,000 resale price). Therefore, XYZ Co. should receive a tax credit of $3,060 on the loss (34% of $9,000). Table 6-3 shows that, in this case, taxes on the sale of the existing machinery are zero, and the tax credit on the sale is $3,060.

When calculating the initial cost of a project, keep in mind that there is neither a tax to be paid nor a tax to be refunded if existing machinery is sold at its book value. For instance, if the existing machinery in the case of XYZ Co. is sold at the book value of $29,000, taxes on the sale of the machinery—as well as tax credits on the sale of the machine—would be zero.

DETERMINING INCREMENTAL CASH FLOW

The preceding section showed how to calculate the initial cost of a project. In order to decide whether the initial cost will pay off, however, it is also necessary to estimate future cash flows. Management should be concerned only with the incremental cash flow. The **incremental cash flow** is the additional cash flow that the firm will receive over the existing cash flow after the project is accepted. Suppose that the existing cash flow of a firm is $100. If cash flow increases to $150 after starting a new project, the incremental cash flow is $50. Therefore, only $50 is considered as the relevant cash flow, or the benefit of the project. There is a simple method to determine the incremental cash flow of a new project for each year.

Determining Incremental Cash Flow

1. Calculate additional net earnings.

Additional net = Estimated net earnings – Estimated net earnings
earnings   (including the new   (without the new
      project)   project)

2. Calculate tax benefits of depreciation.

Additional tax benefit
of depreciation =   Tax rate × Additional depreciation

3. Add additional net earnings and tax benefits of depreciation together.

Incremental cash flow
= Additional net earnings + Additional tax benefits of depreciation

Example 1: Calculating Incremental Cash Flow

PROBLEM   The estimated net earnings for the XYZ Co. in the next 3 years are $100,000, $150,000, and $200,000. The annual depreciation amounts for those years are estimated as $30,000, $40,000, and $45,000. As a result of starting a new project, the estimated net earnings will be $120,000, $165,000, and $230,000; and the annual depreciation will increase to $45,000, $62,000, and $66,000. To make it simple, assume that the tax rate is 40%; calculate the incremental cash flow of the new project.

SOLUTION   **1.** Subtract the estimated net earnings without the new project from the estimated net earnings with the new project for each year. The results are additional net earnings as follows:

Additional net earnings:	Year 1	Year 2	Year 3
	$20,000	$15,000	$30,000

2. Since the annual depreciation increases, so does the tax benefit of depreciation in each year. Subtract to find these benefits:

Additional tax benefit of depreciation (.40 × depreciation increases)	Year 1	Year 2	Year 3
	$6,000	$8,800	$8,400

3. Adding additional net earnings to additional tax benefits of depreciation, determine the incremental cash flow for each year:

Incremental cash flow:	Year 1	Year 2	Year 3
	$26,000	$23,800	$38,400

   In other words, the actual benefits of accepting the new project are $26,000 in the first year, $23,800 in the second year, and $38,400 in the third year. In the next chapter, these annual benefits will be compared against the the initial cost of the project (initial investment), and a decision whether to accept or reject the project will then be made.

Example 2: Calculating Incremental Cash Flows

PROBLEM   The estimated earnings before interest and taxes (**EBIT**) under two conditions are given in Table 6-4:

Table 6–4   EBIT Under Two Conditions

Year	With the Existing Machine	With the New Machine
1	$100,000	$150,000
2	140,000	250,000
3	280,000	350,000
4	400,000	450,000
5	510,000	550,000

The existing machine was purchased 3 years ago at $400,000. A new machine is under consideration for replacement at a cost of $600,000. Depreciation life is 5 years in both cases, and the tax rate is 34%. Determine the incremental cash flow for replacing the existing machine.

SOLUTION   In solving this problem, notice that, if the existing machine is kept, only 2 years are left for depreciation. However, if the new machine is purchased, there are 5 years of depreciation. Therefore, the incremental cash flow should include not only the difference between the EBITs, but also the tax benefits from additional years of depreciation if the company buys the new machine. Tables 6-5, 6-6 and 6-7 show a step-by-step solution to the problem.

In calculating depreciation, you multiply the cost of each machine by 20% for the first year, 32% for the second year, and 19%, 15%, and 14% for the years after, as explained in Chapter 2. In Table 6-5 additional values of EBIT were determined, and in Table 6-6 additional tax benefits of depreciation were calculated. If the additional EBIT and the additional tax benefits are added together, the result is the additional, or incremental, cash flow as reported in Table 6-7.

Table 6–5   Step One: Additional EBIT

Year	New EBIT (a)	Existing EBIT (b)	Additional EBIT (a – b)
1	$150,000	$100,000	$ 50,000
2	250,000	140,000	110,000
3	350,000	280,000	70,000
4	450,000	400,000	50,000
5	550,000	510,000	40,000

Table 6–6   Step Two: Additional Tax Benefits

Year	New Depreciation (a)	Existing Depreciation (b)	Additional Depreciation (a – b)	Additional Tax Benefit 34% (a – b)
1	$120,000	$60,000	$ 60,000	$20,400
2	192,000	56,000	136,000	46,240
3	114,000	0	114,000	38,760
4	90,000	0	90,000	30,600
5	84,000	0	84,000	28,560

Table 6–7   **Incremental Cash Flow in 5 Years**

Year	Incremental Cash Flow = Additional EBIT & Additional Tax Benefits
1	$70,400
2	156,240
3	108,760
4	80,600
5	68,560

From the above example, it can be concluded that
Incremental cash flow
= Incremental EBIT + Incremental tax benefit of depreciation
Incremental cash flow is the *only relevant cash flow* for the capital budgeting decisions that will be made in the next two chapters.

YOU SHOULD REMEMBER

Before deciding about a project, management should determine two important values: initial investment and incremental cash flow. Initial investment is the actual cost of a project after adjusting both for the sale of the existing equipment and for taxes. Incremental cash flows are additional benefits that a project will contribute to the existing cash flows. Incremental cash flow should be considered as the only relevant cash flow in the analysis and comparison of projects.

KNOW THE CONCEPTS

DO YOU KNOW THE BASICS?

1. What is capital budgeting?
2. For tax purposes, which type of expenditure is more favorable to the cash flows of a firm: current expenditures or capital expenditures?
3. What major information (data) do you need for capital budgeting?
4. What is the only relevant cash flow when comparing two projects?

5. Explain the tax consequences of selling an old asset at a price above the depreciated value and also above the original purchase price.

TERMS FOR STUDY

amortization
capital budgeting
capital expenditures
current expenditures
EBIT

incremental cash flow
initial cost
mandatory project
recaptured depreciation

PRACTICAL APPLICATION

COMPUTATIONAL PROBLEMS

1. XYZ Associates are considering the purchase of a new machine for $300,000. Meanwhile, they are planning to sell their old machine for $60,000. The old machine was purchased 3 years ago and its book value is $46,200. Both machines have a depreciation life of 5 years. Delivery expenses are $6,000, and installation expenses are $10,000. Using tax rates of 34% for ordinary income, calculate the initial cost of buying the new equipment.

2. Sara & Associates have estimated the EBIT of its firm under two conditions as follows:

Year	EBIT with Old Equipment	EBIT with New Equipment
1	$150,000	$210,000
2	190,000	290,000
3	340,000	380,000
4	450,000	490,000
5	550,000	710,000

The old equipment was purchased 2 years ago for $500,000. New equipment can be purchased for $710,000. Both pieces of equipment have a depreciation life of 5 years. Using a tax rate of 34%, calculate the incremental cash flow of replacing the old equipment. Explain your findings in your own words.

3. ABC, Inc., is considering replacing a machine that originally cost $40,000 with a new machine that can be purchased for $70,000. The book value of the old machine is $16,800, and it can be sold for $10,000. Installation costs and shipping fees associated with the new machine are $3,500. Using a tax rate of 34%, calculate the cost of purchasing the new machine.

4. XYZ Corporation is considering replacing one of its old machines with a new, more efficient machine. The old machine has a book value of $25,000 and can be sold for $100,000. The new machine has a cost of $500,000. Shipping fees are an additional $5,000. Using a tax rate of 34% for ordinary income, calculate the cost of purchasing the new equipment.

5. Calculate the incremental cash flow for replacing old equipment, given the following information:

Year	EBIT with Old Equipment	EBIT with New Equipment
1	$200,000	$225,000
2	215,000	305,000
3	300,000	315,000

The company's tax rate is 34%, the old machine was purchased 2 years ago for $600,000, the new machine costs $920,000, and both machines have a depreciation life of 3 years.

6. Delicious Daily's is planning on investing in a new food-packaging machine for $600,000 by selling its old one for $60,000. The old machine was purchased 2 years ago and has a book value of $52,000. Both machines have a depreciation life of 5 years. Delivery expenses are $8,000, and the installation expenses are 5% of the cost of machine. Using a tax rate of 34% for ordinary income, calculate the initial cost of buying the new machine.

7. Radiowave, Inc. has an estimated EBIT of their company as follows:

Year	EBIT Old Equipment	EBIT with New Equipment
1	$200,000	$290,000
2	248,000	325,000
3	370,000	410,000
4	420,000	558,000
5	568,000	746,000

Both pieces of equipment have a life of 5 years. The old equipment was purchased 3 years ago for $570,000. The new equipment can be purchased for $740,000. The company uses a tax rate of 34%. Determine the incremental cash flow of replacing the old equipment.

8. Acme Plastic is considering investing in a new machine, which costs $600,000 by selling its old machine for $50,000. Both machines have a depreciation life of 5 years. The old machine was purchased two years ago and has a book value of $52,000. The shipping expenses are $9,000,

and the installation expenses are 4% of the cost of the machine. The company uses a tax rate of 34%. Calculate the initial cost of the new machine.

ANSWERS

KNOW THE CONCEPTS

1. Capital budgeting is the procedure used to evaluate, compare, and select projects with satisfactory cash flows.

2. Current expenditures are more favorable for tax purposes because all expenditures can be written off in 1 year.

3. For capital budgeting, you need to know the initial investment and incremental cash flows.

4. Incremental cash flows are all you need to compare projects.

5. The amount by which the selling price exceeds the original purchase price is considered a capital gain and is taxed as ordinary income. The amount by which the purchase price exceeds the book value is considered a recapture of depreciation and is taxed at the marginal tax rate.

PRACTICAL APPLICATION

1.
Cost of equipment	$300,000
Delivery expenses	6,000
Installation	10,000
Sale of old machine	(60,000)
*Tax on the sale of old machine	4,692
	$260,692

*Tax = 34% of recaptured depreciation

Recaptured depreciation = Selling price − Book value
= $60,000 − $46,200 = $13,800

Therefore, the tax, on the sale of the old machine is 34% × 13,800 = $4,692.

2.
Year	New EBIT	Old EBIT	Additional EBIT
1	$210,000	$150,000	$ 60,000
2	290,000	190,000	100,000
3	380,000	340,000	40,000
4	490,000	450,000	40,000
5	710,000	550,000	160,000

Year	New Depreciation	Old Depreciation	Additional Depreciation	Additional Tax Benefit at 34%
1	$142,000	$95,000	$ 47,000	$15,980
2	227,200	75,000	152,200	51,748
3	134,900	70,000	64,900	22,066
4	106,500	0	106,500	36,210
5	99,400	0	99,400	33,796

Incremental cash flow = Additional EBIT + Additional tax benefit

Year	Incremental Cash Flow
1	$ 75,980
2	151,748
3	62,066
4	76,210
5	193,796

3. Cost of new machine $70,000
Installation and shipping fees   3,500
Sale of old machine   (10,000)
*Tax credit on sale of old machine   (2,312)
   $61,188

*Loss on sale of old machine   = Selling price – Book value
   = $10,000 – $16,800
   = $6,800
Tax credit on sale of old machine   = .34 × $6,800
   = $2,312

4. Cost of new machine $500,000
Shipping fees   5,000
Sale of old machine   (100,000)
*Taxes on sale of old machine   25,500
   $430,500

Recaptured depreciation   = Purchase price – Book value
   $100,000 – $25,000
   = $75,000
Tax on recaptured depreciation   = $75,000 × .34 = $25,500

5.

Year	Additional EBIT
1	$225,000 – $200,000 = $25,000
2	$305,000 – $215,000 = $90,000
3	$315,000 – $300,000 = $15,000

Year	New Depreciation	Old Depreciation	Additional Depreciation	Additional Tax Benefit at 34%
1	$303,600	$138,000	$165,600	$ 56,304
2	404,800	0	404,800	137,632
3	211,600	0	211,600	71,944

Year	Incremental Cash Flow
1	$ 81,304
2	227,632
3	86,944

6.

Cost of equipment = $600,000
Delivery expenses = $8,000
Installation expense = ($600,000 × 0.05) = $30,000
Sale of old machine = $60,000
Tax on sale of old machine = $2,686.00*

Total initial cost = $580,686

*Recaptured Depreciation = Sell price – Book value
= 60,000 – 521,000
= 79,000
Tax = 0.34 × $7,000
= $2,686

7.

Year	New EBIT	Old EBIT	Additional EBIT
1	$290,000	$200,000	$ 90,000
2	325,000	248,000	77,000
3	410,000	370,000	40,000
4	558,000	420,000	138,000
5	746,000	568,000	178,000

Additional Tax Benefits:

Year	New Depreciation	Old Depreciation	Additional Depreciation	Additional Tax Benefits of 34%*
1	$148,000	$85,500	$62,500	$21,250
2	236,800	79,800	157,000	53,380
3	140,600	0	140,600	47,804
4	111,000	0	111,000	37,740
5	103,600	0	103,600	35,224

*Using rates of 20%, 32%, 19%, 15%, and 14% for consecutive years.

Incremental cash flow = Additional EBIT + Additional tax benefits

Year	Incremental Cash Flow
1	$111,250
2	130,380
3	87,804
4	175,740
5	213,224

8. Cost of equipment .... = $600,000
Shipping expenses .... = 9,000
Installation expense = (600,000 × 0.04) = 24,000
Sale of old machines .... = (50,000)
*Tax credit on sale of old machine .... = (680)

Total initial cost .... = $582,320

*Loss on sale of old machine = Sell price – Book value
         = $50,000 – $52,000
         = $2,000
Tax credit on sale of machine = $2,000 × 0.34
         = $680

7

FUNDAMENTALS OF CAPITAL BUDGETING: UNDER THE CONDITIONS OF NO RISK AND RISK

KEY TERMS

after-tax incremental cash flows additional cash flows as a result of replacing an existing machine (or updating an existing project) and after adjustment for all tax effects

average rate of return (ARR) the ratio of average net earnings to average investment

certainty equivalent factor a factor used to convert projected cash flows into certain cash flows

incremental initial investment (III) the true cost of starting a project, which includes the cost of purchasing a new asset, the sale of the old asset, and the tax effect (either tax liability or tax credit) on the sale of the old asset

internal rate of return (IRR) the discount rate that makes the net present value of a project equal to zero

net present value (NPV) the present value of a project's future cash flow less the initial investment in the project

payback period the amount of time required to recover the initial investment in a project

profitability index (PI) the ratio of the present value of the future cash flows from a project to the initial investment in the project

required rate of return (RRR) a discount rate used to convert expected future cash flows into a present value

risk uncertainty; instability, fluctuations

risk-free rate a discount rate equal to the return on a riskless asset

sensitivity analysis a measure of the extent to which one factor varies when another factor changes

simulation the use of a hypothetical situation, similar to the real one, as a help in making a decision

INCORPORATING RISK IN CAPITAL BUDGETING

In real world, there is no capital budgeting project without risk. Risk is synonymous with uncertainty and unexpected fluctuations. Risk, in itself, cannot be labeled either as good or bad; if risk is adequately compensated, it can create value to the firm or the investor. An investment is called **risk free** if its return is stable and reliable. Investors usually think of the treasury bill, which is a U.S. government security, as a risk-free investment, mainly because its return is certain and guaranteed except for the rate of inflation. With the recent downgrades of the U.S. government securities as well as non-U.S. government securities, it is often asked what a risk-free rate is. As a practical answer, in the absence of better proxies, it is still advisable to use the return on the U.S. treasury bill rate as a risk-free rate. Some analysts, depending on their investment horizons, use the 10-year treasury note as a proxy instead.

In capital budgeting, the future cash flows of a project may unexpectedly decrease or increase. The rate at which future cash flows are invested may not remain the same, as was previously assumed. There are many other factors that may reduce expected cash flows: loss of market share, an increase in the cost of goods sold, new environmental regulations, a rising cost of financing. Since there is always risk in capital budgeting, a major job of investment analysts is to select projects under conditions of uncertainty.

CERTAINTY EQUIVALENT APPROACH (CEA)

The idea behind the certainty equivalent approach is to separate the timing of cash flows from their riskiness. Cash flows are converted into riskless (certain) cash flows, which are then discounted at a **risk-free rate**. The rate on a U.S. treasury bill is accepted as risk free and is the rate generally used.

Calculating Certain Equivalents

1. Estimate the expected cash flows of the project.

2. Determine the **certainty equivalent factors**, or the percentages of the expected cash flows that are certain.

3. Calculate the certain cash flows by multiplying the expected cash flows by the certainty equivalent factors.

4. Calculate the present value of the project by discounting the certain cash flows at a risk-free discount rate—the return on U.S. treasury bills, for example.

5. Determine the net present value of the project by subtracting the initial investment from the present value of the certain cash flows.

6. If the *NPV* is either zero or positive, the project is acceptable. Conversely, the project should be rejected if the *NPV* is negative.

Example: Calculating Certain Equivalents

PROBLEM   The XYZ Co. has estimated that annual cash flows in the next 5 years will be $7,000, $6,000, $5,000, $4,000, and $3,000, respectively. The certainty equivalent factors for the same periods are estimated at 95%, 80%, 70%, 60%, and 40%. The initial investment of the project is $11,000. The risk-free rate (return on the U.S. treasury bill) is 10%. Using the certainty equivalent approach, decide if the project is acceptable.

SOLUTION   First, you should convert expected cash flows into certain cash flows. This can be done by multiplying the expected cash flows by the certainty equivalent factors as given:

Year	Expected Cash Flow	Certainty Equivalent Factors	Certain Cash Flow
1	$7,000	.95	$6,650
2	6,000	.80	4,800
3	5,000	.70	3,500
4	4,000	.60	2,400
5	3,000	.40	1,200

Once you have the certain cash flows, discount them at the risk-free rate of 10%. (Note: Certain cash flows should be discounted *only* at the risk-free rate. Remember that these cash flows are supposed to be certain). Using a present value table, you then calculate the present value of the certain cash flows:

Year	Certain Cash Flow	PVIF at 10%	PV of Certain Cash Flow
1	$6,650	.909	$6,044.85
2	4,800	.826	3,964.80
3	3,500	.751	2,628.50
4	2,400	.683	1,639.20
5	1,200	.621	745.20
		PV of total certain cash flows =	$15,022.55

The present value of certain cash flows from this project is $15,022.55. Subtracting the initial investment of $11,000 from $15,022.55, you determine the *NPV* of the project to be $4,022.55. By now, of course, you know that a positive *NPV* means that the project is worth undertaking. Therefore, the XYZ Co. should accept this investment.

YOU SHOULD REMEMBER

The certainty equivalent approach (CEA) converts expected cash flows into certain cash flows and discounts them at a risk-free rate.

SENSITIVITY ANALYSIS

Sensitivity analysis is a popular way to find out how the *NPV* of a project changes if sales, labor, or material costs, the discount rate, or other factors vary from one case to another. In simple terms, **sensitivity analysis** is a "what if" study. For example, you might be interested in knowing what happens to the *NPV* of a project if cash flow increases by 10%, 20%, or 30% each year. Will the *NPV* still be positive if there is no cash flow in the second year? Which project's *NPV* will fall more sharply if the discount rate goes up from 8% to 11%? These are the kinds of questions financial analysts raise when they want to measure the risk of a project through sensitivity analysis. Remember from the preceding chapters that risk is measured by variation. The more variation or change there is in the *NPV* of a project, the more risky that investment would be.

Example: Using Sensitivity Analysis

PROBLEM   Suppose the cash flows of Project A are $1,000 in year 1 and $1,500 in year 2. Project B has expected cash flows of $1,800 in year 1 and $700 in year 2. The initial investment for each project is $1,600. Which project is more risky if the discount rate changes from 10% to 12%?

SOLUTION   To answer this question, first find the *NPV* of each project at 10%. Using the *NPV* method, you determine that the *NPV* of Project A at 10% is $548, and the *NPV* of Project B at the same rate is $614. Review: Multiply the cash flows by the present value factors at 10%, add up the answers, and then subtract the initial investment of $1,600. To see the changes in the *NPV*s of these two projects, you should now calculate the *NPV*s of the cash flows at a new rate. Using the same method, you find that the *NPV* of Project A at 12% is $489, and the *NPV* of Project B at the same rate is $565. Summarize the results:

Project	NPV at 10%	NPV at 12%	Percent Change in NPV
A	$548	$489	–10.77
B	$614	$565	–7.98

By looking at the above figures, you can see that the *NPV*s of both projects decline when the discount rate rises from 10% to 12%. The sensitivity analysis method, however, poses an additional important question that helps to compare the degrees of risk of these two projects: Which project's *NPV* has a higher percentage of change if the discount rate increases from 10% to 12%? Comparing the above figures, you see that the percentage change in the *NPV* of Project A is –12%. While that of Project B is –9%. Therefore, Project A is more sensitive to a change in the discount rate. In other words, Project A is riskier than project B if the discount rate changes in the future.

YOU SHOULD REMEMBER

Sensitivity analysis measures *NPV*, *IRR*, and other indicators of profit or risk as sales, costs, the discount rate, or other variables change. The purpose is to find out how sensitive the *NPV* or the *IRR* is to a change in one variable. Of two projects, the one more sensitive to a change is the project considered to have more risk.

THE CAPM IN CAPITAL BUDGETING

The capital asset pricing model (CAPM) was introduced in Chapter 4, where it was used to find the required rate of return on a stock or portfolio. The calculation is very simple if the return on a risk-free asset, beta (β) of the stock or portfolio, and return on the market portfolio are known. The simple equation given in Chapter 4 was

$$K_e = R_f + \beta(K_m - R_f)$$

Where K_e = required rate of return
β = beta of the stock
R_f = risk-free rate
K_m = return on a market portfolio

In this chapter the same equation, with only slightly different notation, is used:

$$K_p = R_f + \beta_p(K_m - R_f)$$

where K_p = required rate of return on the project being evaluated
β_p = beta of the project

Other notations are the same as before. This method considers a project as it would a share of stock, arguing that the return from a project is linked to the return on the total assets of the company, or to the return in an industry. If you believe that the project being studied has the same basic risk level as a typical project of the company, you can use the beta of the company as the beta of the project.

Example: Using the CAPM in Capital Budgeting

PROBLEM   Suppose you want to find the *NPV* of a project, but you have no idea what discount rate to use. You do know, however, that the beta of the company is 1.50, the risk-free rate is 8%, and the return on a market portfolio, such as Dow Jones, is 16%. You also believe that the risk of the project is not much different from the risk of other company projects.

SOLUTION   Since you believe the risks to be similar, you can say that the beta, or the relevant risk, of the project should be close to the beta of the company, which is 1.50.

Using $K_p = R_f + \beta_p(K_m - R_f)$ and plugging in the given information, you find that the required rate of return on the project will be

$$K_p = .08 + 1.50(.16 - .08) = .20 \text{ or } 20\%$$

Once you have determined the project's required rate of return—20%—the *NPV* calculation is exactly the same as previously discussed. To obtain the *NPV* of the project, discount expected cash flows at 20% and subtract the total present value of cash flows from the initial investment. If the *NPV* is zero or positive, you can accept the project simply because the 20% required rate of return will be maintained.

What happens if a project is not a typical investment of the company? In other words, how can you use the CAPM for a project whose risk and other characteristics are different from average or routine projects that the company undertakes? In this case, you should look into similar projects outside the firm. For instance, if a firm is considering investing in the aluminum industry, the beta for the new project should be the average beta for a group of firms in the aluminum industry. Five other firms in the aluminum industry might have betas of .80, 1.25, 1.10, 1.20, and 1.90. Taking the average of these sample betas, you can say that your project has a beta of 1.25 (.80 + 1.25 + 1.10 + 1.20 + 1.90)/5.

YOU SHOULD REMEMBER

The CAPM calculates the required rate of return for a project. Required rates of return are calculated by the use of the regular equation for the CAPM; of two projects, the one with a higher beta is considered more risky. If a project is similar to other investments in the company, the beta of the company's stock can be used as the beta of the project. Otherwise, the average beta of a group of companies with similar projects should represent the beta of the project.

SIMULATION TECHNIQUES

The word **simulation** comes from the Latin word *similis*, which means "like." Accordingly, the idea behind simulation is basically to make hypothetical situations like real ones. Since the actual cash flows or discount rate that will exist in the future are not known, various cash flows and discount rates are assumed, and the results are studied. These cases based on assumptions are called simulated events. Simulated events in capital budgeting are used to study the *NPV*s or the *IRR*s of a project for different cash flows at different reinvestment rates. After different *NPV*s are computed, the average *NPV* and standard deviation of the project are studied to see if the project is worth undertaking.

If you have more than one project, you can simulate the *NPV* or the *IRR* of each project a number of times and compute the average *NPV*s or *IRSS*s and standard deviations. Then rank the projects, starting with the one that has the highest *NPV* or *IRR* and the lowest standard deviation. Ranking projects is much easier if you first divide the average standard deviation by the average *NPV* of each simulated project. The result, as you may remember from Chapter 4, is the coefficient of variation, giving the highest rank to the project with the lowest coefficient.

Example: Using Simulation Methods in Capital Budgeting

PROBLEM   Suppose the simulated *NPV*s for Project A are $100, $300, $800, $700, and $600, with corresponding standard deviations of 10, 18, 78, 68, and 50. The simulated *NPV*s for Project B are $300, $150, $700, $640, and $800, with corresponding standard deviations of 62, 29, 98, 102, and 130. Based on the simulated figures, which project is more attractive?

SOLUTION   A simple approach is to calculate the average *NPV* and the average standard deviation of each project:

Project	Average Simulated NPV (x)	Average Simulated Standard Deviation (y)	Simulated Coefficient of Variation (y/x)
A	$500	$45	9%
B	$518	$84	16%

The results of the preceding tabulation indicate that the simulated coefficient of variation (CV) for Project A is smaller than for Project B (9% vs. 16%). Since the smaller the CV the better the project from a risk-return trade-off basis, then Project A is more attractive than Project B.

Given the fact that both projects have the same average *NPV*, it is evident that Project A's dispersion away from the average simulated value of *NPV* is smaller than Project B's dispersion (See Figure 7-1, opposite).

The area under curve A is smaller than the one under curve B. This suggest that NPV_B is less certain than NPV_A. By looking at these simulated probability curves, you can see that Project A's *NPV* is less volatile and, therefore, less risky than Project B.

There is a variety of **simulation software** for various personal computers. These programs use variables at random and calculate many more scenarios than anyone would do by hand. These results can also be used to draw curves to show the distribution of the *NPV*s or the *IRR*s. The shapes of distribution curves help financial analysts get a good idea about the riskiness

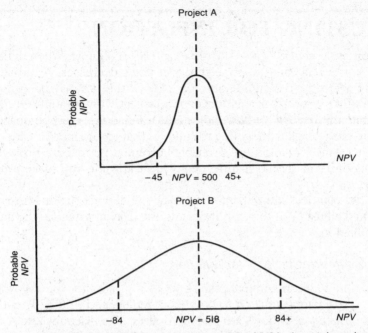

Note that Project B's dispersion away from its *NPV* of 518 is almost twice as large as the dispersion for Project A

Figure 7-1 *NPV* Simulation Curves

of a project. Figure 7-1 shows the distribution curve of simulated *NPV*s for Projects A and B.

Project A has a steeper curve, which indicates less risk and a higher average *NPV* than Project B. The area under curve A is narrow; the probable *NPV*s do not vary very much. Project B has a broader curve, which suggests that its *NPV* is very uncertain. Therefore, by looking at the simulated curves, you can get a clearer idea that Project A is a better choice.

YOU SHOULD REMEMBER

Simulation measures the risk and return of a project. A number of computer packages are currently available to run simulations for project selection. Some of these computer packages will compute results and draw graphs for different assumptions.

ADJUSTING FOR INFLATION

Inflation is a general price increase in the economy. When inflation increases, the real value of expected cash flows decreases. If the analyst does not adjust for risk of inflation, the *NPV* or the *IRR* may be artificially high. In other words, you might accept a project with an adjusted *IRR* or *NPV*, while the real *IRR* or *NPV*, adjusted for inflation, could be unacceptable. Therefore, capital budgeting techniques that ignore inflation are often misleading. Since inflation has probably become a permanent problem in the economy, you should plan to deal with it anytime you make a major decision.

How can you deal with inflation in capital budgeting? The answer is that you should adjust both the cash flows and the discount rate for the annual rate of inflation.

Example: Adjusting the NPV for Inflation

PROBLEM   In 1985, the annual cash flows of a project for the following 3 years are estimated to be $1,000, $2,000, and $3,000. These estimated cash flows are in 1985 dollars. The discount rate is 13%, and the annual rate of inflation is 6%. The initial outlay, or initial investment, of the project is $4,000. What is the *NPV* of this project after adjusting for inflation?

SOLUTION   1. Since the estimated cash flows are in 1985 dollars, you should adjust these amounts for inflation. However, the discount rate of 13% includes a 6% inflation rate. Using a short method, subtract the 6% inflation rate from the discount rate of 13%, getting 7%, which is the real discount rate. Discount the cash flows—which are in 1985 dollars—at 7%, and subtract the initial outlay:

Year	Cash Flow	PVIF at 7%	PV of Cash Flow
1	$1,000	.935	$ 935
2	2,000	.873	1,746
3	3,000	.816	$2,448

Total *PV* at a discount rate of 7% = $5,129
Subtract the initial investment: –4,000
NPV adjusted for inflation = $1,129

SOLUTION   Another way of adjusting for inflation is to increase expected cash flows at a 6% annual rate of inflation, and then discount the inflated cash flows at 13%:

Year	Cash Flow	PVIF at 7%	PV of Cash Flow
1	$1,060	.885	$938
2	2,247	.783	1,759
3	3,573	.693	2,476

Total PV at a discount rate of 13% = $5,173

Subtract the initial investment: –4,000

NPV adjusted for inflation = $1,173

As you can see from the preceding example, the *NPVs* of the project are not necessarily the same using the two methods. The project in this example was found acceptable in both calculations, because the *NPV* is positive. However, it is a good idea to use the two methods and compare the *NPV* results.

When the *NPVs* are different in these two methods, conservative financial analysts usually use the lower *NPV* as a more reliable figure upon which to base decisions.

YOU SHOULD REMEMBER

There are two methods of adjustment for inflation in capital budgeting. One method is to discount deflated cash flows at a deflated discount rate. The second method is to discount inflated cash flows at an inflated discount rate. Both methods should be tried to examine the effect of inflation on the *NPV* of the project.

KNOW THE CONCEPTS
DO YOU KNOW THE BASICS?

1. Explain in your own words why a positive net present value means that a project is worth undertaking.

2. The *NPV* and *IRR* methods may give different answers in terms of accepting or rejecting projects. Explain the reasons for the conflict, and discuss how the conflict can be resolved.

3. Do the *NPV* and *PI* methods give the same answers in terms of accepting or rejecting projects? Discuss.

4. Which method is superior: *NPV* or payback period? Why?

5. Which method is superior: *NPV* or *IRR*?

6. Define risk. How can risk be measured?

7. What is a major different between the CEA and the *NPV* techniques? Do they lead to the same accept/reject decision in capital budgeting?

8. What is sensitivity analysis?

9. How can the CAPM be used in capital budgeting under risk?

10. What is the purpose of simulation in capital budgeting?

11. In practice, how do you find the beta of a project?

12. How can you resolve the problem of inflation in capital budgeting decisions?

TERMS FOR STUDY

average rate of return (ARR)   payback period
certainty equivalent factor   profitability index (PI)
cutoff rate   risk
inflation   risk-free
internal rate of return (IRR)   risk-free rate
maximum return   sensitivity analysis
maximum wealth   simulation
net present value (NPV)   simulation software

PRACTICAL APPLICATION

COMPUTATIONAL PROBLEMS

1. The net earnings of a company for the next 3 years are estimated to be $12,000, $13,000, and $18,000, respectively. Determine the average rate of return if the initial outlay is $80,000.

2. The cash flows of a project are estimated to be as follows:

Year	Cash Flow
1	$2,000
2	4,000
3	6,000
4	5,000
5	1,000

The initial outlay of the project is $14,000. Assuming that the company has a target payback period of 3 years, determine if the project is acceptable.

3. The initial investment of a project is $110,000. Following are the estimated cash flows:

Year	Cash Flow
1	$30,000
2	40,000
3	20,000
4	40,000
5	50,000

Using the *NPV* method and a discount rate of 12%, determine if the project is acceptable.

4. Using the information in Problem 3, determine the profitability index of the project. Explain your findings.

5. A project has annual cash flows of $7,000 for 7 years. The initial investment is $28,500. What is the project's *IRR*?

6. The ABC Co. has to select either Project 1 or Project 2. The projects have the following cash flows:

	Cash Flow	
Year	Project 1	Project 2
0	-$24,000	-$24,000
1	+ 11,000	0
2	+ 11,000	0
3	+ 11,000	0
4	+ 11,000	0
5	+ 11,000	+ 68,000

Using the *NPV* and *IRR* methods, determine which project is preferred. Assume a discount rate of 10%.

7. Using trial and error, determine approximately the *IRR* of the following cash flows:

Year	Cash Flow
0	$1,200
1	780
2	190
3	390

Is this project acceptable if the cutoff rate is 12%?

8. Using the profitability index, rank the following possible investments and discuss their profitabilities:

Investment	Initial Investment	Present Value
A	$100,000	$120,000
B	150,000	180,000
C	200,000	220,000
D	400,000	320,000
E	10,000	30,000
F	280,000	305,000

9. Using the information in Problem 8, rank the listed projects according to their net present values.

10. Suppose the following two individual investment opportunities are available to Spencer, Inc. The appropriate discount rate is 10%.

Year	Project M	Project N
0	-500	-2,000
1	300	300
2	700	1,800
3	600	1,700

(a) Compute profitability index for each of the two projects.

(b) Which project(s) should Spencer, Inc. accept based on *PI* index rule?

11. Project X has a cost of $55,125, and its expected net cash flow is $13,000 per year for 8 years.

(a) What is the project's payback period (to the closest year)?

(b) The required rate of return of the project is 12%. What is the project's *NPV*?

(c) What is the project's *IRR*?

12. The following items are related to the four proposed projects listed below. Each of these projects requires a single initial outlay (CF_0) and produces an incremental annuity for n years (CF_n). The discount rate for these cash flows is 12%.

Project	CF_0	CF_n	Years
A	490	175	4
B	1,100	350	4
C	200	50	6
D	150	45	6

Compute *NPV* and profitability index.

13. Using the certainty equivalent approach, determine whether the following project is acceptable:

Year	Cash Flow of Project	Certain Equivalent Factors
1	$2,000	.93
2	3,000	.91
3	4,000	.80
4	8,000	.75

The initial investment is $15,000. The rate of return on a U.S. treasury bill is 8%.

14. Project M has cash flows of $2,000 in year 1 and $2,500 in year 2. Project N has cash flows of $3,000 in year 1 and $1,500 in year 2. The initial outlay for each project is $2,200. Using sensitivity analysis, determine which project is more risky if the discount rate increases from 12% to 14%.

15. Determine the *NPV* of the following project using the CAPM model:

Year	Cash Flows of Project
0	$10,000
1	+4,000
2	+8,000
3	+2,000

The rate of return on a market portfolio is 14%, the beta of the project is 1.70, and the risk-free rate is 7%.

16. Company ABC has run five simulations for Projects X, Y, and Z. The results are as follows:

Project X		Project Y		Project Z	
NPV	Standard Dev.	NPV	Standard Dev.	NPV	Standard Dev.
$150	12	$100	34	$100	11
250	17	300	41	200	35
450	21	500	27	300	51
650	20	700	31	700	68
850	33	900	18	900	63

Based on these simulations, which project should the company accept?

17. It is estimated that a project will generate cash flows over the next 5 years of $4,000, $8,000, $12,000, $15,000, and $18,000. The discount rate is 12%, annual inflation is 7%, and the initial investment is $10,000. Using both (a) the deflation and (b) the inflation methods to adjust for inflation, find the adjusted *NPV* on which to base your decisions about the project.

18. Eurotrade company is investing $200,000 in a 4-year project that is estimated to generate sales of $90,000 in year 1, $70,000 in year 2, and $60,000 in years 3 and 4. The discount rate is 12%. Managers want to know the maximum percentage drop in sales each year that the company can afford without losing any money on the project.

19. As a manager you are presented with two different projects in which both of the projects happened to have the same initial investment and exact cash flow estimations. The initial payment is $1,000 and the estimated cash flow is $400 annual payments for the next 4 years. The industry beta of the first project is 1.3, whereas the beta of the second project is 2.7. The rate of return on a market portfolio is 13% and the risk-free rate is 6%.

    (a) Calculate the required rate of return for both projects using the CAPM method.

    (b) Calculate the net present values of both projects.

    (c) What is the effect of beta on the required rate of return and *NPV*?

20. What is the effect of an additional 2% inflation on the *NPV* of a project where the initial payment is $10,000 and the cash flow for the next 3 years is $5,000 a year? The current inflation is 3% and the required rate of return is 9%. (Use the inflated cash flow method.)

21. An analyst for Computer Inc. is determining the required risk adjusted return for its upcoming project, whose expected net cash flows are estimated to be $1,000 per year for 5 years. The required investment outlay on the project is $4,000. The industry beta of the project under analysis is 1.4. The risk-free rate of return is currently 9%, and the market risk premium is 5%.

    (a) What is the required risk-adjusted return on the project?

    (b) Should the project under consideration be accepted?

22. The Westerfield Company must decide between two mutually exclusive investment projects. Each project costs $8,000 and has an expected life of 3 years. Annual cash flows from each project begin one year after the initial investment is made. The projects are evaluated at 10%. Which project should the company undertake?

Project A

Year	Cash Flow	Certainty Equivalent Factor
1	$1,500	$0.80
2	4,000	0.94
3	7,000	0.94

Project B

Year	Cash Flow	Certainty Equivalent Factor
1	0	$0.83
2	5,800	0.76
3	7,500	0.91

23. Schwartz Co. plans to invest in any of the four following projects.

(a) Which is the most suitable project for the company in terms of risk?

(b) Which project is the riskiest out of the alternatives?

Project	Average Simulated NPV (x)	Average Simulated Standard Deviation (y)
M	300	27
N	650	43
O	580	40
P	432	30

24. The net earnings of a company for the next 3 years are estimated to be $10,000, $15,000, and $16,000 respectively. Determine the average rate of return if the initial outlay is $65,000.

25. The cash flows of a project are estimated to be as follows:

Year	Cash Flow
1	$1,500
2	3,000
3	4,500
4	5,000
5	2,000

The initial outlay of the project is $20,000. Assuming that the company has a target payback period of 3 years, determine if the project is acceptable.

26. Using the profitability index, rank the following possible investments and discuss their profitability:

Investment	Initial Investment	Present Value
A	$ 50,000	$ 70,000
B	$200,000	$210,000
C	$120,000	$125,000
D	$ 70,000	$210,000
E	$450,000	$425,000
F	$110,000	$150,000

27. Using the certainty equivalent approach, determine whether the following project is acceptable:

Year	Cash Flow of Project	Certainty Equivalent Factors
1	$1,000	.93
2	2,000	.91
3	4,000	80
4	9,000	.75

The initial investment is $14,000. The rate of return on a U.S. treasury bill is 4%.

28. What is the effect of an additional 3% inflation on the *NPV* of a project where the initial outlay is $12,000, and the cash flow for the next 3 years is $6,000 a year. The current inflation is 3%, and the required rate of return is 8%. (Use the inflated cash flow method).

29. It is estimated that a project will generate cash flows over the next 5 years of $5,000, $8,000, $12,000, $16,000, and $18,000. The discount rate is 14%, annual inflation is 6%, and the initial investment is $10,000. Using both (a) the deflation and (b) the inflation methods to adjust for inflation, find the adjusted *NPV* on which to base your decisions about the project.

ANSWERS

KNOW THE CONCEPTS

1. A positive *NPV* means an excess of return over cost. Therefore, projects with positive *NPV*s should be accepted.

2. Possible reasons for a conflict between the *IRR* and *NPV* are as follows: different sizes and/or lives of the projects to be compared, different patterns of cash flows, and faulty assumptions about reinvestment rates. To help resolve the conflict, the reinvestment rate or the selected discount rate must be realistic.

3. *NPV* and *PI* give the same answers in terms of accepting or rejecting a project, yet they can give different orders of ranking.

4. *NPV*, because it considers the time value of money.

5. *NPV*, because it does not have the problem of multiple rates and the assumption of a reinvestment rate.

6. Risk means uncertainty and instability. The future cash flows of a project may unexpectedly decrease or increase. The discount rate in the market may rise or decline, leading to a lower or higher price of stock and other financial securities. Risk can be measured by standard deviation, beta analysis in CAPM, and simulation techniques.

7. In the *NPV* method, uncertain cash flows are discounted at a rate appropriate to the level of risk in the project. In the certainty equivalent approach, certain cash flows are discounted at a risk-free rate. Theoretically, both methods should give the same results.

8. Sensitivity analysis is a technique used to measure risk. The purpose is to estimate net earnings, cash flows, the *NPV*, the stock price, and so on when one or more variables change.

9. When the discount rate is not given, the CAPM can be used to determine a required rate of return: $K_s = R_f + \beta(K_m - R_f)$. This rate ($K_s$) can be used as a discount rate in the *NPV* analysis.

10. The purpose of simulation in capital budgeting is to determine which project has a more stable *NPV*, *IRR*, or *PI* when the values of cash flow, discount rate, and other factors change.

11. The beta of a project is approximately equal to the beta of the company's stock. If the project is not a regular one, then the average beta of several companies engaged in similar projects could be used.

12. The problem of inflation in capital budgeting can be partially resolved by taking one of the following approaches:

(a) Discount deflated cash flows at a deflated discount rate.

(b) Discount inflated cash flows at an inflated discount rate.

PRACTICAL APPLICATION

1. Average net earnings $= \dfrac{(\$12,000+\$13,000+\$18,000)}{3} = \$14,333$

Average investment $= \dfrac{\$80,000}{2} = \$40,000$

Average rate of return $= \dfrac{\$14,333}{\$40,000} = 36\%$

2. After 3 years, only $12,000 of the $14,000 initial outlay is recovered. Therefore, the project is not acceptable.

3. Net present value = Present value – Initial investment
Present value = $30,000(.8929) + $40,000(.7972) + $20,000(.7118) + $40,000(.6355) + $50,000(.5674) = $126,701
Net present value = $126,701 – $110,000 = $16,701
Since the *NPV* is positive, the project is acceptable.

4. $PI = \dfrac{PV}{\text{Initial investment}} = \dfrac{\$126,701}{\$110,000} = 1.15$

The project is acceptable because *PI* > 1.

5. $\dfrac{\$28,500}{\$7,000} = 4.07$. The *PVIFA* table for 7 years shows that the *IRR* is about 16%.

6. *NPV* of Project 1 $= \$11,000(PVIFA)_{10\%,\,5} - \$24,000$

$= \$11,000(3.791) - \$24,000 = \$17,701$
NPV of Project 2 $= \$68,000(PVIF)_{10\%,\,5} - \$24,000$

$= \$68,000(.621) - \$24,000 = \$18,228$

Thus, Project 2 is preferred.

7. *PV* at 10% $= \$780(.9091) + \$190(.8264) + \$390(.7513) = \$1,159$
The *IRR* is close to 10%. Therefore, the project is not acceptable.

8.

Rank	Project	PI
1	E	3
2	A, B	1.2
3	C	1.1
4	F	1.09
5	D	.80

Project D is unacceptable because its *PI* is less than 1. The other projects are acceptable as their *PIs* are greater than 1.

9.

Rank	Project	NPV
1	B	$30,000
2	F	25,000
3	A, C, E	20,000
4	D	−80,000

10. (a) **Project M**

PV of project M $= \dfrac{300}{(1.10)} + \dfrac{700}{(1.10)^2} + \dfrac{600}{(1.10)^3}$

$= 272.73 + 578.51 + 450.79$

$= 1{,}302.03$

$PI \qquad = \dfrac{1302.03}{500}$

$= 2.60$

Project N

PV of Project N $= \dfrac{300}{(1.10)} + \dfrac{1{,}800}{(1.10)^2} + \dfrac{1{,}700}{(1.10)^3}$

$= 272.73 + 1{,}487.6 + 1{,}277.24$

$= 3{,}037.57$

$PI \qquad = \dfrac{3{,}037.57}{2{,}000}$

$= 1.52$

(b) They should accept M as it has a higher *PI*.

11. (a)

Year	Expected Cash Inflows ($)	Total ($)
1	13,000	13,000
2	13,000	26,000
3	13,000	39,000
4	13,000	52,000
5	13,000	65,000
6	13,000	78,000
7	13,000	91,000
8	13,000	104,000

The total in year 4 is closest to the initial cash outflow (55,125). There is a balance of 3,125 to be paid in year 5.

$$\text{Number of weeks in year 5} = \frac{\text{Outstanding balance in year 5}}{\text{Expected cash flow in year 5}}$$

$$= \frac{3,125}{13,000}$$

$$= 0.24$$

$$= (0.24 \times 52 \text{ weeks}) = 12 \text{ weeks}$$

Therefore the payback period is 4 years and 12 weeks.

(b) $NPV = PV_{in}$ – Initial investment
$$= 64,579 - 55,125$$
$$= 9,454$$

(c) $NPV = PV_{in}$ – Initial investment
$$= P = (N/r)(1 - (1 + r)^{-n}) - \text{Initial investment}$$

If we try using $r = 16.75\%$ in the formula above, the $NPV = 0$. This is the IRR of the project (when the present value of the cash inflows is equal to the initial investment).

12.

Project	CF_0	CF_n	Years	NPV	PI
A	490	175	4	41.54	1.08
B	1,100	350	4	–36.93	0.97
C	200	50	6	5.57	1.03
D	150	45	6	35.01	1.23

13.

Year	Cash Flows	Certainty Equivalent Factor	Certain Cash Flows	PVIF at 8%	PV of Certain Cash Flows
1	$2,000	.93	$1,860	.9259	$1,722
2	3,000	.91	2,730	.8573	2,340
3	4,000	.80	3,200	.7938	2,540
4	8,000	.75	6,000	.7350	4,410

PV at 8% $11,012

$NPV = \$11,012 - \$15,000 = \$-3,988$
The Project has a negative NPV. Thus, it is rejected.

14. NPV of Project M at 12% = $1,579
NPV of Project M at 14% = $1,477

% Change in NPV of Project M = $\dfrac{(\$1,477 - \$1,579)}{\$1,579}$ = –6.5%

NPV of Project N at 12% = $1,675
NPV of Project N at 14% = $1,585

% Change in NPV of Project N = $\dfrac{(\$1,585 - \$1,675)}{\$1,675}$ = –5.4%

Project M is riskier because it has a higher percentage change in NPV.

15. $K_s = R_f + \beta(K_m - R_f) = .07 + 1.70(.14 - .07) = 18.9\%$ or 19%

Therefore, cash flows must be discounted at 19% and subtracted from the initial investment of $10,000. $4,000(.840) + $8,000(.706) + $2,000(.593) – $10,000 = $3,360 + $5,648 + $1,186 – $10,000 = $194. Since the NPV is positive, the project is acceptable.

16.

Project	Average Simulated NPV	Average Simulated Standard Dev.	Simulated Coefficient of Variation
X	$470	21	4.5%
Y	500	30	6.0%
X	440	46	10.5%

The lowest simulated coefficient of variation is that for Project X, so that project should be accepted.

17. (a) Deflation Method
12% – 7% = 5%

Year	Cash Flow	PVIF at 5%	PV of Cash Flows
1	$4,000	.952	3,808
2	8,000	.907	7,256
3	12,000	.864	10,368
4	15,000	.823	12,345
5	18,000	.784	14,112

Total *PV* at a real discount rate of 5% = $47,889

Subtract initial investment: –10,000

Adjusted *NPV* = $37,889

(b) Inflation Method

Year	Cash Flow Inflated at 7%	PVIF at 12%	PV of Cash Flows
1	$4,280	.893	$3,822
2	9,159	.797	7,300
3	14,701	.712	10,467
4	19,662	.636	12,505
5	25,246	.567	14,314

Total *PV* at a real discount rate of 5% = $48,408

Subtract initial investment: –10,000

Adjusted *NPV* = $38,408

You would use the lower *NPV*, $37,889

18. When *PV* of cash flows is equal to initial investment, there is no gain or loss from the project.

Year	Cash Flows	% Drop in Sales	Adjusted Flows	PVIF at 12%	PV
1	$90,000	d	d × $90,000	.89286	d × $80,357.40
2	$70,000	d	d × $70,000	.79719	d × $55,803.30
3	$60,000	d	d × $60,000	.71178	d × $42,706.80
4	$60,000	d	d × $60,000	.63552	d × $38,131.20

PV of all Cash Flows = d × $216,998.70

When there is no gain this amount is equal to initial investment of $200,000 and d = 0.9216

A 7.84% (1 – 0.9216) decrease in sales throughout the project will make the *NPV* zero.

19. (a) $K_p = R_f + \beta(K_m - R_f)$

$K_{p1} = 0.06 + 1.3(0.13 - 0.06)$

$\quad = 0.151 = \sim 15\%$

$K_{p2} = 0.06 + 2.7(0.13 - 0.06)$

$\quad = 0.249 = \sim 25\%$

(b) $NPV = $ Present Value – Initial Investment

$NPV_{p1} = \$400\ PVI_{15\%,4yr}\ FA - \$1,000$

$$= \$400 \times \left[\frac{-1}{0.15} - \frac{1}{0.15(1+0.15)4} \right] - \$1,000$$

$= \$400 \times 2.855 - \$1,000$

$\sim = \$142$

$NPV_{p2} = \$400\ PVI_{25\%,4yr}\ FA - \$1,000$

$$= \$400 \times \left[\frac{-1}{0.15} - \frac{1}{0.25(1+0.25)4} \right] - \$1,000$$

$= \$400 \times 2.36 - \$1,000$

$= \sim -\$56$

(c) The higher the beta, the higher the risk. As risk increases, *NPV* decreases, all other variables being the same.

20. 3% inflation

Year	Cash Flow Inflated	PVIF at 9%	PV of Cash Flows
1	$5,150.00	.91743	$4,724.76
2	$5,304.50	.84168	$4,464.69
3	$5,463.64	.77218	$4,218.90

$NPV_{3\%\ Inflation} = \$13,408.35 - \$10,000 = \$3,408.35$

5% inflation

Year	Cash Flow Inflated	PVIF at 9%	PV of Cash Flows
1	$5,250.00	.91743	$4,816.50
2	$5,512.50	.84168	$4,639.76
3	$5,788.12	.77218	$4,469.47

$NPV_{5\%\ Inflation} = \$13,925.73 - \$10,000 = \$3,925.73$

21. (a) $K_s = K_f + \beta(K_m - K_f)$

$\quad = 0.096 + 1.4(0.05 - 0.09)$

$\quad = 0.034$

$\quad = 3.4\%$

(b) $NPV = PV_{in}$ – Initial investment

$= 4,527.87 - 4,000$

$= 527.87$

Since *NPV* is positive, the project should be accepted.

22. **Project A**

Year	Cash Flows	Certainty Equivalent Factor	Certain Cash Flow	PV
1	1,500	0.80	1,200	1,090.91
2	4,000	0.94	3,760	3,107.44
3	7,000	0.75	5,250	3,944.40
				PV = 8,142.75

$NPV = 8,142.75 - 8,000$

$= 142.75$

Project B

Year	Cash Flows	Certainty Equivalent Factor	Certain Cash Flow	PV
1	0	0.83	0	1,090.91
2	5,800	0.76	4,408	3,107.44
3	7,500	0.91	6,825	3,944.40
				PV = 8,770.70

$NPV = 8,770.70 - 8,000$

$= 770.70$

Project B is a better option as it has a higher *NPV*; it should be accepted.

23.

Project	Average Simulated NPV (x)	Average Simulated Standard Deviation (y)	Simulated Coefficient of Variation (y/x)
M	300	27	9.00%
N	650	43	6.62%
O	580	40	6.90%
P	432	30	6.94%

(a) Project N should be accepted as the best option among the alternatives in terms of risk, as it has the lowest coefficient of variance.

(b) Project M is the riskiest, as it has the highest coefficient of variance.

24. Average net earnings = ($10,000 + $15,000 + $16,000) = $13,666

Average net earnings = ($65,000) = $32,500

Average net earnings = $\dfrac{(\$13,666)}{(\$32,500)}$ = 42%

25. After 3 years, only $16,000 of the $20,000 initial outlay is recovered. Therefore, the project is not acceptable.

26.

Rank	Project	PI
1	D	3.0
2	A	1.4
3	F	1.36
4	B	1.05
5	C	1.04
6	E	0.94

Project E is unacceptable because its *PI* is less than 1. The other projects are acceptable as their *PI*s are greater than 1.

27.

Year	Cash Flows	Certainty Equivalent Factor	Certain Cash Flows	PVIF at 4%	PV of Certain Cash Flows
1	$1,000	0.93	$930	0.9615	$ 894
2	2,000	0.90	1,800	0.9246	1,664
3	4,000	0.82	3,280	0.8890	2,916
4	9,000	0.76	6,840	0.8548	5,847
				PV at 4%	$11,321

NPV = $11,321 – $14,000 = –$2,679

The project has a negative *NPV*. Thus, it is rejected.

28. 3% inflation

Year	Cash Flow Inflated	PVIF at 8%	PV of Cash Flows
1	$6,180.00	.9259	$5,722.06
2	$6,365.40	.8573	$5,457.06
3	$6,556.36	.7938	$5,204.44

$NPV_{5\% \text{ Inflation}}$ = $16,383.56 – $12,000 = $4,383.56

6% inflation

Year	Cash Flow Inflated	PVIF at 8%	PV of Cash Flows
1	$6,360.00	0.9259	$5,888.72
2	$6,741.60	0.8573	$5,779.50
3	$7,146.10	0.7938	$5,672.57

$$NPV_{5\% \text{ Inflation}} = \$17,340.79 - \$12,000 = \$5,340.79$$

29. (a) Deflation Method

14% – 6% = 8%

Year	Cash Flow	PVIF at 8%	PV of Cash Flows
1	$ 5,000	0.9259	$ 4,629
2	$ 8,000	0.8573	$ 6,858
3	$12,000	0.7938	$ 9,526
4	$16,000	0.7350	$11,760
5	$18,000	0.6806	$12,251

Total PV at a real discount rate of 8% = $45,024
Subtract initial investment: – 10,000
Adjusted NPV = $35,024

(b) Inflation Method

Year	Cash Flow Inflated at 6%	PVIF at 8%	PV of Cash Flows
1	$ 5,300	0.8772	$ 4,649
2	$ 8,989	0.7695	$ 6,917
3	$14,292	0.6750	$ 9,647
4	$20,200	0.5921	$11,960
5	$24,088	0.5194	$12,511

Total PV at discount rate of 14% = $45,684
Subtract initial investment: – 10,000
Adjusted NPV = $35,684

You would use lower NPV, $35,024.

INVESTING, FINANCING, AND DIVIDEND DECISIONS

8
COST OF CAPITAL

KEY TERMS

cost of capital (cc) the rate of return a firm must pay investors in order to induce them to purchase stocks, bonds, and other securities

expected return the future receipts that investors anticipate from their investments

flotation costs the amount of money an investment banker charges a firm for taking the risk of marketing and distributing new issues of securities

market value weights proportions that bonds and stocks represent (based on their current prices) in the capital structure of the firm

marginal cost of capital the incremental cost of issuing more securities

opportunity cost the rate of return on the best alternative investment that is not selected

required rate of return (RRR) minimum future receipts an investor will accept in choosing an investment

risk-adjusted discount rate (RADR) the rate of return that reflects the riskiness of each project

BASIC CONCEPTS

Individuals have to decide where to invest the income they have saved. The goal, obviously, is to gain the highest return possible. To determine which assets are profitable and which are not, investors need a point of reference. This point of reference is known as the **required rate of return (RRR)**.

Given individual preferences and market conditions, investors establish an expected rate of return for each asset they may purchase. **Expected returns** are the future receipts investors anticipate receiving for taking the risk of making investments. If the expected return from an asset falls below the required rate of return, the investment will not be made. If certain assets

203

are expected to return more than the required rate of return, they will be bought. For example, suppose an investor calculates that the required rate of return on an investment is 10%. Given the opportunity to buy an asset with an expected return of 9%, the investor will refuse to purchase this asset. Conversely, assets will be purchased if they return 11%, 12%, or more.

• *COST OF CAPITAL AS A BENCHMARK FOR INVESTMENT DECISIONS*

A manager of a firm, with the responsibility for making investment decisions, uses a similar point of reference. This point of reference, the firm's required rate of return, is called the **cost of capital**. The firm must earn a minimum rate of return to cover the cost of generating funds to finance investments; otherwise, no one will be willing to buy its bonds, preferred stock, and common stock. The goal of a financial officer is to achieve the highest efficiency and profitability from assets and, at the same time, keep the cost of the funds that the firm generates from various financing sources as low as possible. In other words, the cost of capital is the rate of return (cost) that a firm must pay investors to induce them to risk their funds and purchase the bonds, preferred stock, and common stock issued by the firm.

Factors that determine the cost of capital include the riskiness of earnings, the proportion of debt exposure in the capital structure, the financial soundness of the firm, and the way investors evaluate the firm's securities. If expected earnings or cash flow is volatile, debt is high, and the firm lacks a sound financial record, investors will buy its securities only if high returns are paid to compensate them for taking the risk. In contrast, steadily growing earnings, low debt, and a good financial background will enable the firm to issue securities at low cost.

Clearly, the cost of capital is one of the major factors used in the determination of the value of the firm. In finance, the cost of capital is the same as the discount rate. High risk means a high cost of capital, while low risk means a low cost of capital. Moreover, a high cost of capital (high discount rate) usually means a low valuation for securities, and a low discount rate means a high value for the securities of a firm. Since the sale of these securities provides firms with funds for investments, the cost of financing increases when the value of securities is low, and it decreases when their value is high. The benchmark for determining whether the returns of a firm's securities are high or low is the cost of capital.

• *COST OF CAPITAL AS A MEASURE OF PROFITABILITY*

The role played by the cost of capital in the investment decision process can be explained in another way. When a firm issues securities, it is expected to pay a return to its bond- and stockholders. This payment represents a cost. Funds raised by the issue of stocks and bonds are invested for the purpose of generating income for the firm. This income, usually referred to as cash flow, is measured by calculating the present values of the returns generated from investments and comparing them to the cost of the investments. The role played by the cost of capital in calculating the value and profitability of investments is illustrated below:

$$NPV = (PVCFAT_{(t)}) - I_0$$
$$IRR = (NPV = 0) \text{ or}$$
$$IRR = PVCFAT_{(t)} - I_0 = 0$$

where $PVCFAT_{(t)}$ = present value of cash flows after taxes generated from an investment
NPV = profits from an investment
IRR = internal rate of return (or when $NPV = 0$)
I_0 = original cost of the investment

As discussed in Chapter 6, the profitability of an investment represents the PV of cash flows minus the cost of investment. When the present value of cash flows minus the cost of investment is brought down to zero, the **internal rate of return (*IRR*)** of the investment is obtained.

Because the *IRR* is the rate of return derived from an investment, it is easy to determine whether or not this investment is profitable just by comparing the *IRR* with the cost of capital. When the *IRR* exceeds the cost of capital, the firm gets a higher return than the costs it incurs to raise funds. Conversely, when the *IRR* of an investment falls below the cost of capital, it means that the rate of return of the investment is lower than the cost of acquiring funds, and the investment should not be undertaken.

In summary, there is a very simple relationship between the *IRR*, the cost of capital, and the desirability of a project: When the *IRR* is greater than the cost of capital, the project is profitable; when it is lower than the cost of capital, it is unprofitable.

Example: Cost of Capital as a Measure of Profitability

Figure 8-1 shows how the cost of capital can be used to compare the relative profitabilities of projects. Project, or investment, A is profitable because its *IRR* is 20%, while the cost of capital is only 10%. By investing in this project a firm would make 10% (20% – 10%) more than its required rate of return. Project, or investment, B is unprofitable partly because its *IRR* is less than the cost of capital. This means that *NPV* is negative. Should the firm invest in Project B, it would lose 5% (5% – 10%), because while the cost of funds is 10%, those funds, once invested, would yield only 5%.

The cost of capital can also be viewed in terms of the risk premium that investors in the marketplace assign to a firm or to assets. A **risk premium** is the additional required rate of return that must be paid over and above the risk-free rate. The higher the risk premium, the riskier the firm or the asset. Conversely, the lower the risk premium, the less risky the firm or asset.

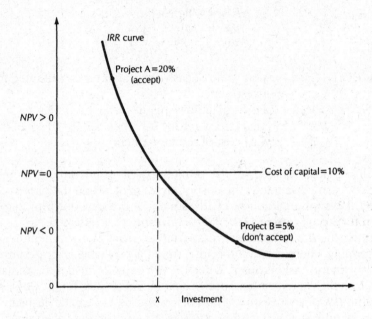

Figure 8–1 Comparing the *IRR*s of Investments to the Cost of Capital (CC)

As shown in Table 8-1, Firm C has been assigned a higher risk premium than Firms A and B. Obviously, the higher the risk premium, the higher the cost of issuing bonds and stocks.

When investors supply a firm with funds for investment purposes, they want to make sure that they are adequately paid for the risk they are taking. For instance, if the yield on an average-risk bond is 10%, a high-risk firm may have to pay investors 12% in order to sell its bonds. Many highly risky firms lack other attractive features, such as the prospect of making technological breakthroughs. They may have a low growth record or may be regarded as unsafe investments. Usually shares of such firms will be assigned a lower value than those of other, more stable companies. As a result, these firms would have to issue more shares to raise needed funds and would therefore incur a higher cost of financing. The reverse is true of a low-risk firm.

Table 8–1   **Risk Premiums and the Cost of Capital (CC)**

	Firm A	Firm B	Firm C
Cost of capital (CC)(%)	0.10	0.08	0.12
Risk-free rate (%)	0.05	0.05	0.05
Risk premium (%)	0.05	0.03	0.07

Although a firm has an average or overall cost of capital (CC), this does not mean that the profitability (net present value) of each project or of each investment decision should be evaluated with reference to that aggregate cost. Individual projects (or divisions) may require different discount rates than the firm's cost of capital, depending on how risky these projects are. This method of adjusting the cash flows of projects and decisions to reflect individual degrees of risk is called the **risk-adjusted discount-rate (RADR)** approach. Unless this approach is used, the *PV* of returns or net present values of these risky projects would be subject to a bias, making them appear more or less profitable than they are. One way to determine the appropriate rate needed to discount the cash flows of a risky project entails finding market-traded companies that have similar financial characteristics as the project under analysis. Then apply the dividend growth model to solve for the discount rate (K_s) of the traded firm or $K_s = (D_1/P_0) + G$. Use this K_s to risk adjust the project's cash flows. Another more subjective approach employs the firm's cost of capital as a reference point and then raises or lowers that figure to account for the riskiness of the project. In any event, the cash flows of each project must be discounted by a rate that reflects the risk associated with that project.

YOU SHOULD REMEMBER

The cost of capital is the required rate of return that a firm must achieve in order to cover the cost of generating funds in the marketplace. Based on their evaluations of the riskiness of each firm, investors will supply new funds to a firm only if it pays them the required rate of return to compensate them for taking the risk of investing in the firm's bonds and stocks. If, indeed, the cost of capital is the required rate of return that the firm must pay to generate funds, it becomes a guideline for measuring the profitabilities of different investments. When there are differences in the degree of risk between the firm and its divisions, a risk-adjusted discount-rate approach should be used to determine their profitability.

• *USING INTERNAL AND EXTERNAL SOURCES TO RAISE CAPITAL*

The funds available to a firm come from internal sources as well as from external ones. The origins of **internally generated funds** can be found on balance sheets and income statements, which report the amounts of funds generated from retained earnings and from depreciation.

These internally generated funds reduce the need for external financing. Because they are alternative source of funds, they should be regarded as having an **opportunity cost**; without them, the firm would have to issue new shares of stocks or bonds, which would mean paying more dividends or more interest. In finance, it is usual practice to assign a cost to these internal sources of funds.

Since retained earnings are considered a proxy for common stock, financing the cost of retained earnings is the same as if new common stock were issued (without making an adjustment for flotation costs). Because depreciation is assumed to be a substitute for all types of financing, it is assigned the firm's cost of capital. As a result, depreciation does not enter into the computation of the overall cost of capital of the firm. Still, directly or indirectly, each internal source of funds plays an important role in determining the overall average cost of capital.

External sources of funds appear on the right-hand side of the balance sheet. The balance sheet indicates the relative importance of long- and short-term funds to the firm. All you have to do is compare the amounts generated from current short-term debt (notes payable), long-term borrowings (mainly bonds), and preferred and common stock.

You might inquire, what happened to short-term borrowing from banks and depreciation? Should these funds be part of the cost of capital? The answer is: yes. Some analysts include the cost of bank and other short-term borrowing in the calculation of the overall cost of capital of firms. The only reason why these short-term borrowing costs are excluded from the calculations is to simplify the presentation. Although depreciation is a noncash item, it certainly represents an opportunity cost that the firm would incur if it had to engage in external financing to cover funds generated from depreciation. As an internal source of funds, however, depreciation is assumed to have the same overall cost of capital of the firm. Therefore, its inclusion in the calculation would not alter the results in any way.

RISK AND THE COST OF CAPITAL

The costs of capital to raise funds from short- or long-term sources are market determined. Investors analyze the degree of risk involved in supplying funds to firms. Obviously, if the risk is high, the return they demand—the firm's cost—will be high; if the risk is low, the cost will be low unless market rates are affected by extreme economic uncertainty.

There is also the uncertainty and risk of time. The longer the funds are invested, the higher the cost of capital because of time-related risks and the risk of loss of principal through failure and default.

Table 8-2 presents a breakdown of current liabilities (notes payable) and long-term external sources of funds made available to the XYZ Co. This table presents the main entries that appear on the right side of the balance sheet, which includes current liabilities, long-term debt, and equity. In each case, the balance sheet tells you the origin of these funds, whether from a bank or from issuing new securities. For example, in most cases, external short-term funds can be assumed to come from bank credit made available to the firm, although trade accounts payable are also an important source of funds until they are repaid. The balance sheet also indicates the external sources of long-term funds, whether these funds come from bank term loans or from issuing bonds or stocks, and internal sources such as retained earnings. Therefore, by referring to the balance sheet of the firm, you can determine the mix of external funds, the book values of these funds, and the importance of each source to the firm. Each source has its specific cost of capital. For example, Table 8-2 shows that new bond issues cost the firm 8%, while stock issues cost 13.5%. Also, note that the costs increase from 7% for short-term bank notes to 13.5% in the case of common stock equity.

Table 8–2   XYZ Co.—External and Internal Sources of Funds Compared to the Cost of Capital

Source of Funds	Dollar Amount	Assumed Cost of Capital* for Each Source of Funds (%)	Percentage of Total Value of each Source (%)
External			
Current liabilities			
Notes payable	1,000,000	7.0	10
Long-term debt			
2,000 bonds @ $1,000 par value	2,000,000	8.0	20
Stockholders' equity			
Preferred stock			
50,000 shares @ $10 par value	500,000	10.0	5
Common stock			
1.0 million shares @ $5.00 par value	5,000,000	13.5	50
Internal			
Retained earnings	1,500,000	13.0	15
Total liabilities and stockholders' equity	$10,000,000		100

*These costs reflect the relative risk associated with each source of capital.

A major reason for this increase is the time factor. Notes payable are usually short-term bank loans that are repaid within one year. The risk is small, and the cost of borrowing is usually lower than that for long-term sources. Long-term debt has the next lowest cost, because it comes due at a definite time and because bondholders are paid off before stockholders in case of bankruptcy. Finally, since common stockholders invest funds for the entire life of the firm, their risk of losing principal is highest, the time involved is longest, and hence investors will claim a high rate of return to compensate them for taking these extra risks. Unlike lenders, however, stockholders participate in the growth, profitability, and wealth of the firm.

YOU SHOULD REMEMBER

Firms use the cost of capital as a break-even point, that is, the cost the firm must cover if it is to stay in business and remain profitable. This means that all projects with rates of return (*IRRs*) lower than the cost of capital are unprofitable, and that those investments with *IRRs* higher than the cost of capital are profitable. A firm cannot stay in business if it does not cover the costs of repaying bondholders. And the market value of the firm's stock will decline if it fails to provide stockholders with an expected rate of return.

A firm can generate capital from both internal and external sources. Because internal sources substitute for external sources, they should be assigned a cost. A firm's balance sheet tells you where funds originated, and it supplies most of the information necessary to calculate the cost of capital for each source. Usually, the lower the risk premium, the lower the cost of capital, and vice versa.

• *COST OF LONG-TERM DEBT*

One example of long-term debt is bonds, which are issued for specified lengths of time. Bonds have prescribed coupons, which usually are paid semiannually and represent payments of interest to bondholders. These fixed-income securities have a **maturity date,** which is when the principal must be repaid. Bonds are usually issued at **par value,** or face value, most commonly $1,000.

The cost of issuing bonds is determined by investors in the marketplace who evaluate the risks involved, assess the financial soundness of the firm, review its solvency record, and evaluate the chances of the firm's defaulting on its promised payments. The cost can also vary depending on whether market interest rates are high or low. When market rates are high, the cost of issuing bonds is greater than when market yields are low. Furthermore, longer maturity periods normally increase the cost of issuing bonds, partly because the chance of default increases with time, and partly because investors prefer short-term repayment dates over long-term repayment dates. In other words, a premium must be paid to overcome the reluctance of investors to commit funds for long periods of time.

MAKING A ROUGH ESTIMATE

The cost of issuing a bond is partly established by **rating agencies**, such as Standard and Poor's and Moody's rating services, which are the largest in this field. These agencies evaluate a company's financial status as well as its past record, and indicate the quality of its bonds by assigning a rating to these securities. These ratings provide measures for comparing the relative riskiness of different fixed-income securities. The two services named above usually—but not always—agree on a particular bond's quality rating.

Another way to find out what a bond will cost a firm is to examine bonds of companies with the same financial structure and risk characteristics. The going yield on long-term bonds can be found in *The New York Times* or the *Wall Street Journal*. If the bonds of similar companies yield 12% and the firm wishes to issue bonds at 12% or more, investors will probably purchase these bonds. However, an offer to pay a coupon rate of 10%, when bond buyers can get 12% for the same type of investment, would not be very successful.

INVESTMENT BANKERS AND FLOTATION COSTS

The stated coupon and corresponding yield on a bond is estimated by investment bankers, who are responsible for sponsoring, distributing, and selling securities. These bankers are expert at determining fair prices for bond issues. They know the prevailing conditions in the market; they are familiar with the financial structure and status of the firm; and they have a fairly good idea, based on prior experience, of the cost or yield at which a bond will sell.

The process of issuing bonds through an investment banker or underwriting house also adds to the expense. The underwriter is a financial house that helps a firm to prepare a prospectus, lines up investors, and has a distribution network. A fee must be paid to the underwriter for this service. Because underwriters usually take risks by guaranteeing sales of the bonds, they want to be compensated. The combined charges for services and risk taking are called **flotation costs**. These costs reduce the receipts that a firm gets from the sale of bonds and stocks. Even though bonds are usually issued at par, the actual net amount paid to the firm is less than par. A firm with a flotation cost of 2% will receive $980, or $1,000(1 − .02), instead of $1,000 per bond.

Because bonds pay interest that is deductible from the firm's income, the cost of issuing debt has to be adjusted for this tax benefit. As a result, the after-tax cost to the firm is always lower than the coupon rate. If the cost of debt is K_d, then the true cost of debt to the firm is

$$K_{dt} = K_d (1 - \text{tax rate})$$

A company with a tax rate of 40% that sells bonds to yield 11% will have a cost of debt equivalent to 6.6%, or .11(1 − .40). The tax benefit usually makes the cost of bonds lower than the cost of financing via other methods of raising funds.

CALCULATING THE COST OF DEBT

Taking all these factors into account, the calculation of the cost of debt to a firm is a relatively simple exercise. Having established the coupon and the annual interest payments that bondholders will receive, all you have to do is relate this coupon cost to the receipts obtained from a single bond:

$$\text{Cost of debt } (K_d) = \frac{\text{Annual coupon on new bond issue}}{\text{Principal}(1 - \text{flotation cost})}$$

There is, however, a distinction between the computation of the cost of debt for outstanding bonds and that for newly issued bonds. In the case of outstanding bonds, the cost principal is not adjusted for flotation costs. Thus, the formula for outstanding bonds is

$$K_d = \frac{\text{Annual coupon on outstanding bond}}{\text{Market value of bond}}$$

Example: The Cost of Debt

A firm that issues a bond paying a $110 coupon per year and incurs a 2% charge for flotation costs would be assigned the following cost of debt:

Outstanding Bonds	Newly Issued Bonds
$\text{Cost of debt} = \dfrac{\$110}{\$1,000} = 11.0\%$	$\text{Cost of debt} = \dfrac{\$110}{\$1,000(1-.02)} = 11.2\%$

The fact that receipts are lower because of flotation costs causes the firm to incur higher costs on newly issued bonds than on outstanding bonds. When the adjustment is made for taxes (assume a 40% rate), the effective cost of long-term debt becomes 6.6%, or 0.11(1 − .40), for outstanding bonds and

6.72%, or 0.112(1 – .40), for newly issued bonds. This is the effective cost the firm incurs when it raises funds by issuing bonds.

The foregoing examples assume the yield has already been determined but do not tell us how it was obtained. This rate can be established by finding some point of reference. That point is a traded bond, which has the same features as the bond being issued. The yield to maturity of that traded bond can be calculated in two ways:

1. Employ the approximate yield-to-maturity formula.

2. Use the regular present bond valuation formula to solve for the yield to maturity.

The approximate yield-to-maturity formula is

$$\begin{array}{c}\text{Approximate} \\ \text{yield to} \\ \text{maturity} \\ \text{(YTM)}\end{array} = \frac{C_{pt} + \dfrac{(Par - P_b)}{N}}{\dfrac{(Par + P_b)}{2}}$$

where C_{pt} = dollar amount of coupon
Par = par value of $1,000
N = number of years to maturity
P_b = current quoted price of the bond

Let's cite some numbers to show how the foregoing formula works. Suppose we have a bond maturing in 10 years that is quoted at $900 on the exchange. Its coupon is $100 and the par value is $1,000. Assume the investment banker charges a flotation fee of $13 per bond. That means we have to reduce the current bond price to $887 to take into account flotation costs. Then, the approximate yield to maturity is

$$\begin{array}{c}\text{Approximate} \\ \text{yield to} \\ \text{maturity}\end{array} = \frac{100 + \dfrac{\$1,000 - \$887}{10 \text{ years}}}{\dfrac{\$1,000 + \$887}{2}}$$

$$\frac{111.3}{943.5} = 11.8\%$$

Having calculated the approximate yield to maturity of 11.8%, we can go on to the second approach, which calls for using the familiar present value bond valuation formula to solve for the yield to maturity. Our goal is to find the discount rate that will produce a present value equal to the current price of the bond (adjusted for flotation costs).

Therefore, a bond with a 10-year maturity date that sells at $887 and has a $100 annual coupon would have the following cost of capital:

$$\text{Bond Price (\$887)} = \sum_{t=1}^{10} \frac{\$100}{(1+R)^t} + \frac{\$1,000}{(1+R)^{10}}$$

Because the price of our quoted bond (adjusted for flotation costs) is $887, that means its yield to maturity should be higher than the coupon rate of 10% at original issue. We already know that 11.8% is close to the actual YTM. But, this discount rate makes the present value of the bond slightly higher than $887. Let's try 12%. That is it! Based on the previous example, we can determine the precise yield to maturity from the following example.

Year		PVIF at 10%	Present Value	PVIF at 12%	Present Value
1 to 10	$ 100	6.145	$ 614	5.650	$565
10th	1,000	.386	386	.322	322
			$1,000		$887

As you can see, a discount rate of 10% is too low, but a 12% rate is about right. At 12%, the present values of the bond would just about equal the current price of the bond. This means that the after cost of debt to a firm in a 40% tax rate bracket would be 7.2% [12% × .60(1 − .40)].

Since bonds represent the lowest cost of capital, why don't firms engage solely in debt financing? The answer is simple: Just as a baby gets indigestion from eating too much candy, a firm with too much debt runs into trouble. Up to a certain point, debt financing is beneficial. Beyond that point, however, the increased risk of insolvency makes further financing via the debt route an unsound practice. Too much debt raises the cost of capital and makes debt securities less marketable.

YOU SHOULD REMEMBER

The cost of debt is lower than the cost of equity. Debt cost increases or decreases in direct relationship to changes in market interest rates. When new bonds are issued, firms incur flotation costs, which raise the cost of debt. However, debt costs are reduced because the interest paid is tax deductible. Too much debt can increase the risk that the firm will become insolvent; it will force the cost of debt to increase and will ultimately make additional debt unmarketable. Two formulas to calculate the cost of debt are: the approximate yield-to-maturity method and the present value method, which solves for the unknown yield to maturity. Remember that the cost of debt must be adjusted for the tax effect or $K_{dt} = K_d (1 - t)$.

• *COST OF PREFERRED STOCK*

Preferred stockholders have prior claim to the assets of a corporation over common stockholders. However, preferred stock has no maturity date; and, in the case of asset liquidation, the holders of preferred stock get paid only after short- and long-term debt holder claims are satisfied.

Whenever a preferred stock is issued, there are usually a number of restrictions to ensure the owners that their dividends will be paid and that the company will strive to maintain a sound and liquid financial position. Although the firm commits itself to pay a fixed annual dividend, this payment need not, in most cases, be made if there are no earnings. If, however, the preferred stock is cumulative, as is usually the case, the dividend must be paid from future earnings before common-stock dividends are paid. Still, compared with bonds, the risk to the firm is less when it raises funds by issuing preferred stock. However, investors require a higher return on preferred stock than with the purchase of bonds.

The features of preferred stock include a fixed dividend payment or a stated percent return on the stock's value at the time of issue. The market plays an important role in establishing the dividend yield on preferred stock. Clues come from the yield that similar preferred issues, quoted on the exchanges, are returning. The underwriter, in consultation with the issuing firm, will finally decide on the terms to be offered.

DETERMINING THE COST OF PREFERRED STOCK

If preferred stock is issued at $100 per share, with a stated annual dividend of $12, the cost of the preferred stock to the firm is

$$\text{Cost of preferred } (K_p) = \frac{\text{Preferred dividend}}{(\text{Market price of preferred}) (1 - \text{Flotation cost})}$$

If the cost of floating the issue comes to 3%, then the actual cost of the preferred stock would be

$$\text{Cost of preferred } (K_p) = \frac{\$12}{\$100(1-.03)} = 12.4\%$$

Unlike the situation with bonds, no adjustment is made for taxes, because preferred stock dividends are paid after a corporation pays income taxes. Consequently, a firm assumes the full market cost of financing by issuing preferred stock.

YOU SHOULD REMEMBER

In case of default, preferred stockholders get paid before common stockholders. Preferred stock is more costly to issue than bonds, but is less costly than common stock. Preferred stockholders receive a fixed dividend and usually cannot vote on the firm's affairs.

• COST OF COMMON STOCK

When individuals need money to pay debts, they can resort to several sources, any one of which may provide a limited amount of funds: they can borrow from banks or finance companies; they can hock their jewelry; they can ask a rich uncle for a loan. The same principle applies to firms—they do not have unlimited access to external funds from any one source. Also, if a firm were to issue only one type of security, it would lose out on the opportunities offered by other types of securities. In the case of bonds, the firm gains financial leverage, which is not available through stock financing. However, by issuing bonds the firm commits itself to fixed financial payments, which can prove dangerous when earnings decline. This implies increased risk. Because the firm strives to achieve an optimal capital structure, it seeks to finance at the most advantageous cost. At times, this calls for the issuing of common stock.

As owners of the firm, common stockholders normally have voting privileges and share in all the gains and losses—and risks—associated with the firm. When the firm makes no profits, stockholders may not be paid any return on their investments. Common stockholders are not guaranteed anything if the firm's assets are liquidated. On the other hand, although they cannot lose more than their original investment, they can gain substantial returns. Because common stockholders take bigger risks than holders of debt and preferred stock, their returns must be higher.

Common stockholders participate mainly in the future returns of the firm, which translate into expected dividends and capital gains (or stock price appreciation). Because these returns accrue in the future, the usual procedure is to discount them by a risk factor. The growth prospects of these returns also affect the valuation of common stock shares. Moreover, the price of the stock reflects investor and market attitudes toward the risk and return prospects of the firm in years ahead.

DETERMINING THE COST OF COMMON STOCK

The cost of common stock, or its discount rate, is determined mainly by three factors: the price of the common stock, the dividends paid by the firm on common stock, and the growth rate of dividends. Chapter 5 indicates that the value of common stock (assuming constant growth of dividends) can be obtained from the following equation:

$$\text{Price of stock} = \frac{\text{Dividend } (1+G)^1}{\text{Discount rate or cost of equity } (K_s) - \text{Constant growth rate } (G)} = \frac{D_1}{K_s - G}$$

The constant-dividend-growth model assumes that the growth rate of dividends remains the same to infinity. Consequently, current dividends need only be adjusted for one year's growth rate, or $D_0(1 + G)^1 = D_1$. To obtain the cost of capital for common stock, all you have to do is to solve for K_s, or the discount rate.

By rearranging the terms in the foregoing equation, the cost of newly issued common stock (K_s) can be calculated by using this equation: Cost of common stock

$$K_s = \frac{D_0(1+G)^1}{\text{Price of stock } (1 - \text{Flotation costs})} + \text{Constant growth rate}$$

If the common stock is outstanding, all you have to do is eliminate the adjustment for flotation costs from the equation.

Where can you get the figures to calculate the cost of common stock? Stock quotation tables in *The New York Times* and other newspapers supply dividends and prices of stocks. The only other factor required to complete the calculation is growth. The growth of dividends can be obtained by looking up the dividends paid by the firm in the last 10 years and calculating the annual growth rate of these dividends.

Example: Calculating the Cost of Common Stock

Suppose the rate of growth for Firm A's dividends was 5% yearly, its stock price was quoted at $20, it paid $2 in dividends per share, and its underwriting costs were 3%. The cost can be easily calculated:

Cost of issuing common stock (K_s) =

$$\frac{\$2.00(1.05)^1}{\$20.00(1-.03)} + .05 = \frac{\$2.10}{\$19.40} + .05 = 15.8\%$$

This 15.8% is not adjusted for taxes because the dividends on common stock are paid out after taxes are deducted.

Can the cost of issuing common stock for the firm differ from the 15.8% calculated above? Yes—if the growth rate and the risk associated with this firm are expected to change in the future. Faster growth, leading to higher dividends, will be reflected in a higher stock price and a lower cost of capital. Lower growth will be reflected in a lower stock price and a higher cost of capital.

It is easy to check the effects on the cost of common stock simply by changing the figures in the preceding example and observing the impact. For example, if the growth rate were raised from 5% to 10%, the cost of common stock would increase from its current level of 15.8% to 21.3%. It is also possible that investor expectations regarding the financial and operating outlook of the firm may become more optimistic. Should this happen, the price of the stock will be bid up and, correspondingly, the cost to the firm of issuing common stock will decline.

An alternate method for deriving the growth rate is to compute the product of return on equity (ROE) and the retention ratio. Therefore, if a firm's ROE is 10% and it usually retains 50% of its earnings, the growth of the firm is estimated to be 5% (.10 × .50).

• CAPM AND THE COST OF COMMON STOCK

The CAPM is another way to determine the discount rate for common stocks which is equal to the cost of issuing common stock. The goal is to calculate the required rate of return using the following SML equation:

$$RRR_s = R_f + (R_m - R_f)\,\beta_s$$

where RRR_s = required rate of return
R_f = risk-free rate
R_m = average market returns
β_s = systematic risk of the stock

Therefore, all we have to do is to determine the parameters that appear in the equation and solve the equation. The first step is to estimate the standard deviations for the stock (σ_s) and the market (σ_m), and to calculate their coefficient of correlation (P_{sm}); this will supply us with beta of the stock.

$$\text{Beta} = \frac{\sigma_s}{\sigma_m} P_{sm}$$

Then we need to establish the return of the market and the risk-free rate. Assume we compute all the separate terms in the equation and come up with the following values.

	Computed Value
Standard deviation of stock	.12
Standard deviation of market	.10
Coefficient of correlation	.8
Return of the market	.11
Risk-free rate	.03

First, we calculate beta

$$\text{Beta} = \frac{.12}{.10} \times .8 = .96$$

And then we substitute all the preceding values in the SML equation to obtain a required rate of return for the stock, which is equal to the cost of capital for issuing stock.

cost of issuing
common stock = .03 + (.11 − .03).96 = .107 or 10.7%
via CAPM

The CAPM then is an alternate method for computing the cost of common stock.

Unfortunately, the CAPM runs into some difficulties. The assumptions are unrealistic; no one really knows which risk-free rate is the correct one at a given time, and the beta may not reflect the true systematic risk of the securities because no one has been able to develop a true market index. Consequently, the CAPM approach should be analyzed carefully before its results are accepted. It can, however, serve as a check against other methods of calculating the firm's cost of equity.

• COST OF RETAINED EARNINGS

Retained earnings are an internally generated source of funds. When dividends are deducted from net income, the funds left over are usually reinvested in the firm. There are no flotation costs associated with retained earnings. Retained earnings do, however, have a cost of capital associated with them. The reason is that, as a source of funds, the alternative to retained earnings would be to issue additional common stock. Consequently, the same cost of capital that applies to common stock applies to retained earnings.

Additionally, stockholders are the owners of the firm. When part of the earnings is retained by the firm, instead of being used to pay dividends, stockholders assume that these retained funds will earn the market-required rate of return on common stock. This market-required rate of return is the cost of common stock.

Because retained earnings are available after taxes, no tax adjustment is necessary. Also, as previously stated, these funds are internally generated and thus are not subject to the flotation cost associated with a new issue of securities.

DETERMINING THE COST OF RETAINED EARNINGS

The cost of retained earnings is the same as the cost of common stock without adjustment for flotation costs.

$$\text{Cost of retained earnings} = \frac{\text{Dividends on common stock}}{\text{Market value of common stock}} + \text{Constant growth rate of dividends} = \frac{D_1}{P_0} + G$$

Example: Calculating the Cost of Retained Earnings

PROBLEM   If a firm pays a $2.00 dividend, which is growing 5% annually, and the price of the stock is $20.00, what is the cost of the firm's retained earnings?

SOLUTION   Using the preceding equation you obtain:

$$\text{Cost of retained earnings} = \frac{\$2.00}{\$20.00} + 5\% = 15\%$$

The cost of retained earnings is generally a little lower than the cost of newly issued common stock, but higher than the cost of debt or preferred stock.

In general, the cost of capital to a firm—no matter what kind of security is involved—reflects the annual payments made by the firm to investors relative to the amounts they invest. The cost of debt is less than the cost of common stock mainly because, in the case of default, creditors are paid before common stockholders. Therefore, investors who purchase debt securities from a firm are subject to less risk than stockholders. Also, common stock dividends, unlike interest on debt, provide no tax benefits.

YOU SHOULD REMEMBER

The cost of issuing new common stock is based on three factors: dividends, growth of dividends, and the market price of common stock. Common stock is the most costly security to issue of any long-term source of capital. It also does not generate a tax benefit as debt does because dividends are paid after taxes. CAPM is an alternative method for determining the cost of common stock.

Retained earnings are considered to have the same cost of capital as new common stock. Therefore, their cost is calculated in the same way as for common stock, except that no adjustment is made for flotation costs.

MEASURING THE WEIGHTED AVERAGE COST OF CAPITAL (*WACC*)

When the cost of capital for different securities has been determined, the next step is to calculate the **weighted average cost of capital (WACC)** for firms with a mixture of debt and stock in their capital structure. To understand this principle, consider how a hypothetical investor, Ms. Jones, might calculate the average return that she obtains from her investments. She keeps $10,000 invested in a time deposit at 5½% and $30,000 in a government bond that yields 10%. To find her weighted average return, it is necessary to determine how important each investment is in Ms. Jones's portfolio and then to assign weights to the returns, as shown in Table 8-3.

Table 8–3 Computing the Weighted Average Cost of Capital of Ms. Jones

Investment	Value of Investment	Weight	Return	Weight × Return
Time deposit	$10,000	$\frac{\$10,000}{\$40,000}$ or .25	5.50%	1.38%
Gov't bond	$\frac{\$30,000}{\$40,000}$	$\frac{\$30,000}{\$40,000}$ or .75	10.00%	7.50%
		Weighted average return of Ms. Jones's portfolio = 8.88%		

As you can see, the procedure for combining and averaging different costs of capital is relatively simple. All you have to do is look at a firm's balance sheet to find out the relative importance of each of the firm's sources of financing.

DETERMINING THE WEIGHTS TO BE USED

To simplify matters, assume that a firm generates funds solely from common stock, preferred stock, and long-term bonds. The balance sheet will show the book values of these sources of funds. As shown in Table 8-4, you can use the balance sheet figures to calculate book value weights, though it is more practicable to work with market weights. Basically, **market value weights** represent current conditions and take into account the effects of changing market conditions and the current prices of each security. **Book value weights**, however, are based on accounting procedures that employ the par values of the securities to calculate balance sheet values and represent past conditions. Table 8-4 illustrates the difference between book value and market value weights and demonstrates how they are calculated.

The book values that appear on the balance sheet are usually different from the market values. Also, the price of common stock is normally substantially higher than its book value. This increases the weight of this capital component over other capital structure components (such as preferred stock and long-term debt). The desirable practice is to employ market weights to compute the firm's cost of capital.

Target weights can also be used. These weights indicate the distribution of external financing that the firm believes will produce optimal results. Some corporate managers establish these weights subjectively; others will use the best companies in their industry as guidelines; and still others will look at the financing mix of companies with characteristics comparable to those of their own firms. Generally speaking, target weights will approximate market weights. If they don't, the firm will attempt to finance in such a way as to make the market weights move closer to target weights.

Table 8–4 Comparison of Book and Market Weights

Value	Dollar Amount	Weights* or Percentage of Total Value	Assumed Cost of Capital (%)
Book Value			
Debt			
2,000 bonds at par, or $1,000	2,000,000	40	10
Preferred stock			
4,500 shares at $100 par value	450,000	9	12
Common equity			
500,000 shares outstanding at			
$5.00 par value	2,500,000	51	13.50
Total value of capital	4,950,000	100	
Market Value			
Debt			
10,000 bonds at $900 (current			
price of bond)	9,000,000	29	10
Preferred stock			
20,000 shares at $90 (current			
price of stock)	1,800,000	6	12
Common equity			
400,000 shares at $50 (current			
price of stock)	20,000,000	65	13.50
Total value of capital	30,800,000	100	

*Weights are derived by dividing the value of each component by the total value of capital.

COMPUTING THE WACC

In any event, whether book value or market value is used, the final goal is to compute the relative importance of each source of external funds in the capital structure of the firm. In other words, weights will show the extent to which each component contributes to the total value of the firm's capital structure.

Given the weights and the costs of capital for each source of financing, it is possible to obtain an average cost of capital of the firm using the following formula:

$$WACC = K_{dt}\left(\frac{\text{Debt}}{D+P+S}\right)$$

$$+K_p\left(\frac{\text{Preferred}}{D+P+S}\right)+K_s\left(\frac{\text{Common}}{D+P+S}\right)$$

where D = debt
P = preferred stock
S = common stock

$WACC$ = weighted average cost of capital of firm
K_{dT} = after-tax cost of debt [or $K_{dT} = K_d (1 - T)$]
K_p = cost of preferred stock
K_s = cost of common stock
T = tax rate

The market weights and the cost of capital as calculated in Table 8-4 are used to compute the weighted average cost of capital of a firm, as shown in Table 8-5.

Table 8–5 Calculating $WACC$ Based on Market Weights

Source of Financing	Cost of Capital (%)	Market Value Weight (%)	Cost of Capital × Market Value Weight (%)
Debt (1 – t)*	6.00	29	1.74
Preferred stock	12.00	6	.72
Common equity	13.50	65	8.78
		Weighted average cost of capital =	11.24

*If the tax rate of the firm is assumed to be 40%, then the cost of debt equals 6.00% (10% × .60).

As you can see, the average cost of capital is influenced by changes in the weights or in the way the firm finances. Up to a certain point, the more debt that a firm issues, relative to common stock, the lower is the average cost of capital. Conversely, if more common stock financing is done, common equity becomes more and more important in the capital structure of the firm, and the average cost of capital increases. And when the cost of capital changes in each security, there will also be a change in the firm's overall cost of capital.

A shift in the weights of the various sources of financing—or a change in their respective costs of capital—can raise or lower the weighted average cost of capital. Clearly, excessive financing through one source can adversely influence the average cost of capital. This is especially true when the firm's debt becomes too high. If this occurs, raising funds by issuing debt may increase the risk of insolvency, causing the cost of debt and the firm's overall cost of capital to rise. The important point to remember is that the average cost of capital establishes the benchmark, or cutoff point, for determining whether or not an investment is profitable.

Although the weighted average cost of capital is a crucial element in a firm's decision-making process, it is necessary to realize that the average cost of capital is only a starting point. It cannot be used indiscriminately to evaluate the profitability of all projects. Some projects are highly risky and require special treatment. In these cases, financial managers have to decide whether they should apply their subjective judgment and raise the discount rate to ensure that it not only reflects the average cost of capital but also includes an additional compensation for risk not taken into account by the *WACC*. The best course of action, especially when future cash flows are highly uncertain, is to use a risk-adjusted discount rate that makes the final assessment of the present values of expected returns more realistic.

YOU SHOULD REMEMBER

The *WACC* is calculated by determining the cost of each source of capital financing and weighting these costs according to the corresponding importance of that capital as a source of funds. It is better to use market weights when calculating the *WACC* because they more accurately reflect market conditions. Book value weights tend to keep the weight assigned to common stock too low, causing a distortion in the *WACC*. Although the *WACC* is used as a guideline to judge the relative merits of individual investments, in many cases each project should be analyzed separately; and, if necessary, the discount rate applied to measure its profitability should reflect its own specific risk rather than that of the overall *WACC*.

MEASURING THE WEIGHTED MARGINAL COST OF CAPITAL (*WMCC*)

Corporations do not have unlimited sources of funds available for investment. Investors in the marketplace are worried when corporations exceed their financial capabilities to meet these financial obligations. The market, being an efficient mechanism, incorporates all information about each firm and then compares the financial merits of one firm against another. Since the market recognizes that resources are limited, investors will not make funds available to a firm beyond a certain limit. If a firm tries to extend its financing beyond such a market-determined limit, investor resistance increases, and more funds are made available only at higher and higher costs to the firm. The incremental cost of financing above a previous level is called the **weighted marginal cost of capital (WMCC)**.

How does a firm determine the point *beyond which* it will incur a higher cost when using a given source of external financing? One way is to consult with an investment advisor or banker who can assess market conditions and estimate how investors would respond to successively higher amounts of financing. The banker will present the firm with a series of ranges (see

Table 8-6) showing the upper limit of financing from each source before the cost of capital increases. In other words, the banker calculates the incremental costs that the firm will incur when its financing passes the maximum limit in each range.

Table 8–6   Ranges of New Financing and Corresponding Levels of the Cost of Capital

Range of New Financing (dollars)	Weighted Marginal Cost of Capital (%)
0 to 1,000,000	8.00
1,000,001 to 3,000,000	9.00
3,000,001 to 5,500,000	9.50
5,500,001 to 8,000,000	11.00
10,000,001 and over	11.90

The weighted marginal cost of capital in any one of the ranges in Table 8-6 increases when its upper limit is breached by an individual source of financing. To illustrate, the rise in the *WMCC* from 9.00% to 9.50% could be due to higher costs of issuing preferred stock, and the increase from 9.50% to 11.00% could occur because the limits for issuing both bonds and common stock were breached. The rising cost of capital reflects the increasing marginal cost of additional capital financing of specific components. This now becomes the cost benchmark against which the profitability of projects can be compared.

USING THE WMCC TO SELECT THE BEST PROJECTS

The most rational investment-decision approach is to select the projects with the highest profitabilities (*IRR*s) and then to move methodically down the profit scale to the ones yielding lower and lower *IRR*s until additional new projects fail to provide rates of return equal to the marginal cost of capital. The idea is based on the concept that the marginal productivity of capital, which says the profitability of projects diminishes as more funds are invested. At the point where declining profitability and rising costs meet, investment should cease. This process is termed diminishing marginal productivity of capital or declining marginal efficiency of capital.

Take a look at how this principle works. The manager of a firm analyzes the merits of several projects and calculates their *IRR*s, or relative profitabilities. The investments required to implement these projects are then compared to the *IRR* of each project by ranking the *IRR*s in the order of their returns, as shown in Table 8-7.

Table 8–7   Ranking Projects by Profitability *(IRR)*

Project	IRR (%)	Investment in Project (dollars)	Cumulative Investment (dollars)
A	18.0	500,000	500,000
B	17.0	500,000	1,000,000
C	15.0	1,500,000	2,500,000
D	12.0	1,500,000	4,000,000
E	11.0	1,000,000	5,000,000
F	9.0	3,000,000	8,000,000
G	8.0	3,000,000	11,000,000

This ranking procedure helps determine which projects are the best. It also indicates the amount of new financing required to implement the most profitable projects. Notice that, as more projects are added, their *IRR*s fall. Also, as more is invested in each project, more funds must be generated. This gradually leads to increased financing beyond the limits established by the investment banker and the market. Consequently, the *WMCC* will continue to increase with additional investments and additional financing. At some point, the rising marginal cost curve and declining *IRR* curve will meet (*IRR* = *WMCC*). Beyond this point, additional financing becomes unprofitable and ceases.

Figure 8-2 demonstrates this principle. The *WMCC* and the *IRR* curves are derived from the values in Tables 8-6 and 8-7. An analysis of Figure 8-2 shows that all of the projects having *IRR*s equal to or higher than 9.5%—including Projects A, B, C, D, and E—will be financed. Total investment and new financing will be $5.0 million.

The *WMCC* principle provides a more realistic measure for choosing the most profitable projects. Because it implicitly recognizes the changing response of investors to increased financing requirements, it takes into account the limits imposed by the market on different levels of new financing. It also recognizes that money is a scarce resource, and that excessive financing leads to successively higher costs of capital.

The explanation for this phenomenon lies in the increased risk incurred by increased financing, especially when debt is issued. This limitation is the investors' response to growing illiquidity, rising risk of insolvency, and eventual deterioration of the value of the firm. As discussed in Chapter 4, this investors' response is an example of the risk/return trade-off which calls for a higher return to compensate for increased risk.

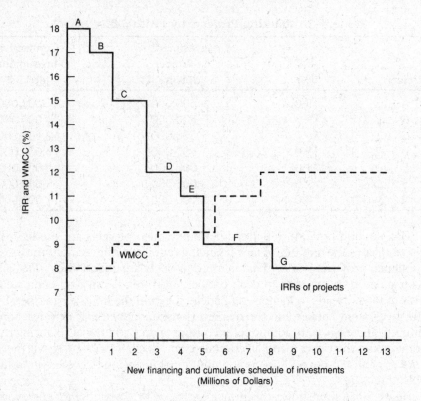

Figure 8–2 Determining Investment Limits Using *IRR*s and the *WMCC*

• *CAPM AND THE COST OF CAPITAL*

The cost of capital can also be computed by using the CAPM. To do so, let's start with the assumption that the firm does all of its financing by issuing stocks and bonds only. We know that the returns of these securities are:

Returns of stocks = Dividend yields + Capital gains
Returns of bonds = Interest yields + Change in the price of the bond

Suppose we calculate a series of the returns for a firm that has outstanding common stocks and bonds. CAPM requires the determination of the betas of these two securities. That can be done by computing the standard deviations of these returns and then solving the following equations.

$$\text{Stock's beta} = \frac{\sigma_s}{\sigma_m} \times P_{sm}$$

$$\text{Bond's beta} = \frac{\sigma_b}{\sigma_m} \times P_{bm}$$

where σ_s, σ_b, σ_m = standard deviations of stock (s), and bond (b), and market (m)

(P_{sm}), (P_{bm}) = coefficient of correlation between the securities and the market

Given the following parameters, we can obtain the respective betas for bonds and stocks. For example, assume you are supplied with the following data:

	σ	P_{sm} or P_{bm}	Amount Invested in Each Security*
Stocks	.12	1.0	$60 million
Bonds	.08	1.0	40 million
Market	.10		

*Market values in the structure of the firm. Assume a R_f of 5%, an average market required rate of return (K_m) of 15%, and a coefficient of correlation of 1.0 for stocks and 1.0 for bonds.

$$\text{Stock beta } (\beta_s) = \frac{.12}{.10} \times 1.0 = 1.2$$

$$\text{Bond beta } (\beta_b) = \frac{.08}{.10} \times 1.0 = .8$$

Just as we described in Chapter 8, the portfolio beta is equal to the sum of the weighted betas; therefore,

$$\text{Average weighted beta } (\beta_{b,s}) = \beta_b \left(\frac{MV_b}{MV_b + MV_s} \right) + \beta_s \left(\frac{MV_s}{MV_b + MV_s} \right)$$

where MV_s = market value of stocks

MV_b = market value of bonds

β_s = beta of stocks

β_b = beta of bonds

$\beta_{b,s}$ = average weighted beta of stocks and bonds.

Referring to the preceding example, we find that the market value invested in stocks is 60% and 40% for bonds. That means the average beta of the firm of these two securities is

$$\begin{matrix} \text{Average beta of} \\ \text{bonds and stocks} \\ \beta(b,s) \end{matrix} = 0.8 \left(\frac{\$40}{\$40 + \$60} \right) + 1.2 \left(\frac{\$60}{\$40 + \$60} \right) = 1.04$$

All that remains is to calculate the required rate of return ($RRR_{b,s}$), which then is the equivalent to the average cost of capital of the firm. This rate can be obtained by using the following formula:

$$RRR_{b,s} = R_f + (R_m - R_f) \, \beta_{b,s}$$

Substituting the appropriate values in the preceding equation we come up with:

$$RRR_{b,s} = .05 + (.10 - .05) \, 1.04 = .102 \text{ or } 10.2\%$$

YOU SHOULD REMEMBER

There is a point beyond which a firm cannot finance without incurring a higher marginal cost of capital. The weighted marginal cost of capital (*WMCC*) principle is useful in determining the total number of additional projects that can be financed because they are profitable. It is important to note that, as more projects are financed, the *IRR*s of these projects decline while the *WMCC* increases. Investment ceases when *IRR* = *WMCC*. Another method to calculate the average cost of capital of a firm is to employ the CAPM. This approach calls for determining the average weighted betas of the firm's stock and bond portfolio. Then, apply this overall portfolio beta to derive a required rate of return using the SML equation.

DIVISIONAL COST OF CAPITAL

The cost of financing for companies with outstanding debt and equity is determined by the market. Consequently, the task of calculating the weighted average cost of capital is almost routine if the steps outlined in this chapter are followed. The cost of capital can then be employed to discount the cash flows of projects that have similar product mixes and risks of the overall company. Unfortunately, the risk and product characteristics of many divisions have little in common with the parent corporation. In these cases, a separate evaluation of the cost of capital is called for. In other words, the risks of individual divisions may turn out to be lower or higher than the parent company. To assign the aggregate cost of capital of the company to discount the future cash flow of these divisions may understate or overstate the true present values of these cash flows. The results could then give a false impression about the true performance of each division leading to a misallocation of scarce funds among divisions.

Biases of this kind can be partially avoided by identifying the risk features of each division. As a result, different discount rates should be assigned to calculate each division's risk-adjusted cash flows and their corresponding present values.

If divisions were able to finance their own projects by issuing stock and bonds in the open market, the calculations of divisional costs of capital would be straightforward. However, this is not the way a corporation finances its investments. Financing is done at the corporate level and then the funds are allocated to divisions.

We are still left with the task of determining individual division cost of capital or required rates of return. One method entails matching a division's products mix with some publicly traded company having similar products and operating features. Then we merely apply the market-assigned costs of equity and debt of a publicly traded company to calculate the opportunity cost of the division, using the capital structure of the parent company as the weights.

Another approach would rely on the CAPM to solve for the required rate of return. Calculate or find the beta of the publicly traded firm reported in several financial services and employ that beta to obtain the required rate of return. Some analysts suggest adjusting the beta for differences in the capital structures of the publicly traded company, but this refinement only complicates the computations.

Determining divisional cost of capital and discount rates is no easy task. In addition to the difficulty of finding a good "match," the manager should recognize the limitations of this approach. Therefore, the mathematical results may have to be modified by the injection of good judgment.

Although these approaches should be regarded as approximations, they are far better than just relying on inappropriate risk measures that make no allowance for differences in divisional risks and returns. In the end, this divisional approach sets a better standard for evaluating the potential contribution of each division to the overall net present value of the firm. Additionally, it establishes a sounder basis for determining the proper allocation of funds to each division.

GLOBALIZATION AND THE COST OF CAPITAL

A few brief comments are in order regarding the effects of foreign exposure on the cost of capital. International diversification by a U.S. firm changes the market's perception of risk. New factors come into play that alter the way the market assesses the risk of a multinational firm. The cost of capital of a global firm gets adjusted up or down depending on the degree of exposure occasioned by new investments abroad.

Normally, diversifying abroad dampens overall risk; however, when investments take place in highly risky countries, the results can be unfavorable to a firm's borrowing capacity. The outcomes of globalization on the cost of capital are not easy to pinpoint.

Theoretically, it is assumed that the economic movements of foreign countries differ from those in the United States. This favorable covariance portfolio effect should diminish overall risk and also lower the cost of borrowing. But the beneficial effects of diversification are not as strong as they once were, largely because of the closer financial and economic ties between countries.

Some consideration must be given to the financing opportunities that become available to foreign subsidiaries of U.S. corporations. In some countries, interest rates are lower than in the domestic market, which gives foreign subsidiaries a financing advantage. The cost of borrowing, especially short-term, is very volatile in many foreign countries and costs may increase dramatically, making refinancing difficult. However, borrowing abroad avoids the risk of changing exchange rates.

The cost of capital of a U.S. multinational corporation is influenced by the interest rates prevailing in foreign countries where the corporation operates. Multinational corporations can be expected to take advantage of lower interest rates and better stock terms abroad, but these benefits could change as risks shift. Although not completely scientific, it is possible to find out the impact of foreign financing on global corporations by comparing the cost of capital with that of purely domestic corporations that have the same features.

In any event, the procedure could entail calculating separate domestic (d) and foreign (f) betas and then weighting these betas according to the importance of financing in the United States and abroad, $B_{df} = (B_d \times W_d) + (B_f \times W_f)$. These worldwide betas become the basis for determining the aggregate beta of the global corporation ($WACC_{df}$). This approach will yield a $WACC_{df}$ as shown below:

$$WACC_{df} = (D_{df} \times W_{df}) + (E_{df} \times W_{df})$$

Obviously, there is no easy method of tracing the impact of foreign exposure on the cost of capital of the global firm, yet capital budgeting analyses cannot ignore differences in domestic and foreign cost of borrowing and risks. There is no precise or formal method to identify foreign and domestic influences on the firm's cost of capital, this will largely depend on the balanced assessment of all factors made by managers.

YOU SHOULD REMEMBER

Because of differences in risks and growth prospects, it is necessary to determine separately the discount rates and risk-adjusted cash flows for each division. That produces more accurate measures of performance and makes possible a better allocation of scarce resources. The cost of capital for global firms should take into consideration the different costs of financing here and abroad. A global firm can benefit from financing in foreign countries when costs of borrowing are lower overseas than the domestic ones. As a result, a global weighted cost of capital for a firm should be considered as follows:

$$WACC_{df} = (D_{df} \times W_{df}) + (E_{df} \times W_{df})$$

KNOW THE CONCEPTS

DO YOU KNOW THE BASICS?

1. List some factors that investors look at when assigning a cost of capital to a firm.

2. How is the value of a firm affected by a changing cost of capital?

3. In what sense does the cost of capital serve as a benchmark for determining the relative merits of projects? Give a graphical example.

4. Calculate the total risk of projects A and B if the risk-free rate is 5% and the risk premium is 3% for project A and 5% for project B. What does this imply?

5. If the maturity period of one bond is 5 years and that of another bond 10 years, why is the cost of capital usually higher in the longer-term bond?

6. What two adjustments are made to calculate the cost of newly issued debt?

7. What happens to a firm's cost of debt when market interest rates increase? Why does this occur?

8. Why is the cost of issuing preferred stock usually lower than the cost of issuing common stock?

9. All other things being equal, what happens to the value of common stock when:
   (a) the growth rate is expected to increase?
   (b) the volatility of earnings is anticipated to increase?

10. How does the calculation of the cost of retained earnings differ from the calculation of the cost of common stock?

11. What is the difference between book value weights and market value weights?

12. What happens to the marginal cost of capital when a firm exceeds its borrowing capacity, and how will this affect its investment decisions?

13. Why does the *IRR* of projects decline while the *WMCC* increases?

14. What does the term (D_1) imply in the constant-dividend-growth model?

15. Why is the risk-adjusted discount-rate (RADR) method used and assigned to different projects or divisions of a firm?

16. Describe two ways to calculate the yield to maturity of bonds.

17. Explain how CAPM can be used to obtain the cost of capital of a firm.

18. Why does it make sense to compute separate divisional and global costs of capital and betas?

TERMS FOR STUDY

book value weights
expected return
external sources of funds
flotation costs
internally generated funds
internal rate of return
market value weights
maturity date
opportunity cost

par value
rating agencies
required rate of return (*RRR*)
risk-adjusted discount rate (RADR)
risk premium
weighted average cost of capital
 (*WACC*)
weighted marginal cost of capital
 (*WMCC*)

PRACTICAL APPLICATION

COMPUTATIONAL PROBLEMS

1. If a company issues a $1,000 par value bond with a $90 coupon and a maturity date of 10 years and flotation costs are 2% of the par value of the bond, calculate the cost of this debt issue, assuming the firm is subject to a 40% tax rate.

2. Drawing on the figures supplied in Problem 1, determine the cost of a new debt issue, using the approximate yield-to-maturity formula, if the price of the original bond has a current quote of $900. (Don't forget flotation costs.)

3. Evaluate the cost of common stock if the current price is $50, the dividend is $2 per share, and dividends grew from $1 to $1.54 over the past 5 years.

4. Given a risk-free rate of 7%, a market return of 12%, and a beta of 1.2, calculate the cost of common stock by using the CAPM. What would happen to the cost if beta was .8 instead of 1.2?

5. A finance company has the following values stated in its balance sheet: debt = $500,000 and common equity = $100,000. Compute the weights of this firm's capital structure. If its cost of debt after taxes is 10% and the cost of common stock is 12%, calculate its *WACC*.

6. The following are the *IRR* and the corresponding investments required by the projects listed below:

Project	IRR	Investment
A	10%	$1,000
B	12%	3,000
C	13%	2,000
D	9%	5,000
E	15%	9,000

The marginal cost of capital is 11%. Indicate which projects will be implemented and the total amount of financing, or investment, that will be required.

7. You are told that the beta of a firm's stock is 1.4 and the corresponding beta for bonds is 0.9. Applying the information given in Problems 4 and 5, compute the average weighted beta of the firm and its cost of capital. (Use book value weights.)

8. If preferred stock has a dividend of $9 and an issue price of $100 and carries a flotation cost of $3 per share, calculate the cost of the stock.

ANSWERS

KNOW THE CONCEPTS

1. Factors include the riskiness (volatility) of earnings, growth of profits, large or small exposure to debt obligations, financial soundness, and the attitude of investors toward management and the company (such as the *P/E* assigned to a stock).

2. If the cost of capital increases, the value of a firm will decline; if the cost of capital decreases, the firm's value will increase.

3. Rate of return (*IRR*)

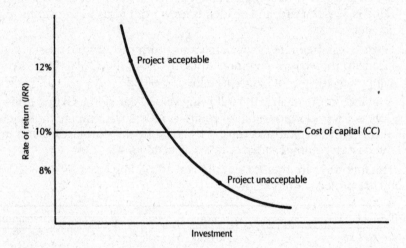

Any project having a rate of return (*IRR*) lower than the cost of capital (10%) will be rejected, and projects having an *IRR* higher than the (*CC*) will be accepted.

4. If total risk equals the risk-free rate plus a risk premium, then Project A is less risky than Project B.

	Risk-free Rate	Risk Premium	Total Risk
Project A	5%	3%	8%
Project B	5%	5%	10%

To compensate for the higher risk premium, Project B has to have a rate of return 2% higher than that of Project A.

5. Because the 10-year bond has a longer maturity period, it has a greater chance of defaulting. As time increases, uncertainty increases. To com-

pensate for this higher degree of uncertainty and increased chance of default, investors will require a higher return.

6. (a) Adjustment for flotation costs: (1 – flotation costs).

   (b) Adjustment for the tax benefits: $K_d(1 - \text{tax rate}) = K_{dT}$

7. If market interest rates increase, all rates move up in sympathy. The result will be a higher cost of issuing debt.

8. The cost of issuing preferred stock is lower than that of issuing common stock because investors are paid a stated dividend and are paid off before common stockholders in case of bankruptcy. This lower risk means that a lower return will be acceptable to investors.

9. (a) When G increases, the value of common stock increases.

   (b) When K_s increases, the value of common stock decreases.

10. The calculations are the same except that in the case of retained earnings the price of the stock is not adjusted for flotation costs.

11. Book value weights are based on the par values of stocks and bonds. Market weights reflect the current prices of common stock and outstanding bonds. Generally, market weights shift in favor of common stock.

12. The marginal cost of capital (*MCC*) increases when borrowing limits are reached, and the *IRR* decreases as more projects are financed. At some point, the *MCC* and *IRR* curves will meet (*MCC* = *IRR*). Beyond this point, investments become unprofitable.

13. The *IRR* of projects declines because of the diminishing marginal productivity of capital. *MCC* increases because the market, or investors, will not supply unlimited amounts of funds. Beyond a certain point, too much debt causes investors to become apprehensive, and they will ask for greater returns. Therefore, excessive borrowing can increase the chances of insolvency; excessive issue of stock leads to dilution of the earnings per share and possible loss of voting control. Hence, a higher cost of capital results.

14. The constant-dividend-growth model assumes that the growth rate remains the same (stays constant) to infinity. If so, the current dividend need only be adjusted upward by one year's growth rate $(D_0(1 + G)^1)$.

15. The overall cost of capital of a firm does not fully reflect the degree of risk that should be assigned to each project or division. If the degree of riskiness is ignored, the *NPV* and the present values of cash flows after taxes will be biased. If the division is riskier than the firm, the profitability of its projects will turn out to be higher than they should be because the discount rate is too low. Thus, each project should be assigned its appropriate RADR in order for it to yield a realistic risk-adjusted *NPV*.

16. The yield to maturity of a bond can be calculated either by using the approximate YTM formula or by solving for the yield-to-maturity or discount rate in the normal present bond valuation formula. Notice that the bond price in these formulas is the quoted price of a similar bond traded on the exchange, which is adjusted for flotation costs.

17. The following steps are required to obtain the cost of capital that employs CAPM as a criterion.

   a. Calculate a series of returns for stocks, bonds, or any other securities.

   b. Derive the betas for stocks and bonds by using:

$$\text{Stock's beta} = \frac{\sigma_s}{\sigma_m} \times P_{sm} \quad \text{Bond's beta} = \frac{\sigma_b}{\sigma_m} \times P_{sm}$$

   c. Compute the weighted sum of the stock and bond betas.

   d. Finally, determine the cost of capital by substituting the values in the following equation:

$$RRR_{b,s} = R_f + (R_m - R_f)\, \beta_{b,s}$$

18. Each division of a firm is subject to its own unique risks and growth potentials. Using the firm's overall discount rate to calculate the present values of divisional cash flows will tend to overstate or understate the results. That is why capital budgeting by divisions requires a separate evaluation of the risks associated with each division.

   The cost of capital of a global firm is influenced by differences in domestic and foreign financing costs. A firm should take advantage of lower costs here or abroad when financing projects. It should also consider borrowing abroad to avoid exchange rate risks. Foreign risks differ from domestic risks, which is why, in capital budgeting, the discount rates employed should reflect their individual degrees of risks.

   Calculations of the global firm's *WACC* ought to include the financing costs of domestic as well as foreign operations (*WACC$_{df}$*).

PRACTICAL APPLICATION

1. Company's cost of bonds $= \dfrac{\$90}{\$1,000(.98)} = \dfrac{\$90}{\$980} = 9.2\%$

$$9.2\%(1 - .40) = 5.52\%$$
after-tax cost of issuing bonds

2. The formula is

$$\text{Approximate YTM} = \frac{C_{pt} + \dfrac{(Par - P_b)}{N}}{\dfrac{Par + P_b}{2}}$$

and the solution is

$$\text{Approximate YTM} = \frac{90 + \left(\dfrac{1,000 - 882}{10}\right)}{\dfrac{1,000 + 980}{2}} = 10.3\%$$

3. Cost of common stock $= \dfrac{\$2.00}{\$50.00} + 9\% = .04 + .09 = 13\%$

4. RRR_s, or cost of common stock (K_s)
Cost of common stock $= .07 + (0.12 - .07)1.2$
$= .07 + .06 = 13\%$
A beta of .8 would yield an RRR_s of 11%

5.

		Weight (W)	Percentage Cost of Capital (CC)	W × CC
Debt	$500,000	.83	.10	8.3%
Equity	100,000	.17	.12	2.0%
	$600,000	1.00		WACC = 10.3%

6.

Projects	IRR (%)	Investment	Cumulative Investment
E	15	$9,000	$ 9,000
C	13	2,000	11,000
B	12	3,000	14,000
A	10	1,000	15,000
D	9	5,000	20,000

Projects E, C, and B will be undertaken, and since the marginal cost of capital is 11%, the total investment in these projects will amount to $34,000.

7. The sum of the weighted betas is

$$\begin{array}{l}\text{Average}\\ \text{weighted}\\ \text{beta } (\beta_{b,s})\end{array} = \beta_b\left(\frac{MV_b}{MV_b + MV_s}\right) + \beta_s\left(\frac{MV_s}{MV_b + MV_s}\right)$$

then

$$\beta_{b,s} = 0.9\left(\frac{500}{500+100}\right) + 1.4\left(\frac{100}{500+100}\right) = .98$$

The firm's cost of capital is

$$RRR_{b,s} = R_f + (R_m - R_f)\,\beta_{b,s}$$

then $RRR_{b,s} = 0.07 + (.12 - .07).98 = .119 = 11.9\%$

8. Cost of preferred stock $= \dfrac{\$9}{\$100-\$3} = \dfrac{\$9}{\$97} = 9.3\%$

9

CAPITAL STRUCTURE

KEY TERMS

agency costs costs, such as bonding and monitoring, incurred by stockholders to induce managers to adopt policies to maximize the wealth of the firm

bankruptcy costs expenses originating in a defaulting firm from legal fees, inefficiencies, liquidation losses, and increased cost of capital

capitalization the sum of debt plus equity

capital structure the financing mix of a firm

debt/capitalization (D/C) the ratio of a firm's debt to its total capitalization

financial leverage the effect of a change in earnings per share as a result of a change in EBIT

insolvency a firm's inability to pay its debts

BASIC CONCEPTS

Capital structure is the financing mix of the firm. Itemized on the right side of the balance sheet, it represents major sources of external funds derived from financing. The capital structure of the firm consists of long-term debt, preferred stock, and common equity.

To simplify the presentation, only long-term debt and common equity will be considered in the following discussion of capital structure. When studying the capital structure of a firm, it is important to calculate the ratio of debt (*D*) to total capitalization: *D/C*. The **debt/capitalization ratio** indicates the proportion of debt and equity issued by the firm. The firm must maintain a certain balance between debt and equity. Too much debt can increase the risk of the firm, making investors apprehensive about the ability of the firm to pay its creditors. This, in turn, may increase the cost of capital.

Up to a certain point, debt financing is beneficial to a firm because it provides financial leverage. That is, the tax deductibility feature of interest paid to creditors enables a firm to achieve higher earnings per share when debt is issued than would be possible by issuing equity. In other words, by issuing debt, the firm achieves higher earnings per share as a result of the tax benefits obtained from the deductibility of interest. This boost in earnings per share is called financial leverage.

• *EXPLAINING FINANCIAL LEVERAGE*

Financial leverage relates to the practice of using debt securities to finance investments and consists of the relationship between EBIT (earnings before interest and taxes) and EPS (earnings per share). When debt is issued, the firm commits itself to pay interest and repay principal sometime in the future. Because this interest is a tax-deductible expense, more of the operating income flows through to investors.

However, the more debt a firm has in its capital structure, the greater the financial risk. This means that, regardless of the level of its operating income, the firm must continue to meet fixed coupon payments plus the payment of principal at maturity. Therefore, the more debt a firm issues, the more fixed financial costs it incurs and the greater the danger that it will not be able to meet these periodic fixed payments. As debt increases, interest payments rise—and although they provide financial leverage, there is an increasing financial risk that interest payments will become too large relative to EBIT. If business activity declines in a business contraction phase, EBIT will also decline, increasing the probability that the firm may not be able to cover the interest payments with existing operating profits. Remember, therefore, that financial leverage is a two-way street. Although it can be beneficial in a cyclical expansion period, it is detrimental in a cyclical contraction phase.

As debt increases, it tends to magnify the swings of EPS. As a result, the benefits of financial leverage must be weighted against the growing financial risk of insolvency. At some point, the tax-adjusted cost of increases in interest exceeds the EPS benefits derived from a smaller number of outstanding shares.

A simple way to explain the way the principle of financial leverage works is to distinguish between an **unlevered** and a **levered firm**. An unlevered firm does its financing by issuing common stock and has no debt on its books. A levered firm finances part of its operation with debt. As a result, it has a mix of debt and common stock in its capital structure. To find out the effects of financial leverage we start by presenting Table 9-1, which compares an unlevered firm with a *D/C* ratio equal to zero and a levered firm with a *D/C* ratio of 50% over two years, 1990 and 1991.

Table 9–1   Financial Leverage

	Unlevered Firm A (D/C = 0)*		Levered Firm B (D/C = 50%)**	
	1990	1991	1990	1991
EBIT	$100,000	$140,000	$100,000	$140,000
Interest on bonds (at 10%)	0	0	10,000	10,000
Earning before taxes	$100,000	$140,000	$ 90,000	$130,000
Taxes (at 40%)	40,000	56,000	36,000	52,000
Net income	$ 60,000	$ 84,000	$ 54,000	$ 78,000
Shares outstanding	10,000	10,000	5,000	5,000
EPS (earnings per share)	$ 6.00	$ 8.40	$ 10.80	$ 15.60

  *Total capital of unlevered firm = $200,000
 **Total capital of levered firm   = $200,000 ($100,000 debt + $100,000 equity)

   The effects of financial leverage on EPS can be seen in Table 9-1. Both firms have the same total capital of $200,000. The unlevered firm's capital of $200,000 represents the issue of 10,000 shares of stock, whereas the levered firm financed its capital with $100,000 of stock and $100,000 of debt, and that means it has only 5,000 shares outstanding. Given these conditions and given the fact that each firm had the same EBIT in 1990, an increase in the D/C ratio from 0 to 50% produced an increase in EPS from $6 to $10.80. What produced this increase in EPS? Clearly, it was the leverage due to debt that allowed the levered firm to deduct interest. We can readily observe that the **degree of financial leverage** can be expressed in the following way and is contingent on the magnitude of interest paid by the levered firm.

$$\text{Degree of financial leverage } (DFL) = \frac{EBIT}{EBIT - I}$$

where $EBIT$ = earnings before interest and taxes
          I = interest expense
Using the figures in Table 9-1, we obtain

$$\begin{array}{l} DFL \\ \text{unlevered} \\ \text{firm} \\ (1990) \end{array} = \frac{\$100,000}{\$100,000} = 1.0 \qquad \begin{array}{l} DFL \\ \text{levered} \\ \text{firm} \\ (1990) \end{array} = \frac{\$100,000}{\$100,000 - \$10,000} = 1.11$$

Referring to Table 9-1 for year 1990, because Firm A has no debt, a change in EBIT produces the same change in income. Firm B has a *D/C* ratio of 50%. For every change in its EBIT, net income increases by 1.11 times that change. This example illustrates how financial managers compare the effects of financial leverage in their firms relative to other firms.

This is the way the degree of financial leverage is calculated at a point in time. When we compare the changes over two periods of time, as was done in Table 9-1, the formula for the degree of financial leverage becomes

$$\text{Degree of financial leverage} = \frac{\% \text{ change in } EPS}{\% \text{ change in } EBIT}$$
$$(1990 \text{ to } 1991)$$

Using the information provided in Table 9-1, we can calculate the DFL for the two firms between 1990 and 1991.

$$\text{DFL unlevered firm} = \frac{.40}{.40} = 1.0 \qquad \text{DFL levered firm} = \frac{.44}{.40} = 1.1$$

Generally, the more debt there is, the higher the degree of financial leverage. However, leverage works in both directions. For example, when the degree of financial leverage has a value of 2.00, a 1% drop in EBIT will produce a 2% decline in EPS. Therefore, the more financial leverage, the more volatile EPS become—and the greater the risk associated with the firm. The value of EPS increases as a result of financial leverage, and this effect is illustrated by the probability curves in Figure 9-1, which compare the dispersion of EPS for an unlevered and levered firm. Note that the dispersion of EPS for the unlevered firm is smaller than for the levered firm. Therefore, we can say that financial leverage occasioned by rising debt increases the risk of the firm and causes its discount rate of common stock to rise.

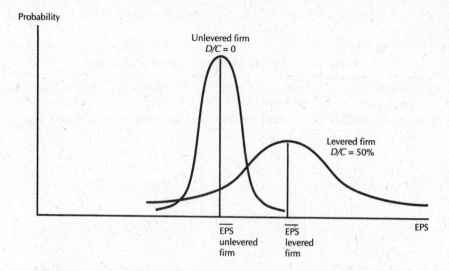

Figure 9-1 Comparing the Dispersion of EPS Between an Unlevered and a Levered Firm

---

YOU SHOULD REMEMBER

Financial leverage arises when a firm issues debt to finance part of its operations. The higher the D/C ratio, the greater the degree of financial leverage. However, while financial leverage produces higher EPS, it also causes EPS to become more volatile. This means risk increases but as long as the D/C ratio remains at manageable levels, it can translate into a higher value for the firm.

CAPITAL STRUCTURE

• *CAPITAL STRUCTURE AND VALUE OF THE FIRM'S STOCK*

The goal of managers is to maximize the value of the firm. One of the important ways to achieve this goal is to strive for the best capital mix or **optimal capital structure.**

Before we discuss this point, we must preface the analysis by explaining how the value of the firm is affected by a change in capital structure. To do so, we have to indicate how the value of the firm is determined and how it is affected by changes in capital structure. The components involved in this valuation process are the amount of debt, the leverage effect of debt on

EPS, and the change in the discount rate resulting from a change in capital structure.

Table 9–2 D/C Ratio and Cost of Financing

Capital Structure (percentage D/C)	Estimated Cost of Common (K_s) (%)	Expected EPS (dollars)	Estimated Price of Stock (P_0)* (dollars)
0	10.5	3.00	28.57
10	11.0	3.50	31.81
20	11.5	4.00	34.78
30	12.0	4.50	37.50
40	12.1	5.00	41.32
50	14.0	5.20	37.14
60	15.5	5.00	32.26
70	16.8	4.80	28.57
80	18.5	4.50	24.32

$$*P_0 = \frac{EPS}{K_s}$$

Note in Table 9-2 that when debt as a percent of total **capitalization** (*D/C*) increases, it imposes a greater financial burden on stockholders to meet fixed payments on that debt. This increased risk is reflected in the discount rate. The benefits of financial leverage from issuing some debt shows up in substantial increases in EPS, which overcome to some extent the adverse impact of a rising discount rate. As a result, the price of the stock increases. At some point debt becomes too burdensome. In our case, this takes place at a *D/C* ratio of 40%. As the *D/C* rises beyond this level, the impact of increased risk (K_s) begins to have serious adverse effects on the value of the stock. So that a *D/C* of 40% produces a maximum stock value of $41.32, and beyond this point it continues to decline until it reaches $24.82 when the *D/C* ratio hits 80%.

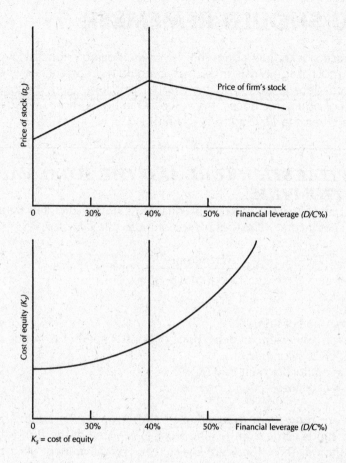

Figure 9–2 Financial Leverage, Risk, Cost of Equity, and Stock Price

Hypothetically, the relationship described in Table 9-2 is shown in Figure 9-2 where we observe that after the *D/C* ratio passes 40%, the cost of issuing equity skyrockets and produces a decline in the value of the firm's stock price.

YOU SHOULD REMEMBER

Because stockholders bear the risk of increasing financial leverage, the cost of equity also increases. Eventually, EPS declines when too much debt is added to the capital structure. And, because the cost of equity increases, the value of the firm's shares will also decline when the D/C ratio is too high.

• CAPITAL STRUCTURE AND THE TOTAL VALUE OF THE FIRM

Theoretically, the value of a firm is equal to the total value of its debt plus capitalized net income. The formula to compute this value follows:

$$V_f = D + \frac{\text{Net income } (E)}{\text{Discount rate } (K_s)} \text{ or } V_f = D + S$$

where V_f = value of firm
D = market value of debt (price of bond × number of bonds sold)
E = Net income (E)
K_s = equity discount rate (K_s)
S = capitalized net income

Funds from **long-term debt** originate in borrowings by issuing bonds, and equity funds come from issuing stock. The value of the firm is determined by the way these funds are invested and by the amount of cash flow they generate. As a result, the total value of the firm is affected by the way the manager combines debt and equity. A change in the proportions of debt relative to equity can alter the value of a firm significantly. This is contingent on the impact that leverage has on EPS and also on the effect that a changing capital structure has on the discount rate.

To demonstrate how the firm value changes in response to changes in the D/C ratio, we have prepared Table 9-3, which is based on the following three assumptions:

Assumption I — D/C = 30%. This rate is below the optimal capital structure; therefore, the financial leverage benefits are greater than the increased cost of K_s, which means there is room for an improvement in the value of a firm's shares.

Assumption II — D/C = 40%. This ratio represents the optimal capital structure of the firm when the EPS is at its highest and the value of its stock reaches a peak.

Assumption III D/C = 50%. This ratio is too high. The firm's EPS declines, the required rate of return of equity rises sharply, and the value of the firm's stock declines.

Table 9-3 shows the capital mix of the firm having a total capitalization of $300,000 under three different assumptions: D/C = 30%, D/C = 40%, D/C = 50%. Observe that the EBIT is unchanged at all three D/C ratios, but interest increases with rising debt, and the value of the firm improves from $88,588 to $896,860 as the D/C rates increase from 30% to 40%, largely because of the benefits of leverage. When the D/C rate increases to 50%, the adverse effects of rising cost of capital and the lower capitalized earnings results in a decline in the value of the firm to $810,714. As a result, when debt increases relative to equity, beyond a certain level, risk and the average cost of capital increase sharply and this produces a lower valuation for the firm.

Table 9–3   Changes in the Value of a Firm, Given Different D/C Ratios (assuming no taxes)

	D/C Ratios		
Capital Structure	30%	40%	50%
Debt	$ 90,000	$120,000	$150,000
Equity	210,000	180,000	150,000
Total Capitalization (C)	$300,000	$300,000	$300,000
EBIT	$100,000	$100,000	$100,000
Interest on debt at 5%	4,500	6,000	7,500
Earnings	$ 95,500	$ 94,000	$ 92,500
Value of Firm (D + E)			
Equity discount rate (K_s)	(12.0)	(12.1)	(14.0)
Value of debt	$ 90,000	$120,000	$150,000
Value of equity	795,833*	776,860**	660,714***
	$885,833	$896,860	$810,714

Value of equity $= \dfrac{E}{K_s}$

* $95,500 ÷ 12.0 = $795,833

** $94,000 ÷ 12.1 = $776,860

*** $72,500 ÷ 14.0 = $660,714

In other words, investors are willing to bear increased risks as long as leverage produces a substantial increase in earnings. When, however, financial leverage makes investors uncomfortable about the firm's ability to maintain solvency, they will sell the stock or demand a substantially higher required rate of return, which precludes further borrowing at reasonable terms.

As a result, managers cannot continue to issue debt beyond a certain point, but they should take advantage of the benefits of financial leverage when the D/C ratio is at a manageable level. Thus, it pays for managers to experiment with the capital structure mix because a reasonable amount of additional debt can help lower the firm's weighted average cost of capital.

Many managers study the capital structure of other companies in the same field and attempt to match their own D/C ratio with the company that has the lowest required rate of return.

There is a relationship between financial leverage, the costs of debt and equity, risk, expected returns, and the value of a firm's stock. Observe that beyond a D/C of 40%, the cost of debt, the cost of common stock, and the average cost of capital increase, partly because risk increases. Consequently, this produces a lower valuation.

YOU SHOULD REMEMBER

The value of a firm in a no-growth state is equal to

$$V_f = D + \frac{E}{K_s}$$

As the D/C ratio increases, so does the required rate of return on equity. Consequently, the value of the firm and its equity is likely to change as more debt is issued. The goal is to aim for a capital mix that allows the firm to meet its fixed financial commitments and still gain the maximum advantages of financial leverage.

CAPITAL STRUCTURE CONTROVERSY

Researchers don't always agree on a given issue. This is a healthy condition because it usually leads to a better understanding of various processes in the field of finance. Capital structure is an area that generated such a difference of opinions. One group of researchers claims that changes in capital structure produce a change in the firm's cost of capital. Another group argues that changes in financial leverage (D/C) or in capital structure do not affect the firm's cost of capital. Both groups have made important contributions to the development of the theory of capital structure.

Credit should be given to Modigliani-Miller (MM), who first developed a very important model on this subject. MM argue that changes in capital structure do not change the value of a firm because cheaper debt is exactly offset by the rising cost of equity. To prove their point, they introduce the concept of **arbitrage** (taking advantage of value differences between two markets), demonstrating that the value of two companies could not be different if the only difference was their capital mix. Should their values differ, investors would sell the overvalued firm and buy the undervalued firm until both firms had the same value.

This theory, however, was based on the assumption of no taxes or chance of bankruptcy. Once these two factors are introduced into the model, MM admit that financial leverage, up to a certain point, does result in a lower discount rate and a higher valuation for the firm. However, as debt increases further, the growing chances of bankruptcy and the loss of tax benefits result in a higher discount rate and a lower valuation for the firm. This MM Theory was a major breakthrough in finance and produced highly fruitful research on this subject, despite the restrictive nature of the assumptions underlying the model.

• *THE NET INCOME (NI) APPROACH*

The group of researchers who associate themselves with the **NI theory** provide a fairly traditional interpretation: they say that changes in capital structure influence the cost of capital and, consequently, the value of the firm. This occurs despite the fact that the costs of debt and of common stock remain constant, regardless of changes in financial leverage.

Because the cost of debt is adjusted for the tax benefits $(1 - t)$, however, it is lower than the cost of issuing common stock. Therefore, when the firm issues more debt, its average cost of capital is lowered, as shown in Table 9-4.

Table 9–4   NI Approach: Effect of Changing Capital Structure on the Firm's Cost of Capital

Method of Financing	Capital Structure (D/C = 50%)			Capital Structure (D/C = 67%)		
	Weight (W)	Cost of Capital (K) (%)	W × K (%)	Weight (W)	Cost of Capital (K) (%)	W × K (%)
Common stock	.50	12	6	.33	12	4
Debt	.50	6	3	.67	6	4
WACC			9			8

If this is what happens, the lower discount rate means a higher value for the firm. Figure 9-3 illustrates this point. Note that the overall cost of the firm's capital declines as the *D/C* increases. When this happens, the lower discount rate raises the value of the firm.

Example: Calculating the Effect of a Change in the Discount Rate on the Value of the Firm.

PROBLEM   Assume that a firm (see Table 9-4) is not growing and that its EPS are $1.00. What will be the effect of a rise in D/C from 50% to 67%?

SOLUTION   Each share will be worth $11.11 ($1.00 ÷ .09), when the D/C equals 50%. When the D/C ratio increases to 67%, the cost of capital decreases to 8%, and the price of the firm's share increases to $12.50 ($1.00 ÷ .08) mainly because the average cost of capital decreased.

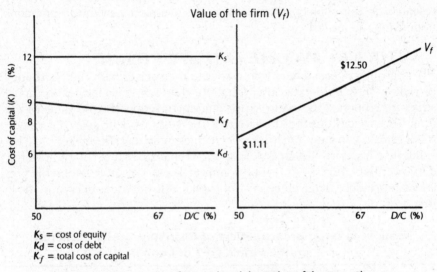

Figure 9–3 How Cost of Capital and the Value of the Firm Change Using the NI Approach

• THE NET OPERATING INCOME (NOI) APPROACH

Although supporters of the NI concept correctly visualized the tax benefits of financial leverage, they failed to take into account the increased risk reflected in the cost of equity as the D/C ratio increases. This development was clearly considered by the supporters of the **NOI theory** (Modigliani-Miller).

Table 9–5 NOI Approach: Effect of Changing *D/C* Ratio on the Cost of Capital

	OriginalCapital Structure (D/C = 50%)			New Capital Structure (D/C = 67%)		
Method of Financing	Weight (W)	Cost of Capital (K) (%)	W × K (%)	Weight (W)	Cost of Capital (K) (%)	W × K (%)
Common stock	.50	10	5	.33	10	4
Debt	.50	6	3	.67	6	4
WACC			8			8

As Table 9-5 shows, even though there is a shift in financial leverage from a *D/C* of 50% to one of 67%, the weighted average cost of capital remains unchanged at 8%.

Figure 9-4 shows graphically what happens to the cost of capital and the price of the stock, given the NOI assumptions. The relative importance of lower-cost debt, as a result of the shift to a 67% *D/C* offsets the higher cost of common stock, so the average cost of capital remains unchanged. Given this condition, $1 worth of earnings should produce a stock value of $12.50 ($1.00 ÷ .08) at a *D/C* of 50%, and the same dollar earnings capitalized by the same discount rate will, therefore, give rise to the same stock value of $12.50 ($1.00 ÷ .08) when the *D/C* ratio increases to 67%.

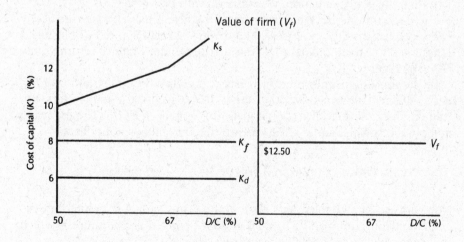

Figure 9–4 How the Cost of Capital and the Value of the Firm Change When Using the NOI Approach

• *THE MODIGLIANI-MILLER THEORY*

The theory explaining the connection between capital structure and the value of the firm was supplied to us by Modigliani-Miller (MM). In its original version, these two academicians developed a model consisting of two propositions in a world of no corporate taxes.

PROPOSITION I stipulates that the market value of a firm is independent of a change in the debt to equity ratio (D/E) or its capital structure (see Figure 9-4). Firms financed solely by equity funds are labeled unlevered (V_u) and firms whose financing consists of both debt and equity are called levered (V_L). Below we present the mathematics upon which the MM theory with no taxes is based.

$$\text{Value of unlevered firm } (V_u) = \frac{EBIT}{K_{su}}$$

where K_{su} = the cost of equity financing
EBIT = earnings before interest and taxes

Add debt to the unlevered firm and you get

$$\text{Value of levered firm } (V_L) = \frac{EBIT}{K_{su}} + D$$

Restating the above equation, we come up with $(V_L) = V_u + D$

The discount rate (K_{su}) and the value of the firm remain unchanged at any D/E level. But, as D/E increases, the growing risk of fixed debt obligations is assumed by stockholders, thus, raising the required rate of return equity (K_s) (see Figure 9-4).

Let's suppose an unlevered firm has $20 million in equity and its *EBIT* is $4 million. The firm's discount rate is 10%. Given these parameters, the value of this unlevered firm (V_u) equals the capitalized *EBIT*. (The following computations will assume all figures are stated in millions of dollars.)

$$\text{Value of unlevered firm } (V_u) = \frac{4}{.10} = \$40 \text{ million}$$

Now, instead of all equity, let's assume the firm's capital structure consists of $10 million equity and $10 million debt financed at 6% interest, which indicates a payment of $600,000 annually.

The value of this levered firm (V_L) is:

$$\text{Value of levered firm } (V_L) = \frac{\$4 - .6}{.10} + \$10 = \$44$$

According to the above calculations, the total value of the firm is ($34 + $10 = $44). However, based on MM's theory, the value of the firm does not change regardless of changes in capital structure. Then why has the value gone up to $44 million? We forgot to take into account the increase in the equity discount rate as the D/E increases. The new discount rate assigned to equity is 11.33%. (see Proposition II for the derivation of this figure).

As shown below, K_s increases and the value of the firm remains unchanged at $40 million.

$$V_L = \frac{4-.6}{.1133} + \$10 = \$40$$

PROPOSITION II stipulates that the cost of equity increases as D/E increases. This is demonstrated by the following equation.

$$K_{SL} = K_{su} + (K_{su} - K_d)\,(D/E)$$

where K_{su} = unlevered firm's cost of equity
K_d = cost of firm's debt
K_{SL} = levered firm's cost of equity

Based on the MM model, the value of the firm remains unchanged ($V_L = V_u$) at any D/E ratio. That being the case, the value of this firm's stock, when there are no taxes involved, is equal to $V_s = (V_L - D)$ or $30 ($40 – $10). Hence, the D/E ratio becomes $10/$30. Substituting the appropriate values in the equation, we come up with

$$K_s = .10 + (.10 - .06)\,(\$10/\$30) = .1133 \text{ or } 11.33\%$$

Observe that K_s rose from 10% to 11.33%. However, because the levered firm benefited from a shift to lower cost of debt, its overall cost of capital remains unchanged. That can be demonstrated by employing the WACC formula developed in Chapter 8.

$$WACC = K_d \times W_d + K_s \times W_s$$

Where $WACC$ = weighted average cost of capital of the firm

If $W_d = \dfrac{D}{D+E}$ and $W_e = \dfrac{E}{D+E}$

then $W_d = \dfrac{\$10}{\$10+\$30}$ and $W_e = \dfrac{\$30}{\$10+\$30}$

The *WACC*, therefore, is

$$WACC = .06\frac{(\$10)}{\$40} + .1133\frac{(\$30)}{\$40} = 10\%$$

The unlevered firm had a discount rate K_{su} of 10% when $D/E = 0$. As the capital structure of the firm (D/E ratio) changed, the increased risk of debt assumed by stockholders raised the market cost of issuing equity to 11.33%. But the overall cost of capital of the firm (*WACC*) remains unchanged at 10%, and neither does the value of the firm change.

• *MM MODEL WITH CORPORATE TAXES*

MM were quick to recognize the benefits of taxes and issued a revised version of their original model. The resulting change in the model (with taxes) is outlined below (assume a marginal tax rate (t) of 40%).

$$V_u = \frac{EBIT\ (1-t)}{K_{su}}$$

Drawing on the same equations used above, the value of the unlevered firm with taxes taken into account is equal to

$$V_u = \frac{\$4.0(1-.40)}{.10} = \frac{2.4}{.10} = \$24.00$$

Once debt becomes part of the firm's capital structure, the interest payment is expensed, thereby reducing the taxes the firm pays. This produces a tax shield that accrues to the firm. Mathematically, that tax shield can be expressed as $D \times T_c$ or the marginal tax rate multiplied by the debt.

The value of the levered firm, therefore, is

$$V_L = V_u + (D \times T_c) \text{ or } \$24 + (\$10 \times .40) = \$28$$

This implies that $V_s = (V_L - D)$ or $\$28 - \$10 = \$18$.

Given these parameters, we are now ready to calculate the cost of equity of the levered firm as follows:

$$K_{SL} = K_s + (K_s - K_d)\ (D/E)\ (1 - T_c)$$

Substituting the appropriate values, we come up with

$$.1133 = .10 + (.10 - .06)\ (\$10/\$18)\ (1 - .40)$$

Although the original cost of equity was 10%, the impact of debt raises the cost of equity to 11.33%.

The next step is to determine the firm's overall cost of capital, bearing in mind that the lower cost of debt, aided by the tax effect, should reduce the WACC. The familiar equation for calculating the WACC of the firm adjusted for the impact of taxes is

$$WACC = K_d(1-t)\frac{D}{D+E} + K_s\frac{E}{D+E}$$

In which case the overall cost of capital of the firm (WACC) is

$$WACC = .06\,(1 - .40) \times \$10/\$28 + .1133 \times \$18/\$28 = .0858 \text{ or } 8.58\%$$

Without debt, the firm's cost of capital was 10%. Adding debt to the capital structure of the firm lowered its cost of capital to 8.58%. As one might expect, stockholders are saddled with the obligation of paying off the debt. This added risk is reflected in an increase of the cost of equity from 10% to 11.33%. But the WACC declines and, in turn (partly because of the tax benefits and benefits of financial leverage), the value of the firm has gone up to $28 million compared to $24 million. All of the pieces now fall into place. MM supply us with an elegant explanation of the effects of debt and the tax shield on the cost of capital of the firm.

YOU SHOULD REMEMBER

The NI and NOI theories are based on many restrictive assumptions. They do not reflect the real world, but each approach enhances your comprehension of the effects of financial leverage on the value of the firm. It is up to the manager to use the insights provided by these theories to make better financial decisions. The theory developed by MM supplies us with a better understanding of the way capital structure influences the cost of capital and the value of the firm.

• CURRENT INTERPRETATION OF CAPITAL STRUCTURE

There has been a gradual reconciliation of different views regarding the way capital structure affects the cost of capital and the value of the firm. Currently, the accepted view is that financial leverage adds tax benefits to a firm—up to a certain point—but too much debt has an adverse effect on the cost of capital and the value of the firm.

As Figure 9-5 shows, an increase in the *D/C* ratio from 0 to 40% may help reduce the average weighted cost of capital simply because of the shift from higher-cost common stock to lower-cost debt (1 – *t*). This indicates that a 40% *D/C* ratio is the optimal capital structure of the firm.

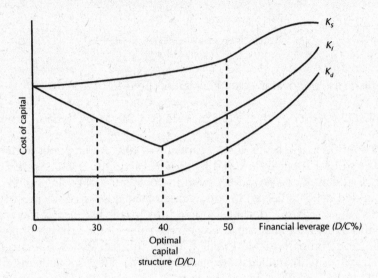

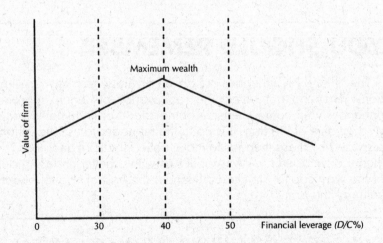

Figure 9–5 Effects of Financial Leverage on the Cost of Capital and Value of the Firm

The benefits derived from financial leverage are reflected in a favorable attitude by investors toward a firm's stock. Investors recognize that up to a certain point an increasing D/C will increase EPS, which in turn will compensate them for the risk of higher financial leverage. Consequently, investors will probably be willing to purchase a firm's stock at higher prices. At some point, however, the D/C ratio becomes too high. Then the risks associated with increasing financial leverage are unacceptable, and, therefore, the price of the stock will decline.

When financial leverage (D/C) passes the optimal capital structure point, which according to Figure 9-5 is 40%, the cost of issuing debt increases and the cost of issuing stock increases more rapidly than before. This is an indication that investors are becoming more apprehensive about the ability of the firm to meet its fixed financial obligations, given available expected resources. As a result, the total cost of capital starts to increase. Among other factors, three reasons can be cited for this development:

1. **Bankruptcy costs** increase

2. **Agency costs** increase

3. **Tax benefits** vanish

Too much debt puts the firm in jeopardy of **insolvency**. Fixed obligations required to meet creditors contractual arrangements become unmanageable at some point, especially if economic activity declines and earnings fall. The firm lacks the financial ability to meet its debt obligations. Managers and investors start to consider the growing probabilities of bankruptcy costs. These costs include increased inefficiencies as good employees leave the firm. Suppliers become alarmed at the prospect of not being paid and start to refuse to grant credit. Customers become worried about the ability of the firm to produce and to deliver goods; hence, they cancel orders. The firm's lack of sufficient funds force it to bypass profitable projects. Also, the firm has to pay too much to borrow, and potential lenders may be reluctant to lend at any return. Potential large legal and court fees loom on the horizon. Because equipment is not replaced, existing equipment becomes obsolete making the firm less efficient and competitive. Interest coverage begins to deteriorate. Finally, the prospects of heavy losses of asset value arising from possible liquidation alarm investors. These increased probabilities of bankruptcy raise the specter of unsolvency and push up the cost of capital. Some investors sell the stock lowering the value of the firm.

Agency costs arise as the goal of stockholders begins to conflict with goal of creditors. Creditors seeking to preserve their investment ma˙ pressure on the firm and the board of directors to adopt more co˙ tive investment policies that preclude maximizing the value of t' Managers now have to pay more attention to meeting creditors' c less attention to stockholders. The efficiency of the firm's op˙

be impaired. Also, stockholders may increase incentives to management thereby increasing costs at a time when the firm can ill afford it. These costs are likely to be observed by investors, and stockholders may sell their stock thereby forcing the price of the stock to decline. At the same time, bondholders will call for more restrictions, which diminish the flexibility of decision-making and constitute an implied agency cost.

All these probable agency and bankruptcy costs result in an increased cost of borrowing and a decline in the value of the firm.

The last reason has to do with the ability of the firm to benefit from lever-age. Leverage is a two-way street, so that a firm with high debt runs into the problem of being saddled with high fixed-interest costs. At some point, debt is so high that any small decline in EBIT produces a very large decline in earnings per share. This is usually looked upon with suspicion by the market, and investors seek to bail out, expecting the adverse effects of risk to result in a lower price of the firm's stock.

Given the increased probability of the occurrence of these events, inves-tors will demand higher returns; this will be followed by an increasing cost of debt. Lenders will be less willing to buy bonds unless they receive a higher return. The advantage of shifting from stocks to bonds will disappear, and the overall average cost of capital for the firm will increase.

When the D/C ratio becomes excessive, the rules of the game are altered. In Figure 9-5 you will notice that beyond a D/C ratio of 60%, the rate of increase in K_s tapers off, and the cost of debt K_d increases rapidly. Why does this occur? Part of this phenomenon can be explained by referring to option theory. When a firm issues debt, it gives prior claim to creditors; in a sense, we can say debt holders became owners of the firm. Stockholders, however, have a call option on the firm. If the firm is successful and generates enough earnings, stockholders can then call the option by paying off the bondhold-ers (the exercise price being the repayment of the debt to reclaim full title to the firm). The other choice stockholders have is "don't exercise" and walk away. You can see that when debt is too high, the chances of default increase substantially. The price of the stock declines. Stockholders may sell the stock at a loss, but the maximum loss is their original investment. That leaves the bondholder with the responsibility of reorganizing the firm ⸺ liquidating it. In some cases, as Mr. Trump did in the Taj Mahal Casino creditors were offered stock in exchange for debt. Whatever the ⸺ of the risk, which was originally borne by stockholders, has ⸺ ndholders. That is why we observe a tapering off of the K_s ⸺ n in the K_d curve when the D/C ratio is too high.

YOU SHOULD REMEMBER

The NOI and NI approaches have produced a compromise position. Academicians have come to recognize that, up to a certain point, financial leverage can produce a lower discount rate and a higher value for a firm. There is, however, a point beyond which the financial risks are too high and the value of the firm will decline because of the growing chances of bankruptcy, rising agency costs and the adverse effects of high fixed financial cost. When the D/C ratio is very high, part of the risk borne by stockholders is shifted onto the bondholders who are left with the responsibility of reorganizing or liquidating the firm at a loss.

SEARCHING FOR THE RIGHT CAPITAL MIX

Financial managers keep trying to develop financing strategies leading to a capital structure that produces optimal results from financial leverage.

The advantages of financial leverage disappear in a firm heavily laden with debt in its capital structure. Too much debt increases risk and raises the potential danger of default. Too much equity financing is not a good policy to pursue, either. It deprives the firm of the full advantages of financial leverage, and the weighted average cost of capital ($WACC$) becomes unnecessarily high. Furthermore, in some cases, issuing an excessive amount of common stock can lead to loss of voting control in the firm. As a result, an unbalanced capital mix (either too much debt or too much equity) can be detrimental to the valuation of a firm.

The primary goal of financial managers, then, is to establish a capital mix that will hold the costs of financing as low as possible, help maintain a stable dividend policy, establish a good earnings record, and maximize the wealth of stockholders. In other words, there is an optimum capital structure that minimizes the $WACC$ while maintaining the firm's credit standing on a level at which it can attract new funds at reasonable terms.

YOU SHOULD REMEMBER

Capital structure refers to the relationship between debt and equity. The more debt a firm has relative to equity, the greater its financial leverage. Financial leverage can be beneficial up to a certain point, but too much debt can mean that the firm may not be able to meet its fixed financial costs. On the other hand, too much common equity can sometimes mean loss of voting control and a higher cost of capital. The goal of a financial executive is to achieve the right capital mix.

Some signals of impending danger are given to managers from the market and the analysis of company operations to indicate when a firm is reaching the optimal D/C ratio and when the D/C ratio is too high. Some firms faced by high business risk, whose operations and earnings are very sensitive to business downturns, should use less debt. Then there are industry constraints. A firm will find that investors compare firms to their industry. That means that the D/C cannot deviate substantially from an industry average or from the debt ratio of a successful competitor. When a firm's bond quality rating is in jeopardy or that of other firms in the same industry has been lowered, this may signal that its debt position is becoming overextended. Hints come from bankers as they become more reluctant to advance credit. Investment bankers will advise the firm that further issues of debt can only be successfully distributed at substantially higher K_d.

The firm can also sense a growing hesitancy by potential stock investors to buy its stock. Other adverse signals can be found in a declining interest coverage ratio and in a growing volatility of EPS that exceed significantly historical patterns.

Fast-growing firms depend on growth opportunities where return on equity (ROE) is higher than the cost of the firm's capital. However, as the marginal cost of capital increase with rising debt, it tends to cut off profitable investment opportunities. That also means that firms who have a large proportion of intangible assets, of little value in a default situation, should borrow less than firms with solid saleable assets.

Depending on the circumstances, the best course of action is to prepare projected or *pro forma* income and balance sheet statements to find out a firm's financial strengths and weaknesses as well as its ability to repay debt in the future. That may call for developing alternative plans. Attention should also focus on **financial slack** because it indicates whether a firm has sufficient funds and adequate capacity to conduct its operations. The financial community is concerned about changes in financial slack because these changes send signals to investors indicating how easily a firm can cope with adverse contingencies and financial distress.

There are no specific rules that managers can use to determine the optimal capital structure of a firm. A great deal depends on how fast earnings are growing and how investors assess the financial soundness of the firm. This assessment can change from firm to firm because of varying investor attitudes toward different firms in regard to the quality of their management and their ability to cope with rising financial risk. Investor attitudes cannot be easily measured, and a great deal of judgment is required before managers sense the way a market will react to a changing capital structure. As you can see, the right financing mix or capital structure is difficult to pinpoint. The final decision represents a compromise. In the long run, all a manager can strive for is a reasonable wealth appreciation that is, if possible, better than that of the industry as a whole and of competing firms.

YOU SHOULD REMEMBER

Theoretically, there is an optimal capital structure that will produce maximum wealth for the firm. Managers get signals from the market and investors when the D/C is becoming too much of a burden. These clues are found in deteriorating financial ratios, declining bond ratings, and a lackluster performance of the stock in arising market. Managers should try to maintain some financial slack, keep the D/C ratio low when business risks are high, and compare their D/C with the industry or some good-quality company in the same field. Also, look for the shrinkage of profitable growth opportunities and investments as the cost of capital rises with an increasing D/C ratio.

KNOW THE CONCEPTS

DO YOU KNOW THE BASICS?

1. What do relatively high fixed financial costs indicate about a capital structure, assuming it has no preferred stock, leases, and so forth?

2. Why can debt produce benefits from financial leverage?

3. What happens to the value of a firm and its cost of capital when it achieves an optimal capital structure? Explain why this occurs.

4. List the factors that make up the total capitalization of a firm.

5. When a firm's D/C ratio gets too high, what is the investors' reaction to risk and their attitude toward the stock?

6. Define a levered and unlevered firm.

7. What happens to the fluctuations in the EPS of a levered firm? How is this viewed by investors who evaluate the merits of stocks for investment purposes?

8. In broad terms, explain the concepts developed by the NI and the NOI theorists.

9. What is the current synthesis of capital structure theory?

10. As a financial manager, what factors would you look at to determine whether a firm's D/C ratio is acceptable to investors?

11. Name two industries that have high D/C ratios and two that have low debt-to-equity ratios. Generally speaking, why do these differences exist?

12. What should a manager do to develop a capital structure that will produce the best results?

13. What reasons can you supply to explain why the cost of issuing debt, common stock, and the overall cost of capital of a firm increases after the D/C ratio exceeds the optimal capital structure point?

14. Explain the option concept that is available to stockholders when the D/C ratio becomes unmanageable. Who bears part of the risk when this happens, and what happens to the cost of debt and equity?

15. Describe some of the clues managers of firms receive from the market and from their own analysis to indicate when the firm's D/C ratio is getting too high. What can a firm do to lower its D/C ratio and still be able to raise more funds for investment purposes?

TERMS FOR STUDY

agency costs
arbitrage
bankruptcy costs
capitalization
capital structure
debt/capitalization (D/C) ratio
degree of financial leverage
financial leverage

financial slack
insolvency
levered firm
long-term debt
NI theory
NOI theory
optimal capital structure
unlevered firm

PRACTICAL APPLICATION

COMPUTATIONAL PROBLEMS

1. If the EBIT of a levered company increased from $100,000 to $200,000, and its EPS increased from $1.00 to $2.50, calculate the degree of financial leverage of the company and explain what this means.

2. A firm's debt is $100,000, and the value of its equity is $200,000. K_s is 12%, K_d is 10%, and the tax rate is 40%. Calculate the weighted average cost of capital of this firm.

3. An unlevered firm ($D/C = 0$) and a levered firm ($D/C = 50\%$) have the same capitalization of $1.0 million, the same EBIT of $1,000,000, a common stock par value of $10 per share, and a tax rate of 40%. Suppose the cost of debt is 7%, calculate the degree of financial leverage of both firms at this point in time. If the unlevered firm has an assigned P/E of 10 times, and the levered firm has a P/E of 9 times, compute the stock prices of these two companies.

4. Assume EBIT = $10,000; debt is $10,000, with an assigned coupon rate of 8%; the cost of common stock (K_e) or required rate of return is 10%. Calculate the value of this firm, whose tax rate is 40%.

5. If a firm's EPS changes from $2.00 to $2.50 per share between 1992 and 1993, and if its EBIT rises from $500,000 to $600,000, calculate the degree of financial leverage and estimate its EPS if EBIT is projected to be $1 million in 1994.

6. Using MM's Proposition I, estimate the cost of issuing equity when the cost of debt is 8% and the cost of an unlevered firm (K_{su}) is 14%. The firm has debt equal to $100,000 and $200,000 worth of equity (assume no taxes).

7. A company is trying to make a decision whether to raise $20 million to finance its future investments and operations. Currently, it has $40 million debt outstanding and $60 million stock outstanding. The firm does a pro-forma income statement analysis and finds out that its EPS would increase to $11 million compared to the current $10 million. Using probabilities, it finds out that the expected standard deviation of EPS, with the new capital structure, would increase to $3 from the current $2.50. After making inquiries, it also finds out that the cost of its equity would increase to 12% from the current level of 10%.

   a. Calculate the existing and the new D/C ratio.

   b. Using the coefficient of variation, indicate whether more debt is appropriate.

   c. Calculate the current price of the firm's stock and the price expected if the new debt financing is undertaken and interpret the findings. (Note: $P/E = 1/K$.)

ANSWERS

KNOW THE CONCEPTS

1. The firm's capital structure has a high proportion of debt.

2. The benefits are derived from the fact that more EBIT filter down to earnings per share because of a lower number of shares. Financial leverage, up to a certain point, helps the firm to reduce its overall cost of capital.

3. A firm attains its highest value when the optimal capital structure is achieved. This occurs when the *WACC* is lowest, which is also the time at which the firm's capitalized value of EBIT is highest.

4. The factors that make up the total capitalization of the firm are long-term debt, preferred stock, and common equity.

5. When *D/C* is too high, investors find that the volatility of earnings per share usually increases and the chances of default rise. This increased risk means the assignment of a higher discount rate to dividends or future returns of the firm. As a result, the present value of these returns declines.

6. A levered firm has a capital structure that has a mix of debt and equity. An unlevered firm finances its operations by issuing stock. Its capital structure consists of common stock only and no debt.

7. A levered firm's EPS are subject to higher volatility than the EPS of an unlevered firm. The higher volatility means the probable dispersion of EPS is wider than that for the unlevered firm. This indicates higher risk for a stock, and investors will require a higher rate of return to be compensated for undertaking this risk.

8. The NI theorists say that financial leverage reduces the cost of capital of the firm, thereby increasing the value of its shares. The NOI theorists say that, no matter how the capital structure of the firm is changed, its cost of capital and the value of its stock will remain unchanged.

9. The current synthesis draws from the contributions made by the NI and NOI theorists and says that, up to a point, financial leverage helps to reduce the cost of capital of a firm. Beyond this point, tax benefits vanish and the chances of bankruptcy increase. Overall risk increases, and the *WACC* will also increase.

10. Look at the *D/C* of the firm versus the industry's *D/C*. Compare the firm's *D/C* and financial structure to the financial structure of the best firm in the industry. Ask investment bankers whether the firm's *D/C* is high or low, and how they feel the market or investors would react to a given capital structure. Finally, try to keep the *D/C* at a conservative level to avoid association with excessive financial risk.

11. Two industries with high *D/C* ratios are utilities and railroads. Two industries with low *D/C* ratios are drugs and travel agencies. (See Morris Associates' data.)

12. Financial managers should avoid excesses. They should study the most successful companies in the industry and try to keep a balance between debt and equity. At all costs, they should avoid debt that increases fixed obligations beyond a reasonable level. To do this, they should calculate the worst situation, such as a recession, and observe whether the payments occasioned by a given debt level could be met. The goal is to maintain a conservative capital structure which yields the lowest possible risk and the best (not necessarily the optimal) value of the firm's common stock.

13. The cost of capital increases when the D/C ratio exceeds its optimal point because the probability of incurring bankruptcy costs increases—that is, there is a growing chance of incurring legal costs, court costs, and asset losses. Agency costs increase because of the increased cost of protecting creditor claims. Also, the value of risk-adjusted EPS deteriorates because the discount rate increases faster than the increase in earnings.

14. Stockholders assume most of the risks faced by the firm. However, when debt is issued, the bondholder has prior claim on the firm and in essence owns the firm until paid off. Stockholders have call options on the firm. If the firm grows and is successful, they can exercise the call by paying off the bondholder thus gaining full claim on the firm's earnings and assets. Stockholders can also waive their right to exercise and walk away when the debt is too high. Their loss cannot exceed their original investment. When this happens, the bondholder assumes the responsibility of reorganizing or liquidating the firm. As a result of these potential losses, creditors bear part of the risk. In this case, the cost of debt increases sharply and increases in the cost of equity tapers off.

15. Some of the signals that indicate when a firm's D/C is too high are:
 a. A reluctance of bankers to lend.
 b. Investment bankers suggest the firm consider alternate types of financing.
 c. The stock fails to increase when the stock market rises.
 d. Other firms in the industry have lower D/C ratios.
 e. Ratio analysis reveals that interest coverage is too thin.
 f. A bond rating agency has just put the firm on its "credit watch" or it lowers its bond rating.

A firm with a high D/C ratio that cannot raise money to finance its operations can merge with another firm that has a low D/C ratio. It may issue preferred stock or sell more common stock. It could consider issuing a convertible bond callable in two years. Or it could enter into a sale-lease-back agreement putting up some of its property as collateral.

PRACTICAL APPLICATION

1. Degree of financial leverage $= \dfrac{150\%}{100\%} = 1.5$. This indicates that a 1% change in EBIT will produce a 1.5% change in the EPS of the firm.

2.

	Capital Structure	Weight (W)	K	(K × W)
Debt	$100,000	.33%	.06	2.0%
Equity	200,000	.67%	.12	8.0%
		100%		WACC = 10.0%

3.

	Unlevered Firm D/C = 0	Levered Firm D/C = 50%
EBIT	$1,000,000	$1,000,000
Interest @ 7%	0	350,000
EBT	$1,000,000	$ 650,000
Taxes @ .40	400,000	260,000
EAT	$ 600,000	$ 390,000
Shares outstanding @ $10 par	$1,000,000	$ 500,000
EPS	.60	.78

$$DFL = \frac{EBIT}{EBIT - I}$$

$$DFL_u = \frac{\$1.0 \text{ million}}{\$1.0 \text{ million}} = 1.0$$

$$DFL_l = \frac{\$1.0 \text{ million}}{\$1.0 \text{ million} - \$350,000} = 1.54$$

Stock price = $P/E \times$ EPS
Stock price (unlevered) $10 \times \$.60 = \$6.00$
Stock price (levered) $9 \times \$.78 = \$7.02$

The favorable impact on price due to additional debt financing implies that (based on this simple hypothetical example) the firm is justified in issuing more debt to finance its operations.

4. $V_f = D + E$

EBIT	$10,000
I	800
EBT	$ 9,200
Taxes @ 40%	3,680
EAT	$ 5,520

$$E = \frac{\text{EAT}}{\text{Discount rate}} = \frac{\$5,520}{.10} = \$55,200$$

Value of firm is $65,200 ($10,000 + $55,200).

5. The degree of financial leverage is:

$$\frac{25\%}{20\%} = 1.25$$

The EPS of this firm in 1994. If EBIT is expected to increase 67%, then EPS in 1994 should reach \$4.67 $\left[\left(\frac{1.25}{.67} \right) \times \$2.50 \right]$.

6. Equation to determine the cost of equity of a levered firm K_s.

$$K_{SL} = K_{su} + (K_{su} - K_d)\,(D/E)$$

then

$$K_{SL} = .14 + (.14 - .08)\,(\$100,000/\$200,000) = .14 + 0.03 = 17\%$$

7. a. Current D/C ratio = \$40 million/\$100 million = 40%
New D/C ratio = \$60 million/\$120 million = 50%

b. Coefficient of variation $(CV) = \dfrac{\sigma_{EPS}}{\text{EPS}}$

$$CV_{\text{current}} = \frac{\$2.50}{\$10} = .25$$

$$CV_{\text{new}} = \frac{\$3.00}{\$12} = .25$$

Because the current and new coefficient of variations are the same, indications are that the risk/return trade-off would remain unchanged by issuing new debt. This result suggests that debt financing may be an appropriate and an acceptable course of action.

c. Given that $P/E = 1/K$ then the current P/E is equal to $1/.10 = 10$ times, and the new P/E after the new debt financing takes place is $1/.12 = 8.33$ times. The price of the stock currently is $(P/E \times \text{EPS})$ $10 \times \$10 = \$100$. The price of the stock with new debt is $\times \$11 = \$91.63$.

10

DIVIDEND POLICY

KEY TERMS

dividend a return on a stockholder's investment usually in the form of cash or stock

dividend yield the rate of return from a dividend relative to the price of a stock

net residual principle stipulation that dividends are to be paid only when *MMC>IRR*

par value the face value of a share of stock or a bond

payout ratio proportion of dividends paid out of total earnings

price earnings ratio relationship between the price of a stock and earnings per share used for stock valuation

record date the date that establishes stock ownership and qualifies stockholders to receive dividends

stock dividend a dividend in the form of additional shares of stock, issued in lieu of a cash dividend

stock repurchase a stock buyback by a firm, with excess cash, to be used for employee stock options and other purposes

stock split the issuing of more shares of stock to current stockholders without increasing stockholders' equity

• *SIGNIFICANCE OF DIVIDEND POLICY*

Dividend policy plays an important role in determining the value of a firm. Stockholders visualize dividends as signals of the firm's ability to generate income. A large number of analysts employ dividends to calculate the intrinsic value of stocks. The returns used to compute the beta of a stock include dividend yields as one of the factors. Consequently, dividends are an important component for calculating the value of a stock.

Although some academicians argue that the decision to pay dividends is independent of investment decisions, dividends can indirectly influence the external financing plans of financial managers. For example, a decision to pay high dividends will leave less internal funds for reinvestment in the firm. This could force the firm to generate funds from new stock or bond issues. In turn, external financing can change the firm's capital structure and cost of capital. Accordingly, financial managers try to strike a balance between paying a reasonable dividend to stockholders (to maintain their loyalty) and reinvesting earnings (to achieve future growth and maximize the price of the firm's shares).

One of the key theories to be discussed in this chapter states that dividends should be paid only after all financing and investment requirements are satisfied. Another theory claims that dividends do not affect the price of shares. Yet others argue that dividends are important for measuring the value of a firm.

Each of these theories helps managers to understand the role played by dividends. A study of each theory will provide better guidelines for finding the best dividend policy for any firm.

ROLE OF DIVIDENDS IN THE VALUATION PROCESS

To the investor, **dividends** represent a return which can be compared to other investment opportunities. This return is called the **dividend yield**. It is the relationship between the dividend payment and the price of a share of stock.

$$\text{Current dividend yield} = \frac{\text{Current dividend}}{\text{Current price of stock}}$$

If a company pays $10 in dividends per share, and its stock is selling for $100, the dividend yield is 10% ($10 ÷ $100). This yield can then be compared with the yields of other stocks or the rates of return offered by fixed income securities and other assets. There are stocks like those of utility companies, which pay out a relatively high proportion of earnings in the form of dividends. These stocks are often favored over bonds because of their high yields and safety.

Dividends provide a basis for calculating the cost of issuing common stock (K_s) as well as the value of a firm's shares. Theoretically, this can be done by employing the *constant-dividend-growth model.* This model assumes that current dividends (D_0) will continue to grow (G) at the same rate each year to infinity. If so, to calculate the value of the firm's common stock (V_s) [or its price (P_0)], one must estimate the growth rate of dividends and the required rate of return or discount rate (K_s). The final step is to adjust (D_0) for one year's growth, or $D_0 (1 + G)^1$. The appropriate equations to determine the discount rate and the value of a share of stock are

$$P_0 = \frac{D_1}{K_s - G}$$

where

$$K_s = \frac{D_1}{P_0} + G$$

Although we are already familiar with the foregoing two equations, it might be useful to review and show how each component in these equations can be determined.

1. The term P_0 stands for the current price of a stock that can be found quoted in the newspapers.

2. D_1 is equal to the current dividends (D_0) paid by the stock, raised by one year's growth rate $(1 + G)'$ of the dividend or $D_0 (1 + G)'$. Example: Assume a firm pays a $5 dividend that has been growing at 10% yearly, then D_1 would be equal to $5 × (1.10) = $5.50.

3. K_s or the discount rate can be calculated by the use of the CAPM equation.

$$RRR_s + R_f + (R_m - R_f)\, \beta_s$$

Example: If a firm's stock has a beta of 1.5, the market's rate of return (R_m) is 15% and the risk-free rate (R_f) is 5%, then the required rate of return (RRR_s) equals

$$RRR_s = .05 + (.15 - .05)\, 1.5 = .20 \text{ or } 20\%$$

The RRR_s term is the discount rate applied in solving the constant dividend growth model.

4. The growth rate of dividends (G) can be obtained by using two methods.

Method I.

$$\text{Growth rate } (G) = ROE \times (1 - \text{Payout ratio})$$

where ROE = return of equity $\left(\dfrac{\text{Net income}}{\text{Equity}} \right)$

Payout ratio = percent of earnings paid out in dividends $\left(\dfrac{\text{Dividends}}{\text{Earnings}} \right)$

PROBLEM   If ROE is 20% and the payout ratio amounts to 50% then the growth rate (G) is equal to

$$G = .20 \times (1-.50) = .10 \text{ or } 10\%$$

Method II. Another way to compute the growth rate of dividends is to find out how dividends changed, let's say, in the past 5 years. So if the dividend five years ago was $3.11 and the current dividend is $5.00, then the growth rate can be derived by computing a factor and relating this factor to the corresponding 5-year period in the future value table, where the growth rate given is 10%.

Example

PROBLEM   The factor for the figures cited above is $\frac{\$5.00}{\$3.11} = 1.61$ (factor).

The corresponding growth rate in the future value table for five years is equal to 10% annually. Note that this growth rate is the same as the 10% rate computed by using Method I. Having outlined the various methods of determining or calculating each component of the dividend model, show how dividends help to determine the price of a share of stock using the equation already cited:

$$P_s = \frac{D_1}{K_s - G}$$

SOLUTION $P_s = \frac{\$5.00(1+.10)^1}{.20-.10} = \frac{\$5.50}{.10} = \$55.00$

This price should be roughly equal to the price quoted on the stock exchange tables published in various newspapers. Based on these parameters, we can now solve for K_s to obtain the implied discount rate of the stock.

$$K_s = \frac{D_1}{P_0} + G \quad \text{or} \quad \frac{\$5.50}{\$55} + .10 = 20\%$$

In other words, a stock that is paying $5.00 in dividends, growing at 10%, and has an assigned discount rate of 20% is worth $55.00.

PAYOUT RATIO AND VALUATION

The **payout ratio** is another important aspect of dividend policy and valuation. It is found by relating dividends per share to earnings per share.

$$\text{Dividend payout ratio} = \frac{\text{Dividends per share}}{\text{Earnings per share}}$$

Assume Company A pays a $5.00 per share dividend and Company B pays $3.00. Also, Company A's EPS are $10.00 and those of Company B are $4.00. Using this equation, the payouts of two companies can easily be compared:

$$\text{Payout ratio of Company A} = \frac{\$5.00}{\$10.00} = 50\%$$

$$\text{Payout ratio of Company B} = \frac{\$3.00}{\$4.00} = 75\%$$

Company A pays out 50% of its earnings in dividends, while Company B's payout is 75%.

The payout ratio is useful for calculating the price/earnings ratio (*P/E*) of a stock.

This can be done as follows:

$$P/E = \frac{\text{Payout ratio}}{K_s - G}$$

As a result, the effect of the payout ratio on stock prices must be considered in conjunction with other factors, such as the discount rate and growth. For instance, as shown previously, the payout ratio of company A is 50% and B's payout is 75%. If both companies had the same K_s (.20) and G (.10), then Company B would have a higher *P/E* than Company A.

$$P/E_a = \frac{.50}{.20 - .10} = 5 \text{ times} \qquad P/E_b = \frac{.75}{.20 - .10} = 7.5 \text{ times}$$

The payout ratio varies from industry to industry and from company to company. Fast-growing companies need all the funds they can get. Therefore, their payout is usually low. Electric utilities, who have highly dependable earnings growth, are known to pay out a high percentage of earnings as dividends.

We may raise the question: Why do companies with a low payout ratio and those of rapid growth potential have high *P/Es*? The answer is found in the denominators where the interaction between growth and the discount rate is observed. Now suppose a company's growth was 15% instead of 10%. This faster growth rate will produce a higher *P/E* than Company B, even though its payout ratio is lower than Company B.

$$P/E_a = \frac{.50}{.20 - .15} = 10 \text{ times}$$

The payout ratio does not indicate anything about the stability of earnings and dividends. As a matter of fact, payout ratios may be misleading: During business contraction phases, the payout ratio may increase sharply, even though earnings are falling because a firm may attempt to pay the same dividends as in good economic periods. However, a steady dividend payout policy telegraphs a message. It tells investors that they can rely, within reason, on the company to maintain its dividends. This message generally attracts a loyal following. Erratic dividend payments create uncertainty. This raises the discount rate and lowers the valuation of a stock. Companies often adopt conservative policies that provide investors with reasonable assurances of receiving stated dividends in good and bad times.

There are several things a manager should do when establishing a dividend policy:

1. Determine the potential growth of future earnings.

2. Find out how sensitive earnings are during various phases of the business cycle.

3. Determine the yields and payouts of other firms in the industry.

These and other considerations provide a basis for setting a dividend policy. The wise course of action is to keep dividend payments fairly low, raising them only when there is an ample earnings cushion. Firms whose earnings are volatile might consider paying a low but steady dividend, accompanied by extra dividends when earnings and times are good. The ultimate goal is to assure the investor that dividend payments will be maintained. Any break in this dividend policy can damage the firm's image and the value of its stock.

YOU SHOULD REMEMBER

Financial managers must pay considerable attention to dividend policy because it influences both investor attitudes toward the firm's stock and the firm's cost of financing investments. The most acceptable policy is determined by judgment and comparison with policies adopted by other companies in the industry. Managers should try to maintain a stable and dependable dividend policy.

DECLARING AND PAYING CASH DIVIDENDS

Common stock dividends are usually paid on a quarterly basis. These cash payments can be high or low depending on different circumstances. Some companies are identified with low-dividend-paying industries and some companies pay high dividends because of the characteristics of their industries. Normally, companies with stable growing earnings pay higher dividends than cyclical companies.

Dividend policy is determined by the board of directors, who evaluate the financial position of the company and assess its investment needs. The board of directors review the prospects for future earnings and, based on these and other considerations, declare a stated amount of cash dividends per share. In addition to setting a date of record and an ex-dividend date, they establish the final payment date, as follows:

Record date. The date that establishes which stockholders of record will receive the dividend.

Ex-dividend date. Four business days prior to the record date. This date establishes who is entitled to the dividend. So that, if December 5th (Friday) is the record date then December 1st is the ex-dividend date. Anyone purchasing the stock before December 1st is entitled to the dividend.

Payment date. The date when the firm mails dividend checks to stockholders.

What happens when the stock goes ex-dividend? The price of the stock declines by the amount of dividend per share. For example, a company's stock is selling for $100 per share, and it declares a $1.00 dividend. On ex-dividend date, the price of the stock will decline to $99. Stockholders now have $99 worth of stock and $1.00 worth of dividend, and their total value is the same as it was before the dividend was paid.

The accounting adjustments include a decline in cash and a reduction in retained earnings on the balance sheet. To see how this works, let's suppose the board of directors establishes the following dividend schedule:

Scheduled Dates	
April 10	Dividend announcement (Cash dividend of $.80 per share.)
May 15	Record date.
July 15	Payment date (Checks are mailed out.)

If the firm has 100,000 shares outstanding, the total dividend paid to stockholders will be $80,000 (100,000 × $.80). The sequence of changes in the balance sheet are:

Before Dividend Announcement

Cash $200,000	Dividend payable:	0
	Retained earnings:	$1,000,000

Dividend Announcement (April 10)

Cash $200,000	Dividend payable:	$80,000
	Retained earnings:	$920,000

Payment of Dividend (July 15)

Cash $120,000	Dividend payable:	0
	Retained earnings:	$920,000

YOU SHOULD REMEMBER

The board of directors determines the dividend policy of the firm. After announcing the dividend, it establishes the record and payment dates. When dividends go ex, the price of the stock declines in value equal to the dividend per share paid by a firm. The balance sheet adjustments for cash dividends call for cash and retained earnings to decline by the amount of dividend paid out to stockholders.

• *NONCASH DIVIDEND PAYOUTS*

Instead of paying cash, firms may decide to make noncash payments to stockholders. Basically, these types of dividend payments include stock dividends and stock splits. What are these dividends like, and how do they influence the value of the firm?

STOCK DIVIDENDS

Stock dividends—that is, dividends in the form of additional shares—may be paid instead of cash dividends to keep stockholders happy when a firm wishes to conserve cash for investment purposes. As long as these stock dividends are small (about 2% to 5%), they do not have any major dilutive effects on earnings. Although stockholders may feel better psychologically when they receive more shares, they don't really gain anything when a stock dividend is declared because the price of the stock declines by the same percentage as the stock dividend.

Example: Calculating the Effects of Stock Dividends on the Value of Stock

PROBLEM   A stock can be purchased for $50 before a 5% stock dividend is declared.

    a. What is the effect on a parcel of 100 shares bought before the dividend was declared?

    b. What can a share of stock be bought for after the sale?

SOLUTION   **a.** Calculate the value of 100 shares before the stock dividend: $50 × 100 shares = $5,000. After the dividend is paid, the parcel contains 105 shares but is still worth $5,000 ($47.62 × 105).

    b. Use the information from the first part of the solution, and you see that the stock can be purchased for $47.62 ($5,000 ÷ 105) when the stock goes ex-dividend.

STOCK SPLITS

Stock splits are similar to stock dividends, but they usually involve the issuance of even more shares. When a firm states that it will split its stock 2-for-1, it is saying that a stockholder who owns 100 shares of the firm's stock will receive another 100 shares. A 3-for-2 split means that 50 additional shares would be issued to a stockholder who owns 100 shares.

• EFFECTS OF NONCASH DIVIDENDS ON THE BALANCE SHEET

Cash and stock dividends produce different changes in the balance sheet of a firm. *Cash dividends,* for instance, result in a reduction of cash in the balance sheet and a corresponding reduction in retained earnings.

The effects of *stock dividends* are illustrated in Table 10-1.

If the market price of the stock is $20, then the value of the new shares amounts to $2.0 million (100,000 shares × $20). This $2.0 million is divided into $500,000 going to common stock ($100,000 shares × $5 par value), and the remaining $1.5 million ($2,000,000 – $500,000) goes into capital surplus. The $2.0 million comes out of retained earnings, leaving $4,000,000 ($6,000,000 – $2,000,000) to retained earnings. Total stockholders' equity, however, remains unchanged.

Table 10–1   Balance Sheet Changes Resulting from a 10% Stock Dividend

	Stockholder's Equity	
	Before Stock Dividend	After Stock Dividend
1.0 million old shares at $5 par value	$ 5,000,000	
1.1 million new shares at $5 par value		$ 5,500,000
Paid-in capital surplus in excess of par*	$10,000,000	$11,500,000
Retained earnings	6,000,000	4,000,000
Total stockholder's equity	$21,000,000	$21,000,000

*Market value of a share of stock = $20.00. 100,000 additional shares (1,000,000 ×.10)

In the case of a stock split, the numbers in the capital account do not change. The only changes are a reduction of par value and an increase in the number of outstanding shares as seen in Table 10-2. Therefore a stock split of 2-for-1 does not change the total value of stockholders' equity. However, the par value is reduced from $5 to $2.50, and the number of outstanding shares doubles to 2.0 million.

Table 10–2   Balance Sheet Changes Resulting from 2-for-1 Stock Split

	Stockholder's Equity	
	Before Stock Split	After Stock Split
1.0 million old shares at $5 par value	$ 5,000,000	
2.0 million new shares at $2.50 par value		$ 5,000,000
Paid-in capital in excess of par value	$10,000,000	$10,000,000
Retained earnings	6,000,000	6,000,000
Total stockholder's equity	$21,000,000	$21,000,000

As indicated, these accounting changes do not change the ownership positions of stockholders in the firm. These payments do, however, allow the firm to keep cash. Also, stockholders are often happier owning more shares than fewer shares. For these reasons, and because of the greater number of shares after a split, the market's response to stock splits and stock dividends is usually favorable.

Some believe that noncash dividends increase the marketability of the stock and allow more investors to buy the stock. Sometimes, these types of dividends provide a signal. That signal might be favorable if it implies that the firm wishes to conserve cash so as to take advantage of growth opportunities. They also might be construed as an unfavorable event because the investors may interpret this action as the inability of the company to raise funds or the firm is strapped for cash.

INTERNAL AND EXTERNAL RESPONSES

In the case of small stock dividends, investors seem to ignore the dilution. As a result, the prices of shares tend to hold up well despite the stock dividend. In the case of stock splits, the anticipation of a dividend increase, for example, usually results in an improving market value of the shares before the stock split. However, if a higher dividend is not declared on the ex-dividend date, there is an unfavorable impact on the price of the shares.

Firms benefit from noncash payments for several reasons. Their shares are more widely distributed, which can facilitate future financing via rights or convertible issues. The firms retain funds internally for investment purposes. Also, although stock dividends or splits cost more to process than cash dividends, they ultimately tend to increase the supply of shares among more shareholders—and this can dampen stock price fluctuations in thin markets.

In the final analysis, remember that, although these forms of dividend payments provide some temporary flexibility, they are no substitute for a sound long-term dividend policy.

YOU SHOULD REMEMBER

If a firm can't pay dividends, there are noncash payments that can be temporarily substituted for cash dividends. Stock dividends change the balance sheet by increasing the total value of common stock par, raising the paid-in capital surplus, and reducing retained earnings. Stock splits reduce par value but do not affect the common equity part of the balance sheet. These non-cash dividends are sometimes used to widen the distribution of the stock ownership, but aside from the psychological benefits to investors, they do not change the value of the firm.

• LIMITATIONS ON DIVIDEND PAYMENTS

There are financial restrictions on the payment of dividends that vary from firm to firm, and there may be legal contractual limitations to the payout of dividends. The main purpose of these restrictions is to conserve liquidity and protect creditor claims in case of insolvency. Payment of high dividends can reduce the amount of funds available to creditors when a firm is liquidated.

FINANCIAL RESTRICTIONS

Financial restrictions are related to a firm's need to maintain a sound financial base, to avoid high costs of financing, and to limit the chances of **insolvency**. The fact that a firm generates good profits does not necessarily mean that it has ready cash to pay dividends to stockholders. Therefore, when a firm considers a dividend policy, it must take into account the investments required to achieve its targeted growth in earnings. Growing firms require substantial amounts of funds. They cannot continually go to the market to generate these funds because the marginal cost of capital will increase. The best course of action is to control the dividend payout in order to minimize external financing.

Dividend payments must also take a back seat to liquidity considerations. If a firm is short of cash and has inadequate net working capital, it may have problems covering its short-term liabilities. Creditors are not easy to get along with when they don't get paid on time. Therefore, prudent managers must make sure—before they make a dividend commitment—that cash and marketable securities are available to cover bills coming due. Financial managers must be concerned with the future potential payment of dividends. Their plans should include projections of earnings so they can establish a long-term policy of stable dividend payments. Remember: companies that maintain stable and steadily growing dividends can expect a stockholder following and a favorable market response.

Stockholders study a firm's past record of dividend payments. Stable and gradually increasing dividends raise investor confidence, reduce uncertainty, and help maintain a high valuation for a firm's stock.

LEGAL RESTRICTIONS

External legal commitments must also be taken into account when the firm develops a dividend policy. In most states, the **capital impairment rule** limits the payment of cash dividends drawn from capital stock or from the par value of the firm. These restrictions are designed to ensure that there is ample equity to protect the claims of creditors.

Dividend payment is, by the same token, restricted to the total of a firm's present and past earnings. Again, the goal is to protect creditors in case of insolvency or liquidation. When a firm cannot meet its liabilities, the law prohibits the firm from paying cash dividends. Otherwise, creditors would suffer and could sue the firm to recover these dividends.

The Internal Revenue Service (IRS) enters the picture when firms accumulate excess earnings. It looks on this strategy as a ploy to avoid paying ordinary income taxes on dividends. Although the value of a firm's shares may increase because of this earnings accumulation, its stockholders will not pay capital gains taxes until they sell their shares. The IRS frowns on this policy, and will investigate a firm which accumulates excessive earnings in the form of cash and marketable securities. It will also penalize such a firm unless it pays out more dividends.

CONTRACTUAL RESTRICTIONS

In addition to these legal constraints on dividends, there are also **contractual obligations** that restrict the payment of dividends. For example, when bonds are issued, the firm may have to promise not to pay dividends if the current ratio, the interest coverage, or other ratios fall below certain levels. Other contracts can require that the amount of dividends paid be limited to a percentage of earnings.

These contractual restraints exist to protect creditors. Any disregard of these obligations can provide grounds for immediate repayment of loans to creditors.

YOU SHOULD REMEMBER

Many states impose restrictions on the payment of dividends to protect the claims of creditors. Creditors are lenders whose positions are protected by contractual promises or covenants in loan agreements to ensure repayment of the loans. There are also financial restrictions that a firm may impose on itself in order to hold the costs of financing as low as possible, to induce lenders to supply more funds, and to limit the chances of insolvency. These self-imposed restrictions ensure readily available sources of external financing. All these constraints on dividends are designed to maintain the firm's ability to meet its fixed financial obligations.

DIVIDEND POLICY AND THE PRICE OF STOCKS

There are those who claim that the value of a firm is unaffected by dividends or changes in dividend policy. Modigliani and Miller (MM) are the leading proponents of this theory. It should be pointed out that MM present a theoretical argument based on the assumption of perfect capital markets and no taxes. Obviously, they realize that taxes and other factors are real-world conditions that can make dividends an important aspect of valuation. Their argument is important, however, in that it produces a fruitful dialogue on an important subject.

Others feel that dividend policy does matter, and that it has an important effect on stock valuation. Myron Gordon was one of the well-known academicians who supported this thesis. As always, different theories and interpretations provide a better basis for understanding the process of valuation.

DIVIDENDS ARE NOT IMPORTANT?

Those who claim that dividends are not relevant to stock valuation argue that dividends do not enter into a firm's decision to invest, and do not influence the outcome of earnings generated from investment strategies. Their contention is that dividends are a residual payment after all investment decisions have been made. Because earnings and the cost of issuing common stock do not change when dividend policy changes, it can be said that the value of the firm does not change. Also, it is assumed that the firm should reinvest all retained earnings, as long as the return is at least equal to or higher than any return the stockholders can get in the market.

At the foundation of their theory, MM postulated that a condition of equilibrium existed between returns from reinvested earnings and the marginal cost of capital ($K_e = MCC$). As long as $K_e > MCC$, it would be inappropriate for a firm to pay dividends mainly because this payment would prevent it from maximizing its value and the wealth of the stockholders. Why? Because when returns from reinvested earnings exceed MCC, net present value is positive. As long as NPV is positive, paying dividends would preclude the firm from maximizing the value of its stock.

Also, MM argue that when the capital gains tax rate is lower than ordinary tax rates, stockholders prefer allowing the stock to appreciate in value as opposed to receiving cash dividends (which are subject to higher taxes).

In their proof, Modigliani and Miller neutralize the influence of dividends on stock valuation by assuming that, if dividends are included in the valuation of a firm, they can easily be offset by issuing more stock or debt to cover the exact value of these dividends, $D(t)$. In a simplified form, the equation for the value of a firm V_f under the MM model (assuming no debt and taxes) is

$$V_f = \frac{D(t) + EBIT_t - \text{Value of newly issued shares}}{\text{Discount rate } (K_0)}$$

Since dividends minus the value of newly issued shares is equal to zero, these two factors drop out of the equation. The value of the firm is therefore determined by investments and the discounted earnings they generate:

$$V_f = \frac{EBIT_t}{K_0}$$

This highly sophisticated and theoretical presentation by MM is designed to show that the firm's decision-making process is based mainly on the evaluation of the relative merits of investments and their profitability. Dividends are a separate policy and do not enter into this decision because they are a derivative of these factors. In neutralizing the role of dividends, MM are merely demonstrating that in the real world the valuation process involves complex strategies. By presenting the theory in this manner, MM pave the way for understanding more clearly the valuation-decision process.

YOU SHOULD REMEMBER

The importance of dividends in the determination of the value of a firm seems to have diminished in the 1990s. Many companies do not pay dividends or generate earnings. We need a new set of rules. Our alternative is to capitalize free cash flows. What we have to do is to rethink our standard valuation approaches and modify them to make them fit the new developments taking place in the market.

DIVIDENDS ARE IMPORTANT?

Another group of academicians says that dividends *do* count in determining the value of a firm. They claim that, if you look at the real world, dividends are important to stockholders, and since that is the case, they play a role in the valuation process.

Supporters of this position indicate that there are three main reasons why investors prefer dividends and why the value of the firm is affected by dividend payments.

First, there is the *"bird in hand"* concept. Current cash dividends are worth more than future cash derived from reinvesting retained earnings. When a firm pays cash dividends, it reduces investor uncertainty. This lowers risk, which, in turn, lowers the discount rate (K_s). In other words, the discount rate assigned to current dividends $(K_{dividends})$ is lower than the discount rate assigned to future retained earnings $(K_{retained\ earnings})$:

$$K_{dividends} < K_{retained\ earnings}$$

If the value of a stock is determined by discounting the future stream of returns, the lower discount rate assigned to dividends will influence the value of shares favorably.

Second, the *informational content* is another important factor that makes dividends relevant in stock valuation. By paying dividends, a firm signals to investors that it expects to generate the earnings to pay these dividends in the future. Conversely, when a firm *stops* paying dividends, it is letting investors know that something is wrong.

Any alteration in dividend policy will influence investors' attitudes toward a firm, and this will affect the market price of its stock. The important thing is to know why this change occurred. Sometimes a firm reduces dividends to maintain its liquidity base, and it may convince investors that the reinvested earnings will produce substantially higher dividends in the long run. If investors are convinced that this represents a good deal, the market value of the shares of the firm may remain unchanged or even increase.

Furthermore, some investors cannot interpret changes in earnings as easily as changes in dividends. They react to dividend changes more easily than to changes in earnings because of lack of financial sophistication or inability to understand how earnings are generated. That part of the decision-making process is left to security analysts. Ordinary investors want to know whether dividends will be paid and whether the firm is doing well. The signals given by the firm's dividend policy produce investor reactions, which lead to changes in valuation.

Third, the *clientele effect* implies that some investors need or prefer current income to future income. This is especially true of low- or moderate- income investors, who are less concerned with the higher returns that may be paid at some future date. This group of dividend followers gravitates toward stocks that pay steady dividends and offer high dividend yields. They search for stocks that provide a return close to that of other assets. Consequently, these stockholders become apprehensive when a company reduces its dividend, and are likely to dispose of their stock, thereby adversely affecting its value.

Let us remind ourselves that the current dividends are taxed when received. Capital gains may be a better alternative because the tax burden can be deferred until the stock is sold. Also, once dividends are paid, the cash is no longer available to the firm should new investment opportunities emerge. Without this cash, the firm might have to engage in costlier external financing. Not to be ignored is the tax savings advantage gained from repurchasing stock in lieu of paying dividends. However, the latest tax code has reduced the maximum tax rate on qualified dividends to 15% making dividends more attractive than in the past. Supporters of both the irrelevance and the relevance theses have something to contribute toward our understanding of the investment and valuation process. The answer probably lies between these two extreme views.

A COMPROMISE POSITION

In the world of theory, it is possible to establish a controlled environment and to present a good case in support of a given position. Theoretically, the decision to invest and to make plans to achieve a certain growth in earnings is independent of dividend policy. After all, dividend policy takes place after the earnings are generated and is a residual decision. The payment of dividends, therefore, should not affect the value of a firm. Realistically, however, investors prefer current gains or dividend income. As long as the potential return that a firm makes available to stockholders is greater than the returns they can receive from outside sources, it is logical to reinvest the earnings. Since there are no flotation costs associated with reinvested earnings, the cost of these funds is lower than the cost of issuing new stock.

But it is not always advantageous for investors to have a firm reinvest all retained earnings. In periods of high inflation, investors may receive a higher return from reinvesting cash dividends in assets other than in the firm in question. Also, during some periods of the business cycle it may be advantageous to pay dividends and finance investments with low-cost debt than by issuing common stock. Hence the argument for irrelevancy does not apply in all cases.

Enough evidence has been presented to indicate that dividends play a role in determining the value of a firm. Analysts and investors do pay a great deal of attention to the way firms invest and generate earnings, but the market also takes into account dividend signals issued by the firm. In the real world, some investors prefer current income and are less concerned with future income. They prefer stocks that pay steadily rising dividends and stocks that provide a good yield. Dividends supply information on the future course of the firm and play a role in the final valuation of the firm. Generally speaking, you should recognize that investment decisions may be completely independent of dividend policy. However, both the independent investment and dividend decisions influence the value of stocks.

YOU SHOULD REMEMBER

Some academicians say dividends are irrelevant, and others say they are relevant, to stock valuations. It all depends on one's interpretation. Some investors prefer the current income of dividends, while others prefer the future income of reinvested earnings. The information value and preference for current income make dividends attractive to some investors, and this in turn influences the value of stocks.

• THE NET RESIDUAL APPROACH

Assuming that all firms seek to achieve an optimal capital structure at the lowest cost of capital, their dividend policies should be influenced by these considerations. This means that dividends should be paid only after all profitable investment opportunities have been undertaken. In adopting a net residual approach to dividend policy, a firm should evaluate how its cost of capital will change as a result of new financing. It should compare this to the returns (*IRRs*) obtained from different projects. Any funds left over can be used to pay dividends. Under these circumstances, the goal is to achieve the lowest cost of capital, which, in turn, will maximize the value of the firm.

$$\frac{\text{Highest } EBIT}{\text{Lowest discount rate}} = \text{Maximum value of firm}$$

Given this scenario, those who support the **net residual principle** claim that a firm should reinvest internally generated funds and not pay dividends, as long as there are profitable opportunities for such investment. Their assumption is that the firm maximizes its value when it has achieved an optimal capital structure. This optimal financing mix should be maintained. To do so, the firm first draws on its retained earnings. Once these are used up (and assuming that there are additional profitable investment opportunities because $IRR>MCC$), then it will have to engage in external financing.

As Figure 10-1 shows, a firm should continue to finance and invest available funds as long as the internal rate of return (IRR) from these investments exceeds its marginal cost of capital (MCC). Under these circumstances, it should not pay dividends because the net present values generated are positive.

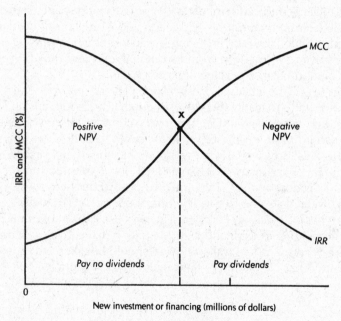

Figure 10-1 Residual Dividend Policy and the Relationship Between *IRR* and *MCC* Curves

At point x, when $IRR = MCC$, financing and investments should cease. Why? Because beyond point x, $IRR < MCC$ and net present value turns negative. Therefore, to the right of point x, any residual funds should become available for the payment of dividends to stockholders.

Since the firm's goal is to maintain the present capital structure, it will continue to issue debt and stock in the same proportion as its present mix. Therefore, if the firm's optimal capital structure is 30% stock and 70% debt, and it has profitable (*NPV* is positive) opportunities amounting to $10 million, the financing will be divided into $3 million worth of stock and $7 million worth of debt. Because dividends are paid to stockholders, these funds should come from surplus funds available to the firm or from retained earnings and not from externally generated (borrowed) funds. Once retained earnings are exhausted, no dividends should be paid if this forces the firm to engage in additional equity financing. Only that part of profitable investment originating from new stock issue is important in the decision either to pay or not to pay dividends.

An example should help to clarify this point. Assume an optimal capital structure of 30% common stock, 70% debt, and retained earnings equal to $4 million. Given profitable investment opportunities of $10 million, new financing will be split into $3 million for equity financing and $7 million for debt. Since there are $4 million in retained earnings, then $1 million ($4 million–$3 million) is the amount of dividends that can be paid to stockholders. If retained earnings were only $3 million and $1 million of dividends were declared, additional equity financing would be required, causing the capital structure mix to move away from its optimal level and thus preventing the firm from maximizing the value of its stock.

Advocates of the residual thesis claim that the rate of return (K_s) that investors require to justify their investment in a stock remains unaffected by a firm's dividend policy. In fact, you have seen that the firm financed more funds than it required, and as a result it could have done as well with less. What this illustrates is that what works well in theory may not work well in practice. There are many other considerations that enter into the determination of dividend policy. The firm's responsiveness to investor attitudes toward dividends is one factor. The return offered by competing assets and similar types of stocks is another. The process is more complicated than simply advocating a residual policy. The fact remains that, in actuality, dividends play a role in stock valuation and should be taken into consideration along with other factors in the final analysis of stock pricing.

YOU SHOULD REMEMBER

In the final analysis, some dividend policies are more effective than others. Financial managers should aim for a stable dividend policy to reduce uncertainty. It should be conservative enough to ensure steady payments without periodic interruptions. Companies whose earnings are highly cyclical and volatile should institute a low dividend payment policy, accompanied by extras when earnings and economic conditions are favorable.

The main goal is to set up a dividend policy that will be accepted by investors as being sound, that will provide them with reasonable returns, and that will result in the highest possible price for the stock of a firm.

• *FREE CASH FLOW APPROACH TO VALUATION*

The fact remains that according to Modigliani-Miller dividends do not play a role in the valuation of a firm. Also, many investors prefer capital gains instead of dividends. A considerable number of firms do not pay dividends. These firms find it advantageous to put earnings to better use by repurchasing their stock in anticipation of receiving higher returns from future capital gains. Or, they reallocate this extra cash to mergers and other profitable investment opportunities. Aware of these changes, corporations are less eager to pay dividends.

The search for other approaches to calculate the value of the firm stem from the several weaknesses inherent in the dividend model. One of them is the assumption that retained earnings are the only source of financing investments. Therefore, the dividend model makes no allowance for external equity and debt financing as well as the effects of a changing capital structure on valuation.

An alternative approach to estimate the value of the firm calls for calculating the present value of cash flows minus new investments and debt. The cash flows consist of the following components:

$$\text{Free cash flows} = EBIT\,(1 - T) + Dep(T) + Ts - New\ I$$

The values of the terms in the above equation are assumed as follows:

		Values
EBIT	= earnings before taxes	$15,000,000
T	= tax rate	.40
Dep	= depreciation	$2,000,000
Ts	= tax shield	$200,000
New I	= new investment	$3,000,000

Note, because the firm has outstanding debt, a tax shield or tax savings arises from the deductibility of interest expense.

Compute the free cash flow of this firm.

Free CF = $15,000,000 (1 – .40) + $2,000,000 (.4) + $200,000 – $3,000,000 = $7,000,000

Suppose we assume the firm's debt amounts to $1.0 million, its discount rate is 15%, and the cash flows are expected to grow at 5% annually. The present value of future free cash flows, based on the above parameters is:

$$PV \text{ of Free Cash Flows } (V_f) = \frac{\text{Free } CF\,(1+G)'}{K-G} = \frac{\$7,000,000\,(1.05)'}{.15-.05} = \$73,500$$

The firm is valued at $73.5 million. However, since debt must be repaid the value of the firm's equity is $(V_f - D)$ or $73,500,000 – $1,000,000 = $72,500,000.

The **free cash flow** method does not require dividends to calculate the value of the firm; it lends itself more easily to the determination of the value of some firms. Additionally, the free cash flow model is more flexible. It adjusts for debt and the benefits of the resulting tax shield.

• EARNINGS APPROACH TO STOCK VALUATION

Earlier in this book, we presented the dividend growth model as a method to determine the price of a stock. That model presupposes that the firm pays dividends. Some firms don't pay dividends. In these cases, the dividend model does not apply. Investors are willing to forego current dividends as long as they can visualize that the firm's decision to reinvest earnings will produce high dividends in the future. In addition, investors will buy or hold non–dividend–paying stocks because they expect high returns from the capital gains generated by the growth opportunities available to a firm. A firm's decision to reinvest earnings is justified because investments in growth opportunities are anticipated to give rise to a higher rate of return than the firm's required rate of return $(ROE > K)$.

For a firm that has growth opportunities the *P/E* equation takes on the following form

$$P/E = 1/K + NPVGO/EPS + QR$$

where K = the discount rate
$NPVGO$ = the profitability of growth opportunities
EPS = earnings per share
P/E = price earnings ratio
QR = rank that measures quality of management and balance sheet strength

As indicated in the above equation, *P/E* is determined by three factors: (1) quality of the balance sheet and management, (2) risk, and (3) growth opportunities. In other words, *P/E* is affected by the soundness of a firm's capital structure, the strength of its balance sheet, and the quality of its management. Companies with good capital structures, conservative accounting practices, and excellent management skills will be assigned a higher *P/E* than firms lacking these financial strengths. Although the market recognizes the importance of these quality differences when assigning *P/E* multiples, investors have trouble quantifying them. One way to get around this problem is to assign ranks to measure the quality factors. For argument sake, a rank of 4 would be assigned to a firm with the best financial and management qualities and a rank of 2 or less is assigned to an average or below average quality firm. From the above equation, we notice that the *P/E* will increase or decrease depending on the assigned rank.

Risk is negatively related to *P/E*, and it appears in the equation as $1/K$, which means that the riskier the firm is, the lower the *P/E* will be and vice versa. We may ask: Why do some high-risk Internet stocks claim such high *P/Es*? The answer is: Investors are willing to de-emphasize risk and focus attention on the prospects for growth opportunities as the dominant factor affecting a *P/E* multiple.

We do not want to minimize the importance of risk and the quality factors in the determination of the current **level** of *P/E* valuation, but because these two factors are expected to remain fairly stable over the short run, they are unlikely to produce any **change** in the *P/E* multiple of a firm. As a result, we concentrate our attention on growth opportunities as the pivotal factor affecting future **changes** in *P/E*. If so, let's set aside risk and quality and proceed to measure growth by employing the following formula:

$$g = \text{Retention ratio} \times ROE$$

where g = growth of earnings
Retention ratio = 1 – Payout ratio
ROE = return on equity

Suppose the *ROE* of the firm is 10%. Since we are analyzing a non-dividend paying firm the retention ratio is 1.0. Therefore, the firm's growth rate is equal to

$$g = 1.0 \times 0.10 = 0.10 \text{ or } 10\%$$

Having established that *ROE* = *g*, let's proceed to estimate *ROE* as it reflects new growth opportunities. One approach is to study the past record of companies that have similar quality and risk characteristics as the firm being analyzed, which we shall refer to hereafter as the firm or stock A. Let's say we discover that when the *ROE* of these companies rose 3 points in response to new investment opportunities, the *P/E* of these companies increased 5 points. If the current *P/E* of our firm is 10 times and the ROE is 10%, then based on new growth opportunities its growth rate (*ROE*) should rise to 13% and its *P/E* can be expected to increase to 15 times earnings.

These upgrades in the growth rate and *P/E* assume no uncertainty. But it is a well-known fact that any investment or research effort is subject to some degree of uncertainty. In the case of stock A, we have assumed that the new growth opportunities depend on the successful development of two major products two years from now. The company's research department informs its CEO that there is a 70% chance of the successful development of these two products. This calls for calculating a probable *P/E* based on the following equation.

$$\text{Probable } P/E = \left(\begin{matrix} \text{Probability of} \\ \text{success} \end{matrix} \right) (P/E) + \left(\begin{matrix} 1 - \text{Probability of} \\ \text{success} \end{matrix} \right) (P/E)$$

Substituting the appropriate figures into the above equation, the probable *P/E* is estimated to be

$$\text{Probable } P/E = (0.70)(15) + (0.30)(10) = 13.5 \text{ or } 14 \text{ times earnings}$$

In order to ascertain (check) whether the above estimates are reasonable, we should explore a different way to calculate growth and *P/E*. For this purpose we start with the premise that the firm knows its own ROE and growth rate which is 10 percent. Then the finance department should be asked to extrapolate the extent to which the two new products will impact the firm's growth rate (*ROE*). Presumably, their findings indicate that the firm's growth rate or *ROE* is expected to increase from 10% to 13% in response to the introduction of the two new products. If so, search for publicly traded companies that are growing at 13% whose quality and risk features are similar to stock A. Find out their *P/E* multiples. Let's assume we discover that other companies with an earnings growth rate of 13 have *P/Es* of about 15 times earnings. Because the two approaches come up with similar results (otherwise it may be necessary to reconcile any differences), we can proceed to estimate the *EPS* and stock prices over the next 5 years. Before we do that, let's establish that last year the company reported the following results.

	Last Year's Results
EPS	$5.00
Growth rate	10%
P/E	10 times earnings
Stock price	$50.00

Suppose the firm decides to announce to the public that two major products are likely to reach market by the beginning of year two. The immediate reaction of the stock market would be to discount this favorable news by raising last year's *P/E* of 10 times to 14 times. The growth rate of *EPS* will remain at 10% over the next 2 years because the new products will still be in the development stage, hence, will not make any contribution to earnings. At the beginning of year 2 and thereafter, earnings and stock prices will depend on the outcome of research and the marketing of the two products. Assume we reached the beginning of year 2 and the research efforts prove successful. In that case, the *P/E* should rise to 15 times, and the growth rate can be expected to increase to 13% annually 2 years thereafter.

To demonstrate the versatility of the earnings approach, let's consider the fact that a high rate of growth is unsustainable for any length of time. After a couple of years, the rate of growth is likely to slow down because of increasing competition and market demand saturation. We therefore assume that by the fifth year the firm's growth rate can be expected to decline to 12% accompanied by a market downgrade of the *P/E* from 15 times earnings to 14 times. These modifications appear in the fifth year as shown in Table 10-3.

Given the above information, we can go ahead and estimate *EPS*, stock prices, and expected returns (capital appreciation) for the next 5 years (see Table 10-3).

Table 10–3   Estimating EPS and Stock Prices for Stock A

	0*	0**	1	2	3	4	5
				Years			
Growth rate, g	10%	10%	10%	13%	13%	13%	12%
EPS, (EPS × g) ($)	5.50	5.50	6.05	6.84	7.73	8.73	9.78
P/E	10	14	14	15	15	15	14
Stock prices (SP), EPS × P/E ($)	55	77	85	103	116	131	137
Expected returns $(SP_t/SP_{t-1}) - 100$			10.4%	21.2%	12.6%	12.9%	4.6%
Present values of expected returns discounted at 10%			9.5%	17.5%	9.5%	8.8%	2.9%

* Current year values before announcement.
** Current year values after announcement (stock prices are rounded-off).

This earnings approach to stock valuation provides important guidelines to a corporate manager. The *EPS* estimates in Table 10-3 can be translated into equivalent cash flows by employing (*EPS* × Outstanding shares). These earnings estimates are important to a manager who may want to find out how much cash will be available to finance new growth opportunities. Stock price estimates should help a manager to gauge the firm's ability to finance future investments by issuing common stock. Moreover, the earnings approach permits the simulation of various outcomes and gives a manager time to work up different contingency plans.

Remember, however, that the results calculated in Table 10-3 depend on several assumptions. Change the assumptions, and you change the results. For example, if at the beginning of year 2 it is discovered that the research effort failed, the growth rate would remain at 10%, the *P/E* would decline from 14 times to 10 times, and the subsequent stream of earnings and stock prices would be lower than the ones in Table 10-3.

Investors will find this approach useful for comparing the relative investment merits of different stocks. The analysis required to make this comparison possible entails estimating the stream of future stock prices for each stock being evaluated by following the same procedures employed in Table 10-3. After calculating the yearly rates of expected returns $[(SP_t/SP_{t-1}) - 100]$ for each stock, they are discounted by the appropriate risk-adjusted discount rate that applies to each stock. Before we present the results of our analysis, you should recall that the calculations in Table 10-3 are for stock A. Also, stock A's annual average return of 9.6%, which appears in Table 10-4, is equal to the sum total of the present value figures that appear in the last row of Table 10-3 divided by 5 years or (48.2%/5). Table 10-4 shows the risk-adjusted expected rates of return for stocks A, B, C, D, and E and their corresponding discount rates.

Table 10–4 Comparison of the Present Values
of the Expected Returns of Five Stocks

Expected Stocks	Discount Rates (%)	Present Values of Rates of Return (%)*
A	10	9.6
B	8	11.0
C	9	8.0
D	13	14.0
E	10	6.8

* Five-year average annual rates of return (Σ PVs% /5).

As Table 10-4 indicates, stock D is the best investment among the five stocks despite its high discount rate. Stocks A and E have the same discount rate, but stock A is a better value than stock E because of its superior risk adjusted rates of return Now, even if we pretended that stocks B and C yielded the same stream of stock prices and expected returns, stock B is a better value because of its lower discount rate. Obviously, stock E is the least attractive investment of any of the other stocks.We have just demonstrated how the earnings approach allows investors to compare the relative invest-ment merits of different stocks. In summary, the earnings approach offers a flexible way to determine stock prices. It not only calculates the current value of a stock ($P/E \times EPS$), but it also permits one to explore several other applications useful for making investment decisions.

Eventually superior investment opportunities tend to diminish as a firm grows in size and reaches some degree of maturation. *ROE* will gravitate toward the firm's required rate of return. At some point, accumulated earn-ings become available for dividend payment. It is at this juncture that the dividend model can be applied to calculate the value of a stock.

STOCK REPURCHASES

• *WHY BUY BACK STOCK?*

Some corporations, such as IBM and General Electric, amass a great deal of excess cash. The question is how to invest these funds profitably. The standard criterion is to put this cash into those projects that will yield the highest net present value. Sometimes there are a number of projects that can be implemented with available excess cash. Merging with other firms may be considered but it is a move that requires careful planning. Investing funds in marketable securities at relatively low returns is only a short-term outlet for idle funds. After weighing these and other options, a corporation may find the buyback of stock an attractive option. There are several reasons for choosing this option.

First, buying one's own shares makes stock available to provide employees with stock options. Some stock must be set aside for employee stock pension plans. Third, faced by the threat of an unwanted takeover by other firms, a company repurchases some of its stock to gain greater control over its voting power.

Perhaps a more important consideration in stock repurchases is the knowledge of the future potential growth and opportunities, which are likely to be reflected in substantially higher earnings and appreciation in the price of the firm's stock. After examining its aggregate outlook, the firm may discover that there are favorable opportunities for capital appreciation accruing to repurchased stock that make this option attractive. Given the efficient market, managers know that a repurchase plan will be scrutinized by the investment community. Properly disseminated information justifying the plan will help condition investors to maintain a favorable outlook. The implication is that the firm considers its shares undervalued and wishes to take advantage of this opportunity.

Obviously, there must be substance behind the company's plans. At times a repurchase strategy backfires because Wall Street interprets it as a last resort when no other good investment opportunities are available. In this case, the repurchased stock may not produce the desired effects.

ACCOUNTING TREATMENT

Stock repurchases reduce the excess cash and equity value of the firm. The shares purchased are set aside as treasury stock. The following table shows what happens to the balance sheet of a firm having set aside $1.0 million in cash to repurchase stock.

Table 10–5 Balance Sheet ($Mil)

Before Repurchased Assets		Liabilities	
Cash	5.0	Debt	2.0
Other assets	10.0	Equity	13.0
Total assets	15.0		15.0
After Repurchased Assets*		Liabilities	
Cash	4.0	Debt	2.0
Other assets	10.0	Equity	12.0
Total assets	14.0		14.0

* If the price of stock is $10, then 100,000 shares will wind up as treasury stock ($1,000,000 divided by $10).

EFFECTS OF REPURCHASES ON EARNINGS AND DIVIDENDS

As indicated above, when a firm repurchases stock, the number of outstanding shares declines and the earnings per share increases. This can be illustrated below assuming Company A reports the following financial figures:

Earnings after taxes	$2,000,000
Number of shares outstanding	1,000,000
Earnings per share	$2.00
Dividend per share	$1.00
Amount of dividend paid	$1,000,000
Price of stock per share	$20.00
Funds for repurchasing stock	$1,000,000

At a market price of $20 per share, Company A can repurchase 50,000 shares ($1,000,000 divided by $20).

If you recall, we indicated that Company A's dividend is $1.00 per share, totaling $1,000,000. The company deals with this situation in several ways. It can continue to pay the $1,000,000 in dividends but the benefit to stockholders would be an increase of 5% in the dividend per share from $1.00 to $1.05 ($1,000,000 divided by 950,000). Stockholders who previously owned 100 shares received $100 in dividends, and now they will receive $105. Should the company decide to keep the dividend per share unchanged, owners of 100 shares of stock would still receive $100 as before but the company retains $50,000 cash it previously paid out in dividends.

What has occurred is a diminution in the supply of shares. If investors should decide to purchase the same dollar amounts as before (especially in the case of dollar averaging plans), upward pressure on the price of the stock may be occasioned by the smaller supply of stock.

Instead of repurchasing stock, a firm can opt to distribute some of the cash allocated for this purpose to the payment of higher dividends, which are subject to ordinary tax rates. By repurchasing stock and foregoing the payment of higher dollar amount dividends, the existing shareholders can defer paying taxes. Should they decide to sell the stock at some future date, they will be taxed at the lower capital gains tax rates.

One last effect bears mentioning. The above balance sheet example indicated that the value of the firm's equity declines when a repurchase plan reaches completion. Consequently, the capital structure of the firm changes and the debt-to-equity ratio increases. Normally the amounts involved are not significant enough to make a big difference. However, a great deal depends on the existing D/E ratio. If it is too high to start with, say relative to its industry and competitors, a further rise in this ratio could adversely impact the cost of capital of the firm. Lenders might construe this move as an increase in risk.

REPURCHASE PROCEDURE

When a company contemplates a repurchase of stock, it is obligated to notify shareholders how it intends to dispose of the additional shares it purchases, either set them aside as treasury stock, for merger purposes, or for stock options. Once the plan is approved by the board of directors, the actual purchase of stock can be accomplished in several ways.

One method is by direct market purchase of the stock. Unfortunately, this approach could put upward pressure on the price of the stock. Since purchases are done over a period of time, the firm may have to buy stock at higher and higher prices.

Another repurchasing technique involves a tender offer. The company announces to brokers and advertises its intentions by mail, newspaper, or perhaps via the Internet. Usually, the selling price per share offered is higher than the prevailing market price. A negotiated deal can be arranged by agreement between the company and other large financial institutions at some mutually agreed price.

In summary, repurchases of stock are increasing especially by large corporations. This trend will probably continue as long as the market maintains its upward momentum. The repurchase plans of companies like IBM and General Electric have proven to be quite lucrative based on the outstanding market performance of the stock of these companies.

YOU SHOULD REMEMBER

Repurchases of stock may be justified if the returns from the expected capital gains exceed the returns from other investments. Repurchases are used to implement stock and other options. When a stock is repurchased, the number of outstanding shares declines and cash and equity also decline from their previous levels. In repurchasing stock, a firm can save cash by paying the same total dividend per share because the number of outstanding shares have declined.

KNOW THE CONCEPTS

DO YOU KNOW THE BASICS?

1. Why are dividends important to investors?
2. Does dividend policy play a role in the investment decision and the valuation process? Explain your answer.

3. From the firm's point of view, what kind of dividend policy is best, and why?

4. What changes occur in the capital account when a stock is split? When a stock dividend is paid?

5. Name two legal restrictions associated with the payment of dividends.

6. What are some contractual agreements with creditors, and in what way can they prevent a firm from adopting the most favorable dividend policy?

7. What tax advantage is available to investors who permit a firm to *reinvest* earnings, rather than pay them out to stockholders? (Assume the tax rate on capital gains is lower than the tax rate on dividends.)

8. How do Modigliani and Miller explain the irrelevance of dividends in stock valuation?

9. Give three reasons why dividends may be relevant to stock valuation.

10. Explain how the residual dividend policy works.

11. What kind of dividend policy is the best one for a firm?

12. Define the ex-dividend and record dates.

13. What happens on the balance sheet to cash and retained earnings on dividend payment date?

14. Define free cash flow and explain why we need to rethink the way we should value a firm.

15. How does the earnings approach calculate the estimated prices of a stock?

16. Why do investors buy and want to own non-dividend–paying stocks?

TERMS FOR STUDY

capital impairment rule
contractual obligations
dividend
price
dividend yield
ex-dividend date
free cash flow
insolvency
net residual principle

par value
payment date
payout ratio
price/earnings ratio
record date
stock dividend
stock repurchase
stock split

PRACTICAL APPLICATION

COMPUTATIONAL PROBLEMS

1. Firm A's dividend payment is $7, and the price of its stock is $40. Compute its dividend yield. If Firm B's dividend yield is 10%, discuss what this difference in yield means.

2. Calculate the dividend payout ratio of a firm with earnings of $10 per share and a dividend payment of $3 per share. And, what is the *P/E* of this firm if it has a discount rate of 15% and a growth rate of 9%?

3. A firm declares a 2-for-1 stock split. Its stock before the split is selling at $50 and has a par value of $10. Indicate the price of the stock and its par value after the split takes place.

4. Firm A reported the following figures on its balance sheet:

	Millions of Dollars
Common stock shares outstanding (5.0 million at $10 par value)	50
Paid-in capital surplus in excess of par	140
Retained earnings	100

Indicate what changes would occur to the above figures if the firm paid a 20% stock dividend and the value of its stock is $40.

5. Using the Myron Gordon dividend model, compute the value of Company X's stock if its earnings grew from $2.00 to $4.00 per share in the past 9 years, the payout ratio is 50%, and the discount rate is 15%. Remember to add 1 year's growth to current dividends.

6. The optimal capital structure of a firm is 35% equity and 65% debt. Retained earnings are $6 million, and shares outstanding equal 100,000. This firm follows the net residual principle in paying dividends to stockholders. Assuming it has a total of $15 million in new profitable investments forthcoming, what is the maximum amount of dividend per share the firm will pay to common stockholders?

7. You are supplied with the following information:

EAT	$5,000,000
Number of shares outstanding	2,000,000
DPS	$1.00
Price of stock	$40
Funds for repurchase	$2,000,000

(a) Calculate the total dividends paid before the repurchase.

(b) How many new shares will be outstanding after the repurchase?

(c) How does the EPS change?

(d) What changes will occur in the balance sheet?

(e) Calculate the cash saved if the firm pays the same dividend per share as before.

8. A firm's financial statements indicate the following:

	Last Year
Equity	$1,500,000
Net income	$200,000
Shares outstanding	100,000
Stock price	$20

On January 1, the firm was licensed to import a new cancer drug that was just developed by a foreign company. Its current *P/E* is 10 times earnings. The firm estimates that the new drug will raise its *P/E* four points and add three points to its *ROE*. What is the firm's stock worth?

9. ABC Company has $1,000,000 in internally generated funds (net income). There are new projects worth $2,000,000 (with positive Net Present Value (*NPV*s)) that have been approved for funding. Forty percent (40%) of the total new projects are required to be financed through internally generated funds (net income). There are 1 million shares of stock outstanding.

Compute the earnings per share (EPS), and compute the dividend per share (DPS) based on these limited data.

ANSWERS

KNOW THE CONCEPTS

1. Dividends are important because they signal to investors the firm's ability to generate income. They serve as a basis for calculating the value of stocks and are used also to calculate the returns of stocks.

2. Investment decisions are independent of a policy to pay dividends. However, the payment of dividends can indirectly influence external financing plans and the cost of capital. In this way, dividends play a role in the decision process of the firm. Dividend is one of the main factors in the dividend valuation model that determines the price of a stock and its discount rate.

3. The best dividend policy is one that attracts investors and maximizes the value of a firm's stock. The main thing is to apply a policy that leads to the payment of stable dividends and that investors will interpret as less risky than volatile dividend payments.

4. A stock split does not change the capital structure of the firm. The higher number of shares is counterbalanced by a commensurate decline in the par value of the common stock. A stock dividend increases the number of outstanding shares, reduces retained earnings, and raises both the common stock par value and paid-in capital surplus in excess of par value.

5. Two legal restrictions associated with the payment of dividends are (1) in most states cash dividends are prohibited when the firm is insolvent, and (2) payment is restricted in cases where dividends are paid out of a firm's equity, thereby reducing the protection given to creditors.

6. There are loan agreements and certain constraints required by creditors, such as limiting the payment of dividends when earnings and/or net working capital fall below certain levels.

7. When the capital gains tax rate is lower than the ordinary tax rate that applies to dividends, investors benefit by allowing the firm to reinvest earnings. The anticipated capital appreciation can be deferred as long as the investor owns the stock. Investors have no control over the payment of dividends. Like any other current income, taxes must be paid when these dividends are paid. The option to defer paying taxes is not available to dividend recipients.

8. Modigliani-Miller say that dividends are a residual. If it is assumed that

$$\text{Return of firm} \geq \text{Return of investor}$$

then it is logical to reinvest earnings. Also, these theorists neutralize the impact of dividends on the valuation of the firm by assuming that dividend payments are offset by issuing an equivalent value of shares. In other words, no matter what dividend policy is adopted, dividends do not play a role in generating income or in determining the value of the firm. Consequently, dividends are irrelevant in the determination of the value of stocks.

9. Three reasons why dividends are relevant to stock valuation are (1) the "bird in hand" principle, (2) the clientele effect, and (3) informational content.

10. The net residual policy says that if a firm has extra funds after it has invested in all profitable projects, then cash dividends should be paid to stockholders.

11. Most managers believe the best dividend policy is one that minimizes the weighted average cost of capital. This policy should provide stable payments, maintain investor confidence, and give good signals to investors about the ability of the firm to maintain and increase its wealth. It should be conservative enough to hold the uncertainty of future payments to a minimum. Cyclical firms should pay low dividends regularly,

and an "extra dividend" when economic conditions are favorable and profits are high.

12. The record date establishes the names of stockholders entitled to the dividend. The ex-dividend date is established four business days preceding the record date. Stockholders of record on or before the ex-dividend date are entitled to the dividend.

13. Cash declines and the same reduction occurs in retained earnings.

14. One definition of free cash flow is

$$EBIT\ (1-T) + Dep\ (T) + Ts\ - \text{New investments}$$

We might want to use this approach because some companies do not pay dividends and also many investors pay less attention to dividends and focus more on capital gains. Our present ways of determining the value of a firm, based on the dividend model, may have to be reviewed in light of these new developments and the changed attitudes of investors toward dividends.

15. The earnings model applied to non-dividend–paying firms begins by estimating the growth rate of earnings ($g = ROE$). Then observe how the ROE and P/E of traded companies changed is response to new growth opportunities. Assume the same changes will occur to the P/E and ROE of the firm under analysis. To estimate EPS apply ($EPS \times g$). To obtain the corresponding stock prices employ ($P/E \times EPS$).

16. Investors find non-dividend–paying stocks attractive because the firm has new growth opportunities that result in $ROE > K$. The capital gains generated from new investments justify owning the stock even though no dividends are received. New growth opportunities usually give rise to a higher P/E and ROE, which should produce higher stock prices.

PRACTICAL APPLICATION

1. Dividend yield $= \dfrac{\$7}{\$40} = \$17.50\%$

A 10% yield would mean that an investor interested in getting a high return—assuming both firms have the same risk level—would buy the stock of Firm A. However, if Firm A is very risky, the investors may look for the safety offered by stock B. Also, Firm B might be a fast-growing firm which prefers to reinvest a large portion of its earnings. As indicated, yield is not in itself a sufficient basis upon which investment decisions are made. Investors must look at many other factors.

2. Dividend payout $= \dfrac{\$3}{\$10} = 30\%$ $P/E = \dfrac{.30}{.15-.09} = 5$ times

3. Stock value after the split equals $25, and the par value is reduced to $5 per share.

4. The following are the changes that would appear on the balance sheet after Firm A paid a 20% stock dividend:

	Stockholders' Equity	
	Before Stock Dividend	After Stock Dividend
Common stock shares outstanding (5 million at $10 par value)	$ 50,000,000	
Common stock shares outstanding (6 million at $10 par value)		$ 60,000,000
Paid-in capital surplus in excess of par value	140,000,000	170,000,000
Retained earnings	100,000,000	60,000,000
Total stockholder's equity	$290,000,000	$290,000,000

5. The Myron Gordon dividend valuation formula is:

$$V_s = \frac{D_1}{K_s - G}$$

Given the appropriate figures, the value of Company X's stock is equal to:

$D_0 = \$2.00 \ (\$4.00 \times .50)$

$G = \dfrac{\$2.00}{\$4.00} = .50$ (look up this value in the present-value table for 9 years and you find that $G = .08$.)

$D_1 = \$2.00 \ (1 + .08) = \$2.16$

$V_s = \dfrac{\$2.16}{.15 - .08} = \dfrac{\$2.16}{.07} = \$30.86$

6. Financing in equity = $(.35 \times \$15,000,000)$
                 = $5.25 million

$6,000,000	Retained Earnings
5,250,000	Equity financing
$ 750,000	Residual or surplus

Maximum dividends per share = $\dfrac{\$750,000}{100,000} = \$7.50$ per share

7. (a) $1.00 × 2,000,000 (Dividends paid to stockholders) = $2,000,000.

(b) $2,000,000/$40 = 50,000 (New shares bought back). This makes total shares outstanding equal to 2,000,000 − 50,000 = 1,950,000 new outstanding shares.

(c) EAT/Number of shares outstanding ($5,000,000/1,950,000) = $2.56 per share compared to $2.50 ($5,000,000/$2,000,000) before the repurchase occurred.

(d) Cash and equity will decline and Treasury stocks will increase.

(e) Cash saved 50,000 shares × $1.00 = $50,000 (Cash savings).

8. Calculate the *ROE*, *EPS*, growth rate (*g*), and *P/E* of this non-dividend–paying firm

ROE or (*g*) = before imports (earnings/equity) or
$200,000/$1,500,000 = 13.3% or 13%
EPS = (earnings/oustanding shares) or
$200,000/100,000 = $2.00
After imports (*g*) = 16%
P/E = $20/$2.00 or 10 times earnings before imports; after imports the *P/E* will increase to 14 times earnings

	Current Year	
	Excluding Imports	Including Imports
g	13%	16%
(*EPS* × g) or *EPS*	$2.26	$2.62
P/E	10×	14×
(*P/E* × *EPS*) or Stock price	$22.60	$36.68

9. Earnings Per Share = $1,000,000 Net Income/(1,000,000 shares) = $1 per share.
Dividend Per Share = [($1,000,000) − (40% × $2,000,000)] / (1,000,000 share) = 200,000/1,000,000 shares = 20 cents per share.

INVESTMENT DECISIONS BASED ON FINANCIAL DERIVATIVES

11

OPTIONS, FUTURES, AND SWAPS

KEY TERMS

basis the difference between the spot price and the futures price

bullish spread where the investor buys a call in the money (at a lower strike price) and sells a call out of the money (at a higher stock price)

call option a contract that gives the buyer the right to purchase an asset at a stated price within a specified time period

credit default swap (CDS) an over-the-counter contract between two parties where credit risk is transferred from one entity to the other

European option an option that can be exercised only at expiration date

exercise price a stated price that allows investors to buy (call) or sell (put) the stock of an option

forward contract a contract to buy or sell a particular good sometime in the future at a predetermined price

futures a contract traded on the exchange whereby two parties agree to buy or sell assets at a stated price and future date

in-the-money call option an option whose stock price exceeds the exercise price

ISDA® (International Swaps and Derivatives Association) a self-regulatory industry organization that recommends criteria and standards for documentation of a CDS

long hedge position buy futures now and cover by selling them at a future date as protection against expected price increases

options a contract that entitles the owner to buy or sell an asset or stock at a stated price within a specified period of time

option writer a party that sells puts and calls for a premium

out-of-the-money call option an option in which the stock price is below the exercise price

put option a contact that gives the buyer the right to sell an asset at a stated price within a specified period of time

short hedge position sell futures now and cover by buying them at a future date as protection against expected price decreases

swaps an exchange of assets or currencies between two parties for a specified period of time

Options and futures are financial instruments that provide managers of firms with more choices when making investment decisions. They are also employed to hedge against the risk of losses. These instruments allow firms to better time the financing of their operations at more favorable costs, and they permit managers to reverse planned investments should conditions change and actual events don't turn out as originally expected.

Financial officers are constantly presented with investment choices. Although the decision to invest depends on projected cash flows and the net present value of a project, there is no guarantee that the projected cash flows or the discount rate assigned to a project will turn out as expected. That risk can be minimized if a firm has the opportunity to buy an option that helps to insure against these unforeseen circumstances. And then there are investments whose implementation is contingent on the outcome of other investment decisions. It is comforting to know that, in many cases, managers can leave the door open to exercise various options. For example, airlines may order planes from a manufacturer like Boeing and put up a deposit. The order is subject to cancellation if traffic conditions deteriorate. Although these airlines may lose the deposit, they do not have to buy the planes, which would add unwarranted capacity that operates at a loss.

Options and futures serve to protect firms against losses incurred when prices change. The goal is to hedge or insure against these adverse price changes, and one way to accomplish this goal is to enter into the appropriate options and futures contracts whose gains will offset losses in price changes. Consequently, it is evident that the study of options and futures markets and the way these instruments are priced is important for understanding how managers can insure the implementation of profitable choices and avoid the unprofitable ones at minimum cost and risk.

YOU SHOULD REMEMBER

Options and futures allow firms to reduce costs, avoid large risks, and achieve better timing of investment decisions. They serve as hedges against adverse price changes and increase the choices available to maximize the risk adjusted returns of the firm.

OPTIONS

Investment decisions involve making choices. These choices can be viewed as **options** that make an investment contingent on other outcomes. For example, a firm may have to borrow and invest in new capacity if the results of current research and development prove successful. It has a choice. Invest in new equipment now or put a deposit on the equipment and purchase it at some future date, should the research experiments be successful. By doing so it has, in essence, purchased a call option on the equipment. Should the research effort fail, the firm can forfeit the deposit and avoid having made a big investment that would prove redundant. Therefore, options allow managers to reverse their investment plans when other developments don't turn out as expected.

When firms decide to modernize or abandon existing projects, they are exercising the option to reverse their original decision. The value of an option increases as more time is involved and the project becomes riskier. The option's value is also contingent on the relationship between the cost of the original equipment (**exercise price**), the final demand for the product, and the profitability of the project. The deposit then is the price of the option, and the exercise price is the cost of the original investment. The chances of exercising the option to purchase the equipment increase the more the expected revenues exceed the original cost.

Having decided that options are an important aspect of planning, we turn our attention to a discussion of the way the option market works and how options are priced.

EXPLAINING CALLS AND PUTS

Before explaining how puts and calls work, it is useful to define some of the terms. There are two main types of options: call options and put options. These options are bought by investors who plan to make a profit. They are sold by **option writers** who charge a premium for selling the option. A **call option** gives the buyer the right to purchase stock from a writer at a specified price (called the exercise price) within a stated period of time. A **put option** gives the buyer the right to sell stock to a writer at a specified price (called the exercise price) within a given period of time. In the case of a call, the buyer anticipates that the price of the stock will rise above the exercise price, and in the case of a put, the buyer expects the price of the stock to decline below the exercise price. The writer, obviously, hopes that the price of the stock will remain unchanged or move in the opposite direction that is anticipated by the buyer.

An option contract is for 100 shares of stock. Therefore, if the writer charges a $10 premium, the total cost of a call or put option would be ($10 × 100) = $1,000. Writers can sell a naked or a covered option. Usually, they sell covered options, which means they own the underlying security and can deliver it to the buyer in case of a call. The only loss the writer can incur, in this instance, is the premium. If writers sell naked calls, they expose themselves to the high risk of having to deliver the stock at a very high price by having to purchase it in the open market.

One problem facing a call or put buyer is the time limitation. Calls and puts usually have a maximum life of 9 to 12 months, and they become worthless upon the **expiration date.** Accordingly, the risk of time has a relationship to the premium paid. The more time there is before the expiration date, the greater the chance that the price of the stock will move favorably for the buyer of calls and puts. Therefore, the more time, the higher the premium, and the less time (or the closer to expiration date), the lower the premium.

YOU SHOULD REMEMBER

Options are important because they provide managers with choices to invest or not invest in projects that are subject to the possibility of success or failure. The decision to modernize or abandon a project is an option available to managers.

There are two basic types of options: calls and puts. The call buyer gambles that the price of the underlying stock will go up, and the put buyer gambles that the price of the underlying stock will decline. The writer of an option hopes that the price of the stock will move in the opposite direction expected by call and put buyers. Usually, to guard against large losses occasioned by big moves in the price of the stock, the writer will buy the stock outright when selling a call and will sell the stock short when selling a put. This is called "covering" the option. Selling options without this protection is called writing naked options.

• *HOW CALLS AND PUTS WORK*

Theoretically, the minimum price of a call and a put depends in part on the relationship between the price of a stock and the exercise price. For call options, we say the price is equal to

	Type		Value
Price of a call	In the money	$P_s > X_p$	Positive
	Out of the money	$P_s < X_p$	0

For a put, we say the price is equal to

Type		Value		
Price of a put	In the money	$P_s < X_p$		Positive
	Out of the money	$P_s > X_p$		0

where P_s = price of stock
X_p = exercise price

In theory, calls have a positive value as long as the price of the stock exceeds the exercise price, and they are worthless when the stock price remains below the exercise price. Theoretically, puts have a positive value as long as the price is lower than the exercise price, and they have no value when the price of the stock is higher than the exercise price. Given these parameters, let's see how option pricing develops and profits are made in different circumstances. The following example assumes that the price of the stock moves from $90 to $120 for calls and from $110 to $80 for puts.

	Call Option	Put Option
Current price of stock	$ 90	$110
Exercise price of option	100	100
Expected future price of stock	120	80
Premium paid	10	10

When our stock price is $90, the value of the call is equal to zero because an investor can purchase the stock at a lower price ($90) in the open market than exercising at $100. At $110, the value of the put is equal to zero because an investor is not about to buy the stock at $110 and exercise it at $100 by selling the same stock to the writer. Now let's suppose the price of the stock goes to $120 for the call and $80 for the put.

We know that the call buyer can buy the stock from a writer at $100. Should the stock price rise to $120, its value is $(P_s - X_p)$ $120 – $100 or $20. The call buyer can ask the writer to deliver the stock at $100. He or she can then sell it in the market for $120. This means a $20 profit. Deduct the original premium paid for the call of $10 and you have a net profit of $10 on a $10 investment.

Put buyers anticipate the price of the stock to decline and if it does, they can buy the stock at $80 on the exchange and put that same stock (sell it) to the writer for $100. The net profit is $10 after deducting the original premium paid to the writer. In the case of the call and put, if the writer had a covered position, the only loss incurred is the $10 premium.

DETERMINING THE VALUE OF OPTIONS

Investors know two things: at expiration an option value is zero and theoretically it is also worthless if the price of the stock is below the exercise price. What produces the value of an option? The answer is: the relationship between the value of an option, its exercise price, and the price of the stock. This relationship is shown in Figure 11-1.

To understand these relationships, we must distinguish between the minimum theoretical value of an option and its market value. The minimum value is equal to $P_s - X_p$. Therefore, as long as $P_s < X_p$, the option theoretically has no value because no one is going to exercise it. If the price of the stock remains below the exercise price, with no possibility of exercising it (which was the reason why it was purchased in the first place), then it is worthless. It offers no probability of a payoff. As shown in Figure 11-1, to the left of the X_p the option is "out of the money." As soon as the price of the stock passes the exercise price $(P_s > X_p)$, the probability of exercise increases, and the further the stock price increases, the greater the chances of exercise. Investors and writers of options know this and that is why the value of the option assumes a positive value. In this case $(P_s > X_p)$, the option is referred to as "in the money." Why does this minimum price continue to rise? The answer is: A very high stock price makes exercise a virtual certainty, and the chances are remote that it will become worthless or $(P_s < X_p)$.

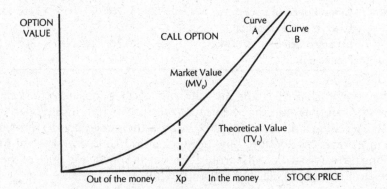

Figure 11-1 Call Option Relationships

The minimum price of an option differs from the market price. Usually, the market price is greater than the minimum price, that is, the area between curve A and curve B. Investors are willing to pay a premium above the minimum price (TV_0) because they expect the price of the stock to rise above the exercise price. Note, however, that curve A collapses toward curve B as the price of the stock continues to increase. This is a rational reaction, partly because no one will pay a premium for an option if the chances of further stock price increases vanish. That is precisely what happens in the marketplace. At some point, the stock becomes overvalued and the probability of continued increases in its price becomes nil. At that point, the market value and minimum value of the option will be equal, and any further stock price increase will produce minimum increases in the value of the option.

The most crucial factor that determines the value of an option is the risk of the stock. As already established in Chapter 4, the risk of a stock is measured by beta (or standard deviation). Consequently, the options of high beta stock are assigned bigger premiums than low beta stocks. This is mainly because investors anticipate the price of a high beta stock to be subject to wider price movements than stock having low betas. Investors who buy call options, for example, do so because they expect the price of high beta stocks to move sharply above their striking prices. A high beta stock has a higher probability than a low beta stock that this will happen. The sellers of calls are aware of this situation and protect themselves by charging higher premiums and setting higher striking prices.

YOU SHOULD REMEMBER

The minimum or theoretical value of an option is equal to $P_s - X_p$. Call options have a positive value when $P_s > X_p$. This is known as an in-the-money call. When $P_s < X_p$, the call is worthless and it is said to be out of the money. Puts have a positive value when they are in the money $(P_s < X_p)$ and out-of-the-money puts are worthless when $P_s > X_p$. The market price of a call is higher than its minimum price because buyers of calls expect the price of the stock to rise above the exercise price. The more **in the money** an **option** is, the greater the chance of exercise and, hence, the higher its value. No **out-of-the-money option** will be exercised because it would be unprofitable to do so.

FACTORS AFFECTING THE VALUE OF OPTIONS
The value of options is linked primarily to the following factors:

• Current stock price relative to exercise price

- Time to expiration

- A risk-free rate

- A risk measure, such as standard deviation

- Exercise price

- Dividend payment on the stock

We have already pointed out that the value of an option depends, in part, on whether the option is in or out of the money. Clearly, the more in the money an option is, the greater its value because of the greater probability of exercise. The more time to expiration, the better the chance that the price of the stock will rise substantially above its current price. An option writer knows this and will charge more the longer the time factor. Because the option expires at some time in the future, we must consider this risk and discount the exercise price by the risk-free rate to obtain its present value. This procedure puts the exercise price on a comparable risk-adjusted basis as the current price of the stock. The risk associated with an option is largely reflected in the volatility of the price of the stock. The greater the volatility, the greater the chance the stock will change and produce a payoff for the buyer of the option.

YOU SHOULD REMEMBER

The value of call and put options depends on the following factors: standard deviation of the price of the stock, time to expiration, risk-free rate, and the relationship between stock price and its exercise price. The relationship between these factors and the fair value of an option is a direct one.

• *OPTION VALUATION AND THE BLACK AND SCHOLES MODEL*

All of the different models used to determine the fair value of an option make use, in one way or another, of the five factors cited previously. One of the better known stock option valuation models is the Black and Scholes model, which is described in this section. Among the various assumptions of this model, we should know that it determines **European call options** (exercisable only at expiration date), and it assumes the underlying stock pays no dividend. The stock price is assumed to increase by very small increments, and the exercise price must be discounted by the risk-free rate.

Because the model also assumes that the price of the stock changes by infinitesimal increments, the continuous discounting method is employed to obtain the present value of the exercise price. Given these assumptions, we can proceed to present the model.

Black and Scholes say that the present value of a call option is equal to

$$PV \text{ call option } = P_s(Nd_1) - \left[\frac{X_p}{e^{rt}}(Nd_2) \right]$$

We have already encountered this valuation model if we set aside the Nd_1 and the Nd_2 terms. If you will recall, our simple formula for the value of a call was: $P_s - (X_p)$. The nuances that Black and Scholes add in their model are probability terms and discounting of the exercise price. Nd_1 stands for the probability that the price of the stock will pay off within the time to expiration assigned to the option. Nd_2 represents the probability that the option will be exercised. Nd_1 and Nd_2 terms are calculated as follows (first compute the d_1 and d_2 values):

$$d_1 = \frac{\text{Log } P_s / X_p + \left(R_f + \frac{\sigma^2}{2} \right) T}{\sigma \sqrt{T}}$$

$$d_2 = d_1 - \sigma \sqrt{T}$$

In the preceeding formula we witness the integration of the factors we discussed before. Note that we see the in and out-of-the-money relationship along with the risk-free rate, the variance of the stock, and the time factor. To translate d_1 and d_2 into Nd_1 and Nd_2 values, we simply look up the corresponding values for d_1 and d_2 in a cumulative normal distribution function table. This table will supply us with the Nd_1 and Nd_2 values that should be plugged into the original formula to obtain the present value of a call option. Although the underlying theory and the mathematics are somewhat complicated, modern computers make the task of solving these equations very easy.

We merely presented this model to familiarize you with the way the valuation of options is determined. It is clear that the model draws on the factors we outlined before and that a call option reflects a direct relationship between these factors and the fair value of the option. That means the higher the value of these factors, the higher the fair value of the call option. The pivotal factor in the determination of option value is the standard deviation of the stock price. Investors who can estimate the right volatility of the stock should be able to get a fairly good estimate of the value of an option.

Let us just follow through on the computation to see how the model works. Assume you determined that the values of Nd_1 was .60 and the value of Nd_2 was .70. Suppose a stock has a current price of $60, an exercise price of $45, a risk-free rate of 5%, and the option expires a year from now, then the fair value of a call option of this stock is

$$V_c = P_s(Nd_1) - \left[\frac{x_p}{e^{rt}} \times (Nd_2)\right]$$

$$= \$60(.60) - \left[\frac{\$45}{e^{.05 \times 1}}(.70)\right] = \$6.04$$

The corresponding formula for deriving the fair value of a put is

$$V_p = V_c + \frac{X_p}{e^{rt}} - P_s$$

where V_p = value of put X_p = exercise price
        V_c = value of call P_s = price of stock

We can observe that the value of a put is determined by the same factors as a call, which has already been captured in the term V_c. At the current stock price of $60, the V_p would be zero. Let's assume the stock price fell to $40, then the V_p would be

$$\text{Value of put } (V_p) = \$6.04 + \frac{\$45}{e^{.05 \times 1}} - \$40 = \$8.84$$

Academicians have found a way of simplifying the mathematics, and the result has been the development of a shorter method for deriving the fair value of calls and puts. This method entails taking into account (see explanation of actual warrant price determination) the relationship between standard deviation and time to expiration compared to the price of the stock relative to its exercise price. This relationship can be more easily translated into the value of an option by referring to a special option table. This table indicates what part of the stock price is represented by the option.

Example:

$$P_0 = \$100$$
$$\alpha\,(t) = .40$$
$$P_0/X_p \div e^{RF,t} = .92$$

Looking up these two values of .40 and .92 in the call option table you obtain a value of .1255. The approximate value of a call that has the foregoing risk, time, and exercise price relative to the stock price is $12.25 ($100 × 0.1225).

In solving these models, the value of a call option or its premium will be high if the current price of the stock is above the exercise price, if the standard deviation is large, if time to expiration is long, if the riskless rate is high, and if dividend payments are small.

THE BINOMIAL MODEL

The binomial model is another method employed to determine the value of options. In some respects, it is superior to the Black and Scholes model; therefore, it deserves discussion. Let's begin by analyzing a one-period (one-year) option.

ONE-PERIOD MODEL

The one period model considers two possible price targets, namely, the stock price could reach $130 a year from now or could drop to $80 as shown in Figure 11-1A. Given these two possible stock price outcomes the goal is to determine the value of their underlying options. To do so, we establish that the exercise price is $100. The year end value of the options is calculated as follows:

Value of option = (Price of stock) – (Exercise price)

If the current price of the stock is $100 and it reaches $130, then

Value of option = ($130 – $100) = $30

If the current price of the stock is $100 and it reaches $80, then

Value of option = ($80 – $100) = $0

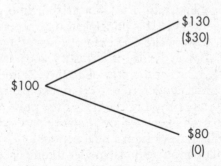

Figure 11–1A One period binomial model. Numbers in parentheses ( ) are option values based on (Stock price – Exercise price). All other numbers are stock prices.

In other words, suppose you knew for certain that the price of the stock would reach $130, the market would place a value of $30 on that option. Should the price of the stock decline to $80, the options would be worthless. Under these conditions, the value of the option is likely to fall within a range of $30 and zero. That is the problem. What is the fair price you should pay for this option ($30, $20, $10, or any other price)? The solution to this problem is to assign probabilities to the two option values. For the purpose of this analysis, we assume there is a .60 chance that the stock price will rise to $130 and a .40 probability that it will decline to $80. Based on these parameters, the expected value of the option is obtained by employing the following equation:

$$\text{Expected value} = [(\text{Probability of rise}) \times (OV_r) \\ + (1 - \text{Probability of rise}) \times (OV_d)]/r$$

where OV_r = Option value assuming stock price rises
OV_d = Option value assuming stock price declines
r = Interest rate

Assigning the above probabilities to each of the option values in the range (assume a 10% borrowing rate), we come up with the following expected value of the option:

Expected value of option = $\{(.60 \times \$30) + (.40 \times \$0)\}/1.10 = \$16.36$ or $16

TWO-PERIOD MODEL

Based on the one-period model, the price of the option is $16. However, the one-period model is not realistic because it considers only two possible price outcomes when we know that there are many others. Consequently, the model allows for other price targets by subdividing the original time period into several subintervals. The shorter the time periods are, the smaller the price range will be. This principle can be observed in the movement of stock prices. We will cite one example. According to the Internet, the price of a share of IBM on the day of August 19, 2005, ranged from a high of $83.30 to a low of $81.16. For the previous 52 weeks, the price range was $99.10 and $71.85. The same pattern applies to all other stocks. The point is that the longer the time period is, the bigger the price range will be. Put differently, stock prices are likely to move in more narrow ranges from day to day compared to quarterly or semiannual periods.

That is what the multiperiod binomial model accomplishes. It dissects the time to expiration of options into very short intervals. In doing so, it considers many possible price outcomes. We can now proceed to demonstrate how a two-period binomial model calculates the value of an option.

First, we postulate that the duration of the option is one year subdivided into two six-month periods. The exercise price is $100, and the semiannual interest rate is 10%. The probability is .45 that the price of the stock will increase and .55 that it will decrease. Figure 11-1B indicates the various stock prices expected at the end of 6 months and at year end.

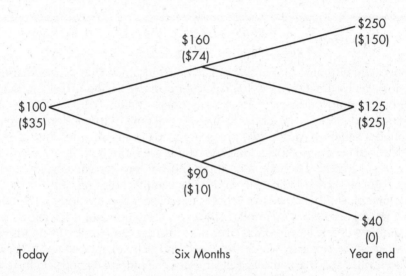

Figure 11–1B Two-period model. Numbers in parentheses ( ) represent option values. All other numbers are stock price stated in dollar amounts.

Recall that the equation to obtain expected option values is

Expected
value $= [$Probability of rise$) (OV_r) + (1 - $Probability of rise$) (OV_d)]/r$
of option

Therefore, if the stock price at the end of 6 months is $160 then there is a .45 chance that the option at year end will be worth $150 ($250 – $100) and a .55 probability that it will have a value of $25 ($125 – $100). In this case the expected value of the 6-month option is

Expected value of
six month option $= [(.45) \times (\$150) + (.55) \times (\$25)] / 1.10 = \$74$

If the stock price at the end of 6 months is $90, then the option at year end should be worth $25 or zero. Under these conditions, the value of the option at the end of 6 months would be

Expected value
of option = [(.45) × ($25) + (.55) × ($0)]/1.10 = $10.22 or $10
at mid year

Combining these two midyear option values and working backward, the expected value of the option today is

Expected value of
option today = [(.45) × ($74) + .55) × ($10)]/1.10 = $35

Notice, the binomial model works backward in time. That is, the year-end option values are the basis for calculating midyear option values, which are then employed to estimate today's option value. To recapitulate, in a multiperiod model, you subdivide the original time of the option into many subperiods each having a two-price target. By doing so, the time of each subinterval becomes shorter, and the results are more realistic. As the number of subperiods become very large, the binomial model results closely approximate those obtained from the Black and Scholes model.

At first blush, the Black and Scholes model seems preferable to the binomial model because it is simpler. However, the binomial model allows one to simulate different outcomes over time. Also, it can handle dividends and American-type options, which the Black and Scholes model is not geared to do. Unlike the Black and Scholes model, the binomial approach involves a large number of computations. Fortunately, the computer can easily deal with this problem. Both models yield the same results and are useful for hedging against adverse price changes.

In summary, managers are discovering that options can protect a firm from rising raw materials and other prices. They have found options to be useful as hedges against adverse changes in exchange rates. A firm may invest large sums of money in a project that may not turn out as well as anticipated. This investment can be postponed until a future date by buying options. Should the project succeed, exercise the option; otherwise, don't invest in the project and be spared the loss of the original investment. Options can also ensure against portfolio losses. For example, a firm may have a substantial portfolio of stocks that it will depend on to finance future growth opportunities. But it has no assurance that these funds will be available in their entirety when needed. To avoid portfolio losses, the firm should buy puts on some market index. Should the value of the portfolio decline, exercising the puts will protect the firm from portfolio losses. There are many ways options can be used to improve the timing of investments and avoid excessive losses when a firm is faced with making uncertain investment decisions.

POPULAR OPTIONS STRATEGIES IN A NUTSHELL

Numerous strategies can be created in using options. Brief descriptions of 9 major strategies used very often in the options market are provided below:

1. **Long call** where the party has the right to buy. The premise behind this strategy is that the investor is expecting that the market is on the rise. With limited investment (paying premium as a fraction of the stock price), an entity may expose itself to the fluctuations of the underlying asset. It is an indirect (synthetic) way of investment in the market.

2. **Short call** where the party sells the right to buy. The premise behind this strategy is that the investor is expecting the market is headed for a decline.

3. **Long put** where the party has the right to sell because the investor is bearish on the future of the market.

4. **Short put** where the party sells the right to sell. In this case, the inventor thinks contrary to what the long put investor is expecting. A "naked" short put (a put sold with no hedging like buying a put) may be used to collect premium (income) and then buy the stock (usually at a low exercise price) if the option is exercised. This strategy might be viable if the underlying stock is the favorite stock of the put seller. In other words, the stock should be the one that the put seller does not mind to own if the option is exercised.

5. **Protective put** consists of having a stock and a simultaneous purchase of the right to sell. This is an excellent strategy if the investor does not want to sell his or her portfolio but plans to hedge against a possible price decline. Protective put (owning a stock and buying a put) is a form of buying insurance and considered a classic hedging strategy. Among users of this strategy could be portfolio managers as well as prospective retirees with 401ks **prior to** the date of retirement.

6. **Covered call** consists of a portfolio of having a stock and selling the right to buy; i.e. owning a stock plus short a call. This strategy is more of enhancing income rather than managing risk. For example, an investor bought 100 shares of IBM at $100 per share and now sells a contract call (for 100 shares) at a strike price of $125 and collects $10 premium per share. Under the worse situation, if the option is exercised, the investor has to sell the stock at the predetermined strike price of $25. In other words, the total proceeds of selling the stock is $135 consisting of $125 strike price plus $10 premium, which was collected before. The net profit per share is $35; computed as $135 minus the original cost of the stock at $100 per share. If the stock price does not go up and the option

expires, the investor keeps the $10 premium. Either way, the investor has enhanced the income. The investor's only opportunity cost is a possible appreciation of the stock price beyond the $135 price level.

7. **Bullish spread** where the investor buys a call in the money (at a lower strike price) and sells a call out of the money (at a higher stock price.) The bullish investor is willing to pay a higher premium in anticipation of a stock price rise. A portion of the higher premium is financed by the sale of a corresponding call with a lower strike price. The reverse of this strategy is called a **bearish spread**.

8. **Volatility trading** where a speculator is anticipating volatility on the upside or downside. Suppose there is evidence or rumors that a company would be acquired by another firm. If the expectation is realized, the stock price may increase; otherwise, there will be a price decline. In this volatile scenario, the speculator may buy a call and buy a put at the same time. Should the rumor turn out to be false, the put option will go in the money if the stock price declines. However, if the company is merged and the price of the target company goes up, the call option will be in the money. In either case, there would be a gain. Of course, if the stock price does not move to the upside or downside, the paid premium will be lost and a loss would incur. In these trading strategies, if the strike prices for both the call and the put are the same, the strategy is called **straddle**. Should the exercise prices be different for the call and the put, the strategy is called **strangle**.

9. **Interest rate caps and floors** are interest rate options. They are popular interest risk management tools. If a bank holds a series of adjustable mortgages in its portfolio, it may buy a **floor** in the derivatives market to hedge itself against an interest rate decline below a certain level. To hedge against increases in the interest rate for liabilities (certificates of deposits and adjustable notes), the bank may buy an interest rate cap to lock itself to a maximum interest rate. Buying a cap and selling a floor at the same time is a **collar strategy** where part of the premium paid for a cap is financed by the premium received by selling a put, or vice versa.

Examples:

Case 1: You bought 10 contracts of a put option with $1 premium each share with an exercise price of $10. At expiration (3 months later), the stock price is worth only $6. What is the total net profit in this strategy if the option is exercised?

Solution:

Gross profits = 10 contracts * 100 shares in each contract *
(Exercise price sold – Stock price) = 10 * 100 * ($10 – $6) = $4,000

Net profits = Gross profits – Premiums paid = $4,000 – $1,000 = $3,000

Note: Each option contract consists of 100 shares.

Case 2: You bought a call option contract with an exercise price of $20 with a premium of $2 per share. The stock price goes up to $40 and you exercise after one month. In this case, compute your net profits, if any.

Solution:

Gross profits = 1 contract * 100 shares in each contract *
(Stock price – Exercise price) = 1 * 100 * ($40 – $20) = 2,000
Net profits = Gross profits – Premiums paid = $2,000 – $200 = $1,800
Note: Each option contract consists of 100 shares.

Case 3: Refer to Cases No. 1 and 2 above. Compute the **rate of return** for the period you held the contracts in each case.

Solution:

The rate of return in Case 1 = Net profits/Premiums paid =
$3,000/$1,000 = 300%

The rate of return in Case 2 = Net profits/Premiums paid =
$1,800/$200 = 900%

A word of caution is in order. **Do not** jump over trading options merely because of these hypothetical rates of return. What happens if the stock price had significantly increased in Case 1 and decreased in Case 2? Your total investment (or speculation money) would have been wiped out. Be excessively careful if you think of trading options. Note that trading options is not a strategy for average investors. It is a highly leveraged and risky venture. Options should be used primarily for managing risk.

APPLYING OPTION THEORY TO CORPORATE DECISIONS

Let us describe two examples to indicate how options can be useful to corporate managers in making investments while providing some degree of protection against risk.

Example 1: A corporate manager has a stock portfolio with a mix of assets similar to the Standard & Poor's 500 Stock Index. The value of this portfolio has appreciated substantially and now has a value equal to a debt obligation, which is coming due in six months. The manager wants to lock in his or her capital gains and avoid a depreciation in the value of the stock portfolio. To ensure against this risk, he or she buys enough put options (expiring in six months), on a market index, to cover the value of the portfolio. In this way, any drop in overall stock market prices will be offset by the gains from the puts when they are exercised. That will ensure that enough funds are available to pay off the debt six months from now.

Example 2: Assume that a firm plans to make a substantial investment in a project that depends on the outcome of current uncompleted research. This product will not be available for another year. The firm can explore an option. It may engage in a pilot study to gain market experience without having to commit funds to a large investment in the new product. At the same time, it will have the opportunity to examine the potential profitability of other products. This strategy is similar to buying a call option (the cost of the pilot). The justification for purchasing the call is the anticipation that the price of the stock will exceed the exercise price, which in this case is the investment required to produce and market the product. Also, the anticipated price of the stock is the present value of cash flows generated by the product, which is expected to equal or exceed the projected target. In other words, the firm is creating an option that allows it to gain information on alternative choices and to arrive at a final investment decision. The cost of the option (pilot) and risk is minimal. Should the facts, a year from now, indicate that the new product turned out to be riskier than originally anticipated and the cash flows are likely to fall short of the original projection, the firm does not have to exercise the option. It can divert the funds to other, more attractive areas. As we can observe, the firm was allowed to explore various choices at low cost and reduced exposure to risk. At the same time, it is given the chance to exercise the option or invest in more profitable areas.

Many option models provide financial managers with insight into the forces that determine the value of corporate assets and the securities held or managed by corporations. The importance of stock options and financial futures is growing steadily, and corporate officers in charge of handling funds must become knowledgeable about the advantages offered by these instruments.

EXECUTIVE OPTIONS

Corporations sometimes offer stock purchase **options** to key management officials as an inducement to keep them with the firm. Conversely, options can also be offered to attract new management skills to a firm. The right to exercise an option is usually given for a specified period of time. Some executive option arrangements are based on performance. In these cases, the number of options and their exercise prices are scaled to reflect results. The option package becomes more lucrative the greater the success achieved by the executive.

Example: Executive Options

Suppose a firm's stock is currently selling for $10. The firm agrees to give key executives the right to buy a certain number of shares at $14 per share. Assume that the price of the stock increases to $20. The executives can then borrow funds, buy the stock from the firm at $14, and sell these shares in the market at $20—making a profit of $6 on each share.

The additional shares issued to executives have a corresponding dilutive effect on the firm's earnings per share. Because the executives don't have to put up any money, the only loss they might incur is one of opportunity—or the inability to exercise and make a profit should the price of the stock fail to exceed $14 per share within the specified period.

Stock options could be worth millions of dollars to an executive. Unfortunately the value of these stock options changes in response to changes in the price of the stock and the exercise price. They also have a limited life. That is why cash salaries, retirement benefits, and annual bonuses sometimes provide attractive alternatives to stock options because there is no guarantee that the price of the stock will rise above the exercise price.

A final note: because corporations view options as a cost of doing business, we have to consider the accounting treatment of executive options. A number of companies have delayed expensing these options against income. The prudent course of action would be to deduct these expenses. The Financial Accounting Standards Board has ruled that these expenses must appear in the income statement and must be deducted from the income of firms. Most companies were in compliance with this GAAP rule by January 1, 2006.

Other options of interest to institutional investors and financial managers include stock market index options and options on interest rate futures. Because many financial officers have the responsibility of supervising, either directly or indirectly, the management of pension and other corporate funds, they should be knowledgeable about the features of these instruments. These securities can be used to reduce portfolio risk and for hedging purposes. Option strategies can be adopted to protect the value of security investments or to increase returns by writing options. Some studies show that options can also influence the volume of trading in the firm's shares and enhance the liquidity of the stock.

YOU SHOULD REMEMBER

The Black and Scholes model is widely used to calculate the fair value of call options. This model requires the computation of a probability factor that the option will pay off (Nd_1) and a probability factor that the option will be exercised (Nd_2). Then these probabilities are assigned to the P_s and the X_p to obtain the price of the call option. The formula is

$$P_s(Nd_1) - \left[\frac{X_p}{e^{rt}}(Nd_2) \right]$$

The Nd_1 and Nd_2 values are dependent on the five main factors that determine the value of options.

There is a shortcut method to obtain the fair value of an option. That method relies on two relationships

$$\sigma \bullet \sqrt{T}$$

$$P_s / \frac{X_p}{e^{rt}}$$

Given the preceding values of these two relationships, we refer to a hedge ratio table that gives us a factor. When this factor is multiplied by the current price of the stock, we obtain the value of the option = (factor $\times P_s$).

The binomial model can be employed to obtain the value of an option. In some respect, this approach is better than the Black and Scholes model when dividends and American-type options are involved.

Executive options are offered as incentives to highly regarded managers to get the best performance from them.

FUTURES

The tool kit for coping with risk should include futures. **Futures** are hedge instruments designed to help managers protect themselves against uncertain developments. **Hedging** is similar to an auto insurance policy. The premium paid is the cost to hedge against heavy casualty losses and other liability claims. Corporations are constantly faced by uncertain price changes, exchange rate risk, etc. It is in their best interest to insure themselves, as much as possible, against losses originating from these risks.

Here is an example of how a firm can attempt to minimize the costs of supplies that have to be purchased in the future. The argument can be made to buy the supplies now for future use. However, what if the price dropped? Then it might have been better to have postponed the purchase. If supplies are purchased now, the inventory might become obsolete by the time it is ready for use. What can managers do? They can buy or sell futures so that losses incurred by waiting are offset by the gains in the futures.

Futures are traded on the exchanges, and they represent contracts to buy or sell a commodity or a financial instrument at some future date. Futures are forward contracts with some differences. A forward contract is an agreement between two parties. One party agrees to purchase a given commodity at a stated price, and the other party agrees to deliver that commodity at a stated price. For example, assume the current price of corn, which is called the "spot price," is $3 per bushel. Party A needs 100 bushels of this corn 6 months from now and wants to pay $3 at that time. Party B agrees to sell the 100 bushels 6 months from now at the current spot price of $3 per bushel. Suppose 6 months elapse and the price of corn per bushel rose to $4 per bushel. Party B would have to deliver 100 bushels at $3 despite the price increase. The problems with this forward contract arrangement is that buyers of futures must find someone who is willing to agree to the contract terms. And, there is no assurance that delivery will take place because either the buyer may refuse to honor the contract or the seller may default.

This cumbersome system of forward contracts was superseded by futures contracts, which are traded on organized exchanges like the Chicago Board of Trade. Buyers and sellers on the exchange know the delivery dates of all contracts. Contracts on a commodity are standardized, and these standards don't change. Orders to buy and sell are executed on the exchange through brokers.

One of the main features of a commodity exchange is the clearinghouse. This arm of the exchange guarantees the consummation of the futures contract. Should any buyer or seller default on the contract, the clearinghouse stands ready to honor and complete the contract. Also, the clearinghouse matches the orders of buyers and sellers and makes sure that all rules are followed.

Traders in futures are required to put up a **margin**, which is established by the exchange. This margin consists of 10% to 15% of the total value of the contract. So that, the 100 bushels of corn worth $3,000 or (100 × $3) having a margin of 10% would require a buyer of the futures contract to put up $300 for the contract. The collateral to cover the margin requirement can be cash or Treasury bills. Should the price of corn drop, the margin becomes deficient and additional cash must be supplied to maintain the original margin.

To make sure that things don't get out of hand and to avoid a disorderly market, the exchange employs a circuit breaker.

1. Daily price limits are established for each commodity. When the price of that commodity exceeds this daily limit, trading ends for that day.

2. The exchange requires investors to engage in the practice of **marking to the market**. That is, each investor is called on to settle their futures account on a daily basis to make sure that things don't get out of hand and losses don't get so large as to cause defaults. As a result, gains from price increases are either credited to the account daily or can be cashed in by the investor. Losses, due to price declines must be settled by having the investor put up more cash to cover the deficiency.

These two requirements prevent abnormal speculative swings in prices, and they help ensure the integrity of futures contracts.

HOW THE SYSTEM WORKS

Trading in commodities essentially is based on the concept that there is a reversing of trades. That means, an initial trade to buy or sell a futures contract must be followed by a covering trade in the opposite direction. So that if a customer buys a futures contract, eventually he or she must cover by selling that contract, and if the contract is sold, the transaction must be completed by an eventual purchase. On the exchange, about 98% of all transactions don't involve actual delivery of the commodity. They are used only to hedge against future unforeseen price changes.

In the futures market, we have three main participants.

1. Buyers of futures who anticipate the prices of commodities to increase, and they establish a long position to hedge against this event.

2. Sellers of futures who anticipate the prices of commodities to decline, and they establish a short position to hedge against this event.

3. The speculator who takes on the risk associated with futures contracts.

As we mentioned before, the clearinghouse matches long and short positions so that the price of a future is established where

$$\text{Long postion} = \text{short position}$$

When long positions don't match the short positions, the speculator steps in to fill the void. Therefore, if

1. Long position > short position, the speculator is induced to take a net short position to cover this deficiency.

2. Long position < short position, the speculator is induced to take a net long position to cover this deficiency.

Clearly, the speculator serves an important function. He/she helps to establish an equilibrium price and is compensated accordingly for taking the risk of buying or selling futures. Speculators take this risk because they expect the price of the futures to move as they predict. That does not always occur. But what is crucial is the way hedging works. By matching buy–sell or long and short positions, the market provides a hedge against future price changes.

YOU SHOULD REMEMBER

The futures market is composed of long and short hedgers. Long hedgers want to insure themselves against price increases, and short hedgers, against price declines. In the marketplace, long and short positions are matched. When an imbalance occurs in these positions (long position ≠ short position), the speculator is given an inducement to fill the deficiency and that reestablishes equilibrium (long positions = short positions). The compensation offered a speculator is designed to cover the risk of the uncertainty of changes in future spot prices.

EXAMPLES OF HEDGING WITH FUTURES

Generally, in the futures market we have more short positions than long positions. That means speculators must be allowed to purchase futures at a discount from current spot prices if we are to maintain equilibrium (long positions = short positions). The difference between the current spot price and the futures price is called **basis**.

$$\text{Basis} = \text{Current spot price} - \text{Futures price}$$

Usually, this difference includes the cost of insurance, inventory carrying charges, and the interest charged on borrowed funds. This basis obviously changes over time, but to simplify the presentation, we assume it remains unchanged. Given this assumption, we can establish what is known as a perfect hedge against any price change.

Now, suppose we have two different hedgers who are concerned about future price changes and want to avoid this risk. Our example involves corn and the two parties are Kellogg and farmers.

Kellogg buys corn and is mainly worried about future increases in the price of corn. Because it periodically purchases corn, it wants to protect itself against expected increases in corn prices. In essence, Kellogg takes a **long hedge position** to avoid the risk of these price increases. This means it will buy futures contracts now and sell these contracts at a later date. Therefore, if the price of corn increases, it will offset the additional cost of buying corn in the spot market by the gain it obtains from reversing the original purchase transaction.

Farmers have to wait until harvest to sell corn. Their main concern is with a decline in the price of corn from the current spot price. Between now and harvest time, farmers can protect themselves against a price decline in corn by taking a **short hedge position** and thereby eliminate that risk. Farmers, therefore, will sell futures contracts now and cover by buying the contract back at harvest time. Should the price of corn decline, the opportunity loss incurred when corn is sold after harvest time, at a lower price than the current spot, is offset by the gain made from having taken the short position.

The two examples of long and short positions are illustrated next. For simplicity's sake, we assume the transaction involves only one bushel of corn, the spot price per bushel is $3.00, harvest time is April, and we are now in January.

Kellogg takes a long futures position on corn.

	Spot Price	Futures Contract Price	Basis (Spot Price − Futures Price)
January	$3.00	$2.80 (buy)	+.20
April	3.50	3.30 (sell)	+.20
Opportunity	− $.50 loss	+ $.50 gain	0

By April we find that the price of a bushel of corn rose to $3.50 per bushel. Kellogg would have to buy corn in April at $3.50 per bushel in the spot market. That means it would pay $.50 more per bushel without the protection of a long position. However, having taken the long position, the extra $.50 it has to pay in the April spot market is made up by the same gain in the futures contract. The purpose was to hedge against a price increase risk. If corn were to sell at a price below $3.00 per bushel, Kelloggs would benefit even more but that was not its goal. The aim was to insure against a price increase, and that is what it accomplished.

In the case of farmers, the transaction is still for one bushel of corn that sells at a spot price of $3.00 in January, and April is still harvest time.

Farmers take a short position on corn.

	Spot Price	Futures Contract Price	Basis (Spot Price – Futures Price)
January	$3.00	$3.20 (sell)	–.20
April	2.50	2.70 (buy)	–.20
Opportunity	–$.50 loss	+$.50 gain	0

The current spot price of corn is $3.00, and by harvest time in April the farmers find the spot price is $2.50. Without the short position, farmers would have to sell their corn at $2.50 in the spot market (or deliver the corn at that price to Kellogg). Having taken the short position, which entails selling in January and buying in April, farmers covered this loss by the gain they made in the futures contract. Because their purpose was to hedge against a price decline, any price increase above $3.00 in April would be frosting on the cake. But that is not the intended goal. The goal was to insure against the risk of a price decline and that was exactly what happened.

Kellogg and farmers are two examples of perfect hedges. Because the basis did not change, the hedge positions accomplished what they were supposed to do. Sometimes the basis changes, which implies that the futures price failed to increase or decrease in sync with the spot price. In those cases, there is no perfect coverage from the futures position; hence, there is only a partial hedge against price risk. The key point we make here, however, is that managers need to have a good understanding of the futures market if they are to operate in an effective manner and keep costs and risk as low as possible.

OTHER POSITIONS ON FUTURE STRATEGIES

There are many other uses for futures and options in the quest to reduce risk. New instruments like interest rate financial futures can be employed by financial managers as risk insurance. Companies with pension funds are likely to sell financial futures contracts to counteract a decline in the value of a pension fund bond portfolio when the expectation is for interest rates to increase. Or, let's assume that a corporation's pension fund manager seeks to lock in a high current yield for some future day when a large sum of money becomes available for investment. Should interest rates decline, the price of bonds would rise, and the current yield would decline. To prevent this from happening, the pension fund manager can take a long hedge financial futures position. Just think of bonds as commodities. In other words, the manager should buy enough futures contracts to cover the amount of expected cash inflow, so that any price increase in the price of bonds will be offset by a gain in the futures contracts when the manager finally covers and sells the contracts. That will allow the manager to buy the same number of bonds and enjoy the current interest yield on those bonds.

And then, there are stock market index options that can be useful in minimizing losses in pension funds with stocks in their portfolios. Think of the stock market index as a composite stock against which you can buy options.

Suppose a corporate pension fund manager has large gains in their stock portfolios and wants to preserve them. If there is a market correction, the manager may want to hold on to the gains. One strategy would be to buy put options so that any decline in the value of the stock portfolio is offset by equivalent gains in the puts.

There are many investment strategies that a firm can adopt by using options and futures. The goal is to keep options open so that the firm can make profitable investments at the right time. The idea is to spread the risk by increasing the choices available. These choices are made possible by the judicious use of options and futures. And, these instruments also serve as hedges against possible adverse events. In this way, they can reduce the risk faced by investors and managers of corporations.

FUTURES TRADING

Financial derivatives trading is not without significant dangers. Sometimes the hedging function of these derivatives becomes overshadowed by the temptation to leverage positions and engage in strategies based on the forecast of future events. Employees assigned the responsibility of hedging may be carried away by attempts to second-guess future price movements. The tragic outcomes of such actions are well documented by those who take liberties beyond the intended hedging function.

It is not unusual for bank trading desks to engage in financial derivatives investments based on a highly questionable forecast of exchange rates. The potential for higher returns associated with these highly leveraged positions are not justified by the enormous risks involved. Many financial institutions and managers of corporate pension funds include provisos in their prospectuses allowing a certain proportion of their portfolios to be invested in financial derivatives. This practice should be avoided as much as possible.

The application of financial derivatives strategies can help a manager to delay the exercise of choices available until more relevant information becomes available. Having waited for this information, the manager is given a better chance to select the best and least risky alternative. It is not practical to insure against all risks because the cost of insuring would be prohibitive. But judicious application of financial derivatives concepts will improve the firm's performance. You should be reminded that, in the final analysis, the value of options is largely dependent on the variability of the outcome. The greater the variability, the more risky the investment and the higher the cost of insurance to protect against this risk.

YOU SHOULD REMEMBER

There are two types of hedgers. Those who want to protect themselves against price increases (long hedgers) and those who want to insure themselves against price decreases (short hedgers). The goal is to use futures to offset any losses that may arise from a change in price. The long hedger buys futures contracts and completes the transaction by selling them at some future date. The short hedger sells future contracts initially and covers the transaction by buying them at a future date. A perfect hedge occurs when the basis (spot price – futures price) remains constant. If this basis changes, there may be only a partial hedge against price risk.

Corporate managers employ options and futures as portfolio insurance to preserve the value of their pension funds or to lock in a high current yield at some future date should the rate of interest decline. Options and futures have expanded the horizons of financial managers and play a key role for those seeking to make intelligent risk and return strategies.

SWAPS

A recent development in the field of finance is the swap agreement. Swap contracts are important for hedging purposes; they also allow firms to benefit from differences in markets. Essentially, a swap contract is similar to a forward contract. A forward contract involves two parties who agree to exchange cash for an asset (such as wheat) at some future date for the spot price of the asset. The swap has similar features. A **swap** is an agreement between firms with good reputations. The chance of default is small and the costs in a hedging transaction with swaps are lower than with futures or forwards. The more common types are currency swaps, interest rate swaps, and commodity swaps. For our purposes, we will confine our discussion to currency swaps.

In the case of currency swaps, two parties—mostly financial institutions or corporations—enter into a contract and agree to exchange a specified amount of one currency for a specific amount of another currency at some future date. One aim is to avoid exchange rate risk and another is to benefit from lower rates of interest.

Example: The Workings of a Currency Swap

Suppose a U.S. multinational firm had a foreign subsidiary in Britain that intends to invest in that country to expand capacity. Normally, the subsidiary would borrow in Britain and make payments in pounds, thereby avoiding exchange rate risk. However, let us assume the parent company, which operates in the United States, has a good credit rating and can borrow at a lower rate of interest than the cost of borrowing in Britain. Although the foreign firm needs pounds to operate in Britain, it borrows dollars in the United States at a lower rate. Conversely, a British company has obligations to make payments in dollars but can borrow in Britain at a lower rate of interest than it would have to pay should it decide to borrow dollars in the United States.

Both companies enter into a swap agreement. The U.S. foreign subsidiary contracts to exchange dollars for pounds and the British company exchanges pounds for dollars at a fixed exchange rate and a specified future period. We can visualize this swap contract as a forward currency contract with a maturity date and having a spot rate as the current exchange rate. Each company will avoid the risk of a change in exchange rates and both will enjoy a lower rate of interest.

Given the trend toward the globalization of firms, there are strong reasons to believe that the market for swaps will increase substantially in the future.

CREDIT DEFAULT SWAP (CDS)

A CDS can be viewed as insurance against credit deterioration on the part of the holder of an asset; i.e. a bondholder. Except for limited CDS indexes traded at a few organized exchanges, a CDS is an over-the-counter contract to transfer risk from one party (who owns the asset) to the other who wants to expose itself to the return and risk of the CDS. Note, in this case, the bondholder who is LONG (owns) a bond becomes SHORT (sells) the credit risk through purchasing a CDS contract.

In a simple CDS contract, Party X, who buys protection, transfers credit risk to Party Y (the protection seller). The protection buyer pays a premium to the protection seller to assume the risk. Using the jargon of the credit market, Party Y becomes "synthetically" long on the credit risk, and Party X is "synthetically" short. Theoretically, any two parties wishing to engage in transferring risk can engage in a CDS. The ISDA®, International Swaps and Derivatives Association, is a self-regulatory industry organization that sets recommended criteria and standards regarding documentation of a CDS. Since CDS is an over-the-contract product, it is all about documentation. Legal risk as how to interpret the provisions of a CDS is a major issue. The "counterparty risk," the problem that one party may not honor its obligations, is another source of uncertainty that creates "snowball effect" in the credit market; once one party becomes insolvent, the rest of the market is inevitably affected. Well-publicized cases of AIG, MBIA, and Assured Guarantee, which could not honor part of their obligations or did not receive the promised premium, are all examples of counterparty risk in the CDS market in 2007–2010. In response to those problems, counterparty risk, in particular, the Chicago Mercantile Exchange (CME), among others, promoted more and more standardized CDS Indexes.

The price of a CDS is quoted in terms of basis points. For example, a CDS could be quoted as 175, meaning the CDS buyer pays 1.75% of an agreed amount (notional) on an annual basis, paid quarterly. The price of a CDS is determined by a number of factors, depending on the model used. In the most basic actuarial approach, the assumption is that the expected value of payments by the insured entity (the protection buyer) should be equal to the expected value of payments by the insurer (the protection seller). In a basic model, the CDS price is affected, among others, by the following five factors:

a. The discount rate (which may vary depending on other parameters)

b. The probability that the insured entity will remain solvent (the probability of survival)

c. The portion of the insured asset that can be recovered after default (the recovery rate)

d. The duration of the contracts or the number of periods involved

e. Accrual adjustments (for the difference between the date of actual cash transactions and obligated dates)

The payment made by the protection buyer is assumed fixed, whereas the payment made by the protection seller is floating (i.e., unknown). Therefore, if the CDS pricing is fair, **the *PV* (present value) of these two expected payments should be the same.** More specifically, we should hold the following two payments equal at inception:

PV of float = ((1–recovery rate) × discount factor × probability of default)

PV of fixed = (premium × discount factor × probability of survival × accrual factors)

The changes in the parameters have different impacts on the *PV* of float and the *PV* of fixed. For example, if the survival probability goes up, the *PV* of fixed is reduced, whereas the *PV* of float increases. Default probability has a reverse effect; namely, when the probability of default goes up, the *PV* of fixed increases and the *PV* of float declines. Consistently, an increase in recovery rates decreases the *PV* of fixed and increases the *PV* of float.

The influence of the interest rate on CDS pricing is not straightforward; it depends on the shape of the yield curve. Generally, when the yield curve is relatively steep, the relationship between the interest rate and the price of the CDS is negative for the fixed leg and positive for the float. When the long-term and short-term interest rates are relatively flat, other factors need to be considered.

YOU SHOULD REMEMBER

The main purpose of futures and options is to hedge against risk and not to speculate on a projected future change in direction of the price of the underlying asset of these financial derivatives. Swap agreements involve commitments between two parties to exchange assets for a specified period of time. Several types of swaps are: currency swaps, commodity swaps, and interest rate swaps. In currency swaps, two firms exchange their own currencies in an effort to avoid exchange rate risk. Interest rate swaps involve an exchange of securities in order to change the composition of portfolios from a fixed-income type to a variable interest rate type, and vice versa, for a given period of time. The goal is to avoid substantial portfolio losses in a given period of time, or to take advantage of some change in interest rates at a future date. These swaps serve as temporary hedges and provide flexibility in financing, which would not be possible under ordinary circumstances or without incurring heavy transaction costs if futures and options were used as hedge vehicles.

KNOW THE CONCEPTS

DO YOU KNOW THE BASICS?

1. Explain how options supply choices available to managers who contemplate an investment that is contingent on the success of other developments, such as the outcome of a research and development project.

2. Cite two situations when investment decisions involve the consideration of option theory.

3. Define a call and a put option. Why do investors pay a premium to buy these two types of options?

4. What do we mean by in- and out-of-the-money calls and puts? And, theoretically, what is the value of an in- and out-of-the-money option? (Use the relationship between P_s and X_p to answer the question, stating whether the value is positive, negative, or zero.)

5. Why does the market value of an option usually exceed the theoretical or minimum price of an option? Why does the market value of an option finally move toward the theoretical value?

6. Cite five factors that determine the value of call options and explain in what way (+ or –) each factor affects this value if we assume each factor increases.

7. The Black and Scholes model calculates the value of options. What type of options is the model designed for and what three assumptions underlie the model?

8. Nd_1 and Nd_2 are essential to the Black and Scholes model. What kind of probabilities do these terms represent?

9. Present the two relationships that are essential for pricing options using the shortcut method. Having established these two relationships, how do we compute the final price of that option?

10. Why are call stock options offered to managers of a corporation? How do they work?

11. What two types of situations can futures serve as hedges against unforeseen price developments?

12. In what way do forward contracts differ from futures contracts?

13. What is meant by (a) marking to the market and (b) reverse trades?

14. Describe the role of the clearinghouse.

15. What happens when the long and short futures positions don't match? How do the speculators help to establish equilibrium between long and short positions?

16. Define basis and note what can happen to a long hedge position (using futures to accomplish this) if the basis declines from the current to a future date?

17. In what way can a corporate pension fund manager reduce the risk of a pension fund portfolio whose securities consist of stocks only? Also, how can futures be employed to hedge against a portfolio that contains bonds only?

18. Describe a swap agreement and indicate some of its advantages.

TERMS FOR STUDY

basis	margin
call option	marking to the market
European option	Nd_1
exercise price	Nd_2
expiration date	options
forward contract	option writer
futures	out-of-the-money option
hedging	put option
in-the-money option	short hedge position
long hedge position	swaps

PRACTICAL APPLICATION

COMPUTATIONAL PROBLEMS

1. An investor purchases a call option when the price of stock is $30 and the exercise price of the option is $35. What is the value of this option and why is that the case?

2. The current stock is selling for $90 and the exercise price of a put option is $100. Calculate the value of this put. What type of put is it when we say: $P_s X_p$?

3. A call option has an exercise price of $45, and the current price of the underlying stock is $55. Originally, the buyer of this call paid a $5 premium to purchase the call. How much profit will this investor make if the call contract is exercised?

4. Using the Black and Scholes model, calculate the fair value of a call option having the following features:

Price of stock	$75
Exercise price	$70
Nd_1	.68
Nd_2	.75
Risk-free rate	.05
Time to expiration	12 months

5. You are supplied with the following information:

Standard deviation of stock	.30
Time to expiration	1 year
Current cost of stock	$40
Exercise price	$37
Risk-free rate	−.10

Using the shortcut method, estimate the value of a call that has the foregoing parameters. The factor in the hedge ratio table corresponding to the two relationships is .203.

6. The futures price is $10.50, and the current spot price is $9.50. Calculate the basis of this relationship.

7. A corporation expects to purchase 5,000 bushels of soybeans 3 months from today. To hedge against a price increase, it establishes a long position and buys a futures contract (standard contract is for 5,000 bushels). Show how it can lock in the current price of $6.80 per bushel if the spot price 3 months from now turns out to be $7.50. The present futures price is $7.00 per bushel. Assume no change in the basis and there are no borrowing or other costs. How much would it pay to buy the soybeans in the spot market 3 months from now?

8. You are asked to analyze a one-period binomial model. The probability is .65 that the price of the stock will reach $140, and there is a .35 chance that it will fall to $60 in 6 months. If the interest rate is 10%, calculate the expected value of this option.

9. What is your expectation about the market trend under the following positions?

    (a) Buy a call option ....

    (b) Sell a call option ....

    (c) Buy a put option ....

    (d) Sell a put option ....

    (e) Simultaneous purchase of a call and put option on the same stock.

10. The value of an option delta shows the sensitivity of the option price to the changes in the price of the underlying stock. Assume you have 3 contracts of a call option (each contract gives you rights on 100 shares) and the value of delta is 0.50. What will happen to the total value of call options if the underlying stock price goes up by $2?

ANSWERS

KNOW THE CONCEPTS

1. Sometimes a corporate manager has to decide whether to make an investment or not make that investment. Let's say the investment involves buying a certain type of equipment to produce a product that is contingent on the outcome of the firm's research and development efforts. To protect against this uncertainty, the manager puts up a deposit on the new machine subject to cancellation should the research fail. The manager will exercise this option call and pay the full price of the equipment if the research works out. But if it does not, he or she will have the option of not buying the equipment, and in that case all that is lost is the deposit (value of the option).

2. The decision to abandon or continue a project is one option. The decision to modernize, rather than abandon, is another option. That is, buying an option to buy a more efficient attachment that will make existing equipment more efficient and profitable again.

3. A call option gives the right to a buyer to purchase stock at a stated price (exercise price) within a specified period of time. A put gives the right to a buyer to sell the stock to a writer at a stated price within a specified period of time. Investors buy calls and pay a premium because they anticipate the stock price will rise above the exercise price before expiration date. Investors will buy puts and pay a premium because they expect the price of the stock to decline below the exercise price of the stock before expiration date.

4. In the case of a call:

		Value of Option
In-the-money	$P_s > X_p$	Positive
Out-of-the-money	$P_s < X_p$	0

In the case of a put:

		Value of Option
In-the-money	$P_s < X_p$	Positive
Out-of-the-money	$P_s > X_p$	0

5. The market value of an option is greater than the theoretical value mainly because investors continue to expect the price of the stock to increase above the X_p and become profitable. At some point, the probability of further increases in the price of the stock becomes very small. That is when the market value of the option collapses toward the minimum value. Because favorable expectations vanish, there is no reason for paying a premium.

6. Five factors that determine the value of options are:

Factors	Value of Options (+ or –)
Increase in standard deviation of the price of the stock	+
Increase in time expectation	+
Increase in risk-free rate	+
Increase in P_s/X_p	+
Increase in cash dividend	–

7. The Black and Scholes model is designed to determine the value of European-type call options, which can be exercised only at the expiration date. The assumptions behind the model are: (1) The stock pays no dividends, (2) the stock price changes by very small increments, and (3) the exercise price is discounted by the risk-free rate.

8. Nd_1 represents the probability that the price of the stock will change sufficiently to provide a payoff and Nd_2 is the probability that the option will be exercised. Usually, the greater the volatility of the stock price, the higher the probability that it will pay off, and the more "in" the money the option, the better the chance of exercise.

9. The shortcut method employs the following two relationships:

$$\sigma\sqrt{\tau}$$

$$P_s \Big/ \frac{X_p}{e^{rt}}$$

If we look up the corresponding factor in a hedge ratio table, we can determine the value of an option by the following formula:

Option value = Factor × Current price of the stock

10. Call options are offered to good managers as incentives to stay with the firm and make every effort to increase the profits of the firm. Because these call options have a low exercise price, they represent a strong inducement to perform. The greater the earnings, the higher the price of the stock and the greater the profit from exercising the option. For example, the board of directors may say to a manager: We will give you a call option to buy the company stock after 5 years at $10. Should the stock rise to $20 per share, the manager can exercise the call option by buying the stock at $10 from the company and selling the stock in the open market at $20, making a $10 profit on each share in the option agreement.

11. Managers may take a long-hedge position or a short-hedge position. For example, suppliers of raw materials may want to lock in the current price of materials and insure against a loss if prices were to fall. They do so by selling futures contracts (taking a short position) now and then buying back these contracts at a future date. Any price decline in the spot market will be offset by a corresponding gain (assuming a perfect hedge) in the futures contracts. Buyers of raw materials want to avoid price increases, and therefore they buy futures contracts now and sell them later. By taking this long position any price increase in the spot market will be offset by the gain made on the futures contracts.

12. Forward contracts are negotiated between two parties, but futures contracts are bought and sold on an exchange where prices are quoted daily. Each forward contract has tailor-made specifications as to the type of goods, quantity, quality, and time. Futures contracts have standard features which don't change. Therefore, each buyer and seller knows the exact description and terms of the commodity for a given contract.

A forward contract relies on the trust and honesty of the two parties who are part of the contract. There is no guarantee that the contract will be consummated. In the futures market, any breach of contract is guaranteed by the clearing house, which stands ready to complete the contract should either party fail to fulfill his or her obligations.

A forward contract usually leads to the physical delivery of the commodity. Most futures contracts do not involve delivery of the commodity. In the futures market, losses and gains due to price changes are settled on a daily basis by the parties involved, whereas forward contracts don't have this arrangement as a safeguard.

13. Marking to the market means that there are daily settlements in futures contract accounts with brokers. An investor who buys futures contracts with a broker establishes an account and must set aside some cash or Treasury bills to cover margin requirements. The prices of futures change daily. That results in a gain or loss in the account. When price changes result in a gain, the account is credited with this gain every day. If price changes produce a loss, the customer is asked to make up this loss on a daily basis. Usually, commodity accounts with brokers require customers to maintain a specified cash balance that brokers draw on to make up any daily deficiencies in the account when losses are incurred.

14. The clearinghouse is an arm of the exchange that acts as a middleman in transactions between broker and customer. Its functions are to make sure that contract agreements are honored. Should any party default on the contract, the clearinghouse uses its own capital to complete the futures contract transaction. The clearinghouse is an overseer of trading practices and makes sure that all the rules are followed by traders in futures.

15. The exchange tries to match long and short future positions, and this allows the hedging process to work efficiently. When there is a net short or a net long position, speculators are called into play. They fill the void or deficiency and must be properly compensated for taking this risk. The risk is the uncertainty of changes in the future expected spot price. Should spot prices change in the direction opposite to the one anticipated by speculators, they bear the risk of that loss. In essence, the speculators buy long futures when hedger positions are net short, and short futures when hedger positions are net long.

    Long positions: buy now and sell futures later

    Short positions: sell now and buy futures later

16. Basis = Spot price – Futures price
    When the futures price fails to increase as much as the spot price, there is only a partial hedge. This means that the gain in futures contracts, used to hedge against an increase in a futures spot price, did not fully cover the opportunity loss that an investor incurs by having to buy the commodity at a higher price in the spot market at some future date.

17. Corporate pension fund managers can reduce the risk of a decline in the value of a stock fund's portfolio by buying stock market index put options. The loss in the portfolio is offset by the gain in the put options. If the fund consists of fixed income securities, the manager can sell financial interest rate futures (regard financial futures contracts

the same as commodity futures contracts) and cover by buying these contracts at a future date. The loss in the portfolio value is offset by the gain in the futures short position established by the manager.

18. A swap is similar to a forward contract. It represents an agreement between two parties to exchange assets, currencies, or commodities for a specified period of time. The agreement allows each party to use the asset for a given period of time and can provide protection against changing values in these assets during the agreement period. For example, a domestic company needs pesos and a Mexican company needs dollars. They both swap their currencies and avoid the exchange rate risks incurred when currency devaluations occur. Similar swaps occur when a firm wants to turn its fixed-income portfolio into a variable rate portfolio. These agreements are entered into by reputable large corporations or institutions with little chance that any party will renege on the agreement.

PRACTICAL APPLICATION

1. The theoretical value of this call is zero because it is out of the money and because no one is going to pay $35 to purchase the stock by exercising the option if the same stock can be purchased for $30 in the open market.

2. The value of the put is positive because

$$P_s < X_p \text{ or } X_p > P_s$$

then

$$\$100 - \$90 = \$10 \text{ Value of put}$$

This put is in the money.

3. A call option contract consists of 100 shares of stock. If the investor exercises this call, he or she will make a profit of $10 per share. Since a $5 premium was paid to buy the option, the net profit is $5, and the total profit on this contract is $5 × 100 shares = $500.

4. The formula is

$$P_s(Nd_1) - \left[\frac{X_p}{e^{rt}}(Nd_2) \right]$$

The solution is

$$\text{Value of call} = \$75(.68) - \left[\frac{\$70}{e^{.05 \times 1}}(.75) \right] = \$1.06$$

5. Shortcut method relationships:

$$\sigma\sqrt{\tau} = .30 \times \sqrt{1} = .30$$

$$\frac{\dfrac{P_s}{X_p}}{\dfrac{}{e^{rt}}} = \frac{\dfrac{\$75}{\$70}}{\dfrac{}{e^{10\times1}}} = \frac{\dfrac{\$75}{\$70}}{\overline{1.1052}} = \frac{\dfrac{75}{63.34}}{} = 1.18$$

Factor × Price of stock

Value of call = .203 × \$75 = \$15.23

6. Basis = Spot price – Futures price
   = \$10.50 – \$9.50 = + \$1.00 (basis)

7. Corporation long hedge position:

Spot price	Futures contract price	Spot price – Futures price
\$6.80	\$7.00 (buy)	–.20
7.50	7.70 (sell)	–.20
– \$.70 loss	+\$.70 gain	0

The corporation would buy soybeans in the spot market at \$7.50 per bushel. It has to pay 70 cents more than the current spot price. But because it gained 70 cents per bushel on the futures contract, the net cost to the corporation is \$6.80. That means that the total cost to purchase 5,000 bushels (disregarding other costs) is 5,000 × \$6.80 = \$34,000 instead of \$37,500, the amount it would have paid had it failed to hedge against a price increase.

8. Expected value of option = [(.65) × (\$40) + (.35) × (0)]/1.10 = \$23.64

9. (a) Buy a call option: Expectation is Bullish.
   (b) Sell a call option: Expectation is Bearish.
   (c) Buy a put option: Expectation is Bearish.
   (d) Sell a put option: Expectation is Bullish.
   (e) Simultaneous purchase of a call and put option on the same stock: Expectation: We are not sure about the direction of the market.

10. 3 contracts × 100 shares × 0.50 × \$2 = \$300 increase in the value of call options

SHORT- AND LONG-TERM CAPITAL SOURCES

12

LEASES

BASICS OF LEASING

A **lease** is a legal contract between two parties, the **lessor**, who owns the asset, and the **lessee**, who uses the asset. The lessor gives the lessee the right to use the asset for a specified period of time. In return, the lessee agrees to pay a certain amount of rent during the lease period. Commonly leased items are computers, equipment, cars, apartments, and offices. Lessors and lessees can be people or companies. Commercial banks, automobile dealers, and lease companies are major lessors in today's market.

The procedure to lease an asset is basically the same as that for borrowing money, though with some significant differences. After selecting the equipment (or other asset), the lessee contacts a leasing company and applies for lease financing. Following the receipt of the lease application, the lessor carefully evaluates the lessee's credit record, prepares a description, and determines the cost of the asset to be leased. Once the application has been approved, the lessor informs the lessee how much the annual rental payments are, the dates when payments are due, the arrangements for the maintenance of the equipment, and other rights and obligations of the lessee during the lease period. If the lessee finds the terms and conditions acceptable, a lease contract is signed and the equipment is delivered to the lessee. At the end of the lease period, the leased equipment is returned to the lessor.

The contract may contain a clause giving the lessee the option to purchase the asset during, or at the end of, the contract period. At the end of the lease period, should the lessee decide to exercise this option, he or she will make an additional payment to the lessor, as stipulated by the contract, and the lessee then becomes the new owner of the asset.

ADVANTAGES OF LEASING

There are a number of advantages to leasing equipment rather than borrowing money to purchase it.

Leases place fewer restrictions on the lessee than on the borrower. Since the title of the leased equipment is in the name of the lessor, a lease is like financing with collateral. In simple terms, if the lessee fails to pay the annual or periodic rent, the lessor can easily reclaim the equipment because it legally belongs to the leasing company. The leasing company does not have to impose many restrictions on the lessee. Applications for leases are usually approved faster, and with more relaxed credit standards, than those for borrowing.

A lessee does not have to raise capital by issuing bonds or new common stock. When issuing bonds and common stock, a firm must follow certain procedures required by regulatory agencies and investment bankers, such as Merrill Lynch. On the other hand, leasing is a straightforward arrangement between the lessor and the lessee. Moreover, leases are not subject to a number of restrictive covenants that are incurred when a firm finances by issuing debt.

Another main advantage of a lease is that the lessee passes the risk of obsolescence (the risk that the equipment becomes outdated) to the lessor. In the business environment of today, innovative ideas and products can become outdated quickly. Even the best equipment today may become obsolete in a short time. Borrowing a lot of money and buying risky equipment may not be an economically sound investment, because the value of this investment will drastically decline if new and more efficient equipment is brought to the market a few years after the purchase. This is especially true in the case of high-technology products, such as computers and precision instruments. In such cases, leasing can be a good alternative to buying the equipment.

Leasing, unlike purchasing, does not require a large initial investment. Lease expenses are paid over a period of time, so there is less financial burden on the lessee. Also, because the lessor receives a tax advantage on the leased equipment, the lease offer may be cheaper than the purchase price charged by a manufacturer. In other words, the lessor may share the tax benefits with customers who regularly lease equipment, and in most cases the annual lease payments are tax deductible.

DISADVANTAGES OF LEASING

The disadvantages of leasing should also be considered whenever there is a choice between leasing and purchasing. A lessee, unlike the buyer of an asset, cannot depreciate the asset, so the tax benefit of depreciation will be lost. The loss of this depreciation benefit can be very costly for a solvent company with a large taxable income and only a small amount of debt.

Another disadvantage is that the lessee has to return the equipment after a certain period. What happens if the lessor decides not to renew the lease contract when the lessee badly needs the equipment to continue the operations of the firm? Because of this possibility, leasing with an option to buy should be considered.

When equipment is leased rather than owned, any major modification to improve the efficiency of the equipment needs the approval of the lessor. Getting the lessor's approval for technical modifications during the period of the lease contract may not be easy. This means that the lessee does not have complete control over the use of equipment that an owner would enjoy.

Another obvious disadvantage of a lease is the loss of salvage value. Salvage value of a purchased asset increases the cash inflow of the company if the asset is sold at the end of its last year. This advantage is lost if the asset is leased.

Small firms often favor leasing rather than borrowing because of the high interest charged by banks or the high coupon rate they have to pay when issuing bonds. The cash that is retained in the firm instead of an up-front full payment to purchase the asset is released for investment in a firm and earns a return. Also, lessees avoid the uncertainty of the risk associated with estimating residual value. This risk is borne by the lessor.

Leases are not a one-way street. The lessor has the opportunity to charge a rental that is high enough to cover most of the risks of leasing. When the contract ends, the lessor can sell or lease the asset to another lessee. The most important advantages accruing to lessors are the tax shield benefits from depreciation and interest expense deductions.

YOU SHOULD REMEMBER

A lease is a contract between two parties: the lessor, who owns the asset, and the lessee, who uses it. From the viewpoint of a lessee, leasing is flexible financing and permits better timing of more permanent investments. By leasing, a firm can keep pace with technological advances and the periodic payments are tax deductible. Lessors benefit from the depreciation and interest expense tax shields.

TYPES OF LEASES

There are four well-known types of leases:

1. Operating or service lease
2. Capital or financial lease
3. Sale-and-leaseback lease
4. Leveraged lease

An **operating lease** has a life span of no more than 5 years. All maintenance and repairs are the responsibility of the lessor. These leases are cancellable at the option of the lessee. They are written for periods that are shorter than the economic life of the asset.

A **capital or financial lease** is a long-term contract between the lessee and the lessor and is noncancellable. The asset is usually fully amortized. Maintenance and repairs are the responsibility of the lessee.

In a **sale-and-leaseback** arrangement, the owner of an asset sells the asset to another company and leases it back for a specified period of time. The original owner of the asset now becomes the lessee. This arrangement allows a company to raise capital and still retain use of the asset. At the end of the contract, the lessee buys back the asset. This type of leasing is a form of temporary borrowing of funds.

Leveraged leasing involves four parties:

1. Lessor
2. Lessee
3. Lender
4. Trustee

The lessor puts up part of the purchase price of the asset, let us say about 20%. The remaining 80% of the purchase price is provided by other lenders, who receive a first mortgage secured loan collateralized by the leased asset. A trustee holds title to the lease contract, and the periodic rental payments are sent to this person. In turn, the trustee pays the interest and principal to the lenders, and the residual is sent to the lessor as a rental payment. When the lease ends, the trustee pays off the creditors and the lessor gains ownership of the asset.

The Financial Accounting Standards Board (FASB) has reviewed this aspect of leasing carefully. Their decision is that an operating lease does not have to be included in the balance sheet. Most companies report these leases in a footnote.

• *FASB AND IRS RULES*

According to FASB rule #13, the present value of a capital lease must be reported as both an asset and a liability on a company's balance sheet. Therefore, the "Board" recognizes that a financial lease is similar to the borrowing of funds or an outright purchase of an asset. To be considered a financial lease for accounting purposes, the FASB rule #13 stipulates that:

- The lessee has an option to purchase the property.

- The contract is for three-quarters (or more) of the life of the property.

- The present value of lease payments is 90% (or more) of the purchase price of the property.

All lease payments are deducted from revenues as annual expenses.

The Internal Revenue Service (IRS) also has its definition of what constitutes a valid lease.

- The asset must be subject to depreciation.

- The lease has economic justification, and the contract is not designed to avoid taxes.

- A lease contract is signed within 90 days after the asset is placed in service.

- The lessee is given the option to purchase the asset on expiration date for an amount equal to 10% or more of the original cost of the asset.

The main concern of the IRS is to make sure that lease contracts are not consummated to avoid taxes.

• *IS A LEASE AN ASSET OR A LIABILITY?*

There has been a great deal of discussion among accountants whether or not a lease should be reported on a balance sheet as an asset. One argument is that the equipment leased is an asset because it is continuously used by the lessee—like any other asset in the company. An opposite argument is that the lessee actually borrows the equipment and uses the leased equipment on a temporary basis; therefore, the lease is a current expenditure like other rentals. If this argument is accepted, a lease should not be reported on the balance sheet and cannot be depreciated. Instead, annual lease payments should be reported as current expenses on the income statement.

Part of this argument has been resolved in the case of capital leases. These long-term lease contracts are viewed as debt equivalents. As a result, they must appear in the balance sheet. The valuation treatment calls for determining the present value of annual rentals, using an appropriate discount rate. This value appears on the asset side of the balance sheet, representing the value of the asset and on the liability side as a long-term obligation of the company. The firm then selects a period to amortize the present value of the lease. At the end of the lease contract, the lease will be fully amortized, and the lease obligation will be wiped off the books.

Unfortunately, no satisfactory accounting rules have been established for operating leases. These short-term contracts appear only in the footnotes of the balance sheet. Some firms do a large part of their financing based on operating leases. That is why certain biases emerge in the calculations of financial ratios unless some adjustments are made to include operating leases when making a financial and comparative analysis of the firm.

YOU SHOULD REMEMBER

In the case of a capital lease, the lessee should estimate the present value of lease payments, reporting that figure both as an asset and as a liability on the balance sheet. If the property is an operating lease, the accounting treatment is more straightforward. They appear in a footnote on the balance sheet. At the end of each year, total lease payments are deducted from revenues—like other annual expenses on the income statement.

CASH FLOWS OF A LEASE

Lease payments are somewhat like an annuity in which the first payment is made before the lease starts. In other words, lease payments are made at the beginning of each time period rather than the end. Since lease payments are made at the beginning of the time period, the lessee usually does not receive a tax benefit in the first period. The IRS does not allow deductions of lease payments covering a period of time before the leased equipment is actually used.

Example: Cash Flows of a Lease

Suppose the ABC Co., which is in the 40% tax bracket, leases equipment for 5 years with annual lease payments of $10,000 starting in January 1985.

In 1985, the ABC Co. pays $10,000, but no tax benefit accrues in that year. The cash outflow of the lease in the first year is $10,000, paid in the beginning of the year. The first tax benefit of $4,000 (40% × $10,000) is realized in the following year, reducing the effective lease payment of 1986 to only $6,000. This $6,000 is the cash outflow of the lease, or the actual cost of the lease after the tax benefit is deducted.

Table 12–1   Cash Flow of the Lease for the ABC Co.

Year	Lease Payment	Tax Benefit	Cash Outflows of Lease
1985	$10,000	0	– $10,000
1986	10,000	$4,000	– 6,000
1987	10,000	4,000	– 6,000
1988	10,000	4,000	– 6,000
1989	10,000	4,000	– 6,000
1990	0	4,000	+ 4,000

The cash outflow of the lease is $6,000 each year from 1986 to 1989. In 1990, the lease contract expires, and no further lease payment is due. However, the ABC Co. has claimed tax benefits for only 4 years, from 1986 to 1989, and has not received the tax benefit of the last lease payment in 1989. Therefore, in 1990 the ABC Co. claims the $4,000 tax credit, which was not taken before.

A word of caution: it has become common practice, especially in thc case of automobile companies, to include in lease contracts a substantial upfront or terminal-period cash payment. This practice masks the true cost of the lease. These cash payments must be added in the appropriate time slots to obtain the actual stream of cash outflows.

The preceding example (Table 12-1) shows that tax benefits can be a major motivation for leasing assets. In reality, though, a company that doesn't have a great deal of taxable income cannot immediately enjoy the tax benefit of a lease. This company can, however, try to find a bank or financial institution with a considerable net income and tax liability. Such a bank has good motivation to purchase an asset and lease it to the company. Once the bank (the lessor) purchases the equipment, it can depreciate the asset and reduce its tax liability. At the same time, the company (the lessee) will expect the bank to share the tax benefits through favorable lease payments and more flexible terms.

Since lease contracts offer a great opportunity for reducing taxes, many lessors are wealthy individuals and profitable corporations with substantial tax liabilities. Congress has tried to weaken the tax motivation of lease contracts. One objective of the Economic Recovery Tax Act of 1981 was to reduce the depreciation lives of various types of assets to make the purchase of an asset more attractive than a lease because of faster depreciation. However, leases are widely used in many industries, and there is no evidence that the growth of this popular form of financing will decline in the future.

• *CALCULATING ANNUAL RENTAL CHARGES*

A lessor must determine the annual payment to charge a lessee. To do this, the lessor must establish the following:

1. Cost of purchasing the leased asset

2. Present value of the benefits derived from outright ownership of the asset

3. Net cost = Cost of leased asset – *PV* of benefits.

Example:

The cost of the leased payment is $2.0 million. The life of the asset is 3 years. The discount rate (K_{dt}) is 9%, and depreciation is based on the ACRS schedule (.33, .44, .23). Calculate the before-tax annual rental of the equipment.

Although other tax shields and benefits may accrue to the lessor, such as salvage value, the presentation can be simplified if we narrow the benefits to depreciation only and assume salvage value is equal to zero at the end of the contract. The present value of the benefits from owning an asset is

$$\text{Present value of benefits} = \sum_{t=1}^{N} \frac{\text{Annual depreciation (T)}}{1+k}$$

In its tabular format, this present value is shown in Table 12-2.

Table 12–2 Present Value of Benefits of Owning

Period	Depreciation	Depreciation (T) @ .40	PVIF @ 9%	PV
1	$660,000	$264,000	.917	$242,088
2	880,000	352,000	.842	296,384
3	460,000	184,000	.772	142,048
				$680,520

* Note: First-year depreciation = $660,000 ($2,000,000 × .33)
Second-year depreciation = $880,000 ($2,000,000 × .44)
Third-year depreciation = $460,000 ($2,000,000 × .23)

The net cost of this leased asset is

Net cost = Cost of asset − PV benefits

$$= \$2,000,000 - \$680,520 = \$1,319.480$$

Because the lease payment is an annuity due (or equal rentals over 3 years), it is necessary to obtain the $(PVIFA_{k,n})$ $(1 + k)$ for 3 years at a discount rate that permits the lessor to obtain a given required rate of return for the risk involved. The term $(1 + k)$ is added to the annuity factor because this is an annuity due that includes a payment right after the contract is signed.

The after-tax lease payments are calculated as follows, if the lessor's required rate of return is 15%:

$$\frac{\text{After-tax}}{\text{annual lease payments}} = \frac{\text{Net cost to lessor}}{(PVIFA_{k,n})(1+k)}$$

In other words, given $k = 15\%$ and $n = 3$ years, the annual lease payments will amount to

$$\frac{\text{After-tax}}{\text{annual lease payments}} = \frac{\$1,391,480}{(PVAF_{.15,3})(1+.15)} = \frac{\$1,391,480}{(2.283)(1.15)} = \$502,659$$

Leasors have the option of quoting annual payments on a before- or after-tax basis, depending on market conditions and how eager they are to rent out equipment. That is why it is useful to calculate lease payments on a before-tax basis. Assuming a tax rate of 40%, the before-tax payments are calculated in the following manner.

$$\text{Before-tax lease payments} = \frac{\text{After-tax payments}}{1 - \text{tax rate}}$$

We have already established that the annual after-tax payments amount to $502,659. Converting to a before-tax basis, we find out that the payments increase to $837,765.

$$\text{Before-tax lease payments} = \frac{\$502,659}{1-.40} = \$837,765$$

Sometimes lease advertising can be deceiving unless properly interpreted. We often see TV ads by auto leasing companies that say: A 3-year car lease has a monthly rental of $399. Less obvious is the requirement of a $1,000 down payment. That $1,000 payment raises the effective rental by about $30 monthly so that the leased car is actually costing $429 a month. This down payment raises the present value of cash out flows and may make the lease a little less attractive than buying an asset.

COMPARING RATES OF RETURNS CHARGED A LESSEE

Suppose you are shopping around for the best deal in a lease and want to compare the rate of return you are being charged with the one charged by others. The procedure in that case would call for solving the annuity due factor and then looking up the required rate of return in a present value annuity due table (or multiply the annuity factor by $1 + k$). Given the previous example, if the leasing firm lets you know that the after-tax annual rental is $502,659 and you calculate the net cost to be $1,319,480. To find the lessor's rate of return, first compute the factor as shown:

$$\text{Factor} = \frac{\$1,319,480}{\$502,659} = 2.625$$

Then look up this factor in the *PV* annuity due table, and the answer is 15%. This tells you that the rate of return charge by the lessor is 15%, which can be compared to the rates charged by other leasing companies.

The question may be raised: Although you know the purchase price, how can you compute the present value of the benefits if the borrowing discount rate (K_d) is unknown? One way of getting around this problem is to find a listed bond of a leasing company and estimate the yield to maturity of that bond. This will be the discount rate applied to discount the depreciation benefits of the lease. The method may not yield the exact rates charged by each lessor, but it will provide a ranking of these rates for comparison purposes.

Now that the lessee knows how to calculate the payments necessary to lease the equipment, the primary concern is to find out whether it is cheaper to lease or to buy the equipment outright. That decision depends on the nature of the outflows. If the net outflows (or costs) are higher for leasing, it makes sense to borrow money to buy the equipment rather than lease it.

YOU SHOULD REMEMBER

Annual rental charges are computed by dividing the net cost to the lessor by the appropriate *PV* annuity due factor. The lessee can compare the rates of returns charged simply by obtaining the factor as follows:

$$\text{Factor} = \frac{\text{Net costs}}{\text{Annual rental}}$$

Then, find the corresponding rate in the *PV* annuity due table. The *IRR* and present value for making a decision to purchase or lease are based on the assessment of cash outflows, not inflows. Therefore, it is the lowest cost that decides which financing should be chosen.

• *LEASE VERSUS PURCHASE: A PRESENT VALUE APPROACH*

Business owners and managers are often faced with the question whether to lease or purchase an asset. When an asset is leased, the lessee does not have to be concerned about raising capital, since the lessor is responsible for financing the project. On the other hand, the lessee loses both the tax savings on depreciation and the salvage value. The loss of these benefits should not be ignored when a comparison is made between the cost of a lease and the cost of a purchase.

In making the final decision whether to lease or to purchase, financial analysts try to pick the less expensive alternative. Since most expenses, such as lease payments, and most benefits, such as tax benefits, occur in the future, a good way to evaluate the lease and purchase options is to compare the net costs of both alternatives in terms of present dollars. This is where the net present value (*NPV*) technique can be helpful.

In other words, the question whether to lease or purchase can be answered if the present values of the expenses for leasing are compared to the purchase price. When you use this technique, the approach is similar to a capital-budgeting problem. However, there is a major difference between capital-budgeting problems and lease problems. In capital budgeting, the project with the *higher NPV* is the preferred one, whereas in the case of lease versus purchase, the option with the *lower* present value of expenditure should be selected.

Example: Choosing Between Leasing and Purchasing

PROBLEM XYZ Inc. is in the 40% tax bracket and plans to buy a precision tool. It employs the ACRS method to compute depreciation. The tool costs $50,000 and has a life of 5 years. The new tool can be financed in two ways:

(a) borrow and buy the tool or (b) lease the tool.

Borrow and Buy Alternative. The first alternative is to borrow $50,000 at 12% and buy the tool. This would mean that over the next 5 years, the XYZ company would have to pay a total of $13,870 annually (see the following calculation), which includes part interest and part principal to amortize the loan.

$$\frac{\text{Annual loan}}{\text{repayment}} = \frac{\text{Amount borrowed}}{PVAF_{k,n}} = \frac{\$50,000}{3.605_{(12\%,5\ yr)}} = \$13,870$$

Because interest is one of the deductible expenses (depreciation being the other), it is necessary to calculate the yearly interest incurred to borrow the funds. That can be done by working out a loan amortization schedule as we have done in Table 12-3.

Table 12–3 Calculating Interest Using the Loan Amortization Method*

Years	Annual Loan Payment	Principal at Beginning	Annual Interest	Repayment of Principal	Principal at End of Period
					$50,000
1	$13,870	$50,000	$6,000	$7,870	$42,130
2	13,870	42,130	5,056	8,814	33,316
3	13,870	33,316	3,998	9,872	23,444
4	13,870	23,444	2,813	11,057	12,387
5	13,870	12,387	1,486	12,384	3

*Interest rate on loan = 12%.

Table 12-3 reveals that interest payments decline from the first to the fifth year because part of the loan is being repaid each year leaving less and less principal on which interest is calculated.

Lease Alternative. After contacting several leasing companies, the firm finds out that the best leasing contract it could sign would call for an annual payment of $11,000.

The decision is to select the best of two alternatives. The aim then is to select the financing method that produces the lowest present value cost.

The tax benefit of lease payments in column 2 of Table 12-4 is calculated by multiplying the lease payments in column 1 by the 40% tax rate. The cash flow in column 3 is the lease payment minus the tax benefit. To calculate present value, 7% is used to discount the cash outflows. Note that this 7% is the after-tax cost of borrowing at 12% (12% × (1 – 40%) = 7.2%). The reason for using the after-tax cost of borrowing of 7% is that the figures for cash flows include the tax benefit. To avoid counting the tax benefit twice, cash flows should always be discounted at an after-tax rate, which in this example is about 7%. The total present value of the lease expenditure is $30,218.

SOLUTION **1.** *Calculating the present value of lease outflows.* Because annual lease costs are deductible the net cost to the lessee is annual rental minus tax benefits.

2. *Calculating the present value of the purchase expenditures.* The way this is done is illustrated in Table 12-4.

Table 12–4 Present Value of the Lease Expenditure

Year	Payment (1)	Tax Benefit* (2)	Cash Outflows (3) = (1) – (2)	PVIF at 7% (4)	Present Value Of Cash Outflows 5 = (3)(4)
0	$11,000	0	$11,000	1.000	$11,000
1	11,000	$4,400	6,600	.935	6,171
2	11,000	4,400	6,600	.873	5,762
3	11,000	4,400	6,600	.816	5,386
4	11,000	4,400	6,600	.763	5,036
5	0	4,400	(4,400)	.713	(3,137)
				Present value of lease expenditure =	$30,218

*Tax benefit = Payment × .40.

In Table 12-5, column 1 is the annual loan repayment from which the tax benefit of interest and depreciation should be deducted. The tax benefit, as reported in column 5, is computed by multiplying the interest and depreciation expenses by the tax rate of 40%. By subtracting the tax benefit from the annual loan repayment, the loan repayment after tax is calculated in column 6. In column 8, the present value of loan repayments has been determined, using the present value factor at 7%, to obtain a total value of $33,556. The decision process then becomes:

1. When *PV* leasing > *PV* purchase, then borrow and buy the equipment.

2. When *PV* leasing < *PV* purchase, then lease the equipment.

Table 12–5 Present Value of the Purchase Expenditure

Year	Loan Repayment (1)	Interest (2)	Depreciation* (3)	Deductible Expenses: Interest + Depreciation (4) = (2) + (3)	Tax Benefit at 40% (5)	Loan Repayment After Tax (6) = (1) – (5)	Present Value Factor at 7% (7)	Present Value of Loan Repayment After Tax (8) = (6)(7)
1	$13,870	$6,000	$10,000	$16,000	$6,400	$7,470	.935	$6,984
2	13,870	5,056	16,000	21,056	8,422	5,448	.873	4,756
3	13,870	3,998	9,500	13,498	5,399	8,471	.816	6,912
4	13,870	2,813	7,500	10,313	4,125	9,745	.763	7,435
5	13,870	1,486	7,000	8,486	3,394	10,476	.713	7,469
								PV = $33,556

*Annual depreciation, computed on the ACRS basis, is 20%, 32%, 19%, 15%, and 14% in years 1 through 5, respectively.

Because the present value of the lease expenditure ($30,218) is lower than $33,556, the lease option is more economical. Broadly speaking, XYZ Inc. would save $3,338 in current dollars by leasing rather than purchasing the equipment ($33,556 – $30,218 = $3,338). Without this analysis, the firm might have decided to borrow $50,000 from a bank, purchased the equipment, and lost the opportunity to save $3,338 by exercising the lease option. *Always work out a step-by-step comparison before making a final decision whether to lease or purchase.*

One more point before we conclude the discussion of leasing versus purchasing. Sometimes it is useful to translate the decision process in terms of relative rather than absolute numbers. Instead of comparing the two dollar amounts of lease and purchase, we might consider determining the rate of discount that would bring the cost of lease down to the cost of purchase. Just as we did in capital budgeting, to obtain the internal rate of return of a project (where $NPV = 0$), all we have to do is lower the discount rate of the lease cash outflows (Table 12-4) to raise the $30,218 cost figure to $33,556. In this case, we find that the after-tax cost of borrowing would be 7% and the corresponding internal rate of return would be 6%. Consequently, using this approach, because the internal rate of return for leasing is less than the borrowing rate, the equipment should be leased.

YOU SHOULD REMEMBER

A step-by-step comparison, using the net present value approach, is recommended to determine which alternative—lease or purchase—is more economical. Unless these analytical techniques are used to study the options available, a firm can pay more than it should. When deciding whether to buy or lease, select the one that yields the lowest present value expenditure. The *IRR* approach can also be employed to make this decision. In this case, the lowest *IRR* between buy and lease should determine the best financing alternative.

KNOW THE CONCEPTS

DO YOU KNOW THE BASICS?

1. What is a lease?
2. What is a major difference between an operating lease and a capital or financial lease?

3. Is a lease an asset or a liability?

4. What are the main advantages of leasing?

5. Describe a method to compare the rate of return charged by different companies to lease a given asset.

6. What kind of cash flows are we talking about in making a buy-lease decision? How does the decision process work when we apply the *NPV* and the *IRR* methods to decide whether to purchase or lease?

7. Explain the difference between leveraged leases and sale-and-leaseback leases.

8. Explain the accounting treatment of a capital versus an operating lease.

9. What are three benefits that accrue to a lessor and represent opportunity losses for a lessee?

TERMS FOR STUDY

capital or financial lease   leveraged leasing
lease   operating lease
lessee   sale and leaseback
lessor

PRACTICAL APPLICATION

COMPUTATIONAL PROBLEMS

1. The XYZ Co., which is in the 40% tax bracket, leases new equipment for 5 years at an annual lease payment of $10,000, due at the beginning of each year. Determine the annual cash outflows of the lease if the after-tax cost of borrowing is $5,900.

2. What decision would you make if the present value of borrowing turned out to be $59,000; the cost of leasing $65,000?

The next problem supplies information to be used in answering Problems 3-6.

George and Associates are planning to buy a machine that costs $80,000. The machine can be purchased or leased. The company is in a 40% tax bracket. If the machine is leased, the company will make equal payments of $19,810 at the beginning of each year. The lease will be for 5 years. If the firm borrows money to buy the machine, it has to pay 15% to issue debt. Annual payments on the loan will be $23,302, and the machine will be depreciated over a period of 5 years under the ACRS. ACRS Factors = 15%, 22%, 21%, 21%, 21%. The salvage value is expected to be $10,000.

3. Calculate the interest payments for the next 5 years if funds are borrowed.

4. Calculate *PV* of cash flows for leasing.

5. Calculate *PV* of cash flows for purchase.

6. State which option (buy or lease) is preferable.

7. Vista Company uses the straight-line depreciation method and has an after-tax cost of borrowing of 6% and is subject to a 40% tax rate. It is contemplating the purchase of a machine for $90,000 and there are no other benefits like salvage value. It wants to lease the machine for 3 years at a required rate of return of 13%. Calculate the net cost of the annual after-tax lease payments Vista will charge a lessee.

8. Would you recommend lease financing if the after-tax cost of borrowing is 10% compared to 12% for leasing?

ANSWERS

KNOW THE CONCEPTS

1. A lease is a legal contract in which the lessor gives the lessee the right to use an asset. The lessee agrees to pay a certain amount of rent each year (period) and to return the asset when the lease contract has expired.

2. An operating lease is an agreement usually for less than 5 years, whereas a capital or financial lease is a long-term contract for longer than 5 years. In an operating lease, the lessor is responsible for maintenance, insurance, taxes, and so on. These expenses are the lessee's responsibilities in a capital lease.

3. A lease is both an asset and a liability. The value of a capital or financial lease equals the present value of its future cash outflows and is included on the balance sheet as an asset and a liability.

4. The main advantages of leasing are 100% financing, avoiding the risk that the asset will become obsolete, and flexible financing.

5. When a lessee wishes to compare the rates of return charged by different lessors, he/she computes the present value annuity due factor and looks up the rate of return in an annuity due table. The formula is

$$\text{Rate of return charged the lessee} = \frac{\text{Net cost to lessor}}{\text{Annual rental}} = \text{Annuity due factor}$$

Look up the rate of return in the *PV* annuity due table corresponding to the number of lease years and the factor.

6. Remember, in the *NPV* method, we are dealing with cash outflows. Therefore, the comparison is being made between the costs of leasing and buying, and not cash inflows. The present value calls for the decision to be:

PV lease > *PV* buy, then buy.

PV lease < *PV* buy, then lease.

The IRR method decision calls for:

IRR lease > K_d then buy.

IRR lease < K_d, then lease.

7. A leveraged lease involves a lessor and a lender. Both put up part of the cash to cover the purchase of an asset. The lender is a creditor who has claim on the asset and receives a return from part of the lease payments, and the lessor also receives a portion of the rentals, which should provide a given rate of return. Sale-and-leaseback arrangements call for the owner (a firm) of an asset to sell the asset to another firm who then becomes the lessor and leases the asset back to the original owner of the asset. At the termination of the lease contract, the asset reverts back to the original owner.

8. Capital leases are carried on the balance sheet as capitalized rentals. These obligations appear on the asset and liability side of the balance sheet and are amortized over time. Operating leases are reported in the footnotes of a balance sheet.

9. Three benefits to the lessor and the corresponding opportunity losses to a lessee are (1) tax shield from depreciation, (2) tax shield from interest expense, and (3) salvage value.

PRACTICAL APPLICATION

1.

Year	Payment	Tax Benefit	Cash Outflows
0	$10,000	$ 0	$10,000
1	10,000	4,000	6,000
2	10,000	4,000	6,000
3	10,000	4,000	6,000
4	10,000	4,000	6,000
5	0	4,000	(4,000)

2. I would borrow rather than lease because the cost of leasing is higher than borrowing.

3. Calculating the *PV* of purchase cash flows:

$$\begin{matrix}\text{Annual}\\\text{loan}\\\text{repayment}\end{matrix} = \frac{\text{Loan}}{PVA_{15\%,\ 5\ yr}} = \frac{\$80,000}{3.352} = \$23,866$$

Deriving Interest from Loan Amortization Method

Year	Payment (1)	Prinicple (2)	Interest (3) = 15% × (2)	Equity (4) = (1) − (3)	Ending Principle (5) = (2) − (4)
1	$23,866	$80,000	$12,000	$11,866	$68,134
2	23,866	68,134	10,220	13,646	54,488
3	23,866	54,488	8,173	15,693	38,795
4	23,866	38,795	5,819	18,047	20,748
5	23,866	20,748	3,112	20,754	−6

4. Calculating the *PV* of cash flows for leasing:

Year	Payment (1)	Tax Benefit (2)	Cash Outflow (3) = (1) − (2)	PVIF @ 9% (4) 13% (0.4)	PV of Cash Outflow (5) = (3) × (4)
0	$19,810	0	$19,810	1	$19,810
1	19,810	$7,924	11,886	0.917	10,899
2	19,810	7,924	11,886	0.842	10,008
3	19,810	7,924	11,886	0.772	9,176
4	19,810	7,924	11,886	0.708	8,415
5	0	7,924	(7,924)	0.650	(5,151)
					$53,157

5. Calculating the present value of borrowing and purchase:

Yr.	Loan Repay- ment (1)	Interest (2)	Depre- ciation (3)	Deduct- ible Expense (4)= (2) + (3)	Tax- Bene- fit @ 40% (5)	Loan Re- payment After Tax (6)= (1) − (5)	PV Factor @ 9% (7)	PV (8)= (6) × (7)
1	$23,900	$12,000	$16,000	$28,000	$11,200	$12,700	0.917	$11,600
2	23,900	10,200	15,600	35,800	14,300	9,500	0.842	8,000
3	23,900	8,200	15,200	23,400	9,400	14,500	0.772	11,200
4	23,900	5,800	12,000	17,800	7,100	16,700	0.708	11,900
5	23,900	3,100	11,200	14,300	5,700	18,100	0.650	11,800

PV = $54,500

*Note: The after-tax cost of debt is 9%. Therefore, cash outflows of purchase are discounted at an after cost of 9%.

6. Because cash outflow of the lease option has a lower present value, the lease option is recommended over the purchase.

7. Annual depreciation $\dfrac{\$90,000}{3} = \$30,000$

$$\text{Benefits} = PV \text{ depreciation } (T)$$
$$= \$30,000 \,(.40) \times 2.673 = \$32,076$$
$$\text{Net cost} = \$90,000 - \$32,076 = \$57,924$$

After-tax annual payments charged by lessor $= \dfrac{\text{Net cost}}{PVAF_{k,n(1+k)}} = \dfrac{\$57,924}{2.361\,(1.13)} = \$21,711$

8. I would recommend borrowing (purchase) rather than leasing.

13

WARRANTS AND CONVERTIBLES

KEY TERMS

conversion price the stock price at which a convertible security may be exchanged for common stock

conversion ratio number of shares exchanged for a convertible bond

conversion value market price of stock multiplied by the conversion ratio

convertible bond a security that gives its owner the option to exchange it for a specified number of shares of common stock

exercise price the pre-established price at which warrant holders may purchase common stock

warrant a security that gives the owner the right to purchase shares of common stock at a stated price within a prescribed period of time

---

Warrants and convertibles give investors the right to purchase common stock at a predetermined price. For this privilege, investors make certain concessions: they agree to accept a lower return on the securities they purchase, and usually they agree to accept less protection than is given to straight bondholders in the case of bankruptcy.

Firms find these securities an attractive source of funds because of their lower cost of capital. Convertibles also provide a certain degree of financing flexibility by allowing a firm to postpone issuing stock until a more advantageous time. Also, in the case of warrants, a firm generates more funds when the warrants are exercised. These forms of financing have become popular, and they play an important role in a firm's financing decisions.

Whether financing is done via warrants or convertibles, the firm gains certain benefits. Also, these securities can successfully be used as "sweeteners" to make a merger more palatable to a target company.

WARRANTS

Warrants ordinarily have a limited lifespan, usually 3 to 5 years, although some warrants are issued in perpetuity. For the purpose of this discussion, warrants are assumed to have a specified expiration date. A **warrant** gives the buyer of a bond or preferred stock the option to purchase a number of shares of common stock at a pre-established price, the **exercise price**. This exercise price is generally 15% to 20% above the current price of the stock. Therefore, if the current stock price is $50, the firm may say to the investor: "When you buy one bond, we will allow you to purchase our shares of common stock, within a specified time (let us say over a 3-year period), at $60." Should the price of the stock rise to $70, the bondholder can exchange, or exercise, the warrants and pay $60 for the stock. The result is a net gain of $10 per share. Obviously, investors will not exchange their warrants for stock unless the price of the stock exceeds the exercise price, because they can purchase the stock more cheaply in the open market.

The terms of exchange can vary over time. Sometimes a firm will raise the exercise price after several years. For example, it may say to investors that they can exercise the warrants at $60 for the next 3 years, but that thereafter the investors have to pay $65 for the stock.

The terms set by the firm indicate how many shares can be purchased at a stated price with one warrant. Some firms will say one warrant is good for the purchase of one share of stock. Other firms may say one warrant can purchase two shares of stock, and so forth. Generally, warrants are detachable. This means that once they are issued to the bond or preferred stock buyer, they can be sold independently, without reference to the security they came with. These warrants trade separately on the stock exchange or over the counter.

• *THEORETICAL VALUE OF WARRANTS*

A warrant derives its value from investors' anticipation that the price of the stock will increase beyond the exercise price, thereby giving them the opportunity to make a profit. If this expectation did not exist, warrants would be worthless, and no one would want to own them. It is also assumed that the firm's earnings will grow in the future, leading to higher dividends. When the dividends are high enough, they will make ownership of the common stock an attractive proposition.

A warrant's value is determined in the same way as a call option. Both derivatives give the owner the right to buy stock at a stated price. A call buyer contracts to purchase 100 shares of stock upon exercise, whereas in the case of a warrant the number of shares a warrant holder can buy is specified at the time a warrant is issued. For example, one warrant entitles the holder to buy three shares of stock. The value of a call, or warrant, then is equal to $N(P_s - X_p)$. Suppose the call option and warrant had the same exercise price of $60 and the current price of the stock is $80. When these two financial derivatives are exercised the call owner would buy 100 shares for $6,000 ($60 × 100), and the warrant owner would buy 3 shares for $180 ($60 × 3).

To recapitulate, the value of a warrant is simply derived by taking the difference between the price of the common stock P_0 and the exercise price E_{xp}, and multiplying this residual by the terms of exchange N. This is called the **theoretical value of the warrant** TV_w.

$$TV_w = N \times [\text{Current price of common } (P_s) - \text{Exercise price } (E_{xp})]$$

Therefore, if a company assigns an exercise price of $60 to the warrants, the current price of its stock is $65, and the exchange terms are two shares for one warrant, the theoretical value of the warrant (or lowest price) is

$$TV_w = 2(\$65 - \$60) = \$10$$

The theoretical value of a warrant is the lowest price at which it will sell. However, warrants are traded on the stock exchanges just like stocks. As a result, they have a market value. The market value is usually higher than the theoretical value because investors are willing to pay a premium based on the anticipation that the price of the stock will continue to increase and exceed the exercise price in the future. The relationship between the theoretical value of a warrant (TV_w), the market value (MV_w) and the exercise price of a warrant is shown in Figure 13-1.

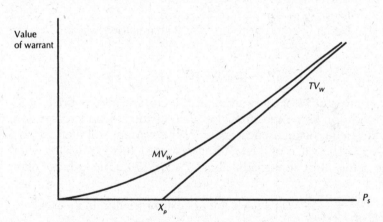

Figure 13–1 Relationship Between Theoretical and Market Value of a Warrant

Just like a call option, when $P_s < X_p$, the TV_w equals zero. The TV_w becomes positive when the warrant is in the money or when $P_s > X_p$. Note, however, that the MV_w is positive even when $P_s < X_p$. This is the premium the warrant buyer is willing to pay because of the expectation that P_s will rise above the X_p, making it profitable to exercise the warrant. As the price of the stock keeps increasing, the probability of further increases in P_s gradually vanish and the MV_w eventually collapses toward the TV_w at which time the premium disappears.

If the market value of the warrant were to fall below the theoretical value, arbitrageurs would buy the warrants, exercise them, and then sell the stock. As more warrants are purchased, the market value would rise to the theoretical value, and arbitrage would cease.

• THE LEVERAGE EFFECT

Warrants have greater leverage than their stocks. By this we mean that a given percentage change in the price of the stock will produce a higher percentage change in the value of the warrant.

$$\text{Leverage of a warrant} = \frac{\% \, \Delta \text{ Price of warrant}}{\% \, \Delta \text{ Price of stock}}$$

Example: Warrants Have Greater Leverage Than Stock

Suppose the market price of a warrant MV_w moves dollar for dollar with the price of its stock. (This often happens after a substantial upward price move in the stock.) And suppose you are given the following information:

Current price of stock:	$70
Exercise price:	$65
Exchange ratio or terms:	2 shares for 1 warrant

Then

$$TV_w = 2(\$70 - \$65) = \$10$$

Assume an investor buys the warrant at the current market price of $5.00 and the stock for $70. Thereafter, the price of the stock increases to $75. The market value, or theoretical value, of the warrant will increase to $20 [2($75–$65)]. The value of the warrant increased 100% ($10/$10) whereas the value of the stock appreciated about 7% ($5/$70). The leverage effect is

$$\frac{\text{Leverage}}{\text{effect}} = \frac{100\%}{7\%} = 14.3 \text{ times the price appreciation in the stock}$$

• FAIR VALUE OF WARRANTS (FV$_w$)

The fair value of a warrant is the intrinsic price of a warrant as it responds to the influences of several factors. This fair value FV_w can be determined by employing two methods:

1. The Black and Scholes model

2. The shortcut call option valuation method

The Black and Scholes method involves the following basic equation:

$$FV_w = P_s \times (Nd_1) - \left[\frac{X_p}{e^{rt}} \times (Nd_2) \right]$$

We can observe, therefore, that the fair value of a warrant is calculated the same way as a call option. To simplify the computations, we assume that Nd_1 and Nd_2 probability terms were already determined. We can now go ahead to show how the fair value of a warrant is obtained based on the following inputs:

P_s	$50.00
X_p	$40.00
Nd_1	.65
Nd_2	.70
R_f	5%
Time to expiration	1 year

Solving the equation we get

$$FV_w = \$50 \times (.65) - \left[\left(\frac{\$40.00}{e^{.05 \times 1}} \right) \times (.70) \right] = \$5.86$$

If the foregoing factors are estimated accurately, the fair value of the warrant is the equilibrium price. That means, any deviation of the market price away from the FV_w will produce arbitrage until $FV_w = MV_w$.

Example: Deriving FV_w Via the Shortcut Method

A simpler method can be used to calculate the approximate fair value of a warrant. To do so, you will require the following information.

Stock price, (P_s)
Risk-free rate, (R_f)
Time to expiration date, (t)
Standard deviation of stock's returns, (σ)
Exercise price (X_p)

The mathematical calculations involve determining the relationship between $\sigma(t)$ *and* $P_s/X_p \div e^{Rf,t}$. In other words, the value of a warrant depends on two relationships

1. the volatility of a stock's returns (σ) and the time to expiration (t)

2. the price of the stock (P_s) relative to its exercise price ($X/e^{Rf,t}$)

Generally speaking, it can be seen that the higher the standard deviation and the more time left to expiration the higher the value of the warrant. Also, the higher the price of the stock relative to the exercise price the higher the value of the warrant.

Example:

Assume you have, or calculate, the following values:

$$P_s = \$50$$
$$\alpha(t) = .35$$
$$P_s/X_p \div e^{Rf,t} = 1.00$$

Look up the amount that corresponds to the foregoing coordinate values in a special option table, and you will find it equals 0.1389. Take the current price of the stock and multiply it by this value, and you will get the fair value of a warrant, $6.94 ($50 × 0.1389).

This is a shortcut method for obtaining the value of a warrant. Note that the fair value of a warrant is usually higher than the theoretical value mainly because it reflects investors' expectations that the price of the stock will increase above the exercise price of the stock.

YOU SHOULD REMEMBER

Warrants are like call options and have a minimum theoretical value determined as follows: $N(P_s - X_p)$. The spread between MV_w and TV_w is the premium investors are willing to pay because they anticipate the price of the stock to rise above the exercise price. Due to leverage, the percent change in warrants is usually greater than a given percent change in the price of the stock. Two methods to determine the fair value of a warrant, just like a call option, are the Black and Scholes model and the short-cut method. These approaches rely mainly on the relationship between time, variability of the stock price, and whether the warrant is in or out of the money.

• *WHAT HAPPENS WHEN WARRANTS ARE EXERCISED*

What are the effects of a combination bond/warrant issue to a firm? First, the firm obtains more money in addition to the funds it received from the original issue of bonds, because investors have to pay for the stock when they exercise the warrant. Second, the firm gains by being able to sell the bond at a lower cost of capital than is incurred by selling straight bonds. Third, there is some dilution of EPS when warrants are exercised because of the increase in the number of outstanding shares. Fourth, both the par value and the capital surplus of the firm increase. Fifth—and very important—the debt stays on the balance sheet.

CONVERTIBLE BONDS

A **convertible bond** is a security that gives its owner the option to exchange it for a specified number of shares of common stock. It normally has a call feature that enables the issuing company to force investors to turn in the bond for a given number of shares of stock at a specified price. For example, suppose a convertible bond is issued at a par value of $1,000. If the call price is set at 10% above par, the 10% call premium will enable the firm to call in their convertible bonds when they reach or exceed a price of $1,100.

A convertible bond has several attractive features. Even though the firm can issue the debenture at a lower cost of debt than a nonconvertible bond, it still retains some of the characteristics of a straight bond. Therefore, a convertible is like a straight bond, but it also has a feature that allows the holder to participate in the growth of the stock. Although convertible bonds may be called in at a given call price, this type of security also has a maturity date—like any other bond. Thus, if convertible bonds are not called in or are not converted, they will mature after a specified time period. A 20-year convertible means that the firm will pay the owners of this debenture par value ($1,000) at the end of the 20th year. In the interim years, of course, the firm agrees to pay a stated coupon on these bonds.

In a number of cases, firms issue convertible debentures in order to postpone the eventual issue of stocks at a more appropriate time. Because convertibles are retired, this debt does not influence permanently the capital structure of the firm. Fast-growing small firms, faced by borrowing restrictions and financing difficulties, fall back on convertibles to finance their growth opportunities. This is an interim solution until they can tap more permanent financing sources.

Because convertibles put less restrictions on the firm than regular bonds, they also minimize the agency problem or conflict between bondholders and stockholders.

• *VALUE OF CONVERTIBLES*

To understand the way convertibles are valued, it is necessary to examine some of the general features that make up this value. Suppose a firm issues a convertible bond when the current price of its stock is $35; the price at which the bond can be exchanged for stock is set at $40. This price of $40 is called the **conversion price**. The difference between the current price of the stock and its conversion price is the **conversion premium**, or $5 ($40 – $35). This premium means that the convertible owners will have to wait until the price of the stock reaches $40 before they can consider converting the bond into stock.

The **conversion ratio** is the number of shares received in exchange for a convertible bond when it is turned in.

$$\text{Conversion ratio} = \frac{\text{Par value of convertible security}}{\text{Conversion price}}$$

Using the foregoing figures, the conversion ratio is

$$\text{Conversion ratio} = \frac{\$1,000}{\$40} = 25 \text{ shares}$$

This means the firm issues 25 shares of common stock when each bond is converted.

Conversion value is a very important feature because it tells you the underlying stock value of the convertible.

$$\text{Conversion value} = \text{Current market price of the stock} \times \text{Conversion ratio}$$

Using the figures in the previous example once more, you get

$$\text{Conversion value} = \$35 \times 25 \text{ shares} = \$875$$

This equation for finding the conversion value makes clear that part of the bond's value originates in the value of the stock. Therefore, par value minus the conversion value ($1,000 – $875), or $125, represents the premium paid by an investor for the option to convert into stock.

Conversion value is the minimum stock value that an investor can receive for a convertible debenture. For instance, should the price of the stock drop to $30, the minimum value behind the convertible debenture is $750 ($30 × 25). In other words, should investors convert into common stock, the least amount they could receive is the conversion value of the bond, or $750. Given that $1,000 was the initial price paid for the bond, you can see clearly why it does not pay to convert until the price of the stock reaches $40 or more. At $35, investors would receive only $875 out of the $1,000 they originally paid. Conversion would result in a loss of $125; hence, it would not pay to convert. At $40, investors would get their $1,000 back ($40 × $25). At $50 the convertible would have a value of $1,250 ($50 × 25), and investors would have a profit of $250 ($1,250 − $1,000).

Since conversion value is the minimum value at which the debenture will sell, a profit can be made by investors when the market value of the convertible bond falls below its conversion value. All they have to do is buy the bond, convert it immediately, and then sell the stock. For example, suppose the market value of a convertible is $1,100 and its conversion value is $1,150. When its holders convert, they get stock worth $50 more than the value of the bond. This imperfection in the market does not last very long. Investors see it as a chance to make an easy profit, and they will continue to purchase the convertible (and make a profit by converting it), putting upward pressure on the market value of the convertible until it rises to, or above, the conversion value of the debenture.

YOU SHOULD REMEMBER

Convertibles have a lower coupon rate than regular bonds because of the conversion feature. Investors should beware of a convertible's call feature because when the call price is below the actual price, they can suffer a reduction in their capital appreciation. Firms issue convertibles to postpone stock and bond financing until a more advantageous time.

STRAIGHT BOND VALUE OF CONVERTIBLES

In addition to having a conversion value, a convertible bond has a floor value, or **investment value**, equivalent to that of a straight bond. This is the price at which the convertible security would sell in the absence of its conversion feature. Consequently, convertible bonds offer more protection than stocks because, while the price of a stock can decline sharply, the market value of a convertible is unlikely to decline below its straight bond value.

The calculation of this value is easy enough. You have, in fact, already done this in Chapter 3 when you found how to obtain the present value of a bond. All you have to do is find a straight bond having the same characteristics and issued by a firm with the same financial structure as that of the issuer of the convertible. The yield to maturity of that straight bond will then serve as a discount rate. The familiar formula for determining the value of a straight bond is

$$\text{Bond value} = \sum_{t=1}^{N} \frac{\text{Coupon}_t}{(1+R)^t} + \frac{P_n}{(1+R)^n}$$

This formula also works for determining the straight bond value of a convertible.

Example: Calculating the Straight Bond Value of a Convertible

PROBLEM   A newly issued $1,000 convertible bond pays an annual coupon of $80 and will mature in 10 years. The straight bond of a comparable company has a yield to maturity of 10%. What is the straight bond value of the newly issued convertible?

SOLUTION

Years	Payments	PVIF at 10%	Present Values
1–10	$80 interest	6.145*	$492
10th	$1,000 par value	.368	386

Bond value = $878

*(PVIFA) 10%, 10 yrs

The preceding present value method shown for calculating the straight bond value of a convertible can be expressed as a formula:

$$\text{Bond value} = \sum_{t=1}^{N} \frac{80(t)}{(1+.10)^t} + \frac{\$1,000}{(1+.10)^{10}} = \$878$$

When market rates increase, the straight bond value of a convertible declines; when market yields decline, the straight bond value increases. The market value of the convertible will not decline below the straight bond value of $878 regardless of any drop in the price of the underlying stock. All these convertible bond features can be more readily visualized in Figure 13-2.

After the price of the stock increases beyond a certain point, say $50, expectations of further price advances in the stock diminish, and the market value curve collapses toward the conversion value, as seen in Figure 13-2. The leverage of the convertible bond disappears. Also, at $50, the convertible has a value of $1,250, which gives investors little protection, because the bond can be called in at $1,100. The more the stock increases, the less investment protection the convertible bondholders have—and the more willing they are to convert.

What other factors induce investors to convert? Sometimes a firm's original agreement states that after a few years the conversion ratio will be lowered. Since this means that investors will receive fewer shares than with the initial conversion ratio, they will be induced to convert before that date so they will not be penalized. Suppose the conversion ratio changed after 3 years from 25 to 23 shares, and the price of the stock reached the $40 conversion price in this period. Since investors would realize only $920 instead of $1,000 (based on a conversion ratio of 23 shares per bond), they would be forced to convert before the change in the conversion ratio occurred. Conversion may also take place when the dividend yield on the common stock is higher than the return obtained from the convertible. Another reason for converting arises from the fact that, as the price of the stock increases, the investor receives less and less protection from the straight bond value. Also, the danger that the bond will be called at a lower price than the conversion value will induce investors to convert the bond into common stock to avoid a potential loss of profit.

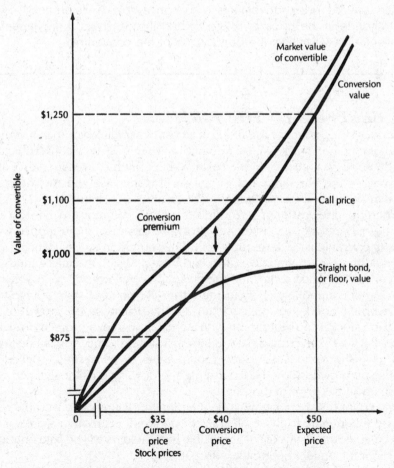

Figure 13-2 Features of Convertible Bonds

YOU SHOULD REMEMBER

Convertibles have two value components: (1) the stock value of the convertible, called the conversion value, and (2) the investment floor value, which represents the straight bond value feature of the convertible. The stock value is equal to market price of the stock × conversion ratio. The bond value is the present value of the coupons and principal discounted by the yield to maturity of other straight bonds that have the same characteristics of the convertible. The convertible's price will move down with the price of a stock until it reaches its straight bond value. At this point, the convertible will start acting like a regular bond and reflect changes in interest rates, and it will no longer be influenced by a decline in the price of the stock. Given these two valuation components, the upward price movements of a convertible is determined by a change in the price of its stock, and the downward movement eventually will reflect the bond value of the convertible.

• *BENEFITS TO THE FIRM*

Besides being able to raise funds at a cost of capital lower than a straight bond or common stock issue, a firm knows when it issues a convertible that the debt will disappear from the balance sheet upon conversion. Also, after conversion, the par value and capital surplus increase and the increased number of shares causes dilution in the earnings per share.

When the price/earnings (*P/E*) ratio of a firm's common stock is too low, it is not advantageous to issue new stock. In this case, the use of convertibles is convenient because they help defer common stock financing to a more advantageous time. The firm can raise a large amount of funds via the convertible bond route, and the final dilutive effects will be less than in the case of common stock financing. From the point of view of investors, a convertible bond gives them a chance to participate in the growth of the common stock. It provides them with a greater degree of protection against losses because convertibles have a floor investment value. Also, while investors have the option of making capital gains by converting, convertible bonds still provide some hedge against the downside risk associated with variability in the price of the stock.

One major disadvantage must be mentioned: Claims of convertible owners are subordinate to those of straight bondholders. In other words, if the firm defaults, the claims of its convertible bondholders will be paid only after the claims of straight debtholders are satisfied.

YOU SHOULD REMEMBER

Warrants and convertibles, which give their holders the right to exchange them for their underlying stock, represent two major alternative sources of financing.

Bonds issued with these "sweeteners" cost less than issues of straight debt. When convertibles are exchanged for stock, although no additional funds are made available to the firm, the debt is wiped from the balance sheet. Conversely, though debt remains part of the capital structure when warrants are exercised, additional funds are generated. Basically, while warrants increase the marketability of bonds, convertibles allow firms some financing flexibility.

The value of warrants to investors is based on the expectation that the stock price will increase. Because of the low price of warrants relative to stocks, they provide substantial leverage.

The market value of a convertible bond will not decline below its investment value, which is equivalent to the value of a straight debt issue with similar characteristics.

• DIFFERENCES BETWEEN WARRANTS AND CONVERTIBLE BONDS

Warrants don't earn interest and are more risky investments than convertibles because they are highly leveraged. They are worthless at their **expiration date** and when the price of their stock declines to very low levels. Convertibles, on the other hand, have a floor investment value; they provide investors with a steady interest income and pay a stated par value at maturity. The cost of capital for issuing a bond/warrant package is a little higher than for a convertible bond. More importantly, when warrants are exercised, they provide additional funds to the firm, whereas the conversion of convertible debentures does not. However, when convertibles are exchanged for stock, the debt is wiped off the books. When warrants are exercised, the debt stays on the balance sheet.

KNOW THE CONCEPTS

DO YOU KNOW THE BASICS?

1. Give several reasons why a firm might choose to issue warrants and convertibles instead of straight debt or common stock.

2. What kind of advantages does an investor receive with a warrant? With a convertible bond?

3. In what way is the capital structure of a firm affected by the exercise of a warrant or the conversion of a convertible bond into stock?

4. What happens to interest and earnings per share when warrants are exercised or when convertible bonds are converted into stock?

5. If the market price of a warrant falls below its theoretical value, what will happen in the marketplace to correct this imbalance?

6. What is meant by the leverage derived from a warrant?

7. Why would a convertible bondholder want to convert into common stock? Include dividends, conversion price, and stock price in your answer.

8. In addition to the conversion value, what other investment feature does a convertible have that is not available with warrants?

9. If the yield to maturity on a straight bond increases, what will happen to the value of the convertible, and what does this mean to the investor?

10. If all other things remain unchanged, how would the value of a call warrant change when the following changes occur in related factors:
    (a) There is a reduction of dividends per share.
    (b) The risk-free rate declines.
    (c) The price of the stock is expected to decline.
    (d) The standard deviation of the stock price declines.
    (e) There is a decline in the life of the call.

11. What is the definition of an in-the-money warrant?

12. Explain the relationship between the theoretical and market value of a warrant (use a graph).

TERMS FOR STUDY

conversion premium	exercise price
conversion price	expiration date
conversion ratio	investment value of convertibles
conversion value	theoretical value of a warrant
convertible bond	warrant

PRACTICAL APPLICATION

COMPUTATIONAL PROBLEMS

1. Calculate the straight bond value and the conversion ratio of a convertible if the current price of the stock is $60, its conversion price is $70, and it matures 5 years from now. A straight bond with similar features has a yield to maturity of 10%, compared to an 8% coupon for the convertible. (Assume par value of the bond is $1,000).

2. The price paid to buy a warrant is $5, the price of the stock is $50, and the exercise price is $40. How much profit or loss would a call buyer make by exercising the warrant if one warrant entitles the owner to buy one share of stock?

3. Calculate the theoretical value of a warrant when the current price of the stock is $50 and the exercise price is $45. The exchange ratio is 3 shares for each warrant.

4. A firm has $10 million of outstanding convertible bonds. The coupon on these convertibles is $100 per bond, and each bond is convertible into common stock at a conversion price of $25. What will happen to the income statement and EPS when all bonds are converted, if the income statement of the firm before conversion was as follows and EBIT remained at $6.0 million after conversions? (Assume the firm originally paid $2.0 million in interest on other outstanding debt before the convertible was issued.)

	Millions of Dollars Before Conversion
EBIT	6.0
Interest (at 10%)	–3.0
Earnings before taxes	3.0
Taxes (at 40%)	–1.2
Earnings after taxes	1.8
Shares outstanding (millions)	1.0
EPS	$1.80

5. A convertible bond has a call price of $1,100. Its underlying stock is selling at $60 per share, and the conversion price is $50. If owners of the convertible bond convert and sell the stock, how much profit or loss will they make on each bond if the convertible is called by the company, given the above conditions?

6. Using the shortcut method, compute the fair value of a warrant FV_w if you are given the following information:

Time to expiration	1 year
Standard deviation of stock price	.30
P_s	$110
X_p	$100
Risk-free rate	.05
Value in call option table	.790

And, what would happen if the market value was 5% higher than the FV_w?

ANSWERS

KNOW THE CONCEPTS

1. Warrants and convertible securities provide a firm with financing flexibility and a lower cost of capital than issuing stock. However, investors usually agree to less creditor protection in case of bankruptcy when they buy convertible bonds instead of straight bonds.

2. A buyer of a warrant participates in the capital appreciation of the stock. An investor can share in the dividends paid to stockholders when the warrant is exercised. Some investors buy warrants for the substantial leverage they provide when the price of the stock increases.

   Investors in convertibles get an interest income, just as they would from a straight bond, and still have downside price protection because of the investment value of convertible bonds. Convertible bond investors have the option to participate in the future growth of the stock and the rising dividend yield paid to stockholders when they decide to convert.

3. When a warrant is exercised in exchange for stock, the debt remains on the balance sheet. When convertible bonds are converted into stock, the debt is wiped off the balance sheet. The D/E decreases when the warrant is traded for stock; equity increases while debt remains the same. The warrant entitles the holder to buy a stated number of shares with the warrant. However, the D/E remains at a higher level when warrants are exercised, whereas it declines when convertible bonds are converted.

4. When warrants are exercised, interest on the income statement remains unchanged but the number of shares increases, causing dilution in EPS. When convertible bonds are converted into common stock, the interest from the convertible bonds disappears from the income statement and the number of shares increases, causing dilution in EPS.

5. The warrant will be purchased and exercised, and the stock will be sold at a profit. This arbitrage will continue until the $MP_w = TV_w$.

6. Leverage of a warrant, or $\dfrac{\% \,\Delta \text{ Price of warrant}}{\% \,\Delta \text{ Price of stock}}$, means that for any given percentage change in the price of the stock, the percentage change in the price of the warrant is greater. In other words, investors receive a bigger relative gain or loss for any dollar invested in warrants than they receive from investing in the underlying stock.

7. A convertible bondholder will convert into common stock when the dividend yield on the stock exceeds the yield from the convertible, when the conversion value and the market price are substantially above the call price, and when the price of the stock moves substantially above the conversion price. At that point, expectations of a further increase in the price of the stock diminish, and the straight bond value protection weakens substantially.

8. A convertible security yields a return, whereas a warrant is only an option to buy stock at a stated price, and thus provides no income.

9. If the yield to maturity increases, the discount factor increases and the investment value of the convertible bond will decline. The investor will find that the straight bond value of a convertible will appreciate when interest rates decline, usually during a recession. A decrease in the yield to maturity may also mean that, because the market value of the convertible bond increases (assume conversion value remains unchanged), it becomes vulnerable to a call by the issuer. Hence, the investor may wish to convert.

10. The value of a warrant would decline with any of the following changes:
    (a) σ declines
    (b) time to expiration declines
    (c) the warrant goes from in- to an out-of-the-money status
    (d) the risk-free rate declines

11. An in-the-money warrant is a condition that arises when the price of the stock exceeds the exercise price.

12. The relationship between the MV_w and the TV_w is shown graphically as follows:

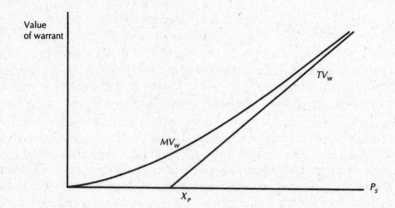

The theoretical value is the minimum price of the warrant. It is zero when $P_s < X_p$ and positive when $P_s > X_p$. The $MV_w > TV_w$ largely because investors anticipate the price of the stock to rise above the X_p. Therefore, they are willing to pay a premium for the option to exercise the warrant and buy the stock at a stated X_p because they expect the P_s to exceed the exercise price of the stock at some future date. As the P_s continues to rise, the probability of a further P_s increase declines. When this expectation vanishes, the premium (spread between the MV_w and TV_w) disappears.

PRACTICAL APPLICATION

1. Conversion ratio $= \dfrac{\$1,000}{70} = 14.29$ shares

This means that investors receive 14.29 shares of stock when they exchange the convertible for common stock.
   Straight bond value of a convertible:

Years	Payment	PVIF at 10%	
1 to 5	$80	3.791	$303
5th	$1,000	.621	621
		Straight bond value of convertible bond =	$924

2. Given that $N = 1$, then

Current value of shares ($50 × 1 share)	$50.00
Value of shares at striking price ($40 × 1 share)	40.00
Net change	$10.00
Cost of call ($5 × 1)	5.00
Net profit	$ 5.00

3. The theoretical value of the warrant is

$$3(\$50 - \$45) = \$15$$

4.

	Millions of Dollars Before Conversion	Millions of Dollars After Conversion
EBIT	6.0	6.0
Interest	–3.0	–2.0
Earnings before taxes	3.0	4.0
Taxes (at 40%)	–1.2	–1.6
Earnings after taxes	1.8	2.4
Shares outstanding (millions)	1.0	1.4
EPS	$1.80	$1.71

Note: After conversion the interest declines by $1.0 million because 10% ($100 coupon) of $10 million is $1.0 million and the original $2.0 million stays on the income statement after conversion. Also, the conversion ratio equals 40 shares ($1,000 ÷ 25). This produces 400,000 additional shares on conversion, and a dilution of 9¢ in earnings per share (from $1.80 before conversion to $1.71 after conversion).

5. Conversion ratio $= \dfrac{1,000}{50} = 20$ shares

Conversion value $= 20 \times \$60 = \$1,200$

$1,200	conversion value of convertible bond
1,100	call price of convertible bond
$ 100	loss to owners on each bond

6. *Shortcut Method*

Formula I $\quad \sigma\sqrt{t} = .30\sqrt{1} = .30$

Formula II $\quad P_s / \dfrac{X_p}{e^{rt}} = 110 / \dfrac{100}{e^{.05 \times 1}} = 1.16$ (rounded)

The formula to calculate the FV_w is

Value of warrant = Price of stock ×
Factor in the call hedge ratio table

The factor found in the call hedge ratio table for call options is .1932. Then the value of the warrant is

$$\$110 \times .1932 = \$21.25 \text{ value of warrant}$$

14

SHORT- AND LONG-TERM FINANCING

KEY TERMS

commercial paper unsecured notes sold at a discount from par value that have maturities up to 270 days

compensating balance part of loans held on deposit that draw no interest and compensate banks for lending and other services

investment banker an advisor and distributor of new issues who takes the risk of distributing a new issue

line of credit bank agreement that allows a firm to borrow a given amount in a specified period of time

nominal interest rate real rate of interest (supply = demand for loanable funds) plus a premium for the expected rate of inflation

preemptive right the right of a stockholder to participate in any distribution of the firm and the right to maintain the same voting power when new shares are issued

primary market arena where original security offerings are sold, usually through an investment banker

prospectus a written document that provides information on an issue of securities being registered and that investors must receive before buying a new issue

secondary market exchange or market where securities are sold, listed, or traded, and their prices determined, after their original issue

secured loan a loan backed by some asset of a firm, which can be sold to pay off the debt in case of default

shelf registration method for registering and getting approval to issue new securities any time within a 2-year period

underwriting syndicate a group of underwriters who share in the distribution and risks of a new security offering

yield curve the relationship between interest rates and different maturities of bonds

zero coupon bond bond issued at a discount from par value that has no coupons, pays no interest, and promises to pay par value at maturity

SHORT-TERM FINANCING

Among other reasons, businesses engage in short-term financing to cover deficiencies of funds when cash inflows fail to cover a sudden surge of expenses. The goal is to borrow temporarily in anticipation of a cash inflow at some future date, which will allow the firm to repay the loan. Many firms are faced by a surge of sales because of the seasonality of their business when sales are concentrated in certain periods of the year, like Christmas, Easter, and special holidays. With summer, air conditioning manufacturers have to build inventories ahead of the surge of sales. These businesses must borrow to produce in advance to meet these seasonal demands. After this seasonal surge of sales, loans incurred are repaid.

The goal in short-term financing is to avoid long-term borrowing, which would make excess funds available when not needed. Short-term borrowing, therefore, fills a temporary void in the financing needs of a firm. In this way, the expenses of carrying redundant funds are avoided.

Short-term borrowing by businesses can be achieved in two ways.

1. The firm can engage in short-term financing by issuing its own paper.

2. The firm can raise funds externally through financial intermediaries.

Most short-term borrowing is done with the help of financial intermediaries, such as banks, finance companies, and money market funds. In other words, it has been found that the financial system of lending and borrowing works more efficiently through middlemen called financial intermediaries. These financial organizations are better equipped to gather savings and lend this money out to borrowers or businesses. They perform the lending function and the matching of the funds of savers and borrowers very efficiently. Some of the ways funds are borrowed by businesses are discussed later.

BORROWING FROM BANKS

Commercial banks borrow funds or are depositories of savings in the form of checking accounts and certificates of deposit. These deposits are the liabilities of banks but are used by banks to finance businesses. More recently, competing money market funds serve a similar function. They facilitate financing by corporations. No matter where these loanable funds originate, the ultimate result is to facilitate borrowing. Let's see how this borrowing process works in the case of banks. Short-term bank credit is referred to as unsecured loans because the money is lent to customers without the need for collateral or asset attachment clauses. These loans are negotiated between the banks and businessmen. The terms vary, depending on the credit status and the financial soundness of the borrower. In many cases these loans are renewed automatically because of long-standing relationships between banks and firms. Banks usually lend for a short period of time and the loan becomes self-liquidating when the firm generates enough funds to repay the loan. A loan agreement usually establishes the time to maturity, the interest to be paid, and a compensating balance. Loan agreements are consummated by the signing of a promissory note, which binds the borrower to repay the loan at a specified date.

Businesses don't have to borrow from banks. As a matter of fact, many firms can finance their operations by less expensive methods. However, firms maintain bank relationships because they provide quick and ready sources of funds when the need arises. To facilitate the loan process, to reduce paperwork and to avoid constant time-consuming negotiations, banks make available **lines of credit** that are designed to set aside a specified amount of money that a firm can borrow against.

Obviously banks charge for making credit available to businesses. Usually, the interest charged to its best quality customers is the prime rate of ½% to 1% more than the rate paid by Treasury bills. This sets the benchmark for the interest charged to other businesses. The rate of interest incurred depends on the risk of the customer, ability to repay the loan, and a ratio analysis of the financial statements of the borrowing firm. The final rate charged a corporation is prime plus a premium that can vary from ½% up to 4% above prime. Once the rate of interest is established, banks have two other loan agreements to cover expenses and make a profit. These are

1. compensating balances

2. commitment fee

A **compensating balance** is that percentage of the loan that a bank requires a borrower to hold on deposit earning no interest. Therefore, the **effective rate of interest** charged by banks is higher than the initial rate quoted by the bank on a loan. The commitment fee is charged a borrower to set up a line of credit. It is generally assessed on the unused portion of the loan. For example, suppose a firm negotiates a loan with a commercial bank at prime rate of 10% plus 1% above prime. The company has to maintain a 10% compensating balance on a $1.0 million loan. A commitment fee to establish a line of credit adds another ½% to the total amount set aside as the line of credit. The effective rate of interest incurred by the firm is

$$\frac{\text{Bank effective}}{\text{rate of interest}} = \frac{\text{Basic interest charge (\%)}}{1 - \text{Compensating balance}} + \text{commitment fee}$$
$$(10\% \text{ of loan})$$

Based on the above charges the effective rate is

$$\frac{.11}{1-.10} + .005 = 12.7\%$$

It is up to the firm to shop around for the best short-term financing deal offered by various banks.

Sometimes a bank will lend a certain amount of money to a customer indicating the amount of monthly payments needed to authorize the loan. The bank will charge a sufficiently high rate of return to make a profit. To find out what that rate is, we solve for the discount rate in the following annuity formula:

$$PVA_{k,n} = \text{Loan} \div \text{Annuity payment} = \text{Factor}$$

where PVA = present value annuity
K = the unknown discount rate
N = number of periods the loan is outstanding

Let us assume the loan is for $2.0 million, which calls for 12 monthly payments in the amount of $353,357 per month. First calculate the factor and then look up this factor in the present value annuity table for 12 periods and you get the corresponding K.

$$\frac{\$2.0 \text{ million}}{\$353,357} = 5.660 \text{ (factor)}$$

The rate of interest charged by the bank for this loan is 14%.

YOU SHOULD REMEMBER

You should remember that a great deal of short-term financing is done to cover seasonal cash needs. The borrowing is done through financial intermediaries like banks and by tapping money markets. Banks arrange unsecured loans, which are not backed by any collateral and are self-liquidating. The interest cost of these loans is the prime rate for the best customers and a premium above prime for other customers. A bank loan is subject to other requirements: a compensating balance and a commitment fee to cover the setting up of a line of credit. Compensating balances call for keeping a certain percentage of the loan on deposit with the bank at no interest. Because of these extra requirements, the effective loan rate charged by the bank is higher than the basic initial rate quoted by a bank.

COMMERCIAL PAPER MARKET

An alternative method of financing short-term loans is to rely on **commercial paper**. This paper is issued by corporations having the best credit ratings and is sold at a discount from par value. Commercial paper is usually sold in $100,000 denominations. By limiting the maturity dates of this paper to less than 270 days, a corporation does not have to register the issue with the Securities Exchange Commission. Commercial paper is backed by the promise of the corporation to buy back the paper at maturity date by paying par value. The rate of interest on this paper varies, but it normally is ½% to 1% above the 3-month Treasury bill rate. This form of borrowing is the preferred method of financing by large corporations because it is relatively easy to issue and is less expensive than borrowing from banks.

Just like bonds, commercial paper is rated or ranked according to quality by Moody's and Standard & Poor's. A great deal of the commercial paper issued by corporations winds up in the portfolio of money market funds. Investors prefer investing in these money funds rather than keeping their money with banks because, in addition to their relative safety, they provide higher yields than bank deposits.

To figure out the interest yield on commercial paper we employ the following formula:

$$\frac{\text{Yield on commercial paper}}{\text{before taxes}} = \frac{\text{Par} - \text{Discount amount}}{\text{Discount amount}} \cdot \frac{365}{N}$$

For example, a company issues $93,000 worth of commercial paper for 182 days. What is the yield on this paper?

$$\text{Yield on commercial paper before taxes} = \frac{\$100,000-\$93,000}{\$93,000} \frac{365}{182} = 15\%$$

TRADE CREDIT

This is another way to finance short term. **Trade credit** is an indirect loan to a customer for purchasing goods from a supplier. The usual procedure is to sell on credit. The seller supplies the goods and expects payment after a certain predetermined period. This credit appears as accounts receivable on the books of the supplier and accounts payable on the books of the purchasing customer. The buying firm is essentially given credit, and it represents cash the firm does not have to give up until the final payment date. The firm has generated a source of funds. The longer it delays payment, the longer it gets to finance its operations with another firm's money.

The implied cost of short-term financing the firm saves depends on the number of days the credit remains outstanding. It could be 30, 60, or 90 days long. Suppose a firm paid cash from borrowed funds, which cost 2% per month, and suppose instead of paying cash, it bought $100,000 worth of merchandise payable in 30 days. In essence, the firm has saved $2,000 by using this delayed method of payment. Suppliers providing this credit recognize the financing role they are playing, but they are forced to grant the credit; otherwise, they could lose the sale. Their goal is to get the customer to pay as quickly as possible so they offer a discount. It is up to the customer to decide whether it is advantageous to take the discount and pay at an earlier date. Generally, it is better to take the discount because the cost of foregoing the discount is very high. The opportunity cost of giving up the discount is significant when computed at an annual rate.

$$\text{Effective annual rate for foregoing trade credit discount} = \frac{\text{Discount Rate}}{1-\text{Discount Rate}} \frac{360 \text{ days}}{\text{Days credit is outstanding} - \text{Discount period}}$$

So, if the terms of the accounts payable credit were 2/10 net 30, the firm receiving the credit is required to pay in 30 days, but it will receive a 2% discount if it pays in 10 days. The effective annual rate of taking the cash discount is

$$\frac{.02}{1-.02} \times \frac{360 \text{ days}}{30-10 \text{ days}} = 36.7\%$$

The decision to take the discount or pay later depends on the benefit derived from the discount compared to the benefits of keeping accounts payable outstanding. Obviously, the longer the credit period, the greater the benefits. Some firms attempt to stretch these payments and request extensions. This can produce a loss of goodwill and damage the firm's credit rating. Normally it is better to take the discount unless borrowing rates are very high.

YOU SHOULD REMEMBER

Commercial paper is sold at a discount and has maturity dates of less than 270 days. Normally, it costs ½% to 1% above the Treasury bill rate to issue this paper, and it is cheaper than borrowing from banks. Another way to finance short term is via trade credit. This is the same as receiving an interest free loan from a supplier. A discount is offered to get customers to pay early. It is usually less costly to take the discount than extend the credit up to its original payment date. Firms should avoid stretching the time of trade credit because it can damage their credit ratings.

SECURED SHORT-TERM LOANS

Often, a corporation can temporarily exhaust some of its sources of short-term credit. It may have used up its line of credit with a bank or find the commercial paper market unreceptive. In these cases a firm may resort to **secured short-term loans,** which employ accounts receivables and inventories as collateral. A Uniform Commercial Code provides a standard list of assets accepted for **pledged collateral**. Usually, pledging accounts receivable and inventories involves a **factor**. Under factoring agreements, the borrower is subject to specific terms of the loan agreement. When there is danger that the loan may not be repaid, the factor can liquidate the collaterized assets to pay off the loan. To insure against this risk, the factor normally applies a **haircut** to the current value of the assets. That is, the loan is an amount substantially less than the face value of the accounts receivable or inventories, so that should the factor liquidate he or she can sell the assets at distressed prices and still get back his or her money.

The secured loan agreement states the type of collateral, the interest, and other fees to be paid, and it has a default provision. The interest rate charged is around 3% to 5% above the prime rate. In the case of accounts receivables, the loan can be arranged to include notification and non-notification. Notification means customers are told to make payments directly to the factor or lender. Non-notification calls for the borrower to collect the receivables and remit the funds to the lender (factor). This last method is used when the borrowing firm does not wish its customers to know it is pledging their payables and putting them under greater pressure of making payments. Another way to borrow from a factor is to sell the accounts payable directly to the factor. In this case the loan is labeled a non-recourse loan because the factor assumes all of the risk and probable bad debt losses.

The costs charged by the factor for the loan include a reserve set-aside, a commission fee, and interest on the loan, all of which are deducted from the face value of the collateral minus a haircut. So that, if we assume the face value of accounts receivable is $130,000, the haircut is 13%, and the total charges including interest amounts to $16,000, then the proceeds of the loan to the borrowing firm are

Face value of accounts receivables × Haircut ($130,000 × .77)	$100,000
Total charges	$ 16,000
Proceeds of loan received by borrowing firm	$ 84,000

Short-term borrowing can be arranged by factoring inventories. Because inventories are the least liquid of current assets, the haircut is higher. Typically, inventory factoring involves a **trust receipt**, which allows the borrower to sell goods out of stock and the proceeds are remitted to the factor. The lender conducts periodic inspections to verify that the assets are on the premise and ready for sale. Factors usually lend up to 80% of the face value of inventories and charge 3% to 5% above the prime rate, depending on financial soundness of the borrower. An example of a trust receipt arrangement is the one between General Motors, which acts as a factor, and its auto dealer. The car manufacturer puts up the cars on the lot as collateral to help finance the dealership.

A warehouse receipt is another type of inventory that factoring uses. This arrangement may require setting up a field warehouse area that marks off the place where the factored inventory is located. When a sale is made, the inventory is released upon presentation of a warehouse receipt. The haircut and interest charge is about the same as in the case of trust receipts.

The effective annual rate of interest depends on the charges assessed by the factor. For instance, assume the face value of inventories is $600,000 and the factor agrees to lend the borrower 70% of the value of the inventory pledged, or $450,000 = ($600,000 × .75). The warehouse fee amounts to $6,000, and the interest rate charge is 10% for 91 days. The proceeds of the loan are

Face value of accounts receivable × Haircut (.75)	$450,000
Warehouse fee	(6,000)
Interest expense ($450,000 × .10) (91/365)	(11,219)
Proceeds of loan	$432,781

Effective annual
rate of interest

$$\left(\frac{\$17,219}{\$450,000}\right) \times 4 = \qquad 15.31\%$$

As indicated, firms can employ several methods to finance their short-term needs. The choice of method depends on market conditions and the risks involved. It is best to rely on a mix of financing alternatives but the recommended sequence is to draw on the trade credit first, then issue commercial paper, followed by a bank line of credit with factoring on the bottom of the priority list. Short-term financing should stress the approach that yields the lowest cost.

YOU SHOULD REMEMBER

Secured loans are based on pledging accounts receivables and inventories as collateral. Factor loans are made for less than the face value of the asset pledged and the interest charged varies between 3% to 5% above prime. A factor will exercise greater or less control over the collateral depending on the type of borrower. Trade credit is the more economical way of financing short-term needs, and factoring is the least preferable way of short-term financing.

THE CASH CYCLE

Firms experience cash inflows and cash outflows that do not occur at the same time. Disbursements to pay for the purchase of raw materials and to carry inventory as well as receivables are turned into cash after the collection of receivables. The goal is to shorten the time cash remains tied up in inventory and receivables and to lengthen the time when accounts payables come due. The less cash is tied up the less external financing is needed. This calls for the analysis of the cash cycle, which is measured in the following way:

Cash cycle = Days in accounts + Days in inventory − Days in accounts
receivables payables

To calculate the number of days cash remains in receivables, inventory, and payables, we employ turnover ratios as shown below:

$$\text{Days in receivables (AR)} = 365/\left(\frac{\text{Credit sales}}{\text{Average AR}}\right)*$$

$$\text{Days in inventory (I)} = 365/\left(\frac{\text{Cost of goods sold}}{\text{Average I}}\right)*$$

$$\text{Days in payables (AP)} = 365/\left(\frac{\text{Cost of goods sold}}{\text{Average AP}}\right)*$$

* Turnover ratios

Let's demonstrate how the cash cycle works if the financial statements of a firm supply the following information:

	In millions $
Credit sales	20.0
Cost of goods sold	15.0
Average accounts receivables	5.0
Average inventory	2.5
Average accounts payables	2.0

Based on the above information the days in receivables, inventory and payables is

$$\text{Days in accounts receivables} = 365/\left(\frac{\$20.0}{\$5.0}\right) = 91 \text{ days}$$

$$\text{Days in inventory} = 365/\left(\frac{\$15.0}{\$2.5}\right) = 61 \text{ days}$$

$$\text{Days in accounts payables} = 365/\left(\frac{\$15.0}{\$2.0}\right) = 49 \text{ days}$$

The cash cycle (days) is

$$\text{Cash cycle (days)} = (91 + 61) - 49 = 103 \text{ days}$$

Indications are that the time between cash disbursements and cash collections is 103 days. Obviously, the shorter the time between payouts, the better off the firm will be and the less the firm will need to borrow from external sources. The days in the cash cycle can be reduced by offering cash discounts to customers to accelerate accounts receivables payments. Inventories can be lowered by offering clearance sales. Requesting time extensions on accounts payables is not a good idea because it may damage the firm's credit rating. In summary, cash cycle analysis is a good way to minimize the need for short-term financing.

LONG-TERM FINANCING

The following are some of the reasons why firms engage in long-run financing.

1. Expected increases in future sales require the funding of marketing and other supportive functions to remain competitive.

2. As the company grows, its capacity needs increase.

3. The firm must continue to modernize and introduce more efficient equipment.

4. Shifts in demand force the firm to abandon obsolete capacity and to invest in a new capacity.

5. Financing long-term research and development projects promotes a healthy life cycle.

6. Over the long run a large part of the **working capital** becomes **permanent** and must be financed on this basis.

The long-term investment needs of a firm depend on how fast the company is expected to grow, the rate of inflation, and the posturing done by the company to compete successfully in the marketplace. In this kind of environment, a firm must be able to develop the right new products, produce them efficiently, maintain a low-cost base through modernization, and come up with the right capacity mix. Recognizing the gradual obsolescence of product lines and equipment and investing to keep abreast with the new developments requires a long-term financing plan.

The implementation of long-term plans will help to maximize the wealth of the firm. In part, that will mean drawing on various sources of financing to minimize the cost of borrowing at the least risk. The two sources of long-term financing are, internal cash flow and external sources of funds.

As the firm grows, it will generate income, and the more it invests the larger the depreciation. These two internal sources of funds generally are insufficient to cover all of the long-term investments required by the firm. As a result, it must develop a strategy to tap various sources of permanent external financing. Remember, even though the firm has various ways of financing investments, it cannot ignore the need to determine the right capital structure mix, which will lead to the lowest average cost of capital. It can't continue to issue debt without having to face the growing probability of bankruptcy and increased agency costs.

Given these considerations, we can divert our attention to the alternatives available to a firm when it engages in planning its long-term financing needs. The discussion in this chapter focuses on the understanding of the market environment, the way new issues are priced, the features of these instruments, and the process of pricing and selling of new issues.

Once a firm determines how much it has to invest, it should evaluate the different ways of financing these investments. Most external financing is done by issuing stocks and bonds. Success in financing depends in part on the value the **stock** and **bond markets** place on these securities. As we have discussed in Chapter 3, the value of securities depends on the future expected returns of bonds and stocks discounted by a risk factor. Firms in a high risk category can finance their long-term operation by issuing stocks and bonds whose expected returns are high enough to attract investors. High-quality and large-size firms, with sound financial bases, can issue new securities more easily than smaller, less-established firms. When all is said and done long-run financing is contingent on the ability of the firm to pay its creditors in the case of a new bond issue and in the case of investors who buy stock the concern is with the firm's ability to generate future earnings, which will be translated into dividends and capital appreciation. If a firm can demonstrate the ability to take advantage of growth opportunities, it has a better chance of selling its stock to investors.

• *BOND FINANCING*

When a firm decides to issue bonds, it assumes the obligation of paying a fixed amount of interest semiannually and promises to pay par ($1,000) at the maturity date.

The cost of issuing these bonds is partly contingent on:

1. the years to maturity

2. the market yield to maturity of similar bonds

3. the coupon rate or rate of interest

4. economic and market conditions

Normally, the longer the maturity, the higher the yield and coupon rate. Also, when the economy is expanding, the cost of borrowing increases, and when it contracts, the cost or yield to maturity declines. This **yield to maturity** is the rate of return a bondholder receives when a bond is held to maturity. It reflects the risk of the firm and is the discount rate that equals the present value of all the bond's returns to the current price of the bond. Therefore, when a firm considers issuing bonds, it must be concerned with the yield to maturity because that is the cost of borrowing by issuing new bonds. This rate does not remain fixed, rather it reflects changes in the overall market rate of interest. Let's see how this rate of interest is determined.

INTEREST RATE DETERMINATION

Interest rates are the cost of borrowing. There are two types of interest rates, namely, a nominal rate and a real rate. The rates you see quoted in the newspapers are nominal rates, which include the following two components:

1. The real rate of interest

2. A premium for the expected rate of inflation

Therefore the nominal rate is equal to

Nominal rate of interest = Real rate of interest + Expected inflation rate

Solving for the real rate, you get

Real rate of interest = Nominal rate − Expected inflation rate

If the real rate is 6% and the inflation rate is 4% then

$$
\begin{aligned}
\text{Nominal rate} &= 6\% + 4\% = 10\% \\
\text{Real rate} &= 10\% - 4\% = 6\%
\end{aligned}
$$

The real rate of interest is determined by the supply and demand for loanable funds. Demand originates in borrowings by consumers, corporations, and the federal government. Supply comes from financial intermediaries who are depositories of savings and lend funds to borrowers. Figure 14-1 shows that the demand curve has a downward sloping shape and the supply curve an upward slope. Generally, strong demand for funds leads to higher interest rates and increased supply to lower interest rates. Demand for funds increases when the economy expands, and it decreases when economic activity contracts. Supply increases or decreases as a result of a loosening or tightening by the Federal Reserve. Higher savings mean more supply, while lower savings indicate a reduction in the supply of loanable funds. Interest rate equilibrium occurs where the supply and demand curves intersect. When the federal government runs a budget deficit, its borrowings increase, causing the demand curve to shift to the right and putting upward pressure on interest rates. The Federal Reserve can influence the supply of funds by raising the federal funds rate. As shown in Figure 14-1, when the supply of money increases, the supply curve shifts from S1 to S2, and all other things being equal, the real rate of interest will decline. If demand for money rises, the real rate of interest will increase, and the demand curve shifts from D_1 to D_2. The nominal rate of interest will move up or down in response to changes in the demand and supply of loanable funds.

Now that we have a general idea of the factors that influence changes in real rates, let's move on to a discussion of the other component of the nominal rate of interest. That component is the expected rate of inflation. No one has been able to forecast the expected rate of inflation with any precision, but we can get a rough idea of its future direction.

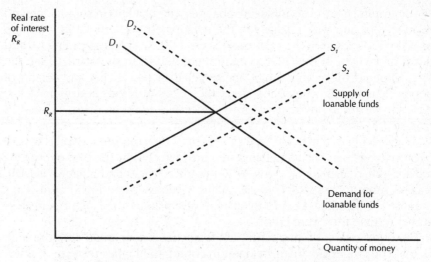

Figure 14-1 Determination of the Real Rate of Interest (General Cost of Borrowing)

General price movements, measured by the Consumer Price Index, tend to increase more rapidly in periods of economic expansion. Barring a major downturn, prices are likely to be contained within acceptable levels when economic activity slows down or declines. So when the economy expands, prices are anticipated to increase. High productivity tends to dampen inflation. And a rapid expansion in money supply will put upward pressure on prices. These are some of the broad factors that impact the rate of inflation.

Some clues regarding the future direction of inflation come from forward contracts or future contracts on the Consumer Price Index. More specifically, the price of futures contracts reflects expectations of investors who believe that the inflation rate will accelerate or decelerate. Therefore, changes in the values of futures contracts give an indication of the direction of the anticipated rate of inflation. Another hint is available from interest rate futures contracts, which reflect investors' belief that the rate of inflation will accelerate or decelerate. Consequently, these contracts provide a general indication of the direction of inflation.

All of the bits of information establish a general basis for arriving at a rough estimate of the future rate of inflation. If so, it is possible to come up with an educated guess about the direction and possible magnitude of the expected rate of inflation.

We have shown how the principles governing the real rate of interest and the expected inflation rate can serve as guidelines regarding future nominal rates. Given this information, a manager can gain a better understanding of why and how interest rates behave the way they do and take appropriate measures to hold the cost of borrowing at the lowest possible level.

To recapitulate, the nominal rate changes with changes in supply-demand relationships and with changes in the anticipated rate of inflation. Any up or down movement in the market rates establishes a corresponding up and down movement in the yield to maturity of bonds. In the marketplace the forces behind the nominal rate are revealed in the buying and selling of bonds. This buying and selling alters the prices of bonds and their yields. Basically we are saying that when the price of a bond goes up, its yield to maturity declines, and when it declines, its yield to maturity increases.

We can observe that from the firm's point of view this interaction is crucial because long-term financing plans are partly affected by the cost of borrowing and the availability of funds. When funds are tight and inflation is high, it costs more to borrow. That can affect adversely some investment plans because the marginal cost of capital increases making some investments less attractive than they were before.

The other aspect of long-term debt financing is concerned with the time factor. The longer the maturity date of a bond, the higher the rate of interest needed to convince investors to buy a bond. The longer the maturity, the greater the uncertainty of payment and the higher the return the bond must offer. This relationship is depicted by what is known as the **yield curve**. Under normal circumstances a yield curve assumes an upward slope as indicated in Figure 14-2, panel A.

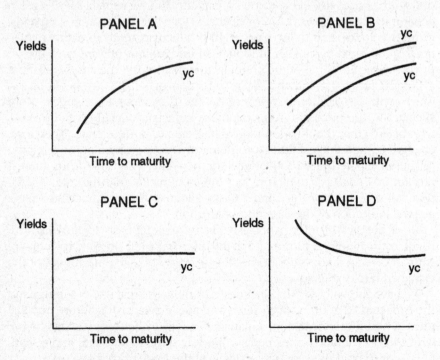

Figure 14–2 Yield curves or the relationship between yields and the time to maturity. yc = yield curve.

Normally, the yields of short-maturity, fixed-income securities, which offer early payback and less time uncertainty, are lower than the yields of longer-maturity bonds. So, when managers plan their long-term financing, they must take into consideration the length of time a debt will remain outstanding. Remember, usually a long-term bond costs more than a short-term, fixed-income security.

Valuable information can be obtained from the analysis of the changing shape of the yield curve. A steeply rising yield curve (see Figure 14-2, panel A), for example, is an indication that interest rates are likely to increase. As the economy expands, the yield curve is likely to shift upward (see Figure 14-2, panel B). Early signs of this shift indicate that it may be a good time to borrow. Eventually the business cycle nears a peak at which time the yield curve assumes a flat shape (see Figure 14-2, panel C). And sometimes the yield curve becomes inverted (see Figure 14-2, panel D). A flat or inverted yield curve suggests that interest rates are expected to decline. At this time, the firm should consider short-term financing, and it ought to postpone long-term borrowing until the curve returns to a more normal upward sloping shape. Some analysts suggest that an upward shift in the yield curve implies an expected increase in the rate of inflation. If so, the firm might consider hedging against future price increases of its factors of production.

As indicated, the information gleaned from changing yield curve shapes may provide useful guidelines for implementing effective financing decisions.

THE TIMING OF FINANCING STRATEGIES

Correct timing of long-term bond issues is of considerable importance to a firm. As we discussed above, the goal is to issue long bonds at the trough of a business cycle when interest rates are the lowest. Unfortunately, that happens to be the time when these funds are least needed. Usually pressure to raise funds by issuing debt increases toward the peak of a cycle when capacity is scarce and there is strong demand for the firm's products. But this is when interest rates are highest. Consequently, managers can finance at high costs and be saddled with this debt for a long period of time. A little planning can help them resolve this dilemma. For example, the firm may consider issuing a convertible bond that is callable in a few years. Should interest rates fall, call the convertible and issue a straight bond at a lower rate of interest.

Another option a firm can exercise is the implementation of an interest rate swap, which involves the use of a floating rate of financing. This flexible method of financing allows the firm to change the bond from a variable rate to a fixed rate. So that, when interest rates decline, the float feature lowers the interest expense incurred by the firm. Should the expectation be that interest rates will decrease, the firm may swap (shift) from a variable to a fixed rate, locking in a lower rate.

• *THE ZERO COUPON BOND ALTERNATIVE*

A less obvious way to avoid heavy interest costs and relieve managers from the interim concern about high fixed charges would be to issue **zero coupon bonds**. These bonds are sold at a discount from face value with a promise to pay par value at maturity. The implied rate of interest of these zero bonds is generally lower than the rate on coupon bonds. By issuing zeros, the firm does not have to make periodic payments of interest, and it postpones final payment at par to a future date when, presumably, the firm will have generated sufficient cash flow from investments to repay the zero coupon bondholder. Because investors who buy zeros are permitted to lock in a long-term return without chance of call, they find these bonds attractive and are willing to accept a lower rate of return.

The valuation of zero coupon bonds is relatively simple. The price of this bond at original issue is equal to the discounted value of the bond, by some predetermined required rate of return:

$$\text{Discounted price of zero coupon bond} = \text{Par value } (PVF_{K,N})$$

Suppose a firm finds that to issue a 10-year-maturity zero coupon bond, it would have to incur a rate of return of 10%. Then the offering price of this zero bond would be

$$\text{Offering price of zero coupon bond} = \$1,000 \, (.319) = \$319$$

$$(K = 10\%, N = 10 \text{ Years})$$

The bond will be issued at $319, and at the end of 10 years that bond will be worth $1,000. A corporation raising $30 million would issue roughly 94,044 bonds ($30 million ÷ $319 = 94,044). At the end of 10 years, it would have to pay bondholders a total of $94,044,000. However, for the time being, it need not worry about interest expense, changes in market rates, and ways to refinance its debt.

Another method of financing involves the use of a sinking fund. This feature allows the firm to retire a stated number of bonds at different periods of time. In addition to allowing the firm to systematically retire the debt, the sinking fund provides a certain degree of financing flexibility. Should the interest rate increase, the price of these bonds will decline, and the firm can buy the bonds at the market price below par value to meet the sinking fund provision. And, when interest rates are low and the prices of bonds are above par, the firm can retire the bonds at par. This flexibility can serve a useful purpose in allowing the firm to achieve more effective and efficient long-term financing.

A firm can postpone issuing bonds until a more advantageous time in the future by trading financial futures. If the strategy is to lock in current low rates of interest and to finance several months from now, then the firm can sell financial future contracts now and cover by buying them at a later date.

Finally, the firm can fall back on shelf registration to achieve more timely long-term financing.

YOU SHOULD REMEMBER

Normally the riskier the bond and the longer its maturity, the higher its coupon rate. Nominal interest rates have two components: the real rates of interest, determined by supply and demand for loanable funds, and an expected rate of inflation. Therefore,

Nominal rate = Real rate of interest + Expected inflation rate

A good time to borrow long is when the yield curve has a steep upward slope. When the curve is flat or inverted, a firm should borrow short term and defer long-term financing. Strategies to keep the cost of borrowing low and issue securities at the right time include, issuing callable convertibles, employing floating rate bonds, and issuing zero coupon bonds. Also, the firm can consider using sinking fund bonds, financial future contracts, and shelf registration.

RISK AND QUALITY OF BONDS

When managers contemplate issuing bonds they must consider the interest and principal payments they will be obligated to make over the life of the bond. The rate of return that is incurred to issue these bonds depends on several important factors:

1. The yield to maturity of other bonds with similar financial characteristics. This establishes the risk of the bond and the discount rate, that must be employed to obtain the present value of that bond.

2. The past default experience of the firm. Investors are concerned with the past record of payments. If the firm has faced past payment problems, investors will require a higher rate of return to compensate them for the higher probability of this risk recurring.

3. Investors analyze the interest coverage ratio or the multiple where operating income exceeds the interest expense. If this coverage is high it will help to reduce the cost of issuing a bond.

4. The marketability and liquidity of a bond and how easily that security trades among investors or on the exchange is an important factor that prospective bondholders consider. The easier it is to buy and sell a bond, the lower the risk and cost of issue.

5. An improving capital structure with the right mix of stocks and bonds is viewed favorably by investors. And, so is the financial soundness of the firm-based financial ratio analysis.

6. Last but not least, the anticipated variability, growth of earnings, and cash flow can make investors more or less inclined to purchase a bond. The greater the variability, the higher the cost.

These are some of the factors, among others, that determine the bond quality rankings assigned to firms by **bond-rating agencies**, such as Standard & Poor's and Moody's. The ratings assigned by these agencies follow:

Ratings of Agencies That Reflect the Quality of Bonds	
Moody's	Standard & Poor's
Aaa	AAA
Aa	AA
A	A
Baa	BBB
Ba	BB

The Aaa and AAA rating are assigned to the best firms with the soundest financial status. These bonds are sold at the lowest rate of interest. All ratings of Baa and BBB or higher are considered investment-grade bonds and are eligible for purchase by banks and other financial institutions. All other lower ratings represent speculative securities and many are referred to as junk bonds. The further down the rating, the higher the chances of default.

What we are saying is that quality ratings serve as guidelines and become a reference point for corporations who want to ascertain the coupon rate to apply to their bonds. All the manager has to do is find rated companies with similar features. This will indicate how his or her company will be rated and what coupon rate the firm must pay.

• COMMON STOCK FEATURES

Another way to finance the long-term requirements of a firm is to issue common stock. When common stock is sold, the stockholders become part owners of the firm. They are entitled to participate in the distribution of earnings (dividends) and the capital gains, which are reflected in the price of the stock when earnings grow. Stockholders assume all of the risks of a firm but have the voting power to elect the board of directors, which sets policy and hires managers to run the firm. Voting by stockholders on company issues can be done directly at the annual meeting, or stockholders can send in **proxies**, which allow someone else to vote at the meeting. It is critical to know that stockholders have last claim on the assets of the firm in case of default and liquidation. However, they also have limited liability, which means stockholders are not responsible for the debts of the firm and their total loss cannot exceed their original investment. One of the benefits of being a stockholder is the **preemptive right**, which by statute gives the stockholders the right to buy new shares of stock before others so that they can maintain the same proportion of ownership they originally had. In addition to being entitled to any cash dividends, stockholders can transfer ownership to another investor. Upon sale of the stock, the stockholder signs the stock certificate, and title is transferred to a new buyer. If the stock is held in "street" name, then the broker sends the stock to the transfer agent (usually a bank) and new stock is issued to the buyer of the stock.

A firm usually has a charter outlining the nature of the business and any applicable rules. In the charter the firm specifies the amount of shares authorized to be issued. Usually only a part of these shares are sold and remain outstanding, and the remainder are held in treasury to be used to compensate managers, to implement reinvestment plans, or to merge with other firms.

NEW COMMON STOCK ISSUES AND TIMING OF THE ISSUES

A firm will prefer issuing lower-cost bonds as long as the debt is manageable and it can safely meet its fixed obligations. But a time comes when the debt-to-equity ratio becomes too high. The market will let the firm know this because the cost of issuing debt begins to reflect the greater probability of default. It is time to consider a new stock offering. The question then is: At what price can the new stock be sold? Fortunately, the value of firms whose shares trade on the organized exchanges is known from the quoted price. The crucial point to consider is whether the timing to issue new stock is correct. This can be established by analyzing market conditions. Obviously, the most favorable time is in a rising market when the P/E is high. In expanding phases there is support for new offerings because of investor optimism. As the market cycle rises, so does the P/E of stocks, which makes financing more favorable. At that time each dollar earned by the firm is likely to have a higher multiple. Therefore, firms prefer offering new stock during expansion rather than contraction phases of the market cycle.

PRICING A NEW ISSUE

Obviously, the amount of shares that a firm will issue depends on the amount of dollars to be financed and the price per share of the stock. For example, if a firm's stock trades at $10 and it must raise $10 million in new funds, then it will have to issue 1,000,000 plus an additional 20,000 shares to cover the 2% flotation costs owed the investment banker who distributes the issue. In other words, a total of 1,020,000 shares will have to be issued at a value of $10,200,000 (1,020,000 × $10). After deducting $200,000 in flotation costs, the firm receives a net of $10,000,000 or ($10,200,000 – $200,000).

What if the firm is issuing stock for the first time and wants to determine its value and the price at which it should issue the common stock. One way is to search for traded securities with similar features to the firm in question.

Another approach is to apply the constant growth dividend model to find out the discount rate the market has assigned a similarly traded company. The formula is

$$K_s = \left(\frac{D_1}{P_s} \right) + G$$

If the traded company has a $D_1 = \$2.00$, its current price is $20, and it is growing at 6% yearly, then K_s is equal to 16%.

$$K_s = \frac{\$2.00}{\$20} + .06 = 16\%$$

This 16% is the discount rate to be used in capitalizing the firm's earnings. However, after making some calculation, the new firm estimates that its earnings will grow at 9%. Given expected earnings of $500,000, the total stock value of the company is $7.1 million based on the following formula

$$\left(P_s = \frac{D_1}{K_s - G} \right)$$

$$P_s = \frac{\$500,000}{.16 - .09} = \$7,142,857$$

If the firm has 500,000 shares outstanding, the price per share of the stock is $14.29 or ($7,142,857 ÷ 500,000). Let us assume it decided to raise $5.5 million, how many shares of stock would this financing require? The answer is 384,884 shares ($5,500,000 ÷ $14.29). Remember the value of a non-traded company cannot differ materially from the price per share of other similarly traded companies. Suppose we want to find out the P/E that will be assigned to the new stock. Based on our calculated price of $14.29 per share and an assumed earnings per share of $1.00, we come up with a P/E of 14.3 ($14.29 ÷ $1.00).

In practice, the pricing of new common stock issues entails some compromises. The issuing firm invariably will seek the highest price it can get while the underwriter of the issue wants to make the price as attractive as possible to prospective investors. That is why many **Initial Public Offerings (IPO)** are underpriced, and upon sale of the stock the early quotes are substantially higher than the initial offer. Investors recognize this condition and the tendency is for new issues to be oversubscribed, putting upward pressure on the price of the stock.

YOU SHOULD REMEMBER

Important features of common stock ownership are the preemptive rights of stockholders who reserve the right to maintain the same ownership in a firm when new financing is done by a firm. Liability is limited to loss of original investment, and stockholders get to elect the board of directors, which is responsible for setting policy and approving all important issues affecting the firm. The cost of issuing stock is higher than debt financing, but when debt obligations are too high, the firm must consider the issue of stock to finance its investments. The value of a common stock is equal to its traded price multiplied by its outstanding shares. Pricing of non-traded common stock involves using the constant growth dividend model to determine the value of the firm, using as a criterion the discount rate of similarly traded companies and the expected growth rate of the firm. Another way to determine a non-traded firm's value is to find out the *P/E* of other traded companies and multiply this *P/E* by the earnings per share of the firm.

PRIVATE VERSUS PUBLIC PLACEMENT

When managers raise long-term funds they have the option to sell a new issue to the public, or the securities can be sold privately to financial institutions, such as insurance companies and pension funds. This later method of financing is known as a **private placement**. There are several advantages in placing an issue directly with an institution. Terms are negotiated with the financial institution and the firm bypasses the tedious and structured process required in going public. It is not required to register the securities with the Securities Exchange Commission (SEC) and avoids the stringent scrutiny of this commission. The issuing firm does not have to make public disclosure of its financial statements, competitive position, and important new product developments. Processing time is reduced, and there are other cost savings. However, the interest cost may be a little higher than going public because the buyer of the issue sacrifices liquidity and marketability.

GOING PUBLIC USING AN INVESTMENT BANKER

The alternative method of financing is to sell the issue to the investing public, which then becomes subject to the scrutiny by the Securities Exchange Commission, a government agency which requires that certain information be divulged and that the information supplied is accurate. The SEC does not pass judgment on the valuation of the security. It just makes sure that its regulations are followed and all statements are correct.

A public placement is finally traded on an exchange, which in turn calls for the company to meet certain criteria. The main advantage of a public placement is that the security is traded, its price is determined, and there is greater marketability of the issue.

A public offering involves the use of an **investment banker** whose main functions are to advise the firm on market conditions, price the issue, undertake the paperwork, and assume the risk of distributing the issue.

When a corporation wishes to raise new funds, it usually contacts an investment banker like Morgan Stanley or Merrill Lynch. Preliminary discussions take place to iron out the broad details of the issue. Once these initial conferences are completed, the firm, in conjunction with the investment banker, prepares a **red herring**, which is a legal document that must be submitted to the SEC for approval.

When the SEC approves the content of a red herring, this document becomes a **prospectus**. A prospectus must be submitted to investors contemplating purchase of the new securities. It contains a description of the issue, the amount and number of shares financed, an income statement, and a balance sheet showing results of the past 4 or 5 years. Statements are included to indicate the products of the firm, its competitive position, and the risks associated with the issue. The names of directors and their compensation are also revealed. The investment banker advises the issuing firm on the timing of issue and helps set the final sale price of a stock or the coupon rate for a bond. The goal is to price the issue so that it will attract buyers. Once all of these details are agreed upon and approval is obtained from the SEC, the issue is ready for distribution.

THE DISTRIBUTION PROCESS

The primary investment banker forms an **underwriting syndicate** composed of various investment houses who become responsible for distributing the new issue in the primary market. This selling group places a "tombstone," which describes the offering price, the size of the issue, and the list of the syndicate members. This tombstone appears in several newspapers announcing the forthcoming issue to the investing public. Each member in the syndicate group is assigned a proportion of the total issue that it must sell. These syndicate members arrange with brokers to get in touch with their customers and generate the direct sale of the securities. The offer of the new security is made by prospectus, which means that investors must receive a prospectus before they are allowed to purchase the security.

In essence, the syndicate members buy the issue from the issuing firm and bear the risk of selling it to the public. Investment bankers incur the costs of advising, expenses of doing the paperwork, and legal costs for these services as well as assume the risk of distributing the securities. There is a charge. That charge is labeled **flotation costs**. The following example illustrates the way these flotation costs are assessed. Suppose a company issues 1.5 million shares of common stock at $10 per share as an initial offering.

Say the flotation costs come to 6% of the value of the share. The amount received by the firm is

> Value of issue
>   (1.5 million × $10.00 per share) $15,000,000
> Flotation costs ($15 million × .06) _____900,000_
> Proceeds received by the firm $14,100,000

There is one more facet to the underwriting process and that entails the alternative methods of negotiating with underwriters. A corporation can sell bonds or shares of stock directly to the public without using an underwriter. A number of new stock issues, especially those of large corporations are done via direct placements. However, most firms avail themselves of the services of an underwriter. One way of doing this is to invite competitive bids by various underwriters. The best bid usually is awarded the underwriting assignment.

Another way to issue stocks and bonds is through negotiated underwriting arrangements. In these cases, a firm and the underwriter negotiate all the terms of the issue, and no other competing underwriter is involved. Finally, there is the **best effort** deal whereby the underwriter agrees to do its utmost to sell the issue to the public but does not guarantee selling the entire issue. Any part of the unsold securities are returned to the firm, and flotation fees are set per security. The best effort arrangement usually involves small and highly speculative securities, which in the opinion of the investment banker are subject to very high distribution risks.

YOU SHOULD REMEMBER

A firm can sell new securities by placing them privately with a financial institution, or it can sell them directly to the public. A private placement does not require SEC approval nor is it necessary to prepare a prospectus. However, these securities lack marketability. A public placement is usually done through an investment banker. In this case, a prospectus must be prepared and approved by the SEC. While selling securities to the public is more expensive, the issue finally is listed and traded on an exchange. An investment banker gives advice on market conditions and the pricing of an issue. This banker takes the risk of distributing the new issue. All the services and risk assumed by the investment banker are covered by a fee called flotation costs. There are three investment banker arrangements. The firm can select one investment banker to distribute a new issue. It can select a banker by competitive bidding and, finally it can arrange a best efforts deal whereby any unsold portion of the securities issued is returned to the firm.

SHELF REGISTRATION

A recent development in the primary market is **shelf registration**, which helps to reduce the highly expensive costs of issuing securities and makes for a smoother and more flexible primary market. The firm, under the SEC Rule 415, goes through the same process of registering with the SEC but is allowed 2 years to issue the securities. In this way, the firm can offer securities at a favorable time and can do so without further disclosures or large underwriting expenses. Shelf registration has also cut down underwriters' fees. Meanwhile, the firm has the option to finance via private placement rather than offering the issue to the general public.

SECONDARY MARKET LISTING OF SECURITIES

Once a new offering of securities (bonds or stocks) is made through the **primary market**, the firm must decide whether to list or not list the new securities on organized exchanges called the **secondary market**. There are substantial advantages in listing a new issue on the secondary market. It provides greater liquidity and marketability of the issue, and, most importantly, it establishes the intrinsic value of the stock through the highly efficient market mechanism. Several firms that can't meet the rigorous requirements of large stock exchanges (like the New York Stock Exchange) have their stock traded on the over-the-counter market. The over-the-counter market has no central trading floor, and all trading is done by electronic communication between what is known as "market makers" or brokerage houses, which make a market in the issue. These market dealers are members of the National Association of Security Dealers (NASD) and must meet certain financial rules and qualify by examination.

The organized stock exchanges consist of members who buy a seat on the exchange and agree to abide by the rules of the exchange. They are the only ones allowed to trade securities. The exchange has a floor where actual sell/ buy orders are executed. Members usually represent brokers through which the public trade stocks for a commission. All securities have specialists who have order books and are ready to buy or sell and execute trades in a security. They have an inventory of the security, make a market, and are supposed to have sufficient capital to maintain an orderly market. Their compensation is the spread between the bid of a buyer and the asked price of a seller.

A firm can be listed on an exchange by applying with the exchange and the SEC. It pays a minimum fee, meets certain requirements, such as agreeing to issue quarterly and annual financial reports. Listing in secondary markets is appealing to investors because of the information they obtain, and it also facilitates the process of pricing and issuing new securities. Listing requirements vary among exchanges, but they generally call for a given level of earnings (assets) and a minimum number of shares to be held by the public.

The institutionalization and globalization of security trading have diminished the role of organized exchanges because they lack the facilities and capabilities to execute large blocks of stocks. This has given rise to a **third market** of private dealers who bypass the exchanges and trade large stocks of listed securities without causing sharp price fluctuations. Many big institutions have also set up trading systems done by a unique electronic network designed to bypass the exchanges.

YOU SHOULD REMEMBER

In shelf registration the firm gets approval to issue securities from the SEC but has 2 years to sell it to the public or place it privately. This approach permits better market timing, is more flexible, and is less costly. After securities are distributed to the public, they are listed on organized exchanges, and the securities are traded through brokers for a commission. The advantage of listing is that the public and the firm know the value of the security at any point in time, and securities can be bought and sold very easily. Securities traded over-the-counter are usually lower in quality and the pricing and trading is done between dealers who are members of the National Association of Security Dealers (NASD). Because financial institutions have become more important in security trading, a third market has emerged. This market allows these institutions to trade large blocks of securities among themselves. This type of trading is done via a unique electronic network system that does not require the use of an exchange to trade.

KNOW THE CONCEPTS

DO YOU KNOW THE BASICS?

1. Explain the role of financial intermediaries.

2. What are the main liabilities of a commercial bank?

3. Differentiate between a secured and an unsecured loan.

4. Why do firms establish a relationship with banks? Can they borrow at lower cost elsewhere and why don't they?

5. Who issues commercial paper, why do they issue it, and what are its features?

6. What do we mean by trade credit and what inducement is given to make debtors pay faster than the usual terms of credit?

7. Describe the process of raising funds via the factoring process and what is a haircut?

8. List four reasons why a firm engages in long-term financing.

9. How does a firm justify financing by making investments to sustain its long-term growth? (Hint: Relate the rate of returns to the cost of borrowing.)

10. Describe three ways a firm can achieve better timing of its financing needs and lower its costs of capital.

11. Explain what factors determine the real rate of interest in the marketplace and how the nominal rate is computed.

12. Describe the shape of a yield curve and indicate the relationship between the price of a bond and its yield to maturity.

13. What happens to *P/E*s, interest rates, and prices of fixed income securities during business expansion and contraction phases?

14. Why would anyone buy a zero coupon bond? How is its price determined at the initial offering?

15. Name two bond rating agencies and indicate, in a general way, five factors they analyze to determine the quality rating of a firm.

16. Define preemptive rights, a proxy statement, and the liability of stockholders.

17. Is it more costly to issue bonds or stocks? Why?

18. What conflict arises in the pricing of new issues between the firm and the underwriter? What usually happens to the IPO pricing of new issues?

19. What are three advantages and two disadvantages of a private placement?

20. Investment bankers play a role when firms issue new securities. What services do they provide, how do they get compensated, and what risks do they face?

21. What is the difference between competitive biddings, negotiated deals, and best efforts arrangements?

22. What are the advantages of shelf registration and how does the firm benefit from this type of procedure?

23. How does the trading mechanism differ between organized stock exchanges and the over-the-counter market?

24. Explain how large institutions trade among themselves and bypass the exchanges. What is the advantage of this type of trading?

25. Explain how the cash cycle works.

TERMS FOR STUDY

best effort
bond market
bond-rating agencies
commercial paper
compensating balance
effective rate of interest
factor
flotation costs
haircut
initial public offerings (IPO)
investment banker
line of credit
nominal rate of interest
permanent working capital
pledged collateral
preemptive rights

primary market
private placement
prospectus (red herring)
proxy
real rate of interest
secondary market
secured loan
shelf registration
stock market
third market
trade credit
trust receipt
underwriting syndicate
yield curve
yield to maturity
zero coupon bond

PRACTICAL APPLICATION

COMPUTATIONAL PROBLEMS

1. A corporation borrows $100,000 at 9% from a bank whose policy calls for a 15% compensating balance and a 1% commission fee. Calculate the bank's annual effective interest charge to the firm.

2. Ajax borrows $5,275,000 million for 5 years from a bank and is making $1,500,000 annual payments. Figure out the effective interest rate that the bank is charging on this loan.

3. A supplier's policy on its accounts receivable is 2/15 net 45. A customer foregoes taking the discount and opts to pay in 45 days. Compute the effective annual rate of interest the customer incurs by not taking advantage of the discount.

4. A factor arranges to lend a borrower $500,000 that calls for a 15% haircut on an accounts receivable. Calculate the proceeds the borrower will receive from the factor if the total charges including interest are $82,000.

5. A firm undertakes financing a $100 million bond issue with a coupon of 10% using the help of an underwriter. The banker charges 2% per bond as its flotation fee, and the bonds are issued at par value. What is the effective rate of interest after taxes to the firm and what proceeds can it expect to receive from the investment banker?

6. The nominal rate of interest is 15%, and the expected rate of inflation is 5%. What is the real rate of interest?

7. Plot a normal and an inverted yield curve. What do these two curves imply and indicate at what point in the business cycle we are likely to see an inverted yield curve?

8. Given market conditions and the quality of a zero coupon bond, a firm finds out that similar zeros have an implied rate of interest of 12%. If the par value of the zero is $1,000 and the bond has a maturity date 5 years from today, estimate the initial discounted price of this zero coupon bond.

9. Compulsive Co. has to finance a new project that will cost $6.0 million. The current price of its stock is $15 per share. How many shares will the company have to issue to raise $6.0 million if the investment banker will charge $500,000 as flotation costs, but will take the equivalent of this amount in stock?

10. Lodi Corporation has earnings of $1.0 million and pays 50% of its earnings in dividends. The firm is growing at 10% per year and its discount rate is 15%. Calculate the value of the firm. Use the constant growth dividend model formula.

11. A firm's payout ratio is 40%, its discount rate is 10%, and it is growing at 5% yearly. Calculate the *P/E* and the price of the firm's stock if its earnings are $1.2 million and it has 480,000 shares outstanding [formula for *P/E* = Payout ratio/$(K - G)$].

12. You are supplied with the following information:

	$ millions
Credit sales	25
Cost of goods sold	20
Average accounts receivables	10
Average inventory	5
Average accounts payables	3

Calculate the cash cycle days.

ANSWERS

KNOW THE CONCEPTS

1. Financial intermediaries are institutions that act as middlemen. They gather the savings of the economy and make them available to investors and borrowers. The suppliers of loanable funds are paid a return, and the financial intermediaries receive a given compensation (rate of return) depending on market conditions from borrowers of loanable funds.

2. The main liabilities of a commercial bank are its deposits.

3. A secured loan is backed by the collateral that a borrower puts up. This collateral could be accounts receivable, inventories, or other major tangible assets like property. An unsecured loan has no backing and relies on the credit standing and the reliability of the borrower. An example of an unsecured loan is a bank line of credit.

4. Firms establish a relationship with banks because they wish to have a ready source of cash to take care of their temporary needs for cash and working capital. They could borrow at lower cost by issuing commercial paper or short-term notes, but it is always helpful to have a line of credit with a bank without having to do the paperwork and arrange a public or private offering. Also, banks provide many services that are important to a firm.

5. Commercial paper is issued by large corporations with high credit ratings. It is paper having a maturity date less than 270 days, and the cost of borrowing by this method is lower than borrowing at a bank. The firm sells this paper at a discount from face value and it usually costs ½% to 1% more than the rate paid on a 3-month Treasury bill.

6. Accounts payable are a form of trade credit. This is an indirect way of financing the purchase of goods and services for a specified period of time. If a firm paid cash, it would have to draw on internal or external sources of funds to finance these purchases. We can consider this credit a loan that must be paid after a short period of time. Suppliers provide trade credit to attract customers, and they give discounts of 1% to 3% of the value of the goods bought if the customer pays up before the designated payment date.

7. The factoring process involves borrowing from a financing firm by putting up some form of collateral. The collateral usually involves accounts receivables or inventories. The value of the loan is generally less than current market value of the assets being used as collateral. This is known as a haircut. Therefore, if a firm collaterizes $100,000 of its receivables the factor may arrange a loan equal to 70% of the value of the accounts receivables. This would mean the amount of the loan would be $70,000 or ($100,000 × .70).

8. Five reasons why firms borrow for long-term financing are
   (a) to expand capacity and change the capacity mix.
   (b) to modernize operations and increase the efficiency of machinery.
   (c) to finance research and development.
   (d) to cover permanent working capital needs.
   (e) to meet growing demand for the firm's products.

9. A firm will continue to grow as long as its return on equity exceeds its average cost of borrowing. As long as there are profitable investments ($ROE > K$), it pays the firm to borrow and invest in projects that have an internal rate of return that is higher than its cost of capital.

10. A firm can achieve better timing of its financing at lower costs by using the following methods:

    (a) Issue convertible bonds with a call feature. When interest rates drop they can call the convertible and issue straight bonds at a lower rate of interest.

    (b) Use floating rate financing so that a decline in interest rates will be reflected in a decline of interest paid to creditors.

    (c) Sell interest rate futures contracts now and cover by buying at the time when financing takes place, if the issuance of debt must be delayed and interest rates are expected to increase. In this way a hedge is created whereby the future higher rate is reduced by the gain achieved from the futures contracts.

11. The real rate of interest is computed as follows:

    Real rate of interest = Nominal rate − Expected inflation rate

    In the marketplace, the real rate of interest is determined at the point of intersection between the supply of loanable funds and the demand for loanable funds. The nominal rate of interest is the sum of the real rate of interest plus a premium reflecting the expected rate of inflation at some future date.

12. A normal yield curve represents the relationship between the yields of fixed income securities and their years to maturity. Normally, the longer the maturity date, the greater the risk and the higher the yield. A normal yield curve says: Low maturities usually pay low yields, and long maturities pay higher yields. A normal yield curve is upward sloping, and yields increase at a decreasing rate as maturities lengthen. The relationship between a bond's price and its yield to maturity is an inverse one. When yields go up, bond values decline and vice versa. The yields of an inverted yield curve are higher for short maturities than longer maturities. This phenomenon usually occurs at the peaks of business cycles.

13.

Business Expansion Phases	Business Contraction Phases
*P/E*s increase	*P/E*s decline
Interest rates increase	Interest rates decrease
Prices of bonds decrease	Prices of bonds increase

14. The reason why investors buy a zero coupon bond is to match the cash inflows of that bond with the liability payments incurred at some future date. Also, the low discounted price of the bond has a certain attrac-

tion. The initial offering price of a zero coupon bond is determined as follows: Determine the number of years and the yield to maturity of the zero; then calculate the discounted price by using the following formula: $1,000 par value $\times$ $(PVAF_{K,N})$.

15. Two bond rating agencies are Standard & Poor's and Moody's. Five factors analyzed by these credit agencies are:

    (a) interest rate expense coverage.

    (b) marketability and liquidity of the bond.

    (c) capital structure of the firm or how high its debt is relative to equity.

    (d) the financial ratios of the firm.

    (e) the default history of the firm.

16. A preemptive right means that stockholders are given the right to purchase additional shares when offered by a firm, so that their voting power and their proportional ownership in the firm remains unchanged. A proxy statement duly signed empowers a party other than the original owner of the stock to vote on important company issues, like electing directors at the annual meeting. Stockholders assume the risks of the corporation, and creditors are paid before stockholders, in case of default. Stockholders have limited liability which means they can lose only their original investment and are not responsible for the debts of the firm. The benefits that accrue to stockholders are participation in the earnings and dividends paid by the firm. When the stock increases in price stockholders participate in capital gains. Stockholders get to elect the board of directors of a company and therefore have a vote in the determination of key issues affecting the company.

17. It is more costly to issue stocks than bonds because ownership of bonds gives precedence of payment to creditors before any payment is made to stockholders in the case of insolvency. Also, the cost of issuing bonds to a firm is lower because of the deductibility of interest payments or cost of debt equals yield to maturity $(1 - T)$.

18. The firm wants the issue to be priced as high as possible so that it can obtain the highest possible proceeds. Investment bankers want to assign a low price to a new issue to insure a successful distribution. The initial pricing of issues is usually set at a lower price than the intrinsic value of the stock. Investors recognize this underpricing. As a result, the issue is oversubscribed and the price increases above the IPO price.

19. A private placement avoids the scrutiny and rigid regulations of the SEC. There is less disclosure of the financial status of the firm. The cost of processing and arranging a private issue is lower than for a public issue. There are no flotation costs. The disadvantages are: the issue has less marketability, the cost of capital for a private issue may be higher than "going" public, and there is no public trading of the securities.

20. Investment bankers advise the firm on the timing and pricing of a new issue, help in the preparation of the prospectus, and investigate the legal aspects of a new issue. The investment banker usually bears the complete risk of distributing and selling a new issue. This function entails a compensation to the investment banker called flotation costs. The percentage cost to a firm diminishes as the dollar amount of the issue increases. Usually, the investment banker gets the spread between the offering price and the price it pays the issuing firm.

21. Competitive bidding calls for the issuing firm to contact various leading investment bankers and request that they submit bids for the issue. The best or highest bid in the case of stocks or the lowest interest rate bid in the case of bonds will be awarded the issue. Negotiated deals represent a direct contact with an investment banker to negotiate the final terms of a new issue. This does not involve other bankers and may result in a higher cost of issuing new securities. Best efforts is an arrangement between the issuing firm and the investment banker. The investment banker agrees to do its best to sell the new issue, but part of the distribution risk is borne by the issuing firm. If investors cannot be found to buy part of the issue, the unsold securities are returned to the firm.

22. Shelf registration involves preparation of a prospectus and getting SEC approval. Once this is done, the firm has 2 years to issue the securities to the public or to place it privately. This approach permits better timing of the issue; it reduces the cost of issuing new securities because once approved the issue can be sold quickly with little paperwork.

23. The stock exchanges are a formal place where trading of securities takes place between members of the exchange. Listing on the exchanges requires the firm to pay an initial fee and to meet certain requirements of the exchange. Prices on the organized exchanges are determined by the bid and asked quotes of different investors. A specialist is available with an order book. It is the specialist's responsibility to match, buy and sell orders and to maintain an orderly market.

    The over-the-counter market has no formal trading floor or membership arrangement. It consists of a number of dealers, linked to an electronic network, that makes a market and determines the prices of each security. These dealers belong to the National Association of Security Dealers who must meet certain financial requirements and pass a qualifying exam.

24. Large financial institutions can bypass the exchanges and trade among themselves. This so-called third market system consists of trades in large blocks of securities via a unique electronic network linking one institution to another. The advantage of this third market is lower costs of trading without causing substantial price fluctuations that might occur if that trading took place on organized exchanges.

25. The cash cycle estimates the number of days cash remains tied up in accounts receivables and inventories minus the number of days accounts payables are outstanding. The most important determinants of the cash cycle are the turnover ratios. One way to find out whether a firm is managing cash effectively is to compare its cash cycle days with competing companies in the industry. Should the cash cycle of a firm be higher than other companies, the firm should investigate the reasons why this is so. To bring the days in the cash cycle in line with other companies, a firm might consider offering a cash discount to induce early payments of accounts receivables. Or, it may advertise an inventory clearance sale. Attempts to have sellers agree to delay payments of accounts payables is not a prudent policy because it many damage the credit rating of the firm. The goal is to minimize the number of days in the cash cycle.

PRACTICAL APPLICATION

1. Bank effective rate of interest

$$= \frac{\text{Bank interest charge}}{1- \text{ Compensation balance}} + \text{Commission fee}$$
$$\text{(\% of loan)}$$

$$= \frac{.09}{1-.15} +.01 = 10.6 +.01 = 11.6\%$$

2. Calculate factor

$$\frac{\$5,275,000}{\$1,500,000} = 3.517 \text{ (factor)}$$

Look up the factor for a period of 5 years in the present value table, and you get 13% as the annual interest rate charged by the bank.

3. Effective rate of interest

$$= \frac{.02}{1-.02} \times \frac{360}{45-15} = 24.48\%$$

4. Haircut × Value of accounts receivables

($500,000 × .85)	$425,000
Total charges (including interest)	82,000
Proceeds loaned to firm	$343,000

5. Effective rate of interest

$$= \frac{\$100}{1000 \times (1 - .02)} = \frac{\$100}{\$980} = 10.2\%$$

After tax cost of bonds = $.102 \times (1 - .40) = 6.12\%$

Total value of bond issue	$100 million
Flotation costs	
($100 million × .02)	2 million
Proceeds firm receives	
from underwriter	$98 million

6. Real rate of interest = Nominal rate of interest − Expected rate of inflation 10% = .15 − .05

7. The normal yield curve tells us that the yield increases as the years to maturity increase. The inverted yield curve indicates that short-term yields are higher than long-term yields. An inverted yield curve rises toward the peak of a business expansion phase.

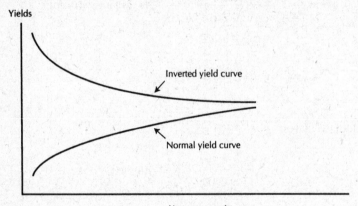

8. Discount price of zero = Par value × $(PVAF_{K,N})$
(where $K = 12\%$ and $N = 5$)

then
Initial price of zero bond = 1,000 (.567) = $567

9. Number of shares raised equals:

$6.0 million/$15 = 400,000 Shares that have to be issued
$500,000/$15   = 33,333 Additional shares to cover the flotation costs
            433,333 Total shares to be issued to raise $6.0 million

10. Value of firm:

$$(\$500,000 \times 1.10) = \frac{550,000}{.15 - .10} = \$11.0 \text{ million}$$

11. $P/E = \dfrac{\text{Payout ratio}}{K - G} = \dfrac{.40}{.10 - .05} = 8 \text{ times}$

EPS = 1.2 million ÷ 480,000 = $2.50 per share
Value of firms shares = $P/E \times EPS$ = 8 × $2.50 = $20

12. The standard equation to calculate the days in receivables, inventories, and payables is

$$\text{Days} = 365/\text{Turnover ratio}$$

Then

Days in account receivables	365/($25/$10) = 146
Days in inventory	365/($20/$5) = 91
Days in accounts payables	365/($20/$3) = 55

Cash cycle (days) = (146 + 91) − 55 = 182 days

INTRODUCTION TO FINANCIAL ANALYSIS

15
FINANCIAL PLANNING

THE IMPORTANCE OF FINANCIAL PLANNING

Financial planning is the process of estimating the amount of financing required to continue a company's operations, and of deciding when and how the needed funds should be financed. Without a reliable procedure to estimate financing needs, a company may run out of sufficient funds to pay obligations such as interest on loans, suppliers' bills, rental expenses, and the cost of utilities. A company is in default if it is unable to pay its contractual obligations, such as interest on loans. Therefore, the lack of sound financial planning may cause lack of liquidity and then bankruptcy—even when total assets, including nonliquid assets, such as inventory, plant, and equipment, are well in excess of liabilities.

The success and solvency of a firm cannot be guaranteed merely by profitable projects and increasing sales. "Liquidity crisis," that is, a shortage of cash to pay financial obligations, always threatens a company. Since the problem is more critical when credit is limited, small and medium-sized firms are in greater danger of possible cash shortages than larger corporations, which usually have a wider range of financing alternatives. This does not mean that large firms never have liquidity problems. A good example is the Chrysler Corporation, which suffered badly from a shortage of cash in the 1970s.

Be aware that even accounts receivable don't have liquidity unless they are readily convertible into cash. A supernormal growth rate of sales does not protect a firm from possible bankruptcy, either. Management has to do regular financial planning to estimate future financing needs. The timing of different types of financing is also critical to financial planning. For instance, in a time of rising interest rates, a long-term, fixed-rate loan is preferred to a short-term loan. When the interest rate is expected to decline, however, a financial officer is better off borrowing temporarily, and then refinancing the loan at a lower rate once the interest rate has fallen.

Financing sources include short- and long-term debt, preferred and common stock, and retained earnings. Retained earnings, which are accumulated profits after tax and dividends, are an especially desirable source of financing. The ability to expand business operations by using retained earnings is a sign of financial solvency, because these funds make the firm financially self-sufficient. In the absence of adequate retained earnings, however, management has a more difficult decision to make, and needs to find the best combination of debt and equity. In the following sections, the emphasis will be on the methods used to estimate financing needs and the analysis of sources and uses of funds.

YOU SHOULD REMEMBER

Financial planning is referred to as the process of estimating future financing needs and identifying how previous funds were financed and for what purposes they were spent. Through financial planning and control, the management of a company can evaluate whether the existing patterns of financing and spending funds are in line with the overall goals of the company. The timing as well as the amount of required funds can be determined through financial planning techniques.

METHODS TO ESTIMATE NEEDS

There are several methods to estimate the financial needs of a firm. Although none of the methods can predict future needs precisely, a financial manager must use some method to roughly estimate the amount of cash required for at least one year ahead. The basic methods for this purpose are discussed below.

PERCENT-OF-SALES METHOD

The purpose of the percent-of-sales method is to show how financing needs for working capital can be calculated. The percent-of-sales method assumes that changes in sales affect the amount of assets to be maintained in a company. By definition, an asset that changes as a result of increases or decreases in sales is called a **spontaneous asset**. In other words, sales or revenue basically determines how much financing is required to run a business. There is a logical connection between expected sales and various types of assets. For instance, if sales are expected to rise, the company needs more cash and inventory and should expect more accounts receivable to accumulate. On the other hand, if sales are predicted to decline, inventory levels should be reduced. Sales also determine the amount of liabilities, or debt, a company maintains. As sales go up, the company increases its trade debt and borrows more money to purchase goods and raw materials to ensure that the level of inventory is sufficient. Accounts payable and short- and long-term debts will then tend to increase, enabling the company to acquire more assets and expand operations.

By looking into previous financial statements, a financial analyst can determine the ratios of different types of assets and liabilities to sales. Suppose the ratio of changing assets to sales is 60% and the ratio of changing liabilities is 40%. These ratios indicate that when sales increase by $100, assets and liabilities of the company will probably go up by $60 and $40, respectively. Subtracting 40% from 60%, you get 20% net assets as percent of sales. In simple words, if the company plans to expand its sales by $100, it needs $20 in new financing, part of which can be financed internally—through expected profits—though the rest must be raised from outside. For instance, if the firm can generate $5 in net earnings after dividends, $15 must be financed through borrowing and by issuing preferred or common stock. On the basis of the above line of reasoning, the following equation to determine the external financing needs of a company is easily developed:

$$\text{External required financing} = \frac{A}{S}(\Delta S) - \frac{L}{S}(\Delta S) - rS$$

where A = assets that change with sales
ΔS = expected change in sales forecast for the year
L = liabilities that change with sales
r = ratio of net profits after dividends to sales

Example: Percent-of-Sales Method

PROBLEM   The historical ratio of assets that spontaneously change with sales is 70% for the ABC Co. The ratio for liabilities is 30%. Sales are expected to increase by $200,000 in the next year. The company has historically maintained 3% of its sales revenue as net earnings after dividends. Assuming that expected sales are $1,000,000, predict the amount of external required financing for the next year.

SOLUTION   Inserting the given information into the equation gives

$$\text{External required financing} = 70\%(\$200,000) - 30\%(\$200,000)$$
$$- 3\%(\$1,000,000)$$
$$= \$140,000 - \$60,000$$
$$- \$30,000 = \$50,000$$

Therefore, the ABC Co. has to arrange for external financing of $50,000 if it plans to increase sales by $200,000, as assumed in this case. Without that external financing, the company will be unable to buy more inventory, acquire other assets and meet its sales target.

CASH BUDGET METHOD

A major part of financial planning is liquidity management. In simple terms, the purpose of **liquidity management** is to ensure that the company will never run out of cash. The cash budget technique is commonly used to achieve this objective.

Using this technique, a financial analyst compares future cash receipts with future cash payments on a monthly basis and determines the financing surplus or deficit for each month. The result is a cash budget through which future financing of the firm can be predicted. Table 15-1 shows a format that can be used to estimate the required cash.

In Table 15-1, net monthly cash flow is determined by subtracting estimated payments from estimated receipts, as shown in column 3. The amount of cash at the end of each month, found by adding the cash at the beginning of each month to the net cash flow, is reported in column 5. Column 6 is the minimum cash reserve that a company maintains to avoid running out of cash. Adding the minimum cash reserve to the ending cash reported in column 5 gives the estimated cash surplus or deficit. If there is a surplus in column 7, the company may think of investing the excess cash in an interest-bearing security. Should column 7 show a deficit, the company must plan in advance to determine how and where to borrow the money needed to cover the deficit. Note that the cash surplus/deficit computed in column 7 is different from the expected earnings or losses reported in an income statement. Despite a substantial amount of earnings, a company may run into cash deficit problems if accounts receivable are not properly collected. Therefore, cash budgeting is absolutely necessary to forecast and arrange for future financing.

This method of projecting cash flow is very popular in practice. However, the estimated cash flow is reliable only if receipts and payments are correctly estimated. Cash receipts result mainly from cash sales; collection of

Table 15–1   A Format to Estimate Required Cash

Month	Receipts (1)	Payments (2)	Net Monthly Cash Flow (1) – (2) (3)	Beginning (Cash) (4)	Ending Cash (3) + (4) (5)	Cash Reserve (6)	Cash Surplus or Deficit (5) + (6) (7)
January							
February							
March							
April							
May							
June							
July							
August							
September							
October							
November							
December							

accounts receivable, interest, and dividends (from investments); the sale of old equipment; and lease revenues. The major components of cash payments are cash purchases and payments of accounts payable, wages, salaries, taxes, interest charges, rental expenses, insurance premiums, cash dividends, and other operating expenses. By looking into both old and current data for receipts and payments, a financial analyst can prepare a cash budget similar to that shown in Table 15-1 to get a clear idea about the future cash requirements of the firm.

CASH TURNOVER METHOD

In the cash turnover method, the minimum amount of cash needed by a company to run its operation is determined by the use of the following equation:

$$\text{Minimum cash required} = \frac{\text{Annual operating expenditures}}{\text{Cash turnover}}$$

This equation assumes that there are no significant changes in operating expenditures from one period to another. Annual operating expenditures are defined here as total cash expenditures, or expenditures such as purchases of goods and raw materials and payment of salaries, wages, interest, and dividends.

Cash turnover is the number of times that a firm's cash is collected, or turned over, in a year. Cash turnover is calculated as follows:

$$\text{Cash turnover} = \frac{360 \text{ days}}{\text{Days between purchase of raw materials and collection of sales proceeds}}$$

or, simply,

$$\text{Cash turnover} = \frac{360 \text{ days}}{\text{Cash cycle}}$$

Note that **cash cycle** refers to the number of days that pass between the purchase of raw materials and collection of sales proceeds.

Example: Using the Cash Turnover Method

PROBLEM   Suppose the cash cycle of a company is 72 days. Assuming that the company has annual expenditures of $600,000, determine the minimum required cash of the company.

SOLUTION   Using the equation given above, calculate the cash turnover:

$$\text{Cash turnover} = \frac{360 \text{ days}}{72} = 5$$

To determine the minimum cash required, you divide the annual expenditures of $600,000 by the firm's cash turnover:

$$\text{Minimum cash required} = \frac{\$600,000}{5} = \$120,000$$

Therefore, the firm must keep a minimum cash balance of $120,000 throughout the year to maintain its liquidity. Keeping a balance below $120,000 will create a shortage of cash and possibly lead to bankruptcy. On the other hand, maintaining a balance significantly above the level of $120,000 would be costly to the company, since interest has to be paid on borrowed funds. Note that this method is recommended only if the flow of funds is maintained at a steady, even pace.

YOU SHOULD REMEMBER

The three basic methods to estimate future cash needs are the percent-of-sales method, cash budget method, and cash turnover method.

ANALYSIS OF SOURCES AND USES OF FUNDS

In financial planning and control, it is essential to understand how funds have been generated and where they have been used. This study is called the **analysis of sources and uses of funds**. Without a good understanding of the sources and uses of funds, and of the changes that occur in these sources and uses, management cannot evaluate what the company has done or in what direction it is going. A thorough analysis of the sources and uses of funds will determine the extent to which the company is relying on debt or equity. It also gives a good indication whether generated funds are being used effectively to maintain sufficient cash, purchase inventories, expand fixed assets, reduce liabilities, pay dividends, and so on.

Once the sources and uses of funds have been determined, management can decide whether or not the sources are reliable and what changes must be made to ensure future cash inflows. It can also be determined whether or not the uses of funds are consistent with the overall objectives of the firm, and, if not, corrective measures can be taken.

Sources of Funds

a. *A decrease in assets*, such as the sale of assets.

b. *An increase in liabilities*, such as borrowing money.

c. *An increase in capital*, such as reinvestment of profits.

Uses of Funds

a. *An increase in assets*, such as the purchase of new equipment.

b. *A decrease in liabilities*, such as the payment of debts.

c. *A decrease in capital*, such as the payment of dividends and various expenses.

Table 15-2 illustrates how a change in a balance-sheet account could be either a source or a use.

Table 15–2   Sources and Uses of Funds

Transaction	Source	Use
If asset ↑		✔
If asset ↓	✔	
If liabilities ↑	✔	
If liabilities ↓		✔
If capital ↑	✔	
If capital ↓		✔

Example: Analyzing Sources and Uses of Funds

PROBLEM The balance sheets of the Brown Company are given for 2 consecutive years in Table 15-3. Analyzing the sources and uses of funds, determine how the funds were generated and for what purposes they were spent.

SOLUTION The analysis in Table 15-3 indicates that the sources of funds for the Brown Company were cash, marketable securities, accounts receivable, depreciation, long-term debt, and retained earnings. The generated funds were spent to acquire more inventories and fixed assets and to repay accounts payable, notes payable, and accruals. Note that depreciation has a negative sign, which means that the value of assets has decreased. Since depreciation is a decrease in asset value and a noncash expenditure offset in retained earnings, it is viewed as a source of funds.

With further analysis, you can pinpoint which accounts absorbed most of the funds and which accounts contributed most to the generated funds. This can be done by calculating the percentage of the total for each source and use, as in Table 15-4.

To determine the relative significance of each account in generating or using funds, the sources and uses in Table 15-4 are then ranked—based on their percentages—as shown in Table 15-5.

Table 15-5 is very informative, as it clearly reveals the main sources and uses of funds. For instance, in the case of the Brown Company, depreciation generates 43% of the total sources. Second to depreciation as a main source of funds is long-term debt, which contributes 22% of all generated funds. Note that depreciation, long-term debt, and retained earnings together account for 79% of the total funds and, therefore, are the major sources of funds on which the financing of Brown Company relies. If the management thinks that any of these major sources are not very reliable for future operations, the company should take corrective actions and arrange for new sources of financing in advance.

Table 15–3 Balance Sheets of Brown Company
(values in thousands of dollars)

	Year 1	Year 2	Source	Use
Assets				
Cash	12	7	5	
Marketable securities	30	20	10	
Accounts receivable	20	15	5	
Inventories	15	55		40
Fixed assets	140	180		40
Accumulated depreciation	−40	−80	40	
Total assets	177	197		
Liabilities				
Accounts payable	8	7		1
Notes payable	17	7		10
Accruals	13	11		2
Long-term debt	47	67	20	
Preferred stock	14	14		
Common stock	50	50		
Retained earnings	28	41	13	
Liabilities and capital	177	197		

Table 15–4 Percentages of Sources and Uses of Funds for the Brown Company

	Dollar Amount	Percentage
Sources		
Cash	5	5
Marketable securities	10	11
Accounts receivable	5	5
Depreciation	40	43
Long-term debt	20	22
Retained earnings	13	14
	93	100
Uses		
Inventories	40	43
Fixed assets	40	43
Accounts payable	1	1
Notes payable	10	11
Accruals	2	2
	93	100

Table 15–5 Ranking of Sources and Uses of Funds for the Brown Company

Rank	Source	Percentage	Rank	Use	Percentage
1	Depreciation	43	1	Inventories	43
2	Long-term debt	22	2	Fixed assets	43
3	Retained earnings	14	3	Notes payable	11
4	Marketable securities	11	4	Accruals	2
5	Cash	5	5	Accounts payable	1
6	Accounts receivable	5			

Table 15-5 also indicates that the generated funds are spent mainly to increase inventories (63%), purchase new assets (63%), and pay outstanding notes payable (11%). If this pattern of spending funds is not a desired one, management should correct the situation before the shortage of funds for other purposes becomes a problem. Because it can reveal such vital information, the analysis of sources and uses of funds is an integral part of any sound financial planning and control system. The final results of such analysis are also needed to prepare and present the financial sections of the annual reports of publicly held companies.

YOU SHOULD REMEMBER

Analysis of sources and uses of funds reveals how a firm has been financed and how its resources have been spent. This analysis is an integral part of financial planning and control.

Decreases in assets, increases in liabilities, and increases in capital are the sources of funds. Increases in assets, decreases in liabilities, and decreases in capital are the uses of funds.

KNOW THE CONCEPTS

DO YOU KNOW THE BASICS?

1. What are the main purposes of financial planning and control?
2. Name three techniques of financial planning used to estimate external financing needs.
3. What information is required before you can make an analysis of the sources and uses of funds?
4. Give an example of an actual company that suffered badly from lack of financial planning in the past.
5. How do you determine cash surplus/deficit in the cash budget method?
6. How do you determine the required external financing in the percent-of-sales method?

TERMS FOR STUDY

cash cycle	liquidity management
cash turnover	sources and uses of funds analysis
financial planning	spontaneous asset

PRACTICAL APPLICATION

COMPUTATIONAL PROBLEMS

1. Using the following information, determine the amount of external financing required by the MBO Co.

Estimated sales for the next year	$400,000
Current sales	$350,000
Ratio of net profit after dividends to sales	3%

Assets that change with sales have a ratio of 80% of sales Liabilities that change with sales have a ratio of 40% of sales

2. Using the following data, compute the sources and uses of funds and interpret your results:

Balance Sheets of the ABC Co.

	Year 1	Year 2
Assets		
Cash	100	200
Marketable securities	50	110
Accounts receivable	40	42
Inventories	80	110
Fixed assets	90	95
Depreciation	(30)	(34)
	330	523
Liabilities		
Accounts payable	45	46
Notes payable	45	45
Long-term debt	20	210
Common stock	100	100
Retained earnings	120	122
	330	523

3. Determine the minimum cash required if a firm's total annual expenditures are $2,000,000 and the cash cycle is 60 days.

4. Determine the cash surplus/deficit for a particular month, given the following information: receipts, $100,000; payments, $60,000; beginning cash, $10,000; and cash reserve, $5,000.

ANSWERS

KNOW THE CONCEPTS

1. The main purposes of financial planning and control are estimating future financing needs, deciding how to finance, identifying sources and uses of funds, and taking corrective actions as to how funds are allocated.

2. Percent-of-sales method, cash budget method, and cash turnover method.

3. To make an analysis of the sources and uses of funds, you will need the balance sheets and income statements for at least the past 2 years.

4. The Chrysler Corporation in the 1970s.

5. The equation is

Cash surplus/deficit = Ending cash + Cash reserve

where

Ending cash = Net cash flow + Beginning cash
Net cash flow = Receipts – Payments

(See Table 16-1.)

6. The equation is

$$\text{External required financing} = \frac{A}{S}(\Delta S) - \frac{L}{S}(\Delta S) - rS$$

where A = assets that change with sales
ΔS = expected change in sales forecast for the year
L = liabilities that change with sales
r = ratio of net profits after dividends to sales

PRACTICAL APPLICATION

1. The equation is

$$\frac{A}{S}(\Delta S) - \frac{L}{S}(\Delta S) - rS$$

Using the given values, you have

80%($50,000) – 40%($50,000) – 3%($400,000) = $8,000

2.

Account	Source	Use
Cash		100
Marketable securities		60
Accounts receivable		2
Inventory		30
Fixed assets		5
Depreciation	4	
Accounts payable	1	
Notes payable	0	
Debt	190	
Retained earnings	2	
	197	197

This company borrows heavily to have inventory and liquidity.

3. Step 1. Cash turnover $= \dfrac{360 \text{ days}}{\text{Cash cycle}} = \dfrac{360 \text{ days}}{60} = 6$

Step 2. Minimum cash required $= \dfrac{\text{Annual expenditures}}{\text{Cash turnover}}$

$$= \dfrac{\$2,000,000}{6}$$

$$= \$333,333$$

4. Net cash flow $\quad=\quad$ Receipts − Payments

$\quad=\quad \$100,000 - \$60,000 = \$40,000$

Ending cash $\quad=\quad$ Net cash flow + Beginning cash

$\quad=\quad \$40,000 + \$10,000 = \$50,000$

Cash surplus/deficit $=\quad$ Ending cash + Cash reserve

$\quad=\quad \$50,000 + \$5,000 = \$55,000$

The company has a cash surplus of \$55,000 in that month.

MANAGING WORKING CAPITAL

16
FINANCING WORKING CAPITAL

KEY TERMS

contribution margin selling price less variable cost

economic order quantity (EOQ) the quantity of an item that, when ordered regularly, minimizes ordering and storage costs

inventory management the process of determining and maintaining the optimal inventory level

net working capital current assets minus current liabilities

NET WORKING CAPITAL

By definition, **net working capital** is the amount of money left after current liabilities have been subtracted from current assets:

$$\text{Net working capital} = \text{Current assets} - \text{Current liabilities}$$

Therefore, net working capital can also be thought of as the portion of current assets that should be financed through long-term borrowing or owners' equity.

If current liabilities remain the same, net working capital rises as current assets increase. Between two firms in the same industry and with equal amounts of assets, the one with higher net working capital is more liquid because more liquid assets are available to cover short-term debts. Because of this line of reasoning, net working capital is often viewed as an indicator of liquidity in working capital management.

MANAGING CURRENT ASSETS

Current assets usually fluctuate from month to month. During months when sales are relatively high, firms usually carry a lot of inventory, accounts receivable, and cash. The level of inventory declines in other months when there is less selling activity. The timing of high and low inventory levels basically depends on the nature of the product. For example, sporting goods stores will generally have larger inventories of ski equipment in November than in July. These inventory fluctuations mean that the current asset values of the firms also vary.

Management should be aware of the expected minimum and maximum levels of current assets each year. The minimum level can be viewed as the permanent portion of current assets, while the difference between the minimum and maximum levels is called the seasonal portion. For instance, if the highest level of current assets from January to December is $50,000 and the lowest level is $30,000, by definition the permanent portion of current assets is $30,000 and the seasonal portion is $20,000 ($50,000 – $30,000). These figures play a large part in financing decisions. Since the fixed portion of $30,000 remains on the book for a relatively long period of time, it should be financed like a fixed asset, through long-term debt or equity. On the other hand, the seasonal requirement of $20,000 can be financed by short-term borrowing.

Example: Calculating Permanent and Seasonal Financial Needs

PROBLEM The total value of current assets of the XYZ Co. fluctuates: $80,000 in February; $100,000 in April; $140,000 in June; $40,000 in August; $60,000 in October; and $90,000 in December. The company's fixed current assets are estimated to be $50,000 from January to December. How should the company's assets be financed?

SOLUTION To solve this problem, you should break the total financing into two portions: **permanent financing** and **seasonal financing**. The permanent portion is the minimum level of current assets plus fixed assets. The seasonal portion is the amount of current assets exceeding the minimum level. The following equations help illustrate these relationships:

Permanent financing = Minimum level of current assets + Current fixed assets

Seasonal financing = Current assets – Minimum level of current assets

Table 16-1 shows both the permanent and seasonal financing needs of the XYZ Co. Follow the calculations column by column. For instance, the value of current assets in April is $100,000. When the minimum level of $40,000 is subtracted, the April seasonal financing requirement is $60,000. The seasonal requirement goes up to $100,000 in June, then drops to zero in August, and so on. Since these financing needs are not permanent or stable, they are usually arranged through short-term bank loans. In contrast, the permanent financing requirement of $90,000 in Table 16-1 should be provided through a combination of long-term debt and equity. If the $90,000 permanent needs were borrowed for a short period, the lender might not renew the loan at maturity, and the company would face liquidity problems and possibly bankruptcy.

Table 16–1   Analysis of Financing Assets for the XYZ Co.

	Feb.	April	June	Aug.	Oct.	Dec.
Current assets (A_c)	$80,000	$100,000	$140,000	$40,000	$60,000	$90,000
Minimum level of current assets (M)	–40,000	–40,000	–40,000	–40,000	–40,000	–40,000
Seasonal financing ($A_c - M$)	40,000	60,000	100,000	-0-	20,000	50,000
Current fixed assets (A_f)	50,000	50,000	50,000	50,000	50,000	50,000
Permanent financing ($M + A_f$)	90,000	90,000	90,000	90,000	90,000	90,000

RISK AND PROFIT: CHOOSING THE RIGHT MIXTURE

The decision whether to finance assets with short-term or long-term loans is a choice between minimizing risk and maximizing profits. Under normal economic situations, long-term loans are more costly than short-term loans. The reason is that lenders who extend credit for a longer period are faced with more uncertainty than lenders who collect their original loans after a short period of time. The risk of default and inflation is usually more significant for long-term loans, since the loss of principal investment is greater for loans of longer maturity if the interest rate rises. An increase in interest rate produces a bigger discount in the value of a long-term bond because the time to maturity is relatively long. Therefore, the higher costs of long-term loans are partly a compensation for risk. Another reason for costly long-term financing is that the borrowers are assured of being able to use the funds for a long period of time without having to renew the loans from year to year. Remember that, if short-term loans are not rolled over on time, the firm may run out of cash, and business activities may be disrupted. Long-term financing, although very costly, is a conservative approach to ensure the continuous liquidity of the firm. On the basis of this line of reasoning, conservative financial managers meet most future financial needs through long-term loans, borrowing only a very limited amount of funds through short-term loans.

Figure 16-1 illustrates three different approaches to financing: very conservative, conservative, and aggressive. In a very conservative approach, fixed current assets, the minimum level of current assets, and a portion of seasonal requirements are all financed through long-term loans and equity. Only a portion of seasonal requirements is financed by short-term loans. As a result, the cost of this type of financing may be high, but the risk of running out of cash is minimal. In a **conservative approach**, long-term loans and equity are used to finance fixed assets and the minimum level of current assets. The seasonal requirement is financed through short-term loans. In an **aggressive approach**, fixed assets and only part of the minimum level of current assets are financed by long-term debt and equity. All seasonal requirements, plus a portion of the minimum level of current assets, are provided through short-term financing. Therefore, the cost of financing is minimal but the risk of running into liquidity problems is relatively high. (See the graphic illustrations in Figure 16-1.)

Depending on the attitude of financial managers toward risk, each firm takes a specific approach to finance its assets. If a firm is confident that its short-term loans are easily renewed, an aggressive approach will save considerable interest expense. On the other hand, if there is no assurance that loans will be available in the future, a conservative approach, or sometimes a very conservative approach, may be a better solution.

YOU SHOULD REMEMBER

In a very conservative approach to financing working capital, fixed assets, the minimum level of current assets, and a portion of seasonal requirements are all financed by long-term debt and equity. In a conservative approach, equity and long-term debt are used to cover fixed assets and the minimum level of current assets. In an aggressive approach, fixed assets and only part of the minimum level of current assets are financed by long-term sources; the rest are arranged through short-term funds.

MANAGING ACCOUNTS RECEIVABLE

The volume of accounts receivable is basically determined by the credit standards of the company. If these standards are rigid, fewer customers are qualified for credit, sales decrease, and, as a result, accounts receivable decline. On the other hand, if credit standards are relaxed, more customers are attracted to the firm, sales increase, and higher accounts receivable are generated. Relaxing credit standards to increase accounts receivable has both advantages and disadvantages. The advantages are increases in sales and profits. The disadvantages are reflected in the probability of more bad debts and the additional financing cost of accounts receivable.

Accounts receivable are like interest-free loans to customers because sellers must pay interest expenses as long as their capital is tied up in accounts receivable. Before making a decision to lower credit standards, the cost of additional accounts receivable and the benefit of more sales should be compared. If the result of this cost/benefit analysis is a net profit, the firm should relax credit standards.

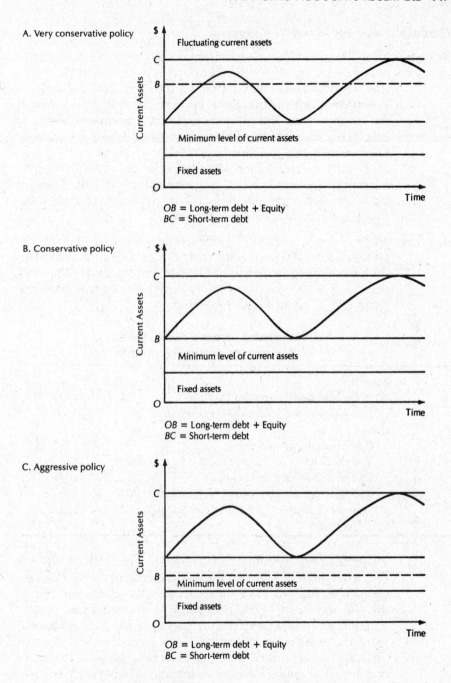

A. Very conservative policy

OB = Long-term debt + Equity
BC = Short-term debt

B. Conservative policy

OB = Long-term debt + Equity
BC = Short-term debt

C. Aggressive policy

OB = Long-term debt + Equity
BC = Short-term debt

Figure 16–1 Financing Approaches

Example: Managing Accounts Receivable

PROBLEM   Jones Electronic Manufacturing has current sales of 100,000 units of electronic signal devices. Each unit is sold for $50. The variable cost per unit is $40; therefore, the contribution margin is $10. (**Contribution margin** is equal to the selling price minus the variable cost.) The existing volume of accounts receivable is expected to increase by $500,000 if credit standards are relaxed. Sales should also increase by 30,000 units, from which 5% is expected to be an additional loss from bad debts. Assuming that the cost of goods sold is 80% of sales and that the cost of financing is 12%, determine whether relaxing credit standards would be a profitable decision for Jones Electronic.

SOLUTION   The solution is a simple cost/benefit analysis. The benefits are profits of $300,000 from additional sales (30,000 additional units sold × contribution margin of $10); the costs are additional bad debts of $75,000 and a $48,000 financing cost of new accounts receivable, as calculated in Table 16-2.

Table 16–2   Cost/Benefit Analysis for New Accounts Receivable

Benefits	
Profits from additional sales	$300,000
(30,000 units × $10 contribution margin)	
Costs	
Cost of additional bad debts	(75,000)
[(30,000 units × $50 unit price) × (5% bad debt)]	
Cost of additional financing costs	(48,000)
[($500,000 additional accounts receivable × 80% cost	
of goods sold) × (12% cost of financing)]	
Net profit	$177,000

Subtracting costs from benefits shows that Jones Electronic will earn a net profit of $177,000 if it lowers credit standards. But lowering credit standards doesn't always have this effect. Sometimes the additional cost of bad debts and the financing cost of new accounts receivable more than offset the profits from additional sales. The result is a combination of new receivables and an accumulation of old ones because of slower collections. In that case, of course, the right decision is to leave the credit policy alone—that is, not to relax standards.

> # YOU SHOULD REMEMBER
>
> The benefit of lowering credit standards is the profit from additional sales; the costs are additional bad debts and greater financing costs for additional accounts receivable.
>
> The benefits of raising credit standards are reduction of bad debts and lower financing costs for accounts receivable; the cost is reduction of profits from sales.

MANAGING INVENTORY

The main purpose of **inventory management** is to determine and maintain the level of inventory that will ensure that customer orders are satisfied in sufficient amounts and on time. However, holding inventory is costly because it ties up money on which no interest or income is generated. In other words, the cost of inventory precludes other profitable opportunities for investment. If there is an opportunity to make 15% profit on an investment, maintaining a level of inventory at $10,000 costs $1,500 annually. Put another way, the firm would make $1,500 profit if it could invest $10,000 rather than using it to purchase inventory. Understanding this concept is essential in solving a number of problems in the area of inventory management.

WHEN TO INCREASE INVENTORY

The level of inventory should be increased if the added benefits will be greater than the cost of maintaining additional inventory. Suppose a company saves $10,000 in ordering goods if the average inventory is increased from $450,000 to $600,000. If the firm has an opportunity to earn 16% on its money, is the proposal to raise the level of inventory acceptable? In answering this question, you would compare the additional profits of $10,000 against the lost opportunity to earn profit on the money tied up in the additional inventory of $150,000.

Since the $24,000 cost of additional inventory (16% × $150,000) exceeds the savings of $10,000, the decision should be to *not* increase the level of inventory. If inventory is increased to a new level of $600,000, the company would have a net loss of $14,000 ($24,000 loss – $10,000 savings). The firm may also decide to decrease the level of inventory if savings of inventory cost outweigh profits.

ECONOMIC ORDER QUANTITY (EOQ)

The **economic order quantity**, better known as **EOQ**, is the quantity of an item that, when ordered regularly, results in minimum ordering and storage costs. Costs of ordering include salaries and wages paid to full- and part-time employees working in the purchasing department and the cost of computer time and supplies to prepare purchase orders. The more frequently orders are placed, the more costly is the ordering process. Ordering costs will be minimal if annual requirements are all ordered at one time in the beginning of the year. Figure 16-2 shows the general relationship between order quantity (number of units in each order) and ordering cost.

Storage costs include the various expenses associated with warehouse operations and stocking items. As the number of units in each order increases, storage costs rise. Therefore, storage cost is maximum when the annual consumption is requested through a single order. By the same token, storage cost declines as items are ordered in smaller amounts. The relationship between storage costs and the order quantity (number of units in each order) is illustrated in Figure 16-3.

The economic order quantity (*EOQ*) can be determined if Figures 16-2 and 16-3 are projected side by side, as shown in Figure 16-4.

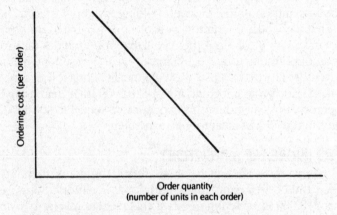

Figure 16–2 Ordering Cost and Order Quantity

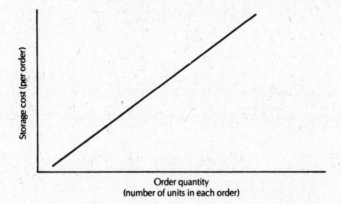

Figure 16-3 Storage Cost and Order Quantity

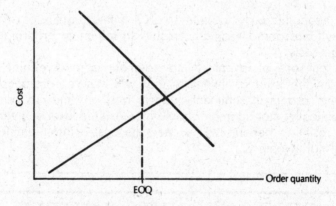

Figure 16-4 The Economic Order Quantity (*EOQ*)

The *EOQ* can also be determined by the use of the following equation:

$$EOQ = \sqrt{\frac{2RO}{W}}$$

where R = required number of units in each time period
O = ordering cost per order
W = cost of warehouse/storage

Example: Calculating the EOQ

The annual consumption of an item is 10,000 units, the ordering cost per order is $120, and the storage cost per unit is $4. Under these assumptions, the *EOQ* can quickly be found with the given equation:

$$EOQ = \sqrt{\frac{2RO}{W}} = \sqrt{\frac{(2)(10,000)(120)}{4}} = \sqrt{600,000}$$
$$= 774 \text{ units}$$

The firm will minimize the total cost of ordering and storage if 774 units are requested with every purchase order. Since the annual consumption is 10,000 units, the firm should order 13 times, each time requesting 774 units:

$$\text{No. of orders per year} = \frac{\text{Annual consumption}}{EOQ} = \frac{10,000}{774} = 12.91, \text{ or 13 times}$$

YOU SHOULD REMEMBER

The economic order quantity (EOQ) is the quantity of an item that, when ordered regularly, results in minimum ordering and storage costs.

The purpose of inventory management is to determine and maintain the level of inventory that will ensure satisfaction of customer orders in sufficient quantity and on time. To operate economically, management should increase the level of inventory if the resulting benefits will exceed the cost of maintaining the additional inventory.

MANAGING ACCOUNTS PAYABLE

Accounts payable can be viewed as free loans from suppliers. In the absence of accounts payable, the firm has to borrow money or use its own equity to pay suppliers' bills. Therefore, the benefit of accounts payable is in the saving of interest expenses that would have to be paid if credit weren't given by the supplier. However, accepting credit and using accounts payable are not always in the best interests of the purchasing company. Suppliers usually offer generous cash discounts if bills are paid either on delivery or within a few days after the receipt of an invoice. In this case, a crucial question is whether to take the cash discount and pay immediately or to purchase on credit and use accounts payable. If the cash discount is taken, the advantage is the cash discount itself and the disadvantages are the cost of borrowing money to pay cash and the loss of a free loan. The cash discount offer should be accepted if the benefit exceeds the cost.

Example: Managing Accounts Payable

PROBLEM   ABC Co. is eligible for a 3% cash discount if a merchandise bill of $100,000 is paid in cash immediately. However, the company also has the option of using its credit and paying the bill within 60 days. ABC Co. has contacted its local bank and learned that money to pay the bill can be borrowed at a rate of 14%, which would allow ABC Co. to take advantage of the 3% cash discount offer. Which option is more economical: using the cash discount or paying through accounts payable?

SOLUTION   Table 16-3 compares the benefit of taking the cash discount, which amounts to $3,000, versus the cost of the cash discount, $2,263.

Table 16–3   Using Cash Discounts or Account Payable

Benefit of cash discount	$3,000.
(*3% cash discount* × *$100,000 bill*)	
Cost of cash discount	– 2,263
(*Interest expenses on $97,000 for 60 days at 14%*)	
interest rate: $97,000 × $\left(14\% \times \dfrac{60 \text{ days}}{360 \text{ days}}\right)$	
Net benefit	$ 737

Note: Since the 3% cash discount is used, the company has to borrow only $97,000, rather than $100,000.

Using accounts payable rather than taking the cash discount, in this case, is somewhat similar to rejecting a free cash offer of $737 from the supplier.

Since the net result is a saving of $737, ABC Co. should take the cash discount. Taking the cash discount of 3% requires an immediate payment of $97,000, which must be borrowed or taken from existing funds.

The benefit of a cash discount can also be calculated using standard terms like 2/10 net 30. This means that a buyer can receive a 2% cash discount if the bill is paid within 10 days; otherwise, the full amount— without discount—is due in 30 days. If the bill is paid immediately, the benefit of this cash discount is 2% for 30 days and approximately 24% in 1 year (2% × 12 months). In the preceding example, the cash discount should be accepted if the borrowing rate is less than 24%, since the benefit of the cash discount would outweigh the cost of borrowing to pay the bill within 10 days.

There is a precise formula by which the cost of not using the cash discount (the benefit of the cash discount) can be calculated:

Cost of not using cash discount

$$= \frac{\text{Cash discount}}{1 - \text{Cash discount}} \times \frac{360 \text{ days}}{\text{Days credit outstanding} - \text{Discount period}}$$

According to this formula, the precise cost of not using the cash discount is 36.7%:

$$\left(\frac{2\%}{1 - 2\%} \right) \times \left(\frac{360 \text{ days}}{30 - 10} \right) = 36.7\%$$

YOU SHOULD REMEMBER

A cash discount is an acceptable offer if its benefit (or the cost of not using the cash discount) exceeds the cost of borrowing. If, however, the benefit of the cash discount is less than the cost of borrowing, the firm is better off using accounts payable and paying the bill at a later time.

KNOW THE CONCEPTS

DO YOU KNOW THE BASICS?

1. Give two definitions of net working capital.
2. What is the difference between seasonal and permanent working capital?
3. Describe a conservative approach to financing working capital.
4. Under what conditions should a cash discount offer be accepted?
5. What does the term 3/10 net 45 mean?
6. What does the *EOQ* strive to minimize, and what does it strive to maximize?

TERMS FOR STUDY

aggressive approach	inventory management
conservative approach	net working capital
contribution margin	permanent financing
economic order quantity (*EOQ*)	seasonal financing

PRACTICAL APPLICATION

COMPUTATIONAL PROBLEMS

1. Management at Brown Mfg. has determined that relaxing credit standards would add $14,000 to profits, but that the average investment in accounts receivable would increase by $20,000. As a result of lowering the credit standards, the cost of bad debts is expected to increase from $5,000 to $13,000. The required return on investment is 14%. Determine whether a policy to relax credit standards should be recommended.

2. The Ajax Co. has the following options: (a) borrow at 15%, pay the purchase invoice of $100,000 immediately, and take a 3% cash discount; or (b) use accounts payable and pay after 90 days. Which option is more economical?

3. LI Bolts and Nuts purchases 10,000 units of a particular item per month. The monthly storage cost per item is $0.10, and each order costs $50. Determine the *EOQ* of this company.

4. Determine the average level of inventory and the number of orders per month in Problem 3.

5. Determine the precise cost of not using a cash discount under the terms 3/10 net 40.

ANSWERS

KNOW THE CONCEPTS

1. Two definitions of net working capital are: (a) Current assets – Current liabilities, and (b) the portion of current assets financed by long-term sources.

2. The minimum level of current assets is "permanent," whereas the amount over the minimum level is "seasonal."

3. A conservative approach would be to finance permanent current assets and a good portion of seasonal working capital through long-term debt or equity.

4. A cash discount offer should be accepted if its benefit (the amount of discount) is greater than the cost of borrowing to be able to pay cash.

5. The customer is entitled to a cash discount of 3% if the bill is paid within 10 days of receipt of the invoice. Otherwise, the customer must pay the full price within 45 days.

6. The *EOQ* strives to maximize order quantity while minimizing ordering and storage costs.

PRACTICAL APPLICATION

1. Additional profit from new sales $14,000
   Cost of investment in accounts receivable   (2,800)
   Additional bad debts because of new sales   (8,000)
       Net profit $ 3,200

   The proposal should be recommended because it leads to additional profit.

2. Benefit   3% ($100,000) = $3,000
   Cost   15% ($97,000 borrowed) (3 months/12) = $3,637
   The cost of borrowing is greater than the benefit of discount. Obviously, option (b) is preferable.

3. $EOQ = \sqrt{\dfrac{2(10,000)(50)}{.10}} = 3,162$

4. Average level of inventory $= \dfrac{3,162}{2} = 1,581$

   No. of orders per month $= \dfrac{10,000}{3,162} = 3$ orders

5. Cost of not using cash discounts $= \left(\dfrac{3\%}{1-3\%}\right)\left(\dfrac{360}{40-10}\right) = 37\%$

ANALYZING FINANCIAL STATEMENTS

17

FINANCIAL STATEMENTS AND RATIOS

KEY TERMS

balance sheet an accounting statement that displays the assets, liabilities, and equity of a firm

current ratio current assets divided by current liabilities (a liquidity measure)

debt/equity (D/E) ratio debt divided by equity (a financial leverage measure)

dividend yield the rate of return on dividends obtained by dividing dividends by the price of the stock

income statement an accounting statement of a firm's sales, operating costs, and financial charges

net profit margins the rate of return obtained from sales calculated by dividing net income by net sales

P/BV ratio the price of a stock related to the book value (net worth) per share of a firm

P/Ec/P/Em a method for comparing a firm's price earnings ratio(P/Ec) to the market (P/Em). This ratio helps to determine whether a P/Ec is selling at a premium or at a discount to the market.

price/earnings (P/E) ratio the price of a stock divided by the earnings per share, or the price multiple investors are willing to pay for a dollar of earnings

replacement cost the current purchase price of an asset used to replace an existing asset

> **return on investment (ROI) ratio** net profits divided by assets (a measure of overall effective use of assets)
>
> **times interest-earned ratio** EBIT divided by annual interest expense (a measure of how well the firm meets its fixed interest payments)

FINANCIAL STATEMENTS

There are several ways to evaluate the performance of a firm. One approach is to analyze its financial statements. You can accomplish this in three ways:

1. study the contents of the income statement and the balance sheet.

2. analyze the statement of cash flows.

3. examine the relationship between the income statement and the balance sheet by engaging in ratio analysis.

The ultimate purpose of analyzing financial statements by these three procedures is to help managers achieve sound planning. By studying income and balance sheet statements, managers can spot areas of weakness in financial operations and take appropriate remedial action. It is through the analysis of these statements that managers can establish a more effective way of allocating funds and resources. They can also control the future direction of the firm's operations and help maximize its wealth.

INCOME STATEMENT

Income statements report the flows of receipts generated by a firm and the flows of expenses incurred to produce and finance company operations. An abbreviated version of an income statement appears in Table 17-1. It starts by reporting the sales generated from the assets and liabilities reported in the balance sheet. The company then incurs certain expenses. These expenses include cost of goods sold (including labor and materials) and other operating expenses, mainly depreciation, selling, and administrative expenses. By deducting these expenses from sales, operating profits are found. Beyond this point, the income statement shifts and considers financial costs, such as interest and taxes. Subtracting these financial costs from operating profits gives net profits and retained earnings. As a generalization, then, income statements provide a picture of the sales, costs, and profitability generated by a firm during a certain period of time.

It is customary to translate net income into earnings per share (EPS) (outstanding shares of the firm divided into net income) because this measure informs stockholders and investors how much profit is behind a share of stock and helps to establish a common basis for deriving the valuation (*P/E*) and price of one company's share versus other companies.

Chapter 13 indicated that in addition to regular bonds and stocks, some firms raise money by issuing special types of securities that can be converted into stock. When warrants are exercised, convertible bonds and convertible preferred stocks are converted, the number of shares outstanding increases. As a result, it is customary to report both so-called primary earnings per share, and secondary earnings per share on a fully diluted basis. This is done to appraise investors of the impact, which these additional shares will have on the EPS of a firm. As Table 17-1 shows, if we assume that an additional 100,000 shares will have to be issued to investors exercising all warrants and convertible securities, the number of outstanding shares will increase to 400,000 and the EPS of the firm will decline to $2.93 per share versus $3.91.

Table 17–1 Typical Income Statement for Year Ending December 31

Sales	$20,000,000
Less cost of goods sold	16,000,000
Depreciation ($500,000)	
Gross profits	4,000,000
Less operating and	2,000,000
other expenses	
Operating profits (EBIT)	2,000,000
Less net interest (at 10%)	44,000
Profit before taxes	1,956,000
Less taxes (at 40% rate)	782,400
Profits after taxes (N)	1,173,600
Less common stock dividends	588,000
Retained earnings	$ 588,000
Number of outstanding shares	300,000
Earnings per share (ESP) $\left(\dfrac{\text{NI}}{\text{Number of shares}} \text{ or } \dfrac{\$1,173,500}{300,000} \right)$	$3,91
Fully diluted outstanding shares	400,000
Fully diluted EPS ($1,173,600 ÷ 400,000)	$2.93

BALANCE SHEET

Figures appearing in the balance sheet (see Table 17-2) represent the historical value of the stock of assets available to the firm to generate sales and profits. Because the value of assets are based on original purchase price, they tend to understate the real value of these assets if they had to be replaced. In high inflationary periods, the cost of replacing existing assets is relatively high. As a result, by understating the value of these assets, the returns on these assets become overstated. Attempts have been made to state assets on a replacement basis, but accountants have been unable to resolve this problem to everyone's satisfaction.

Generally speaking, however, the **balance sheet** is a statement of assets, liabilities, and stockholders' equity. As of a certain date, the left side of this statement shows a breakdown of current assets in the form of cash and other assets that constitute the working capital of the firm. Fixed assets are mainly long-term investments, including plant and equipment.

The right side of the balance sheet shows current liabilities, consisting of accounts payable, notes payable, and other short-term liabilities. From this point on you find long-term debt, which has a maturity date of over 1 year. This part of the balance sheet may also include the capitalized value of financial leases. After you deduct the liabilities from the assets, the remaining value is the net worth of the firm. The components of net worth include the par value of common stock outstanding, paid-in capital surplus, and retained earnings accumulated from previous profits generated by the firm after the deduction of dividend payments. If the firm were liquidated and all creditors' claims paid off, the net worth is what would be left over for distribution to stockholders.

As a statement of assets and liabilities, a balance sheet allows investors to observe the mix of these components and to decide whether the allocation is sound. By deducting current assets from current liabilities, you can find out something about the liquidity of the firm, and by matching profits against the assets invested in the firm, you can gain some idea of how effectively the firm has utilized assets to generate profits.

Table 17-2   Typical Balance Sheet

Assets		Liabilities and Common Stockholders' Equity	
Cash	$ 40,000	Accounts payable	$ 150,000
Marketable securities	50,000	Notes payable	50,000
Accounts receivable	320,000	Other current assets	20,000
Inventory	250,000	Total current liabilities	220,000
Total current assets	660,000	Long-term debt	440,000
Net fixed assets	550,000	Common stock	350,000
		Retained earnings	200,000
Total assets	$1,210,000	Total liabilities and equity	$1,210,000

CURRENT STATEMENT OF CASH FLOWS

FASB statement number 95 requires firms to prepare and report a **Statement of Cash Flows**. In addition to the cash budget, the income statement and the balance sheet, this statement provides a more comprehensive analysis of the process by which firms generate cash from operations, investments, and financing activities. It also traces the ways this cash is put to use by the firm.

Cash-flow analysis has taken on greater significance in financial analysis because the reported earnings of a firm can be biased by the way costs and other accounting entries are treated in the income statement. In a sense, the Statement of Cash Flows represents a restructuring and a more detailed presentation of entries found in other financial statements. It helps to pinpoint areas of weakness in a firm's cash positions and in its ability to meet debt obligations.

Usually, the cash flow statement breaks down the cash inflow and outflow activities of a firm into three broad categories:

1. Cash from operating activities

2. Cash from investing activities

3. Cash from financing activities

Cash from operating activities relates net income to the way cash is generated in the operation of a firm. It presents the actual cash receipts and payments made by the firm in its normal business operations and indicates how effectively this cash is utilized. Cash from investments allows an analyst to observe the direction of the firm's policy on plant and equipment and its net working capital. Analysis of this category's flows can indicate what assets are purchased and whether expansion plans are geared to more risky assets and a changing product mix. Cash from financing activities pinpoints the firm's ability to raise cash in financial markets and indicates the ease with which it can pay debts and interest.

Inflows and outflows don't necessarily have to be equal, because a firm's cash can increase or decrease in a given period of time depending on the circumstances. The flow chart (Figure 17-1) presents the items which may be included in the calculation of the Statement of Cash Flows.

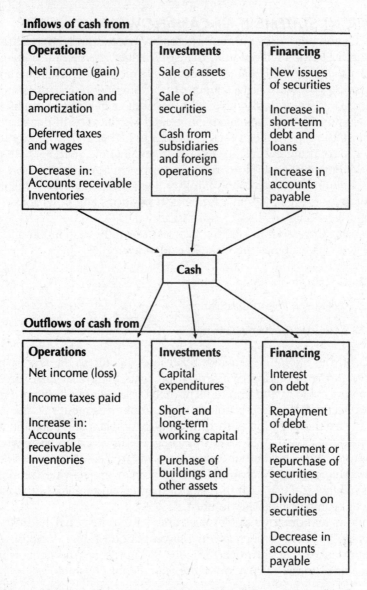

Figure 17–1 Flow Chart Indicating Cash Inflow and Outflow Entries Included in the Statement of Cash Flows.

Entries shown in Figure 17-1 can be obtained from the cash budget, sources and uses of funds analysis, the balance sheet, and the income statement, but the results here are presented in a neat and concise package. Below is a mock-up of a Statement of Cash Flows which indicates the cash inflows and outflows generated by each of the three activities.

Table 17–3   Statement of Cash Flows
Figures Without Brackets Represent Inflows
and Bracketed Figures ( ) Represent Cash Outflows

Operating Activities	1992	1993
Net income	X	X
Depreciation and amortization	X	X
Deferred taxes and wages	(X)	X
Change in:		
Accounts receivable	X	(X)
Inventories	(X)	X

Investment Activities	1992	1993
Capital spending	(X)	(X)
Change in working capital	(X)	(X)
Purchase of other assets	(X)	(X)
Sale of assets	X	X

Financial Activities	1992	1993
New issues of securities	X	X
Change in short-term debt	X	X
Repayment of debt	(X)	(X)
Retirement or purchase of outstanding securities	(X)	(X)
Payment of dividends	(X)	X
Change in accounts payable	(X)	X
Total Net Change in Cash and Marketable Securities	X	(X)

The cash flow statement reports actual cash generated at a point in time, thus avoiding the problem of accruals, and it supplies more detailed break-downs of entries which also appear in the balance sheet. Some financing activities, such as capital leases, do not appear in this statement, nor do cash flow changes from discontinued operations. The statement of cash flows, while subject to several deficiencies, is an important tool because it brings to light some of the biases in income and balance sheet statements that arise from accounting practices. The "statement" can serve other purposes as well. For example, it is helpful in determining the quality of earnings, how much cash is backing these earnings, and the ease with which the firm can pay interest and dividends. Moreover, a decline in accounts receivable could mean an improving collection policy and an increase in accounts payable could indicate that suppliers are more willing to finance the firm's purchases. These and other features of the cash flow statement spotlight areas for further investigation into why changes in the statement have occurred.

> # YOU SHOULD REMEMBER
>
> The balance sheet and income statements provide basic accounting information for preparing a Statement of Cash Flows and a table of the sources and uses of funds. Different financial statements indicate how a firm allocates its resources, produces profits and makes effective use of the cash it generates. Analysis of these statements helps the firm to spot areas of financial weakness and strength.

• USES OF FINANCIAL STATEMENTS

One important use of financial statements is to determine the efficiency of a firm's cost control or profit production. This can be done by comparing the income statement of the firm to the income statement of the industry or to the best firm in the industry.

Income statements can also tell you how a firm's profits are affected by changes in its fixed charges like interest, depreciation, and fixed costs. Balance sheets help managers of firms to find out if certain assets and liabilities are utilized effectively. For example, assume that a firm has higher inventories than are usual for its industry. This might indicate that it is carrying too much stock and is incurring excessive carrying costs. Or the analysis of the balance sheet might indicate that the firm's net fixed assets are too high for the sales it generates. This might mean that it has excess capacity or that it uses assets inefficiently. Also, the firm may be carrying excess liabilities, which would make it vulnerable to insolvency. And, finally, the Statement of Cash Flows draws attention to the way cash is generated and used in the conduct of operations, investments, and financing activities. These statements provide additional tools for developing effective and efficient ways of controlling inflows and outflows of cash.

In summary, financial statements lend themselves to a great deal of analysis, and they can reveal the operating and financial strengths and weaknesses of a firm. It is up to the firm's manager to interpret the figures in the financial statements properly and to institute corrective actions when required.

Two approaches for analyzing, comparing, and interpreting financial statements are

1. standardizing financial statements, and

2. financial ratio analysis.

• STANDARDIZING FINANCIAL STATEMENTS

Managers should always be searching for ways to improve the utilization of assets and controlling costs. They can gain insights by comparing the relative structures and changes in financial statements, especially those of similar companies.

No two companies have the same product lines, and they are likely to differ in size. It is not possible to compare the dollar amounts of several companies' financial statements. Also, the problem is complicated when a foreign company's statement is expressed in its currency, while that of a domestic company is reported in dollars. One way of getting around these problems is to restate the balance sheet's individual assets as a percentage of total assets and recalculate the income statement's components as a percentage of total sales. Not the ultimate solution but certainly a highly useful one. Tables 17-4 and Table 17-5 present the standardized financial statements of two companies (A and B) for periods 1996 and 1999.

The first thing we notice is the breakdown of the relative importance of assets in the balance sheet. For example, we can observe that each company has about the same percent of assets invested in net plant and equipment. But Company B has more debt relative to Company A. Of significance is the change in the relative importance of inventories. Company A's inventories have declined between 1996 and 1999; Company B's inventories remained unchanged. Does this mean that Company A has achieved greater control over inventories? This situation warrants investigation. We also notice that Company B has a larger debt structure that has increased over the last four years. Has this company benefited from financial leverage? Also, is it possible that Company A has lengthened the days of its accounts receivables?

Going on to the income statements, Company A has higher profit margins and they have improved from 1996 to 1999, while those of Company B remained unchanged. Part of the answer can be observed in cost of goods sold. Relatively speaking, Company A enjoyed a decline in this expense category and this percentage has fallen below Company B's. As a result, only 56% of Company A's sales constitute cost of goods sold whereas these costs remained unchanged at 58% for Company B. Company B may want to investigate how Company A accomplished this cost control. Notice that Company B has higher interest costs than Company A because its debt is higher.

Table 17–4   Company A and B Balance Sheets 1996–1999

	Company A		Company B	
	1996	1999	1996	1999
Assets	%	%	%	%
Cash	1.0	2.0	1.0	1.0
Accounts receivables	6.0	8.0	2.0	7.0
Inventories	12.0	10.0	12.0	12.0
Net plant and equipment	81.0	80.0	80.0	80.0
Total assets	100.0%	100.0%	100.0%	100.0%
Liabilities and Equity				
Accounts payable	10.0	11.0	12.0	11.0
Notes payable	8.0	9.0	9.0	10.0
Long-term debt	18.0	18.0	20.0	24.0
Equity	64.0	62.0	59.0	55.0
Total liabilities and equity	100.0%	100.0%	100.0%	100.0%

Table 17–5   Company A and B Income Statements 1996–1999

	Company A		Company B	
	1996	1999	1996	1999
	%	%	%	%
Sales	100.0	100.0	100.0	100.0
Cost of goods sold	59.0	56.0	58.0	58.0
Other expenses	11.0	12.0	10.0	10.0
EBIT	30.0	33.0	32.0	32.0
Interest	6.0	7.0	8.0	9.0
Taxable income	24.0	26.0	24.0	23.0
Net income	16.0	17.0	14.0	14.0

We have cited enough examples to indicate the advantage of standardizing financial statements. When differences are spotted, they might warrant further investigation.

YOU SHOULD REMEMBER

You can analyze a company's financial statements by engaging in ratio analysis and/or by standardizing the financial statements. Ratio analysis helps managers to evaluate performance and make comparisons of various components of the financial statements at a point in time and over time. Because comparisons of financial statements of different-size companies are not possible, it is necessary to standardize these statements by size, translating the dollar amounts into percentages of assets in the balance sheet and computing the percentages of sales for each item in the income statement.

FINANCIAL RATIOS

Responsible management of a firm requires constant monitoring of operations. For example, financial executives have to know whether or not they have enough liquidity; that is, they must ensure that sufficient funds are available to pay liabilities on time. Firms also establish guidelines regarding acceptable amounts of debt and fixed financial commitments.

Accordingly, managers are concerned about trends and degrees of their firms' efficiency and profitability. One way to measure the liquidity, debt position, and profitability of a firm is to engage in financial ratio analysis. This analysis can serve as a basis for financial planning and can provide a tool for monitoring performance.

• *USES AND TYPES OF RATIOS*

Ratio analysis helps to reveal the overall financial condition of a firm. It helps analysts and investors spot whether a firm is subject to the risk of insolvency and whether the firm is doing well compared to its industry or its competitors. Investors look at ratios to help them evaluate a company's performance and growth. Accordingly, poor financial ratios generally lead to higher financing costs, while good ratios usually mean that investors will be willing to make funds available to the company at more reasonable costs. Banks use ratios to determine whether to grant credit and how much credit to grant a firm.

Creditors worry when a firm does not generate enough earnings to make periodic payments of interest on outstanding debt. They also become concerned about firms that are top-heavy in debt, since a downward trend in business activity may lead to insolvency. Security analysts constantly monitor different financial ratios of the companies they follow by using ratio spreadsheet computer programs. By this analysis they can detect strengths and weaknesses in different companies.

Managers use financial ratios to monitor operations, to make sure their firms are using available resources effectively, and to avoid insolvency. The idea is to find out whether the firm's financial and operating status is improving over time and whether its overall ratios are better or worse than the ratios of competing companies. When these ratios fall below certain standards, it is the responsibility of the manager to regain control before serious problems arise.

Ratio analysis allows you to better understand the relationship between the balance sheet and the income statements. For instance, to compute a firm's return on investment, you need the total assets figure from the firm's balance sheet and the net income from its income statement. In addition, some ratios can indicate how effectively assets are being used and whether the liability mix is a good one. Clearly, the use of financial ratios is an important tool in modern financial planning.

Although there are a substantial number of individual ratios, they are usually lumped into five major categories:

- Liquidity ratios
- Activity ratios
- Debt ratios
- Profitability ratios
- Market ratios

LIQUIDITY RATIOS

An asset's degree of liquidity depends on how quickly that asset can be converted into cash without incurring a substantial loss. Liquidity management consists of matching debt claims with asset maturities and other cash flows in order to avoid technical insolvency. The measurement of liquidity is important. The main question, therefore, is whether or not a firm can generate sufficient cash to pay its suppliers and creditors.

In essence, liquidity ratios test a firm's degree of solvency. Two well-known ratios used to measure the liquidity of a firm include the current and the acid-test (quick) ratios.

CURRENT RATIO

The **current ratio** is the relationship between current assets and current liabilities:

$$\text{Current ratio} = \frac{\text{Current assets}}{\text{Current liabilities}}$$

Example: Current Ratio

A firm with $20 million in current assets and $10 million in current liabilities is said to have a current ratio of 2.0 times:

$$\text{Current ratio} = \frac{\$20,000,000}{\$10,000,000} = 2.0 \text{ times}$$

The current ratio roughly indicates the margin of safety available to a firm to meet short-term liabilities. The ratio can vary, depending on the industry and the type of company. A ratio of 2.0 times or better may be good for a manufacturing firm, while a ratio of 1.5 may be acceptable for a utility, because of its highly predictable cash inflow and small current liabilities.

The current ratio does not always measure a firm's true liquidity. Obviously, a firm with large cash reserves and marketable securities is more liquid than a firm with large inventories and high collection period receivables. A more refined ratio to deal with the asset mix problem would be to eliminate the component in current assets that is the least liquid.

ACID-TEST RATIO (QUICK RATIO)

By eliminating the less liquid inventory category and concentrating on assets more easily converted into cash, the **acid-test** (or **quick**) **ratio** determines whether a firm could meet its creditor obligations if sales were to drop catastrophically.

$$\text{Acid-test ratio} = \frac{\text{Current assets} - \text{Inventories}}{\text{Current liabilities}}$$

Example: Acid-test Ratio

In the preceding example, current assets were valued at $20 million. But what if $5.0 million were tied up in inventories? The acid-test ratio would indicate the following:

$$\text{Acid-test ratio} = \frac{\$20,000,000 - \$5,000,000}{\$10,000,000} = 1.5 \text{ times}$$

This figure might tell you that the firm can easily meet its short-term obligations because it would have no trouble generating cash from other current assets. On the other hand, this firm might have some doubtful receivables or be in a very highly sensitive industry in which creditors get paid quickly. Thus, this firm might require a quick ratio of 2.0 times, and the

1.5 times ratio would indicate that the firm should attempt to either reduce inventories or raise the value of its other liquid assets. Also, it should be pointed out that one clue to a buildup of inventories can be observed when the current ratio increases while the quick ratio remains unchanged.

YOU SHOULD REMEMBER

The intelligent use of ratios requires that you apply them in association with other information. Current ratios don't tell the whole story. We must study the mix. Even though two firms have the same amount of current assets the one with a higher concentration in more liquid current asset components like cash and marketable securities would be in a better liquidity position to meet its short-term debt obligations.

ACTIVITY RATIOS

Activity ratios determine the speed with which a firm can generate cash if the need arises. Clearly, the quicker a firm can convert inventories and accounts receivable into cash, the better off it is. The following ratios and computations assume that a year has 360 days.

AVERAGE COLLECTION PERIOD

Finding the **average collection period** of a firm will tell you how long that firm must wait before receivables are translated into cash. Note that cash sales are excluded from total sales.

$$\text{Average collection period} = \frac{\text{Accounts receivable}}{(\text{Annual credit sales}/360 \text{ days})}$$

Example: Average Collection Period

If a firm's balance sheet shows an accounts receivable figure of $700,000 and its income statement shows credit sales of $5,500,000, then

$$\text{Average collection period} = \frac{\$700,000}{(\$5,500,000 / 360 \text{ days})} = 45.8 \text{ days}$$

As with other ratios, the average collection period must be examined against other information. If this firm's policy is to extend credit to customers for 38 days, then a period of 45.8 days implies that the firm has trouble collecting on time and should review its credit policy. Conversely, if the firm's usual policy is to set a 55-day collection period for customers, then the 45.8-day average indicates the firm's collection policy is effective.

Remember that the average collection ratio is only *an average,* which can be misleading. For example, consider Firm A and Firm B, which have the same amount of accounts receivables but different collection schedules.

Table 17–6   Time Needed to Collect Payment

	% Collected Within 10 Days	% Collected Within 30 Days	% Collected Within 60 Days
Firm A	10	30	60
Firm B	60	30	10

Table 17-6 shows the percentage of the two firms' accounts receivable collected in each time period. Clearly, Firm B is in a better position because 60% of its receivables are collected within 10 days, compared to only 10% for Firm A. If Firm A and Firm B have the same number of customers and the same amount of receivables, their average collection periods will be the same. But the *distributions* of collections, a factor not shown in the ratio, clearly favor Firm B. Again (because this bears repeating), *financial ratios are useful, but you have to be careful how you interpret them.*

AVERAGE PAYMENT PERIOD

The counterpart to accounts receivable is accounts payable. To find out the **average payment period** for accounts payable, you simply do the same thing you did for accounts receivable—that is, divide annual purchases into accounts payable:

$$\text{Average payment period} = \frac{\text{Accounts payable}}{(\text{Annual credit purchases}/360 \text{ days})}$$

However, annual credit purchases are not reported in a financial statement. To obtain this figure, estimate the percentage of cost of goods sold that are purchased on credit.

Example: Calculating the Average Payment Period

PROBLEM   Assume an accounts payable figure of $275,000. If cost of goods sold is $3,000,000 and it is estimated that 80% of these goods are purchased on credit, what is the average payment period?

SOLUTION   The figure to use for annual credit purchases is $2,400,000 ($3,000,000 × .80). The average payment period for accounts payable can now be computed:

$$\frac{\text{Average payment}}{\text{period}} = \frac{\$275,000}{(.80 \times \$3,000,000 / 360 \text{ days})} = 41.3 \text{ days}$$

The average payment period (for accounts payable) of the firm is 41.3 days. Anything lower might mean that sellers give a discount or that they consider the firm a poor risk and therefore hold it to stricter terms. Anything higher might indicate that the firm can receive good credit terms, or that it is "a slow payer"— that is, it is using suppliers as a source of financing.

Sellers—who generally want their money as soon as possible—calculate this ratio to obtain an idea of how long it may take to collect from a firm. And since delaying payment is usually beneficial to the firm, the manager who controls payments is placed in the position of having to strike a balance between the two extremes.

If the industry average exceeds the firm's ratio, the manager may want to find out why the credit that the firm receives is limited and what can be done to obtain better or longer credit terms from suppliers.

CONVERTING INVENTORIES TO CASH

Inventory turnover is important to a firm because inventories are the most illiquid form of current assets. Because the firm must tie up funds to carry inventories, it is advantageous to sell inventories as quickly as possible to free-up cash for other uses. Generally, a high inventory turnover is considered to be an effective use of these assets.

The **inventory turnover ratio** is calculated as follows:

$$\text{Inventory turnover} = \frac{\text{Cost of goods sold}}{\text{Average inventory}}$$

Example: Inventory Turnover

If a firm's annual cost of goods is $3,000,000 and an average inventory value is $300,000, then the firm's inventory turnover ratio is 10 times.

$$\text{Inventory turnover} = \frac{\$3,000,000}{\$300,000} = 10 \text{ times}$$

Another way of analyzing the ability of a firm to convert inventories into cash employs the **inventory conversion ratio**, which tells us how many days it takes to convert inventories into cash. The formula for this ratio is

$$\frac{\text{Inventory conversion}}{\text{to cash period (days)}} = \frac{360 \text{ days}}{\text{Inventory turnover}}$$

Example: Inventory Conversion

We note from the previous example that the inventory turnover is ten times and inventories are $300,000. The following inventory conversion period ratio says that inventories are converted into cash every 36 days.

$$\frac{360}{10} = 36 \text{ days}$$

The same results can be obtained as follows:

$$\frac{\text{Inventory conversion}}{\text{to cash period (days)}} = \frac{\text{Inventories}}{\text{Cost of goods sold}/360} =$$

$$\frac{\$300,000}{\$3,000,000/360} = \frac{\$300,000}{8,333} = 36 \text{ days}$$

These inventory ratios should be compared with the industry average before any interpretations can be made, because ratios can vary widely between industries. Companies selling perishable goods, such as vegetables, will normally have a high turnover rate and low conversion days, while a bulldozer manufacturer's inventory turnover will be much lower and their day conversion will be high. If a firm's ratio is substantially lower than its industry average, however, the manager should probably investigate why this discrepancy exists.

Be careful when interpreting the inventory turnover and conversion figures. A high turnover ratio does not necessarily imply that a firm is effective in moving inventories. A high ratio can occur when a firm continually runs out of stock because it does not produce or purchase enough goods. In this case, a high ratio actually implies poor planning or control of inventories. As a result, unless the inventory policy of a firm is studied in detail, a ratio alone does not provide enough information about the ability of that firm to generate cash from inventories.

DEBT STATUS OF THE FIRM

A firm may borrow money for short-term purposes, mainly to finance working capital, or for long-term reasons, mainly to buy plant and equipment. When a firm borrows for the long run, it commits itself to make periodic payments of interest—and to repay the principal at maturity. To do this, it has to generate sufficient income to cover debt payments. One way to find out the debt position of a firm is to analyze several debt ratios.

DEBT RATIO

The debt ratio indicates the percentage of total assets that is financed by debt. The lower the debt ratio, the less financial leverage; the higher the debt ratio, the greater the financial leverage.

$$\text{Debt ratio} = \frac{\text{Total liabilities}}{\text{Total assets}}$$

Example: Debt Ratio

If a firm's balance sheet shows liabilities at $1,000,000 and assets of $5,000,000, then

$$\text{Debt ratio} = \frac{\$1,000,000}{\$5,000,000} = .2, \text{ or } 20\%$$

A high ratio tends to magnify earnings and a low ratio could mean inefficient use of debt.

DEBT/EQUITY (D/E) RATIO

A more familiar debt ratio involves the relationship between long-term debt and stockholders' equity. This is called the **debt/equity ratio**:

$$\text{Debt/equity } (D/E) \text{ ratio} = \frac{\text{Long-term debt} + \text{Value of leases}}{\text{Stockholders' equity}}$$

Thus, if long-term debt and leases on the balance sheet is $2,000,000 and stockholders' equity is $5,000,000, the debt/equity ratio is ($2,000,000 ÷ $5,000,000), or 40%. Electric utilities, which have steady inflows of receipts, can safely afford to have high D/E ratios, whereas cyclical companies usually have lower ones. In other words, the customers of electric utilities make periodic payments to these companies. Because these utilities know just about how much they will be paid and are allowed to raise customer charges when their rates of return fall below a certain level, they can estimate profits fairly well. Knowing this, they feel more confident about issuing bonds because the income they will generate in the future will ensure that they can meet interest and principal payments without much danger of default. Cyclical companies, on the other hand, enjoy high operating profits in good economic periods but must endure low operating profits in periods of economic contraction: If they issue substantial debt, they may not be able to cover interest payments when profits deteriorate. As a result, these companies must adopt a more conservative debt policy and issue more equity, which does not require payment of dividends in poor business periods.

LONG-TERM DEBT/TOTAL ASSET (*LD/TA*) RATIO

The long-term debt/total asset ratio (*LD/TA*) relates debt to the total assets of a firm, and can provide useful information regarding the degree to which that firm finances its assets with long-term debt.

$$LD/TA \text{ ratio} = \frac{\text{Long-term debt}}{\text{Total assets}}$$

This ratio can serve as a proxy for evaluating financial leverage.

TIMES INTEREST-EARNED RATIO

It is also important to find out how well a firm can pay its interest. For this purpose, you can use the **times interest-earned ratio**. This ratio measures how well a firm's interest payments are covered by the operating income of the firm (EBIT). Obviously, the higher the ratio, the better situated the firm is to pay off its creditors.

$$\text{Times interest earned ratio} = \frac{\text{EBIT}}{\text{Annual interest expense}}$$

Example: Times Interest-Earned Ratio

If EBIT is $8,000,000 and annual interest charges are $3,000,000, then

$$\text{Times interest earned ratio} = \frac{\$8,000,000}{\$3,000,000} = 2.67$$

In other words, income is 2.7 times higher than interest charges.

A low interest coverage indicates a dangerous position because a decline in economic activity could reduce EBIT below the interest a firm must pay, thus leading to default and ultimate insolvency. This danger, however, is mitigated by the fact that EBIT is not the only source of coverage. Firms also generate cash flows from depreciation, which can be used to pay off interest. What a firm should aim for is a big enough cushion so that it is in a position to pay its creditors.

The interest-earned ratio is deficient because the denominator does not consider other fixed payments such as principal repayments, lease expenses, and preferred stock dividends.

OVERALL COVERAGE RATIO

To deal with the problems associated with the times interest-earned ratio, an overall coverage ratio can be computed:

Overall coverage ratio

$$= \frac{\text{Cash inflows}}{\text{Lease expenses} + \frac{\text{Interest}}{\text{charges}} + \left(\frac{\text{Debt repayment}}{1-t} \right) + \left(\frac{\text{Preferred dividend}}{1-t} \right)}$$

All charges in the denominator are fixed and must be taken into account. Obviously, a firm and its investors would like to see the highest coverage possible, but this depends partly on the profitability of the firm.

When debt ratios get out of line, the firm may find that its cost of capital increases. The value of its stock may also deteriorate in response to the higher degree of risk associated with the firm. Therefore, financial managers must be careful to avoid carrying excessive debt in their capital structures. Important sources of industry data related to interest coverage and overall coverage can be found in the SEC quarterly financial statements of manufacturing, retail, and mining industries. You can also refer to Dun and Bradstreet, Moody's, and Standard and Poor's reports for similar composite industry figures.

PROFITABILITY RATIOS

Investors, stockholders, and financial managers pay a great deal of attention to the profitability of firms. Profit analysis begins with an examination of the way the asset mix of a firm is employed. Good managers make efficient use of their assets. Through increased productivity, they are able to reduce or control expenses. The rates of return achieved by any firm are important if its managers expect to attract capital and to engage in successful financing for the firm's growth.

If the rates of return for a given firm fall below an acceptable level, the *P/E* and the value of the firm's shares will decline—which is why the measure of profit performance is crucial to any firm.

GROSS PROFIT MARGINS

Gross profit margins show how efficiently a firm's management uses material and labor in the production process.

$$\text{Gross profit margin} = \frac{\text{Sales} - \text{Cost of goods sold}}{\text{Sales}}$$

Example: Gross Profit Margin

If a firm has $1,000,000 in sales and cost of goods sold amounts to $600,000, its gross profit margin would be

$$\text{Gross profit margin} = \frac{\$1,000,000 - \$600,000}{\$1,000,000} = 40\%$$

When labor and material costs increase rapidly, they are likely to lower gross profit margins unless the firm can pass these costs on to customers in the form of higher prices. One way to find out whether these costs are out of line is to compare the margins of comparable companies. If the margins of competitors are higher, the firm should realize that it must do something to gain better control over labor and material costs.

OPERATING PROFIT MARGINS

Operating profit margins show how successful a firm's management has been in generating income from the operation of the business.

$$\text{Operating profit margin} = \frac{\text{EBIT}}{\text{Sales}}$$

The numerator of this ratio represents earnings calculated after deducting the cost of goods sold and operating expenses from sales (EBIT).

Example: Operating Profit Margin

If EBIT amounted to $200,000 compared to sales of $1,000,000, the operating profit margin would be

$$\text{Operating profit margin} = \frac{\$200,000}{\$1,000,000} = 20\%$$

This ratio is a rough measure of the operating leverage a firm can achieve in the conduct of the operational part of its business. It indicates how much EBIT is generated per dollar of sales. High operating profits can mean effective control of costs, or they can mean that sales are increasing faster than operating costs. It behooves managers to trace the causes of high or low operating profit margins so that they can determine whether a firm is operating efficiently or inefficiently, or whether its prices have increased faster or slower than costs.

NET PROFIT MARGINS

Net profit margins are those generated from all phases of a business. In other words, this ratio compares net income with sales.

$$\text{Net profit margin} = \frac{\text{Net profits after taxes}}{\text{Sales}}$$

Example: Net Profit Margin

If a firm's after-tax earnings are $100,000 and its sales are $1,000,000, then

$$\text{Net profit margin} = \frac{\$100,000}{\$1,000,000} = 10\%$$

Some firms have high profit margins of over 20%, and others have low profit margins of around 3% to 5%. The level of these margins varies from industry to industry. Usually, the better managed companies record higher relative profit margins because they manage their resources more efficiently. From an investor's point of view, it is advantageous for a firm to hold profit margins above the industry average and, if possible, to demonstrate an improving trend. Also, the more effectively a firm holds its expenses down—at any level of sales—the higher its net profit margin ratio will be.

RETURN ON EQUITY (*ROE*) RATIO

The **return on equity (*ROE*)** ratio measures the rate of return to stockholders. Security analysts, as well as stockholders, are especially interested in this ratio. Generally, the higher the return, the more attractive the stock. This ratio is one way of assessing the profitability and the rate of returns of the firm, which can be compared to those of other stocks. The ratio is computed as follows:

$$ROE = \frac{\text{Net profits after taxes}}{\text{Stockholders' equity or tangible net worth}}$$

RETURN ON INVESTMENT (*ROI*) RATIO

The **return on investment (*ROI*)** ratio was developed by the Du Pont Company for its own use, but is now used by many major firms as a convenient way to measure the combined effects of profit margins and total asset turnover.

$$ROI = \frac{\text{Net income}}{\text{Sales}} \times \frac{\text{Sales}}{\text{Total assets}} = \frac{\text{Net income}}{\text{Total assets}}$$

The purpose of this formula is to compare the way a firm generates profits, and the way it uses its assets to generate sales. If assets are used effectively, income (and *ROI*) will be high; otherwise, income (and *ROI*) will be low.

YOU SHOULD REMEMBER

Financial statements can be interpreted by calculating financial ratios, which are divided into four major categories: liquidity ratios, activity ratios, debt ratios, and profitability ratios. Creditors pay close attention to these ratios in order to assure themselves that a firm can meet its short-term and long-term fixed interest and principal obligations. Bank lending policies are based heavily on the evaluation of relevant ratios, and financial analysts use them to compare the relative merits of different companies.

Liquidity ratios tell you how easily a firm can pay its short-term liabilities. *Activity ratios* indicate how fast the firm collects its accounts receivable or pays its bills, and the speed with which accounts payable, inventories, and accounts receivable are turned over. The faster it collects and the slower it pays, the better off the firm is—within certain limits. *Debt ratios* reveal what the financial leverage of the firm is and whether debt is becoming too top-heavy. Debt ratios can alert management to the need for altering the firm's financing mix before insolvency problems develop. *Profitability ratios* reveal how effectively a firm uses its assets to produce sales; to keep costs in line, and to generate net income.

MARKET RATIOS

Firms are concerned with investor responses to their stock. They do so by comparing certain market ratios to find out the value assigned to their stock. This value also allows them to determine the cost of issuing stock. Some of these market ratios include *P/E,* dividend yield, payout ratio, and price-to-book-value ratio.

P/E RATIO

Besides the constant growth dividend model, discussed in Chapter 5, a widely employed stock valuation measure is the ***P/E* ratio**. Broadly, *P/E*s rank the value of firms relative to their earnings per share. This ratio reflects investors' assessments of the growth of earnings, the risk of the firm, its efficiency, and its financial status all in a simple ratio package. The *P/E* is the price multiple investors are willing to pay for each dollar of earnings per share. A high-performance company that is growing rapidly and has good management and relatively low risk usually has a high *P/E,* and a poor performing company is given a low *P/E.* The actual computation of a *P/E* involves:

1. Estimating the future expected *EPS* of a firm

$$EPS = \frac{\text{Expected earnings}}{\text{Number of outstanding shares}}$$

2. Current price of the stock

3. Payout ratio = Dividend ÷ Earnings

4. A measure of risk (*K*) derived from CAPM

The assumption is that a firm uses its resources to generate income. When this is done efficiently and effectively, it is recognized in the *P/E* valuation. The formula is

$$P/E = \frac{\text{Payout ratio}}{K_s - G}$$

where $\text{Payout ratio} = \dfrac{\text{Dividend}}{\text{Earnings}}$

K_s = Discount rate assigned to the stock

G = Expected growth of earnings

Example: P/E Ratio

Suppose a company pays 50% (Payout ratio) of its earnings to stockholders, the market determined *K* (using CAPM) is 15%, and its earnings are expected to grow 9% annually, then the *P/E* of this company is

$$P/E = \frac{.50}{.15 - .09} = 8.3 \text{ times}$$

This *P/E* of 8.3 implies that investors are willing to pay 8.3 times each dollar earned per share by the company. Assume the estimated earnings are $1.0 million and the number of shares outstanding are 500,000 then the price of the stock is:

$$EPS = \frac{\$1,000,000}{500,000 \text{ shares}} = \$2.00$$

$$P/E \text{ of stock} = \frac{\$16.60}{\$2.00} = 8.3 \text{ times}$$

$$\text{Price of stock} = EPS \times P/E$$
$$= \$2.00 \times 8.3 = \$16.60$$

In addition to the P/E ratio, some security analysts rely on several other measures to evaluate the investment merits of a company. As we have already established, the profitability of projects are determined by the discounted cash flows that the project is expected to generate in coming years. Consequently, these analysts study the present value of cash flows of a company relative to the price of a stock.

$$\text{Cash flow ratio} = \frac{\text{Price of stock}}{\text{PV cash flow } (CF) \text{ per share}}$$

where

Cash flow is equal to the present value of EBIT $(1 - T)$
plus depreciation (T).

This ratio, supposedly, is a better measure of the value of firms.

A number of companies in their early development stages do not have earnings or their earnings are too small to permit the calculation of a meaningful *P/E*. In their case, the price-to-sales ratio may be employed.

A market ratio that is frequently computed and studied is the **price/book value ratio (P/BV)**.

$$P/BV = \frac{\text{Price of stock}}{\text{Book value per share}}$$

If the price is $20 and *BV* is $20, it is said that this ratio is equal to

$$P/BV = \frac{\$20}{\$20} = 1.0$$

Another version of this ratio, called the Tobin Q, divides the market value of a firm's debt and its equity by the replacement value of the firm's assets. A Tobin Q ratio lower than 1.0 means that the firm is unable to generate sufficient value for its stockholders to warrant investments. It might pay the firm to acquire assets by merging with another firm rather than investing in its own operations. A ratio greater than 1.0 implies that investors believe the firm has good investment opportunities.

In many instances, the interpretation and comparison of these market ratios is difficult to do; therefore, the tendency is to develop relative measures of market performance. For example, it is said that the earnings in the denominator of the *P/E* ratio fail to take into account the full growth potential of these earnings. Usually, the *P/E* is computed on the basis of the earnings of the past four quarters. While it is true that analysts project earnings and then plug these earnings projections to derive an estimated *P/E*, this approach does not fully capture the true earnings potential of a firm. To deal with this problem, the *P/E* ratio is standardized by an estimated growth rate that reflects potential increases in future earnings.

Also, analysts study the *P/E*s of companies (*P/Ec*) relative to a market index (*P/Em*). In other words, the market *P/E* becomes a benchmark against which company *P/E*s are measured. So, if we say firm A's *P/E* is 20 times and the market *P/E* (based on the Standard & Poor's market index) is selling at 20 times, we can view the company's performance as about equal to the market. Firm B may have a *P/E* of 30 times. This premium may be warranted because of the higher quality and growth rate of firm B's earnings and other financial strengths. A firm's *P/Ec/P/Em* ratio is usually analyzed in its historical context, so, when we hear about a stock selling at a 20% discount to the market, reference is being made to the fact that historically it may have sold on a one-to-one basis relative to the market and now it is considered attractive because the presumption is that the firm's *P/E* is historically low and will again move up to its historical norm.

We can now visualize why the relative analysis of market ratios, as measures of value, makes sense.

YOU SHOULD REMEMBER

Some companies have no earnings or dividends to report, making the analysis of market ratios impossible. That is why a Price/cash flow ratio, Price/sales or a Price/book value ratio (P/BV) maybe employed to analyze market performance. In the case of P/BV ratio, a ratio less than 1.0 means money should be invested in more attractive areas. A ratio higher than 1.0 indicates that the company has good investment opportunities.

A better basis for evaluating the merits of a stock is to relate the company's P/Ec to a market index P/Em. Remember, it is useful to state earnings per share on a fully diluted basis to determine how much dilution is likely to occur when new shares are added to the outstanding stock from the issuance of stock options and when convertible bonds are converted into common stock sometime in the future.

DIVIDEND YIELD

Stockholder dividends are paid out of net income. Stockholders participate in the dividends and capital gains of the stock they own. So one of the important returns they look at are dividends and the yield received from these dividends. By comparing the **dividend yields** of stocks (all other things being equal), investors will purchase the stock with the highest yield. Comparison is also made between dividend yields and bond yields. The yields on many utility company stocks are relatively high and attract a certain clientele of investors who look for those high returns and the possibility of capital gains. In combination, these features may induce investors to buy utility stocks instead of bonds.

Dividends also are indicative of the firm's ability to generate earnings and are a measure of financial stability. That is why dividend-paying stocks have an investor following. To find out how much a company pays out we merely employ the following ratios:

$$\text{Payout ratio} = \frac{\text{Dividend per share } (DPS)}{\text{Earnings per share } (EPS)}$$

So that a company with dividends per share of $1.50 and earnings per share of $6.00 is said to have a payout ratio of 25% or ($1.50/$6.00). Because dividend yield relates dividends to the price of the stock (DPS/P_s), then given the preceding information for a stock selling at $15, its dividend yield is

$$\text{Dividend yield} = \frac{\$1.50}{\$15.00} = 10\%$$

Dividend yields vary from industry to industry, but generally cyclical industries and small, fast-growing companies are low-dividend-yielding stocks while utilities and highly stable steadily growing companies tend to pay higher dividend yields. Dividend yields of a stock that change dramatically from their historical pattern produce adverse price reactions in the stock. The best course of action is to maintain a stable dividend policy. Otherwise, investors may become disappointed, and that can result in an adverse stock price reaction.

YOU SHOULD REMEMBER

The *P/E* is a measure of stock value, and it reflects the price multiple investors are willing to pay for each dollar of earnings per share. A *P/E* reflects the growth rate, the risk, and the efficiency of a firm, and it is computed as follows:

$$P/E = \frac{\text{Payout ratio}}{K - G}$$

Remember, however, it is expected earnings and not historical earnings that count in calculating *P/Es*.

Dividends are important because they are a source of current income to investors. Managers should strive to maintain a stable dividend policy, and they should recognize what the yield on dividends is compared to the returns from other investments. When dividend yields are too low relative to bonds, investors may sell stocks and reinvest their funds in bonds.

• *USING RATIOS TO ANALYZE PERFORMANCE*

Each of the ratios just discussed provides some insight into the effective way a firm is run. As you know, however, financial analysis is most meaningful when you have some standards against which a firm's ratios can be measured. Not only do you want to find out whether a firm's profitability, liquidity, debt positions, and activity relationships are high or low and whether they are improving or deteriorating, you should also determine how well a firm is performing relative to competitors, the industry, or the best firm in the industry.

Although the manager of a firm can compute the ratios of other companies, this information is readily available from published sources, such as *The Almanac of Business and Industrial Financial Ratios, Dun and Bradstreet Key Business Ratios, Value Line Service,* and *Standard and Poor's Corporation Financial Sheets.* These sources provide industry and individual company ratios to be used for comparison purposes. The *Robert Morris Associates Standard Ratios* even breaks down these ratios by sizes of firms.

Once the ratios for a company and industry are computed, managers usually employ three main approaches to analyze these ratios.

1. Cross-sectional analysis

2. Time series analysis

3. Comparative analysis

Cross-sectional analysis compares ratios at a point in time and is used to find out whether they are high or low relative to other companies or the industry. This type of analysis helps to rank performance and indicates whether ratios are higher or lower than competitors at a point in time. But sometimes a single year's ratio can become distorted by unusual developments, such as extraordinary expenses and unusual price changes that are unlikely to reoccur. That is why managers must also analyze changes in these ratios over time.

Time series analysis allows managers to trace the trend of ratios over time and thus provides a way of observing improvements or deterioration in performance. Also, some firms may have recorded poor ratios in the past but their ratios may be catching up to the industry. Should a current ratio be abnormally high or low relative to the past trend, it might be a one-time occurrence that should be ignored. There are deviations from past trends, and they should be investigated to ascertain whether the shifts are permanent or just a one-time occurrence. And then, there may be some ratios that are better than the industry or other competitors but if the trend is declining, we should find out why they are falling and if this trend will continue.

Comparative analysis refers to a study of company ratios relative to the ratios of an industry or other companies. It is important to analyze the reasons why certain ratios lie above or below certain benchmarks and why other ratios are gaining or declining on a relative basis.

Table 17-7 presents selected hypothetical ratios for a firm compared to its industry. Let's see how we might apply these three types of analysis to the hypothetical ratios shown in Table 17-7.

At a glance, the figures in Table 17-7 tell you that over the 7-year period, the improvement in the liquidity and profitability of the firm was greater than that for the industry as a whole. The firm's times interest-earned ratio declined, partly because the D/E ratio increased sharply, but was still higher than the industry level. Also, you find that, generally speaking, the levels of liquidity, profitability, and interest coverage were better than those for the industry. Somewhat less favorable was the change in the firm's financial leverage (D/E), which rose to 45% and in 1991 was noticeably higher than the financial leverage in the industry. This indicates that in the future it might be advisable to issue stock rather than debt to bring the D/E ratio in line with the industry. Table 17-7 also indicates that although the firm's growth rate is the same as the industry's, its P/E ratio is higher—probably because the overall liquidity and soundness of the firm is better than that of the industry. However, the firm's risk/return trade-off in 1991 was the same as its industry's, as revealed by the coefficient of variation. Investors apparently viewed the increase in the D/E ratio with alarm; consequently, the price/earnings ratio declined from 10.5 in 1991 to 10.0 in 1998. The industry's P/E remained unchanged in this period of time.

Table 17–7   Comparing Firm and Industry Ratios

Ratio	Firm		Industry	
	1991	1998	1991	1998
Current ratio	2.0 times	2.5 times	1.8 times	1.9 times
Average collection period	51.3 days	60.0 days	43.0 days	45.2 days
Debt/equity ratio	30%	45%	40%	38%
Times interest-earned ratio	4.1 times	3.8 times	3.0 times	3.0 times
Net profit margin	6.2%	8.3%	5.1%	6.0%
Return on investment	12.3%	13.4%	10.4%	11.0%
Coefficient of variation $\left(\frac{\sigma}{\varepsilon}\right)$	.90	.81	.90	.90
Growth rate of earnings (7-year avg.)	—	.09%	—	.09%
Price/earnings Ratio	10.5 times	10.0 times	8.0 times	8.0 times

Breakdowns of ratios similar to those presented in Table 17-7 help firms pinpoint areas of strength and weakness in their operations. As a result, the analysis of these ratios provides managers with tools for improving the overall performances of their firms.

YOU SHOULD REMEMBER

Financial ratios are more meaningful when they are compared with the averages of competitors, an industry, or the best companies in the industry. Industry and other external ratios provide the benchmark measures for determining whether or not a firm is better off financially or more profitable than others, at one particular moment or over a period of time.

By monitoring changes in these ratios, managers can spot developing areas of strength and weakness and can take appropriate action.

• THE QUALITY OF EARNINGS

One of the major tests of a firm's performance is its ability to generate future earnings that are sufficient to pay off debt obligations and maximize the wealth of the firm. We have noticed that a number of ratios require the use of earnings. But, can we assume that profitability ratios and market ratios like the *P/E* ratio supply us with a good picture of the income generation capabilities of the firm? If the reported earnings have biases, then the ratios that employ earnings can be misleading.

Many of the biases in the earnings figures originate in different accounting practices adopted by firms. Some firms employ conservative accounting rules and are concerned with the long-run sustainability of their firm's earnings. Others take a shorter point of view and sacrifice sound accounting practices for immediate earnings results. Therefore, because of the importance of earnings, analysts and investors should delve more deeply into the quality of earnings and not simply take profitability ratios at their face value.

Look at the income statement. It reports sales at the time the transaction takes place and not when cash is actually received. A company with short-term accounts receivable collection periods and heavy cash sales is said to enjoy better economic income than another company whose collection periods are very long. Long delays in these payments mask an element of weakness and tell us something about the quality of earnings.

And then, there is a question of inventory valuation. Accounting standards allow firms to value inventories on a first in first out basis (FIFO) or on a last in last out basis (LIFO). The FIFO method tends to inflate reported earnings because in inflationary periods, the costs of previously purchased inventories are usually lower than goods purchased in more recent periods. Earnings derived from employing the FIFO method of valuation include extra gains from price appreciation in the final goods and fail to take into account the cost that is incurred if those inventories were purchased now. That is why we should be aware of inventory valuation differences. LIFO accounting is more conservative and provides a closer measurement of replacement costs. At times, companies change inventory policy. When that shift involves a change from LIFO to FIFO, we should recognize the resultant overstatement of earnings, and take this into consideration when making comparisons with other companies using a LIFO method.

Depreciation policies can create biases in earnings. Some companies employ accelerated depreciation schedules (ACRS) and others use a straight-line method for depreciating fixed assets. The use of accelerated depreciation dampens early years' earnings and the straight-line method tends to inflate earnings. While a faster write-off may produce a large cash inflow from depreciation, it makes for a more conservative reporting of earnings. If we have two companies with the same features and same earnings, the earnings of the company that uses accelerated depreciation can be said to be of better quality than the other company that employs the straight-line method.

Pension fund reporting is a complex phenomenon. Most of this reporting is done in the footnotes of financial statements. A number of companies use these funds to cover internal operations and the unfunded liability continues to grow putting the fund in jeopardy. Also, by getting a high rate of return, the company can contribute less to the fund. But that merely defers the inevitable. At some time in the future, it must make up the deficiencies. Recently the tendency was to rely on high interest rates to maintain adequate amounts in the fund, but when interest rates fell sharply, many companies were caught short and had to make substantial contributions to keep the pension fund solvent. This affected earnings adversely.

Some consideration has to be made for the impact of inflation on earnings. Because financial statements fail to consider rising prices and figures are based on book value, there is a tendency for earnings to become overstated. That is why many accountants advocate the use of replacement costs accounting. But unless all corporations adopt this method, the result could be a great deal of confusion. Adjustments for inflation must be made; otherwise, the tendency is to overstate earnings. For example, some companies include the earnings of discontinued operations. These should be ignored. Some consolidate the operations of subsidiaries and some do not, especially when losses are involved. These financial results should be included in a parent company's income statement.

There are many cosmetic adjustments made to mask the true earnings' power of the firm. The market is very efficient, and sophisticated analysts usually tend to discount these attempts to doctor up financial statements. More specifically, operating leases are reported only in the footnotes of the balance sheet. But capital leases are reported like debt and amortized over time. A firm with all capital leases will report a higher asset base than one that has all operating leases. That means that if both firms had the same earnings, the one with operating leases will report a higher rate of return on assets than the one that has capital leases. This gives a false impression of the profitability of the firm. Also, because capital leases are amortized, the extra charges against income tend to lower the earnings of the firm. These distortions must be recognized and the biases corrected.

Other practices employed by firms to make financial statement reporting more attractive than it is include the deferral of taxes in an attempt to report higher earnings. Or, sales can be inflated by the temporary infusion of funds generated from the sale of assets. This method of reporting is adopted sometimes to meet the expected earnings target of analysts. Attention should be given to reserves that companies may draw on to smooth earnings fluctuations and to meet preannounced targets. These reserves help to bolster a shortfall in earnings but tend to give a false view of the true earning power of a company. They also distort the historical volatility of earnings, giving a false impression of the risk-return performance of a company.

Care should be taken to spot sudden reductions of expenditures such as those allocated to research or marketing. These cutbacks may bolster earnings but they also undermine the ability of the company to compete successfully in the future. As we can observe, financial statements require constant vigilance. The uncovering of unorthodox accounting treatments and figure manipulations are very helpful in making the analysts aware of unacceptable practices.

It is, therefore, important to delve into the reasons why some accounting practices have been adopted and whether these changes distort the reported income figures in the financial statements.

So, the interpretation of financial statements and earnings is not an easy task. Different accounting methods can lead to the overstatement or understatement of earnings. And unless proper adjustments for these biases are included in the analysis, profitability ratios are not likely to be comparable. Therefore, we should be paying more attention to the quality of earnings when conducting ratio analysis.

YOU SHOULD REMEMBER

Ratio analysis of the profitability of a firm is not complete unless we recognize differences in the quality of earnings. Beware of changes in earnings that result from temporary changes in accounting practices. Study the figures and adjust for biases arising from different valuation of inventories, the use of accelerated compared to straight-line depreciation, the way a company contributes to a pension fund, and whether some of these funds are used for the conduct of internal operations. Earnings should also take into consideration the impact of inflation on the costs and the pricing policies of the firm. When analyzing the quality of earnings, more attention should be given to replacement costs as opposed to the historical costs that are reported in the financial statements. Don't forget to search for the reasons why ratios and the quality of earnings have changed.

• LIMITATIONS OF RATIO ANALYSIS

Financial ratios supply only part of the information necessary to evaluate the overall performance and efficiency of a firm. Other statistical measures—such as risk—should be taken into account to obtain a full picture of a firm's financial status.

Furthermore, comparisons of ratios can be misleading on several counts. A firm may have adopted new accounting standards; that is, it may have shifted from a FIFO to a LIFO valuation of inventories. It may have changed from a straight-line method to an **accelerated method of depreciation**. Through mergers, the firm may be identified with a new industry. Also, the value of the firm's assets may be understated because of high inflation. Some industry figures may also be distorted, especially if the averages include many small firms with specific financial weaknesses.

You should be careful to determine the type of debt incurred by the firm you're studying. If funds were raised by issuing convertible debentures that are due to be called or may be converted soon, the interpretation of the D/E ratio will be different than when the debt represents straight bond issues. Also, some companies finance their investments with short-term leases. As a result, several financial ratios will be understated as a result of these financial arrangements. This is especially true in the case of ROI.

Also be wary when using reported data, because industry figures sometimes represent only the best and most financially sound companies. In addition, the classification of specific companies into an industry is difficult, because most companies have diverse product lines. This problem may distort the comparison of the firm's ratios with industry ratios.

Watch out for companies that try to manipulate their figures by selling assets or by understating certain replacement costs. Although the accounting profession attempts to deal with some of these problems, there are different interpretations and methods for compiling financial statements which can mask the true strengths or weaknesses of a company. Therefore, when engaging in financial statement and ratio analysis, it is necessary to realize that interpretations can vary among managers and analysts. All in all, be careful when analyzing a firm on the basis of financial ratios. Make allowances for the limitations associated with these ratios.

YOU SHOULD REMEMBER

Make sure that ratios are consistent and comparable. Some firms employ different inventory valuation methods or depreciation policies. Other firms may report on a different fiscal basis. Industry averages could be biased in favor of small or large companies.

Therefore, to ensure that ratio comparisons are as representative as possible, make a careful analysis of the accounting interpretations of standards and the different methods employed by firms to calculate charges (e.g., using straight-line depreciation or accelerated depreciation methods) in their financial statements. *This must include a careful reading of the footnotes that follow these statements.*

KNOW THE CONCEPTS

DO YOU KNOW THE BASICS?

1. Describe the information you can get from reading the income statement and the balance sheet.

2. What can the analysis of the statement of cash flows tell you about the financial activity of a firm?

3. Define cash flow and explain its contribution as a source of funds.

4. Define book value. What does the *P/BV* ratio tell us about a firm's investment opportunities?

5. How do you compute a firm's average collection period? If it turns out to be 40 days, while the industry average is 30 days, what does this mean?

6. How is it possible for a firm to incur a loss even when sales increase?

7. How will profits and cash flow in a firm that employs straight-line depreciation differ from those of another firm that uses accelerated depreciation?

8. What does a times interest-earned ratio of 1.0 mean?

9. If a firm's *D/E* ratio is too high compared to the ratios of its industry and competing companies, what may you conclude about this firm? What should the financial manager attempt to do?

10. What things should an analyst look for in financial statements to ensure that the financial ratios they compute are as accurate as possible?

11. What are several problems to consider when using industry ratios as norms?

12. Explain the difference between *ROI* and net profit margins.

13. Are there differences in the quality of earnings reported by different companies? Cite three accounting practices that tend to overstate earnings.

14. What kind of values are reported in the balance sheet? Indicate how accountants and economists prefer to have them calculated and reported.

15. List three approaches employed to analyze a firm and compare its financial status with that of other firms and its industry. Cite a weakness that applies to each approach.

16. Indicate why it is advisable to standardize financial statements for size differences.

TERMS FOR STUDY

accelerated method of depreciation
acid-test (or quick) ratio
average collection period
average payment period
balance sheet
current ratio
debt/equity ratio
dividend yield
income statement
inventory conversion ratio

inventory turnover ratio
net profit margins
operating profit margins
price/book value ratio
price/earnings ratio
return on equity ratio
return on investment ratio
times interest-earned ratio
statement of cash flows

PRACTICAL APPLICATION

COMPUTATIONAL PROBLEMS

1. If a firm's current assets are $1,000,000 and its current liabilities $500,000, calculate its current ratio. What does this ratio tell you?

2. You are given the following balance sheet and income statement for 1992 and 1993:

Table A Balance Sheet for 1992 and 1993
(All Values in Thousands of Dollars)

	1992	1993
Assets		
Cash	200	300
Marketable securities	300	200
Receivables	800	1,000
Inventory	1,200	1,000
Fixed assets	3,300	3,700
Total assets	5,800	6,200
Liabilities and common equity		
Accounts payable	300	200
Notes payable	200	300
Other current liabilities	1,000	800
Long-term debt	1,000	1,200
Common equity	3,300	3,700
Total liabilities and common equity	5,800	6,200

Table B Income Statement for 1993

Sales	$1,000,000
Operating and other costs	– 700,000
EBIT	300,00
Interest	– 100,000
Profits before taxes	200,000
Tax at 40% rate	– 80,000
Profits after taxes	120,000 *

*Depreciation amounts to $50,000 in 1993.

Using the financial information given in Table A, calculate the changes that occurred to assets, liabilities, and equity from 1992 to 1993, and indicate whether these changes were sources or uses of funds.

3. Using the financial information presented in Table A (Problem 2), calculate the following ratios for 1992:
   (a) the current ratio
   (b) the debt/equity ratio
   (c) the acid-test or quick ratio State what each ratio might imply

4. Analyzing both the income statement (Table B) and the balance sheet (Table A) in Problem 2, calculate the following ratios for 1993:
   (a) times interest-earned ratio
   (b) net profit margins
   (c) return on investment

5. If the firm in Table A (Problem 2) had 100,000 common shares outstanding, its stock sold for $20 per share, and it paid $0.50 per share in dividends, calculate its *EPS, P/E,* and dividend payout ratio (dividend ÷ net income).

6. Selected financial ratios for a firm and its industry are as follows:

	Firm Ratio	Industry Ratio
Current ratio	2.5	3.0
Debt/equity ratio	30%	40%
Times interest-earned ratio	3.0	2.0
Net profit margins	10%	8%
Average collection period	45 days	35 days
Return on investment	5%	3%
Inventory turnover ratio	10 times	12 times
Average payment period	30 days	40 days

Compare the financial ratios of the firm and the industry and discuss their strengths and weaknesses.

7. Robbins Company's earning are $4.00 per share, and dividends are $2.00 per share. The company expects to grow at 8% annually in the future. The beta of the company is calculated to be 1.2, the risk-free rate is 6%, and the market expected return is 12%. Calculate the *P/E* of this company. Then use this *P/E* to determine the market price of Robbins' stock.

8. A firm's earnings are $1.0 million. It has 400,000 shares outstanding and pays $400,000 in dividends. If the *P/E* of this stock is 12 times, calculate the payout ratio and the dividend yield of this firm.

9. A firm reports the following financial figures:

Present value of cash flows	$ 200,000
Shares outstanding	100,000
Price of stock	$20
Assets	$3,000,000
Liabilities	$1,000,000

Calculate the cash flow ratio and the *P/BV* ratio. If another company had a *P/BV* ratio of 1.5, would this be better or worse than 1.0?

ANSWERS

KNOW THE CONCEPTS

1. When you read an income statement, you find out the sales generated by the firm, the cost breakdown of the business. By deducting all costs—including interest and taxes—from sales, you obtain the net income available for common stockholders. The income statement also reveals the dividends paid by the firm and the amount of profits available for reinvestment.

   The balance sheet records the mix of current and fixed assets. It indicates the liabilities incurred by the firm in the form of short-term and long-term obligations. This statement also reveals the net worth, or common stockholder's equity in the firm (assets – liabilities).

   In short, the income statement indicates the profitability of the firm, and the balance sheet indicates the sources of funds and the assets into which these sources are invested.

2. The statement of cash flows helps the firm to identify the sources of cash inflows and the uses of cash outflows. It establishes a basis for determining the most efficient allocation of scarce cash or funds.

3. Cash flow is defined broadly as net profits after taxes plus depreciation. Depreciation charges permit the firm to reduce tax payments and thus retain more funds in the firm for investment purposes. The more cash flow, the easier it is for the firm to finance investments from internal sources and the less funding it has to generate from external sources.

4. Book value = assets minus liabilities. The *P/BV* ratio indicates a firm's ability to generate wealth for its stockholders. A ratio lower than 1.0 implies that a firm can't generate enough wealth to attract investors. A ratio greater than 1.0 indicates a good investment opportunity.

5. The average collection period is computed by dividing accounts receivable by (annual credit sales ÷ 360). If the industry has a 30-day collection period versus 40 days for a particular firm, generally speaking, the firm's customers are not paying their bills as fast as the customers of other firms in the industry. A longer collection period could be due to the fact that the firm has a more liberal customer payments policy, or it could mean that the firm has trouble collecting accounts receivable. A long collection period usually leads to higher interest costs and bad debt write-offs for the firm.

6. An increase in sales does not guarantee a profit. This increase may occur at a time when capacity is limited; as a result, substantially higher costs can be incurred by the firm to supply customers with goods or services. In this case, the increase in costs may be so high that it produces losses.

7. All other things being equal, profits will be higher in the early years and lower in later years with straight-line depreciation. Higher depreciation does, however, mean lower tax payments. From a present value point of view, accelerated depreciation is more valuable to a firm than the straight-line method.

8. An interest-earned ratio of 1.0 indicates that the firm barely generates enough EBIT to cover its fixed financial obligations. Any small decline in EBIT would put the firm in danger of becoming insolvent, unless it found some reserves or other sources of funds to match debt payments in the short run.

9. If the firm's *D/E* ratio is greater than the ratios for the industry and competing companies, investors may feel that it is out of line, and the cost of capital of the firm may increase. When this situation arises, the firm may want to change its capital structure by issuing more common stock, by merging with a company that has a lower *D/E* ratio, or by retiring (buying back) some of its debt.

10. Analysts should seek to adjust for differences in inventory policy (LIFO vs. FIFO), differences in methods of depreciating assets, differences in charging off research and development costs, and differences in leasing policies. Also, analysts should examine the composition of industry averages used for comparison purposes.

11. Industry ratios may include factors that can produce an upward or downward bias in the ratios. For example, the liquidity ratios may be better if the industry average gives a greater weight to large, well-run companies. If, on the other hand, the averages are heavily weighted in favor of small companies, the liquidity ratio may have a downward bias.

12. *ROI* provides a measure of how effectively the firm uses assets to produce income. Net profit margins indicate how well a firm controls its costs and how much it benefits from financial leverage. In some industries, like services, the asset base is small compared to other factors. Therefore, in those cases, net profit margins are a more meaningful measure of profitability and efficiency than *ROI*.

13. Some companies adopt conservative accounting practices that are designed to maintain the long-run sustainability of earnings and that reflect more accurately the efficient and effective utilization of the resources available to them. Other companies choose to adopt accounting policies that tend to inflate earnings and thus mask the true ability of a firm to generate profits. As a result, many profitability ratios tend to overstate the true capabilities of the firm to generate profits. Three accounting practices that overstate earnings and produce lower quality of earnings are calculating inventories on a FIFO compared to a LIFO basis, employing straight-line depreciation instead of ACRS schedules, and using operating leases that are not included as assets in the balance sheet, and therefore, overstate the *ROI* of the firm.

14. The balance sheet states assets on a historical basis or the original cost of purchase. The longer the life of the asset, the less it reflects the current replacement value. Accountants and economists prefer that assets be stated at their replacement cost or the price to buy that equipment currently. However, replacement cost complicates the preparation of the balance sheet and would require difficult valuation decisions that firms are unwilling to undertake.

15. Ratio analysis can be done in three ways:
    (a) cross-sectional analysis
    (b) time series analysis
    (c) comparative analysis

    One of the weaknesses in applying cross-sectional analysis is that it is done at a point in time. That period may not be appropriate for a company that has had abnormal charges, unusual accounting changes, or certain non-repetitive developments that might tend to overstate or understate the ratios. Time series analysis helps spot changes in an industry that may no longer be representative of the company's operations. Also, the product mix of the company may have changed altering the features of the company in such a way that its current product line is no longer comparable with its past products.

    Comparative analysis runs into trouble when attempts are made to select a representative industry. Because most industries consist of an aggregation of companies with a variety of products, it may be difficult to find and identify the appropriate industry that would permit the making of a valid comparison with a company.

16. It is not possible to compare the dollar amounts of the financial statements of different-size corporations. That is why we standardize these statements by restating them in percentage terms. Each item in the balance sheet is stated as a percentage of total assets and each expense (and other components) of an income statement is calculated as a percentage of total sales. When doing cross-sectional analyses, we can then observe the relative importance of components between several companies and industries in their financial statements. That means, for example, that we can compare whether costs are high or low in some companies and so forth. Or in the balance sheet, we can observe whether items such as inventories and account receivables are high or low. When time series analysis is undertaken, these standardized statements allow a manager to analyze changes in the various components of financial statements over time. That is, whether a particular component is increasing or decreasing over a period of time. Once these differences are spotted, the next step is to find out why they exist.

PRACTICAL APPLICATION

1. Current ratio $= \dfrac{\$1,000,000}{\$500,000} = 2.0$ times

This current ratio indicates that the firm can meet its current, or short-term, obligations because it has twice the amount of cash from liquid assets as it does current liabilities.

2.

Table A (All Values in Thousands in Dollars)

	1992	1993	Sources	Use
Assets				
Cash	200	300		100
Marketable securities	300	200	100	
Receivables	800	1,000		200
Inventory	1,200	1,000	200	
Fixed assets	3,300	3,700		400
Total assets	5,800	6,200		
Liabilities and common equity				
Accounts payable	300	300		100
Notes payable	200	300	100	
Other current liabilities	1,000	800		200
Long-term debt	1,000	1,200	200	
Common equity	3,300	3,700	400	
Total liabilities and common equity	5,800	6,200	1,000	1,000

Note that in 1993 combined cash flow [Depreciation ($50,000) + Profits after taxes ($120,000)] amounted to $170,000, and this sum represents a source of funds.

3. (a) $\dfrac{\text{Current ratio}}{\text{(for 1992)}} = \dfrac{\text{Current assets}}{\text{Current liabilities}} = \dfrac{\$2,500}{\$1,500} = 1.67 \text{ times}$

This implies that the company has inadequate working capital to cover its liabilities. The ratio should be more than 2 times.

(b) $\dfrac{\text{Debt equity ratio}}{\text{(for 1992)}} = \dfrac{\text{Long-term debt}}{\text{Common equity}} = \dfrac{\$1,000}{\$3,300} = 30\%$

This seems to be a reasonable mix between debt and equity for a manufacturing corporation, but electric utilities will allocate much higher proportions to debt than 30%.

(c) $\dfrac{\text{Acid test ratio}}{\text{(for 1992)}} = \dfrac{\text{Current assets} - \text{Inventories}}{\text{Current liabilities}} = \dfrac{\$1,300}{\$1,500} = .86 \text{ times}$

The current asset coverage in this case is inadequate, suggesting that the company needs to generate more current assets, excluding inventories.

4. (a) Times interest earned ratio =

$$\frac{\text{EBIT}}{\text{Annual interest expense}} = \frac{\$300,000}{\$100,000} = 3.00 \text{ times}$$

(b) Net profit margins $= \dfrac{\text{Net profits after taxes}}{\text{Sales}} = \dfrac{\$120,000}{\$1,000,000} = 12\%$

(c) Return on investment $= \dfrac{\text{Net income}}{\text{Total assets}} = \dfrac{\$120,000}{\$6,200,000} = 1.9\%$

5. $EPS = \dfrac{\text{Net income}}{\text{Outstanding shares of common}} = \dfrac{\$120,000}{100,000} = \$1.20$

$P/E = \dfrac{\text{Price per share of stock}}{\text{Earnings per share}} = \dfrac{\$20}{\$1.20} = 16.67$

Dividend payout ratio $= \dfrac{\text{Dividends per share}}{\text{EPS}} = \dfrac{\$0.50}{\$1.20} = 41.7\%$

6. The *industry current ratio* is better than the firm's indicating that the firm is less liquid than some of its competitors. Nevertheless, a ratio indicates a satisfactory level of liquidity. The firm has a lower *D/E ratio* than the industry, indicating an opportunity to issue more debt without incurring too much financial risk, especially since its times interest-earned ratio is 3.0 versus 2.0 for the industry.

The *times interest-earned ratio* is better than the industry's, probably because of the lower debt/equity ratio. The firm appears to have ample coverage of interest expense and less danger of defaulting than the industry, on average.

Net profit margins are better for the firm than for the industry, indicating either that the firm may have more effective cost controls, better salespersons or that it charges higher prices because of a differentiated product line.

Average collection period for the firm appears too high, suggesting that the firm should institute discount policies or other collection procedures to get customers to pay their accounts receivable earlier.

The firm's *return on investment,* like its net profit margins, is higher than the industry's, indicating that it is making more effective use of available resources or assets.

The firm has a slower *inventory turnover rate* than the industry, suggesting that it is carrying too much inventory. However, if this extra inventory is helpful in satisfying customer needs and in enabling the firm to charge slightly higher prices, it may be worth the additional investment.

The firm's *average payment period* of 30 days indicates that the firm is paying its accounts payable faster than the industry at large. The firm might consider having suppliers provide it with longer credit terms so that it can retain this source of funds longer and thereby reduce its borrowing requirements at banks. This lower payment period could also be due to the fact that the firm is paying its bills faster because it is getting a higher discount for doing so.

7. The formula to compute the *P/E* of the Robbins Company is

$$P/E = \frac{\text{Payout ratio}}{K_s - G}$$

Using CAPM, we compute K_s

$$\text{Payout ratio} = \frac{\text{Dividends per share}}{\text{Earnings per share}}$$

that means

$$\text{Payout ratio} = \frac{\$2.00}{\$4.00} = .50$$

$$P/E = \frac{.50}{0.132-.08} = \frac{.50}{.052} = 9.62 \text{ times}$$

The price of Robbins' stock is

$$\text{Price of share} = P/E \times EPS$$

$$9.62 \times \$4.00 = \$38.48$$

8. The payout formula is

$$\text{Payout ratio} = \frac{\text{Dividends}}{\text{Earnings}} \text{ or } \frac{\$400,000}{\$1,000,000} = .40 \text{ or } 40\%$$

$$\text{Dividend per share} = \frac{\$400,000}{400,000 \text{ shares}} = \$1.00 \text{ per share}$$

$$\text{Earnings per share} = \frac{\$1,000,000}{400,000 \text{ shares}} = \$2.50 \text{ per share}$$

then

$$\text{Value of Share} = P/E \times EPS$$
$$= 12 \times \$2.50 = \$30$$

$$\text{Dividend yield} = \frac{\text{Dividend per share}}{\text{Price per share}}$$

The answer is

$$\text{Dividend yield} = \frac{\$1.00}{\$30} = .033 \text{ or } 3.3\%$$

9. (a) $\text{Cash flow ratio} = \frac{\text{Price of stock}}{PV \text{ cash flow per share}}$

$$\frac{\$20}{\$200,000 / 100,000} = 10\times$$

$$P/BV = \frac{\$20}{(\$3,000,000 - \$1,000,000) / 100,000} = \frac{\$20}{\$20} = 1.0$$

(b) A *P/BV* of 1.5 is better than 1.0 because it indicates that investors consider a firm with a 1.5 ratio as having more attractive investment opportunities.

SPECIAL
TOPICS

18

MERGERS, INVESTMENT BANKING, AND IPOs

KEY TERMS

book value (of a firm) assets minus liabilities

consolidation a combination of two firms, ending the existence of the two firms as separate units. A new company is formed and new stock is issued

corporate restructuring the altering of the product mix or asset composition to upgrade operations, hoping to receive a favorable evaluation from investors

economies of scale the returns derived from spreading output over a fixed amount of assets, capacity, or investment

exchange ratio price per share offered a target company divided by current price per share of acquiring company

golden parachute compensation that officers of target companies set up for themselves to insure against loss of jobs from a merger

horizontal acquisition a combination of two firms producing similar goods and services

licensing agreement an agreement in which one firm allows another firm to use its technology or methods for a fee

merger a combination of two firms, with one firm maintaining its identity

poison pills actions taken by the target company to make the merger less attractive

synergism economies and other gains created by the combination of companies in a merger

tender offer an offer from an acquiring firm to purchase a number of shares from target firm stockholders at a stated price per share

tracking stock the issuing by a parent company of a new stock that trades on its own to gain market recognition for a highly valued division

value of merged company *PV* acquiring + *PV* target + *PV* synergism

vertical acquisition a firm purchases a target company that operates on a different stage of production from the acquiring firm

white knight target company's attempt to avoid an unfriendly takeover by offering to sell out to a compatible and friendly buyer

TYPES OF MERGERS

The following are some of the types of arrangements that emerge from a combination between two companies:

1. Merger
2. Consolidation
3. Horizontal merger
4. Vertical merger

Although the term merger is applied to any combination of two companies, it also has a more retrictive meaning. Specifically, a **merger** refers to the agreement between an acquiring company and an acquired company (target company) to join businesses. The acquiring company assumes control over the assets and liabilities of the target company and only the acquiring firm retains its name and identity.

In the case of **consolidation**, a new firm is formed from the combination of two companies. The legal existence of both companies comes to an end and a completely new company is born with the issue of new stock.

Both merger and consolidation agreements produce the same results except that a merger is usually less costly and less complicated.

A **horizontal acquisition** takes place between two firms in the same line of business, while a **vertical acquisition** involves a takeover or joining of two firms in completely different stages of production. Horizontal mergers facilitate integration because both companies understand the problems of their businesses and industry. Sometimes, vertical arrangements give rise to conflicts of interest and difficulty of getting managements to resolve their differences. In any event, a horizontal merger may arise in cases when a small company in possession of advanced technology cannot finance its expansion adequately or lacks the production facilities to produce and market its products. In these cases, a larger firm could supply the money and the scale advantages to that company simply by a takeover.

Customarily, we will not find the distinction made between domestic and global mergers, yet it is an important consideration. For example, the integration of the operations of two domestic waste management companies is fairly easy and can produce substantial benefits. However, global mergers face entirely different problems than domestic ones. The DaimlerChrysler merger, for example, should be advantageous to both companies; however, making the two companies work as a unit is a big task.

Some of the considerations that surface in global mergers are as follows:

- Global conbinations mean reconciling different accounting standards, tax laws, and management styles.

- They entail finding ways to adjust to different labor relationships and how to deal with dissimilar health, pension, and other employee plans.

- Domestic marketing and advertising approaches may not work well in foreign countries.

- Attitudes toward capital structure and financing differ.

Reconciling these differences may take time, therefore, preventing the merged firm from achieving the full advantages of the synergies anticipated by the combined operations of the two companies.

WHY COMPANIES MERGE

There are almost as many reasons why companies merge as there are mergers. Some firms do so because they believe that the combination will bring faster and steadier growth of earnings per share. This growth can often be achieved with less cost and with less risk than by starting from stratch. If an attractive buy that can provide new products and new capacity is available, the merger may quickly produce the desired results.

A firm may have a high D/C ratio and may want to bring better balance to its capital structure. A quick way to adjust the capital structure of the firm is to acquire a firm with a low debt base so as to lower the D/C ratio to a more acceptable level.

There are advantages in purchasing companies for certain managerial skills not available to the acquiring firm. Also, the cost of setting up new regional distribution systems may be prohibitive. Therefore, why not acquire a successful firm operating in the region into which you wish to expand? Not only do you gain a good sales force, but you also eliminate head-on competition with the acquired firm and achieve immediate access to additional plant capacity.

An acquiring firm may have excess funds for investments but finds that it does not have sufficient growth opportunities. In part, this may be because it is reaching a maturation stage. As a result, it may search for target firms to merge with that have considerable growth prospects. The justification might be that the target (t) firm has better profitability than the acquiring (a) firm because the target (t) firm's $(ROE_t - K_t) > (ROE_a - K_a)$ of the acquiring firm. We might argue that this excess cash should be paid as dividends to the stockholders of the acquiring company. Remember, however, that cash dividends are taxable. The firm might use the cash to acquire its stock in the open market and negotiate a stock deal with the target company. In this way, no taxes are incurred by stockholders, and the dividends paid by the target company are 70% exempt from taxes.

Sometimes there are technological advantages in merging. For example, a manufacturer of computers might consider acquiring a software programming company to enhance the marketability of its products and gain competitive advantage.

And then there are synergistic benefits resulting from **economies of scale**, higher sales from improved competitive advantages, and lower costs occasioned by greater efficiency and the elimination of duplication in departments.

More specifically, the merged company benefits from a larger fixed-cost base, which may help to lower unit costs. For example, the computer and accounting departments of the two companies can be consolidated into one unit. This can eliminate duplication and should lead to lower per-unit costs of operation. Extra employees and administrative functions can be eliminated, and savings may be generated at the corporate headquarters level.

In addition, a merger may reduce the volatility of earnings. For example, consolidating the operations of two companies whose earnings are subject to different co-movements can lower the overall variability in earnings. This steadier earnings pattern is likely to be recognized by investors, which could mean a lower discount rate and a higher value for the firm's stock. A firm with a low ROI and a low P/E may seek to improve its image and valuation by acquiring another firm with a higher ROI and a higher P/E.

• *TAX BENEFITS OF MERGERS*

Sometimes a merger will occur because of tax considerations. A company with a large **tax-loss carry-forward** may be acquired by a firm with substantial profits. In this case, the losses can be used to reduce taxable profits.

The tax benefits of a merger can be shown more clearly in the following example.

Example: Tax Benefits of Mergers

Company T has incurred $600,000 in tax losses during the past 4 years. Company A has achieved earnings of $400,000 in each of the past 4 years. As a result, Company A acquires Company T to gain a tax benefit. Table 18-1 shows what happens to the income of Company A once it acquires Company T.

Table 18–1   Sample Tax Benefits of a Merger

Year	Earnings before Taxes	Taxes before Merger (Taxes at 40%)	Tax-Loss Carry-Forward	Taxable Income	Taxes after Merger (Taxes at 40%)
1	$400,000	$160,000	$400,000	0	0
2	400,000	160,000	200,000	$200,000	$ 80,000
3	400,000	160,000	0	400,000	160,000
4	400,000	160,000	0	400,000	160,000
Total taxes		$640,000			$400,000

*Note: The Internal Revenue Service allows firms to carry back and carry forward losses. According to the tax law, losses can be carried back up to 3 years and firms are permitted to carry these losses forward for as many as 15 years. In this way, carryback losses provide the firm with a tax refund and carryforward losses reduce future tax liabilities.

The tax benefits from this merger should be evident. Whereas Company A would have paid a total of $640,000 before the merger, it pays only $400,000 after the merger.

These tax advantages play a role in the search for suitable merger candidates. In the final analysis, however, tax reduction features are short-term considerations and should not be the only factor influencing the decision to merge. The success of a merger depends on many considerations, not the least of which is the price paid for the acquisition—in terms of money *and* personnel.

YOU SHOULD REMEMBER

Some of the reasons why mergers take place are to reduce paying taxes, to gain technological expertise, to increase the liquidity of the acquiring firm, to diversify into new product lines, to expand into new regional markets, to bring a better balance to the acquiring company's debt/equity structure, to acquire new managerial skills, and to achieve economies of scale. The merged firm may also benefit from diminished volatility of earnings because of favorable covariance effects and higher target company's return on investment.

A merger combines two companies, and one company retains its identity, while consolidation means forming a new company that issues new stock, retiring the old. In a horizontal acquisition, both companies are in the same business; vertical mergers combine companies engaged in different production stages.

SOME MERGER CONSIDERATIONS

Both acquiring and target company can engage in a thorough analysis of each others financial statements and they can employ very sophisticated mathematical formulas to determine the right exchange of values. However, we should consider that present value approaches rely on estimates of future cash flows, which can be substantially off target. This is why a merger is based not only on the determination of company values and what the merger is worth but also, and equally as important, on the way the two managements can work together. After all, good management plays a major role in any merged company's success.

Unless the managers of the two companies can get along, key personnel may be lost. This is especially a problem when the acquiring company's executives attempt to run the newly acquired firm or to "second-guess" its management. Although the extremely complex field of management cannot be summarized in a few paragraphs, this factor should be considered along with financial statement analysis.

In many cases, successful mergers include firms that have compatible product lines and problems of a similar nature. Why? Because the management of both acquiring and target company have a good appreciation of, and are responsive to each others' needs. A less desirable fit, such as would generally occur when a steel company merged with a food company, creates more problems than it solves.

• *METHODS OF ACQUISITION*

The acquisition of a firm entails the evaluation of key variables such as earnings per share, market prices of shares, book value, and operating and financial risks of the target company. The idea is to assess the risk associated with the merger so that a discount rate can be assigned to the future flows of these returns. In addition, some attempt must be made to predict the future trend of these variables and their effect on the merged company.

Given the required information on these variables, the acquiring company can employ several techniques to evaluate the merits of a merger. The acquiring company can buy the target company by making a cash payment or it can exchange common stock in a tax-free transaction. Cash is paid to acquire other companies, especially when the acquiring firm has a sizable liquid base that cannot be put to very profitable use. Conversely, when firms are on the brink of insolvency they will often sell out for the value of their assets, rather than go through the expense and trouble of bankruptcy. In this way, they may get a better price than the liquidation value of their assets.

Some acquiring companies employ a form of mixed payments, which can include a combination of one of the foregoing techniques plus some form of financial incentive, such as issuing preferred stock or convertible securities. Management of the acquired company may also be induced to stay on by the use of stock options.

• *THE THEORETICAL JUSTIFICATION OF MERGERS*

The total value of a merger is determined by adding up the present value of the acquiring and the target companies plus any additional gains or benefits that accrue from the mergers. In other words, the theoretical justification of a merger depends on the benefits that are called synergistic effects. Therefore, we can say that the **value of a merger is equal to**

$$PV_{a,t,s} = PV_a + PV_t + PV_s$$

where PV_a = present value of the acquiring company's cash flows
PV_t = present value of the cash flow of the target or company being acquired
PV_s = incremental cash flows resulting from synergistic benefits
$PV_{a,t,s}$ = sum of the above three present values.

We already know how to derive the present value of a series of cash flows based on normal capital budgeting techniques. The following example assumes the hypothetical present values of acquiring and target companies and determines the value of a merged firm.

$$PV_a = \$1,000,000$$
$$PV_t = 500,000$$
$$PV_s = \underline{100,000}$$
$$PV_{a,t,s} = \$1,600,000$$

The present value of the two companies operating as separate units is $1,500,000, but the merger produced several efficiencies and other benefits called synergistic effects having a value equal to $100,000 so that the total value of the merged firm is $1,600,000.

CALCULATING THE SYNERGISTIC EFFECTS

Synergistic benefits represent the incremental cash flows generated by the merger that could come from the following sources:

1. Sales (S) of the merged company could increase more than $S_a + S_t$ mainly because of better advertising, improved product quality, and more effective distribution systems.

2. Increased efficiencies, reductions of workers by combining departments, economies of scale, and lower costs.

3. There is an increase in depreciation due to a revaluation of assets.

Additional synergistic benefits from a merger stem from the elimination of overlapping managerial functions. In many cases, mergers justify the layoff of a sizable number of employees, something that might not have occurred had the merger failed to take place.

Increasing the growth rate of sales and earnings is another motivation for merging. This can be accomplished partly by acquiring faster-growing companies. Also, technological advantages may arise when both companies exchange each others' research or expertise. Internal expansion may be too costly. Instead, a merger can supply the added capacity at substantially lower costs. A merger can also lead to a restructuring of the asset or product mix of a corporation, and upgrade its image toward product lines to which the market assigns a high valuation.

Obviously, these synergy effects do not occur overnight. The managements of the two companies must learn how to compromise and it takes some time before the operations of all divisions adjust to the new arrangement and can run smoothly and efficiently.

Ultimately, a merger should produce synergistic benefits, measured by positive incremental cash flows accruing to the combined companies. In other words, the merged company's PV cash flows should exceed the sum of the PV of cash flows generated by the target and acquiring companies when they operated as separate entities.

Table 18-2 illustrates the method employed to calculate these incremental cash flows.

Table 18–2   Cash Flows Before and After Merger

Year	Before Merger Cash Flows $(a + t)(1)$	After Merger Cash Flows $(a + t)*(2)$	Net Cash Flows** $(2 - 1)$	PVF @ 10%	PV
1	$500,000	$ 600,000	$100,000	.909	$ 90,900
2	600,000	800,000	200,000	.826	165,200
3	700,000	1,000,000	300,000	.751	225,300
4	800,000	1,150,000	350,000	.683	239,050
5	900,000	1,300,000	400,000	.621	248,000
				Σ PV =	$968,450

*Includes synergistic benefits.
**= IVCF

The discount rate should reflect the cost of capital of the merged company because both firms should benefit from the merger.

NEGOTIATING THE PURCHASE PRICE

The results of the incremental cash flow analysis provide the maximum premium above the present value of the target company, which the acquiring company should pay. So that any cash offer should include payment for the PV_t and any part of the synergistic benefits (PV_s). As a result, the net cost to the acquiring firm would be

$$\text{Net cost} = \text{Cash or purchase price } (t) - PV_t$$

where the purchase price includes the PV_t plus any part of the synergistic gains.

We have already determined the present value of the synergistic benefits of the merger to be $968,450. The remaining task at hand is to compute the present value of the target company. The procedure involves a simple capital-budgeting analysis that calls for forecasting the target company's cash flows after taxes and discounting them by its risk-adjusted required rate of return.

Example:

Assume that the discount rate assigned to the target company is 12%. Cash flows after taxes are estimated as shown below, and the growth of these cash flows after the fifth year is 5% annually. The target company's liabilities equal $1,258,950, and it has 100,000 shares outstanding. The acquiring company has 200,000 shares outstanding.

Period	CFAT	PVIF @ 12%	PV
1	$ 100,000	.893	$ 89,300
2	150,000	.797	119,550
3	200,000	.712	142,400
4	250,000	.636	159,000
5	300,000	.567	170,100
5-*	4,500,000	.567	2,551,500
			$3,231,850

$$\text{*Value of the CFAT after 5 years} = \frac{\$300,000\,(1+.05)}{.12-.05}$$

$$= \frac{\$315,000}{.07} = \$4,500,000$$

If all the estimates and calculations are correct, then the minimum price that must be paid for the target company is $3,231,850. This part of the analysis is especially important when the target company is not traded publicly. Should it be traded on an exchange, the current quoted price per share ought to be roughly $32.32 or ($3,231,850 ÷ 100,000 shares).

Put in another way, the minimum price is the actual price of the target company's stock, as quoted in the market, times the number of its shares outstanding. Although the target company sells in the marketplace at this price, most of its stockholders would not part with their shares for that price. If the acquiring company tries to purchase shares in the open market, it would drive the target's stock price upward. The minimum price, however, represents the lowest value in the negotiating range and furnishes a starting point for negotiation.

The next step is to come up with a maximum price that the acquiring company might be willing to pay for the target company. That maximum price should follow capital-budgeting rules and takes into account the total synergistic benefits stemming from the merger. In other words, the acquiring firm should protect the interests of its own stockholders, and any investments it makes must yield a positive net present value (NPV). That NPV is none other than the PV_s – Net cost, or

$$NPV \text{ of merged company} = \sum_{t=1}^{N} \frac{\Delta\,CFAT_t}{(1-K)_t} - \text{Net Cost}$$

This decision is based on sound financial principles; otherwise, the cash should be invested elsewhere. However, it is true that in the majority of merger cases the price paid for target companies is unjustifiably high and makes little economic sense.

We can then establish the maximum price to be

$$PV_t + PV_s$$

Employing the previously calculated figures, we obtain

Maximum offer price = $3,231,850 + $968,450 = $4,200,300

We now have a **negotiating range**.

Minimum Price	Maximum Price
PV_t $3,231,850	$4,200,300

The final acquisition price will depend on the bargaining strength of the target company relative to the acquiring firm. If the target company is strong financially and unwilling to settle except for a high premium over the minimum price, its final acceptance will be closer to the maximum price.

The acquiring company's offer will consist of the lowest possible price within the negotiating range. Assume the final agreement is for a premium of 20% over the current price. The acquiring firm would pay $3,878,220 ($3,231,850 × 1.20) in cash for the target company. That means that the stockholders of the target company would get $38.78 ($3,878,220 ÷ 100,000) per share in a straight cash deal.

Although the above two approaches establish a basis for negotiating a merger, many times the urge to merge leads to unwarranted competitive bidding. In these cases, the price paid for a target company is usually too high. Prices paid for target companies are at times exhorbitant by any standard. Egos enter into the equation with a resulting loss of perspective.

At any rate, usually a contemplated merger is accompanied by sharp rises in the price of the company being taken over. We might argue that this increase in valuation occurs because the target company is undervalued, but this explanation runs counter to the efficient market hypothesis. It suggests that the market failed to recognize the true value of the target company. A more rational answer is that the merger gives rise to new information and the anticipated synergies from the merger are translated into a higher valuation for the target company. Apparently, the merger brings these facts to the surface. That still does not explain why, in most cases, the benefits of a merger are mostly received by target company shareholders. In many cases, both companies contribute to the gains occasioned by a merger. Unfortunately, no satisfactory answer has been given to explain why most of the benefits are received by the target company shareholders.

PAYMENT BY EXCHANGE OF STOCK

When a merger involves the exchange of stock, the crucial factor to be determined is how many shares does the acquiring company offer the target company to induce its stockholders to surrender their original holdings? In the bargaining process, the acquiring company attempts to give up the minimum number of shares, and the company being acquired tries to get as many shares as possible of the acquiring company. This difference is generally resolved through negotiations in which the company with the greater wish to consummate the merger should be willing to make concessions.

One way of determining the number of shares to be exchanged is to calculate the **exchange ratio**. Going back to the previous example, let us assume that the current price of the *acquiring* company is $48. Obviously, the acquiring company will not be willing to make an even swap (or share for share) for the target company stock because its stock is selling for twice the current price of the target company stock. The share exchange ratio in a stock transaction can be calculated as follows:

$$\text{Share exchange ratio} = \frac{\text{Price per share offered to target company}}{\text{Price per share of acquiring company}}$$

Referring to the previous computations and example, the negotiated and settlement price offered and accepted by the target company was $38.78 per share. The share exchange ratio will tell us how many shares target stockholders will receive in exchange for all their shares.

$$\text{Share exchange ratio} = \frac{\$38.78}{\$48} = .81$$

This means that to consummate the merger, the acquiring company will give up .81 shares of its own stock for each share of the target company. The total number of shares received by the target company will be 81,000 (100,000 × .81). Because the acquiring company had 200,000 shares outstanding, the merged company will have a total of 281,000 shares outstanding (200,000 acquiring + 81,000 target).

THE MODIFIED EPS APPROACH

What if the two merger parties are privately held or the target company has no publicly owned stock? In either case it may be necessary to apply the modified EPS approach. Some analysts compare the earnings per share of both companies to obtain an exchange ratio. Unfortunately, a simple comparison of EPS is subject to several flaws. It assumes that the growth rate, the timing of cash flows, and the risks of the target and acquiring companies are roughly the same. Should the two companies have disparate growth and risk characteristics, one way of resolving these differences (and to give these factors adequate consideration) would be to employ a constant growth dividend model.

$$V_A = \frac{EPS_A \ (1+g)^1}{ks-g}$$

$$V_T = \frac{EPS_T \ (1+g)^1}{ks-g}$$

Once these values are calculated, the exchange ratio would then be

$$\text{Modified EPS exchange ratio} = \frac{V_T}{V_A}$$

Example:

You are given the following:

	Target Company	Acquiring Company
EPS	3.95	5.25
ks	.10	.12
g	.05	.08

Based on these factors, the EPS of each company becomes adjusted for growth and risk:

$$V_T = \frac{3.95 \ (1.05)^1}{.10-.05} = \frac{\$4.15}{.05} = \$83.00$$

$$V_A = \frac{5.25 \ (1.08)^1}{.12-.08} = \frac{\$5.67}{.04} = \$141.75$$

The current value of the target company as computed previously (V_T) represents its current **intrinsic value**. A premium is usually paid above this value. Through negotiations, both parties might agree to a premium of 25% above the current value. That means an offer price of $103.75 ($83 × 1.25) per share for the target company. This would make the modified EPS exchange ratio equal to

$$\text{Modified EPS exchange ratio} = \frac{V_T}{V_A}$$

$$= \frac{\$103.75}{\$141.75} = .73$$

That is, the acquiring company would exchange .73 of its shares for each share of the target company. The modified EPS approach provides an alternate method for determining the exchange ratio.

YOU SHOULD REMEMBER

The value of a merged firm is equal to $PV_a + PV_t + PV_s$. The minimum price of a target company is the PV_t or its current stock price. The maximum price that should be offered for a target company is $PV_t + PV_s$. The actual cash price paid for the target company should fall within the minimum and maximum price range. The final offer depends on the bargaining strength of the target and an acquiring company. In an exchange of stock, the exchange ratio is obtained by dividing the price offered the target firm by the current price of the acquiring company. This ratio indicates the number of shares the acquiring company exchanges for the shares of the target company's shares. The constant growth dividend model exchange establishes the value of the acquiring and the target companies and provides alternative method for determining the exchange ratio of a merger.

AFTER-MERGER EPS

A concise formula for estimating the after-merger *EPS* of the combined company's earnings follows:

$$\text{After-merger } EPS_{A+T} = E_{a+T} \bigg/ \left(N_a + \frac{P_T \times N_T}{P_a} \right)$$

where,

EPS_{A+T} = the sum of the current earnings per share of the target and acquiring companies plus any synergistic gains

E_{A+T} = combined earnings of target and acquiring companies

N_a = acquiring company's outstanding shares

P_T = offered price for target company

N_T = number of target company's outstanding shares

P_A = current price of acquiring company's stock

Example:

Looking up the stock price quotations on the Exchange, it is discovered that the share price of the acquiring company is $20 and the price offered to the target company is $16 per share. Total earnings of the merged company are estimated at $920,000 plus estimated synergistic gains of $100,000, occasioned by several cost reductions. Assuming N_a = 100,000 shares and N_T = 100,000 shares, then the after-merger EPS_{A+T} is equal to

$$EPS_{A+T} = \frac{1{,}020{,}000}{\left(100{,}000\right) + \left(\dfrac{16 \times 100{,}000}{\$20}\right)}$$

$$= \$1{,}020{,}000 / 180{,}000 = \$5.67$$

Merger negotiations don't always work out as neatly as outlined here, however. In some cases, a good merger candidate may get a bid from a second firm that is higher than the offer of the first firm. Many times the bidding gets out of hand, so that the price paid for the shares of the target company bears little relationship to the intrinsic value of the target firm's stock.

MIXED PAYMENT

Financial arrangements other than the payment of cash or exchange of common stock may be agreed upon by the merging companies. While some stockholders of a target company prefer common stock because they wish to participate in the growth of the merged firm, other stockholders are concerned with interest and dividend income. In addition, cash payment of shares held may result in substantial tax payments by some target shareholders to the Internal Revenue Service. Therefore, to avoid taxes and to retain certain options for the future, some target firms ask for a package deal involving some cash and the rest in convertible preferred stock or convertible bonds. These convertible securities provide steady income and leave the door open for the target stockholders to participate in the future growth of the merged company. This arrangement also has the advantage of reducing the dilutive effect that occurs when common stock is the medium of exchange.

Other inducements used to get target companies to agree on a merger include issuing options to management which can be exercised to purchase stock at a stated price. Some target officials may be offered bonuses or profit-sharing arrangements when the earnings of the target subsidiary exceed a certain level. These so-called **contingency payments** are offered to overcome the reluctance and resistance of target company management toward the merger. In a way, this is not a bad strategy for assuring both continuity of management and continued productivity of target company officials. Moreover, these special inducements are especially important to target companies that rely on a few key individuals. Unless these individuals can be induced to stay on, the future of those target companies may be in jeopardy.

A takeover must not generate bad feelings, which usually lead to the defection of key personnel and, sometimes, to increased competition from those who leave to start competing businesses.

• OTHER CONSIDERATIONS IN MERGER DEALS

In the process of evaluating the relative merits of a merger, other factors are taken into consideration. One of these might be the difference in the prices of the stock. For example, suppose two firms have the same earnings per share, but the acquiring firm's stock is quoted in the market at $65, compared to $40 a share for the firm being acquired. This indicates that there are other favorable factors the market is taking into account, which is why a higher *P/E* may be assigned to the acquiring than to the target firm. Under these conditions, the merger terms are influenced by this difference in valuation. Given this situation, the more appropriate guideline for establishing an exchange ratio is found in the prices of the two stocks. As a result, negotiations might begin with a ratio of .62 ($40 ÷ $65), which indicates that the acquiring company would be willing to exchange .62 share for each share of the target company. Reaching a final exchange ratio will obviously depend in part on the willingness of each side to make concessions.

Book value is another factor to consider. **Book value** per common share is obtained by dividing total assets, minus the sum of liabilities and preferred stock, by the number of outstanding common shares of the firm. This measure becomes relevant in negotiations when the book value is higher than the quoted price of a share. In other words, if the market price per share of the target company is $50 and its book value per share is $60, this indicates that an acquiring company can buy the shares of the target company at a bargain. As long as book value exceeds market value, the merger favors the acquiring company.

Another factor that might be considered in a merger is the net current assets of the firm being acquired. This measure of liquidity could help determine the bargaining positions of the two firms. A target company with substantial net working capital would make an important contribution to the liquidity of the acquiring firm. For example, marketable securities would be an important source of funds to the acquiring firm and might be used to reduce debt.

In the merger process, the acquiring company cannot overlook the costs involved. In addition to the costs of searching for the proper candidate, there are legal fees for determining potential antitrust actions or court costs associated with target company stockholders who object to the merger. Many times, instead of utilizing direct negotiations, the firm uses an investment banker to perform the search, carry on the negotiations, and consummate the final deal. There are, of course, paperwork expenses, costs of transactions in issuing new shares and registering stock in the name of new stockholders, and expenses incurred for handling other financial matters. Parties entering into negotiations should be serious about their intentions; otherwise, they will incur useless expenditures of time and money.

YOU SHOULD REMEMBER

The final merger terms or agreement depend on the bargaining power of each participant in the negotiations. The initial basis for arriving at a value depends on the method of payment. Usually, the amount of cash paid for the target company entails the use of capital budgeting techniques to determine the present value of expected returns of the target company over a stated number of future years.

Whatever the terms, the acquiring company will usually pay a premium over the existing value of the target company to induce target stockholders to turn over their stock. Attractive terms, however, don't always determine whether a target company is willing to merge. Consideration must also be given to whether the two companies are compatible, whether the two managements can work together, and whether the acquiring company can assure the target company managers that their jobs will not be in jeopardy after the merger is consummated.

ACCOUNTING ASPECTS OF MERGERS

When a merger takes place, the accounting procedure used is called the purchase acquisition method. If the purchase price equals the net worth (assets – liabilities) of the target company, the consolidated balance sheet is restated by adding up the assets and liabilities of the two firm. Usually, however, the price paid exceeds the net worth of the acquired company and two things will happen: There will be an upward valuation of assets and an additional adjustment will be made to cover an appreciation of intangible assets called **goodwill**. Therefore, in the consolidated balance sheet statement, the asset and the equity values are raised to take these changes in valuation into account. If the price paid for a target company is $70,000 and its book value is $50,000, the additional value is $20,000 ($70,000 – $50,000). The accountants will figure how the $20,000 is divided between assets and goodwill. Table 18-3 shows how these changes in values are allocated when the division is half ($10,000) for revaluation of assets and half ($10,000) for goodwill.

The income statement is also adjusted when these valuation changes occur. The upward revaluation of fixed assets gets depreciated, as any other assets—by applying the depreciation schedules used by the firm. That means that if the firm used a 10-year straight-line depreciation policy, the additional depreciation charge would be $1,000 per year. Goodwill can be amortized over a period not to exceed 40 years. Because goodwill is a non-taxable item, it is written off after net income is determined in the income statement. It does, however, dilute the net earnings of a merged firm as well as its EPS. Assuming the firm decides to amortize goodwill over a 5-year period, then the income statement will show a deduction of $2,000 yearly from net earnings.

This is a simplified explanation of the accounting techniques employed in consolidating the balance sheets of merged firms when the purchase acquisition method is used by the acquiring company.

Table 18–3   Balance Sheet According to the Purchase Acquisition Method (All Values in Thousands of Dollars)

	Firm A (1)	Firm B (2)	Merged Company Purchase Method A + B (3)
Current assets	$100	$50	$150
Fixed assets	100	60	170*
Goodwill	0	0	10
Total assets	$200	$110	$330
Debt	$ 80	$ 30	$110
Common equity	150	50	220**
Total liabilities and net worth	$230	$ 80	$330

* This number ($170) includes $10,000 worth of revalued assets.
** This $220 number includes $10,000 worth of goodwill and $10,000 worth of revalued assets.

YOU SHOULD REMEMBER

When a merged company uses the pooling method, it merely adds up the income and balance sheet statement figures of both companies to obtain their combined financial statements. The purchase method makes two basic adjustments in the financial statement. Goodwill is created when the purchase price > net worth of the target company, and it is amortized and charged off in the income statement of the merged company. Also, an upward valuation of fixed assets raises the depreciation expense charged off in the income statement.

ANTI-MERGER STRATEGIES

If the negotiations are friendly, there is little problem in arriving at mutually satisfactory terms. The actual negotiations may take place directly between the two management teams.

A friendly takeover involves a negotiated exchange ratio and acceptance by the target company of certain financial policy changes after the merger. When the two parties agree, they present the terms to the stockholders and ask for their approval.

At other times, the target company may feel that a merger will not be in the best interest of its management or stockholders, and negotiations may break down. This may also occur when the acquiring company tries to exert too much pressure and impose too many conditions. Sometimes target company management may become apprehensive about job security and put up a fight to remain independent. In this case, it will appeal to its own stockholders for support or may look for a more suitable partner.

Generally, when a target company is faced with an unfriendly takeover attempt by an acquiring company, it employs several defensive tactics, which might include

1. poison pill

2. golden parachute

3. white knight

4. legal action

In a number of cases, a target company agrees to pay large compensation packages to senior managers in case of a merger that would result in the loss of jobs by these managers. These so-called **golden parachutes** were getting out of hand, consequently, legislation was passed to restrict payments to no more than three times the annual compensation of the executive.

A target company may also try to avoid a takeover by resorting to the courts, claiming violation of anti-trust security laws. Another defense is called a **poison pill**. This action is designed to make the buyout less attractive. It includes selling a highly profitable division and giving the proceeds to stockholders, and paying the stockholders a large cash dividend, thereby reducing the liquidity of the target firm.

To thwart an unfriendly takeover, the target company may seek a **white knight**. This means finding another more friendly company (whose compatible management would make a better fit) that would be willing to merge with the target company.

In cases involving unfriendly mergers, either the negotiations are terminated or the acquiring company makes a direct appeal to the stockholders of the target company in the form of a **tender offer**. The goal is to gain controlling interest of the target company. A successful tender offer consists of offering a premium above the current price of the target company's stock. Stockholders are told of this offer through direct mail or by newspaper announcements. When this happens, the price of the target company will generally rise to the newly offered price. If the target company's shareholders continue to balk, the price offering may be raised even further. Should financial institutions have large blocks of target company stock, they may offer the acquiring firm a buyout at attractive terms—with the acquiring firm getting the company it wants, and the sellers of the stock receiving a nice profit—without transaction costs.

A tender offer does not require approval by the target company management. Because of certain abuses, legislation has been enacted that requires the acquiring company to notify the target company and the Securities Exchange Commission in advance that it intends to make a tender bid. Some target companies then resort to state courts to block tender offers, in the hope that the legal delays will prove too costly and cumbersome for the acquiring company.

Being too persistent in seeking a tender of stock from a target company's stockholders, then, can backfire, leaving the acquiring company in the unenviable position of having bought overpriced stock in an amount insufficient for control. This may pose a problem for the acquiring company when it attempts to dispose of these shares in the market. Obviously, if the price of the stock is bid too high—even if this does lead to a merger—the initial advantages for having entered into the merger negotiation will have been lost.

FINANCING MERGERS

Over the years, investment bankers and other institutions have come up with many innovative ways of financing acquisitions. In the 1980s, the most notable development was the widespread use of **junk bonds**. These bonds are low in quality, unsecured debentures, usually assigned a Baa or lower quality rating, and their yield is substantially higher than high-quality bonds. Because acquiring firms may not have sufficient collateral to buy out the target company, they issue large amounts of these low-quality bonds. All too often, their debt-to-capitalization ratio increases to dangerously high levels. The classical example of a brokerage house involved in this type of financing is Drexel Burnham Lambert under the direction of Michael Milken, who was indicted for violations of federal securities laws in 1989.

These junk bonds tend to weaken the position of existing creditors and sometimes lead to inexcusable excesses. Investors in fixed-income securities have thus begun to require firms to introduce protective clauses in the indentures of new bond issues. Some creditors may even forbid junk bond financing unless they receive appropriate protection. Recent experience shows that some firms have relied on junk bond financing and have over-extended their fixed financial commitments. The major test for these firms will come in a recession, when many will be faced with reduced cash flows. Will these firms be able to meet the interest payments on the debt when economic activity is contracting?

Some of the financing of mergers takes place via *leveraged buyouts,* whereby part of the debt is financed and paid by selling off some of the target company's divisions or assets. In a leveraged buyout, the acquiring firm merely puts up a small percentage of the total purchase price. The remainder of the financing is arranged through financial institutions that agree to assume the debt in exchange for a piece of the action, namely, the right to receive a substantial stake in the ownership of the merged firm.

And then, there are the *Employee Stock Ownership Plans* (ESOP). These plans call for a firm to tender its own stock, paying for it by borrowing at a bank. The firm then repays the loan from the employee stock fund. Avis and Polaroid engaged in this type of financing. Because of several special tax advantages, these types of financing are attractive. They are also used to increase controlling stock ownership, hence, prevent hostile takeovers.

Another practice involves a corporate raider purchasing a large stake in a target company and threatening a takeover. Often the directors of such a company will succumb to **greenmail**, signing a repurchase agreement whereby the greenmailer sells his or her stock to the firm at a price far higher than he or she paid for it. In addition, the greenmailer agrees not to purchase shares of the target company for a stated period of time. This fictitious increase in the price of the stock is unsupported by any change in the financial or asset structure of the firm. The greenmail arrangement is a dubious practice that is likely to be curbed by future government legislation.

All in all, the financing of many mergers leaves a great deal to be desired because it allows acquiring firms to issue huge amounts of debt that cannot be fully backed by the resources available to the acquiring company. In addition, there are many abuses involving special concessions with large compensation packages, labeled *Golden Parachutes.* They involve large awards to the senior managers of target companies, who insist on being protected against adverse developments arising from a merger. Payments include large salaries, options on stocks, bonuses, and pre-established long-term payments. Some companies go so far as to assume the tax payments for the managers who reap the benefits of these golden parachutes.

The payment in the leveraged buyout of RJR Nabisco to F. Ross Johnson, the company's chief executive officer, included a package amounting to $53.8 million. Gerald Tsai, chairman of Primerica, was guaranteed a total of $46.8 million in case of a takeover. One wonders whether these arrangements are in the best interest of stockholders.

YOU SHOULD REMEMBER

There are two ways to negotiate a prospective merger. The acquiring company can approach the target company's management directly and negotiate terms, or it can appeal to stockholders via a public tender offer. If negotiations are friendly, the ultimate result is a merger by cash payment or exchange of securities. When the negotiations are unfriendly, the cost of fighting a takeover via mail, newspaper advertising, or court action can be substantial. Some target firms raise dividends or tell their stockholders not to sell to the acquiring company. Recent legislation requires that advance notice be given to the Securities Exchange Commission and to the target company. A target company can defend itself against a takeover by resorting to poison pills, golden parachutes, taking legal action to prevent the merger, or seeking a white knight. All these defensive maneuvers are costly and can prove damaging to the target company if carried to excessive limits.

DO MERGERS WORK?

Are mergers a fad or are they here to stay? Recently, there was a surge of activity by large firms acquiring other large firms and large firms acquiring small, fast-growing, and innovative companies. The justification for some of these past mergers was less than sound, and the conglomerate wave of the 1960s left many companies in a fragmented state without the means to deal effectively with different unrelated businesses.

In theory, mergers are supposed to generate **synergism**—that is, the value of a merged firm is greater than the sum of the two separate firms. If this argument is carried to the extreme, the conclusion might be that there should be only one firm in the economy, and that this would be the most efficient system. In reality, the large size of the merged firm can create management problems. The early success of many small firms comes from entrepreneurs who manage and control them efficiently. When these small firms are acquired, their managers may lose the drive and incentive needed to compete aggressively in the marketplace because they feel protected by the umbrella of the greater resources available from the acquiring firm. They no longer feel the pressure or need to struggle for survival and may not operate as successfully as they did when they were on their own.

Also, the management of an acquired company may become demoralized or disenchanted by directives from the top that put restraints on former methods of operation. This can lead to the eventual departure of the best managers or to loss in their motivation needed to maintain the acquired firm's efficiency. The urge to retire or leave grows, especially when generous golden parachutes are available to the target firm's managers.

A combination of many small companies into a large company may pose additional problems of fragmentation. Top management does not usually have the expertise or time to monitor each individual small company, and this can lead to poor control over costs and profitability.

A merger should be based on long-term considerations. Management should consider whether or not the merger will result in a favorable future growth trend for the merged company, whether it leads to a healthy diversification of product lines and lower risk, whether it improves the capital structures of the firm, and whether it results in wealth maximization for the merged firm.

• *MERGERS IN THE 1990s*

The urge to merge was strong in the 1990s. Below we comment on several mergers that took place in the 1990s.

Lucent's attempt to achieve superior growth by acquiring a number of companies has not yielded the desired results. It hopes to resolve some of its problems by merging (a merger of equals) with Alcatel, a larger firm having a compatible product mix. Whether this latest strategy proves successful only time will tell.

An illustration of a horizontal merger took place between Waste Management, Inc. and U.S. Waste. Besides cost savings and an upgrade in management, Waste Management has had access to new landfill collection sites, along with additional transfer stations that has permitted the combined company to gain share of market and streamline operations.

A similar lateral union occurred when Honeywell and Allied Signal entered into a $25 billion acquisition, which should integrate complimentary businesses and help develop a strong market base. The new Honeywell Company should have greater financial flexibility and establish a stronger basis for rapid growth and expansion into more profitable areas, such as avionics, space, and commercial jet areas. The merged company feels that the synergistic cost savings of this merger promise to produce a substantially higher present value of cash flows than the cash flow generated by each individual company prior to the merger.

Exxon and Mobil Corporations have combined into the largest oil and gas company in the world. The globalization of this merger promises substantial economies of scale and cost savings from the elimination of duplicative gas station investments.

Compaq Computer has grown in size by its acquisition of Tandem Computer in 1997 and Digital Equipment in 1998. It now lays claim to a wide line of hardware products as well as related computer services and software. Compaq hopes that these mergers will standardized services and enhance the reliability of its personal computers. Working together, these companies are likely to broaden their customer base for their products and services.

United Healthcare combined with Humana, Inc. in order to strengthen its pricing policies via its ability to raise premiums. This arrangement has eliminated overlapping markets that competed with each other in the past. Both companies should benefit from more effective advertising and an enlarged membership base.

One of the biggest mergers in recent years is the union between Chrysler Corporation and Daimler-Benz in a $92 billion deal. Each expected to broaden its product and customer base on a worldwide basis. Besides synergistic benefits, Chrysler expected to profit from its ability to draw on its German counterpart's technology in the luxury end of the auto market. A management conflict of interest has emerged, and it is still not certain if these two companies can work out their differences.

The largest of all mergers involved the deal between America Online (AOL) and Time Warner (TW), worth an all-time high acquisition price of about $165 billion. By agreeing to this merger, AOL relinquished its image as a fast-paced pure Internet player in exchange for a more stable, financially sound, and less glamorous identity. AOL gave up the high *P/E* assigned by investors to Internet companies and is likely to receive a more traditional valuation partly because the new company is not likely to grow as rapidly as the old AOL.

As it turned out the merger ran into difficulties from the start and was followed by large write-offs and loss of prestige. AOL failed to live up to expectations partly because of its inability to keep abreast with competitors like Google, Yahoo, and Microsoft. Lacking its own Internet search technology, AOL is playing catch up. Attempts are being made to put more life into AOL, but such a plan will require a substantial financial commitment by TW with the outcome still anyone's guess. Meanwhile TW has become the dominant player. We don't believe that the final purchase price of this acquisition was determined by the principles outlined in this chapter.

These are a few of the mergers that took place in the 1990s. In some cases, the mergers seem to be working out as planned, while in others the outcome is still uncertain.

• *MERGERS IN THE 2000s*

In 2005 Proctor and Gamble stockholders approved the acquisition of Gillette for $57 billion. The products of these two companies compliment each other, and this merger appears to be a good fit. A merger between Chevron and Unical involved a purchase price of $18 billion. Chevron's motivation for acquiring Unical was to broaden its capacity mix. Despite sharp increases in oil prices, Chevron has not been able to capitalize fully on favorable developments in its industry because of the lack of an appropriate mix of production facilities. It would have been possible for Chevron to invest in new facilities, but the costs of such a decision were considered to be too high. The merger accomplished the same results in a much shorter period of time.

Some big mergers have been consummated in the financial sector with the aim to increase size and expand into lucrative related fields. A case in point is the takeover of MBNA, a prime credit card company, by Bank of America. The shares of MBNA surged 24%, while Bank of America stock declined. As often happens the benefits of a merger accrue to the target company. This purchase was preceded by the acquisition of Fleet Boston for $48 billion at a 40% premium. One wonders if Bank of America paid too much for these two companies.

The motivation for some mergers may be called into question, for example, the combination between two financially weak retailers: Sears and Kmart. This $11 billion get-together involves Kmart, which just emerged from bankrupty, and Sears, which was gradually losing market share to competing retailers. These two firms have valuable real estate properties and other assets, which if sold could raise substantial cash. Given present circumstances, we can only hope that the newly formed Sears Holding Corporation will eventually solve its problems. Other notable acquisitions included the purchase by AT&T (for about $64 billion) of Bell South. Cingular acquired AT&T Wireless. Sprint bought Nextel and J. P. Morgan took over Bank One. These acquisitions make some sense because they are in related fields.

Merging does not guarantee success. Some merged firms are still seeking to resolve problems like desertions among top executive and loss of highly prized technical personnel. Paying unjustified high premiums for target firms has many disadvantages; one being the squandering of scarce resourses, which could have been used to invest in more profitable growth opportunities. Some analysts point to the benefits of size as a means to reduce competition and gain from economies of scale. Whatever the motivation, some mergers were successful, while others failed to produce the desired results. For the time being, the trend toward mergers is likely to continue.

Certain lessons can be learned from recent merger experiences. Usually, when both companies share information about their strengths and weaknesses, when they carefully evaluate their future expected cash flows, and when they are satisfied that they can benefit each other in different ways, the outcome is likely to be good.

As stated earlier, one of the more worrisome trends in the merger field has been the issuing of junk bonds to finance these transactions. Junk bonds per se are not the problem; rather, it is the high debt created by this type of financing that is of significance. It indicates a diminishing concern with financial soundness and could create problems for merged firms in the future. The jury is still out on this one, but the test will come during a business recession, when earnings decline and interest coverage becomes a problem. Historically, excesses of this kind seem irrelevant until a crisis emerges. As in the case of the savings and loan associations, current merger excesses may come to roost unless more fiscally and financially sound practices are adopted.

Mergers are here to stay, but the mistakes of some large companies in the recent past should provide acquiring companies with food for thought. No doubt there will still be chief executives who seek personal aggrandizement through mergers, but in many cases they will regret their actions later on. When seeking a merger candidate, an acquiring company must determine how both companies will work out the future patterns of geographic distribution, the technological base, and their management skills. The two companies should complement each other to make the merger work. Attempts to interject corporate politics and to override each other's decisions can lead only to frustration and poor results.

There are no well defined rules on which to base mergers. In most cases, success comes from careful analysis, advance planning, and the application of modern decision-making techniques to calculate a fair exchange of values and long-run benefits for the combined company.

• ALTERNATIVES TO MERGERS

As companies grow and expand their operations, they may require the backing of systems and expertise, which cannot be developed without enormous investments. The alternative is to have other companies fill the void. While this gap can be filled via the merger route, there is no guarantee a marriage of this kind would work out. Furthermore, a merger might mean acquiring superfluous assets and undesirable product lines. The acquiring company might have to assume the large debt of a target company and there is no guarantee that the managements of the merged company could work in harmony. This means finding alternatives to a merger. For example, America Online had to gain access to a higher-speed communication system. It could have searched for a merger candidate in the telecommunications field but the cost probably would have been prohibitive, so it decided to invest about $1.5 billion in Hughes Satellite communications systems for its Internet connections.

This arrangement supplied Hughes an important source of cash to develop new systems. In exchange, America Online was to receive, based on a security agreement with General Motors, Hughes' tracking stock series H at 24% above the current price. This was equivalent to a 5% interest in Hughes' equity. America Online would then work with Hughes to develop a box allowing customers to access the Internet through their television sets. This and other America Online steps to develop a direct TV and direct PC high-speed Internet service is a defensive move to ensure that it will have a delivery system for its Internet should cable TV companies, that own high-speed delivery systems, decide to preclude America Online from access to their system.

The merger route may not always be the best alternative partly because there are no available target companies that meet the specifications of an acquiring company. That is why some companies choose to enter into licensing agreements and joint ventures. There are instances when a project is too big for one company to handle. The next best option in this case is to join into partnerships to share research and other costs. In this way they participate in the success of a project and minimize their losses when the venture does not pan out.

YOU SHOULD REMEMBER

Mergers have produced mixed results in the past. Some experiences have been good, others less than satisfactory. The trend seems to show a continued movement toward mergers. It is hoped that more careful attention will be given to the goal of maximizing the wealth of both participants in the merger deal.

Alternatives to mergers include licensing agreements, joint ventures, sharing research costs, and making partial investments.

• *CORPORATE RESTRUCTURING*

Competition and constantly changing external environments are forcing companies to alter their asset and product mixes. Merging with other companies is one approach to adjust to these changes. Restructuring a firm can also be accomplished by divestitures or spin-offs. Divestiture entails the sale of specific assets, whereas in the case of a spin-off, a division becomes a separate and independent firm and the parent company issues shares to its stockholders. A new company is formed and its stock trades on its own. One reason for a spin-off is the expectation that the new firm will receive a higher valuation from the market than it is getting as part of the parent company. Divestiture also takes place when a unit of the company no longer fits into a parent company's long-range plans.

On a purely financial basis, the disposition of a unit or group of assets can be justified when the sum of the present value of the future cash flows of that unit are lower than the selling price. In other words, the cash generated by the sale of the units can be invested in more productive assets. Or, the profits of the unit fail to meet the standard internal rate of return established by the parent company.

A firm may also seek to streamline its operations or change the nature of its business. In these instances, some assets become redundant and are sold. Recently, a great deal of emphasis has gone into attempts to upgrade the image of companies. The name of the game is to convince investors that the company's asset mix is shifting into high valuation areas that merit substantially higher *P/E*s.

DuPont is an example of a company seeking to change its image by divestiture and restructuring of its asset base. Although well regarded in its own field, management is convinced that investors keep identifying DuPont with the cyclical chemical industry. DuPont is now in the process of developing a new identity. It rid itself of Conoco, its large oil subsidiary, and by disposing of several product lines, it wants Wall Street to associate its future with the more glamorous area, which it labels "Life Sciences."

Other companies are selling or shifting operations to areas having greater potential and that are given a high valuation by investors. Some companies are finding existing products and assets falling behind market changes. The trend then is to restructure the firm's assets base to establish a new image. The investment is toward those areas associated with high valuation because of their rapid growth, high profitability, stability of earnings, and favorable investor attitudes. By changing the assets and products from low to high P/E mixes, companies are making a conscious effort to highlight those operations that have not received the appropriate valuations they deserve.

TRACKING STOCK AND REVERSE MERGERS

The tracking stock is a recent ingenious strategy designed to gain recognition for the value of specific assets of a company. Investors tend to associate large companies with specific industries. If these industries are assigned low values, the highly regarded growth segments of that firm fail to receive the kind of superior valuation they merit. That is why a number of companies have issued tracking stock. A tracking stock is likely to receive a much higher P/E than the parent company's stock.

Examples of companies that have issued tracking stocks are

Parent Company	Tracking Stock
Georgia Pacific	Georgia Pacific Group
U.S. West	Media Group
Ralston Purina	Continental Baking
DuPont	Life Sciences
Genzme Corp.	Molecular Oncology Division

Brokerage companies are beginning to realize the potential in this field and are establishing separate units to capitalize on this development.

Technically, a tracking stock is still part of the parent company. When the stock is issued, it is not subject to capital gains taxes. These type of operations do not have their own separate board of directors or require parent stockholder approval to issue this stock. It can be issued by pro-rate distribution (distributing stock to parent stockholders), an initial public offering, or exchange of stock. Dividends are paid by the tracking stock company based on its earnings. Usually, there is no adjustment in the financial statements or the creation of goodwill. However, the parent company generally publishes addendums to the parent company's financial statements indicating the contribution made by the tracking stock division to the net worth of the parent company reflecting the price of the tracking stock's price.

Tracking stock provides a good opportunity to be used in new acquisitions or for paying dividends. It focuses investors' attention to highly prized parts of a company's business that would not have received recognition if the unit was still part of the parent company. Stockholders of the parent company benefit from the higher valuation of the tracking stock and usually the price of the parent firm is unaffected by this new issue, while that of the tracking stock is given a much higher valuation. Stockholders of the tracking stock do not have any voting rights.

Where this trend toward the issue of tracking stock will lead is not yet clear. If widely used, tracking stock could complicate the problem of issuing stock by the parent company, which no longer enjoys the benefits of the highly regarded unit as an integral part of its asset structure.

Some conglomerates have come to the realization that bigger does not necessarily mean better. These firms have been disappointed by the poor valuations given to their stocks. Sometimes diverse businesses are difficult to control and manage. Analysts and investors find it hard to evaluate these types of companies, and thus the valuation suffers. In an attempt to gain more recognition, some conglomerates have switched gears by employing a process we call **reverse merger**. This strategy involves breaking up a conglomerate into separate and independent companies. Witness the case of Viacom, which plans to divide the company into two units, namely, CBS and its cable TV companies. The goal is to focus attention on smaller and more efficient businesses that are likely to be assigned higher *P/E* multiples.

Cendant is a prime example of a conglomerate that expanded by acquiring well-known companies like Century 21, Days Inn, Orbit, and Budget Car Rental among other target companies. The decision is to break up this conglomerate into four independent companies: real estate, travel, hotels, and vehicle rentals. In this way, Cendant is attempting to have investors give full recognition to the growth potential of each unit.

Several companies are finding out that the investments they made in mergers have not worked out as originally planned. It is difficult for a firm to admit a mistake was made and to reverse course. Maintaining the status quo is the easy way out, even though a decision to break up the firm into separate units might be in the best interest of the stockholders.

Also, CEOs may be reluctant to propose a reverse merger for fear they may wind up in a less prestigious position by heading a smaller company once the separation takes place. However, should some of the current reverse mergers strategies prove successful, we may expect more firms adopting similar break-up decisions.

This development gives us pause to rethink whether acquiring firms should devote more attention to increasing internal efficiency and channeling investments into areas that match the managerial skills of their executives rather than spending precious time and resources toward the acquisition of unrelated businesses of dubious merit.

In summary, we are finally witnessing certain restructuring changes in corporate strategy geared to take full advantage of a possible upgrade of stock valuations that are likely to prove beneficial to existing stockholders.

The current drive to merge seems to be partly based on the premise that "big is good." Large corporations do gain from economies of scale and lower purchasing costs. However, one must wonder if there may not be a downside to this movement. It should be noted that some gains are one-time events, such as the elimination of duplicative functions. We wonder also whether the emergence of these powerhouse companies means a lessening of the competitive spirit to differentiate, strive for market share, upgrade products, and accelerate new product introductions. The tendency toward complacency and emphasis on maintaining harmony between divisions of merged companies can dim the sparks, which would have produced the rapid progress when companies operated separately.

YOU SHOULD REMEMBER

Instead of merging, some companies seek to make a partial investment in another firm to gain access to its expertise and technology. Or, they may enter into licensing agreements and joint ventures that are less costly should the arrangement fail. Corporations can also restructure by divestitures and spin-offs. A recent development has been the issuing of tracking stock. The stock trades on its own and is designed to gain recognition for a high-performance unit of a parent company. In this way, the tracking division capitalizes on a higher valuation, which would not have been possible if the unit remained a part of the parent company. A reverse merger means breaking up a company into several independent firms to achieve greater efficiency and, hopefully, each new entity will get full recognition and a better valuation.

INVESTMENT BANKING

A BRIEF HISTORY

Investment banking in the United Stated can trace its roots back to colonial times when European firms controlled the U.S. banking system. Commercial banks and investment banks were entirely different, where commercial banks covered the issuing of small loans, and investment banks handled a broad range of financial activities that were highly profitable. Eventually, commercial banks began taking on some of these financial activities as well, creating an almost fully integrated financial system by the early 1930s. However, after the stock market crash of 1929, federal regulators got involved in an effort to prevent any future financial collapse. The **Glass-Steagall Act of 1933** was passed, and separated the investment banking activities and commercial banking activities.

The Glass-Steagall Act prevented commercial banks from underwriting and trading stocks and bonds, which was one of the most important parts of the bill that helped to keep investment banking separate from commercial banking. The act was also passed to help alleviate some of the fear surrounding bank failures by keeping the risky activities (investment banking activities) separate from the activities that affect our personal wealth through commercial banking activities. The act also required that commercial banks and investment banks hold their operations separately as an effort to prevent possible conflicts of interest in their day-to-day activities and strategies.

INVESTMENT BANKING ACTIVITIES

Investment banking is one of the most important activities involved with bringing financing capabilities to companies. Investment banks bring about new funding to the **indirect market** by way of issuing debt or securities on behalf of a firm. After the investment bankers issue the new securities or debt, they also help create a **secondary market** by acting as **brokers** and **dealers** of the securities and debts. By acting as the dealer, they become market makers. Their role of market maker means that their profit depends on the bid-ask spread. The **bid-ask spread** is the difference between the bid price, and the ask price of a stock, and is the profit that the market makers make by acting as an intermediary or "middleman."

Investment banks are at the heart of the underwriting business, and one of the core services that investment banks provide is the bringing of new debt or securities to the market as a way of providing funds for a firm or governmental agency. The way that large amounts of funds are raised for corporations and governments is by a form of investment banking. The way that an investment bank brings a firm's equity to market depends on whether or not the firm already has securities trading in the market. If the firm already has equities trading in the market, the new issuing of equity would be called a **secondary offering**, or a seasoned offering. If the firm's equity is new to the market, the offering of this equity is called an **initial public offering (IPO)** or sometimes known as the unseasoned offering, as explained in the next section.

INITIAL PUBLIC OFFERING

An **initial public offering** (or *unseasoned offering*) is the first sale of stock(s) to the public by a private company that has never had securities accessible to the public, and is not currently being traded in the secondary market. A *secondary market* is where previously issued stocks, bonds, options and futures have been sold and purchased in the market from investors who issued the securities themselves, instead of companies. An example of a secondary market would be the New York Stock Exchange (NYSE) or the NASDAQ. When companies want to raise capital and expand their company, they usually make their stocks available to the public. When a private company has stocks and makes the decision to offer it to the public for the first time, it is said that company is going public.

There are several types of IPOs, and they all represent the different management and owner compensation in companies. Different types of initial public offerings include: venture capital-backed IPO, reverse-leveraged buyout IPO, and spin-off IPO.

A **venture capital-backed** IPO is an arrangement through which shares previously sold by a company's management to private investors are now available for sale to the public. Another option of this IPO is an acquisition purchased by another firm. Both choices are known as "exit strategies," giving venture capitalists an opportunity to receive return on their investments. During poor economic times, investors' interest is low and certainty in venture capital-backed IPOs is high. For example, when the economy was hit by the financial crisis in 2008, there was a record low of venture capital-backed IPOs both in the U.S. and global markets.

A **reverse-leveraged buyout** IPO is usually taken by a privatized company undergoing difficulties in paying back its debt from a previous leveraged buyout (LBO) or operational activities. In order for the firm to pay back its debt, it chooses to raise capital through a reverse leverage buyout. New offerings of shares become available to the public. By choosing to do a reverse leveraged buyout, a company is trying to have a more manageable level of debt and maintaining a lower debt-to-equity ratio. A reverse-leveraged buyout IPO can be viewed as a form of repairing or enhancing the capital structure.

Finally, when a parent company decides to create a new independent subsidiary firm and sell it to the public, it is called a **spin-off IPO**. It also allows a chance to capitalize any mispricing from the parent company and subsidiary if the market is not as productive as it should be.

When a business wants to centralize its operations, it is usually because it is selling below the level of productivity that it wishes, so a spin-off is created. The spin-off is expected to lead to a higher value than the one associated with and attached to the larger entity. But empirical research shows mixed results on expectation of a higher value after the spin-off IPO. The IPO issuers or prospective IPO firms may also consider offering plain vanilla options to its managements and newly hired executives to attract better employees and keep retention high. A plain vanilla option is one with a straightforward expiration date and strike price with no unique characteristics; i.e., nothing "exotic."

PRICING AN IPO

Investment bankers undertake risk in underwriting new securities. Their decisions are based on a number of assumptions and analytics, both quantitative and qualitative, that determine the price of the equity that they bring to the market. However, coming to an exact price for an initial public offering (IPO) is not straightforward; in practice there is no universal method to follow. Many firms involved in an initial public offering may underprice their securities, and some deliberately so as to prevent a lack of demand.

One popular way of pricing an initial public offering is to use a **dutch auction**. A dutch auction is a way of bringing a new equity to the market but with no set price. The buyers then place their bids, which include a price they are willing to pay and the quantity of the equity that they wish to purchase. Once all of the bids, are received, the price is determined. Dutch auctions are good in the sense that they get a preview of the bids that the market has to make. It is also beneficial because if a prospective buyer places a bid of $100 per share for 100 shares of stock, and the bankers decided to charge $80 per share, the buyer would only have to pay $80 per share. This, in a way, gives the buyer the ability to buy at discount compared to the true value of the asset.

As an example, Google was brought to market on August 14, 2004, in an initial public offering of 22.5 million shares at the price of $85 per share through an auction-based IPO. The auction-based IPO was selected for going public in an effort to reduce stock price volatility, avoid initial jumps in share price, and control speculation. This auction-based IPO assumed that the more bids received, the higher the IPO price would be set, and vice versa. Eventually, the price of $85 per share was deemed by the investment bankers to be a fair initial price to the public; only a few months earlier Google was expecting to price its IPO at more than $120 per share. So, Google, in consultation and agreement with its underwriters, readjusted the price to $85 accordingly. Since the driving force of the market is supply and demand, on the very first day of trading, the share price rose to more than $100 per share approaching the original estimated price of $120 per share. This simple—and—real example demonstrates the difficulties involved in computing and recommending a fair and reasonable price for a successful initial public offering.

AFTER THE INITIAL PUBLIC OFFERING

After a successful completion of the initial public offering, the investment bankers start with helping to create a secondary market for the securities that they issued by becoming brokers and dealers. A broker helps bring together buyers and sellers of securities, and charges a commission for matching the two together. A dealer makes a market of the securities, and trades on its own account for profits.

Investment banks don't only act as brokers and dealers, and help to bring new securities to market. They give advice on business activities, participate in arbitrage activities, act as providers of venture capital, and participate in mergers and acquisitions (M&A) activities. The merger and acquisition activities can be either friendly or hostile. One of the most important types of merger and acquisition activities is management buyouts.

ISSUING DEBT AND MANAGEMENT BUYOUTS

The greatest risk associated with being an investment banker responsible for the issuance of debt is the guarantees provided to the firm by the banker. The firm is promised by the investment bankers that they will get the firm a certain amount of capital. This promise is made after the bankers perform due diligence and research to see what a reasonable interest rate on the bond would be. However, it leaves the investment bankers vulnerable to adjustments in the market of interest rates and demand for debts. Since interest rates and bond prices move inversely, if interest rates were to rise, this would then mean that bond prices were falling. A dramatic increase in yields and a drop in bond prices could leave an investment bank to take a big financial hit on the sale of these bonds to the public, as the bank would need to pay the difference between the promised amount and the amount that the public was willing to pay.

Management buyouts occur when a firm's existing management and executives acquire a large portion or all of the firm's stock as to be in control of the firm, and take it private. The reason that the management would take over the company to take it private would be to further advance the business in its specialty while maintaining better control over its decisions than stockholders would be. A firm that is specialized in a particular industry may be taken private by the management to focus its business on one particular area that it believes it is exceptional at or in which they have an advantage over the competition. Management can also be motivated to participate in a management buyout by their personal experience and expertise that they feel leaves them with an upper hand over the market, and would be better off with self-governance rather than the corporate stockholder bureaucratic system to which a public company must adhere to.

When management participates in a management buyout, they are essentially acquiring the firm the same as another company would—by purchasing the stock of the company. However, the management acquiring the stock is a difficult and expensive process and often requires large sums of capital. This is where venture capitalists become key players because they often team up with the management as providers of the capital for a non-voting equity stake in the company.

A good example of a global management buyout is the case of Equistone Partners Europe, which used to function as the private equity arm of the U.K's financial giant Barclays Capital. Through a management buyout, the management acquired Equistone by way of Barclays Private Equity from Barclays Capital. The management teamed up with Barclays Private Equity because of its need for funds to acquire the stock in Equistone. Although the firm is now independent, Barclays Capital, the owner of Barclays Private Equity, is still the largest investor in the firm and its private equity funds. Equistone Partners continues to provide advisory and managerial consulting services, equity and debt valuation and acquisitions in the area of investments in global markets. The reasoning behind the management buyout of Equistone was based on the proven track record and winning strategies of the management, which could lead to a stronger company than if controlled by the shareholders of Barclays Capital.

YOU SHOULD REMEMBER

An **initial public offering** (or *unseasoned offering*) is the first sale of stock(s) to the public by a private company that has never had securities accessible to the public, and is not currently being traded in the secondary market. There is no set formula for coming up with a perfect stock price for an initial public offering. When there is an initial or unseasoned offering, it is difficult to get a gauge of what price will be acceptable to the market. This then causes many stocks to be underpriced when initially offered to the public. Pricing seasoned offers, which are issuances of new stock for already publicly traded companies, is much easier to do. It is easier to do because all that is required to get an idea of the acceptable market price is to look at the listed price of the already trading stock. Management buyouts occur when a firm's existing management and executives acquire a large portion of or all of the firm's stock so as to be in control of the firm, and take it private.

KNOW THE CONCEPTS

DO YOU KNOW THE BASICS?

1. Give six major reasons why firms merge.

2. What is meant by the term *synergism*?

3. When a firm buys another firm for cash, what technique does it use to appraise the value of the target firm and establish a maximum and minimum price range for negotiating the merger?

4. Will the calculated share exchange ratio determine the ultimate terms of a merger? What other factor plays a key role in the final negotiations?

5. Why do some target companies ask for convertible securities as a condition for a merger?

6. When does book value become a significant factor in negotiations, and why?

7. How does the debt/capitalization ratio play a role in the selection of a likely merger candidate by an acquiring company?

8. Besides cash and common stock, what methods of exchange can be used to consummate a merger? Why are these methods attractive to management and stockholders?

9. Indicate some of the ways a target company can attempt to thwart a merger with an unfriendly acquiring firm. What are these practices called?

10. What should the parties to a merger expect in terms of short-range results from the merged firm?

11. What are the tax benefits of acquiring a firm with tax losses?

12. Define the negotiating range and how would you calculate the upper and lower limits of the range?

13. What happens to the balance sheet and income statement when the purchase method is employed?

14. Define a tracking stock and why is this strategy adopted by some firms.

15. Why does a firm seek to restructure its asset and product lines?

16. What is a reverse merger and how does it work?

17. Define an Initial Public Offering (IPO) and secondary offering. Explain the differences between the two.

18. How do investment banks price initial public offerings?

19. How did market forces affect Google's initial public offering price and the price after one day of trading? What does this say about the market forces?

20. What services do investment banks provide?

21. What was the Glass-Steagall Act?

22. What do managers do to complete a management buyout?

23. Why do managers participate in a management buyout?

TERMS FOR STUDY

book value (of a firm)	merger exchange ratio
consolidation	negotiating range
contingency payments	poison pill
corporate restructuring	purchase acquisition method
economies of scale	reverse merger
golden parachute	synergism
goodwill	tax-loss carry-forward
greenmail	tender offer
horizontal acquisition	tracking stock
intrinsic value	value of merged company
junk bond	vertical acquisition
licensing agreement	white knight
merger	

PRACTICAL APPLICATION

COMPUTATIONAL PROBLEMS

1. The expected cash flow of a target company is $10,000 annually for the next 10 years, the corresponding discount rate is 15%, and the growth rate of cash flow is 10% after the tenth year. Also, the *PV* of synergistic benefits accruing to the merged company amount to $80,000. The outstanding shares of the target company equal 1,000, and the price of its stock is $10. Calculate the minimum and maximum negotiating range.

2. The acquiring firm's stock price is $30, and the target company's stock price is $20. Calculate the share exchange ratio and state what the results mean.

3. An acquiring company has agreed to an exchange ratio of 1.75 for 100,000 shares of the target company.

a. How many shares will the acquiring company exchange for the target company's shares?

b. What will be the total price paid for the target company if the acquiring stock is selling in the market at $60 per share?

4. You are supplied with the following financial data:

	Target Company	Acquiring Company
Earnings	$100,000	$200,000
Outstanding shares	10,000	20,000
Price of stock	$24 (offered target Co. to merge)	$50

5. Firm A acquires Firm B. The exchange ratio is 2 shares of Firm B's stock for 1 share of Firm A's stock. Also, you are given the following:

	Firm A	Firm B
Earnings available to common stockholders	$200,00	$100,000
Number of shares outstanding	100,000	50,000

   (a) Calculate the EPS of the merged company.
   (b) If the exchange ratio was 5 for 1, what would the combined EPS of the merged company be?

6. Firm A purchases Firm B for $1,600,000 in cash. Given the following premerger balance sheets of the two firms, indicate how the merged firm's balance sheet will look like now that goodwill is created and fixed assets are revalued upward by $200,000. Also, show what happens to the income statement.

Balance Sheet (all values in thousands of dollars)

	Firm A	Firm B
Current assets	$ 850	$ 975
Fixed assets	1,500	1,200
Total assets	2,350	2,175
Debt	1,000	800
Equity	1,350	1,375
Total liabilities and net worth	2,350	2,175

Assume that goodwill is amortized over 25 years.

ANSWERS

KNOW THE CONCEPTS

1. Here are six major reasons why companies merge:
   (a) to achieve synergistic effects.
   (b) to gain tax advantages.
   (c) to reduce the overall risk of the firm.
   (d) to improve the capital structure of the firm.
   (e) to acquire talent or managerial skills.
   (f) to obtain the technology of the target firm.

2. Synergism originates in more effective advertising and better quality products, which provide competitive advantages and higher sales. It also stems from economies of scales and reduced costs by combining departments and from an upward revaluation of fixed assets, larger depreciation charges, and a net incremental cash flow over and above the cash flow of the two companies when operating as separate entities.

3. The method used to calculate the value of a target company is based on capital-budgeting techniques. The minimum price is the present value of the target company (PV_t) or its current stock price quoted on the exchange times the number of its outstanding shares. The maximum price is the sum of: $PV_t + PV_f$. The final negotiated price is determined by the bargaining strength of each party negotiating the merger.

4. The share exchange ratio is equal to the price offered or paid for the target company's share divided by the current price of the stock of the acquiring company. It determines how many of the acquiring company's shares the target shareholders will receive in exchange for each share of the acquiring company's shares. This ratio will be high or low depending on the bargaining strength of the companies negotiating the merger.

   The exchange ratio represents a starting point for negotiations. The final terms depend on the respective bargaining powers of the two negotiating firms. If the target company is eager to merge, it will accept a lower exchange ratio than it would if it were reluctant to merge. A great deal depends on market conditions, the relative P/Es of the two companies, their comparative growth, and their comparative stock prices.

5. Some target companies prefer convertible securities as a condition for a merger because the stockholders want the income from these securities. They also want the option of investing in the stock of the merged firm at a future date, should the merger prove successful.

6. Book value becomes especially important when it exceeds the market price of the target company's stock. In this instance, the net worth of the target company is higher than its market value. The price of the target company is a bargain because its shares can be purchased for less than its book value or net worth.

7. The candidate's debt/capitalization ratio may help the acquiring company to modify its capital structure. For example, assume that the acquiring company's D/C ratio is too high by its industry and all other standards. In that case it may seek to acquire a company with a low D/C ratio to bring its own ratio down to a more acceptable level.

8. The acquiring firm can issue convertible securities or options to purchase its stock. Contingency payments may be arranged to permit the target company management to share in the profits of the merged company.

9. To stop an unfriendly merger, the target company can appeal to state courts to block the tender offer. It can sell out to a friendlier partner, or so-called white knight. It can also raise the dividend so that shareholders will be reluctant to tender their stock. In a poison pill defense, the target company can make its stock much less attractive to a takeover specialist by creating a new class of stock or requiring special dividends in the event of a buyout.

10. In the short run, it is possible that the growth of the merged compa-ny's EPS could fall below the premerger growth rate of the acquiring firm. It takes time for the merged companies to work out their differences. Also, the initial payment to the firm's stockholders may have been high. The acquisition can only be justified over the long run. Merging for short-term gains will not result in wealth maximation of the postmerged company.

11. The taxes paid by the postmerged company can be reduced when the acquiring company has profits and the target company has carryforward losses.

12. The negotiating range is the minimum and the maximum price an acquiring company is willing to consider in discussion with a target company. The minimum price is calculated as the current price of the stock times the outstanding shares of the target company. The maximum range is the present value of discounted cash flows (plus a value of the target company to infinity) minus all liabilities of the target company, plus the present value of the incremental cash flows arising from the merger.

13. When the purchase method is adopted, two things happen in the balance sheet. There is an upward valuation of the fixed assets when the purchase price exceeds book value. Also, intangible assets increase in a category known as goodwill. This goodwill is amortized over a number of years and the annual amount of amortization is deducted from goodwill and in the income statement. The upward valuation of assets means a higher depreciation charge-off in the income statement as well.

14. A tracking stock is issued by employing an initial public offering or an exchange of stock. It is a method of allowing a subsidiary of a parent company to trade on its own so that investors will give it the recognition it deserves. Actually, it is a device employed to get a separate valuation for a part of a parent company's business that is growing rapidly and has many attractive technological and product innovations. If it remained part of the parent company, the subsidiary would not receive the market attention it deserves. While it trades as any other stock, it is still part of the parent company, although it pays dividends according to its own earnings. Its assets, liabilities, and income are part of the parent company; however, the usually higher stock price valuation enjoyed by

this tracking stock increases the net worth of the parent company and supplies it with stock that can be employed in merger deals.

15. A company can restructure by spinning off a division, divesting itself of a subsidiary, investing in different assets, and altering its product mix. The main purpose is to change the identity of the company in an attempt to draw investor attention toward an upgrading of the firm's product line. In other words, the goal is to convince investors that the firm is becoming sounder, is growing more rapidly, and becoming more efficient.

16. A reverse merger occurs when a conglomerate decides to break up the firm into separate and independent companies. This process takes place when a firm realizes that as a combined firm the target companies it acquired don't receive full valuation from investors. By dividing the firm into several companies, it hopes to draw investor attention to the individual merits of each unit and thus assign them a better valuation. In this way, the sum total of the values assigned to each individual company should exceed the valuation given to the conglomerate.

17. An initial public offering is the first issuing of a security for a private firm. A secondary offering is the issuing of a security for a firm that already has publicly traded securities. The major difference between the two is the pricing of an IPO is more difficult, whereas the pricing of a secondary offering is simpler since the market has already determined the price of its existing shares.

18. There is no set method for pricing an initial public offering and is, in fact, one of the most difficult tasks of an investment bank. Investment bankers use market analysis and research to try and decide on what the market would consider to be a reasonable price for the securities. Using dutch auctions is a popular way for investment banks to receive bids before the security actually goes to market. Dutch auctions are popular because the received bids act as a preview for the market, which allows them to come to a more accurate price, and are often used to prevent volatility of newly public equities.

19. Demand in the market affected Google's public offering price by creating a sense of fear in the investment banker issuing the stock. Since the initial price expected to be around $120 per share gave the investment bankers a fear of a lack of demand, the price was then reduced to be $85 per share. After one day of trading, the share price increased $15 per share, which shows that getting an accurate measure of market demand is difficult for investment bankers to do.

20. Investment banks underwrite new debt and equity, act as brokers and dealers, give advice on business activities, perform arbitrage activities, and participate in M&A activities.

21. The Glass-Steagall Act of 1933 was a piece of federal legislation that separated the commercial banking and investment banking arms of banks.

22. In order to complete a management buyout, the management of a firm must acquire a controlling portion of or all of the stock of the firm. After that, they can choose to take the firm private in an effort to better run the firm.

23. Managers may wish to participate in a management buyout because they feel that the firm would be better run if it were completely under their control, without the votes of stockholders. The management may also feel that its expertise and experience is not being used to its fullest potential with the firm structured the way it is. Taking the company private alludes to the likeliness that the firm being private would then lead to the managers' skills and expertise to be taken advantage of fully, thusly leading the firm to be more profitable and competitive.

PRACTICAL APPLICATION

1. $\$10,000 \times 5.019 = \$50,190$ *PV* cash flows in first 10 years

$$\frac{\$10,000\,(1.10)}{.15-.10} = \frac{\$11,000}{.05} = \$220,000(0.247) = \$54,340 \text{ } PV \text{ cash flow}$$
$$\text{beyond tenth year}$$

$\$54,340 + \$50,190 = \$104,530 \text{ } PV_t$

Maximum price $= PV_t + PV_s$:
$= \$104,530 + \$80,000 = \$184,530$

Minimum price $= 1,000 \times \$10 = \$10,000$

2. $\dfrac{\$20}{\$30} = .67$ Exchange ratio

This means that the acquiring company will give up .67 of each share of its stock for each share of the target company.

3. **a.** $1.75\,(100,000) = 175,000$ shares

The acquiring company will exchange 175,000 of its shares for 100,000 of the target company's shares.

b. $175,000 \times \$60 = \$10,500,000$

The target company is acquired for a total price of $\$10,500,000$.

4. $\text{Earnings}_A = \$200,000$
$\text{Earnings}_T = \underline{\quad 100,000\quad}$
$\text{Earnings}_{A+T} \;\; \$300,000$

$$EPS_{A+T} = E_{A+T}/[N_a + (P_T \times N_T)/P_A]$$
$$= \$300,000/[200,000 + (\$25 \times 100,000)/\$50]$$
$$= \$300,000/(200,000 + 50,000)$$
$$= \$1.20 \text{ (earnings per share of merged company)}$$

5. (a)

	Firm A	Firm B	Merged A + B
Earnings available for common stockholders	$200,000	$100,000	$300,000
Number of outstanding shares	100,000	50,000	
Original *EPS*	$2.00	$2.00	
Merger exchange ratio is 1 share of A for 2 of B			$2.40*
(b) 1 share of A for 5 of B			$2.73†

*The number of shares outstanding after the merger would be 125,000.

†The number of shares outstanding after the merger would be 110,000.

6. Since the purchase price exceeds the net worth of Firm B, goodwill is created in the amount of $225,000 ($1,600,000 – $1,375,000). The balance sheet of the merged company will be as follows:

Balance Sheet (all values in thousands of dollars)

	Firm A	Firm B	Merged A + B
Current assets	850	975	1,825
Fixed assets	1,500	1,200	2,900*
Goodwill			225
Total assets	2,350	2,175	4,950
Debt	1,000	800	1,800
Equity	1,350	1,375	3,150**
Total liabilities and net worth	$2,350	2,175	4,950

 * Figure includes an additional $200,000 worth of revalued assets.
 ** Figure includes both revalued assets ($200,000) and goodwill ($225,000).

The income statement will show a goodwill write-off of $9,000 ($225,000 ÷ 25) each year for the next 25 years.

19

BASICS OF INTERNATIONAL FINANCE

KEY TERMS

arbitrage taking advantage of temporary differences in market prices to make a profit

balance of payments a document showing all payments and receipts of a country vis-à-vis the rest of the world for a year

banker's acceptance a very popular method of raising funds in export financing, issuing debts through banks by submitting export or import bills

consignment the shipment of goods from an exporter to the importer, in which the title of the goods is held until the amount is fully paid

Eurodollars U.S. dollars traded outside U.S. borders

factoring a financial arrangement in which the exporter outsources its receivables to a factoring firm to raise funds

foreign exchange rate the price at which the currency of one country can be bought with the currency of another country

forfaiting a special form of factoring for medium-term accounts receivables

letter of credit a contract between the banks representing the exporter and the importer including all the terms and conditions of the sale

multinational corporation a firm with significant operations outside its national borders

open account an account in which an exporter ships the goods to an importer and bills the importer's account with the transaction amount to be paid within a specified period of time

INTRODUCTION TO INTERNATIONAL FINANCE

An **international firm** can be defined as a company that is involved in the export/import of goods and services, or a company that has at least a business branch (subsidiary) in a foreign country for business purposes. An international firm with substantial operations (usually over 30% of its total activity) in one or more foreign countries is called a **multinational corporation (MNC)**. There is no universal definition for an MNC. Some academicians argue that the term "multinational" is misleading unless the firm is actually owned and managed by people or institutions of more than one country. According to this view, a true multinational is a firm that has international operations, international management, and international ownership. Since this is not a realistic definition, we refer to any firm with significant operations outside its national borders as a multinational company. Therefore, a multinational corporation is the outgrowth of an international firm. For the sake of simplicity in this chapter, the term "international firm" refers to any company with some type of business outside its home country.

Among the unique problems of international firms are fluctuation of the U.S. dollar and foreign currencies, international taxation laws, political events outside the home country, and, most important, the need to understand and respect foreign cultures. If we lived in a world where there was only one international currency, no export and import barriers, and no taxation, the main differences between domestic business and international business would be reduced to cultural factors. The reality is that we are in a complex world with different national currencies, export and import regulations, and tax laws, and diverse cultural and political systems. Therefore, knowledge of domestic finance is not sufficient to cope with the problems of international finance. You need to understand how the value of a foreign currency is determined and why it fluctuates from day to day. You need to learn about the balance of payments, which shows the payments and receipts of a country in relation to the rest of the world. Understanding of international financial markets such as the Eurodollar market, the Eurobond market, futures markets, and option markets is essential to an international financial officer. In view of this need, the basic principles of international finance are explained in this chapter to supplement foregoing discussion of corporate finance.

WHAT DETERMINES THE VALUE OF A FOREIGN CURRENCY?

Like any other asset, the value of a foreign currency is determined by demand and supply. For instance, if the total of U.S. imports from Japan go up, we need more Japanese yen to pay our import bills. Since our demand for that currency goes up, its value must go up also. On the other hand, if the Japanese buy more U.S. goods, their demand for dollars goes up and they have to sell local currency to obtain dollars. This would lead to more supply of their currency in the market. An increase in the supply of Japanese yen will bring its price down.

The price of a currency, where demand equals supply, is called the market price of a currency (see Figure 19-1). This market mechanism works in the existing currency system, where the values of major international currencies are continuously floating. That is why the current system is called a floating system. Since governments periodically intervene in the market to control drastic fluctuations, however, it is more precise to call the existing system a managed floating system. This system has been in effect since the early part of the 1970s.

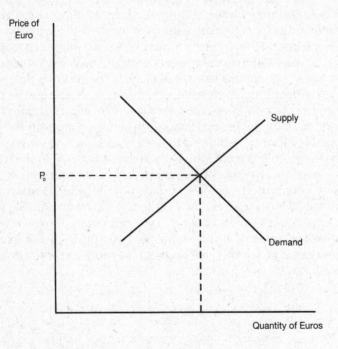

Figure 19-1 The Market Price of Euros

From the end of World War II up to the early 1970s, a different system, called a fixed currency system, was in effect throughout most of the world. In the fixed system, the values of currencies were connected to the value of the U.S. dollar, which was, in turn, defined in terms of a fixed quantity of gold (1 oz. of gold = $35.00 U.S.). The U.S. government could print as many dollars as it wanted, but it had an obligation to convert dollars into gold for other governments that were holding dollars. By the late 1960s, however, the Vietnam War and other monetary expansion policies had created a huge supply of dollars both domestically and overseas. Clearly, there was not nearly enough gold to back up all of these "wandering dollars." The French government was among the first to suspect the true state of affairs and claimed redemption of gold in exchange for their dollars. Other countries began to follow suit. Washington had benefited from free credit, printing as many dollars as the demand called for in the 1950s, but now the bills were coming due, and there was not enough gold in vaults to honor the obligations. The situation can be imagined as if a major bank was unable to pay back the money of its own depositors.

This was a very unsettling experience for the United States in international markets because a currency system (like any credit system) is based on full faith and trust. And trust in the U.S. dollars was significantly diminished in the late 1960s and early 1970s. Consequently, in 1972, the fixed monetary system, which had been operating according to the Bretton Woods agreement of 1944, collapsed. A new mechanism, the managed floating system, which still exists, replaced the old system. Thus, the values of major currencies are now determined by supply and demand and by periodic government interventions. Indeed, there is every indication that this existing system, which basically lets the markets set the rates, within limits, will continue to operate for many years to come.

After the collapse of the old Soviet Union, the economic liberalization in Eastern Europe, and the privatization efforts in many regions in the world (e.g. South America, the Middle East, Southeast Asia, and the Persian Gulf region), there has been a tendency on the part of many countries to float their national currencies. In many cases, currency floating became part of the requirements of borrowing from international financial institutions such as the World Bank and International Monetary Fund. It is important to remember that a "cookie-cutter" approach to currency flotation is not a wise public policy decision for every country at all times. Currency flotation may lead to an immediate devaluation (lower value) of the local currency. While devaluation makes the country's exports cheaper and may help foreign exchange revenues, it also makes imports very expensive. If the country that devalues its currency is heavily dependent on imports (and in many countries that is the case), then currency flotation and subsequent devaluations will lead to higher domestic prices and a rise in the rate of inflation in the economy. This creates dissatisfaction among large sectors of the population, especially those living on fixed incomes, and contributes to political problems and unrest in the country. This has been a typical negative side-effect of shifting to a floating currency system in many developing countries in the late 1980s and 1990s. Therefore, government officials of countries in transition must weigh the advantages and disadvantages of a currency flotation system carefully. As a rule of wisdom, currency flotation must be implemented gradually and cautiously to avoid social/political problems such as the crisis in Russia, in the case of Yeltsin and others in 1993.

YOU SHOULD REMEMBER

A currency is a financial asset, and its value is expressed in terms of another currency. If a foreign currency is quoted in terms of local currency, we call it a direct quotation. If the domestic currency is quoted in terms of foreign currencies, we call it an indirect quotation. The market price of a currency is its value when supply and demand are equal. After the collapse of the fixed exchange rate system in 1972, the current managed floating exchange rate system emerged and replaced the old one.

TERMINOLOGY AND CONCEPTS

In this section, we define five important terms and then explain four major concepts in international finance:

1. The spot rate is the price of a currency for immediate delivery.

2. The **forward rate** is the price for delivery in the future. When you buy a currency in a forward market, you sign a paper but nothing is exchanged until the specified delivery time.

3. The nominal interest rate is the actual rate and includes a premium based on the rate of inflation. The rate you receive on your certificate of deposit and the interest rate you pay on your mortgage are examples of nominal interest rates.

4. The real interest rate is a more accurate measure of the value of interest payments because it excludes inflation. Once you subtract the rate of inflation from the nominal interest rate, you arrive at a real interest rate. Thus, if the rate of inflation is 5% and you receive 9% on your certificate of deposit, the real interest rate you enjoy is approximately 4% (9% − 5%).

5. A currency is said to be at premium if its forward rate is higher than the spot rate; if the forward rate is lower, the currency is at discount. Let us explain it differently. Currencies that are more expensive for future than for immediate delivery are called "at premium." If it is cheaper to buy and wait for future delivery, usually three, six, or nine months in future, the currency is "at discount."

Read the above five terms again before you continue. Once you know these terms, you are ready to understand the following four major concepts:

1. *The purchasing power parity:* According to this theory, there is a relationship between inflation rates and the values of currencies in different countries. If the U.S. rate of inflation is 5% more than that of Japan, the U.S. dollar should lose value (depreciate) by approximately 5%. If two countries have equal rates of inflation, the values of their currencies, relative to each other, should remain the same. This theory suggests that currencies fluctuate because rates of inflation change. The higher the rate of a country's inflation, the less valuable would be its currency in the international currency markets. Why? Because inflation erodes the value, or purchasing power, of money.

2. *Interest rate parity:* Generally speaking, the difference between interest rates in two countries is equal to the premium or discount of their currencies. For example, if the interest rate in the U.S. is 2% more than that in another country, the U.S. dollar should be sold at 2% discount compared to the other currency. Note that according to this theory, the country with a higher interest rate must bear a discount on its currency, and vice versa. In other words, what you gain as an extra interest rate in X country is offset out by a discount on its currency when you sell it in the currency market. This is partly consistent with the concept of market efficiency, which suggests that investors cannot beat the market.

3. **International Fischer effect:** Between two countries, the one with a higher rate of inflation must have a higher interest rate. If the rate of inflation in England is 2% more than that of the U.S., banks in England must pay approximately 2% more on deposits.

4. *Foreign exchange expectation:* According to this theory, the forward rate of a currency is the same as what we expect the currency to be worth in the future. If you want to get a sense of what will happen to the value of the U.S. dollar 6 months from now, simply look up the six-month forward rate of the U.S. dollar, published daily in the *Wall Street Journal*. This theory suggests that the forward rate reflects the future value of a currency. Why? Because future is basically a realization of what people expect today.

• *BALANCE OF PAYMENTS*

The **balance of payments** of a country is a document that shows all pay-ments and receipts of the country vis-à-vis the rest of the world for a year. Table 19-1 illustrates a numerical example of a balance of payments reported in the local currency, P, of an imaginary country named Parsland.

Table 19–1   Country: Parsland
Balance of Payments for the Year 1989
(Figures in Millions of P)

Export of goods	+100	
Import of goods	– 80	
Trade account		+20 P
Export of services and other intangibles	+ 40	
Import of services and other intangibles	– 10	
Service account		+30
Current account		+50 P
Export of long-term capital	+ 20	
Import of long-term capital	– 40	
Export of portfolio and other short-term capital	+ 30	
Import of portfolio and other short-term capital	– 20	
Capital account		–10
Overall account		+40 P
Foreign exchange inflow		–30
Gold inflow		–10
Total inflow of funds		**–40 P**

A balance of payments has five major accounts: trade account, service account, current account, capital account, and overall account. Each account is described separately in the following sections.

TRADE ACCOUNT

The **trade account** shows the difference between the exports and the imports of goods and services of a country in its local currency. Other, equivalent terms for the trade account are merchandise balance and exter-nal gap or surplus. In Table 19-1, Parsland has a surplus of 20 million P in the trade account, which means that the country exported 20 million P more than it imported in 1989. As a result of this surplus, Parsland has generated 20 million P worth of foreign currencies in the economy. In other words, the country has a claim, equal to 20 million P, against other countries that purchased goods from Parsland.

SERVICE ACCOUNT

Technical know-how, financial services, trade and military aids, gifts, and other intangible items are reported in the **service-and-other-intangible account.** Countries around the world not only export and import goods, buy actively trade services as well. The plan and design of manufacturing facilities, consultations for military affairs, permission to copy patents (licensing), financial services (including arrangements to borrow from foreign banks or to issue bonds and stocks in foreign markets), marketing research, and various other similar activities are all reflected in the service account. A country that renders more services than it receives ends up with a surplus in this account. In Table 19-1, Parsland has generated a surplus of 30 million P in the service-and-other-intangible account.

CURRENT ACCOUNT

The **current account** is the algebraic sum of the trade account and the service account. Because of the combined effect, a negative trade account may completely or partially offset a surplus balance of the service account. For instance, a negative trade account of $100 and a surplus service account of $100 lead to a zero balance in the current account. In the case of Parsland, both the trade account and the service account are positive; therefore, the balance of the current account, +50 million P, is derived from adding the +20 million of the trade account and the +30 million of the service account.

CAPITAL ACCOUNT

The **capital account** shows the net inflows and outflows of various types of capital, such as direct investment and portfolios. **Direct investment** refers to over-10% ownership of an investment in a foreign country. Ownership of a foreign project by less than 10% is called **portfolio investment.** For instance, if General Motors invests in 40% of a $100 million project to manufacture cars in Brazil, the capital account of the U.S. balance of payments would reflect a $40 million outflow in the form of direct investment overseas. Meantime, the capital account would include $1 million worth of the foreign portfolio if U.S. residents buy 1% of the project in the form of Brazilian stock. Capital may also be imported or exported by short- and long-term borrowings between two countries. French corporations may use the U.S. market to issue bonds, American or Japanese firms may use the Swiss financial market to raise funds, and so on. All these lending and borrowing activities are reported in the capital account of each country's balance of payments. Borrowing from other countries generates an inflow of funds, while lending to other countries creates a cash outflow in the balance of payments of the lending country.

OVERALL ACCOUNT

The **overall account** is the net of all other accounts in the balance of payments. In a simple form, the overall account is the sum of the current account and various capital accounts. For instance, Parsland has an overall account of +40 P, derived from the 50-P surplus in the current account and the 10-P deficit in the capital account. The overall account reflects the net inflow or outflow of funds as a result of various short- and long-term transactions of a country with the rest of the world. In Table 19-1, Parsland receives its surplus overall account in the form of foreign exchange and gold. Precisely speaking, Parsland received 30 P in foreign exchange and 10 P in gold, resulting in a 40 P surplus in its overall account. Note that a surplus overall account is always equal to the total inflow of funds, and that a deficit overall account is always equal to the total outflow of funds. Inflow and outflow of funds may occur in the form of foreign currencies, gold, or special drawing rights (SDRs).

• *SPECIAL DRAWING RIGHTS (SDRs)*

In the late 1960s, neither gold nor major foreign currencies were available in sufficient quantities to support the growing volume of international transactions. In 1967, therefore, an agreement was reached among the industrial and developing countries to create an artificial currency named Special Drawing Rights (SDRs). **SDRs** are credits extended to importing countries, and are monitored by an international organization called the International Monetary Fund (IMF), located in Washington, D.C. Each country has a credit quota depending on the volume of its exports and imports. SDRs are exchanged only among central banks and are convertible into other currencies. Although there are currently over $30 billion (U.S.) worth of SDRs outstanding in international transactions, they constitute—excluding gold—less than 8% of world international reserves.

The value of an SDR was initially determined by 16 major currencies, each of which had a different weight depending on its volume in international trade. The method of valuation was changed in 1981, and the value of an SDR now is basically the weighted average of a basket of several currencies subject to periodic adjustments. The U.S. dollar has the most influence, with a weight of over 40% in the valuation of the SDR.

YOU SHOULD REMEMBER

The balance of payments of a country reports all payments and receipts of the country, in a given year, in relation to the rest of the world. The balance of payments has five major accounts: trade account, service account, current account, capital account, and overall account. The overall account is the net of all other accounts, and its balance equals the total inflow or outflow of funds.

An agreement was reached among the industrial and developing countries to create Special Drawing Rights (SDRs) in 1967. The purpose of the SDRs is to increase liquidity in world financial transactions.

UNDERSTANDING FOREIGN EXCHANGE

In recent years, the **foreign exchange rate** has experienced sharp fluctuations as a result of the increased volatility of relative currency values and the increased volume of world trade. The two major types of foreign exchange risk consist of transaction risk and translation risk.

Transaction risk exists when future foreign currency cash flow is exposed to a possible adverse currency movement before the transaction can be completed. For instance, suppose a U.S. exporter has export proceeds in Italian lire to be collected 6 months from now. In this case the U.S. exporter has transaction risk because she/he may lose part of the credit if the Italian lire depreciates in value vis-à-vis the U.S. dollar.

Translation risk arises from the need to translate the assets and liabilities of a foreign subsidiary, expressed in local currency, into the currency of the home country. This is necessary for consolidating the financial statement of the subsidiary with that of its parent company.

Many foreign exchange transactions arise in connection with the importation or exportation of goods or raw materials. However, such transactions are also performed for numerous other purposes, including acquisition of foreign facilities, financing of operations of foreign subsidiaries, repayment of foreign borrowings, pursuit of attractive short-term investment opportunities, and diversification of securities holdings.

There is no organized exchange to establish a market for these rates. The market in foreign currencies exists in every large financial center in the world and consists primarily of trading by the world's international banks.

Foreign exchange rates are established through instantaneous communication facilities, and as a result these rates tend to be very similar worldwide. However, when dispersion occurs, traders in foreign currency will quickly bring rates back into alignment.

Foreign currency rates involving the U.S. dollar may be quoted in one of two ways: as the cost of the foreign currency in U.S. dollars, or as the cost of the U.S. dollar in the stated foreign currency. In the U.S. interbank market, exchange rates for most currencies are quoted in U.S. dollars.

• *INSTRUMENTS OF FOREIGN EXCHANGE*

Instruments available to traders of foreign exchange consist of spots, forwards, futures, and options. In addition, a method employed strictly by corporations to avoid currency losses is a direct swap with a foreign business. The precise arrangements are widely varying and complex, but the principle is simple: Instead of buying and selling currencies directly, corporations locate a foreign business with opposite needs and work out a set of loans to each other.

THE SPOT MARKET

The **spot market** establishes the current price of a specific foreign currency. This rate is the underlying basis for evaluating forwards, futures, and options.

Spot rates of the currencies of the major industrial countries are determined mainly by supply and demand. If an excess amount (in comparison to demand) of domestic currency is offered, the value of that currency will tend to decline. Conversely, when demand for a certain currency exceeds the supply, the value of that currency will increase.

The demand for a country's products and raw material plays a principal role in determining the demand for its currency-and, subsequently, its exchange rate. In other words, a country's balance of payments has an important impact on the value of its currency. Factors affecting the level of demand for a country's products include its supply of raw materials, the efficiency of its manufacturing facilities, the size and skills of its labor force, and the price levels of its products. The level of investment in foreign plants and financial assets also has an impact on the exchange rate. If foreign facilities are acquired by a country, that country's demand for foreign currencies may increase. The fiscal and monetary policies of a government also are important determinants of exchange rates because of their effects on inflation, interest rates, and income levels. With a sharp increase in the money supply unaccompanied by comparable growth in the gross national product (GNP), inflationary conditions can be created that will lower the value of the currency.

Short-term rates are affected by additional factors, and because of the complex interrelationships and unpredictability of these factors, forecasting short-term exchange rates is very difficult.

In the spot market the dealers usually do not charge any commissions on the transactions; however, they make their profit from the difference between the ask and the bid prices of the exchanged currency. The ask price represents the price at which the dealer sells the currency, and the bid price represents the price that the dealer pays to buy the currency. The price difference between the bid and ask is called the spread. Spread can also be quoted as a percentage of the ask price using the following formula:

$$\text{Percent Spread} = \{(\text{Ask price} - \text{Bid price})/\text{Ask price}\} \times 100$$

Note that that the percentage spread will always be positive since the dealers will not offer to sell the currency for less than they offer to buy.

Example:
A dealer in New York buys British pound (£) for $1.5931/£. Calculate the spread for British pound.

$$\text{Spread} = \text{Ask Price} - \text{Bid Price} = \$0.0014/£$$
$$\text{Percentage Spread} = 0.0014/1.5945 \times 100 = 0.0878 = 8.78\%$$

FORWARDS
In a **forward transaction**, the seller sells any specified amount of foreign currency, at a fixed rate, for delivery on a future date. The exchange rate is fixed when the transaction is agreed upon, just as it is in spot transactions. The buyer and seller determine the dollar size of the contract because there are no standardized amounts. Forward delivery dates are computed as the number of months from the spot delivery date. "Spot" indicates delivery at the time of transaction. In practice, "forward" is counted after "spot"; for example, 3 months forward means 3 months after spot. Contracts providing for delivery in 1 month, 3 months, 6 months, 9 months, or 12 months are the most common; however, contracts with maturities of more than a year can be obtained in the major currencies. Forward contracts normally require no cash outlay until the delivery date. If the creditworthiness of a customer is in doubt, a deposit of cash or other collateral may be required.

FUTURES
Foreign currency futures are different from forward contracts. Futures contract prices are determined by open auction markets. The sizes of these contracts are also standardized. Each German mark contract is for 125,000 marks; each British pound contract, for 25,000 pounds; each Canadian dollar contract, for 100,000 Canadian dollars; each Japanese yen contract for 12,500,000 yen; and each Swiss franc contract, for 125,000 Swiss francs. In addition, delivery dates are standardized.

An active futures market exists for a few major currencies on the International Monetary Market (IMM). Futures contracts differ from forward contracts in that transactions are made through a clearinghouse. The clearinghouse becomes the buyer to every seller, and the seller to every buyer, in the futures market. As a result, a trader is not concerned about the creditworthiness of the other party, and foreign currency futures-contract positions can be closed out more easily than can foreign currency forward contracts. Most futures contracts are liquidated by an offsetting purchase or sale and never reach delivery. If delivery occurs, the procedure is identical to that used in the interbank market.

OPTIONS

Foreign currency options give their buyer the right—but not the obligation—to buy (or sell) a fixed amount of currency at a fixed rate, or **strike price**, on or before an expiration date. The right to buy the currency is known as a call, and the right to sell is a put. The two parties to a currency option contract are called the option buyer and the option writer.

The time period for delivery of foreign currency option contracts is limited to several weeks or a month. This type of option is merely a variation of a foreign currency forward contract.

There are two types of currency options: call options and put options. A **call option** gives the right to buy, and a **put option** gives the right to sell.

PROFIT AND LOSS IN OPTION TRANSACTIONS

BUY A CALL

The investor who thinks a foreign currency's price is likely to rise may want to buy a call. As the foreign currency price rises, the buyer of a call will have capital gains. If the foreign currency price decreases, only the premium is lost. Because the call buyer invested only the amount of the writer's premium, a large rate of return on the investment can be realized if the price of the foreign currency rises substantially.

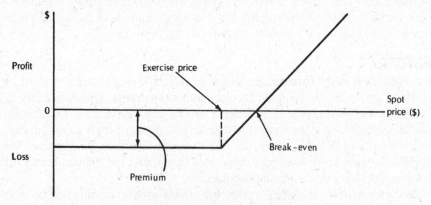

Figure 19–2 Buy a Call

In Figure 19-2 the call option buyer has a loss, equal to the premium paid, up to the point where the exchange rate rises above the exercise price. When the exchange rate exceeds the exercise price by enough to cover the premium, the option buyer's profit is zero. If the currency price rises still further, the buyer makes a profit.

Example:

PROBLEM   A computer-manufacturing firm has bought computer memory for ,¥6,250,000. The firm has to pay the balance in 90 days. The company can buy a yen call option to minimize its currency risk. A call option will give the company the right (without any obligation to exercise the option) to buy ¥6,250,000 after 90 days at a prespecified strike price. The strike price is $0.00928/¥ and the option price is $0.000149/¥. Calculate the firm's gain (or loss) on the transaction if the spot rate after 90 days turns out to be $0.00956/¥.

SOLUTION   Liability according to the spot rate at the end of the 90 day:

$$¥6,250,000 \times \$0.00956/¥ = \$59,750$$

Liability according to the strike rate at the end of the 90 day:

$$¥6,250,000 \times \$0.00928/¥ = \$58,000$$

Price of the option;

$$¥6,250,000 \times \$0.000149/¥ = \$931.25$$

Total cost of the option = $58,000 + $931.25 = $58,931.25

The firm has saved $818.75 ($59,750 − $58,931.25) by buying and executing the option at the strike price.

SELL A CALL

A speculator who expects the value of a foreign currency to fall may wish to sell a call. The writer of a call has a profit graph opposite to that of a call buyer. Profit is limited to the premium received from the call buyer, and risk is unlimited (see Figure 19-3).

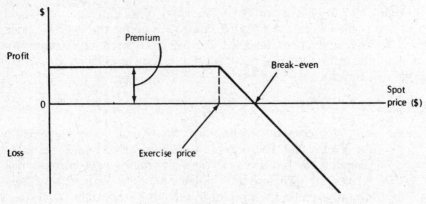

Figure 19–3 Sell a Call

BUY A PUT

The buyer of a put, like a call writer, hopes the foreign currency price will fall. But unlike the call writer, the buyer has limited losses (only the premium) if the foreign currency rises. If the foreign currency price falls, the put owner's profit cannot exceed the exercise price times the unit size of the contract.

SELL A PUT

An investor who feels a foreign currency will rise has a choice of buying a call or selling a put. If the foreign currency falls, the writer of a put cannot lose more than the exercise price times the unit size of the contract. If the price of the foreign currency rises, the writer gains no more than the premium.

YOU SHOULD REMEMBER

In a foreign exchange transaction the currency of one country is bought or sold with the currency of another country. Instruments available to traders of foreign exchange are spots, forwards, futures, and options.

The spot market establishes the current price of a specific foreign currency. In a forward market, the seller sells a certain amount of foreign currency at a specific rate for delivery at a future date. A future market is an organized forward market in which prices are determined by open auctions. Currency options convey to the purchaser the right (but not the obligation) to buy or sell a fixed amount of currency at a specified rate on or before a particular expiration date.

• *ARBITRAGE*

Arbitrage means taking advantage of temporary differences in price. The person who does arbitrage is called an arbitrageur. Arbitrage in foreign currencies can take different forms. A simple form of arbitrage is **geographical arbitrage**, which exploits the difference in the price of a foreign currency between two markets at the same time. If transaction costs allow, an arbitrageur can buy the foreign currency in the market at a lower price and sell it immediately at a higher price in the other market. The **spread** (the difference between the selling price and the buying price), after the transaction cost has been subtracted, is the net benefit of the arbitrage.

Example:

PROBLEM   Assume that the ask price of yen (¥) is $0.009189/¥ in Tokyo, and the bid price of yen is €0.06103/¥ in Paris. At the same time you can sell Euros (€) for $0.1524/€ in New York.

An investor from New York exchanges $25,000,000 for yen in Tokyo. With this money he or she buys Euros in Paris, and sells the Euros in New York. Calculate the arbitrage gain (loss) on this transaction.

SOLUTION   In Tokyo, $25,000,000 = ¥(25,000,000/0.009189) = ¥2,720,644,249

In Paris, ¥2,720,644,249 = €(2,720,644,249 × 0.06103) = €166,040,918

In New York, €166,040,918 = $(166,040,918 × 0.1524) = $25,304,635

Therefore, the amount of profit is the difference between $25,304,635 and $25,00,000: $25,304,635 − $25,000,000 = $304,635 (profit)

This kind of opportunity rarely exists in practice because of transaction costs and market efficiency. First, transactions are subject to certain commissions due to the ask-bid spread, assumed to be zero in this example. Second, due to the efficiency of the market, the information about the prices of foreign currencies is transmitted across the borders so quickly that any temporary differences between prices disappear before a person or an institution can benefit, or at best the temporary price differences will disappear right after the first arbitrageur (traders who benefit from temporary profits in the market) takes advantage of the opportunity. In the above example, the extra demand for yen in Tokyo will increase the ask price of yen in dollars (less yens for the same amount of dollars), and in Paris the same phenomenon will be observed on the € ask price in terms of yen (less € for the same amount of yens). In New York, the dealers will increase the ask price of dollars against €, meaning less dollars for the same amount of €. The price adjustment will continue until there will be no arbitrage opportunity.

Arbitrage may also become possible if there is a difference between the interest rates in two countries, and if there is a difference between the spot rate and the future rate of their currencies.

Example: Arbitrage

Suppose interest rates in the United States and England are 8% and 10%, respectively, and the U.S. dollar is sold at a 4% premium over the British pound in the future market. In this case arbitrageurs can borrow British pounds in London at 10%, invest in U.S. dollars at 8%, and then sell their future dollar proceeds at a 4% premium. The result is a 2% net profit, as shown in Table 19-2. This kind of arbitrage could also become unprofitable in practice because of transaction costs, market efficiency, and the difference between the investment rate and borrowing rates.

Table 19-2   Procedure for Arbitrage

Transaction	Cost/Benefit
Borrow British pounds in London in 10%	−10%
Convert British pounds into U.S. dollars and invest in U.S. dollars at 8%	+8%
Sell dollar proceeds for British pounds in the future market at 4% premium	+4%
Net benefit	2%

YOU SHOULD REMEMBER

Arbitrage takes place when there are temporary differences in price between two markets at the same time. Arbitrage is also possible if there is a difference between the interest rates in two countries and a difference between the spot rate and the future rate of a currency.

The International Money Market (IMM) in Chicago is an active market where contracts for future delivery of foreign currencies are purchased and sold.

Arbitrage opportunity disappears in a relatively short period of time as information spreads around and more investors try to benefit from the situation. Otherwise, there would be an endless money machine open to public!

• *INTEREST RATE OPTIONS*

An **interest rate option** is a financial instrument to control interest rate fluctuations by both domestic and international investors. Since these options are used by global investors at large, it is appropriate to introduce the interest rate options as a global financial instrument. The Telerate System, Inc., a major international supplier of financial data, provides quotes for interest rate options. Similar to currency option, an investor may take four basic positions:

1. Buy an interest rate call if the interest rate is expected to go up

2. Sell an interest call if the interest rate is expected to go down

3. Buy an interest rate put if the interest rate is expected to go up

4. Sell an interest rate if the interest rate is expected to go down

An investor can use these instruments to express an opinion about the direction of the market. The interest rate options are offered on the U.S. Treasury securities. They are availalbe in short-, medium- and long-term rates. These options are traded on the Chicago Board Options Exchange. Following are the major interest rate options currently traded.

- IRX is a ticker symbol for option on the interest rate of a 13-week Treasury bill. The Treasury bills are auctioned on a weekly basis.

- FVX is a ticker symbol for option on a 5-year Treasury note. The Treasury notes are auctioned every month.

- TNX is a ticker symbol for options on a 10-year Treasury note. The notes are usually auctioned four times a year in February, May, August, and November.

- The symbol for a 30-year Treasury bond interest rate option is TYX.

Example:

Suppose the XYZ International Hedge Fund is expecting the 30-year Treasury bond yields to rise. What strategy should we recommend? As a hedging strategy, the XYZ International Hedge Fund might choose to buy a TYX call options. If the interest rate goes up, the value of the TYX will increase. This gain would offset and reduce the loss that the XYZ International may have in borrowing at a higher interest rate. In other words, profits through the interest rate call option will neutralize or control the loss of borrowing at a higher rate. The investor has hedged its position in the market.

MANAGING TRANSACTION RISK

Companies that plan to have any form of cash flow in a foreign currency are subject to (or exposed to) translation risk. As long as the exchange rate fluctuates, the exposed company may gain or lose from the movement of the exchange rate. However, the company can enter into an offsetting transaction in order to minimize its risk. Hedging is taking a position against the expected cash flows in order to offset any gain or loss that may arise from exchange rate changes in the future.

PRICING AND THE CHOICE OF CURRENCY

In international markets, exchange rates between currencies fluctuate both in anticipated and unanticipated ways. The management of an international firm should investigate the forward exchange rates before negotiating on a price for the goods and services. An American firm planning to sign a contract to buy goods from a British company in the next two months may explore basing its pricing policy according to the forward exchange rates. For instance, an American company A is ordering £1,000,000 of commercial equipment from a British company to be delivered after two months. The current exchange rate is $1.6092/£ and the two months forward rate is $1.5948/£. If company A requests to be quoted in dollars, £1,000,000 is equal to $1,609,200 at the spot rate. Since company A will pay the total amount after two months, it may negotiate to pay $1,594,800 which is equal to £1,000,000 at the time of transaction.

Multinational companies can also protect themselves or try to gain advantage from anticipated strengthening or weakening of a currency by accepting spot payments for a currency expected to depreciate (lose value) or appreciate (gain value). In the previous example, the British firm could have gained benefits by quoting the price in U.S. dollars at the spot rate if the U.S. firm was willing to accept such an offer.

TRANSFERRING RISK

Instead of trying to take a better position against the other party by selecting the appropriate currency, both companies can enter into an agreement to share the exchange rate risk. In this method the company that profits from the exchange rate movement gives up part of the extra profit in order to compensate the loss of the other party. In a $1,000,000 transaction, where the dollar appreciates 2% against the Euro (€), the party who benefits $20,000 ($1,000,000 × .02) agrees to give some part of this profit to compensate a portion of the $20,000 loss of its counterpart.

FORWARD MARKET

Using the currency forward market, a company can totally offset the exchange risk it is experiencing with the future cash flows in foreign currencies. For instance, an American company dealing with a French company can sell its future cash flows in € in the forward market to hedge (protect) its income in terms of the U.S. dollars.

Example:

An American company is expecting to receive €5,000,000 after three months. The forward rate for a three-month contract is $0.5068/€. The company can buy a forward contract that delivers $2,534,000 (€5,000,000 × $0.5068/€) after three months in exchange for €5,000,000. This simple strategy, sometimes called "currency immunization," stabilizes the future cash flows in terms of the U.S. dollars.

• *THE FUTURE CURRENCY MARKET*

The International Monetary Market (IMM) in Chicago is a typical future currency market. In the IMM, an American exporting firm with future income in foreign currencies can sell those foreign currencies at a certain rate with the promise of delivery at a certain time. On the other hand, an importing company needing foreign currencies to pay its import bills may buy those foreign currencies for future delivery. Through this technique, both the exporting and importing firms are hedged (protected) against an unfavorable currency fluctuation.

Example: The Future Currency Market

The ABC Export Co. is supposed to collect £100,000 from a British firm 6 months from now. At the present rate, 1 British pound (£) = $1.20. However, there is a possibility that the value of the British pound will decrease.

By using the future currency market, the ABC Export Co. sells its £100,000 at the rate of £1 = $1.15. After 6 months, the company will collect $115,000 (£100,000 × $1.15/£) and deliver £100,000 to the other party of the contract. Regardless of what occurs to the value of the British pound during the next 6 months, the total income of the company is guaranteed, by a forward contract, for $115,000. The actual cost of this contract that locks the exporting company into a certain rate is $0.05 per British pound. The reason is that the British pound was undersold by $0.05 for future delivery ($1.20 − $1.15 = $0.05). Another way to look at the cost of this arrangement is that the actual cost depends on the value of the British pound after 6 months. If the value of the pound rises to $1.25 by the time of the delivery, the export company has lost $.10 per pound, because the contract rate of $1.15 is $.10 below the market value of the British pound. According to this line of reasoning, the company saves money, rather than pays costs, if the value of the British pound falls below the contract rate of $1.15 at the time of delivery.

The *Wall Street Journal* and the financial sections of *The New York Times* and many other daily journals are good sources of information about the rates of major foreign currencies in different future markets.

MONEY MARKET

Companies can hedge their future cash flows by using the money market and lock the dollar value of a future cash flow. In order to use the money market hedge, the company should be able to borrow in dollars and lend in a foreign currency.

Example:

Let us assume that General Motors (GM) is expecting £10,000,000 from a customer in the UK after 6 months. In order to engage in a money market hedge, GM borrows in the British pound in a way that the principal and interest amounts of the loan equal 10 million pounds. In this case, the total cash flows (future assets) in British pounds will match a corresponding cash outflows (future liabilities) in the same currency. A little arithmetic shows that this company must borrow £9,523,809 at 10% annually or 5% semiannually (£10,000,000/1.05) to be paid back with its interest in 6 months. GM then converts £9,523,809 to $15,325,713 in the spot market at the rate of $1.6092/£. As a next step, GM puts $15,325,713 in an interest-bearing account in the United States. Using the future market for the U.S dollar and the British pound, this company can guarantee the delivery of its British pound loan in six months.

OPTIONS ISSUED ON FOREIGN CURRENCIES

For uncertain cash flows, a firm can also use options instead of forward or future contracts. Note that a major advantage of the option is the fact that there is no obligation to exercise the option if the currency trend is not in the favor of the company. Assume that a firm is expecting to sign an overseas contract in the next two months. At this point, the firm cannot take the risk to get into a forward or a future contract. However, the firm can buy an option in the foreign currency option market to sell its expected cash inflows (or to buy against expected cash outflows) at a predetermined exchange rate.

• *INTERNATIONAL FINANCIAL MARKETS*

The term "international financial markets" refers to various financial institutions around the world in which multinational firms and governments participate to borrow money or invest their surplus funds. The two major international financial markets are the Eurodollar market (Euromarket) and the international bond (Eurobond) market.

THE EUROMARKET

The Eurodollar market offers short-term and intermediate loans denominated in the U.S. dollar. The maturity date of Eurodollar loans is usually less than 5 years. **Eurodollars**, by definition, are U.S. dollars traded outside U.S. borders. The Eurodollar market is an alternative to domestic banks for financing the business operations of international firms. Instead of using commercial banks in the United States, an American firm may find it cheaper and easier to borrow dollars outside this country to finance its foreign or domestic subsidiaries. Borrowing through the Euromarket has become very popular because the banking procedure is not controlled by the host governments and credit terms are more flexible and sometimes cheaper than those for domestic loans. These flexible and relatively cheaper terms are sometimes attributed to greater availability of funds and more efficiency in the Euromarket as compared to domestic banking.

THE INTERNATIONAL BOND MARKET

Whereas the Euromarket deals with short-term and intermediate loans, the international bond market lends long-term funds outside the country of the borrower. For instance, a firm in Brazil may issue long-term bonds denominated in the U.S. dollar in European countries. Such bonds, denominated often in most major currencies and issued outside the borrowing country, are called **international bonds** or Eurobonds.

HOW EURODOLLARS ARE CREATED

Eurodollars are created when deposit holders in the United States transfer their deposits outside the country and maintain the denomination in the U.S. dollar. Suppose the XYZ Corporation in New York decides to transfer $50,000 of deposit from Citibank in New York to Westminster Bank in London. If this deposit is maintained in terms of the U.S. dollar, the XYZ Corporation becomes the owner of 50,000 Eurodollars. As a result, Westminster in London becomes liable to the XYZ Corporation, and Citibank to Westminster. Note that Eurodollars, despite being traded outside the United States, keep their origin with a bank in this country.

Another characteristic of Eurodollars is that they may continuously create more credit. To illustrate, the Westminster Bank in London may lend the 50,000 Eurodollars obtained in the above example to a firm in or outside England. Suppose the borrowing firm is located in France, and it decides to keep the loan in the form of a deposit with Credit Lyonnais in Paris. What happens in the United States is simply a change in liability of the Citibank from Westminster to Credit Lyonnais. As long as deposits are maintained in the U.S. dollar, Eurodollars may grow without limit in the form of new loans. The reason is that Eurodollar banks need not maintain reserve requirements. The absence of reserve requirements could be a major reason for the substantial growth of Eurodollar loans in the last decade.

The beginning of Eurodollar markets can be traced to the late 1940s, after World War II. Many scholars believe that the Soviet Union and some Eastern European governments were among the first active participants in this market; the Soviet Union placed its dollar deposits with Soviet banks in Europe, and these banks rechanneled the deposits in the form of loans to other European banks. Substantial growth of the Eurodollar and international bond markets occurred in the mid-1970s, when American and European commercial banks aggressively started to lend the deposits of the OPEC countries to both developed and developing countries.

Although the Eurodollar market has served the financial needs of both American and non-American firms, some scholars argue that it was responsible for the double-digit inflation rates in the 1970s. The spectacular growth of Eurodollars led to a significant increase in the money supply in that period, which, in turn, raised price levels both domestically and overseas. Although this economic reasoning makes sense to some extent, proof would require thorough empirical research.

YOU SHOULD REMEMBER

International financial markets consist of various financial centers around the world in which governments and international firms participate to raise capital or invest money. The international bond market and the Eurodollar market are the two major categories of these markets.

Eurodollars are U.S. dollars traded outside the geographical boundaries of the United States. Eurodollars are created when a deposit is transferred outside the United States and maintained in U.S. dollars. The origin of Eurodollars always remains with a bank in this country. Eurodollars may grow continuously as long as Eurodollar loans are not converted into other currencies.

EXPORT FINANCING

Every company that is involved in exporting goods or services abroad needs to secure some kind of financing during international transactions. The same is also valid for the companies that are involved in import transactions.

The trade cycle of an export/import transaction is longer than a similar domestic transaction and it also carries additional risks. Some of the factors that make these kinds of transactions longer and riskier than their domestic counterparts are longer transit time, different custom regulations for each country, different business or banking rules and regulations, creditworthiness of the buyer/seller, and exchange rate risk, as well as political risk of a specific country.

METHODS OF PAYMENT

One of the complicated aspects of international finance is the system of payments or settlements. An exporter cannot claim that he or she has actually sold merchandise until the sales proceeds are received and deposited in a bank account. In export financing there are a number of payment methods with varying flexibility in terms and conditions for the buyer and the seller. These methods differ in a number of ways including the timing of the legal transfer of ownership, the date of the payment, the risk exposure of the buyer, and the risk exposure of the seller.

1. *Cash in Advance or Payment in Advance.* Payment in advance or cash in advance carries the least degree of risk for an exporter. In this scenario the exporter receives the payment before shipping the goods, and with this method, the exporter is protected from any default of the buyer as well as all other risks. Although this method seems to be reasonable in some specific cases such as highly customized product orders, high credit risk customers, or politically unstable countries, it is not perceived as the best arrangement by importers, especially in established economics or markets since it shifts all the risks to the importer.

2. *Letter of Credit (better known as an L/C).* As opposed to cash in advance payment, which shifts most risks to the importer, the **letter of credit** provides a means of safety to both parties. A letter of credit is a contract between the banks representing the exporter and the importer and including all the terms and conditions of the sale. In a basic letter of credit transaction, the buyer (importer) sends a request to a bank to open an account (letter of credit) and to notify the bank of the seller (exporter) that the total amount of sales will be paid upon submission of certain documents. Among the documents required are the bill of lading, a detailed invoice, and a third-party inspection report (if stated in the contract). Thus, the exporter is

assured that once the documents are submitted the export proceeds will be paid by the importer's bank and the importer is assured of the delivery of the ordered goods. While the documents related to the transaction are examined by the banks, the goods are not inspected by any party in this process.

There are different types of letter of credit that vary the risk exposure of the exporter and the importer:

- Irrevocable letter of credit: The purpose of an irrevocable letter of credit is to ensure that the arrangement is not canceled or changed by either the buyer or the seller; therefore, irrevocable letters of credits cannot be canceled or amended without the consent of all parties involved, whereas revocable letters of credit can be changed any time by the issuer bank without any notification to the seller.

- Confirmed letter of credit: In this case both the issuing bank and a third party are obligated to make the export payments upon submission of certain documents. Since the seller usually works with a domestic bank, it is always safer for the exporter to have the domestic bank assume the responsibility of the payment. This is a double-insured export financing arrangement. A confirmed, irrevocable letter of credit provides even a greater protection to the exporting party. In an advised letter of credit, the second bank does not guarantee the funds, but acts as an advisor to the exporter in its relations with the foreign bank that has issued the letter of credit and guaranteed the payment. Advising activities consist of reviewing and submitting the documents to the issuer bank. In case the issuer bank defaults on its obligations, the exporter's bank does not take any action; therefore, the degree of protection to the exporter is relatively lower.

- Revolving letter of credit: To avoid repetitious requests to open letters of credit, the importer may request, under certain terms and conditions, that a revolving letter of credit be opened for a number of orders for the same supplier and at the same time.

3. *Drafts.* After establishing a credit line with the bank, an importer can send a notification to the exporter requesting that payments be made upon submission of a draft. A draft is basically a formal collection request through a bank. Note that the bank is only an intermediary and it simply serves as a collection agent; therefore, unlike the case of a letter of credit, the bank has no obligation for final payments. Sight drafts are common among firms with years of business relations and established trust. From the buyer's point of view, the draft eliminates the risk of accepting goods before checking that the goods are received in

proper condition and agreed quantity. On the other hand, a sight draft creates an extra risk for the seller in the event that the buyer does not honor the payments. In this case, the seller has to pay for the shipment of the goods back to the warehouse or dispose the goods in certain situations.

A time draft is a specific draft in which the buyer is given an extra period of time before the buyer submits the payment for this transaction. This gives the buyer an opportunity to check and try the goods before any payment is made. At the same time, this opportunity for the importer (buyer) increases the cost and risk for the exporter (seller).

4. *Open Account.* An **open account** is the opposite side of a cash in advance option in terms of sharing risk between the buyer and the seller. In an open account, an exporter ships the good to an importer and bills the importer's account with the transaction amount to be paid within a certain period of time. This transaction places all the risk on the seller's side.

5. *Consignment.* An exporter can also send the goods on **consignment** where the exporter holds the title of the goods until it is fully paid. A consignment arrangement expedites the sale of goods and increases the turnover ratio of the inventory. However, the exporter takes full risk if the buyer decides not to buy the shipment. A well-established business relationship and mutual trust are needed for successful arrangements in the case of consignments in international trade. If the importer does not sell the goods, the exporter can either ship the goods back to the warehouse or dispose of them at their entire cost.

FINANCIAL TOOLS

1. *Banker's Acceptance.* A very popular method of raising funds in export financing is issuing debts through banks by submitting export or import bills. Depending on the future cash flows involved, commercial banks may accept the documents and lend a portion of the future proceeds to the exporter/importer. The instrument generated through this process is called a **banker's acceptance**, which can be traded in a secondary market.

2. *Financing through Receivables.* An exporter can borrow money against the export receivables and pay it back with the interest at the end of the term. If the exporter insures the receivables, it may negotiate with the lender for a lower interest rate on the loan. Borrowing against receivables is generally used for increasing the working capital, and it does not decrease any of the risks imposed on the exporter.

As long as the exporter can find a bank to buy its receivables, it can totally liquidate them. However in this case, the bank that buys the receivables will contact the customer directly on the due date, and the exporter should evaluate the consequences of this process in terms of its customer relationship and future transactions.

3. *Factoring or Outsourcing Receivables.* **Factoring** firms offer services to the exporters who want to outsource their receivables departments by paying a factored fee per receivable. Factoring firms buy the receivables and carry out the tasks of credit investigation, collection, bookkeeping, and statements. The exporter contracts a local factoring firm and transfers the receivables; in turn, the local factoring firm begins to work with an associate factoring firm in the foreign country. This arrangement provides access to the credit records of the importer leading to a more efficient collection process for all parties involved.

4. *Forfaiting (Customized Factoring).* **Forfaiting** is basically a form of factoring customized to finance medium-term accounts receivables based on a fixed interest rate. It has been a major instrument used in Europe, and is becoming popular among American financial institutions. Forfaiting offers a simpler documentation process compared to contracts. The importer issues a series of semiannual notes in the form of drafts against the balance. The forfaiting firm finds a bank or a guarantor who endorses the note itself, thereby avoiding the costs of preparing and signing a contract.

5. *Private and Public Financing Agencies.* The Private Export Funding Corporation (PEFCO) is an example of a private agency that may finance foreign importers of U.S. products under certain terms and conditions. An example of a public agency that facilitates financing of foreign firms buying U.S. products is the Overseas Private Investment Corporation (OPIC). The OPIC also provides insurance programs to exporters/importers for currency risk and political risk.

YOU SHOULD REMEMBER

Along with numerous opportunities, international trade brings extra risks including longer transactions times, different trade regulations in each country, different business or banking rules and reporting systems, credit status of the buyer/seller, exchange rate risk, and political risk. There are different kinds of payment methods in international trade: cash in advance, letters of credit, drafts, consignment, and open accounts. There are special financial tools and services that can be utilized in international trade, including banker's acceptance, borrowing against or sale of receivables, factoring, forfaiting, and special agencies servicing the export/import sector.

KNOW THE CONCEPTS

DO YOU KNOW THE BASICS?

1. Define a multinational corporation.

2. List some of the problems unique to firms operating in an international environment.

3. Define the balance of payments, and list its major accounts.

4. What is the difference between direct and indirect quotations of foreign currencies?

5. What obligation could the U.S. government not fulfill in the previous fixed currency system? What happened next?

6. Fill in the missing words:
   a. Approximately, nominal interest rate minus the rate of inflation equals _____ .
   b. If the forward rate exceeds the spot rate, the currency is at _____ .
   c. If you want to "lock in" a certain currency rate for a future delivery, you can buy the currency in the _____ .

7. Fill in the missing words:
   a. Purchasing power parity connects _____ and _____ .
   b. Interest rate parity connects _____ and _____ .
   c. International Fischer effect connects _____ and _____ .
   d. The forward rate reflects _____ .

8. Define a currency option, and explain the major difference between it and a future contract.

9. What is arbitrage?

10. What is the difference between a portfolio investment and a direct investment?

11. In what forms does a surplus overall balance flow into an economy?

12. What is the maximum loss/gain of a call option buyer?

13. What is the maximum loss/gain of a put option seller?

14. What is the cost of hedging in a future currency market?

TERMS FOR STUDY

arbitrage
balance of payments
banker's acceptance
call option
capital account
consignment
current account
direct investment
Eurodollars
factoring
foreign currency futures
foreign currency options
foreign exchange rate
forfaiting
forward rate
forward transaction
geographical arbitrage
interest parity theorem
international bonds

international firm
international Fischer effect
letter of credit
multinational corporation
open account
overall account
portfolio investment
purchasing power parity
put option
SDRs (Special Drawing Rights)
service-and-other-intangible
  account
spot market
spread
strike price
trade account
transaction risk
translation risk

PRACTICAL APPLICATION

COMPUTATIONAL PROBLEMS

1. Calculate the arbitrage opportunity in the following situation. In Paris the ask price for euros is $0.1524/€, in Zurich the ask price for Swiss francs is CHF 0.29816/€, and in New York the ask price for dollars is $0.51675/CHF. As an investor you have $50,000. (Hint: First convert dollars into €.)

2. A computer-manufacturing firm has bought computer memory for ¥6,250,000. The firm has to pay the balance in 90 days. The company can buy a yen "call" option to minimize its currency risk. A "call" option will give the company the right to buy without any obligation ¥6,250,000 after 90 days at the strike price. The strike price is $0.00928/¥ and the option price is $0.000149/¥. We have already calculated the firm's gain (or loss) on the transaction if the spot rate after 90 days turns out to be $0.00956/¥.

   (a) Calculate the firm's gain (or loss) on the transaction if the spot rate after 90 days turns out to be $0.00928/¥.

   (b) Calculate the firm's gain (or loss) on the transaction if the spot rate after 90 days turns out to be $0.00874/¥.

ANSWERS

KNOW THE CONCEPTS

1. A multinational corporation is a firm with substantial operations (usually 30% of its total activity) in a foreign country.

2. Some of the problems unique to firms operating internationally are foreign currency fluctuations, tax laws of different countries, political events outside the home country, and the need to understand and respect foreign cultures.

3. The balance of payments report is a document showing all receipts and payments, in 1 year, of a country in relation to the rest of the world. Major accounts are the trade account, current account, service account, capital account, and overall account.

4. In a direct quotation, the value of a foreign currency is expressed in terms of a local currency; in an indirect quotation, the value of the local currency is defined in units of a foreign currency.

5. The United States did not have enough gold to support and pay for dollars. As a result, in the early 1970s the fixed currency system collapsed.

6. **a.** the real interest rate

    b. premium

    c. forward market

7. **a.** inflation and currency fluctuations

    b. interest rate and currency premium/discount

    c. inflation and interest rates

    d. the value of a currency in the future (the trend of a currency)

8. A currency option is the right, with no obligation, to buy or sell a certain amount of foreign currency at a certain rate on or before a certain date. In a future contract, the buyer has the obligation to buy or settle the account as determined in the contract.

9. Arbitrage involves taking advantage of different prices of the same commodity or currency, in two markets at the same time, to make a profit.

10. Investment in a project with over 10% ownership is direct investment.

11. Investment with less than 10% ownership is portfolio investment.

12. The maximum loss that can be incurred by a call option buyer is the premium paid when the option was purchased. There is no maximum gain.

13. The maximum loss that can be incurred by a put option seller is the value of the currency. The maximum gain is the premium collected when the option was sold.

14. The cost of hedging in a future currency market is the difference between the spot rate and the future rate. Another possible answer is the difference between the actual future price and the spot rate.

PRACTICAL APPLICATION

1. In Paris, $50,000 = €(50,000/0.1524) = €328,083.98$
   In Zurich, $€328,083.98 = CHF (328,083.98 \times 0.29816) =$
   CHF 97,821.52
   In New York, CHF 97,821.52 = $(97,821.52 \times 0.51675) = $50,549.27$

$$\$50,549.27 - \$50,000 = \$549.27 \text{ (profit)}$$

2. Liability according to the strike rate at the end of the 90 days:
   ¥6,250,000 × $0.00928/¥ = $58,000$
   Price of the option (already paid sunk cost):
   ¥6,250,000 × $0.000149/¥ = 931.25

   (a) Spot rate equal to the strike rate. There is no difference between exercising the option or using the spot rate. Liability equal to $58,000 plus the option price. The firm could have saved $931.25 (cost of the option) by not buying this option.

   (b) Liability according to the spot rate at the end of the 90 days:

$$¥6,250,000 \times \$0.00874/¥ = \$54,625$$

Do not exercise the option; exchange the currency in the spot market, but do not forget to add on the sunk cost of the option to the total cost of the transaction.

20

INTRODUCTION TO FINANCIAL SOFTWARE, SOCIAL MEDIA, AND DATABASES

KEY TERMS

Bloomberg Terminals computer software system developed by Bloomberg L.P. that gives financial professionals the ability to access financial market data and make trades on the electronic trading platform through a subscription service.

Capital IQ Compustat a Standard and Poor's database for equity research used in industry and academic centers that contains historical prices, financial statements, relevant company information and composition, and other financial data.

data mining computing process to discover patterns and correlations of data in large data sets through statistics machine learning, and database systems.

financial data banks compilations of historical financial statements, prices, and dividend data that is easily accessible for analysis and manipulation.

hypertext markup language (HTML) a simple language that is employed to code webpages.

stock screeners tools used to filter through stocks based on user-defined metrics, such as target p/e ratios, market cap, industry, dividend yield, etc.

spreadsheet programs programs that facilitate the construction of financial statements and lend themselves to ratio analysis, cash flow consumption, and the study of changes that occur in "what if" situations.

statistical package for the social sciences (SPSS) a special package of programs to help solve statistical and financial problems.

Yahoo! Finance a website that provides financial market information, historical prices, news, and more for free.

FINANCIAL SOFTWARE INTRODUCTION

The ability to perform complex analyses is a main purpose of **financial software**. These programs permit comparisons of performance and preparation of detailed financial statements, and they also aid in problem solving at unheard-of speed. Therefore, today's managers must familiarize themselves with the types of software available and what these facilitator packages can accomplish, yet they must also recognize their limitations. It is the duty of a manager to implement a software system that meets the goals of the organization, as these financial software programs serve as starting points for making final decisions, which, in the end, must rest on the manager's judgment. Every company utilizes a financial software system to house and analyze its data for competitive advantage.

Some software programs are useful in solving accounting problems, others provide a set of outcomes for making sound choices, and some simply represent data banks that serve as inputs for solving financial problems. Despite the ability to "crunch numbers" and establish relationships, financial software is of little help unless a manager has a sound understanding of the basic principles of finance.

No one expects managers to comprehend the detailed mathematical complexities of financial programs, but managers should know how to interpret the output generated by these packages. A variety of financial software programs is available in the marketplace. For our purposes, we have identified the following broad categories of financial software:

1. Data filing, retrieval, and management

2. Statement and spreadsheet analysis

3. Statistical solving packages

4. Financial data banks

• MANAGEMENT FILES

The better known data filing, retrieval, and management programs can be seen on display at computer and retail stores. These programs are designed to file, store, and permit speedy access to information on market features and customer profiles. Software of this type is recognized by such well-known names as Paradox, Filemaker II, and S Base IV. Each of these systems performs roughly the same functions once the data are filed and stored in the program, and they can be combined in any way desired.

For example, a company might want to identify the address and telephone numbers of customers with incomes above $50,000 annually who live in a particular region and are a certain gender. Records can be kept on inventories by type of product and location. The due dates and amounts of accounts receivables and accounts payable can be easily retrieved at high speeds. These data files serve a highly useful purpose; they enable a user to analyze the structure of quickly accessing important information, which helps that user to make important decisions regarding the effectiveness of advertising.

• *SPREADSHEET ANALYSIS*

The most widely used software program utilized to prepare and analyze financial statements is Microsoft Excel. This program can be geared toward preparing balance sheets, income statements, cash flow statements, and cash budgets. Companies use spreadsheet programs to break down the major categories in financial statements in order to analyze areas deserving special attention.

Once these spreadsheets are prepared, the program permits the manager to set up "what if" assumptions that indicate how each item in a financial statement might change, given various economic scenarios, asset changes, and sales projections. They can be used to trace how statements change when a decision is made to reduce labor costs or raise prices by different amounts. A firm can visualize the impact of a change in capital structure on earnings. These spreadsheet programs lend themselves to the analysis of company performance via the computation of useful ratios, or they can help reconstruct cash flows used to calculate net present values, the internal rates of returns, and growth rates. These spreadsheets can have code written into them through an application known as Visual Basics Application (VBA) to improve the use of spreadsheets, run simulations, and streamline processes and calculations. While it is not necessary for a manager to have a mastery in coding through VBA to be effective, it is important to recognize its potential to increase efficiency. The use of VBA can significantly reduce the amount of labor necessary for tasks when used properly, which in turn can increase employee efficiency.

This type of software is very helpful for comparing industry and competitive company ratios. Spreadsheets and statement analysis have become indispensable tools for accountants and managers seeking to analyze the internal financial structure of their companies and to identify areas requiring improvement. Spreadsheet analysis via the computer has virtually eliminated the tedious and time-consuming calculations of the past.

• *STATISTICAL PACKAGES*

There are more complex financial problems that require highly sophisticated programs. These programs provide the basis for forecasting various operations of a firm, given certain parameters, and in some cases, they provide alternative strategies that allow the manager to choose the most probable or feasible outcome. Companies like IBM and Microsoft—and more specifically, universities—have programs originating in operations research, the physical sciences, space simulation techniques, and the social sciences, which include Monte Carlo simulations, linear programming, and quadratic programming. These software models can be used to simulate probable net present values under numerous sets of assumptions. Through the use of simultaneous solutions of a large matrix of equations, it is possible to determine, via linear programming, the best combination for a project that will maximize the profitability of the firm. Although very complex, the linear programming technique produces a distribution of probabilities corresponding to various expected net present values for given investment plans. The goal is the optimization of resource allocation to produce the highest increase in the firm's wealth. Some of these models—more specifically, quadratic programming—can help determine the proportions to invest in given projects and how much capacity is needed to implement these projects.

• *MATH PACKAGES*

A few of the better-known statistical software packages are the **Biomed package**, the **statistical package of social sciences (SPSS)**, and **statistical analysis system (SAS)**. Among their features are multiple variable regression techniques that establish the basis for forecasting sales, cash flows, and earnings. The regression package allows a statistician to establish relationships between a dependent variable and several independent variables. In this way, it is possible to determine the relative importance to each factor in the equation or how significant it will be in the final outcome. More complicated models for volatility, such as different versions for GARCH, can be solved through SAS and a newer software called eviews (econometric views).

• *FINANCIAL DATA BANKS*

Statistical programs cannot work without the input of relevant historical data. Software packages consisting of **financial data banks** supply this missing link. Among the many sources of historical data, there are two major categories of financial data. One type is the securities prices series; the other contains financial statements and related statistical information. The files compiled by the **Center for Research in Security Prices (CRSP)** provide monthly and daily prices and dividend data adjusted for splits. These files form the basis for calculating the risk and return measures outlined in this book. By accessing these files one can apply SPSS to compute the best and required rates of return that can be assigned to different companies. These risk measures can then be used as a basis for evaluating the risk/reward relationships of investments. They establish the basis for constructing an efficient frontier against which managers can compare their own risk/return performance and perhaps diversify investments to achieve the optimal or best risk/return combinations—namely, any point that falls on the efficient frontier curve.

Suppose you are searching for companies that have superior financial records, and you want to ascertain why they were able to achieve these results. Just think how cumbersome and time-consuming this task would have been before the advent of PCs and the availability of financial data files. In the past, it was necessary to sift through a large number of annual reports, 10 releases, the yellow sheet reports published by Standard & Poor's, and Moody's manuals. Fortunately, easy and speedy access to this information is possible via financial data banks, and the most notable ones are Standard & Poor's Capital IQ, Compustat, PDE files, and the Value Line Service on disks. These data banks contain financial statistics on earning and sales broken down by domestic and foreign sources. This information can easily be retrieved and analyzed by using the Capital IQ file. These files lend themselves to the statistical verification of different relationships and can be manipulated to select companies that have certain characteristics or a combination of performance factors. For instance, we may obtain a list of companies paying high dividends, while sales are growing annually and with 20% returns. These and other combinations can be retrieved, and the numbers could readily be printed out, listing the companies in any order.

Capital IQ has further use for evaluating companies and counterparties as a manager. The credit quality of a firm can easily be accessed through this database, while any recently issued bonds and credit reports are made available. This can be beneficial to a manager, as it gives them a nonobjective point of reference on a firm and the starting point of analysis to make strategic business decisions. In conjunction with high-speed PCs, they provide managers with financial data ranging from competitors' performances to evaluation and selection of merger candidates that meet certain specifications. They can provide invaluable insights and a basis for comparing and evaluating operations leverage, financial leverage, and the proportion of profits benefiting from various cost items and the income statement. It is also possible to visualize the structure of balance sheets in order to pinpoint whether certain companies are doing a better job of controlling inventories and accounts receivables, and utilizing idle flows. The debt policies of firms originating in their capital structures are evident from these software packages. The pro forma income and balance sheet statements can readily be calculated for quick comparison, regardless of the size of the firm.

Technological advancement has been remarkable in the past quarter of a century and has been reflected throughout the finance industry. One such example is the popularity of Bloomberg L.P. and its status in the finance industry as a widely trading platform (both in industry and academia), providing market data, news, and analysis in real time through its Bloomberg

Terminals. These terminals and databases have become integral not only for the major financial organizations but also for businesses for the purposes of market access and transparency, trade execution, and research. Although these terminals and databases are not cheap, their value to an organization may surpass their costs. A realistic cost benefit analysis, however, should be done before investing in this technology. There are a number of inexpensive or free alternative platforms on the Internet that may serve the purpose of some users.

YOU SHOULD REMEMBER

Financial software comes in different forms. Some programs can be employed to store, retrieve, and manage efficiently working capital assets and accounts payables. Excel and other spreadsheet programs allow managers to construct financial statements and engage in ratio analysis to evaluate performance. They allow managers to observe the changes that might occur to financial statements in "what if" situations—that is, managers can evaluate the changes in financial statements by assuming different investment and forecasting strategies. There are data banks that allow access to an enormous amount of financial data for comparing performances. And, finally, a number of programs supply the mathematical tools required to manipulate data, make forecasts, and develop emulation models. When used in tandem, these financial software systems can improve the efficiency of employees and an organization. In summary, software packages are great tools for analyzing and controlling operations but are not a substitute for the judgment required to make final investment decisions.

THE INTERNET AND SOCIAL MEDIA

The Internet has transformed the business landscape of the past several decades, creating an environment with instant access to consumers. Through the Internet, firms can improve their productivity and lower their costs while providing customers with greater information on products at lower costs. By expanding the demand for products, increasing accessibility, and providing alternative purchasing options, the Internet has become a giant directory covering all types of information that help consumers be informed about products and businesses. The Internet facilitates the process of shopping, delivery, and payments efficiently. Some research shows that it may improve the "consume surplus," a value-added feature of online shopping. Yet, the value-added feature is not universal (not true in every case) across all platforms of online shopping. Disadvantages include possible loss of private data and personal information hacking.

• *THE RISE OF COST-EFFICIENCIES*

There are many opportunities for cost reductions on the Internet, but entry into the Internet system is not without cost. Once a firm decides to operate on the Internet, it is faced with several challenges. One is to learn a new programming languages, such as **HTML (hypertext markup language)**, the language used to code webpage documents, or **Java**, a programming language developed by Sun Microsystems for the Internet. These languages are needed to set up a Communication Gateway Interface (CGI) program to collect, store, transmit, and receive data. A webmaster will probably be needed to handle day-to-day operations on the Internet, deal with technical problems, respond to a deluge of email inquiries, and keep the system working smoothly. Some people will have to be hired to constantly update the company information. Obviously, the design of a **website** is important and calls for investments in sophisticated hardware and software.

Among the benefits for having an Internet presence are:

1. Firms are able to market products at lower costs and save on costly television and newspaper advertising.

2. Search time for relevant information important to the firm shrinks significantly. At the same time, labor costs previously required to gather this information are reduced considerably.

3. The use of email may reduce mailing costs and bring customers into closer communication with the firm, which was not feasible prior to the Internet.

Corporations are constantly uncovering new cost-cutting Internet applications. For example, stockholders are now assigned PIN numbers to be used to vote on issues and elections via the Internet. Also, many corporations are choosing to send out quarterly and annual financial reports by requests only. Corporations are relying on stockholders to use the Internet as a resource to access the financial information, which, in turn, provides substantial savings for firms in handling, mailing, and printing costs.

According to the United States Census Bureau, the amount of online transactions has reached over $4 trillion, with the amount of global online transactions topping $10 million annually. This surge in e-commerce and online transactions has led to a correlating surge in job growth. The consulting firm McKinsey & Company reported that the Internet has created 2.6 jobs for every job it has eliminated. McKinsey & Company also reported that between 1998 and 2008, the number of IT jobs in the United States grew by 26%, which is four times faster than U.S. employment as a whole. Forecasted job growth in the IT field is expected to grow by another 22% by 2018 and represent 20% of the economy.

With the Internet's role in business increasing exponentially, managers must develop innovative approaches in order to take advantage of the Internet's efficiency. The Internet offers this opportunity to expand sales and tap mass markets on a global basis at much lower costs. In other words, emphasis has shifted from the industrial age to the information and distribution age.

Simple tools such as an **email** system and social media have opened new avenues of communication and interaction between buyers and sellers. There are internal and external benefits of the Internet. Internally, a firm's employees are provided with more effective research and marketing tools for selling products. The time and cost spent in generating sales is reduced because more information is available to assess market demand potentials. Managerial information on the Internet adds a new dimension on the capital budgeting decision-making process.

If a firm has not already made its presence on the Internet, it is at a huge disadvantage to its competitors who reach the ever-growing number of people who choose to make transactions on this medium. Retail stores are now getting a large portion of their sales from online transactions, while many brick-and-mortar storefronts are experiencing laggings sales due to their online competitors. The Internet has become a partial substitute for catalog sales, and it increases the motivation of users to buy because more information on pricing and product descriptions, as well as customer-generated product reviews, is supplied by this system.

Just think of the impact the Internet will have on outdoor advertising and telephone marketing! There is likely to be a continuing diminution in cost allocated to 1-800 phone numbers and a rise in the interaction between well-trained competent employees and customers via the Internet. How many times have we gone to department stores to buy an electronic product, only to find the salesperson ill equipped to answer our questions and unable to supply the information we need to make a purchase or make an intelligent selection among several choices of products? The Internet brings well-informed employees closer to the customer so they can be convinced of the merits of a product. This medium is becoming more personal in approach, as many products are sold by a live presentation, which permits the exchange of information, along with questions and answers, through email.

In addition to the many ways the Internet allows consumers, corporations, and retailers to communicate with each other, another development is emerging that enables corporations to share and exchange information via the Internet. The goal is to achieve better cost-effective business-to-business relationships.

• *BLOOMBERG TERMINALS*

Technological advancement has been remarkable in the past quarter of a century and has been reflected throughout the finance industry. One such example is the rise of Bloomberg L.P. and its status in the finance industry as the preeminent trading platform, providing market data, news, and analysis in real time through its Bloomberg Terminals. They have become integral not only for the major financial organizations, but also for businesses for the purposes of market access and transparency, trade execution, and research. Although Bloomberg Terminals are not cheap, with one terminal subscription costing approximately $20,000 per year, their value to an organization can far surpass their costs.

• *YAHOO! FINANCE AND STOCK SCREENERS*

The businesses and individual investors who may not find value in the purchase of a Bloomberg terminal do have other options. One of the prominent websites used for researching companies and easily accessing important stock information and historical performance is Yahoo! Finance. This website provides a range of information from earnings before interest depreciation and taxes (EBITDA) margins to corporate performance and important employees within the organization. When used in conjunction with a stock screener, such as FINVIZ, it can provide an investor with substantial information to make investment decisions and acquire insight into the market on a continuous basis.

• *SOCIAL MEDIA*

The rise of social media over the past decade has been astronomical. Facebook, Twitter, LinkedIn, Instagram, and other social media platforms have become so ingrained into the fabric of society like no other product ever has before. Aided by the smartphone, social media connects people around the globe and has contributed to the globalized economy of today. Users are able to reach markets, consumers, and other users with relative ease and at low costs. Integral to the success of companies is to have an active social media presence on platforms such as Twitter, Facebook, and LinkedIn. These provide potential customers with an opportunity to examine the company, products, services, and other necessary information, including the parties with whom they do business. It is an opportunity to connect and forge a relationship that goes beyond the good or service offers. However, the benefits are not only external; having an active social media presence can cultivate employees' enthusiasm to see their business succeed by highlighting employees, business practices, and philanthropic events sponsored by the firm.

Social media and the smartphone made it possible for consumers to personalize their financial profiles. With a plethora of information available at the click of a button, consumers are as knowledgeable as ever (granted, they can disseminate accurate and inaccurate information). This has led to increased autonomy in personal finance. For example, on Twitter, users can follow well-known traders who share their opinions on stocks, trading strategies, and the market in general. On Instagram, if users want to follow the market, but may not have the time to do so, they can follow accounts that provide quick, easy-to-read graphs on stock performance, market data, and market projections through personal accounts. LinkedIn is the preeminent professional networking platform for business professionals. It connects business professionals with each other as they build their professional network, while also allowing employers to have a presence and post job openings through their platform. Many employers use LinkedIn as a way to connect with potential candidates and conduct due diligence on applicants.

Personal finance has become increasingly specialized for the consumer and more entrepreneurial than ever before. With the rise of apps making personal finances, budgeting, and saving much easier, consumers are taking control over their finances like never before. Robinhood is one of the most popular apps, marketed mainly toward young investors who want to try their hand at investing for the first time. Robinhood provides a platform for investors to invest in stocks on the New York Stock Exchange without any fees. With an award-winning interface, Robinhood gives users access to historical stock performance through easy-to-read graphs, important ratios, and recent news and conversations regarding stocks that are of interest to them. Mint, a web-based personal financial management service, integrates all bank accounts and bills and provides an easy way to manage money and set budgets. Mint even provides suggestions on how to stay on budget or curb spending habits that are preventing savings. Another popular app is Acorns, which rounds up every purchase on a debit or credit card linked to your account to the nearest dollar and invests that spare change into personalized mutual funds that match your investment strategies and goals.

• *THE RISE OF CRYPTOCURRENCY*

One of the hottest topics being discussed in financial circles over the past decade has been the astronomical rise of Bitcoin, the popularized form of cryptocurrency. Utilizing blockchain technology (sometimes abbreviated as BCT) to encrypt and encode virtual currencies, Bitcoin not only prevents hacking but also almost entirely eliminates the ability to trace the external factors. The demand and popularity of bitcoin rose out of the financial crisis as distrust in the market and government rose. The belief behind bitcoin is a completely virtual monetary system, transcending currencies and countries, which self-regulates and eliminates the current financial systems. This radical idea birthed the notion of cryptocurrency and is the foundation of Bitcoin today.

While the original purpose and foundation of Bitcoin is admirable, its use hasn't always been as positive. With Bitcoin's birth shrouded in secrecy, with questions over who created it, the anonymity of users trading Bitcoin through blockchain technology has intrigued those trying to hide their identity. Many terrorist organizations use Bitcoin to move money around and pay for illegal substances and weaponry without leaving a money trail. An online black market known as the Silk Road rose to prominence through its use of Bitcoin. This has led many to be suspicious of Bitcoin and its uses. Recently, there has been efforts to have Bitcoin regulated by the federal government—a move that may help or hinder the very purpose of a digital currency. Even so, as many prominent investors and bank executives denounce its value, Bitcoin has continued to rise. Many financial experts question the value of Bitcoin, reporting that their trading modes and platforms will not change because of the new cryptocurrencies. Some economists and investors have stated that Bitcoin and other cryptocurrencies will be the next bubble, as they find it difficult to quantify its price relative to its worth and believe consumer and market sentiment have been driving the price to unsustainable levels. By December 2017, Bitcoin had risen to over $15,000/Bitcoin, with a huge momentum, especially through trading a new Bitcoin Exchange Traded Funds. Yet, the daily volatility of Bitcoin is extremely high. NASDAQ recently confirmed that they will begin a Bitcoin futures index as soon as 2018. Many argue that the value of Bitcoin is not in the Bitcoin itself, but in the blockchain technology. In fact, blockchain technology is used in banking today, with the best example being Venmo, a peer-to-peer payment app used mainly on mobile devices. Through the use of blockchain technology, the sensitive banking information is encrypted and separate from the information available to all users. In our opinion, the use of blockchain technology in businesses is endless and will probably have greater potential and prominence in the coming years. Students of finance and technology are encouraged to remain updated on the evolution of this technology.

• MORE TO COME

People are now connected to each other very closely, with a huge amount of information available at the palm of their hands (i.e., mobile phones). Organizations have access to information regarding their consumer base like never before. But the question is, where do we go from here? The answer seems to lead toward the intersection and integration of the world around us and the world on the Internet. "Augmented" and "virtual reality" are the buzzwords, as we experience and see things that have either artificially been created or have been captured to present to us as reality. Facebook, for instance, has revealed its future vision for the company—namely, implementing augmented virtual reality into everyday life. While this may be disturbing for some, and reminiscent of many sci-fi films, the business opportunity is endless. As technology continues to improve, businesses will find new ways to cut costs and increase efficiency. It is important for managers to be open-minded to new technology and find ways to integrate it into their organizations. This is also a subject for finance and technology students to follow and remain up to date on.

YOU SHOULD REMEMBER

The Internet and social media have dramatically changed the marketing industry for business while completely rethinking the shopping experience for consumers. The ease of access to vast amounts of information via the Internet has created much more informed consumers. Through sites such as StockWiz and Yahoo! Finance, coupled with the rise of personal investment platforms such as Robinhood, investors are taking more control of their personal finances. The future of the Internet and the incredible amount of personal information available via the Internet are not completely predictable, but we can imagine an intersection of reality and the Internet and the use of just-in-time information in most daily decisions far beyond finance and investments decisions.

• *SELECTED FINANCIAL WEBSITES*

Below are 20 popular finance- and investment-related websites that every finance student and finance practitioner should be familiar with so they can use them in their daily work and research:

1	Yahoo! Finance	finance.yahoo.com
2	Bloomberg	www.bloomberg.com
3	Wall Street Journal	www.wsj.com
4	Motley Fool	www.fool.com
5	Standard & Poor's Capital IQ	www.capitaliq.com
6	Moody's	www.moodys.com
7	FinViz Stock Screener	finviz.com
8	Market Watch	www.marketwatch.com
9	Investopedia	www.investopedia.com
10	Trading Charts	tradingcharts.com
11	Internal Revenue Service	www.irs.gov
12	E*Trade	www.etrade.com
13	Seeking Alpha	seekingalpha.com
14	Forbes	forbes.com
15	TurboTax	turbotax.intuit.com
16	Quicken	www.quicken.com
17	Mint	www.mint.com
18	Acorns	www.acorns.com
19	Oanda Currency Convertor	www.oanda.com/currency/converter
20	Reuters	www.reuters.com

KNOW THE CONCEPTS

DO YOU KNOW THE BASICS?

1. Sarah is a finance manager and wants to know the impact that increased sales of one product has on the bottom line. What kind of financial software would be most beneficial for this, and why?

2. When contemplating the implementation of a new financial management system, what are some concerns that managers should have?

3. The smartphone and the Internet have changed the way we interact with the world. What impact has it had on the finance industry, from a personal finance perspective?

4. Describe issues with Bitcoin.

TERMS FOR STUDY

Bloomberg Systems
Capital IQ
Cryptocurrency
Data mining
Eviews system
Financial data banks

Hypertext markup language (HTML)
SAS system
Stock screeners
Spreadsheet programs
SPSS system

ANSWERS

KNOW THE CONCEPTS

1. Sarah should use spreadsheet analysis and modeling. With a fully functioning dynamic model, Sarah would easily be able to see the impact it would have on revenues, profit margins, and net income through the use of "what if" functions and scenarios.

2. Managers must think of how to effectively implement a new financial management system into their current work practices in an efficient way and evaluate the effect it will have on the business. It is also important to forecast the potential for future development and changes in business practices and figure out if the new system will have the ability to effectively adapt.

3. The rise of personal finance apps, such as Robinhood and Acorns, has led to increased investment in the market by millennials. Consumers are taking greater control of their finances through apps that make it easier to keep track of money and invest.

4. Bitcoin seems to be overpriced, relative to the intrinsic value, and the concern is that its value will collapse. Through its anonymity, Bitcoin has attracted users that are engaging in illegal activity. Since Bitcoin is not regulated, it allows that activity to take place.

APPENDIX
TABLES

Table A–1   Future Value Interest Factor

Period	1%	2%	3%	4%	5%	6%	7%	8%	9%	10%
1	1.010	1.020	1.030	1.040	1.050	1.060	1.070	1.080	1.090	1.100
2	1.020	1.040	1.061	1.082	1.102	1.124	1.145	1.166	1.188	1.210
3	1.030	1.061	1.093	1.125	1.158	1.191	1.225	1.260	1.295	1.331
4	1.041	1.082	1.126	1.170	1.216	1.262	1.311	1.360	1.412	1.464
5	1.051	1.104	1.159	1.217	1.276	1.338	1.403	1.469	1.539	1.611
6	1.062	1.126	1.194	1.265	1.340	1.419	1.501	1.587	1.677	1.772
7	1.072	1.149	1.230	1.316	1.407	1.504	1.606	1.714	1.828	1.949
8	1.083	1.172	1.267	1.369	1.477	1.594	1.718	1.851	1.993	2.144
9	1.094	1.195	1.305	1.423	1.551	1.689	1.838	1.999	2.172	2.358
10	1.105	1.219	1.344	1.480	1.629	1.791	1.967	2.159	2.367	2.594
11	1.116	1.243	1.384	1.539	1.710	1.898	2.105	2.332	2.580	2.853
12	1.127	1.268	1.426	1.601	1.796	2.012	2.252	2.518	2.813	3.138
13	1.138	1.294	1.469	1.665	1.886	2.133	2.410	2.720	3.066	3.452
14	1.149	1.319	1.513	1.732	1.980	2.261	2.579	2.937	3.342	3.797
15	1.161	1.346	1.558	1.801	2.079	2.397	2.759	3.172	3.642	4.177
16	1.173	1.373	1.605	1.873	2.183	2.540	2.952	3.426	3.970	4.595
17	1.184	1.400	1.653	1.948	2.292	2.693	3.159	3.700	4.328	5.054
18	1.196	1.428	1.702	2.026	2.407	2.854	3.380	3.996	4.717	5.560
19	1.208	1.457	1.753	2.107	2.527	3.026	3.616	4.316	5.142	6.116
20	1.220	1.486	1.806	2.191	2.653	3.207	3.870	4.661	5.604	6.727
21	1.232	1.516	1.860	2.279	2.786	3.399	4.140	5.034	6.109	7.400
22	1.245	1.546	1.916	2.370	2.925	3.603	4.430	5.436	6.658	8.140
23	1.257	1.577	1.974	2.465	3.071	3.820	4.740	5.871	7.258	8.954
24	1.270	1.608	2.033	2.563	3.225	4.049	5.072	6.341	7.911	9.850
25	1.282	1.641	2.094	2.666	3.386	4.292	5.427	6.848	8.623	10.834
30	1.348	1.811	2.427	3.243	4.322	5.743	7.612	10.062	13.267	17.449
40	1.489	2.208	3.262	4.801	7.040	10.285	14.974	21.724	31.408	45.258
50	1.645	2.691	4.384	7.106	11.467	18.419	29.456	46.900	74.354	117.386

Period	11%	12%	13%	14%	15%	16%	17%	18%	19%	20%
1	1.110	1.120	1.130	1.140	1.150	1.160	1.170	1.180	1.190	1.200
2	1.232	1.254	1.277	1.300	1.322	1.346	1.369	1.392	1.416	1.440
3	1.368	1.405	1.443	1.482	1.521	1.561	1.602	1.643	1.685	1.728
4	1.518	1.574	1.630	1.689	1.749	1.811	1.874	1.939	2.005	2.074
5	1.685	1.762	1.842	1.925	2.011	2.100	2.192	2.288	2.386	2.488
6	1.870	1.974	2.082	2.195	2.313	2.436	2.565	2.700	2.840	2.986
7	2.076	2.211	2.353	2.502	2.660	2.826	3.001	3.185	3.379	3.583
8	2.305	2.476	2.658	2.853	3.059	3.278	3.511	3.759	4.021	4.300
9	2.558	2.773	3.004	3.252	3.518	3.803	4.108	4.435	4.785	5.160
10	2.839	3.106	3.395	3.707	4.046	4.411	4.807	5.234	5.695	6.192
11	3.152	3.479	3.836	4.226	4.652	5.117	5.624	6.176	6.777	7.430
12	3.498	3.896	4.334	4.818	5.350	5.936	6.580	7.288	8.064	8.916
13	3.883	4.363	4.898	5.492	6.153	6.886	7.699	8.599	9.596	10.699
14	4.310	4.887	5.535	6.261	7.076	7.987	9.007	10.147	11.420	12.839
15	4.785	5.474	6.254	7.138	8.137	9.265	10.539	11.974	13.589	15.407
16	5.311	6.130	7.067	8.137	9.358	10.748	12.330	14.129	16.171	18.488
17	5.895	6.866	7.986	9.276	10.761	12.468	14.426	16.672	19.244	22.186
18	6.543	7.690	9.024	10.575	12.375	14.462	16.879	19.673	22.900	26.623
19	7.263	8.613	10.197	12.055	14.232	16.776	19.748	23.214	27.251	31.948
20	8.062	9.646	11.523	13.743	16.366	19.461	23.105	27.393	32.429	38.337
21	8.949	10.804	13.021	15.667	18.821	22.574	27.033	32.323	38.591	46.005
22	9.933	12.100	14.713	17.861	21.644	26.186	31.629	38.141	45.923	55.205
23	11.026	13.552	16.626	20.361	24.891	30.376	37.005	45.007	54.648	66.247
24	12.239	15.178	18.788	23.212	28.625	35.236	43.296	53.108	65.031	79.496
25	13.585	17.000	21.230	26.416	32.918	40.874	50.656	62.667	77.387	95.395
30	22.892	29.960	39.115	50.949	66.210	85.849	111.061	143.367	184.672	237.373
40	64.999	93.049	132.776	188.876	267.856	378.715	533.846	750.353	1051.642	1469.740
50	184.559	288.996	450.711	700.197	1083.619	1670.669	2566.080	3927.189	5988.730	9100.191

Period	21%	22%	23%	24%	25%	26%	27%	28%	29%	30%
1	1.210	1.220	1.230	1.240	1.250	1.260	1.270	1.280	1.290	1.300
2	1.464	1.488	1.513	1.538	1.562	1.588	1.613	1.638	1.664	1.690
3	1.772	1.816	1.861	1.907	1.953	2.000	2.048	2.097	2.147	2.197
4	2.144	2.215	2.289	2.364	2.441	2.520	2.601	2.684	2.769	2.856
5	2.594	2.703	2.815	2.932	3.052	3.176	3.304	3.436	3.572	3.713
6	3.138	3.297	3.463	3.635	3.815	4.001	4.196	4.398	4.608	4.827
7	3.797	4.023	4.259	4.508	4.768	5.042	5.329	5.629	5.945	6.275
8	4.595	4.908	5.239	5.589	5.960	6.353	6.767	7.206	7.669	8.157
9	5.560	5.987	6.444	6.931	7.451	8.004	8.595	9.223	9.893	10.604
10	6.727	7.305	7.926	8.594	9.313	10.086	10.915	11.806	12.761	13.786
11	8.140	8.912	9.749	10.657	11.642	12.708	13.862	15.112	16.462	17.921
12	9.850	10.872	11.991	13.215	14.552	16.012	17.605	19.343	21.236	23.298
13	11.918	13.264	14.749	16.386	18.190	20.175	22.359	24.759	27.395	30.287
14	14.421	16.182	18.141	20.319	22.737	25.420	28.395	31.691	35.339	39.373
15	17.449	19.742	22.314	25.195	28.422	32.030	36.062	40.565	45.587	51.185
16	21.113	24.085	27.446	31.242	35.527	40.357	45.799	51.923	58.808	66.541
17	25.547	29.384	33.758	38.740	44.409	50.850	58.165	66.461	75.862	86.503
18	30.912	35.848	41.523	48.038	55.511	64.071	73.869	85.070	97.862	112.454
19	37.404	43.735	51.073	59.567	69.389	80.730	93.813	108.890	126.242	146.190
20	45.258	53.357	62.820	73.863	86.736	101.720	119.143	139.379	162.852	190.047
21	54.762	65.095	77.268	91.591	108.420	128.167	151.312	178.405	210.079	247.061
22	66.262	79.416	95.040	113.572	135.525	161.490	192.165	228.358	271.002	321.178
23	80.178	96.887	116.899	140.829	169.407	203.477	244.050	292.298	349.592	417.531
24	97.015	118.203	143.786	174.628	211.758	256.381	309.943	374.141	450.974	542.791
25	117.388	144.207	176.857	216.539	264.698	323.040	393.628	478.901	581.756	705.627
30	304.471	389.748	497.904	634.810	807.793	1025.904	1300.477	1645.488	2078.208	2619.936
40	2048.309	2846.941	3946.340	5455.797	7523.156	10346.879	14195.051	19426.418	26520.723	36117.754
50	13779.844	20795.680	31278.301	46889.207	70064.812	104354.562	154942.687	229345.875	338440.000	497910.125

Period	31%	32%	33%	34%	35%	36%	37%	38%	39%	40%
1	1.310	1.320	1.330	1.340	1.350	1.360	1.370	1.380	1.390	1.400
2	1.716	1.742	1.769	1.796	1.822	1.850	1.877	1.904	1.932	1.960
3	2.248	2.300	2.353	2.406	2.460	2.515	2.571	2.628	2.686	2.744
4	2.945	3.036	3.129	3.224	3.321	3.421	3.523	3.627	3.733	3.842
5	3.858	4.007	4.162	4.320	4.484	4.653	4.826	5.005	5.189	5.378
6	5.054	5.290	5.535	5.789	6.053	6.328	6.612	6.907	7.213	7.530
7	6.621	6.983	7.361	7.758	8.172	8.605	9.058	9.531	10.025	10.541
8	8.673	9.217	9.791	10.395	11.032	11.703	12.410	13.153	13.935	14.758
9	11.362	12.166	13.022	13.930	14.894	15.917	17.001	18.151	19.370	20.661
10	14.884	16.060	17.319	18.666	20.106	21.646	23.292	25.049	26.924	28.925
11	19.498	21.199	23.034	25.012	27.144	29.439	31.910	34.567	37.425	40.495
12	25.542	27.982	30.635	33.516	36.644	40.037	43.716	47.703	52.020	56.694
13	33.460	36.937	40.745	44.912	49.469	54.451	59.892	65.830	72.308	79.371
14	43.832	48.756	54.190	60.181	66.784	74.053	82.051	90.845	100.509	111.119
15	57.420	64.358	72.073	80.643	90.158	100.712	112.410	125.366	139.707	155.567
16	75.220	84.953	95.857	108.061	121.713	136.968	154.002	173.005	194.192	217.793
17	98.539	112.138	127.490	144.802	164.312	186.277	210.983	238.747	269.927	304.911
18	129.086	148.022	169.561	194.035	221.822	253.337	289.046	329.471	375.198	426.875
19	169.102	195.389	225.517	260.006	299.459	344.537	395.993	454.669	521.525	597.625
20	221.523	257.913	299.937	348.408	404.270	468.571	542.511	627.443	724.919	836.674
21	290.196	340.446	398.916	466.867	545.764	637.256	743.240	865.871	1007.637	1171.343
22	380.156	449.388	530.558	625.601	736.781	866.668	1018.238	1194.900	1400.615	1639.878
23	498.004	593.192	705.642	838.305	994.653	1178.668	1394.986	1648.961	1946.854	2295.829
24	652.385	783.013	938.504	1123.328	1342.781	1602.988	1911.129	2275.564	2706.125	3214.158
25	854.623	1033.577	1248.210	1505.258	1812.754	2180.063	2618.245	3140.275	3761.511	4499.816
30	3297.081	4142.008	5194.516	6503.285	8128.426	10142.914	12636.086	15716.703	19517.969	24201.043
40	49072.621	66519.313	89962.188	121388.437	163433.875	219558.625	294317.937	393684.687	525508.312	700022.688

Table A–2   Future Value Interest Factor Annuity

Period	1%	2%	3%	4%	5%	6%	7%	8%	9%	10%
1	1.000	1.000	1.000	1.000	1.000	1.000	1.000	1.000	1.000	1.000
2	2.010	2.020	2.030	2.040	2.050	2.060	2.070	2.080	2.090	2.100
3	3.030	3.060	3.091	3.122	3.152	3.184	3.215	3.246	3.278	3.310
4	4.060	4.122	4.184	4.246	4.310	4.375	4.440	4.506	4.573	4.641
5	5.101	5.204	5.309	5.416	5.526	5.637	5.751	5.867	5.985	6.105
6	6.152	6.308	6.468	6.633	6.802	6.975	7.153	7.336	7.523	7.716
7	7.214	7.434	7.662	7.898	8.142	8.394	8.654	8.923	9.200	9.487
8	8.286	8.583	8.892	9.214	9.549	9.897	10.260	10.637	11.028	11.436
9	9.368	9.755	10.159	10.583	11.027	11.491	11.978	12.488	13.021	13.579
10	10.462	10.950	11.464	12.006	12.578	13.181	13.816	14.487	15.193	15.937
11	11.567	12.169	12.808	13.486	14.207	14.972	15.784	16.645	17.560	18.531
12	12.682	13.412	14.192	15.026	15.917	16.870	17.888	18.977	20.141	21.384
13	13.809	14.680	15.618	16.627	17.713	18.882	20.141	21.495	22.953	24.523
14	14.947	15.974	17.086	18.292	19.598	21.015	22.550	24.215	26.019	27.975
15	16.097	17.293	18.599	20.023	21.578	23.276	25.129	27.152	29.361	31.772
16	17.258	18.639	20.157	21.824	23.657	25.672	27.888	30.324	33.003	35.949
17	18.430	20.012	21.761	23.697	25.840	28.213	30.840	33.750	36.973	40.544
18	19.614	21.412	23.414	25.645	28.132	30.905	33.999	37.450	41.301	45.599
19	20.811	22.840	25.117	27.671	30.539	33.760	37.379	41.446	46.018	51.158
20	22.019	24.297	26.870	29.778	33.066	36.785	40.995	45.762	51.159	57.274
21	23.239	25.783	28.676	31.969	35.719	39.992	44.865	50.422	56.764	64.002
22	24.471	27.299	30.536	34.248	38.505	43.392	49.005	55.456	62.872	71.402
23	25.716	28.845	32.452	36.618	41.430	46.995	53.435	60.893	69.531	79.542
24	26.973	30.421	34.426	39.082	44.501	50.815	58.176	66.764	76.789	88.496
25	28.243	32.030	36.459	41.645	47.726	54.864	63.248	73.105	84.699	98.346
30	34.784	40.567	47.575	56.084	66.438	79.057	94.459	113.282	136.305	164.491
40	48.885	60.401	75.400	95.024	120.797	154.758	199.630	259.052	337.872	442.580
50	64.461	84.577	112.794	152.664	209.341	290.325	406.516	573.756	815.051	1163.865

Period	11%	12%	13%	14%	15%	16%	17%	18%	19%	20%
1	1.000	1.000	1.000	1.000	1.000	1.000	1.000	1.000	1.000	1.000
2	2.110	2.120	2.130	2.140	2.150	2.160	2.170	2.180	2.190	2.200
3	3.342	3.374	3.407	3.440	3.472	3.506	3.539	3.572	3.606	3.640
4	4.710	4.779	4.850	4.921	4.993	5.066	5.141	5.215	5.291	5.368
5	6.228	6.353	6.480	6.610	6.742	6.877	7.014	7.154	7.297	7.442
6	7.913	8.115	8.323	8.535	8.754	8.977	9.207	9.442	9.683	9.930
7	9.783	10.089	10.405	10.730	11.067	11.414	11.772	12.141	12.523	12.916
8	11.859	12.300	12.757	13.233	13.727	14.240	14.773	15.327	15.902	16.499
9	14.164	14.776	15.416	16.085	16.786	17.518	18.285	19.086	19.923	20.799
10	16.722	17.549	18.420	19.337	20.304	21.321	22.393	23.521	24.709	25.959
11	19.561	20.655	21.814	23.044	24.349	25.733	27.200	28.755	30.403	32.150
12	22.713	24.133	25.650	27.271	29.001	30.850	32.824	34.931	37.180	39.580
13	26.211	28.029	29.984	32.088	34.352	36.786	39.404	42.218	45.244	48.496
14	30.095	32.392	34.882	37.581	40.504	43.672	47.102	50.818	54.841	59.196
15	34.405	37.280	40.417	43.842	47.580	51.659	56.109	60.965	66.260	72.035
16	39.190	42.753	46.671	50.980	55.717	60.925	66.648	72.938	79.850	87.442
17	44.500	48.883	53.738	59.117	65.075	71.673	78.978	87.067	96.021	105.930
18	50.396	55.749	61.724	68.393	75.836	84.140	93.404	103.739	115.265	128.116
19	56.939	63.439	70.748	78.968	88.211	98.603	110.283	123.412	138.165	154.739
20	64.202	72.052	80.946	91.024	102.443	115.379	130.031	146.626	165.417	186.687
21	72.264	81.698	92.468	104.767	118.809	134.840	153.136	174.019	197.846	225.024
22	81.213	92.502	105.489	120.434	137.630	157.414	180.169	206.342	236.436	271.028
23	91.147	104.602	120.203	138.295	159.274	183.600	211.798	244.483	282.359	326.234
24	102.173	118.154	136.829	158.656	184.166	213.976	248.803	289.490	337.007	392.480
25	114.412	133.333	155.616	181.867	212.790	249.212	292.099	342.598	402.038	471.976
30	199.018	241.330	293.192	356.778	434.738	530.306	647.423	790.932	966.698	1181.865
40	581.812	767.080	1013.667	1341.979	1779.048	2360.724	3134.412	4163.094	5529.711	7343.715
50	1668.723	2399.975	3459.344	4994.301	7217.488	10435.449	15088.805	21812.273	31514.492	45496.094

Period	21%	22%	23%	24%	25%	26%	27%	28%	29%	30%
1	1.000	1.000	1.000	1.000	1.000	1.000	1.000	1.000	1.000	1.000
2	2.210	2.220	2.230	2.240	2.250	2.260	2.270	2.280	2.290	2.300
3	3.674	3.708	3.743	3.778	3.813	3.848	3.883	3.918	3.954	3.990
4	5.446	5.524	5.604	5.684	5.766	5.848	5.931	6.016	6.101	6.187
5	7.589	7.740	7.893	8.048	8.207	8.368	8.533	8.700	8.870	9.043
6	10.183	10.442	10.708	10.980	11.259	11.544	11.837	12.136	12.442	12.756
7	13.321	13.740	14.171	14.615	15.073	15.546	16.032	16.534	17.051	17.583
8	17.119	17.762	18.430	19.123	19.842	20.588	21.361	22.163	22.995	23.858
9	21.714	22.670	23.669	24.712	25.802	26.940	28.129	29.369	30.664	32.015
10	27.274	28.657	30.113	31.643	33.253	34.945	36.723	38.592	40.556	42.619
11	34.001	35.962	38.039	40.238	42.566	45.030	47.639	50.398	53.318	56.405
12	42.141	44.873	47.787	50.895	54.208	57.738	61.501	65.510	69.780	74.326
13	51.991	55.745	59.778	64.109	68.760	73.750	79.106	84.853	91.016	97.624
14	63.909	69.009	74.528	80.496	86.949	93.925	101.465	109.611	118.411	127.912
15	78.330	85.191	92.669	100.815	109.687	119.346	129.860	141.302	153.750	167.285
16	95.779	104.933	114.983	126.010	138.109	151.375	165.922	181.867	199.337	218.470
17	116.892	129.019	142.428	157.252	173.636	191.733	211.721	233.790	258.145	285.011
18	142.439	158.403	176.187	195.993	218.045	242.583	269.885	300.250	334.006	371.514
19	173.351	194.251	217.710	244.031	273.556	306.654	343.754	385.321	431.868	483.968
20	210.755	237.986	268.783	303.598	342.945	387.384	437.568	494.210	558.110	630.157
21	256.013	291.343	331.603	377.461	429.681	489.104	556.710	633.589	720.962	820.204
22	310.775	356.438	408.871	469.052	538.101	617.270	708.022	811.993	931.040	1067.265
23	377.038	435.854	503.911	582.624	673.626	778.760	900.187	1040.351	1202.042	1388.443
24	457.215	532.741	620.810	723.453	843.032	982.237	1144.237	1332.649	1551.634	1805.975
25	554.230	650.944	764.596	898.082	1054.791	1238.617	1454.180	1706.790	2002.608	2348.765
30	1445.111	1767.044	2160.459	2640.881	3227.172	3941.953	4812.891	5873.172	7162.785	8729.805
40	9749.141	12936.141	17153.691	22728.367	30088.621	39791.957	52570.707	69376.562	91447.375	120389.375

Period	31%	32%	33%	34%	35%	36%	37%	38%	39%	40%
1	1.000	1.000	1.000	1.000	1.000	1.000	1.000	1.000	1.000	1.000
2	2.310	2.320	2.330	2.340	2.350	2.360	2.370	2.380	2.390	2.400
3	4.026	4.062	4.099	4.136	4.172	4.210	4.247	4.284	4.322	4.360
4	6.274	6.362	6.452	6.542	6.633	6.725	6.818	6.912	7.008	7.104
5	9.219	9.398	9.581	9.766	9.954	10.146	10.341	10.539	10.741	10.946
6	13.077	13.406	13.742	14.086	14.438	14.799	15.167	15.544	15.930	16.324
7	18.131	18.696	19.277	19.876	20.492	21.126	21.779	22.451	23.142	23.853
8	24.752	25.678	26.638	27.633	28.664	29.732	30.837	31.982	33.167	34.395
9	33.425	34.895	36.429	38.028	39.696	41.435	43.247	45.135	47.103	49.152
10	44.786	47.062	49.451	51.958	54.590	57.351	60.248	63.287	66.473	69.813
11	59.670	63.121	66.769	70.624	74.696	78.998	83.540	88.335	93.397	98.739
12	79.167	84.320	89.803	95.636	101.840	108.437	115.450	122.903	130.822	139.234
13	104.709	112.302	120.438	129.152	138.484	148.474	159.166	170.606	182.842	195.928
14	138.169	149.239	161.183	174.063	187.953	202.925	219.058	236.435	255.151	275.299
15	182.001	197.996	215.373	234.245	254.737	276.978	301.109	327.281	355.659	386.418
16	239.421	262.354	287.446	314.888	344.895	377.690	413.520	452.647	495.366	541.985
17	314.642	347.307	383.303	422.949	466.608	514.658	567.504	625.652	689.485	759.778
18	413.180	459.445	510.792	567.751	630.920	700.935	778.504	864.399	959.485	1064.689
19	542.266	607.467	680.354	761.786	852.741	954.271	1067.551	1193.870	1334.683	1491.563
20	711.368	802.856	905.870	1021.792	1152.200	1298.809	1463.544	1648.539	1856.208	2089.188
21	932.891	1060.769	1205.807	1370.201	1556.470	1767.380	2006.055	2275.982	2581.128	2925.862
22	1223.087	1401.215	1604.724	1837.068	2102.234	2404.636	2749.294	3141.852	3588.765	4097.203
23	1603.243	1850.603	2135.282	2462.669	2839.014	3271.304	3767.532	4336.750	4989.379	5737.078
24	2101.247	2443.795	2840.924	3300.974	3833.667	4449.969	5162.516	5985.711	6936.230	8032.906
25	2753.631	3226.808	3779.428	4424.301	5176.445	6052.957	7073.645	8261.273	9642.352	11247.062
30	10632.543	12940.672	15737.945	19124.434	23221.258	28172.016	34148.906	41357.227	50043.625	60500.207

Table A–3   Present Value Interest Factor

Period	1%	2%	3%	4%	5%	6%	7%	8%	9%	10%
1	.990	.980	.971	.962	.952	.943	.935	.926	.917	.909
2	.980	.961	.943	.925	.907	.890	.873	.857	.842	.826
3	.971	.942	.915	.889	.864	.840	.816	.794	.772	.751
4	.961	.924	.888	.855	.823	.792	.763	.735	.708	.683
5	.951	.906	.863	.822	.784	.747	.713	.681	.650	.621
6	.942	.888	.837	.790	.746	.705	.666	.630	.596	.564
7	.933	.871	.813	.760	.711	.665	.623	.583	.547	.513
8	.923	.853	.789	.731	.677	.627	.582	.540	.502	.467
9	.914	.837	.766	.703	.645	.592	.544	.500	.460	.424
10	.905	.820	.744	.676	.614	.558	.508	.463	.422	.386
11	.896	.804	.722	.650	.585	.527	.475	.429	.388	.350
12	.887	.789	.701	.625	.557	.497	.444	.397	.356	.319
13	.879	.773	.681	.601	.530	.469	.415	.368	.326	.290
14	.870	.758	.661	.577	.505	.442	.388	.340	.299	.263
15	.861	.743	.642	.555	.481	.417	.362	.315	.275	.239
16	.853	.728	.623	.534	.458	.394	.339	.292	.252	.218
17	.844	.714	.605	.513	.436	.371	.317	.270	.231	.198
18	.836	.700	.587	.494	.416	.350	.296	.250	.212	.180
19	.828	.686	.570	.475	.396	.331	.277	.232	.194	.164
20	.820	.673	.554	.456	.377	.312	.258	.215	.178	.149
21	.811	.660	.538	.439	.359	.294	.242	.199	.164	.135
22	.803	.647	.522	.422	.342	.278	.226	.184	.150	.123
23	.795	.634	.507	.406	.326	.262	.211	.170	.138	.112
24	.788	.622	.492	.390	.310	.247	.197	.158	.126	.102
25	.780	.610	.478	.375	.295	.233	.184	.146	.116	.092
30	.742	.552	.412	.308	.231	.174	.131	.099	.075	.057
40	.672	.453	.307	.208	.142	.097	.067	.046	.032	.022
50	.608	.372	.228	.141	.087	.054	.034	.021	.013	.009

Period	11%	12%	13%	14%	15%	16%	17%	18%	19%	20%
1	.901	.893	.885	.877	.870	.862	.855	.847	.840	.833
2	.812	.797	.783	.769	.756	.743	.731	.718	.706	.694
3	.731	.712	.693	.675	.658	.641	.624	.609	.593	.579
4	.659	.636	.613	.592	.572	.552	.534	.516	.499	.482
5	.593	.567	.543	.519	.497	.476	.456	.437	.419	.402
6	.535	.507	.480	.456	.432	.410	.390	.370	.352	.335
7	.482	.452	.425	.400	.376	.354	.333	.314	.296	.279
8	.434	.404	.376	.351	.327	.305	.285	.266	.249	.233
9	.391	.361	.333	.308	.284	.263	.243	.225	.209	.194
10	.352	.322	.295	.270	.247	.227	.208	.191	.176	.162
11	.317	.287	.261	.237	.215	.195	.178	.162	.148	.135
12	.286	.257	.231	.208	.187	.168	.152	.137	.124	.112
13	.258	.229	.204	.182	.163	.145	.130	.116	.104	.093
14	.232	.205	.181	.160	.141	.125	.111	.099	.088	.078
15	.209	.183	.160	.140	.123	.108	.095	.084	.074	.065
16	.188	.163	.141	.123	.107	.093	.081	.071	.062	.054
17	.170	.146	.125	.108	.093	.080	.069	.060	.052	.045
18	.153	.130	.111	.095	.081	.069	.059	.051	.044	.038
19	.138	.116	.098	.083	.070	.060	.051	.043	.037	.031
20	.124	.104	.087	.073	.061	.051	.043	.037	.031	.026
21	.112	.093	.077	.064	.053	.044	.037	.031	.026	.022
22	.101	.083	.068	.056	.046	.038	.032	.026	.022	.018
23	.091	.074	.060	.049	.040	.033	.027	.022	.018	.015
24	.082	.066	.053	.043	.035	.028	.023	.019	.015	.013
25	.074	.059	.047	.038	.030	.024	.020	.016	.013	.010
30	.044	.033	.026	.020	.015	.012	.009	.007	.005	.004
40	.015	.011	.008	.005	.004	.003	.002	.001	.001	.001
50	.005	.003	.002	.001	.001	.001	.000	.000	.000	.000

Period	21%	22%	23%	24%	25%	26%	27%	28%	29%	30%
1	.826	.820	.813	.806	.800	.794	.787	.781	.775	.769
2	.683	.672	.661	.650	.640	.630	.620	.610	.601	.592
3	.564	.551	.537	.524	.512	.500	.488	.477	.466	.455
4	.467	.451	.437	.423	.410	.397	.384	.373	.361	.350
5	.386	.370	.355	.341	.328	.315	.303	.291	.280	.269
6	.319	.303	.289	.275	.262	.250	.238	.227	.217	.207
7	.263	.249	.235	.222	.210	.198	.188	.178	.168	.159
8	.218	.204	.191	.179	.168	.157	.148	.139	.130	.123
9	.180	.167	.155	.144	.134	.125	.116	.108	.101	.094
10	.149	.137	.126	.116	.107	.099	.092	.085	.078	.073
11	.123	.112	.103	.094	.086	.079	.072	.066	.061	.056
12	.102	.092	.083	.076	.069	.062	.057	.052	.047	.043
13	.084	.075	.068	.061	.055	.050	.045	.040	.037	.033
14	.069	.062	.055	.049	.044	.039	.035	.032	.028	.025
15	.057	.051	.045	.040	.035	.031	.028	.025	.022	.020
16	.047	.042	.036	.032	.028	.025	.022	.019	.017	.015
17	.039	.034	.030	.026	.023	.020	.017	.015	.013	.012
18	.032	.028	.024	.021	.018	.016	.014	.012	.010	.009
19	.027	.023	.020	.017	.014	.012	.011	.009	.008	.007
20	.022	.019	.016	.014	.012	.010	.008	.007	.006	.005
21	.018	.015	.013	.011	.009	.008	.007	.006	.005	.004
22	.015	.013	.011	.009	.007	.006	.005	.004	.004	.003
23	.012	.010	.009	.007	.006	.005	.004	.003	.003	.002
24	.010	.008	.007	.006	.005	.004	.003	.003	.002	.002
25	.009	.007	.006	.005	.004	.003	.003	.002	.002	.001
30	.003	.003	.002	.002	.001	.001	.001	.001	.000	.000
40	.000	.000	.000	.000	.000	.000	.000	.000	.000	.000
50	.000	.000	.000	.000	.000	.000	.000	.000	.000	.000

Period	31%	32%	33%	34%	35%	36%	37%	38%	39%	40%
1	.763	.758	.752	.746	.741	.735	.730	.725	.719	.714
2	.583	.574	.565	.557	.549	.541	.533	.525	.518	.510
3	.445	.435	.425	.416	.406	.398	.389	.381	.372	.364
4	.340	.329	.320	.310	.301	.292	.284	.276	.268	.260
5	.259	.250	.240	.231	.223	.215	.207	.200	.193	.186
6	.198	.189	.181	.173	.165	.158	.151	.145	.139	.133
7	.151	.143	.136	.129	.122	.116	.110	.105	.100	.095
8	.115	.108	.102	.096	.091	.085	.081	.076	.072	.068
9	.088	.082	.077	.072	.067	.063	.059	.055	.052	.048
10	.067	.062	.058	.054	.050	.046	.043	.040	.037	.035
11	.051	.047	.043	.040	.037	.034	.031	.029	.027	.025
12	.039	.036	.033	.030	.027	.025	.023	.021	.019	.018
13	.030	.027	.025	.022	.020	.018	.017	.015	.014	.013
14	.023	.021	.018	.017	.015	.014	.012	.011	.010	.009
15	.017	.016	.014	.012	.011	.010	.009	.008	.007	.006
16	.013	.012	.010	.009	.008	.007	.006	.006	.005	.005
17	.010	.009	.008	.007	.006	.005	.005	.004	.004	.003
18	.008	.007	.006	.005	.005	.004	.003	.003	.003	.002
19	.006	.005	.004	.004	.003	.003	.003	.002	.002	.002
20	.005	.004	.003	.003	.002	.002	.002	.002	.001	.001
21	.003	.003	.003	.002	.002	.002	.001	.001	.001	.001
22	.003	.002	.002	.002	.001	.001	.001	.001	.001	.001
23	.002	.002	.001	.001	.001	.001	.001	.001	.001	.000
24	.002	.001	.001	.001	.001	.001	.001	.000	.000	.000
25	.001	.001	.001	.001	.001	.000	.000	.000	.000	.000
30	.000	.000	.000	.000	.000	.000	.000	.000	.000	.000
40	.000	.000	.000	.000	.000	.000	.000	.000	.000	.000

Table A–4   Present Value Interest Factor Annuity

Period	1%	2%	3%	4%	5%	6%	7%	8%	9%	10%
1	.990	.980	.971	.962	.952	.943	.935	.926	.917	.909
2	1.970	1.942	1.913	1.886	1.859	1.833	1.808	1.783	1.759	1.736
3	2.941	2.884	2.829	2.775	2.723	2.673	2.624	2.577	2.531	2.487
4	3.902	3.808	3.717	3.630	3.546	3.465	3.387	3.312	3.240	3.170
5	4.853	4.713	4.580	4.452	4.329	4.212	4.100	3.993	3.890	3.791
6	5.795	5.601	5.417	5.242	5.076	4.917	4.767	4.623	4.486	4.355
7	6.728	6.472	6.230	6.002	5.786	5.582	5.389	5.206	5.033	4.868
8	7.652	7.326	7.020	6.733	6.463	6.210	5.971	5.747	5.535	5.335
9	8.566	8.162	7.786	7.435	7.108	6.802	6.515	6.247	5.995	5.759
10	9.471	8.983	8.530	8.111	7.722	7.360	7.024	6.710	6.418	6.145
11	10.368	9.787	9.253	8.760	8.306	7.887	7.499	7.139	6.805	6.495
12	11.255	10.575	9.954	9.385	8.863	8.384	7.943	7.536	7.161	6.814
13	12.134	11.348	10.635	9.986	9.394	8.853	8.358	7.904	7.487	7.103
14	13.004	12.106	11.296	10.563	9.899	9.295	8.746	8.244	7.786	7.367
15	13.865	12.849	11.938	11.118	10.380	9.712	9.108	8.560	8.061	7.606
16	14.718	13.578	12.561	11.652	10.838	10.106	9.447	8.851	8.313	7.824
17	15.562	14.292	13.166	12.166	11.274	10.477	9.763	9.122	8.544	8.022
18	16.398	14.992	13.754	12.659	11.690	10.828	10.059	9.372	8.756	8.201
19	17.226	15.679	14.324	13.134	12.085	11.158	10.336	9.604	8.950	8.365
20	18.046	16.352	14.878	13.590	12.462	11.470	10.594	9.818	9.129	8.514
21	18.857	17.011	15.415	14.029	12.821	11.764	10.836	10.017	9.292	8.649
22	19.661	17.658	15.937	14.451	13.163	12.042	11.061	10.201	9.442	8.772
23	20.456	18.292	16.444	14.857	13.489	12.303	11.272	10.371	9.580	8.883
24	21.244	18.914	16.936	15.247	13.799	12.550	11.469	10.529	9.707	8.985
25	22.023	19.524	17.413	15.622	14.094	12.783	11.654	10.675	9.823	9.077
30	25.808	22.397	19.601	17.292	15.373	13.765	12.409	11.258	10.274	9.427
40	32.835	27.356	23.115	19.793	17.159	15.046	13.332	11.925	10.757	9.779
50	39.197	31.424	25.730	21.482	18.256	15.762	13.801	12.234	10.962	9.915

Period	11%	12%	13%	14%	15%	16%	17%	18%	19%	20%
1	.901	.893	.885	.877	.870	.862	.855	.847	.840	.833
2	1.713	1.690	1.668	1.647	1.626	1.605	1.585	1.566	1.547	1.528
3	2.444	2.402	2.361	2.322	2.283	2.246	2.210	2.174	2.140	2.106
4	3.102	3.037	2.974	2.914	2.855	2.798	2.743	2.690	2.639	2.589
5	3.696	3.605	3.517	3.433	3.352	3.274	3.199	3.127	3.058	2.991
6	4.231	4.111	3.998	3.889	3.784	3.685	3.589	3.498	3.410	3.326
7	4.712	4.564	4.423	4.288	4.160	4.039	3.922	3.812	3.706	3.605
8	5.146	4.968	4.799	4.639	4.487	4.344	4.207	4.078	3.954	3.837
9	5.537	5.328	5.132	4.946	4.772	4.607	4.451	4.303	4.163	4.031
10	5.889	5.650	5.426	5.216	5.019	4.833	4.659	4.494	4.339	4.192
11	6.207	5.938	5.687	5.453	5.234	5.029	4.836	4.656	4.487	4.327
12	6.492	6.194	5.918	5.660	5.421	5.197	4.988	4.793	4.611	4.439
13	6.750	6.424	6.122	5.842	5.583	5.342	5.118	4.910	4.715	4.533
14	6.982	6.628	6.303	6.002	5.724	5.468	5.229	5.008	4.802	4.611
15	7.191	6.811	6.462	6.142	5.847	5.575	5.324	5.092	4.876	4.675
16	7.379	6.974	6.604	6.265	5.954	5.669	5.405	5.162	4.938	4.730
17	7.549	7.120	6.729	6.373	6.047	5.749	5.475	5.222	4.990	4.775
18	7.702	7.250	6.840	6.467	6.128	5.818	5.534	5.273	5.033	4.812
19	7.839	7.366	6.938	6.550	6.198	5.877	5.585	5.316	5.070	4.843
20	7.963	7.469	7.025	6.623	6.259	5.929	5.628	5.353	5.101	4.870
21	8.075	7.562	7.102	6.687	6.312	5.973	5.665	5.384	5.127	4.891
22	8.176	7.645	7.170	6.743	6.359	6.011	5.696	5.410	5.149	4.909
23	8.266	7.718	7.230	6.792	6.399	6.044	5.723	5.432	5.167	4.925
24	8.348	7.784	7.283	6.835	6.434	6.073	5.747	5.451	5.182	4.937
25	8.442	7.843	7.330	6.873	6.464	6.097	5.766	5.467	5.195	4.948
30	8.694	8.055	7.496	7.003	6.566	6.177	5.829	5.517	5.235	4.979
40	8.951	8.244	7.634	7.105	6.642	6.233	5.871	5.548	5.258	4.997
50	9.042	8.305	7.675	7.133	6.661	6.246	5.880	5.554	5.262	4.999

Period	21%	22%	23%	24%	25%	26%	27%	28%	29%	30%
1	.826	.820	.813	.806	.800	.794	.787	.781	.775	.769
2	1.509	1.492	1.474	1.457	1.440	1.424	1.407	1.392	1.376	1.361
3	2.074	2.042	2.011	1.981	1.952	1.923	1.896	1.868	1.842	1.816
4	2.540	2.494	2.448	2.404	2.362	2.320	2.280	2.241	2.203	2.166
5	2.926	2.864	2.803	2.745	2.689	2.635	2.583	2.532	2.483	2.436
6	3.245	3.167	3.092	3.020	2.951	2.885	2.821	2.759	2.700	2.643
7	3.508	3.416	3.327	3.242	3.161	3.083	3.009	2.937	2.868	2.802
8	3.726	3.619	3.518	3.421	3.329	3.241	3.156	3.076	2.999	2.925
9	3.905	3.786	3.673	3.566	3.463	3.366	3.273	3.184	3.100	3.019
10	4.054	3.923	3.799	3.682	3.570	3.465	3.364	3.269	3.178	3.092
11	4.177	4.035	3.902	3.776	3.656	3.544	3.437	3.335	3.239	3.147
12	4.278	4.127	3.985	3.851	3.725	3.606	3.493	3.387	3.286	3.190
13	4.362	4.203	4.053	3.912	3.780	3.656	3.538	3.427	3.322	3.223
14	4.432	4.265	4.108	3.962	3.824	3.695	3.573	3.459	3.351	3.249
15	4.489	4.315	4.153	4.001	3.859	3.726	3.601	3.483	3.373	3.268
16	4.536	4.357	4.189	4.033	3.887	3.751	3.623	3.503	3.390	3.283
17	4.576	4.391	4.219	4.059	3.910	3.771	3.640	3.518	3.403	3.295
18	4.608	4.419	4.243	4.080	3.928	3.786	3.654	3.529	3.413	3.304
19	4.635	4.442	4.263	4.097	3.942	3.799	3.664	3.539	3.421	3.311
20	4.657	4.460	4.279	4.110	3.954	3.808	3.673	3.546	3.427	3.316
21	4.675	4.476	4.292	4.121	3.963	3.816	3.679	3.551	3.432	3.320
22	4.690	4.488	4.302	4.130	3.970	3.822	3.684	3.556	3.436	3.323
23	4.703	4.499	4.311	4.137	3.976	3.827	3.689	3.559	3.438	3.325
24	4.713	4.507	4.318	4.143	3.981	3.831	3.692	3.562	3.441	3.327
25	4.721	4.514	4.323	4.147	3.985	3.834	3.694	3.564	3.442	3.329
30	4.746	4.534	4.339	4.160	3.995	3.842	3.701	3.569	3.447	3.332
40	4.760	4.544	4.347	4.166	3.999	3.846	3.703	3.571	3.448	3.333
50	4.762	4.545	4.348	4.167	4.000	3.846	3.704	3.571	3.448	3.333

Period	31%	32%	33%	34%	35%	36%	37%	38%	39%	40%
1	.763	.758	.752	.746	.741	.735	.730	.725	.719	.714
2	1.346	1.331	1.317	1.303	1.289	1.276	1.263	1.250	1.237	1.224
3	1.791	1.766	1.742	1.719	1.696	1.673	1.652	1.630	1.609	1.589
4	2.130	2.096	2.062	2.029	1.997	1.966	1.935	1.906	1.877	1.849
5	2.390	2.345	2.302	2.260	2.220	2.181	2.143	2.106	2.070	2.035
6	2.588	2.534	2.483	2.433	2.385	2.339	2.294	2.251	2.209	2.168
7	2.739	2.677	2.619	2.562	2.508	2.455	2.404	2.355	2.308	2.263
8	2.854	2.786	2.721	2.658	2.598	2.540	2.485	2.432	2.380	2.331
9	2.942	2.868	2.798	2.730	2.665	2.603	2.544	2.487	2.432	2.379
10	3.009	2.930	2.855	2.784	2.715	2.649	2.587	2.527	2.469	2.414
11	3.060	2.978	2.899	2.824	2.752	2.683	2.618	2.555	2.496	2.438
12	3.100	3.013	2.931	2.853	2.779	2.708	2.641	2.576	2.515	2.456
13	3.129	3.040	2.956	2.876	2.799	2.727	2.658	2.592	2.529	2.469
14	3.152	3.061	2.974	2.892	2.814	2.740	2.670	2.603	2.539	2.477
15	3.170	3.076	2.988	2.905	2.825	2.750	2.679	2.611	2.546	2.484
16	3.183	3.088	2.999	2.914	2.834	2.757	2.685	2.616	2.551	2.489
17	3.193	3.097	3.007	2.921	2.840	2.763	2.690	2.621	2.555	2.492
18	3.201	3.104	3.012	2.926	2.844	2.767	2.693	2.624	2.557	2.494
19	3.207	3.109	3.017	2.930	2.848	2.770	2.696	2.626	2.559	2.496
20	3.211	3.113	3.020	2.933	2.850	2.772	2.698	2.627	2.561	2.497
21	3.215	3.116	3.023	2.935	2.852	2.773	2.699	2.629	2.562	2.498
22	3.217	3.118	3.025	2.936	2.853	2.775	2.700	2.629	2.562	2.498
23	3.219	3.120	3.026	2.938	2.854	2.775	2.701	2.630	2.563	2.499
24	3.221	3.121	3.027	2.939	2.855	2.776	2.701	2.630	2.563	2.499
25	3.222	3.122	3.028	2.939	2.856	2.776	2.702	2.631	2.563	2.499
30	3.225	3.124	3.030	2.941	2.857	2.777	2.702	2.631	2.564	2.500
40	3.226	3.125	3.030	2.941	2.857	2.778	2.703	2.632	2.564	2.500
50	3.226	3.125	3.030	2.941	2.857	2.778	2.703	2.632	2.564	2.500

GLOSSARY

accelerated method of depreciation an accounting method whereby part of the cost of a fixed asset is charged off yearly at faster rates than under the straight-line method, where equal amounts are charged off each year over the life of the asset

Acceleration Cost Recovery System the depreciation method that must be used for tax purposes on all assets acquired later than 1980

acid test or quick ratio current assets, less inventories, divided by current liabilities

after-tax incremental cash flows additional cash flows as a result of replacing an existing machine (or updating an existing project) and after adjustment for all tax effects

agency costs costs incurred by stockholders to induce managers to adopt policies designed to maximize the wealth of the firm

aggressive approach a method of financing in which fixed assets and only part of the minimum level of current assets are financed by long-term debt and equity

amortization the gradual, planned reduction in value of capital expenditures

arbitrage taking advantage of temporary differences in market prices. This is done by buying in the cheap market and then selling in the higher-priced market.

arbitrage pricing theory (APT) an alternate method to compute the required rate of return of an asset. The return is a function of several factors and equilibrium is maintained by arbitrage.

average collection period the number of days required, on average, to collect accounts receivable (a measure of how effectively the firm is getting customers to pay the credit it gives them when they purchase merchandise)

average payment period the number of days, on average, within which a firm pays off its accounts payables

average rate of return (ARR) the ratio of average net earnings to average investment

balance of payments a document showing all payments and receipts of a country vis-à-vis the rest of the world for a year

balance sheet an accounting statement that displays the assets, liabilities, and equity of a firm

bankruptcy costs expenses occasioned by a defaulting firm, such as legal fees, inefficiencies, liquidation losses, and increased cost of capital

basis spot price minus the future price

beta an indicator of the riskiness of a stock's returns, as compared to the riskiness of general market returns. A beta of 1.0 indicates the same risk as the general market; a beta lower than 1.0 is less risky, and a beta higher than 1.0 is more risky, than the market.

bond a long-term debt security issued by a borrower, either a public or private institution

book value (of a firm) assets minus liabilities

book value weights valuation of a firm's financial structure according to the book values of its securities

break-even approach a method used to evaluate the point where sales equal operating costs. It serves as a guideline to determine the profitability of a firm.

bullish spread where the investor buys a call in the money (at a lower strike price) and sells a call out of the money (at a higher stock price)

call option an option that gives the holder the right to buy

call option buyer an investor who speculates that the price of a stock will increase beyond a strike price

call price the price at which an issuing firm may call in its bonds. Usually the call price is set above the par value and in the case of convertible bonds is a feature used to force conversion into common stock.

capital the net worth of a company's assets

capital account an account in the balance of payments that shows the net capital inflows and outflows resulting from various types of investment

capital appreciation the percentage upward change in the price of an asset, such as a stock, from one period to another

capital asset pricing model (CAPM) a theoretical concept that measures the required rate of return of an asset by taking into account the sensitivity of other assets' returns to market returns

capital budgeting a method for evaluating, comparing, and selecting projects to achieve the best long-term financial return

capital expenditures long-term expenditures that are amortized over a period of time determined by IRS regulations

capital gains profits from the resale of assets that have been held longer than 6 months

capital impairment rule a requirement in most states that firms limit the payment of cash dividends. This is generally done to protect the claims of creditors in case of insolvency.

Capital IQ Compustat a database for equity research used in industry and academic centers, containing historical prices, financial statements, and other financial data; part of Standard and Poor's

capitalization rate the discount rate employed to determine the value of earnings as dividends

capital lease a long-term lease, usually extending over 6 years or more

capital structure the financing mix of a firm. The more debt in relation to equity, the more financial leverage the firm is said to have.

cash cycle the number of days between the purchase of raw materials and the collection of sales proceeds for finished goods

cash flow a measure of a company's liquidity, consisting of net income plus noncash expenditures (such as depreciation charges)

cash turnover the number of times a firm's cash is collected in a year

certainty equivalent factor a factor used to convert projected cash flows into certain cash flows

coefficient of variation a statistical factor that measures the relative variability of risk and return; it is calculated by dividing the standard deviation of outcomes by the mean expected value of returns

commercial paper unsecured notes sold at a discount from par value that have maturities of less than 270 days

common equity the value of common stock issued by the firm. Common stockholders are the owners of the equity in the firm and are the last to receive payment in case of insolvency.

compensating balances part of bank loans held on deposit that draw no interest

Compustat a giant file containing detailed (historical) financial statements and other company financial statistical data

conservative approach a method of financing in which long-term loans and equity are used to finance fixed assets and the minimum level of current assets

consolidation the formation of a new firm by issuing new stock and ending the existence and identity of the two merged firms

contingency payments monetary incentives offered to target company managers as inducements to merge

contractual obligations restrictions on dividend payments that a firm may agree to in a contract with a creditor

contribution margin selling price less variable cost

conversion premium the difference between the current price of a firm's stock and the conversion price of a convertible security

conversion price the stock price at which a convertible security may be exchanged for common stock. It is found by dividing the par value of the security by the conversion ratio.

conversion ratio the number of shares of stock for which a convertible security can be exchanged. It is calculated by dividing the par value by the conversion price.

conversion value the current market price of a firm's stock multiplied by the conversion ratio

convertible bond a security that gives its owner the option to exchange it for a specified number of shares of common stock

corporate restructuring altering the product mix or asset composition of the firm to increase efficiency and achieve a favorable evaluation from investors

corporation a form of organization that is a legal entity and whose owners have limited liability

correlation coefficient a measure of the degree of relationship between one variable and another

cost of capital (*CC*) the rate a firm must pay to investors in order to induce them to purchase the firm's stock and/or bonds

coupon rate the rate of interest received by a bondholder on an annual, semiannual, or quarterly basis

covariance the degree of correlation between the returns of one asset and those of another asset

credit default swap (CDS) an over-the-counter contract between two parties where credit risk is transferred from one entity to the other

current account a combined account in the balance of payments that reflects the sum of the trade account and service account balances

current expenditures short-term expenditures that are completely charged to income the year in which they occur

current ratio current assets divided by current liabilities (a liquidity measure)

cutoff rate the standard discount rate chosen by a firm, against which the profitabilities of potential projects are measured

debt/capitalization (*D/C*) ratio the ratio of a firm's debt to its capitalization. The higher this ratio, the greater the risk and the financial leverage.

debt equity (*D/E*) ratio the ratio of a firm's debt to its equity. The higher this ratio, the greater the financial leverage of the firm.

degree of financial leverage the extent to which EPS will change, given a change in EBIT. High financial leverage means high financial exposure and a greater risk that the firm may not be able to meet its debt obligations.

depreciation the allocation of an asset's cost, for tax or management purposes, based on its age

direct investment investment in a foreign asset representing at least 10% ownership

discount rate the required rate of return that a firm must achieve to justify its investments

distress debt a security in government entities or companies that are already in default, under bankruptcy protection, or heading toward default

dividend a return on an investment, usually in the form of cash or stock. Directors decide periodically to declare (or to forgo) dividends, and they set the amount to be paid and the form of the dividend.

dividend income income generated by the receipt of dividends from another company's stock held by the firm

dividend yield the annual dividend payment divided by the market price of a share of the stock

double-declining balance method a method that uses a constant rate (usually double the straight-line ratio) to depreciate the book value of an asset

e-mail transmitting system for sending letters, messages, and other information electronically from one computer to another

EBIT earnings before interest and taxes

economic order quantity (*EOQ*) the quantity of an item that, when ordered regularly, minimizes ordering and storage costs

economies of scale the increasing returns derived from spreading output over a fixed amount of assets, capacity, or investment. These gains are derived from research or from highly efficient machinery.

efficient frontier sophisticated mathematical curve, using quadratic programming, that calculates the optimal maximum expected returns at different levels of risk or standard deviations.

efficient market (*EM*) market in which stock prices reflect all information and these prices represent their fair value. Understanding the EM process will help managers supply the market with the kind of information that should help raise the price of a firm's stock.

EPS earnings per share

equity the dollar value of the total assets after subtracted from debt

Eurodollars U.S. dollars traded outside U.S. borders

European option option exerciseable only at expiration date

exchange ratio price per share offered a target company divided by the current price per share of the acquiring company

ex dividend without dividend; used with reference to a share of stock purchased after a dividend was declared

exercise price the pre-established price at which warrant holders may purchase common stock. The initial exercise price is usually above the current market price of the stock at the time the warrant or option is issued.

expected return the future receipts that investors anticipate from their investments

expiration date the date when a call or put option comes due. After the expiration date, options become worthless.

external sources of funds current debts, long-term borrowing, preferred stock, and common stock

face value the value of a bond at maturity, also called the nominal, or par value

finance the application of a series of economic principles to maximize the wealth, or overall value, of a firm

financial analysis evaluation of the income and balance sheet statements

financial data banks compilations of historical financial statements, prices, and dividend data easily accessible for analysis and manipulation

financial lease See **capital lease.**

financial leverage the use of debt to finance investments

financial planning the process of estimating a firm's fund needs and deciding how to finance those funds

financial software programs designed to manage data, undertake spreadsheet analysis, and supply data banks and financial statements for solving complex mathematical problems

flotation costs fees paid to intermediaries who help a firm issue stocks and bonds

foreign currency futures a formal contract to sell or to buy a certain amount of foreign currency at a specified rate for delivery at a future time

foreign currency option a contract that gives the purchaser the right to buy or sell a fixed amount of currency at a fixed rate on or before a specified expiration date

foreign exchange rate the price at which the currency of one country can be bought with the currency of another country

forward transaction a transaction that involves the buying or selling of a foreign currency at a specified price for delivery at a future date

free cash flows net income adjusted for all noncash expenditures as well as estimated increases or decreases in capital expenditures and working capital

futures contracts traded on the exchange whereby the parties agree to buy or sell an asset at a stated price and at a future date

future value the value of an initial investment after a specified period of time at a certain rate of interest

general partnership a partnership in which all partners have unlimited liability for future obligations

geographical arbitrage a type of arbitrage that occurs when the price of a given foreign currency in one market is different from the price in another market

global firm a firm that has asset investments and operations on a worldwide basis

golden parachute large compensation package given to senior management; it provides generous benefits if the firm is taken over and the executive loses his or her job. Payment guaranteed top officers.

goodwill the intangible assets of a firm, calculated as the excess purchase price paid over book value

greenmail payment made by a takeover target company to a holder of a large block of company stock who is regarded as a corporate raider. To induce the raider to go away, the company offers to buy his shares at a price substantially higher than the current market value.

horizontal acquisition a combination of two firms producing similar goods and services

HTML a simple language employed to code web pages

image building attempts by firms to change their product lines and financial performance in order to obtain a favorable investor valuation

in-the-money call option option in which the stock price exceeds the exercise price

income statement an accounting statement of a firm's sales, operating costs, and financial charges

incremental initial investment (III) the true cost of starting a project, which includes the cost of purchasing a new asset, the sale of the old asset, and the tax effect (either tax liability or tax credit) on the sale of the old asset

inflation a general price increase in the economy

insolvency the inability to repay debt

internal rate of return (*IRR*) the discount rate that makes the net present value of a project equal to zero

internally generated funds monies that a firm generates from retained earnings and depreciation

international firm a firm that exports or imports goods and/or services or has overseas activities

Internet a communication system that allows suppliers and users of information to exchange that information on computers

intrinsic value the value of an asset or a firm, as perceived by an investor, a manager, or anyone else, based on the person's judgment of all the facts at hand; also, the difference between the exercise price of a put or call option and the market value of the underlying stock

inventory management the process of determining and maintaining the optimal inventory levels

inventory turnover ratio the costs of goods sold divided by the inventory. Usually, the faster the turnover, the better for a firm.

investment banker an advisor and distributor of new security issues who takes the risk of selling the securities

investment value of convertibles the straight bond value of convertibles; the price at which a convertible would sell in the absence of its convertibility

ISDA® (International Swaps and Derivatives Association) a self-regulatory industry organization that recommends criteria and standards for documentation of a CDS

junior debt a type of debt that has a lower priority or ranking than another debt claim within the same asset or property; usually unsecured; also known as subordinate debt

junk bond unsecured debenture with an assigned rating of Baa or lower. It features yields 3% to 5% higher than good quality bonds. Many of these bonds are issued by acquiring companies to finance a merger.

lease a legal contract under which the owner of an asset gives the right to use the asset to another party for a certain period of time in return for a specified payment

lessee the user of an asset that is leased from another party

lessor the owner of an asset that is leased to another party

leverage leasing involves a lessor who does not buy the equipment outright. The lessor puts up roughly 20% to 25% of the purchase price; the rest of the funds are supplied by lenders.

limited partnership a partnership in which one or more partners may have limited liability provided that at least one partner has unlimited liability

line of credit bank agreement which allows a firm to borrow a given amount of money within a specified period of time

liquidity a measure of how easily assets can be converted into cash

liquidity management the process of ensuring adequate cash for the operation of a firm

long hedge to buy futures contracts now and sell them at a later date as protection against a price increase

long-term debt borrowing over a long period of time, usually through bank loans or the sale of bonds. On a balance sheet, any debt due for more than one year is classified as long term.

macro factors factors that pertain to developments in the general economy and government fiscal policy

marginal cost of capital the incremental cost of financing above a previous level

market efficiency a theory that prices of securities or foreign currencies reflect all information, transmitted so quickly that differences between prices are corrected before arbitrage can take place

market value weights valuation of a firm's financial structure according to the market prices of its securities

marking to the market procedure for the daily settlement of gains and losses on futures contracts

maturity, maturity date the date on which the issuer of a bond is obligated to pay the principal or face value of the bond

maximize the wealth to achieve the highest level of profits attainable at a given risk level

maximum return the highest possible profit

maximum wealth the highest possible stock price attainable at the least risk

merchandise balance See **trade account**.

merger a combination of two firms, with one firm maintaining its identity

merger exchange ratio a ratio derived by dividing the EPS of the acquired company by those of the acquiring company. The result is the number of shares that the acquiring company will accept to consummate a merger.

micro factors factors that pertain to supply, demand, and pricing

multinational corporation a firm with significant operations outside its national borders

negotiating range the minimum and the maximum price an acquiring company is willing to consider when entering in merger negotiations with a target company

net present value (*NPV*) the present value of a project's future cash flow less the initial investment in the project

net profit margins net profits after taxes divided by sales

net residual principle a rule for determining dividend payments, based on investing retained earnings to the point where the *IRR* and *MCC* curves meet, and distributing the remainder as dividends

net working capital current assets minus current liabilities; it may be used as an indication of liquidity from one year to another

NI theory the theory that changes in a firm's capital structure affect its value or its cost of capital

NOI theory the theory that changes in a firm's capital structure does not affect its value or its cost of capital

nominal rate of interest real rate of interest plus a premium for the expected rate of inflation

nominal value See **face value**.

operating lease a lease, usually lasting for 5 years or less, in which the lessor handles maintenance and servicing

operating profit margins the rates of profits earned from operations, excluding taxes and interest from consideration

opportunity cost the rate of return on the best alternative investment that is not selected

optimal capital structure the theoretical structure of debt and equity that results in the lowest cost of capital and the maximum wealth of a firm

option the right to purchase stock at a specified price

option writer an investor who enters into a contract to sell stock (in case of a call) or buy stock (in the case of a put) at a stated price for a specified time in exchange for a premium

ordinary income income from the main activities of a firm and from the sale of assets that have been held for less than 6 months

out-of-the-money call option option in which the stock price is lower than the exercise price

outsourcing a firm decides to invest and produce goods abroad (or rely on imports) rather than invest and produce those goods domestically

overall account an account in the balance of payments that reflects the sum of the balances in the current account and various capital accounts

par, par value the face value of a share of stock or a bond. In the case of stocks, par value is merely a bookkeeping entry and serves no other purpose.

partnership an operation owned by two or more persons and conducted for a profit

payback period the amount of time required to recover the initial investment in a project

payout ratio the cash dividend per share divided by the earnings per share

P/E ratio the price of stock divided by either the current or expected earnings per share

permanent financing the minimum level of current assets plus fixed assets

perpetuity an annuity forever; periodic equal payments or receipts on a continuous basis

poison pill defensive practices by a target company to make an unfriendly merger less attractive to the acquiring company

portfolio the sum total of all the assets owned by a firm or an individual investor

portfolio investment an investment in a foreign asset in which there is less than 10% ownership

preemptive rights the rights of stockholders to participate in any security distributions of a firm and to maintain voting power when new shares are issued

preference for liquidity the assignment of more value to available cash than to future income

preferred stock a kind of equity whose owners are given certain privileges over common stockholders, such as a prior claim on the assets of the firm. Preferred stockholders usually have no voting rights and are paid a fixed dividend.

present value the cash value, today, of future returns

price/book value (*P/BV*) a market ratio that relates the stock price of a company to its book value

price/earnings (*P/E*) ratio the price of a firm's stock divided by its EPS. It is usually stated that stock price is a multiple of earnings per share.

probabilities the chances that specific events will occur. Probabilities are used to weight an estimated range of outcomes in order to reduce the range to a single figure.

profitability index (*PI*) the ratio of the present value of future cash flows from a project to the initial investment in the project

proprietorship an operation owned by one person and conducted for a profit

prospectus written document which provides financial and other information about a new issue of securities

purchase acquisition method payment of cash for another corporation, taking into account goodwill (or cost over book value)

put option an option that gives the holder the right to sell

put option buyer an investor who speculates that the price of a stock will decline

quick ratio See **acid test**.

rating agencies agencies that study the financial status of a firm and then assign a quality rating to securities issued by that firm. Standard and Poors and Moody are leading rating agencies.

recaptured depreciation the selling price of a used asset minus the book value and capital gain (if any)

replacement cost the current purchase price of an asset used to replace an existing asset

repurchase of shares a situation in which a firm buys back its stock with excess cash

required rate of return (*RRR*) the minimum future receipts an investor will accept in choosing an investment

return the gains or losses incurred by the owner of an asset over a period of time; usually measured as the sum of the periodic payments (dividends or interest) and the capital appreciation of the asset (total return)

return on equity (*ROE*) net profits after taxes divided by stockholders' equity

return on investment (*ROI*) net profits after taxes divided by assets. This ratio helps a firm determine how effectively it generates profits from available assets.

reverse merger a conglomerate breaks up into several independent companies to improve its valuation

risk (*n.*) instability; uncertainty about the future; more specifically, the degree of uncertainty involved with a project or investment

risk-free rate, riskless rate a discount rate equal to the return on a riskless asset. A U.S. Treasury bill is usually considered a riskless asset, and its yield provides a riskless rate.

risk premium an additional required rate of return that must be paid to investors who own risky assets. The riskier the asset, the higher the premium.

risk/return trade-off the relationship between the riskiness of an asset and its expected returns. This can be measured by using the coefficient of variation or the SML model.

sale and leaseback leasing arrangement whereby a firm that owns a piece of equipment sells it to another firm and leases it back, agreeing to pay periodic annual rentals. The contract provides for the original owner of the equipment to buy the equipment back at the termination of the lease.

salvage value the estimated selling price of an asset once it has been fully depreciated

SAS a package of programs to help solve statistical and financial problems

SDRs (Special Drawing Rights) credit extended by the International Money Fund to importing countries. SDRs are exchanged only among central banks and are convertible into other currencies

seasonal financing the amount of current assets minus a minimum (fixed) level of current assets. In other words, seasonal financing can be viewed as that portion of current assets that fluctuates from one month to another.

securities company assets guaranteed to lenders to ensure repayment of loans

security market line (SML) a way to measure the relationship between beta (systematic risk) and expected returns. All points on the SML represent required rates of return for a given beta.

senior debt debt with a higher ranking or priority than all subordinate or junior debt in the same asset or property

sensitivity analysis a measure of the extent to which one factor varies when another factor changes; a "what-if ..." technique

service-and-other-intangible account an account in the balance of payments that reflects transactions involving technical know-how, financial services, trade and military aid, and other intangible items

service lease See **operating lease**.

shelf registration method of allowing a firm to expedite registration within a two-year period

short hedging locking in the value of an asset by selling futures contracts

simulation the use of a hypothetical situation, similar to the real one, as a help in making a decision

simulation software computer programs that randomly generate variables for simulations and calculate the results of these simulations, creating useful distribution curves

Small Business Administration an organization established by Congress in 1958 to assist small companies in solving their financial (e.g., borrowing) problems

sources and uses of funds analysis analysis of how a firm generates and applies funds

spontaneous asset an asset that changes in value as a result of increases or decreases in sales

spot market the market for buying and selling a specific commodity or foreign currency at the current price for immediate delivery

spreadsheet programs like Excel, programs that facilitate the construction of financial statements and lend themselves to ratio analysis, cash flow computations, and the study of changes that occur in a "what-if ..." situations

SPSS a statistical package of programs to help solve complex financial (mathematical) problems

standard deviation the volatility of returns, or the average deviation from an expected value or mean

standardized financial statements a method for comparing the balance sheets and income statements of companies having different sizes of assets, liabilities, incomes, and expenses. Each asset component of the balance sheet is restated as a percentage of total assets, and each component of the income statement is restated as a percentage of total sales.

statement of cash flows financial statement that traces the cash inflows and outflows originating in operating, investment, and financing activities

stock dividend a dividend in the form of additional shares of stock, issued in lieu of a cash dividend. It increases the common stock par value and capital surplus and is taken out of retained earnings.

stock repurchase a firm uses its available cash to repurchase its own stock, which then becomes treasury stock

stock split the issuing of more shares of stock to current stockholders without increasing stockholders' equity. It reduces the par value of common stock but does not alter the equity values in the balance sheet.

straight-line depreciation depreciating an asset by equal dollar amounts each year over the life of the asset

strike price the price at which an option to purchase stock can be exercised

sum-of-the-years'-digits method an accelerated depreciation method whereby a greater portion of an asset is depreciated in the early part of its life

swaps exchange of assets, securities, or currencies between two parties for a specific period of time

synergism economies and other gains created by the combination of companies in a merger

tax-loss carry-forward a situation that allows a firm to charge off ordinary losses for 3 years against the past and for 15 years forward against income. Capital losses can be carried back 3 years and forward 5 years.

tender offer an offer from an acquiring firm or any other source to purchase a number of shares from stockholders at a stated price per share

theoretical value of a warrant the current price of a share of common stock less the exercise price, multiplied by the terms of exchange

Thomson One Integrated a database consisting of First Call, DataStream, IBES, and a few other subsets of data for financial research used both in industry and academic centers

times interest-earned ratio EBIT divided by annual interest expense (a measure of how well the firm meets its fixed interest expenses)

tracking stock new stock issued by a parent company that trades on its own. This strategy is adopted to gain recognition for a highly valued division (subsidiary) and to have the market recognize its superior performance via the price of the tracking stock.

trade account an account in the balance of payments, also called the merchandise balance, that shows exports and imports of goods and services in the local currency

transaction risk a type of foreign exchange risk arising when a future foreign currency cash flow is exposed to a possible adverse currency movement before the transaction can be completed

translation risk a type of foreign exchange risk arising from the need to translate the assets and liabilities of a foreign subsidiary into the currency of the home country

underwriting syndicate a group of investment firms buys an issue of securities from a company and then take the risk of selling the issue to investors

variance the standard deviation squared; See **standard deviation**.

vertical acquisition acquiring a target firm in a different stage of the production cycle

volatility the degree of fluctuations that occur away from a common denominator such as the mean, or average value, of a series of figures. The greater the volatility in returns, the higher the risk.

warrant a security that gives a bond or preferred stock buyer the right to purchase shares of common stock at a given price

web site a number of web pages linked together

weighted average cost of capital (*WACC*) a measure of a firm's overall cost of capital, based on the percentage values of the components comprising its financial structure

weighted marginal cost of capital (*WMCC*) See **cost of capital**.

wealth maximization selecting those investments that produce the best risk/return tradeoff

white knight in cases of unfriendly takeover bids, the target company seeks out other more compatible firms to merge with, hence preventing the original bidder from acquiring the target company

yield curve relationship between bond yields and corresponding maturity dates

yield to maturity yield on a fixed income security if held to maturity

z-score statistical index or variable used to predict a firm's potential probability of financial problem or bankruptcy

zero coupon bond bond issued at a discount from par value that pays no coupon and promises to pay par value at maturity

INDEX